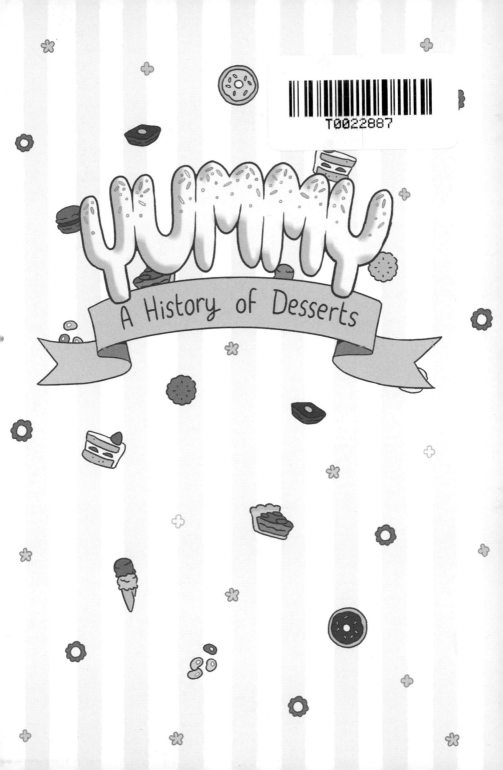

# YUMMY
## A History of Desserts

*Yummy* was illustrated, colored, and lettered digitally.
All recipes were made and enjoyed by the author.

All rights reserved. Published in the United States by RH Graphic, an imprint of
Random House Children's Books, a division of Penguin Random House LLC, New York.

RH Graphic with the book design is a trademark of Penguin Random House LLC.

Visit us on the web! RHKidsGraphic.com • @RHKidsGraphic

Educators and librarians, for a variety of teaching tools, visit us at RHTeachersLibrarians.com

Library of Congress Cataloging-in-Publication Data is available upon request.
ISBN 978-0-593-12437-6 (hc) — ISBN 978-0-593-12438-3 (pb)
ISBN 978-0-593-12542-7 (lib. bdg.) — ISBN 978-0-593-12439-0 (ebk)

Designed by Patrick Crotty

MANUFACTURED IN CHINA
10 9 8 7 6 5 4 3
First Edition

**A comic on every bookshelf.**

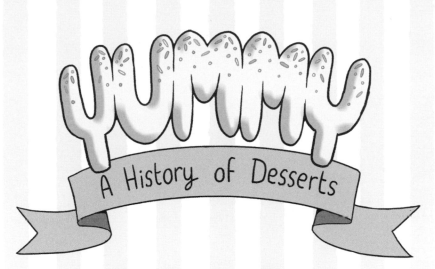

# A History of Desserts

Victoria Grace Elliott

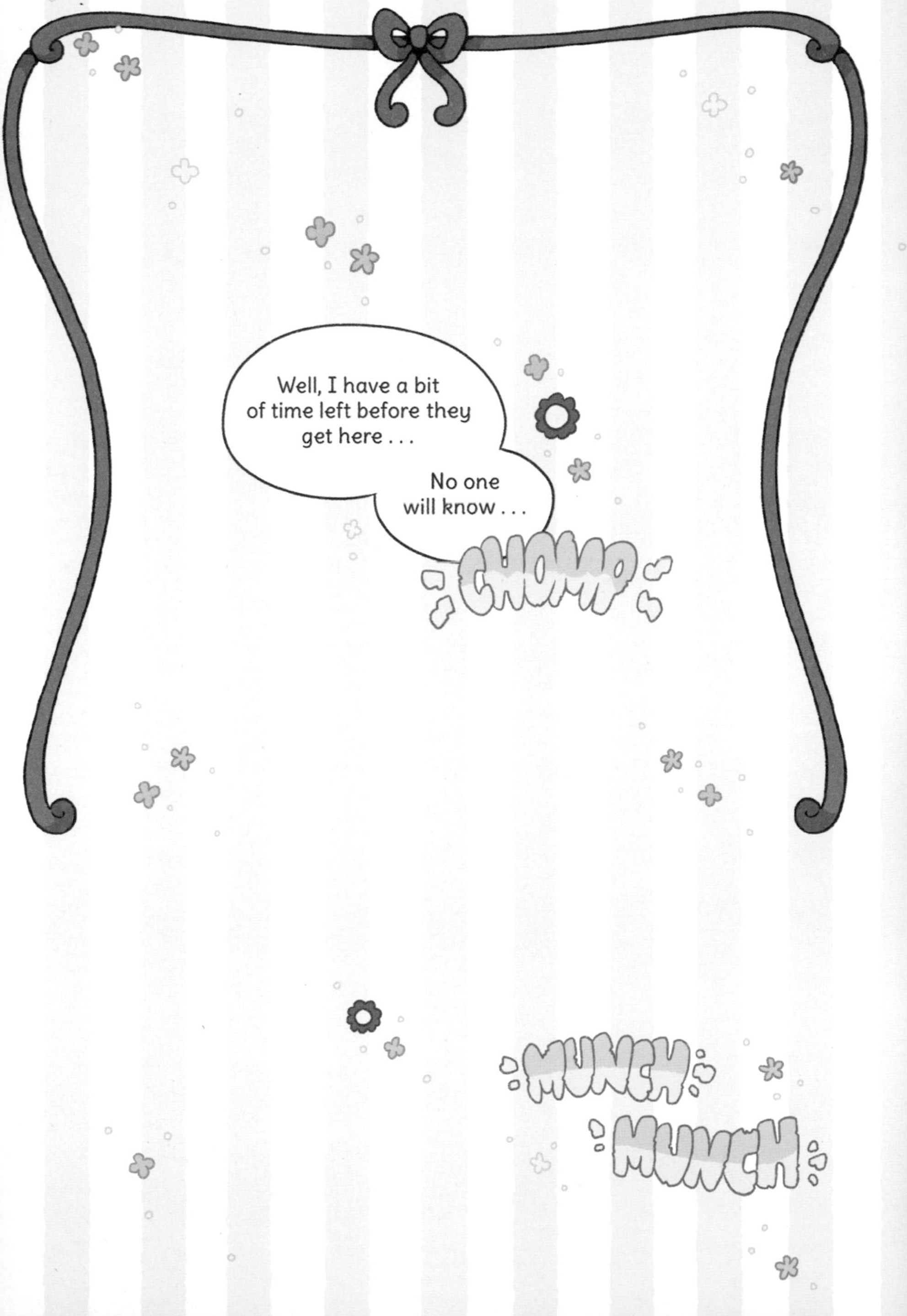
Well, I have a bit of time left before they get here . . .
No one will know . . .
CHOMP
MUNCH
MUNCH

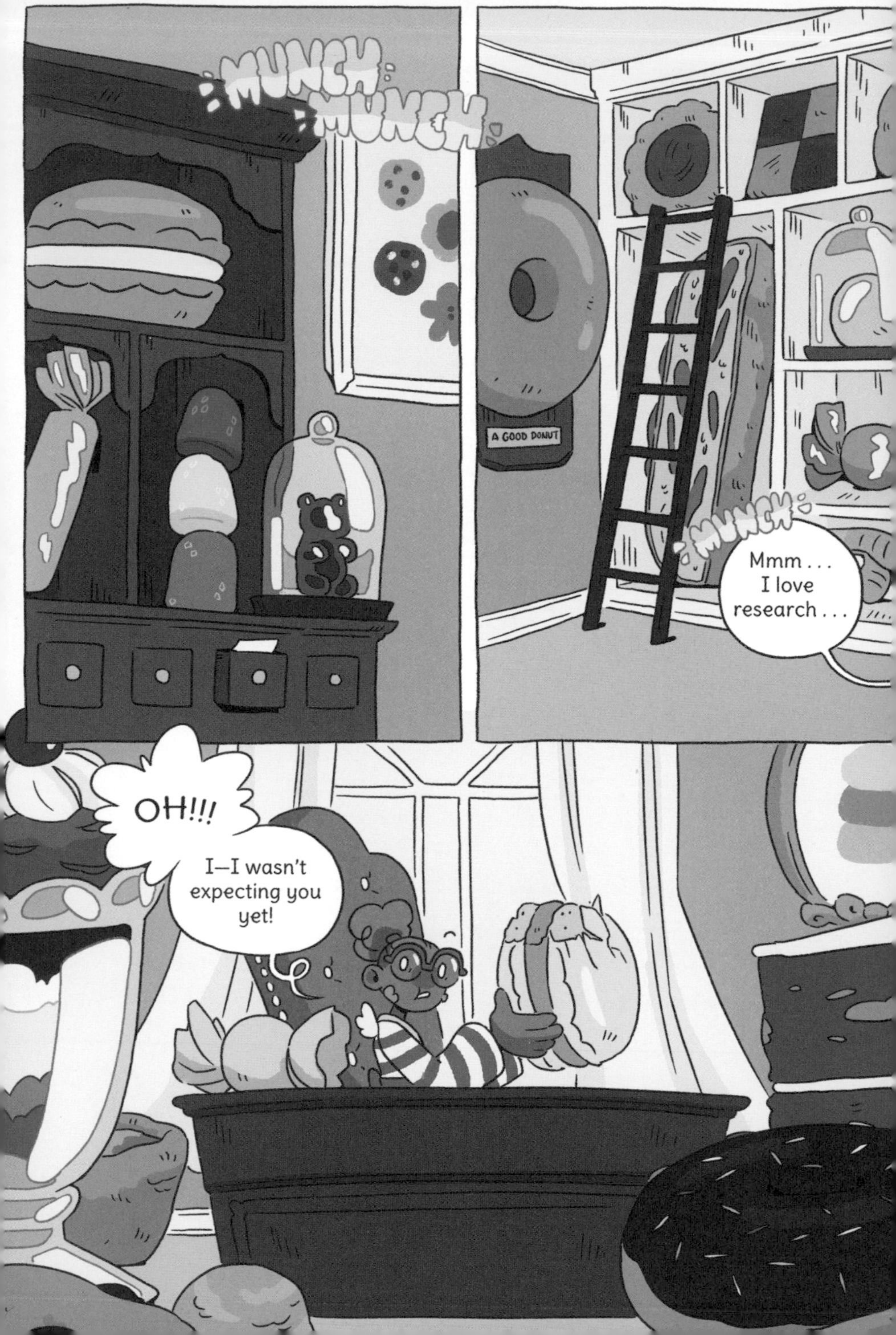
MUNCH
MUNCH
A GOOD DONUT
MUNCH
Mmm . . . I love research . . .
OH!!!
I—I wasn't expecting you yet!

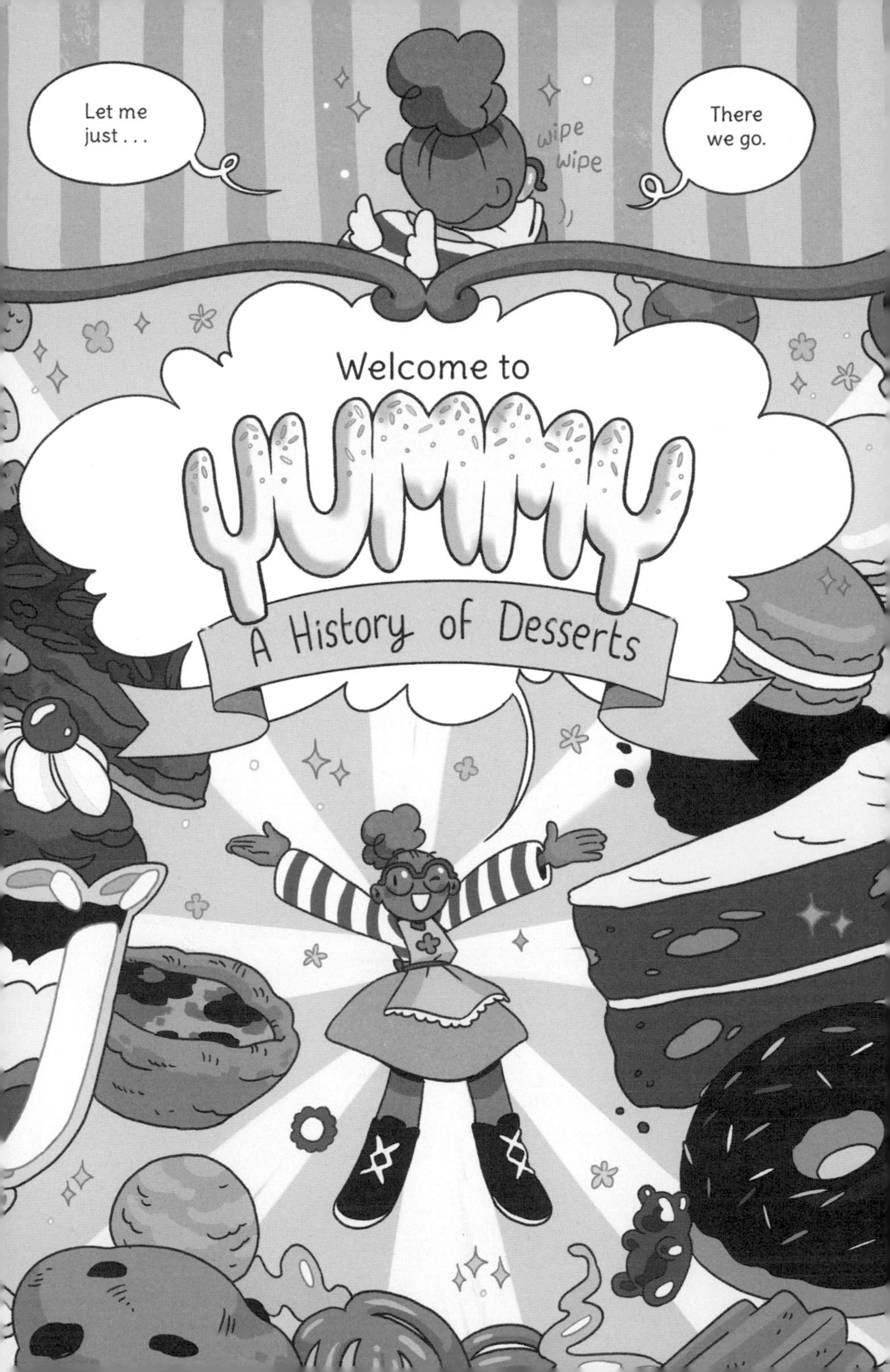
Let me just . . .
wipe wipe
There we go.
Welcome to
YUMMY
A History of Desserts

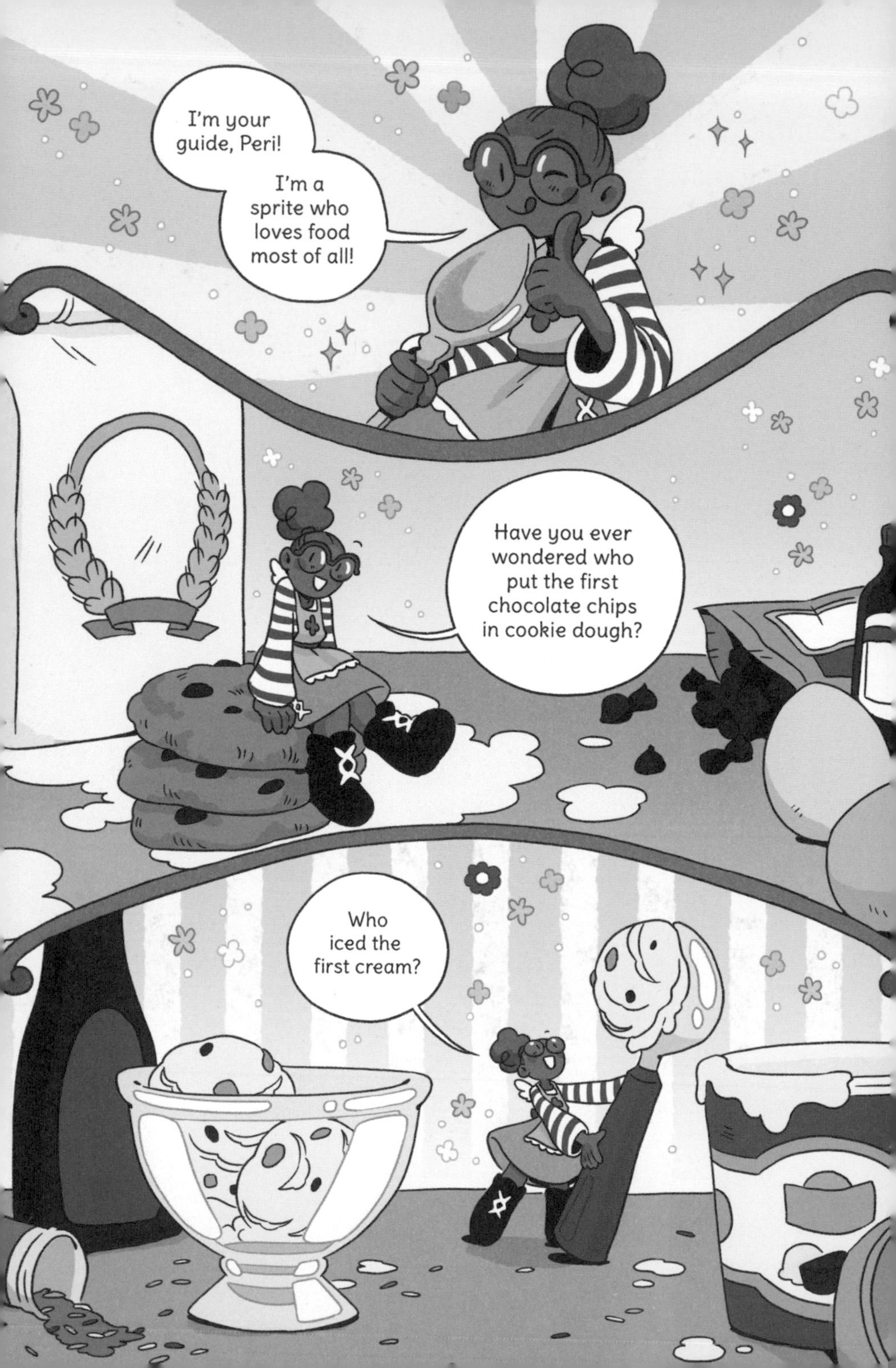
I'm your guide, Peri!
I'm a sprite who loves food most of all!
Have you ever wondered who put the first chocolate chips in cookie dough?
Who iced the first cream?

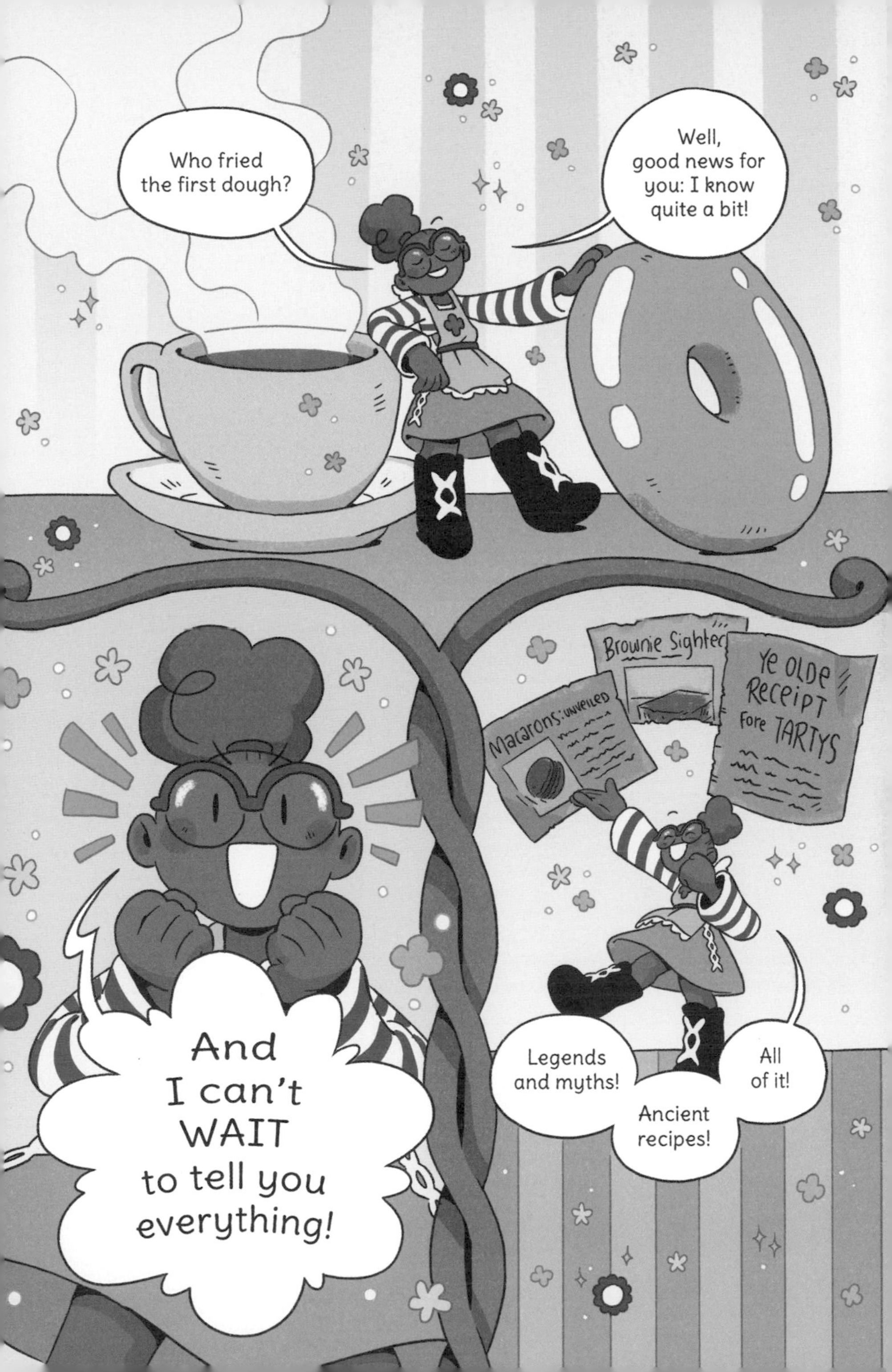
Who fried the first dough?
Well, good news for you: I know quite a bit!
And I can't WAIT to tell you everything!
Brownie Sighted
Macarons: unveiled
Ye Olde Receipt Fore TARTYS
Legends and myths!
Ancient recipes!
All of it!

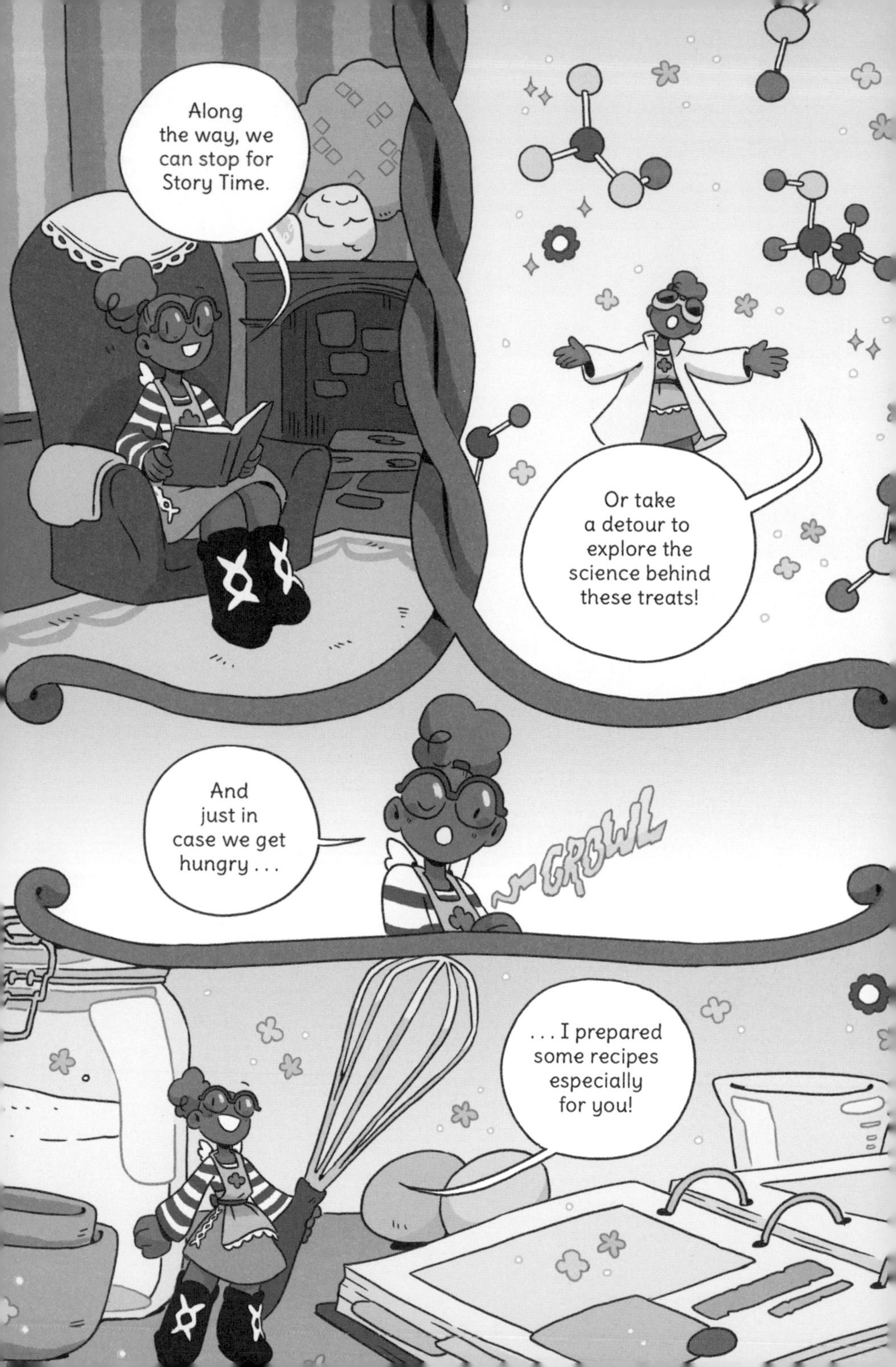

Along the way, we can stop for Story Time.
Or take a detour to explore the science behind these treats!
And just in case we get hungry . . .
GROWL
. . . I prepared some recipes especially for you!

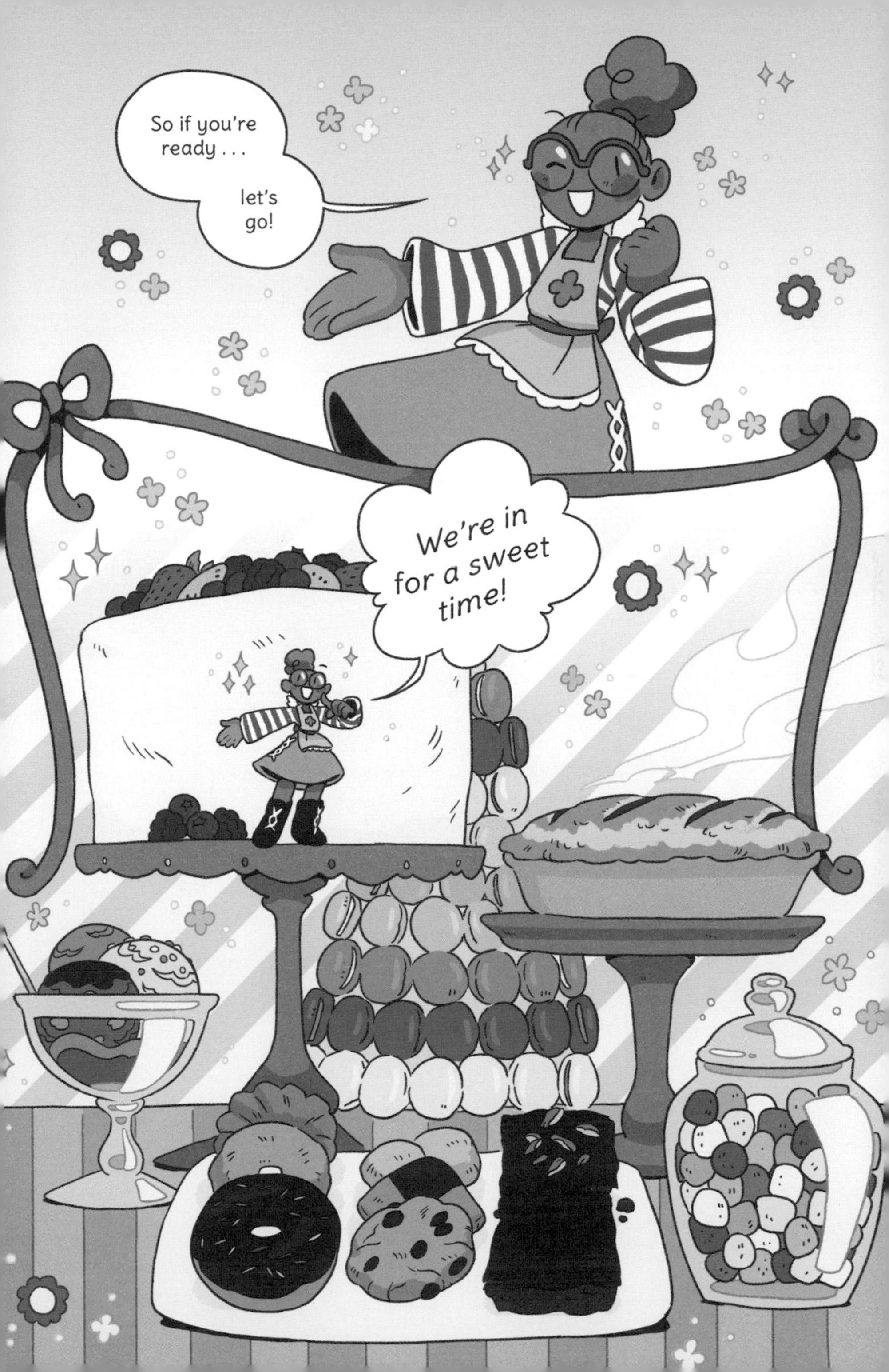
So if you're ready . . .
let's go!
We're in for a sweet time!

# The Abridged
# Atlas of Ice Cream History

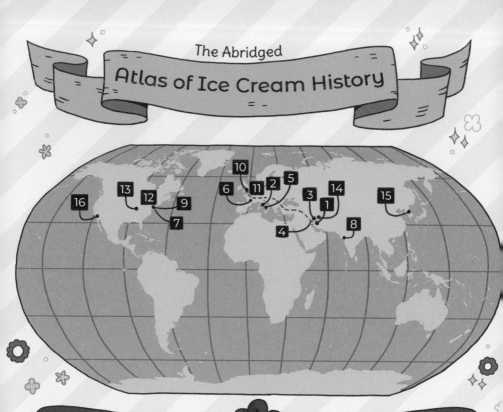

1. Ancient Persian Yakhchāl
2. Roman Emperor Nero's Favorite Iced Treat
3. Ibn Sina's *Canon of Medicine* and Sharbat
4. The Journey from Sharbat to Sorbetto to Sorbet to Sherbet
5. Antonio Latini's *The Modern Steward*
6. Monsieur Emi's *Book of Ices*
7. Eliza Leslie's *Seventy-Five Receipts for Pastry, Cakes and Sweetmeats*
8. Salt and Ice Freezing Technique
9. Nancy Johnson's Ice Cream Maker
10. Thomas Masters's Ice Cream Maker
11. Ice Cream Cart Vendors
12. American Ice Cream Sundae
13. St. Louis World's Fair Waffle Cone
14. Iranian Bastani Sonnati
15. Korean Bingsu
16. Japanese American Mochi Ice Cream

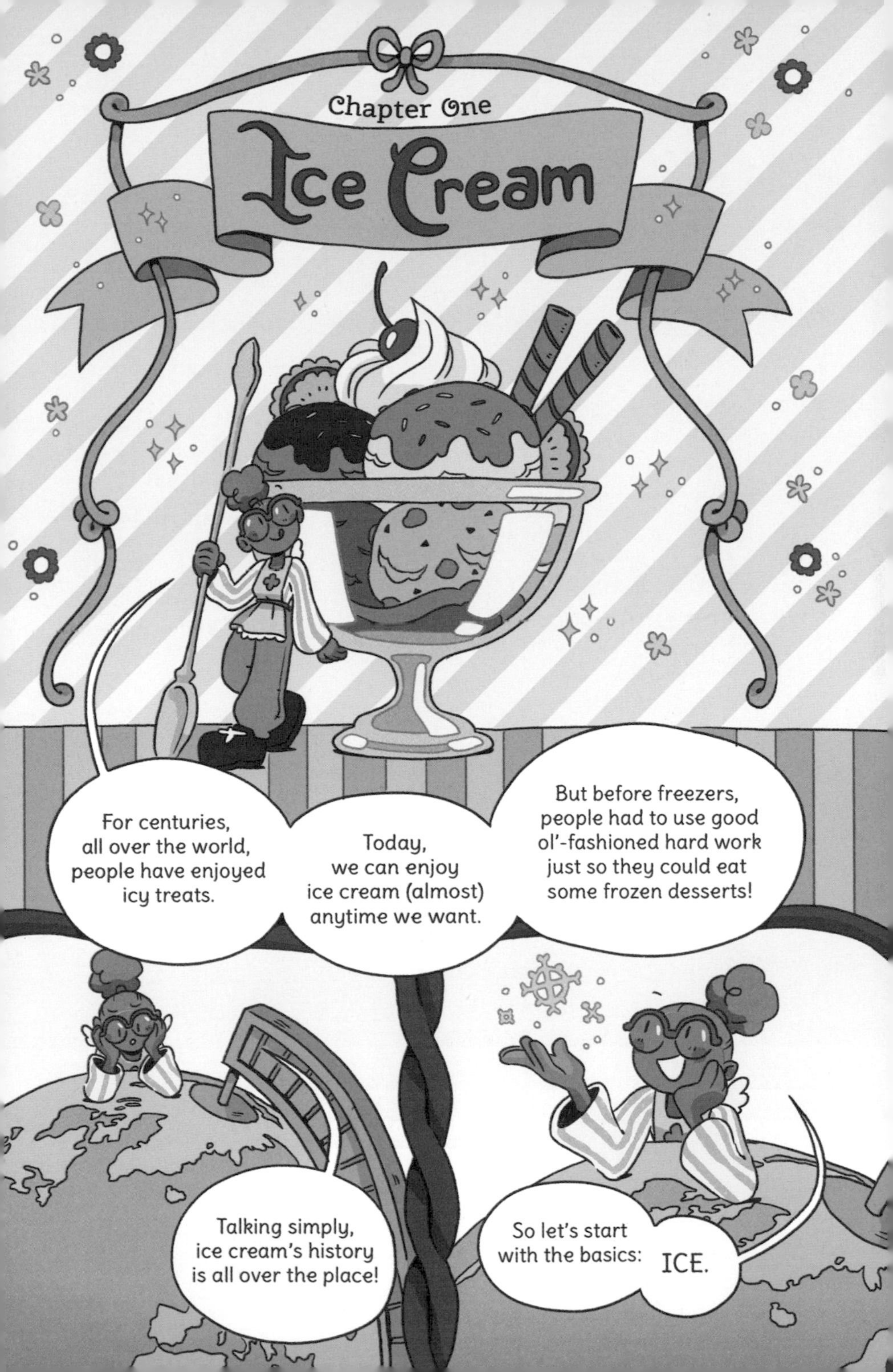
Chapter One
Ice Cream
For centuries, all over the world, people have enjoyed icy treats.
Today, we can enjoy ice cream (almost) anytime we want.
But before freezers, people had to use good ol'-fashioned hard work just so they could eat some frozen desserts!
Talking simply, ice cream's history is all over the place!
So let's start with the basics:
ICE.

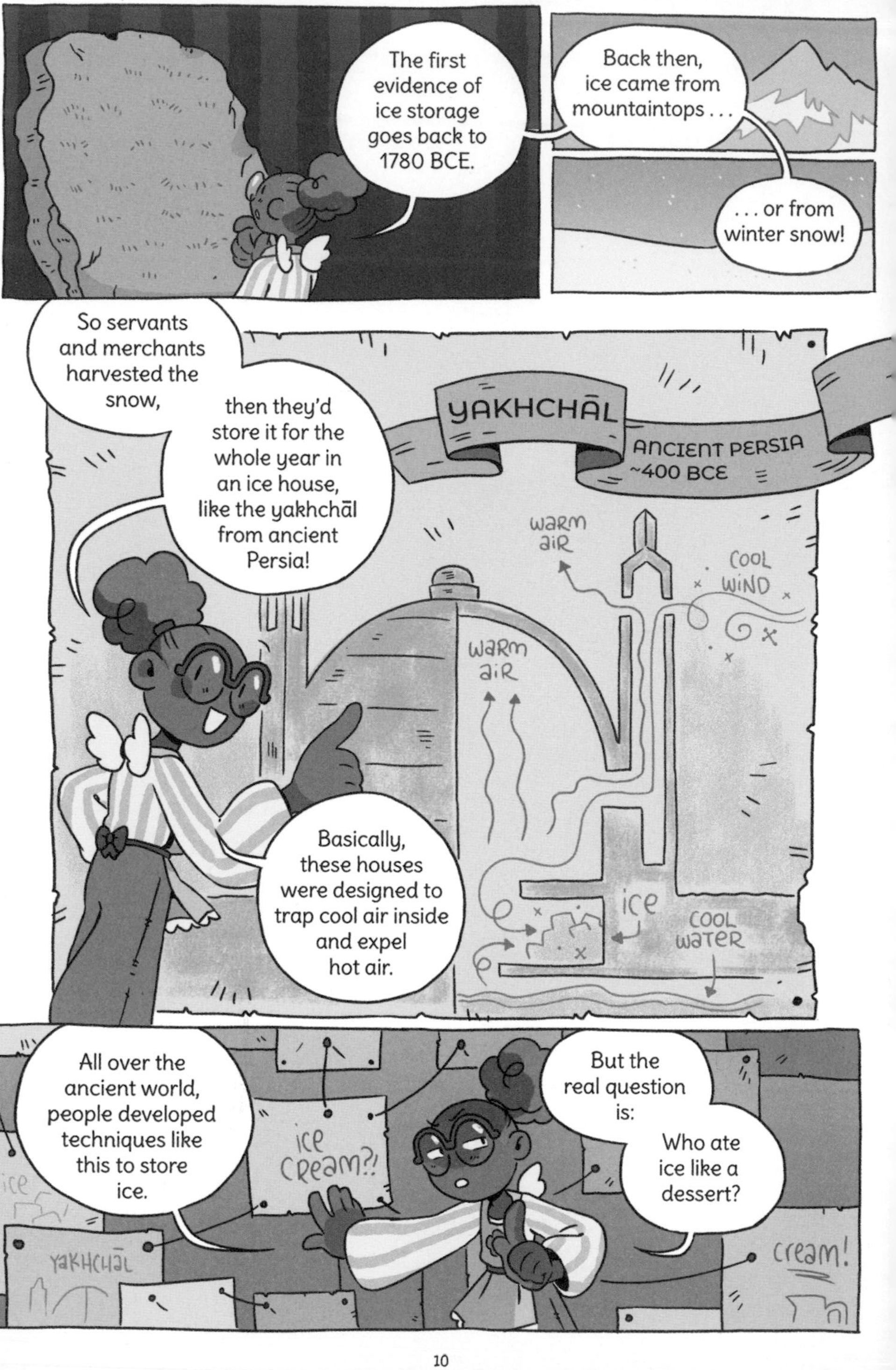
The first evidence of ice storage goes back to 1780 BCE.
Back then, ice came from mountaintops . . .
. . . or from winter snow!
So servants and merchants harvested the snow,
then they'd store it for the whole year in an ice house, like the yakhchāl from ancient Persia!
YAKHCHĀL
ANCIENT PERSIA ~400 BCE
warm air
cool wind
warm air
ice
cool water
Basically, these houses were designed to trap cool air inside and expel hot air.
All over the ancient world, people developed techniques like this to store ice.
ice cream?!
yakhchāl
ice
But the real question is:
Who ate ice like a dessert?
cream!

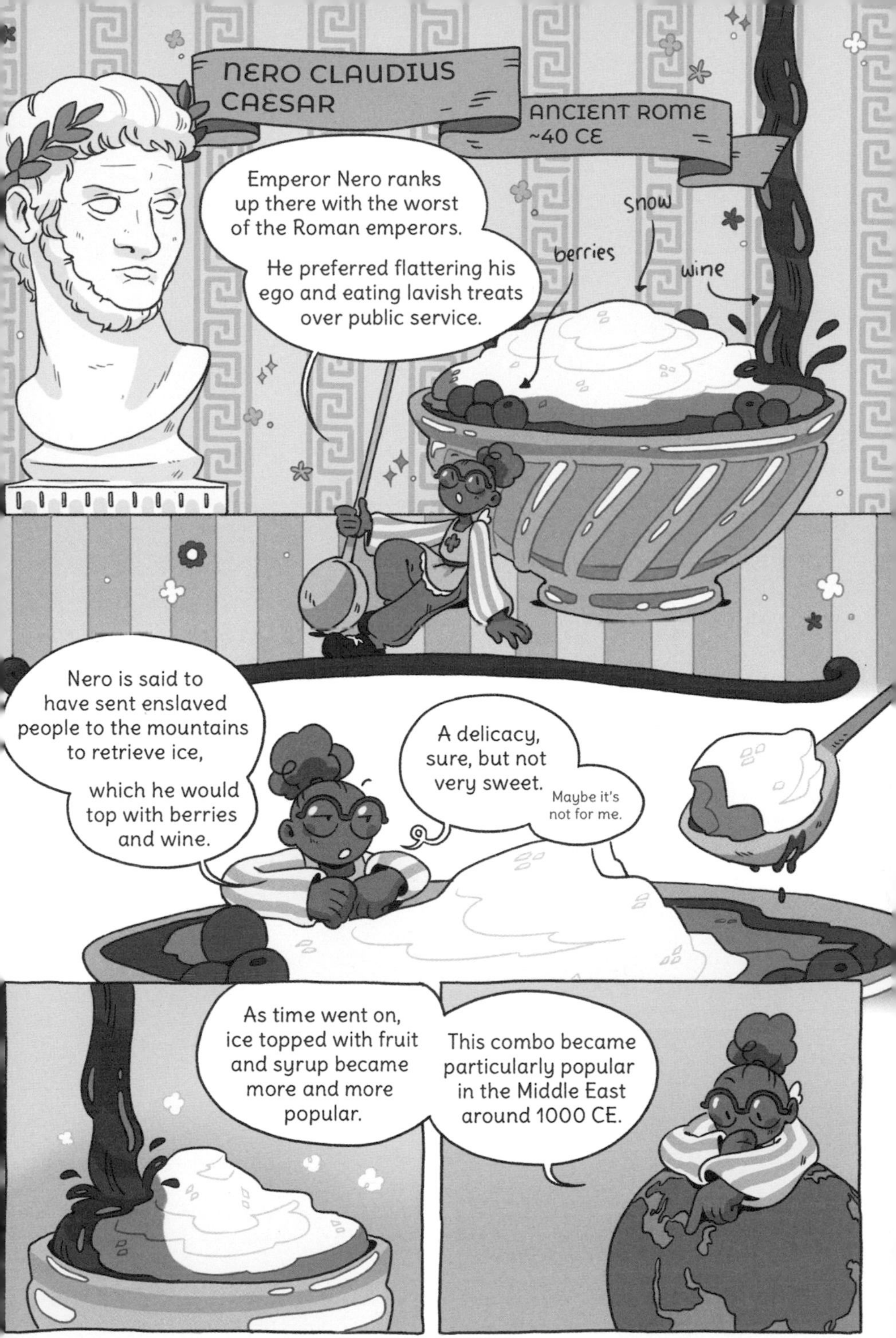
NERO CLAUDIUS CAESAR
ANCIENT ROME ~40 CE
Emperor Nero ranks up there with the worst of the Roman emperors.
He preferred flattering his ego and eating lavish treats over public service.
snow
berries
wine
Nero is said to have sent enslaved people to the mountains to retrieve ice,
which he would top with berries and wine.
A delicacy, sure, but not very sweet.
Maybe it's not for me.
As time went on, ice topped with fruit and syrup became more and more popular.
This combo became particularly popular in the Middle East around 1000 CE.

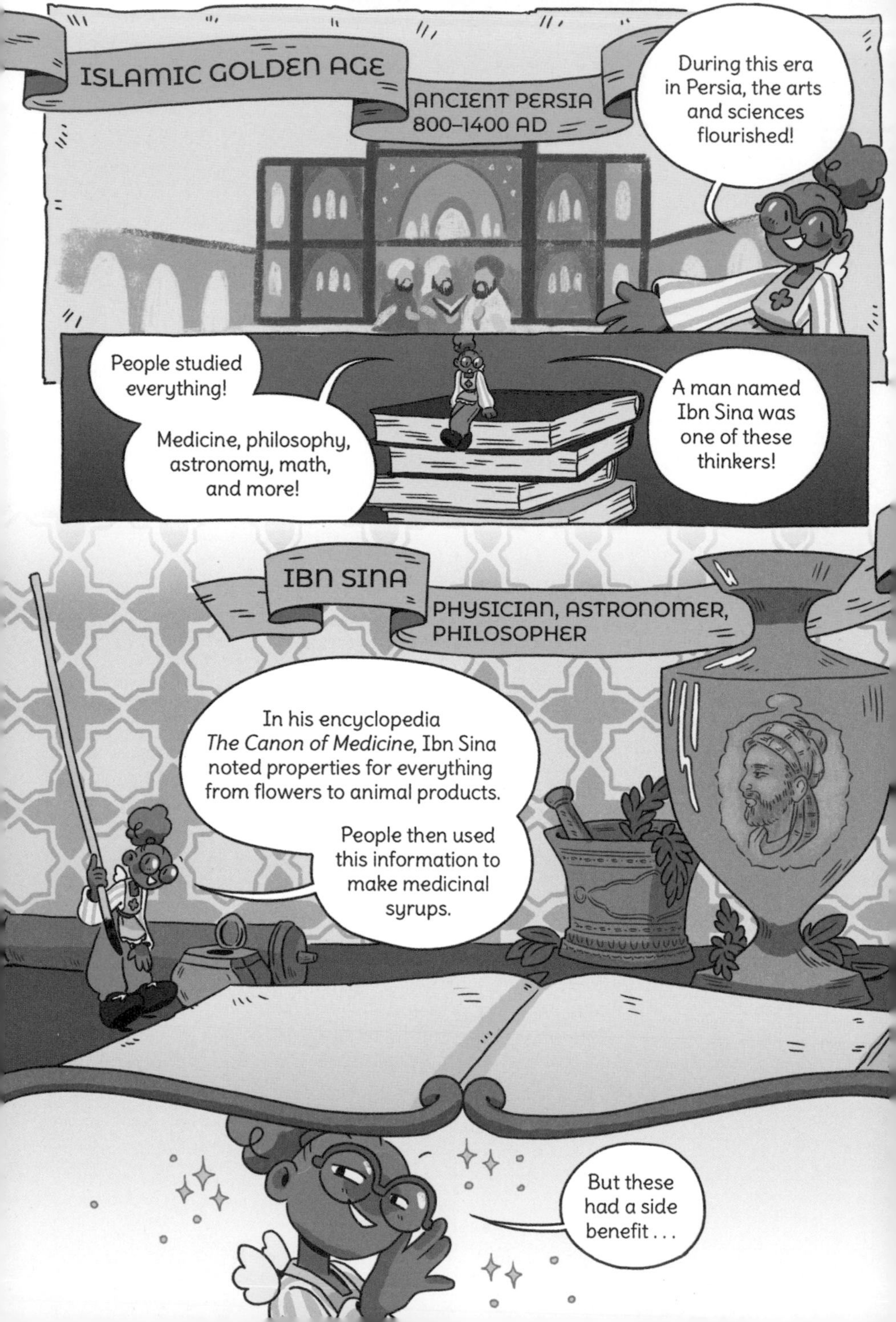
ISLAMIC GOLDEN AGE
ANCIENT PERSIA 800–1400 AD
During this era in Persia, the arts and sciences flourished!
People studied everything!
Medicine, philosophy, astronomy, math, and more!
A man named Ibn Sina was one of these thinkers!
IBN SINA
PHYSICIAN, ASTRONOMER, PHILOSOPHER
In his encyclopedia *The Canon of Medicine*, Ibn Sina noted properties for everything from flowers to animal products.
People then used this information to make medicinal syrups.
But these had a side benefit . . .

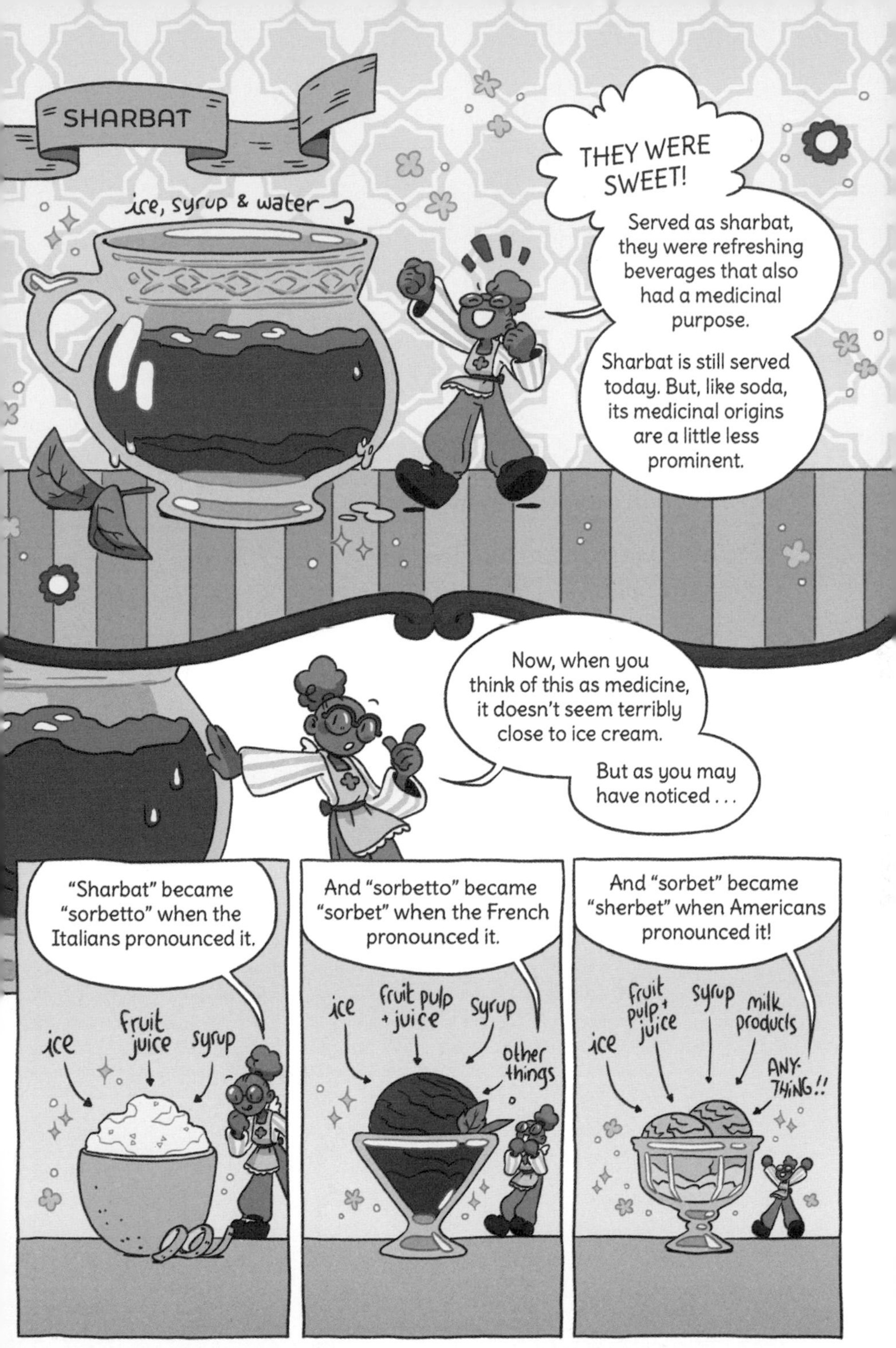

SHARBAT
ice, syrup & water
THEY WERE SWEET!
Served as sharbat, they were refreshing beverages that also had a medicinal purpose.
Sharbat is still served today. But, like soda, its medicinal origins are a little less prominent.
Now, when you think of this as medicine, it doesn't seem terribly close to ice cream.
But as you may have noticed . . .
"Sharbat" became "sorbetto" when the Italians pronounced it.
ice
fruit juice
syrup
And "sorbetto" became "sorbet" when the French pronounced it.
ice
fruit pulp + juice
syrup
other things
And "sorbet" became "sherbet" when Americans pronounced it!
ice
fruit pulp + juice
syrup
milk products
ANY-THING!!

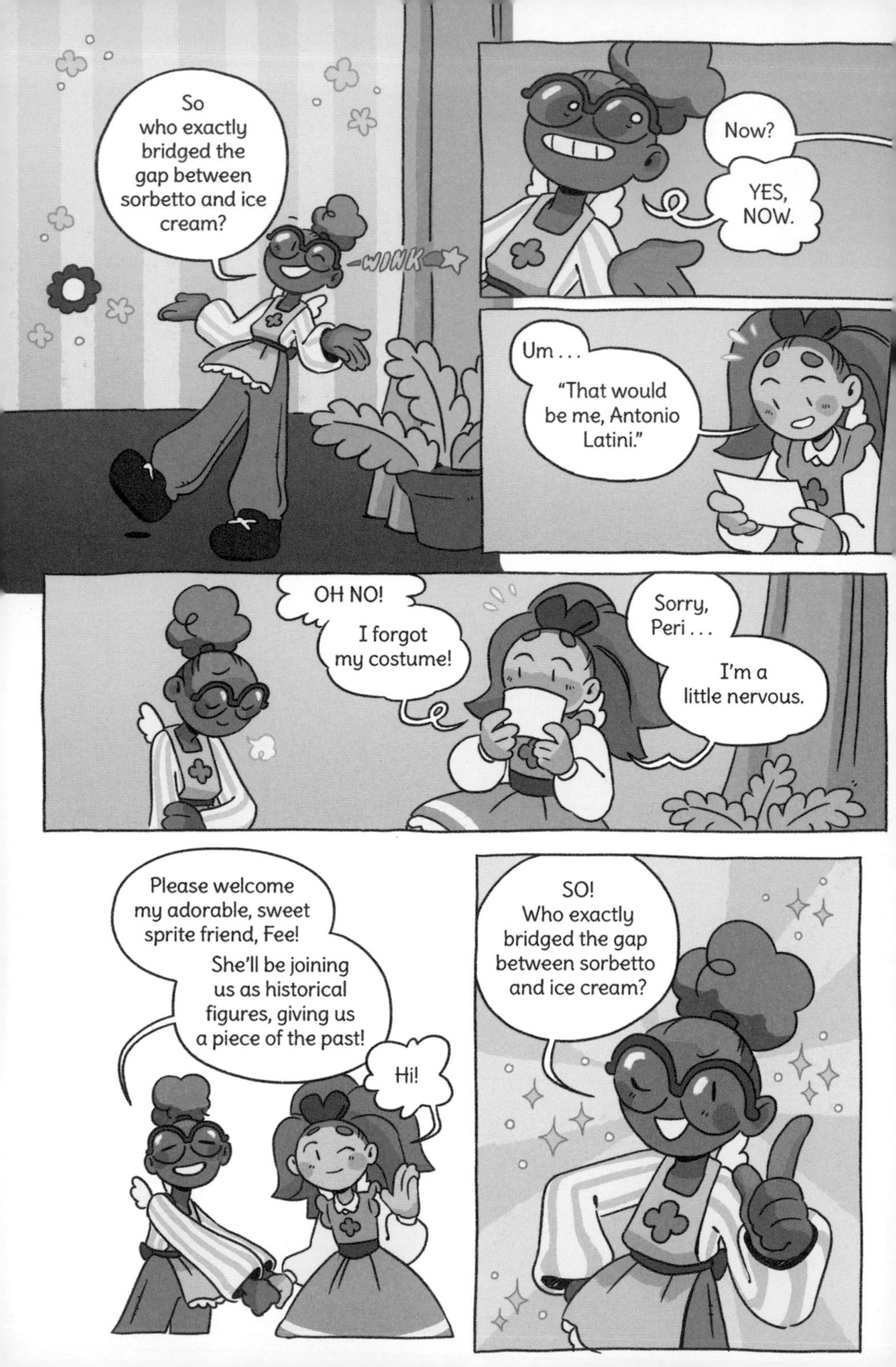
So who exactly bridged the gap between sorbetto and ice cream?
WINK
Now?
YES, NOW.
Um . . .
"That would be me, Antonio Latini."
OH NO!
I forgot my costume!
Sorry, Peri . . .
I'm a little nervous.
Please welcome my adorable, sweet sprite friend, Fee!
She'll be joining us as historical figures, giving us a piece of the past!
Hi!
SO! Who exactly bridged the gap between sorbetto and ice cream?

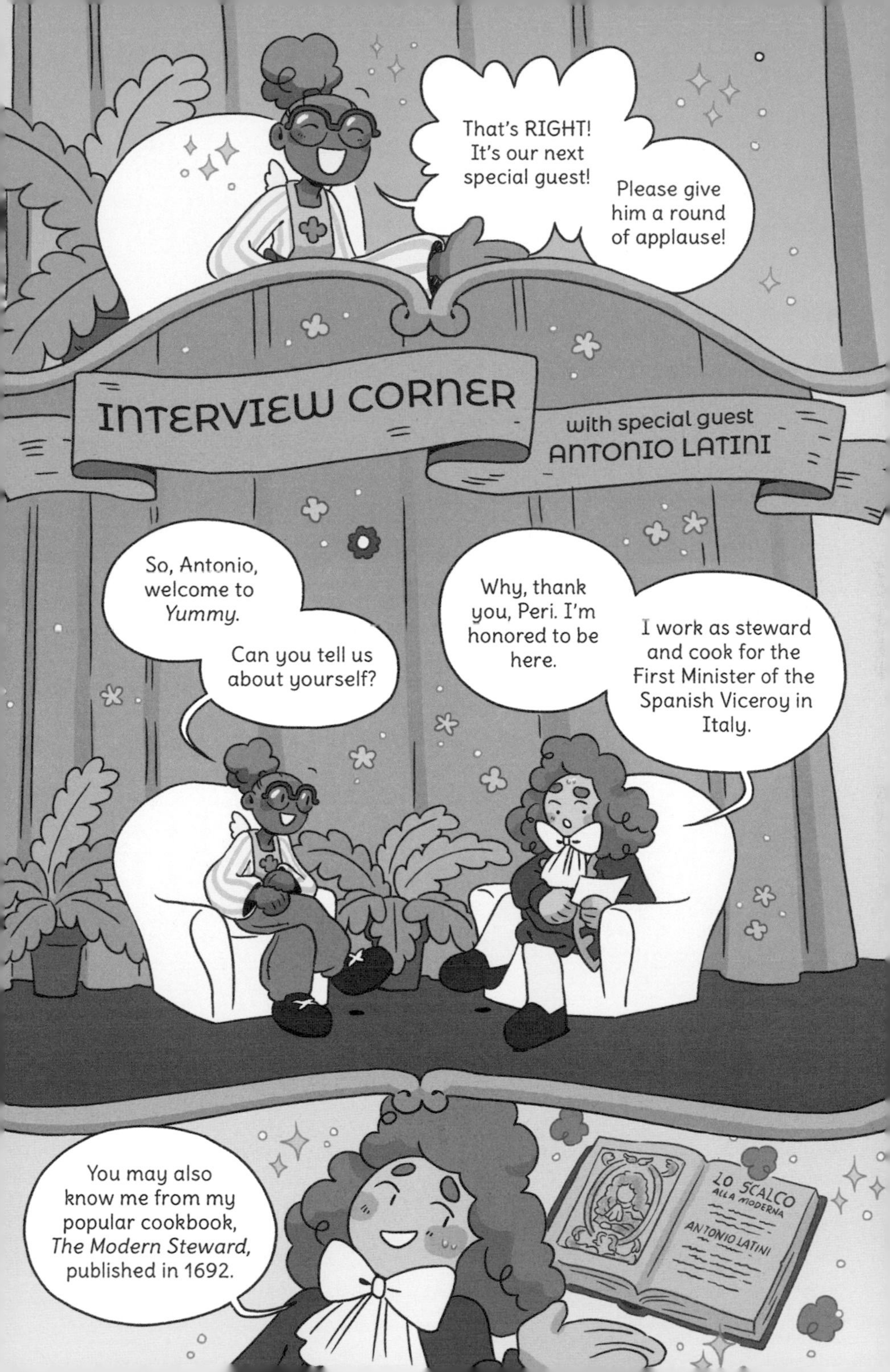
That's RIGHT! It's our next special guest!
Please give him a round of applause!
INTERVIEW CORNER
with special guest ANTONIO LATINI
So, Antonio, welcome to *Yummy*.
Can you tell us about yourself?
Why, thank you, Peri. I'm honored to be here.
I work as steward and cook for the First Minister of the Spanish Viceroy in Italy.
You may also know me from my popular cookbook, *The Modern Steward*, published in 1692.
LO SCALCO ALLA MODERNA
ANTONIO LATINI

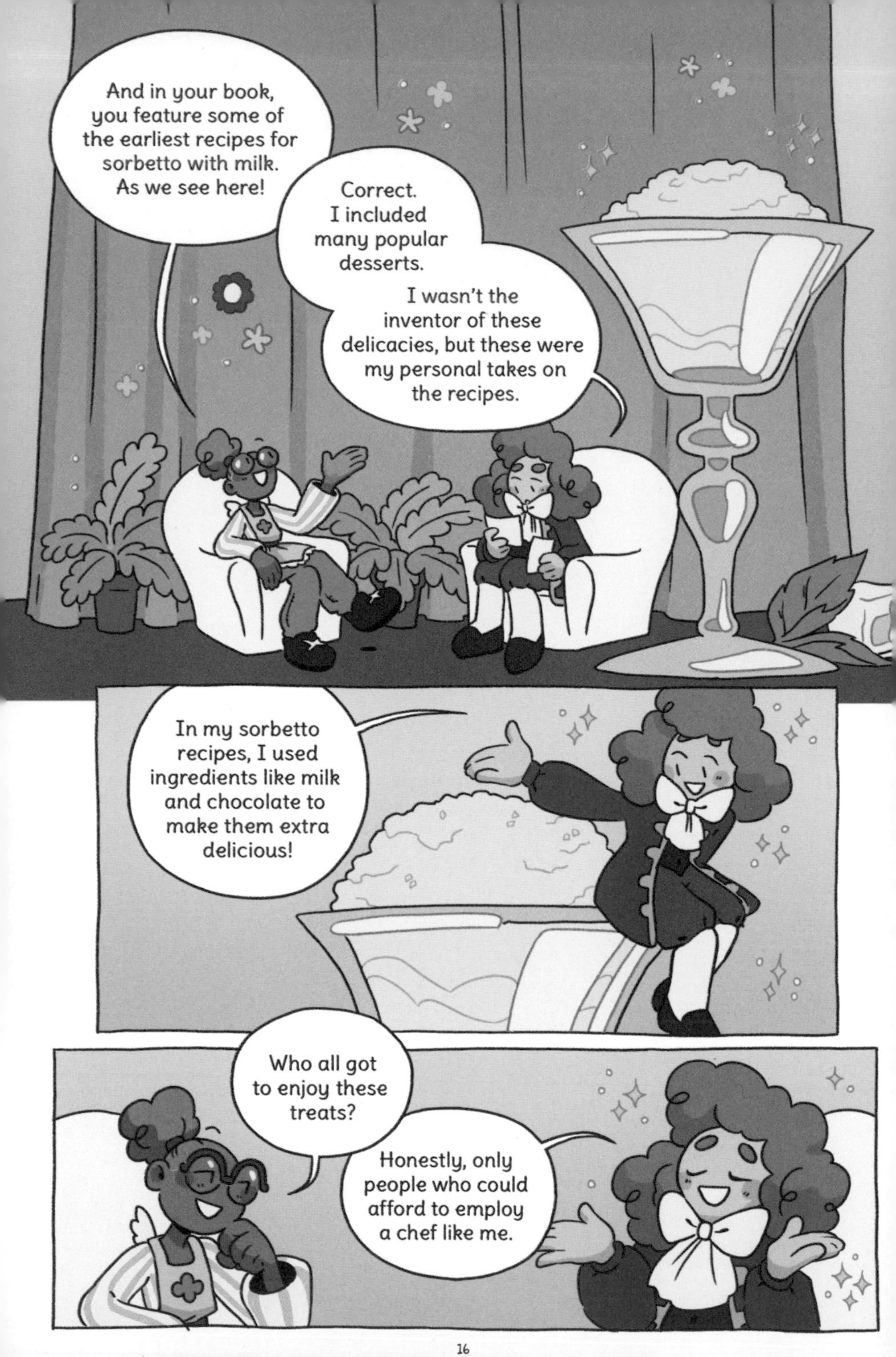
And in your book, you feature some of the earliest recipes for sorbetto with milk. As we see here!
Correct. I included many popular desserts.
I wasn't the inventor of these delicacies, but these were my personal takes on the recipes.
In my sorbetto recipes, I used ingredients like milk and chocolate to make them extra delicious!
Who all got to enjoy these treats?
Honestly, only people who could afford to employ a chef like me.

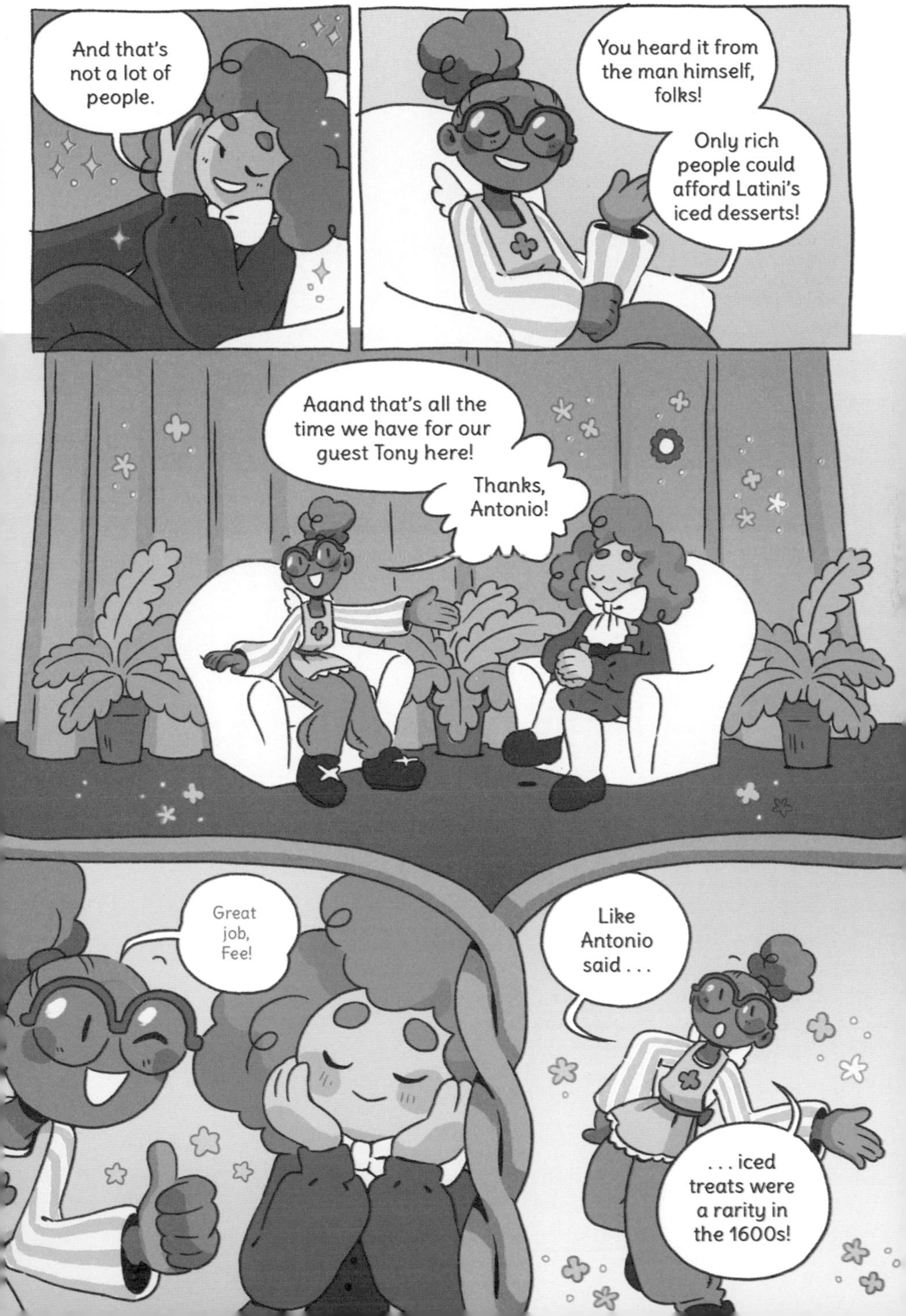
And that's not a lot of people.
You heard it from the man himself, folks!
Only rich people could afford Latini's iced desserts!
Aaand that's all the time we have for our guest Tony here!
Thanks, Antonio!
Great job, Fee!
Like Antonio said . . .
. . . iced treats were a rarity in the 1600s!

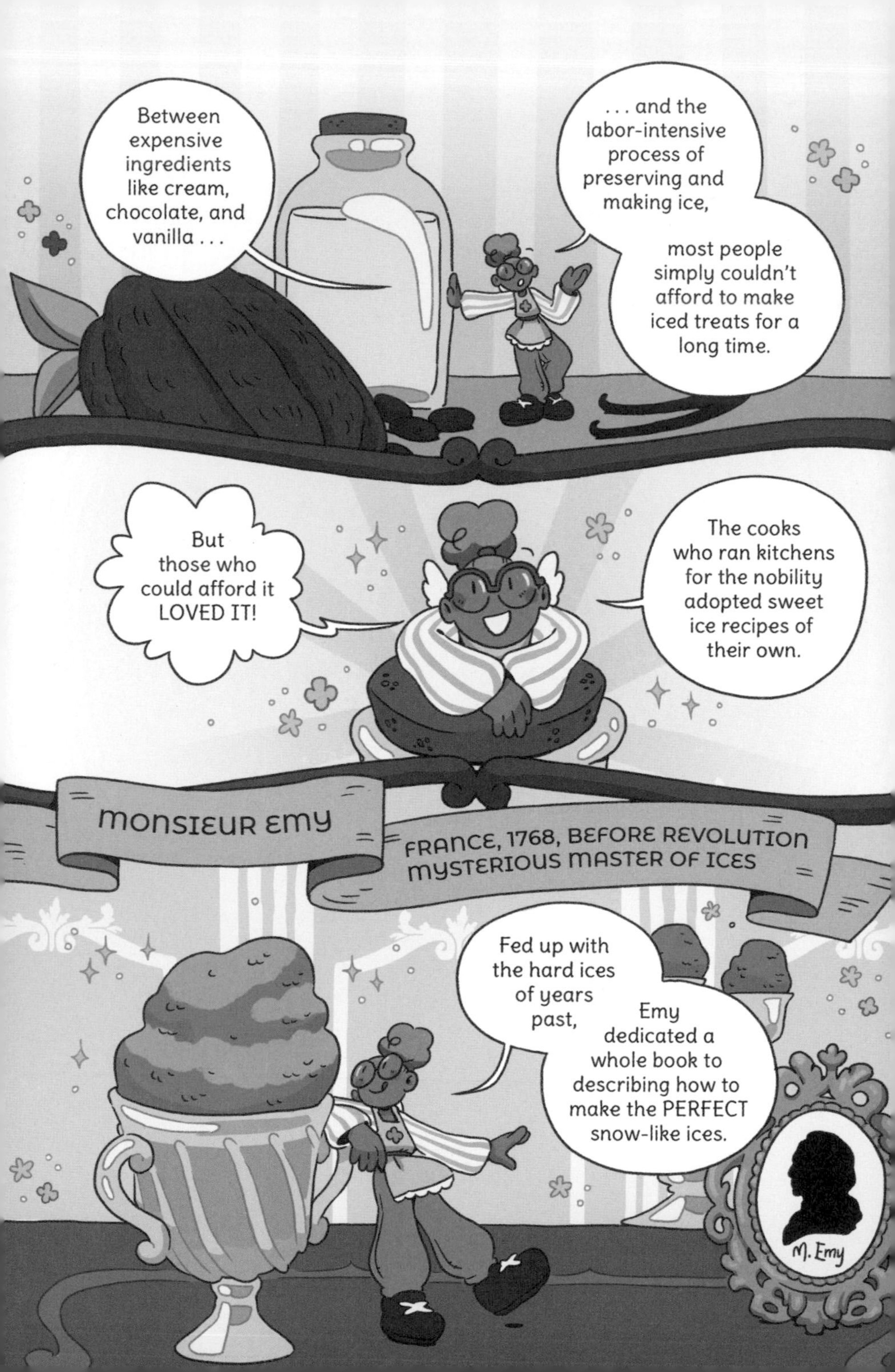

Between expensive ingredients like cream, chocolate, and vanilla . . .
. . . and the labor-intensive process of preserving and making ice,
most people simply couldn't afford to make iced treats for a long time.
But those who could afford it LOVED IT!
The cooks who ran kitchens for the nobility adopted sweet ice recipes of their own.
MONSIEUR EMY
FRANCE, 1768, BEFORE REVOLUTION
MYSTERIOUS MASTER OF ICES
Fed up with the hard ices of years past,
Emy dedicated a whole book to describing how to make the PERFECT snow-like ices.
M. Emy

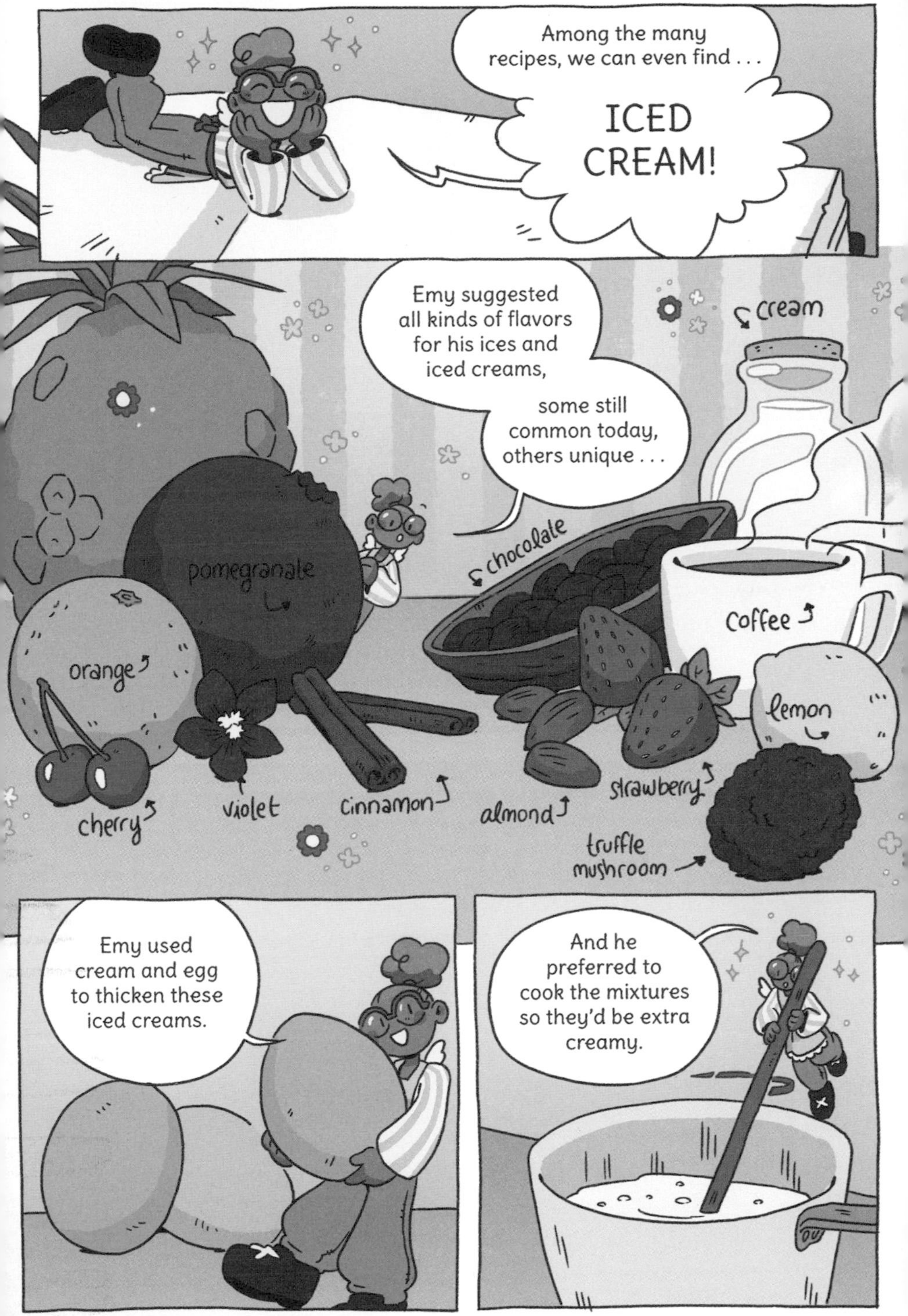

Among the many recipes, we can even find . . .
ICED CREAM!
Emy suggested all kinds of flavors for his ices and iced creams,
some still common today, others unique . . .
cream
chocolate
pomegranate
coffee
orange
lemon
strawberry
violet
cinnamon
almond
cherry
truffle mushroom
Emy used cream and egg to thicken these iced creams.
And he preferred to cook the mixtures so they'd be extra creamy.

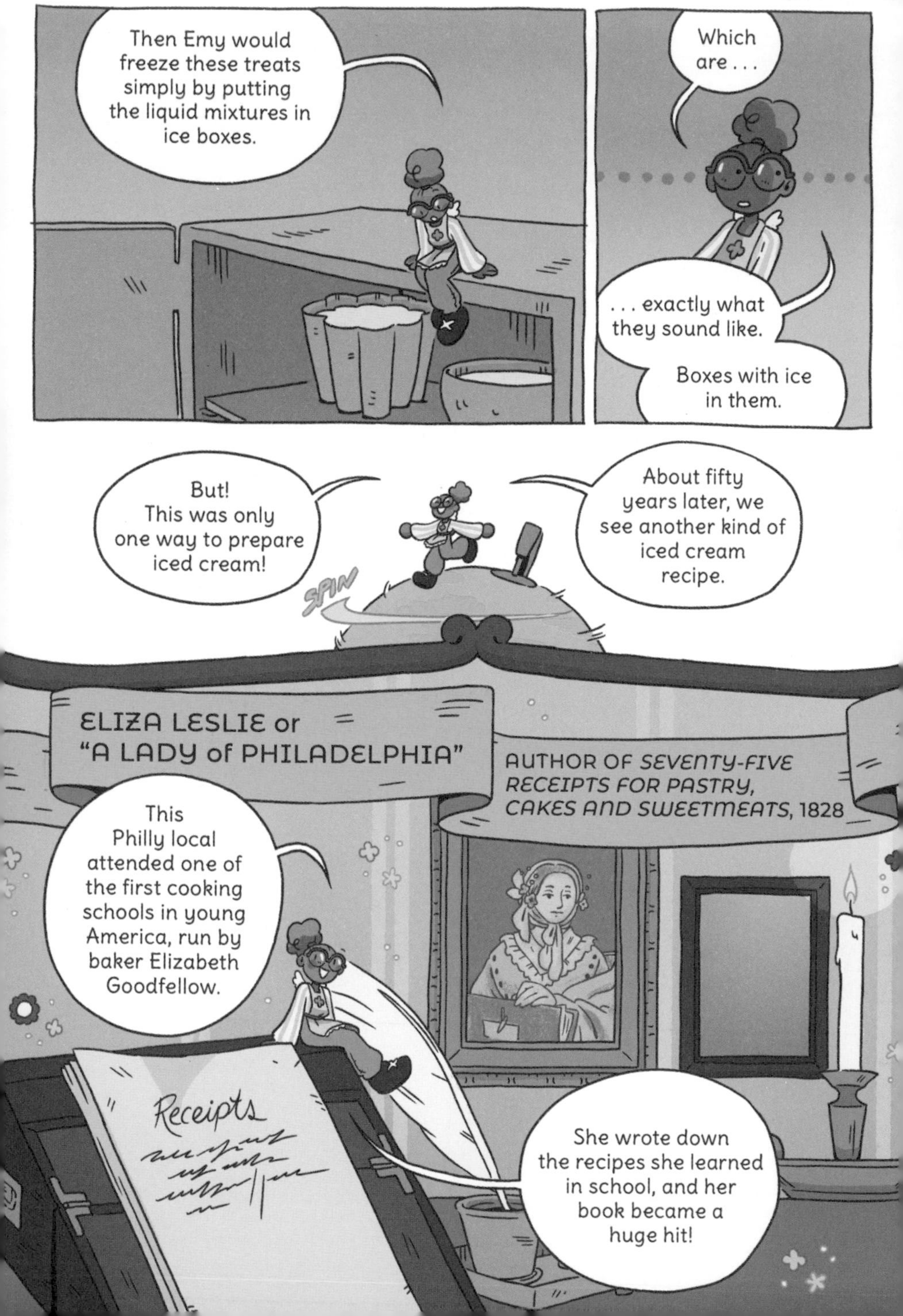
Then Emy would freeze these treats simply by putting the liquid mixtures in ice boxes.
Which are . . .
. . . exactly what they sound like.
Boxes with ice in them.
But! This was only one way to prepare iced cream!
SPIN
About fifty years later, we see another kind of iced cream recipe.
ELIZA LESLIE or "A LADY of PHILADELPHIA"
AUTHOR OF SEVENTY-FIVE RECEIPTS FOR PASTRY, CAKES AND SWEETMEATS, 1828
This Philly local attended one of the first cooking schools in young America, run by baker Elizabeth Goodfellow.
Receipts
She wrote down the recipes she learned in school, and her book became a huge hit!

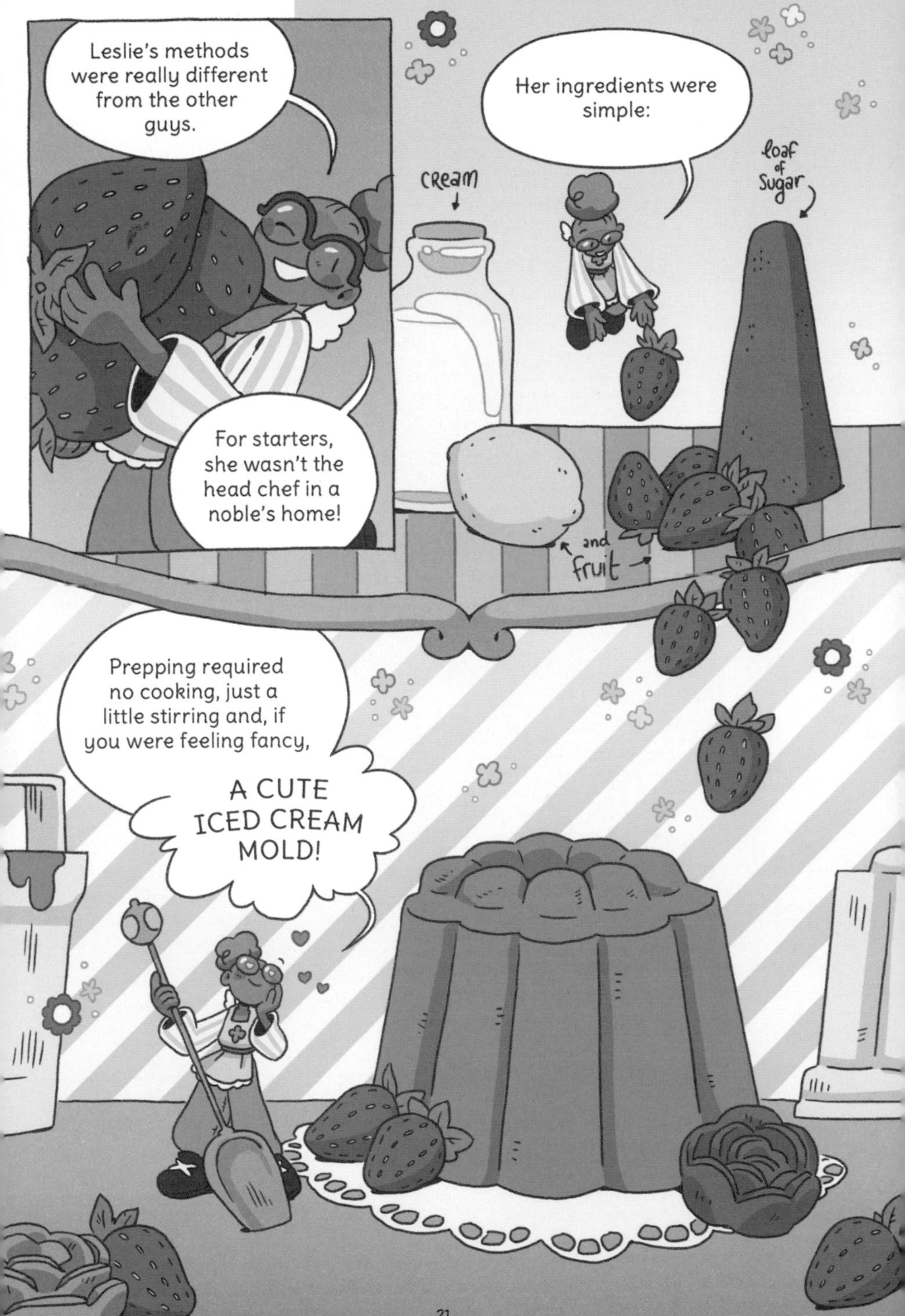

Leslie's methods were really different from the other guys.
For starters, she wasn't the head chef in a noble's home!
Her ingredients were simple:
cream
loaf of sugar
and fruit
Prepping required no cooking, just a little stirring and, if you were feeling fancy,
A CUTE ICED CREAM MOLD!

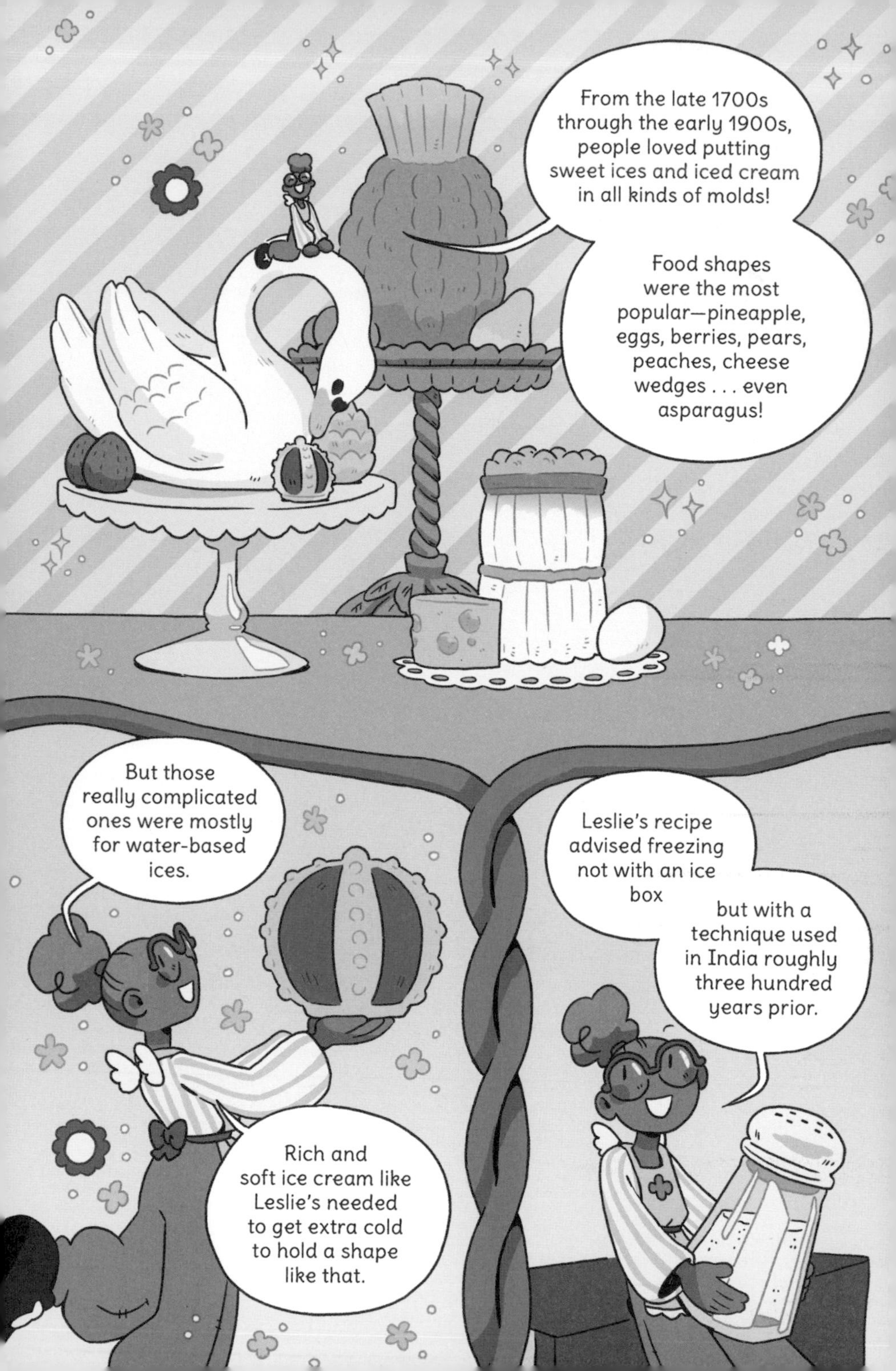
From the late 1700s through the early 1900s, people loved putting sweet ices and iced cream in all kinds of molds!
Food shapes were the most popular—pineapple, eggs, berries, pears, peaches, cheese wedges . . . even asparagus!
But those really complicated ones were mostly for water-based ices.
Rich and soft ice cream like Leslie's needed to get extra cold to hold a shape like that.
Leslie's recipe advised freezing not with an ice box
but with a technique used in India roughly three hundred years prior.

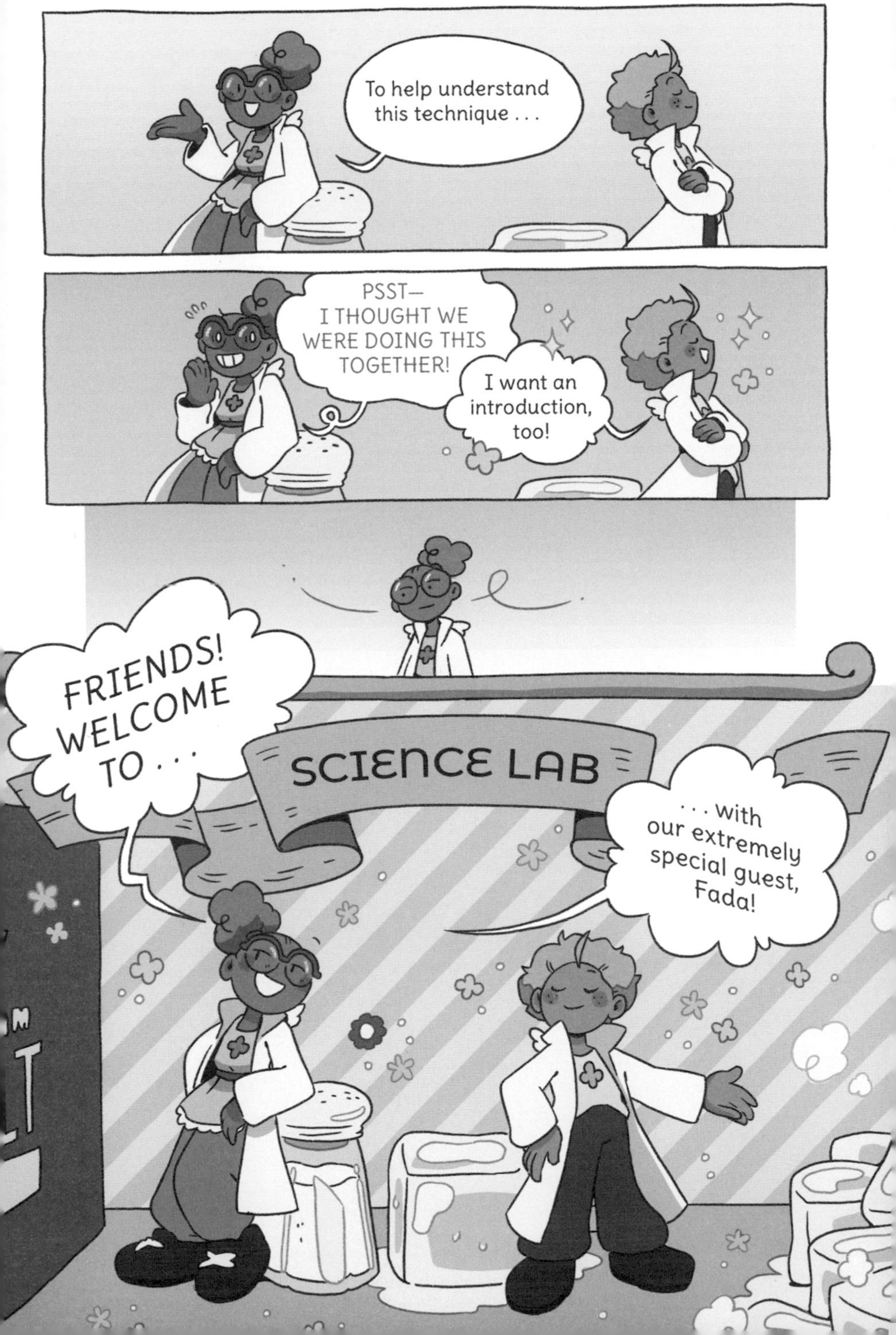

To help understand this technique . . .
PSST— I THOUGHT WE WERE DOING THIS TOGETHER!
I want an introduction, too!
FRIENDS! WELCOME TO . . .
SCIENCE LAB
. . . with our extremely special guest, Fada!

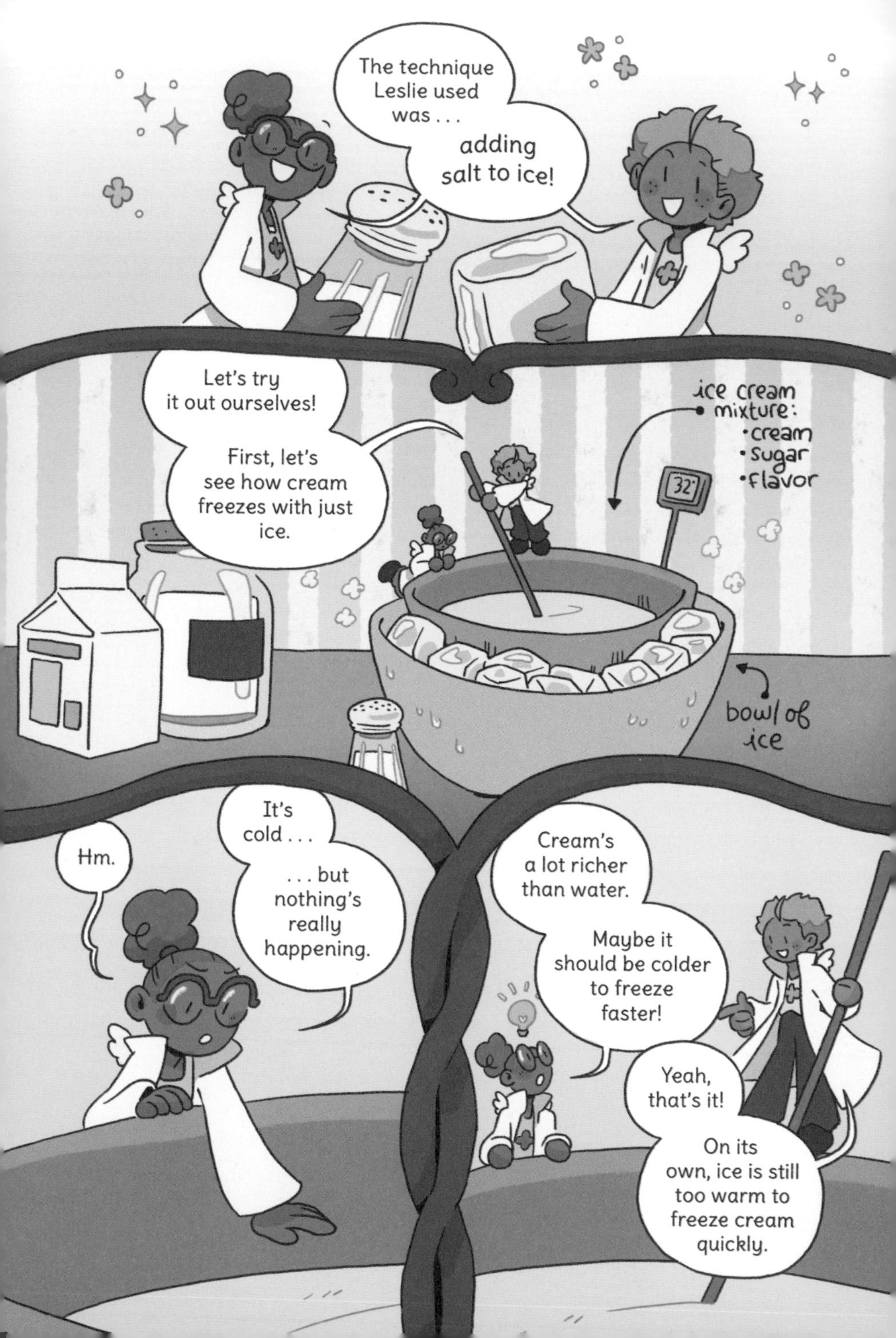

The technique Leslie used was . . .
adding salt to ice!
Let's try it out ourselves!
First, let's see how cream freezes with just ice.
ice cream mixture:
•cream
•sugar
•flavor
32°
bowl of ice
Hm.
It's cold . . .
. . . but nothing's really happening.
Cream's a lot richer than water.
Maybe it should be colder to freeze faster!
Yeah, that's it!
On its own, ice is still too warm to freeze cream quickly.

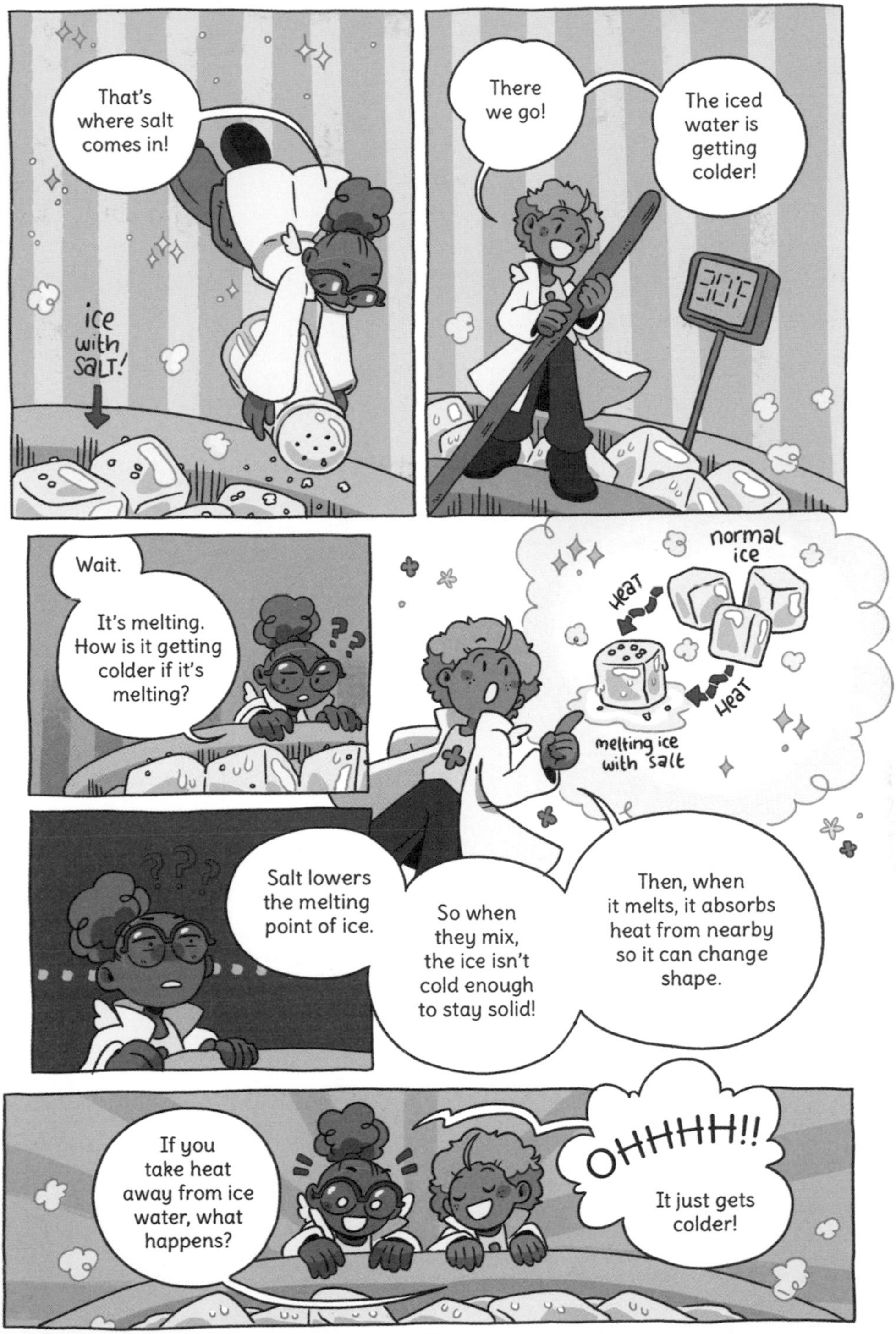
That's where salt comes in!
ice with SALT!
There we go!
The iced water is getting colder!
30°F
Wait.
It's melting. How is it getting colder if it's melting?
normal ice
HEAT
HEAT
melting ice with salt
Salt lowers the melting point of ice.
So when they mix, the ice isn't cold enough to stay solid!
Then, when it melts, it absorbs heat from nearby so it can change shape.
If you take heat away from ice water, what happens?
OHHHHH!!
It just gets colder!

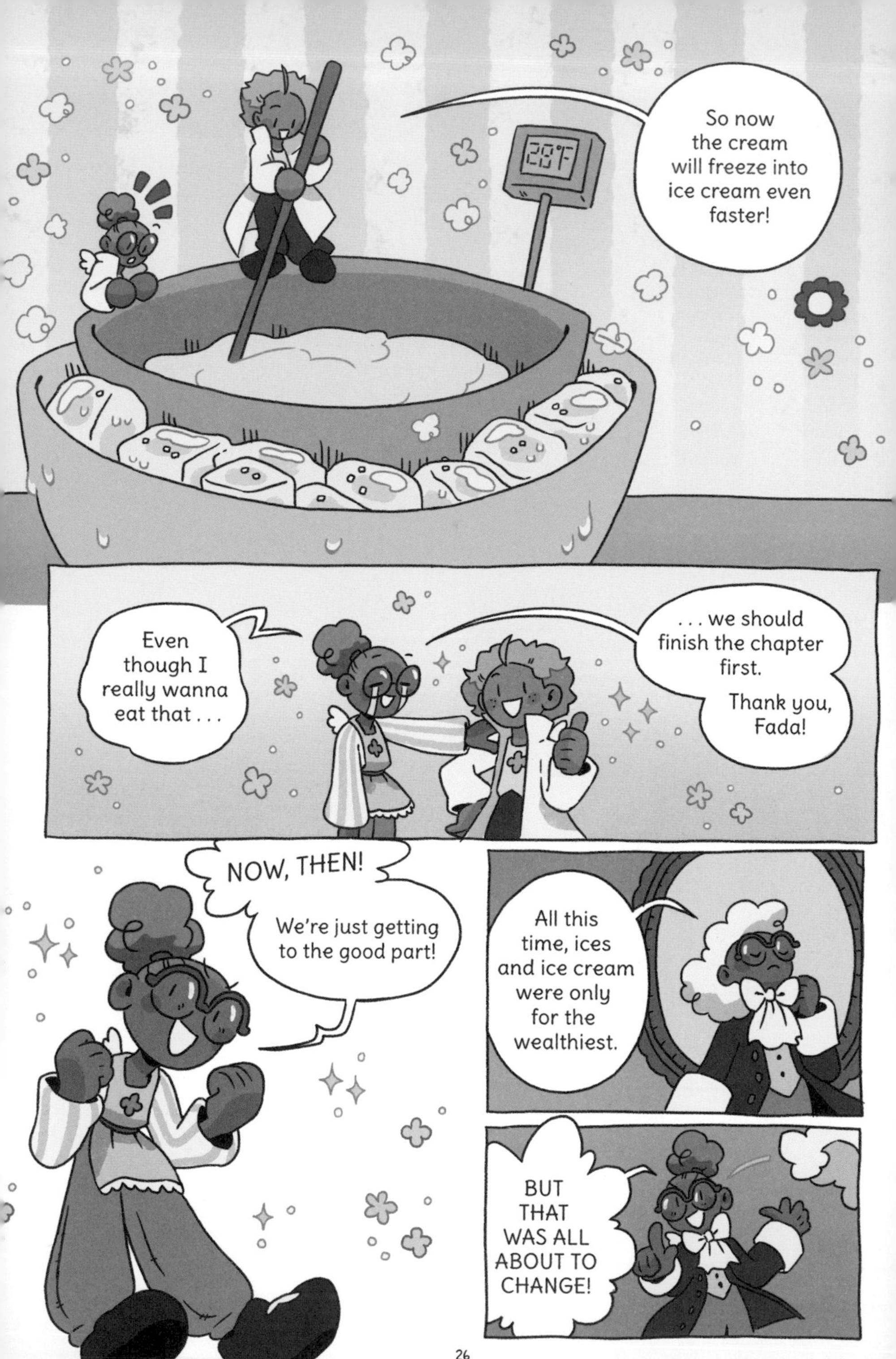

So now the cream will freeze into ice cream even faster!
28°F
Even though I really wanna eat that . . .
. . . we should finish the chapter first.
Thank you, Fada!
NOW, THEN!
We're just getting to the good part!
All this time, ices and ice cream were only for the wealthiest.
BUT THAT WAS ALL ABOUT TO CHANGE!

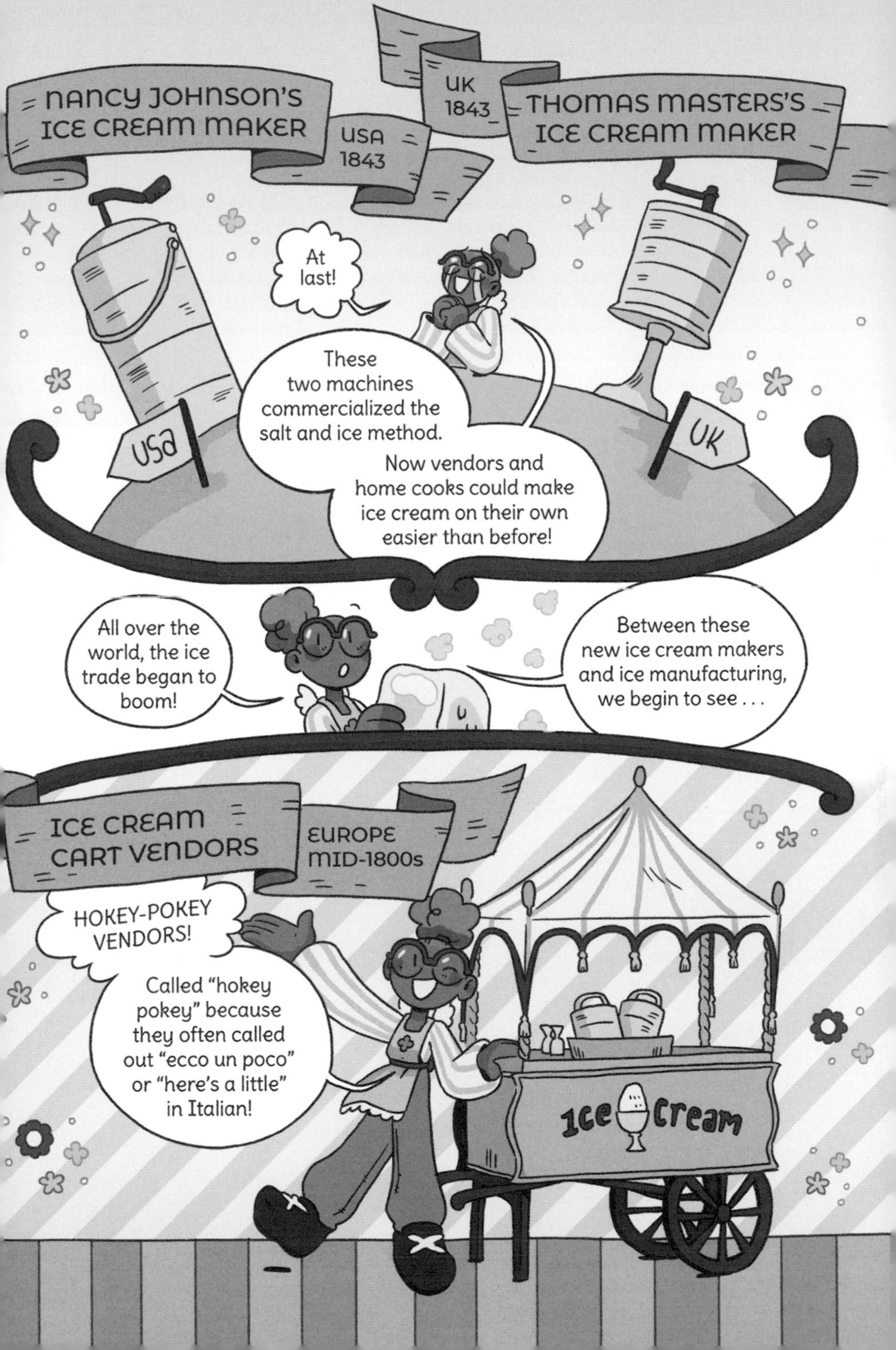
NANCY JOHNSON'S ICE CREAM MAKER
USA 1843
UK 1843
THOMAS MASTERS'S ICE CREAM MAKER
At last!
These two machines commercialized the salt and ice method.
Now vendors and home cooks could make ice cream on their own easier than before!
USA
UK
All over the world, the ice trade began to boom!
Between these new ice cream makers and ice manufacturing, we begin to see . . .
ICE CREAM CART VENDORS
EUROPE MID-1800s
HOKEY-POKEY VENDORS!
Called "hokey pokey" because they often called out "ecco un poco" or "here's a little" in Italian!
Ice Cream

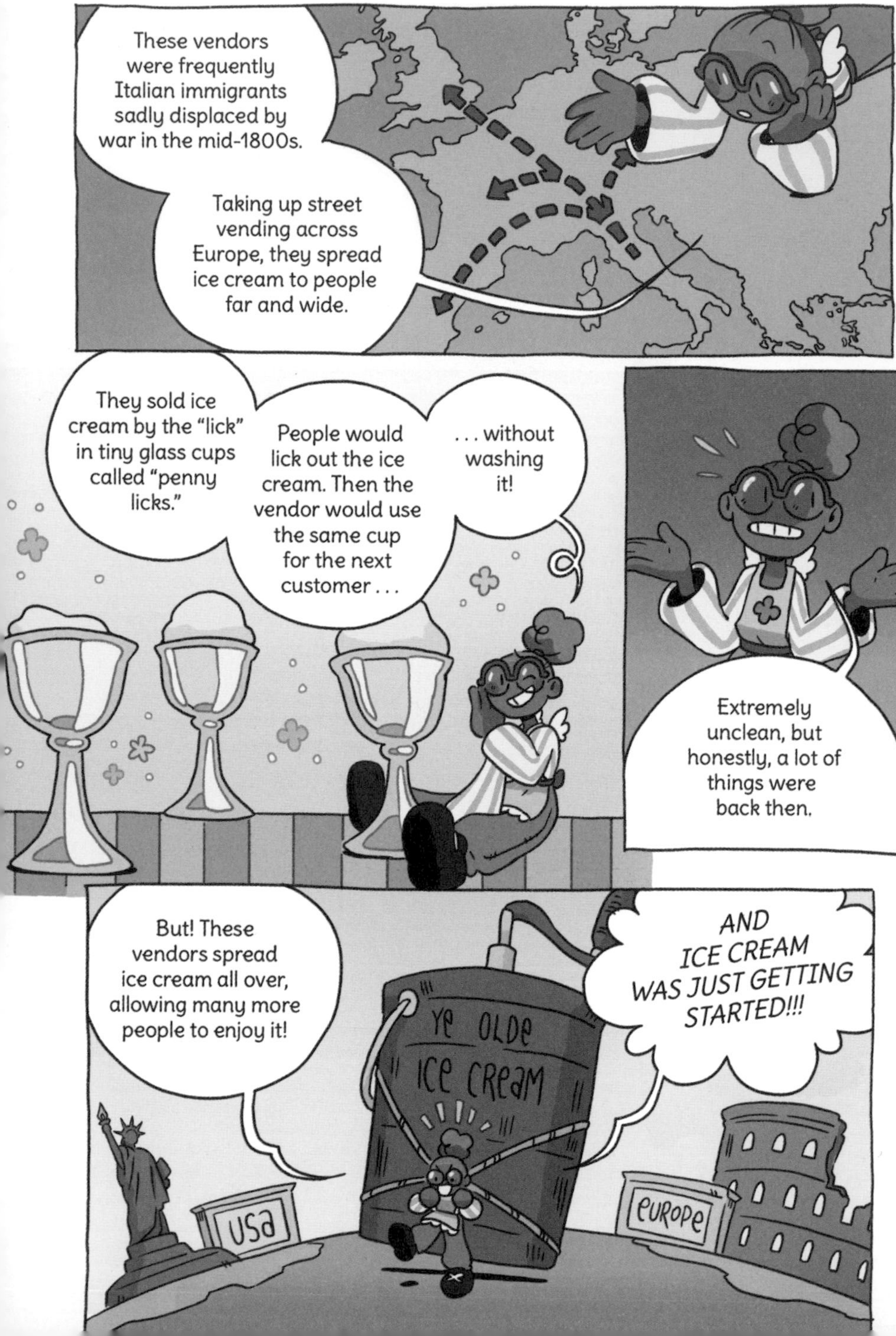
These vendors were frequently Italian immigrants sadly displaced by war in the mid-1800s.
Taking up street vending across Europe, they spread ice cream to people far and wide.
They sold ice cream by the "lick" in tiny glass cups called "penny licks."
People would lick out the ice cream. Then the vendor would use the same cup for the next customer . . .
. . . without washing it!
Extremely unclean, but honestly, a lot of things were back then.
But! These vendors spread ice cream all over, allowing many more people to enjoy it!
AND ICE CREAM WAS JUST GETTING STARTED!!!
YE OLDE ICE CREAM
USA
EUROPE

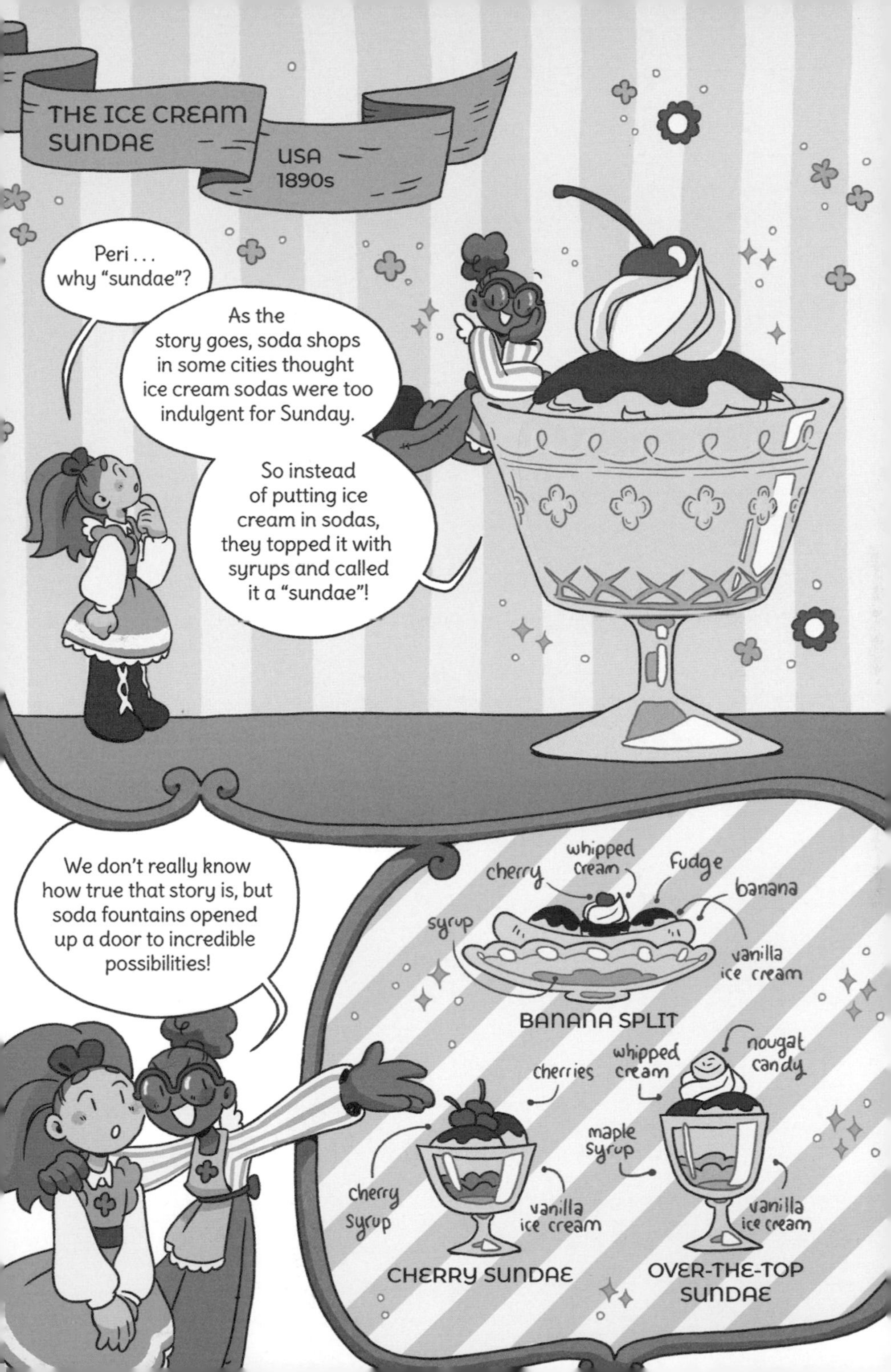
THE ICE CREAM SUNDAE
USA 1890s
Peri . . . why "sundae"?
As the story goes, soda shops in some cities thought ice cream sodas were too indulgent for Sunday.
So instead of putting ice cream in sodas, they topped it with syrups and called it a "sundae"!
We don't really know how true that story is, but soda fountains opened up a door to incredible possibilities!
whipped cream
cherry
fudge
banana
syrup
vanilla ice cream
BANANA SPLIT
cherries
whipped cream
nougat candy
maple syrup
cherry syrup
vanilla ice cream
vanilla ice cream
CHERRY SUNDAE
OVER-THE-TOP SUNDAE

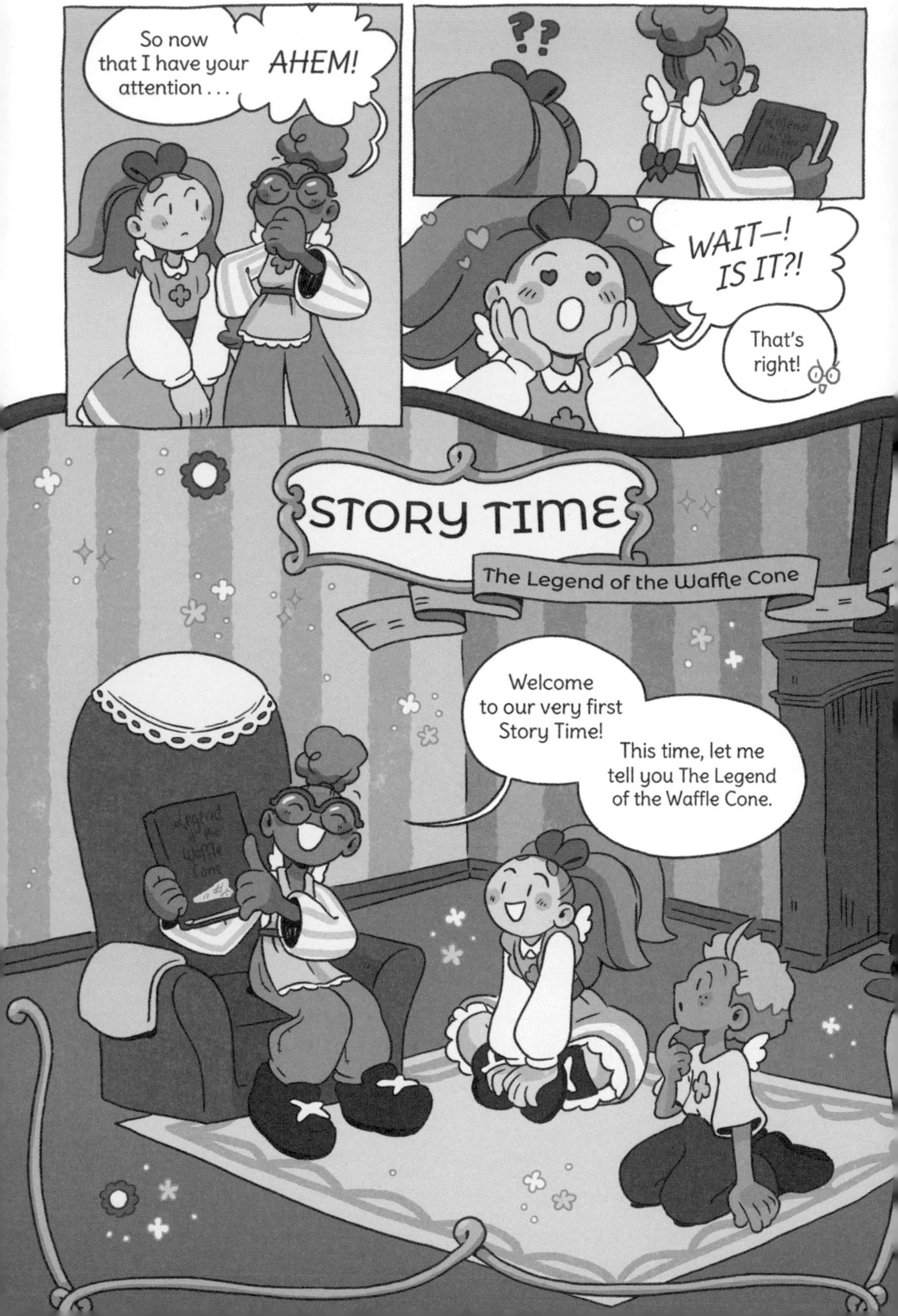

So now that I have your attention . . .
AHEM!
??
WAIT—! IS IT?!
That's right!
STORY TIME
The Legend of the Waffle Cone
Welcome to our very first Story Time!
This time, let me tell you The Legend of the Waffle Cone.

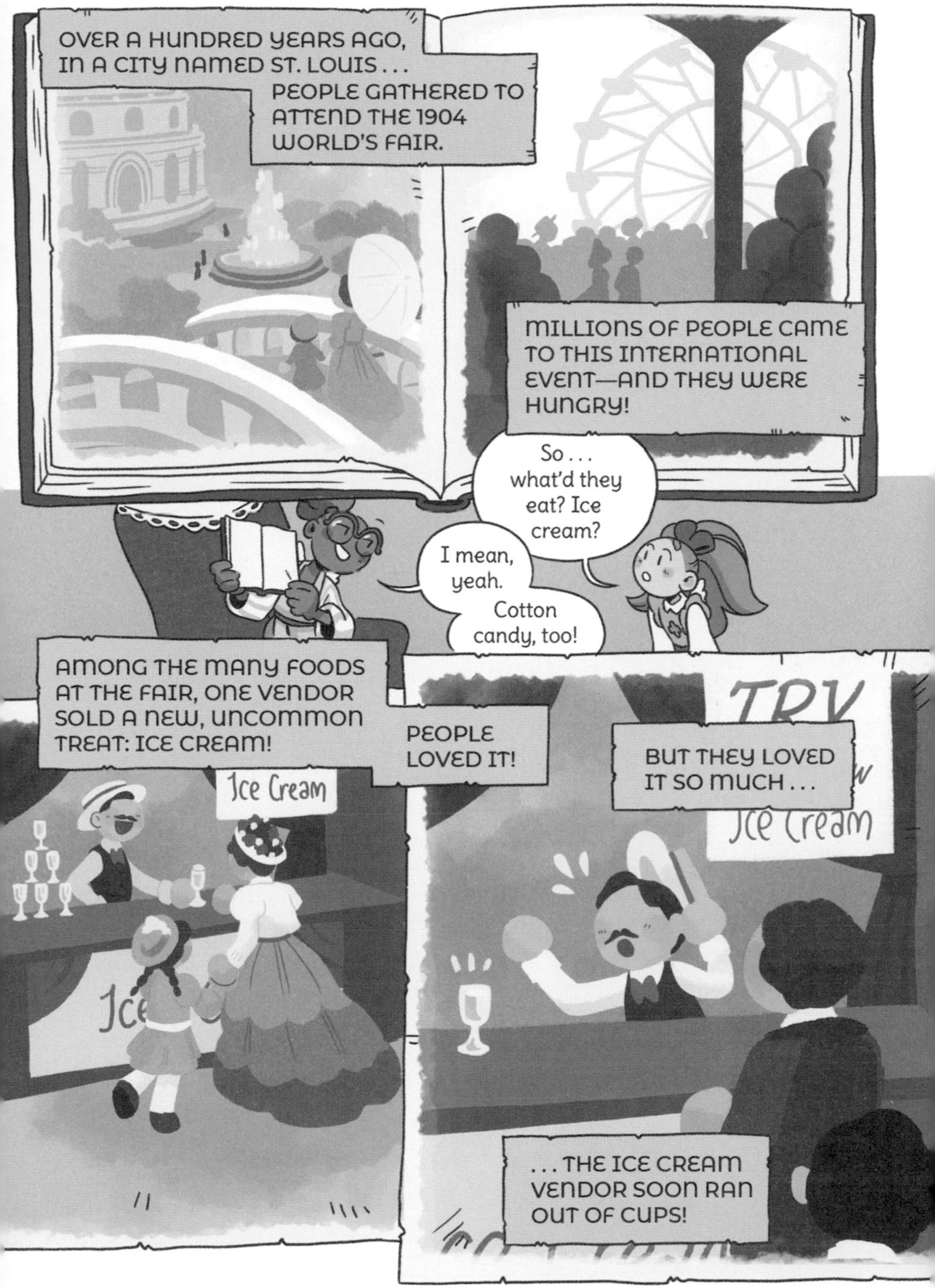
OVER A HUNDRED YEARS AGO, IN A CITY NAMED ST. LOUIS . . .
PEOPLE GATHERED TO ATTEND THE 1904 WORLD'S FAIR.
MILLIONS OF PEOPLE CAME TO THIS INTERNATIONAL EVENT—AND THEY WERE HUNGRY!
So . . . what'd they eat? Ice cream?
I mean, yeah.
Cotton candy, too!
AMONG THE MANY FOODS AT THE FAIR, ONE VENDOR SOLD A NEW, UNCOMMON TREAT: ICE CREAM!
PEOPLE LOVED IT!
Ice Cream
BUT THEY LOVED IT SO MUCH . . .
Ice Cream
. . . THE ICE CREAM VENDOR SOON RAN OUT OF CUPS!

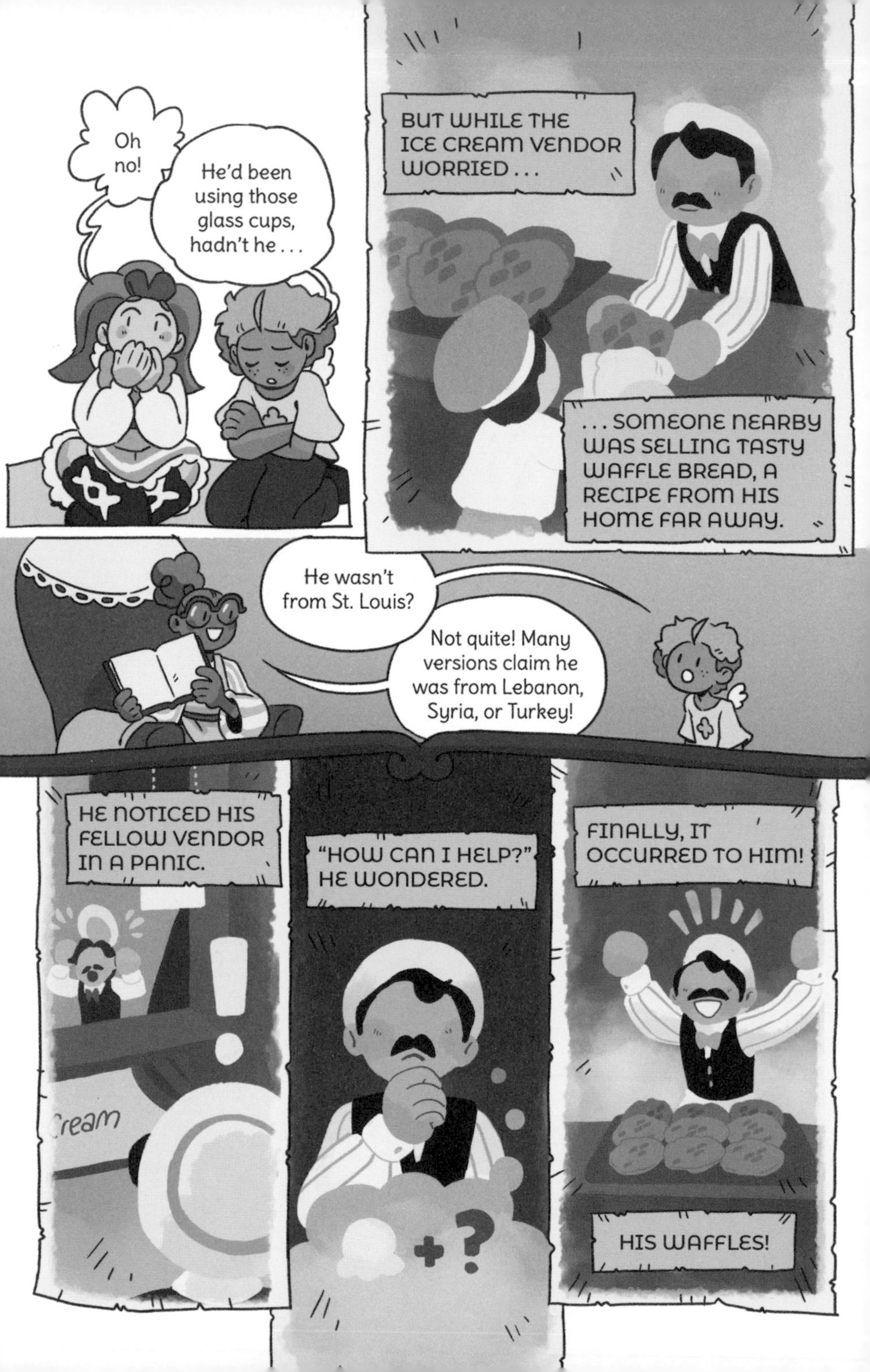
Oh no!
He'd been using those glass cups, hadn't he . . .
BUT WHILE THE ICE CREAM VENDOR WORRIED . . .
. . . SOMEONE NEARBY WAS SELLING TASTY WAFFLE BREAD, A RECIPE FROM HIS HOME FAR AWAY.
He wasn't from St. Louis?
Not quite! Many versions claim he was from Lebanon, Syria, or Turkey!
HE NOTICED HIS FELLOW VENDOR IN A PANIC.
Cream
"HOW CAN I HELP?" HE WONDERED.
FINALLY, IT OCCURRED TO HIM!
HIS WAFFLES!

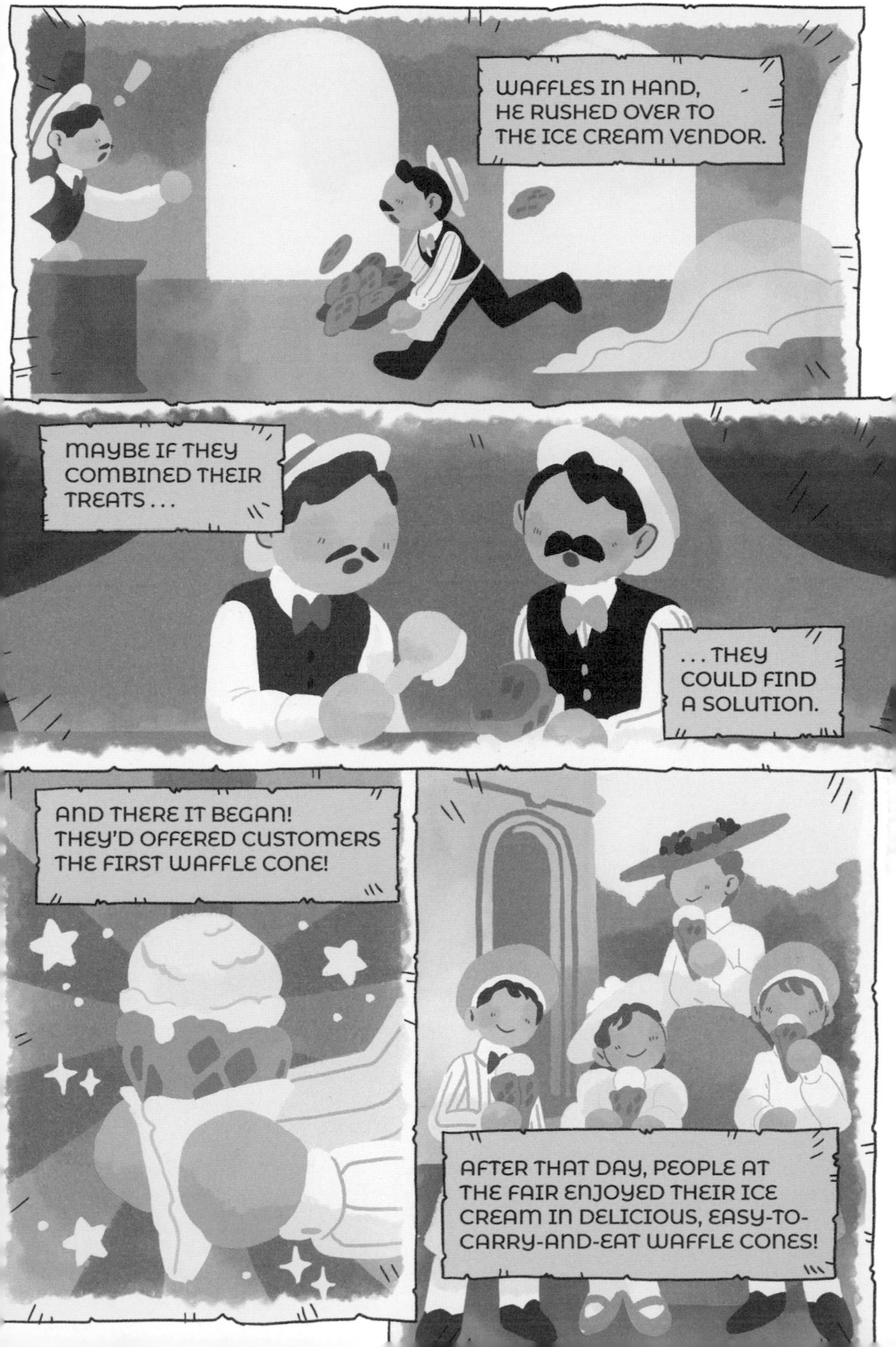
WAFFLES IN HAND, HE RUSHED OVER TO THE ICE CREAM VENDOR.
MAYBE IF THEY COMBINED THEIR TREATS . . .
. . . THEY COULD FIND A SOLUTION.
AND THERE IT BEGAN! THEY'D OFFERED CUSTOMERS THE FIRST WAFFLE CONE!
AFTER THAT DAY, PEOPLE AT THE FAIR ENJOYED THEIR ICE CREAM IN DELICIOUS, EASY-TO-CARRY-AND-EAT WAFFLE CONES!

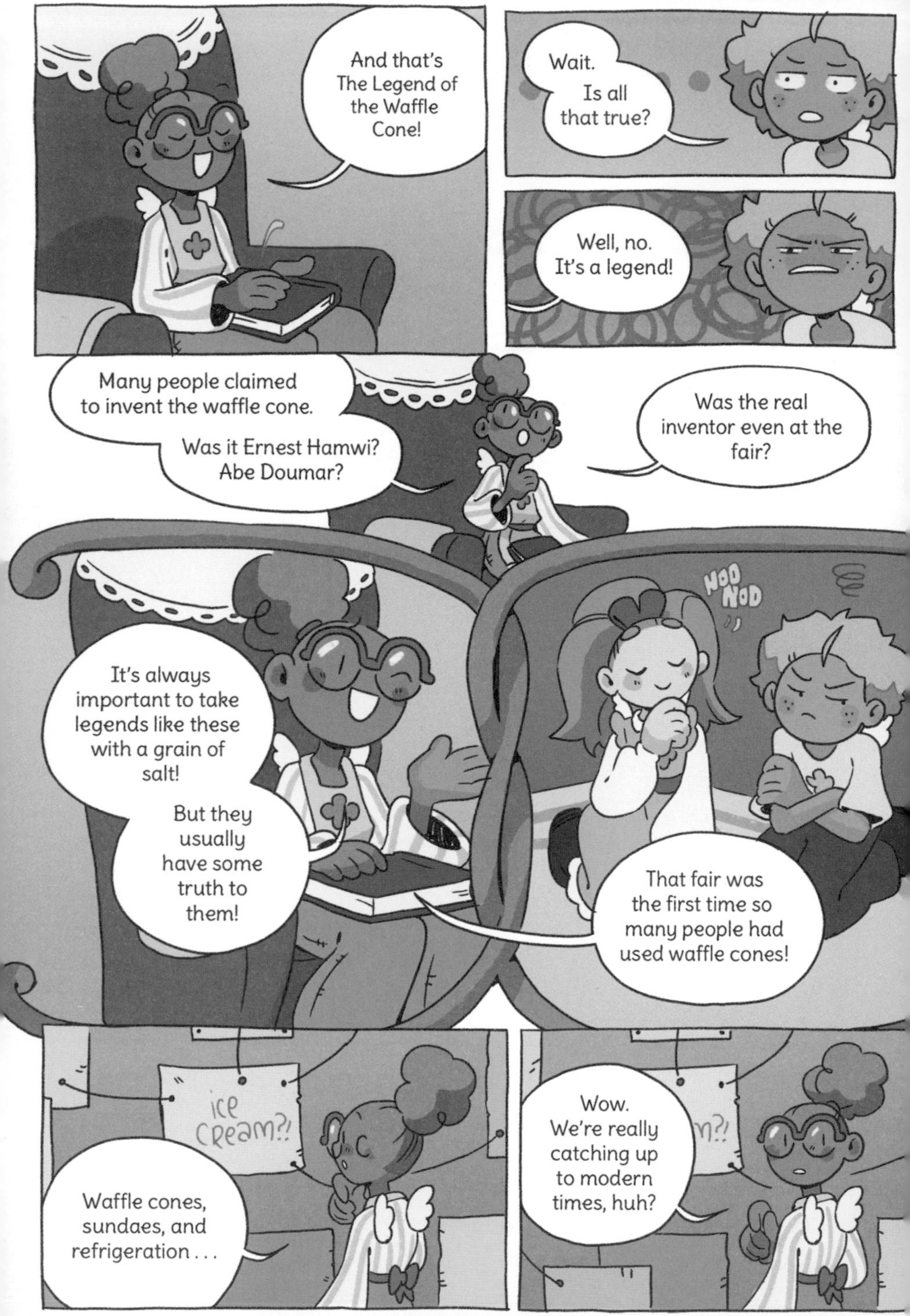
And that's The Legend of the Waffle Cone!
Wait.
Is all that true?
Well, no. It's a legend!
Many people claimed to invent the waffle cone.
Was it Ernest Hamwi? Abe Doumar?
Was the real inventor even at the fair?
NOD NOD
It's always important to take legends like these with a grain of salt!
But they usually have some truth to them!
That fair was the first time so many people had used waffle cones!
ice CReam?!
Waffle cones, sundaes, and refrigeration . . .
Wow. We're really catching up to modern times, huh?

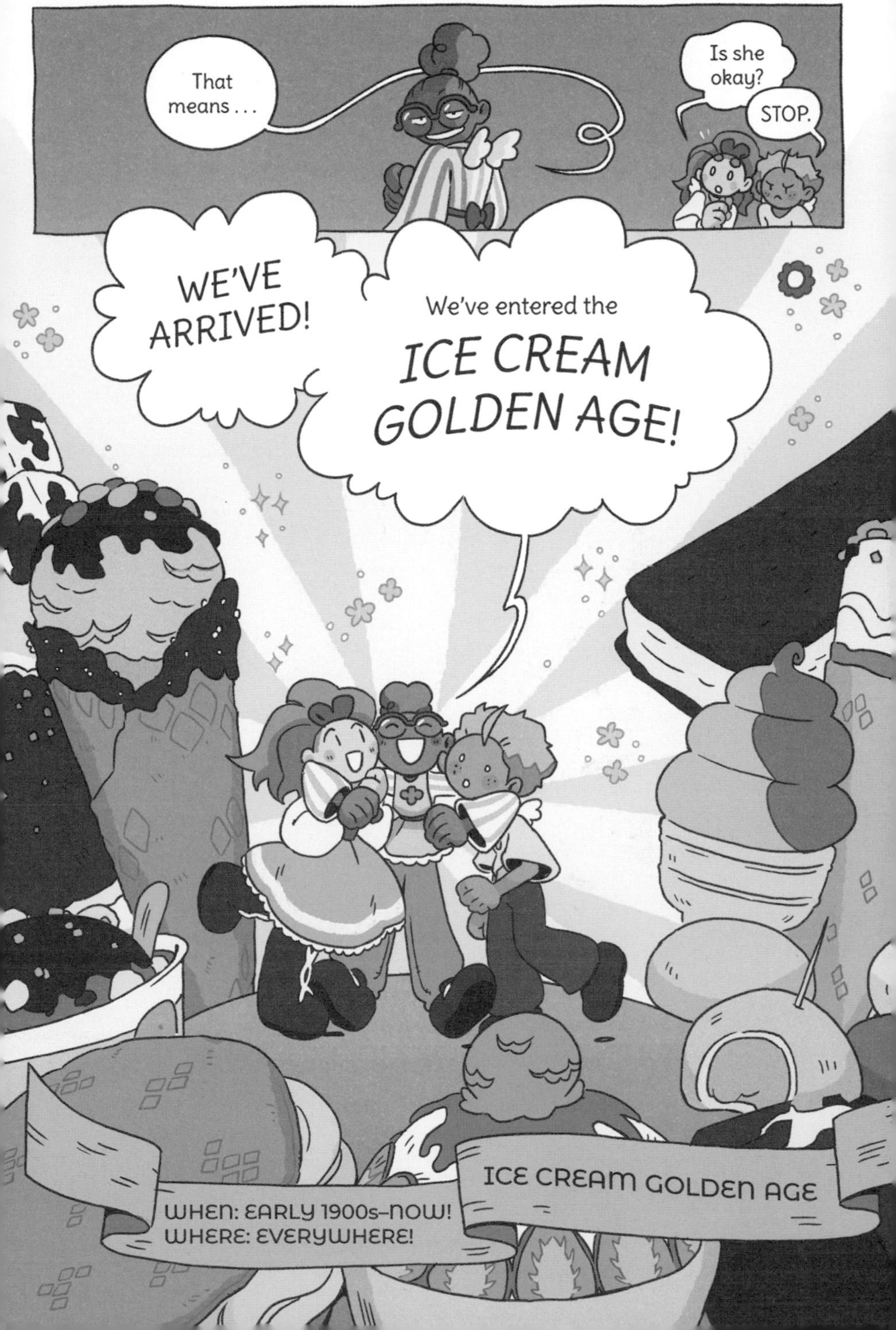

That means . . .
Is she okay?
STOP.
WE'VE ARRIVED!
We've entered the ICE CREAM GOLDEN AGE!
ICE CREAM GOLDEN AGE
WHEN: EARLY 1900s–NOW!
WHERE: EVERYWHERE!

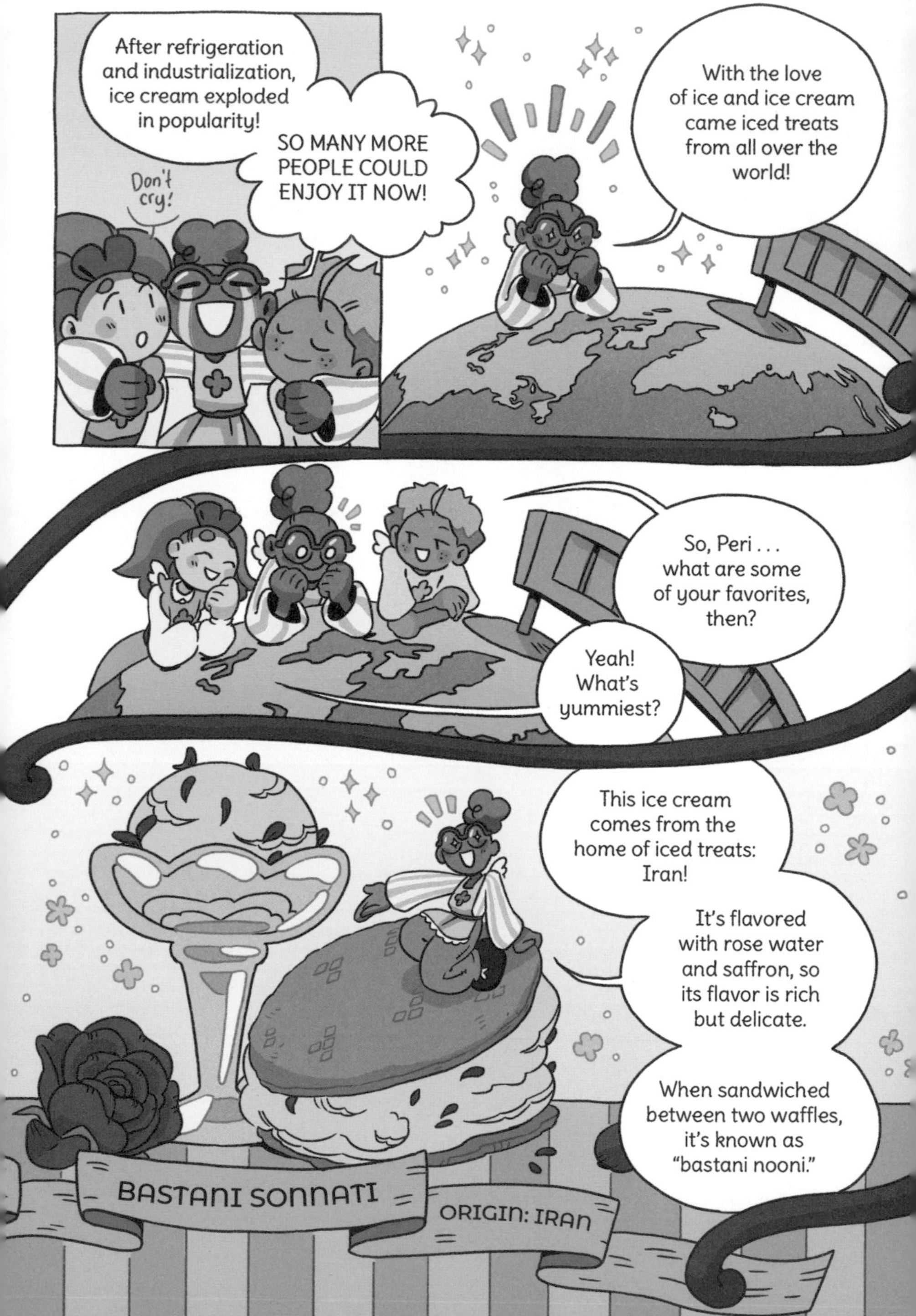
After refrigeration and industrialization, ice cream exploded in popularity!
SO MANY MORE PEOPLE COULD ENJOY IT NOW!
Don't cry!
With the love of ice and ice cream came iced treats from all over the world!
So, Peri . . . what are some of your favorites, then?
Yeah! What's yummiest?
This ice cream comes from the home of iced treats: Iran!
It's flavored with rose water and saffron, so its flavor is rich but delicate.
When sandwiched between two waffles, it's known as "bastani nooni."
BASTANI SONNATI
ORIGIN: IRAN

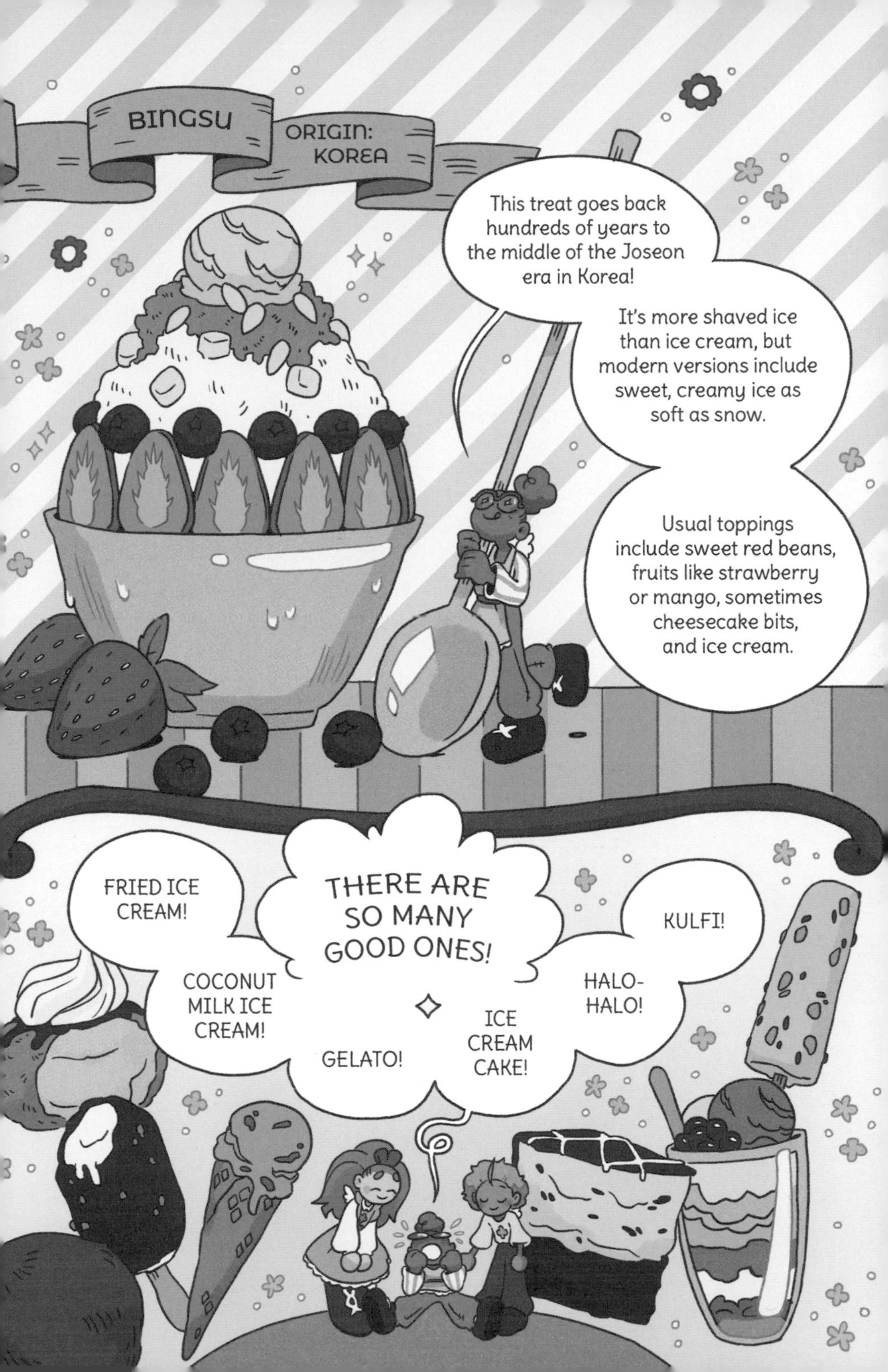
BINGSU
ORIGIN: KOREA
This treat goes back hundreds of years to the middle of the Joseon era in Korea!
It's more shaved ice than ice cream, but modern versions include sweet, creamy ice as soft as snow.
Usual toppings include sweet red beans, fruits like strawberry or mango, sometimes cheesecake bits, and ice cream.
THERE ARE SO MANY GOOD ONES!
FRIED ICE CREAM!
COCONUT MILK ICE CREAM!
GELATO!
ICE CREAM CAKE!
HALO-HALO!
KULFI!

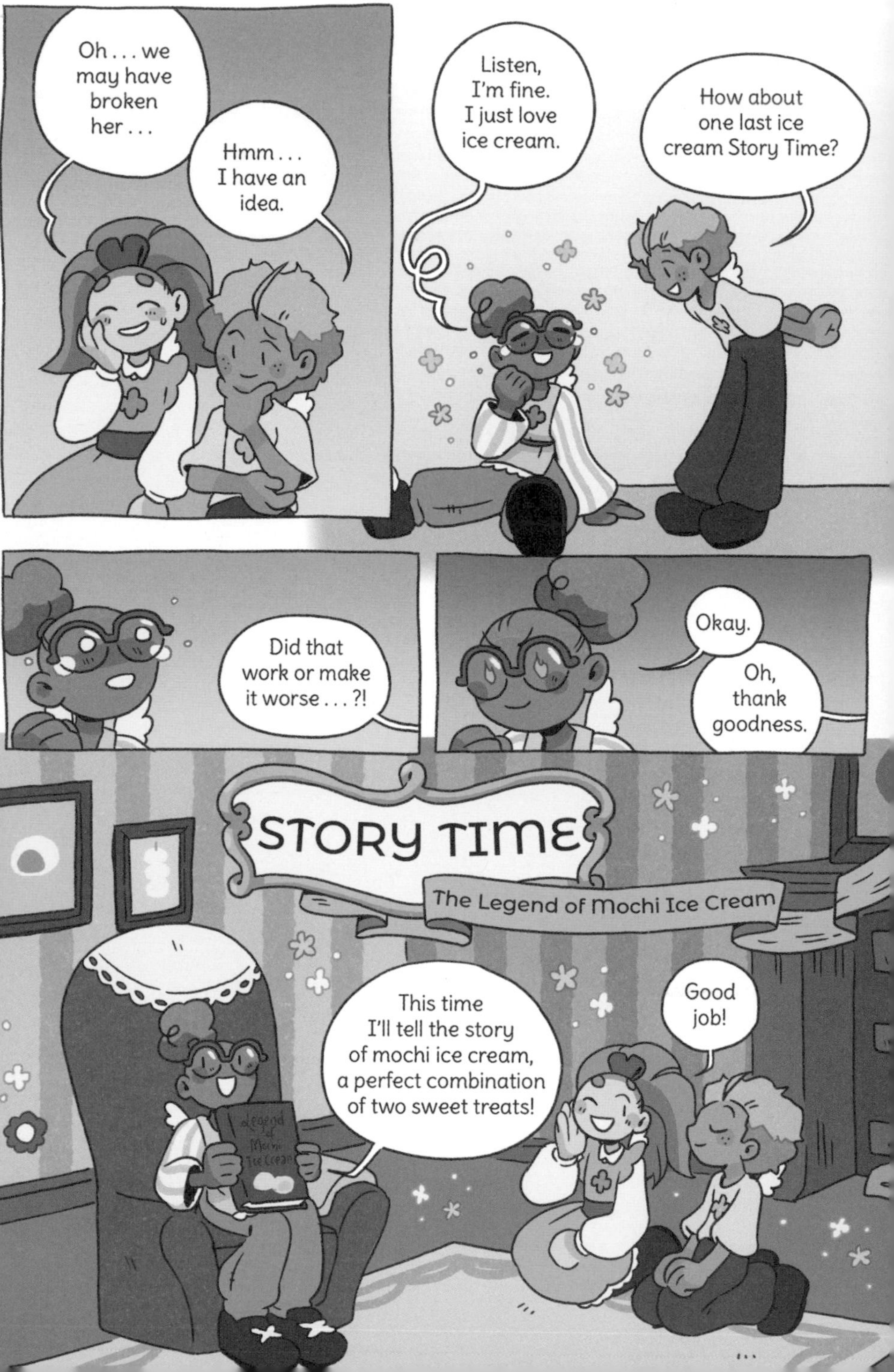

Oh . . . we may have broken her . . .
Hmm . . . I have an idea.
Listen, I'm fine. I just love ice cream.
How about one last ice cream Story Time?
Did that work or make it worse . . . ?!
Okay.
Oh, thank goodness.
STORY TIME
The Legend of Mochi Ice Cream
This time I'll tell the story of mochi ice cream, a perfect combination of two sweet treats!
Good job!
Legend of Mochi Ice Cream

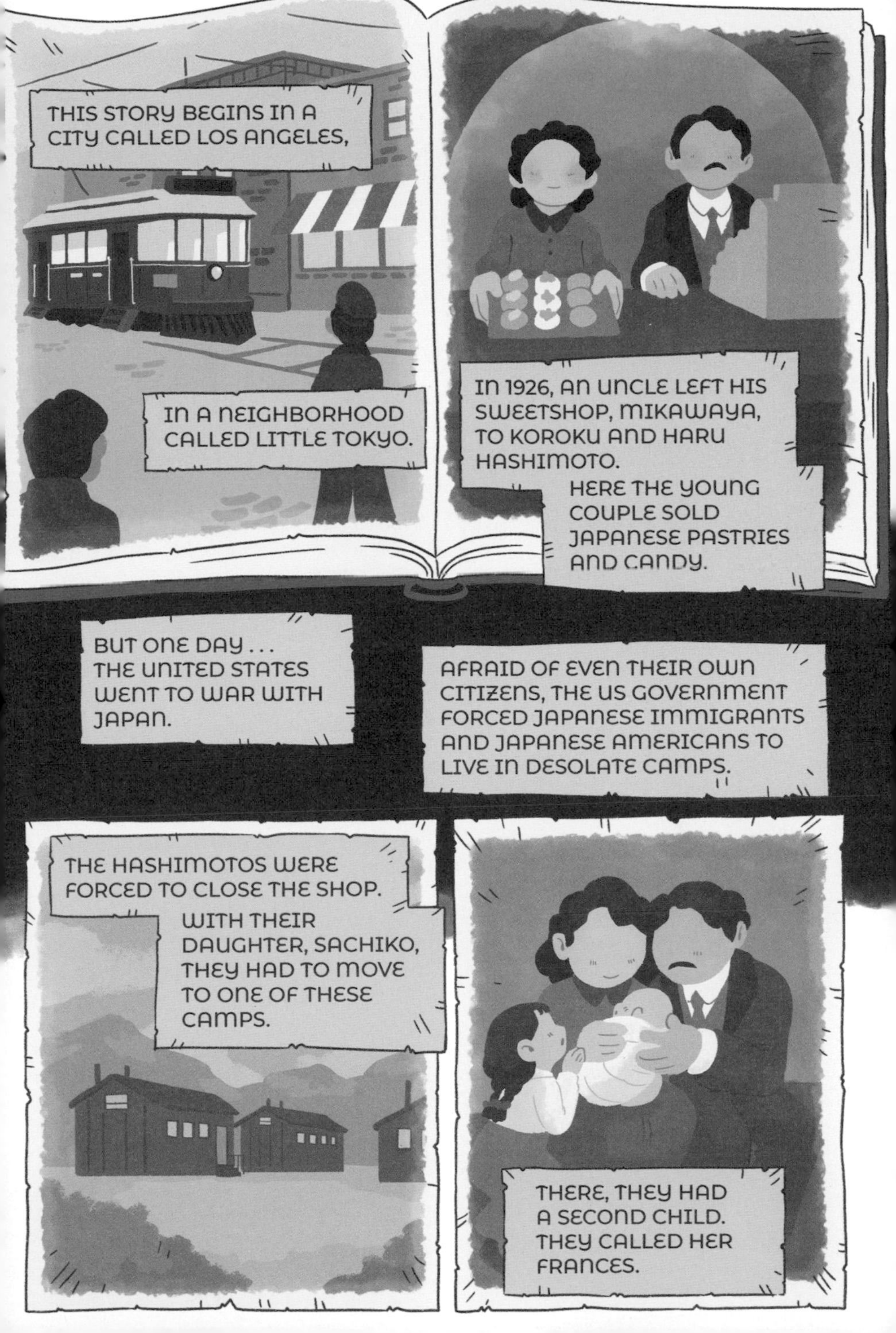
THIS STORY BEGINS IN A CITY CALLED LOS ANGELES,
IN A NEIGHBORHOOD CALLED LITTLE TOKYO.
IN 1926, AN UNCLE LEFT HIS SWEETSHOP, MIKAWAYA, TO KOROKU AND HARU HASHIMOTO.
HERE THE YOUNG COUPLE SOLD JAPANESE PASTRIES AND CANDY.
BUT ONE DAY . . . THE UNITED STATES WENT TO WAR WITH JAPAN.
AFRAID OF EVEN THEIR OWN CITIZENS, THE US GOVERNMENT FORCED JAPANESE IMMIGRANTS AND JAPANESE AMERICANS TO LIVE IN DESOLATE CAMPS.
THE HASHIMOTOS WERE FORCED TO CLOSE THE SHOP.
WITH THEIR DAUGHTER, SACHIKO, THEY HAD TO MOVE TO ONE OF THESE CAMPS.
THERE, THEY HAD A SECOND CHILD. THEY CALLED HER FRANCES.

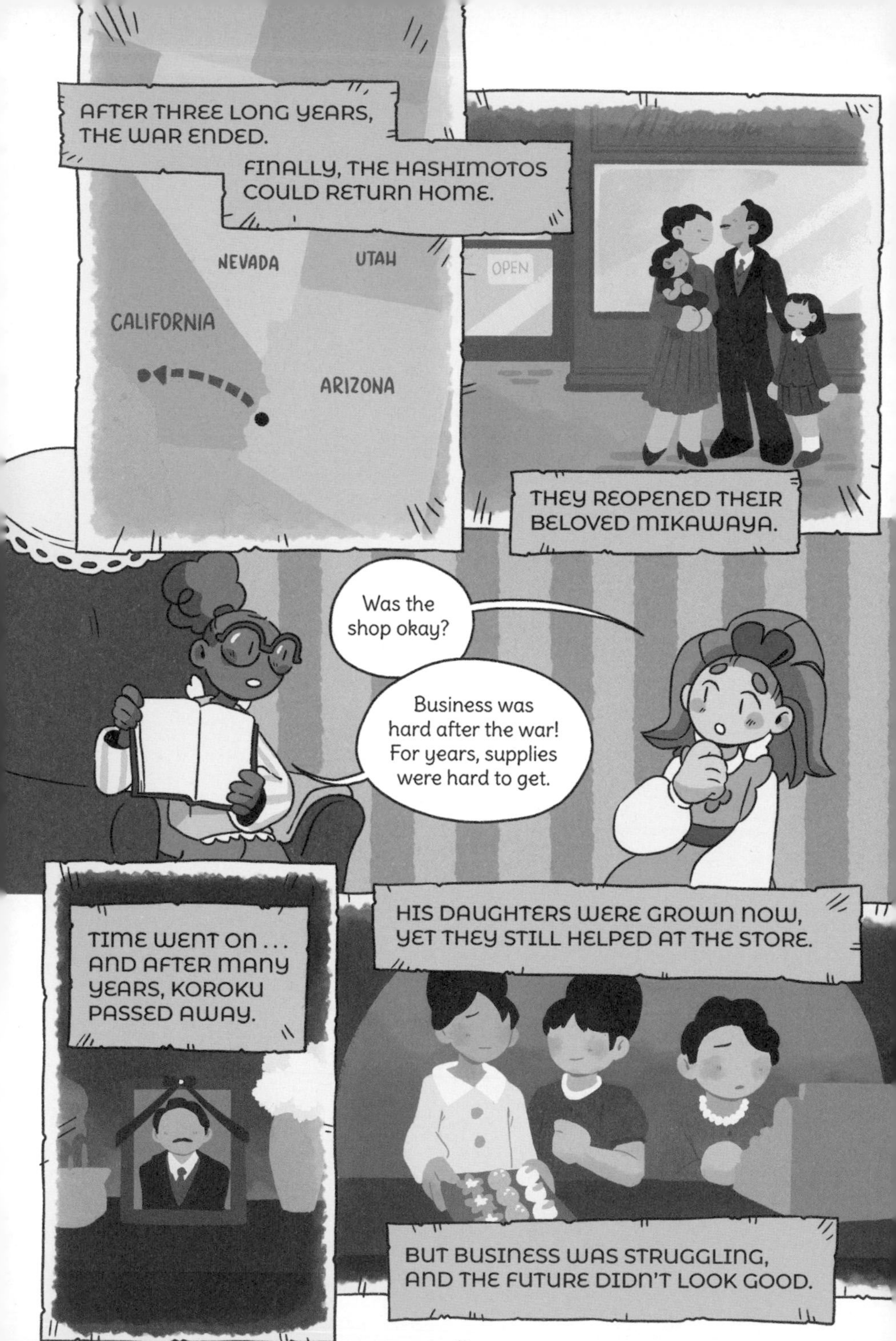
AFTER THREE LONG YEARS, THE WAR ENDED.
FINALLY, THE HASHIMOTOS COULD RETURN HOME.
NEVADA
UTAH
CALIFORNIA
ARIZONA
OPEN
THEY REOPENED THEIR BELOVED MIKAWAYA.
Was the shop okay?
Business was hard after the war! For years, supplies were hard to get.
TIME WENT ON . . . AND AFTER MANY YEARS, KOROKU PASSED AWAY.
HIS DAUGHTERS WERE GROWN NOW, YET THEY STILL HELPED AT THE STORE.
BUT BUSINESS WAS STRUGGLING, AND THE FUTURE DIDN'T LOOK GOOD.

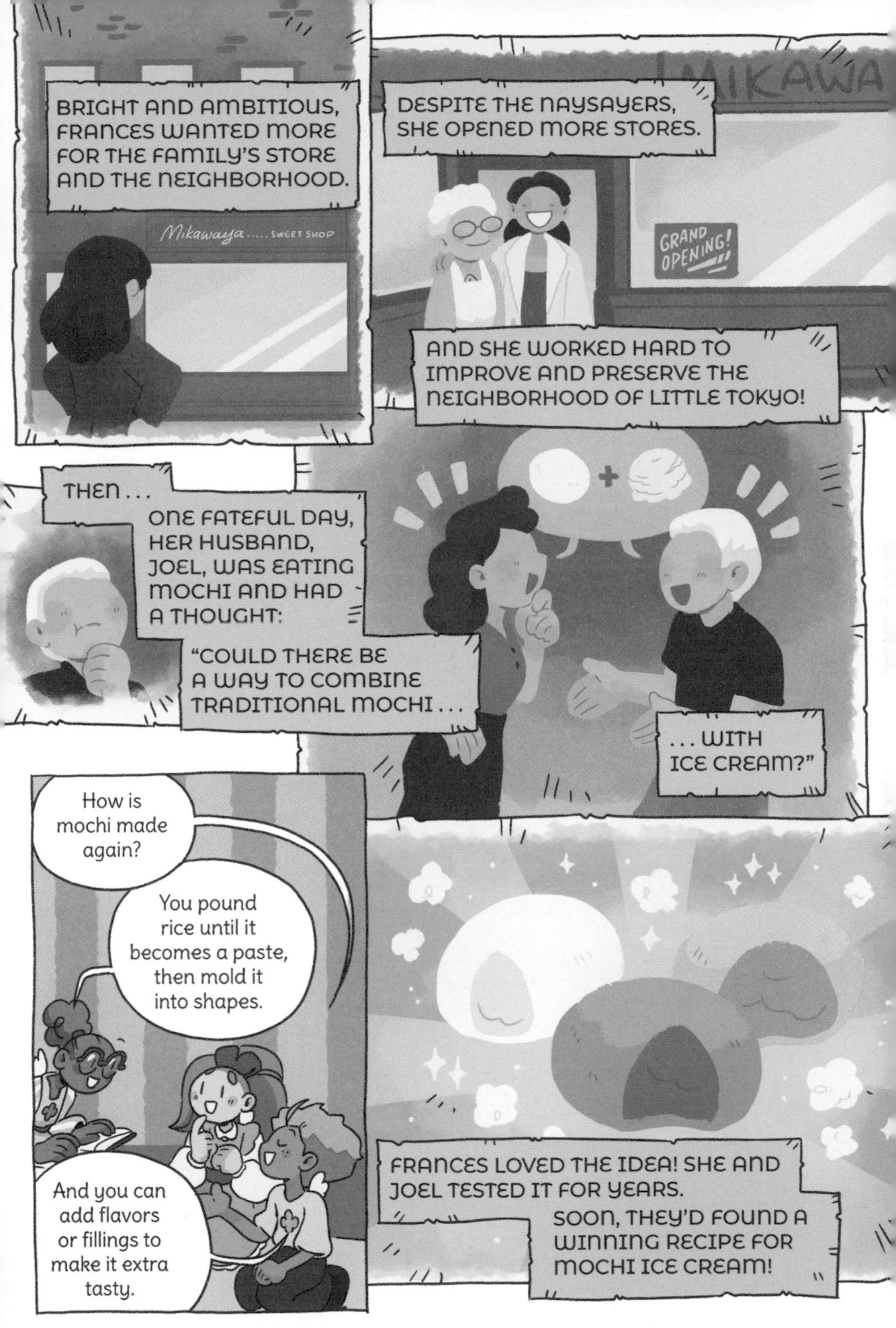
BRIGHT AND AMBITIOUS, FRANCES WANTED MORE FOR THE FAMILY'S STORE AND THE NEIGHBORHOOD.
Mikawaya ..... SWEET SHOP
MIKAWA
DESPITE THE NAYSAYERS, SHE OPENED MORE STORES.
GRAND OPENING!
AND SHE WORKED HARD TO IMPROVE AND PRESERVE THE NEIGHBORHOOD OF LITTLE TOKYO!
THEN . . .
ONE FATEFUL DAY, HER HUSBAND, JOEL, WAS EATING MOCHI AND HAD A THOUGHT:
"COULD THERE BE A WAY TO COMBINE TRADITIONAL MOCHI . . .
. . . WITH ICE CREAM?"
How is mochi made again?
You pound rice until it becomes a paste, then mold it into shapes.
And you can add flavors or fillings to make it extra tasty.
FRANCES LOVED THE IDEA! SHE AND JOEL TESTED IT FOR YEARS.
SOON, THEY'D FOUND A WINNING RECIPE FOR MOCHI ICE CREAM!

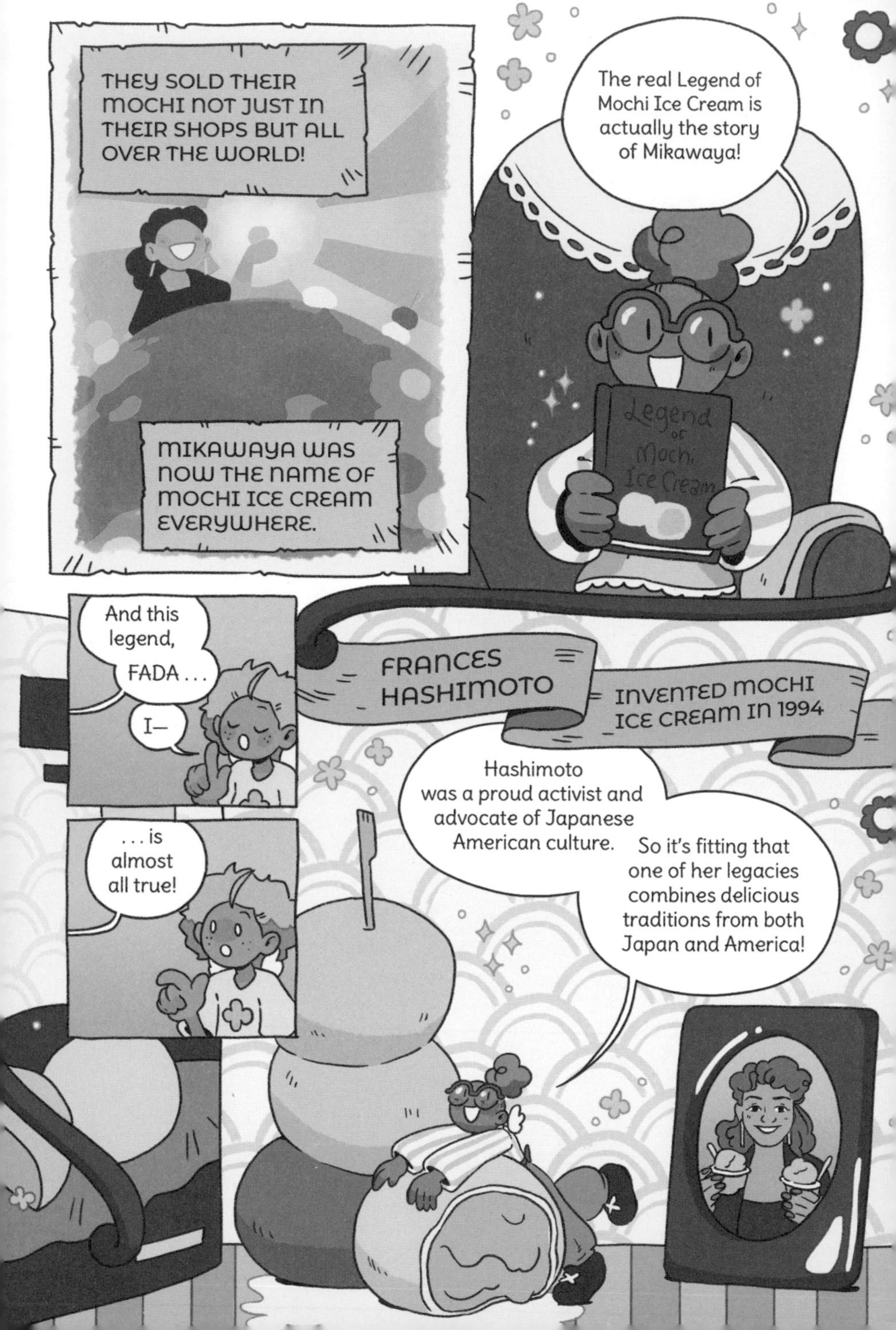

THEY SOLD THEIR MOCHI NOT JUST IN THEIR SHOPS BUT ALL OVER THE WORLD!
MIKAWAYA WAS NOW THE NAME OF MOCHI ICE CREAM EVERYWHERE.
The real Legend of Mochi Ice Cream is actually the story of Mikawaya!
Legend of Mochi Ice Cream
And this legend,
FADA . . .
I—
. . . is almost all true!
FRANCES HASHIMOTO
INVENTED MOCHI ICE CREAM IN 1994
Hashimoto was a proud activist and advocate of Japanese American culture.
So it's fitting that one of her legacies combines delicious traditions from both Japan and America!

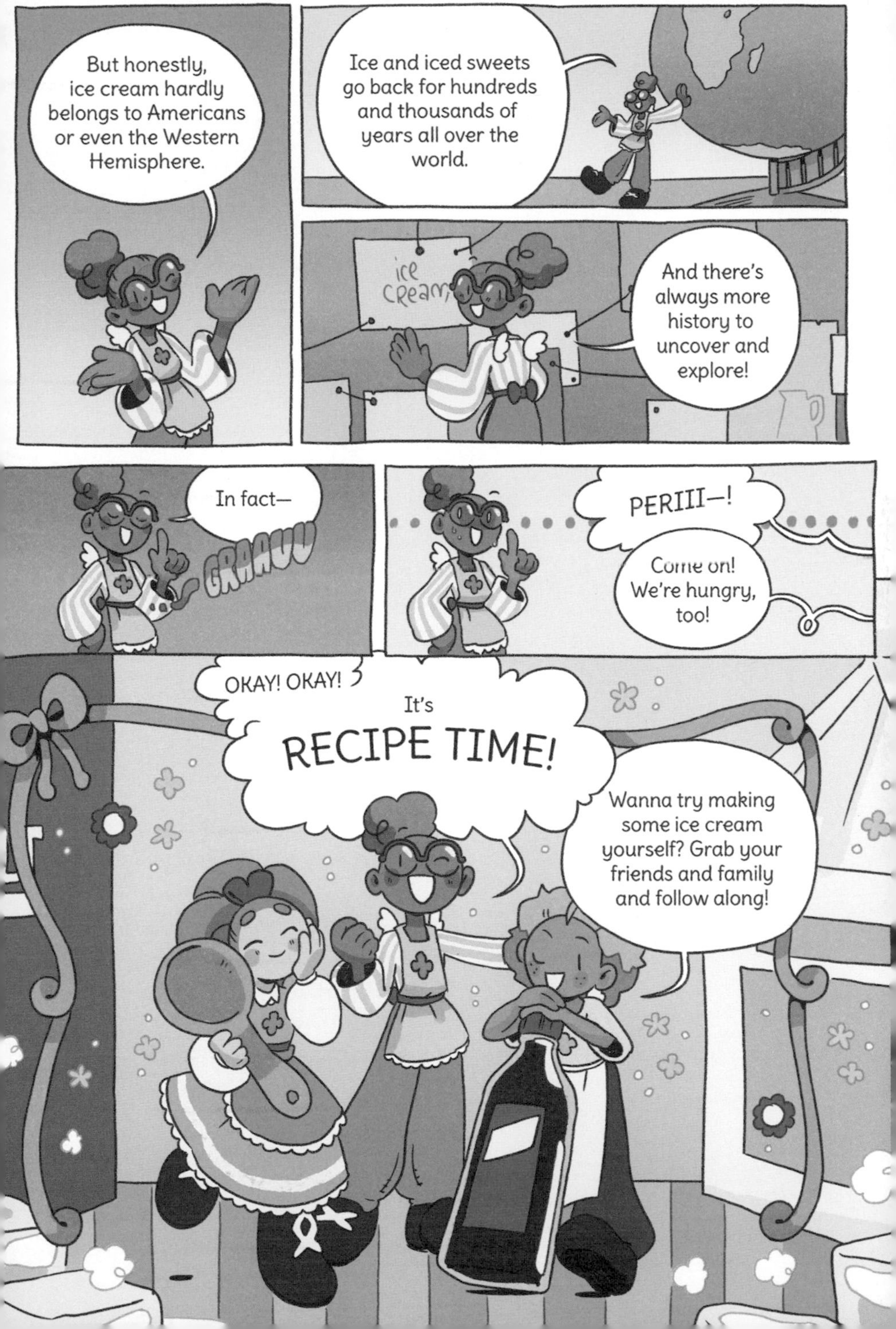
But honestly, ice cream hardly belongs to Americans or even the Western Hemisphere.
Ice and iced sweets go back for hundreds and thousands of years all over the world.
ice cream
And there's always more history to uncover and explore!
In fact—
GRAAUU
PERIII—!
Come on! We're hungry, too!
OKAY! OKAY!
It's RECIPE TIME!
Wanna try making some ice cream yourself? Grab your friends and family and follow along!

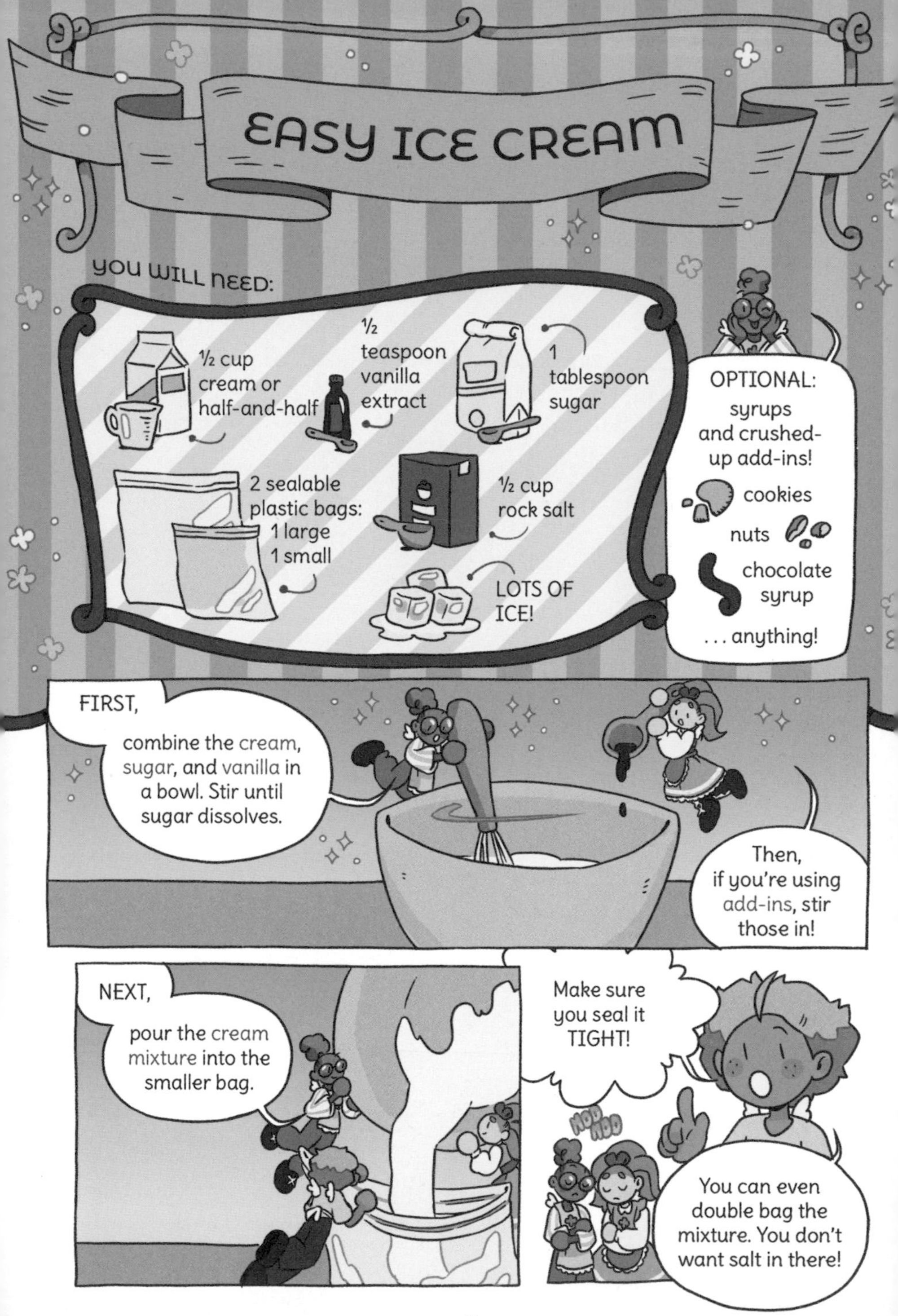
EASY ICE CREAM
YOU WILL NEED:
½ cup cream or half-and-half
½ teaspoon vanilla extract
1 tablespoon sugar
2 sealable plastic bags: 1 large 1 small
½ cup rock salt
LOTS OF ICE!
OPTIONAL: syrups and crushed-up add-ins!
cookies
nuts
chocolate syrup
. . . anything!
FIRST,
combine the cream, sugar, and vanilla in a bowl. Stir until sugar dissolves.
Then, if you're using add-ins, stir those in!
NEXT,
pour the cream mixture into the smaller bag.
Make sure you seal it TIGHT!
NOD NOD
You can even double bag the mixture. You don't want salt in there!

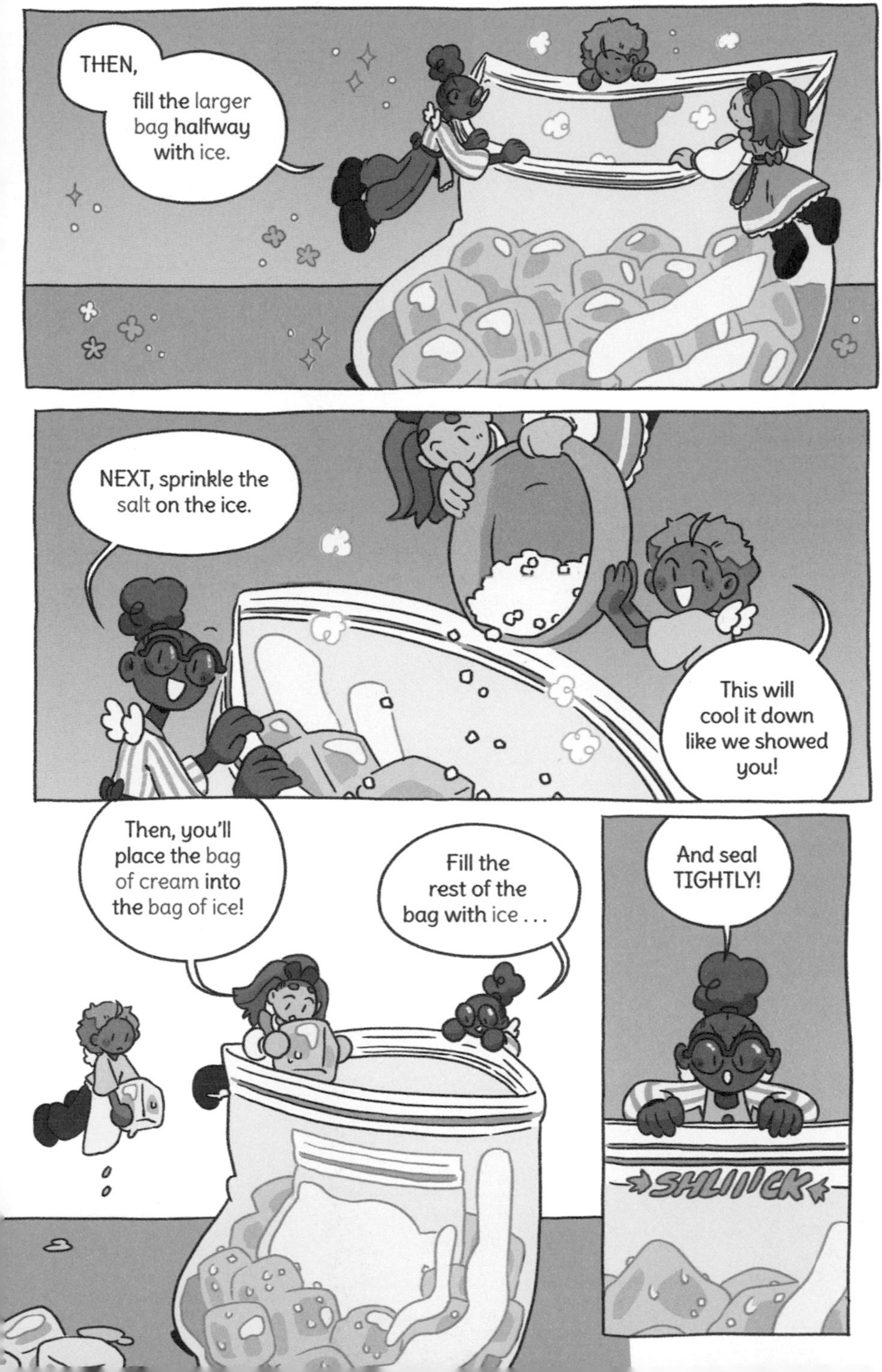
THEN,
fill the larger bag halfway with ice.
NEXT, sprinkle the salt on the ice.
This will cool it down like we showed you!
Then, you'll place the bag of cream into the bag of ice!
Fill the rest of the bag with ice . . .
And seal TIGHTLY!
SHLIIICK

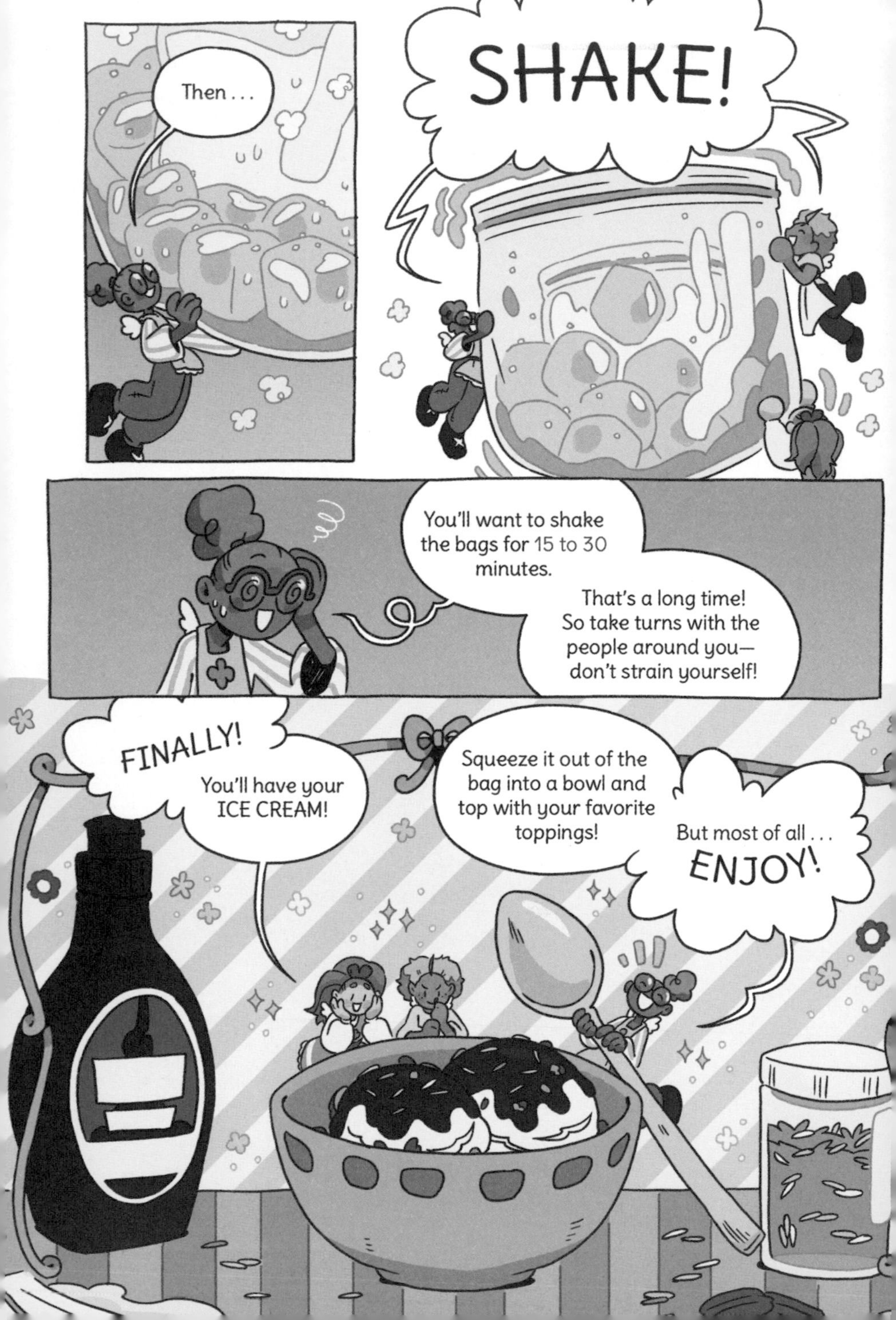
Then . . .
SHAKE!
You'll want to shake the bags for 15 to 30 minutes.
That's a long time! So take turns with the people around you—don't strain yourself!
FINALLY!
You'll have your ICE CREAM!
Squeeze it out of the bag into a bowl and top with your favorite toppings!
But most of all . . .
ENJOY!

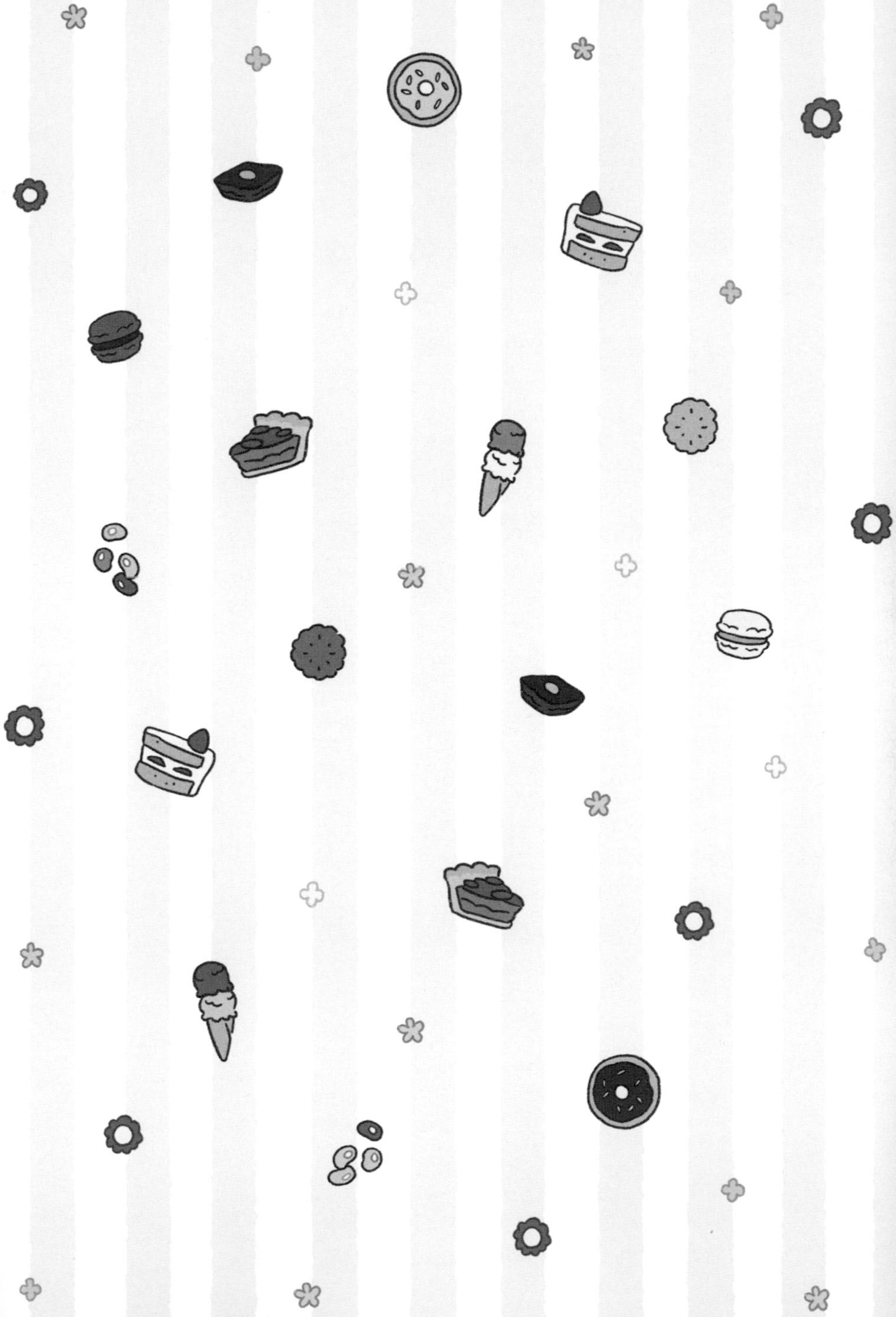

# The Abridged
# Atlas of Cake History

1. Prehistoric Egyptian Sweet Bread

2. Ethiopian and Eritian Himbasha/Ambasha

3. Ancient Greek Plakous

4. Ancient Roman Placenta

5. Chinese Mooncakes

6. Martino da Como's *The Art of Cooking*

7. Origin of Refined Sugar

8. Origin of Cinnamon

9. Origin of Chocolate and Vanilla

10. German Gugelhupf

11. Western European Pound Cake

12. Spanish Sponge Cake

13. Japanese Castella Cake

14. Indonesian, Singaporean, and Southeast Asian Pandan Cake

15. Austrian Chocolate Torte

16. Fannie Farmer's *Boston Cooking-School Cook Book*

17. Baking Soda and Baking Powder

18. Boxed and Canned Cake Mixes

19. John A. Adams's Red Velvet Cake

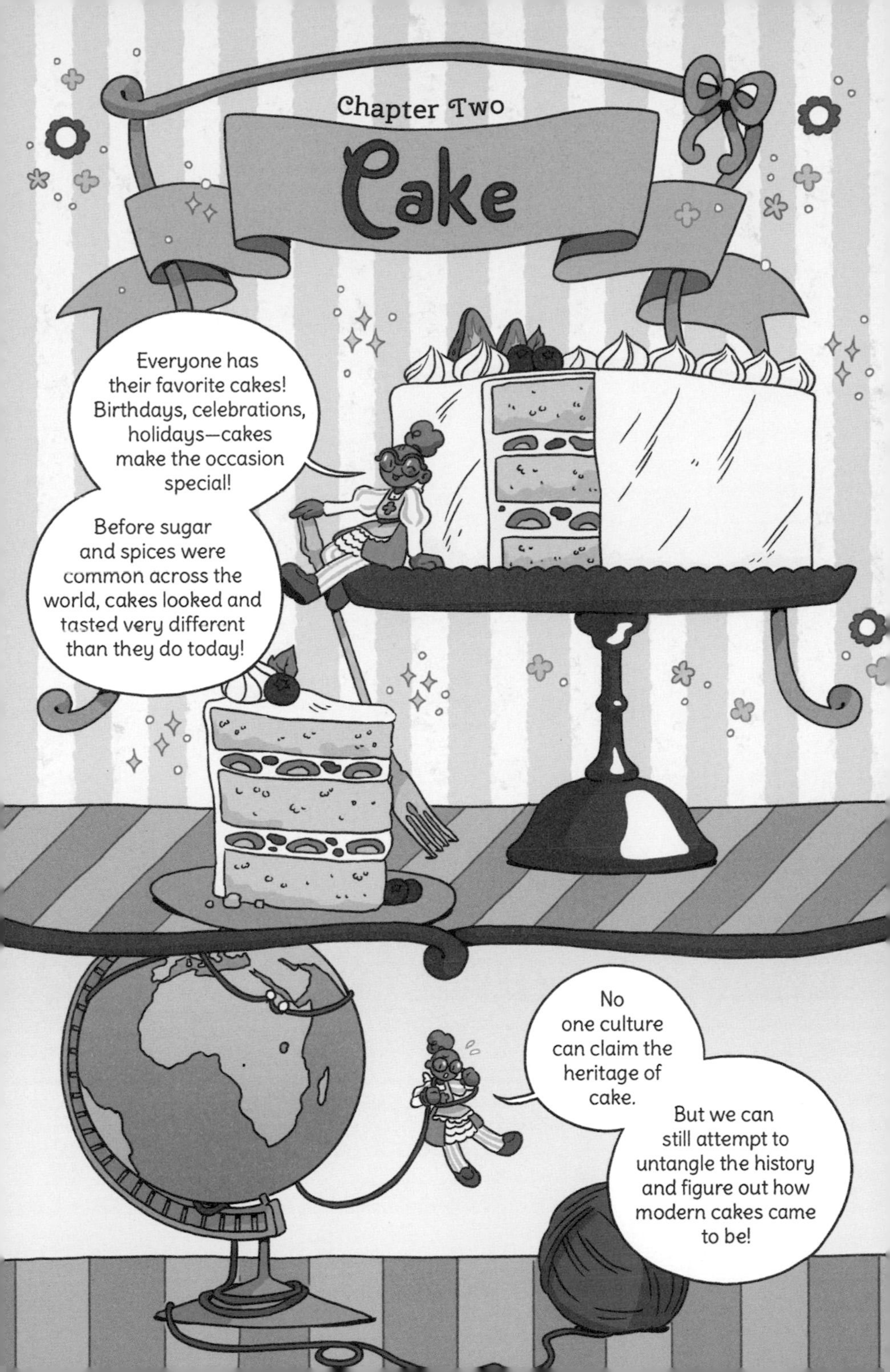
Chapter Two
Cake
Everyone has their favorite cakes! Birthdays, celebrations, holidays—cakes make the occasion special!
Before sugar and spices were common across the world, cakes looked and tasted very different than they do today!
No one culture can claim the heritage of cake.
But we can still attempt to untangle the history and figure out how modern cakes came to be!

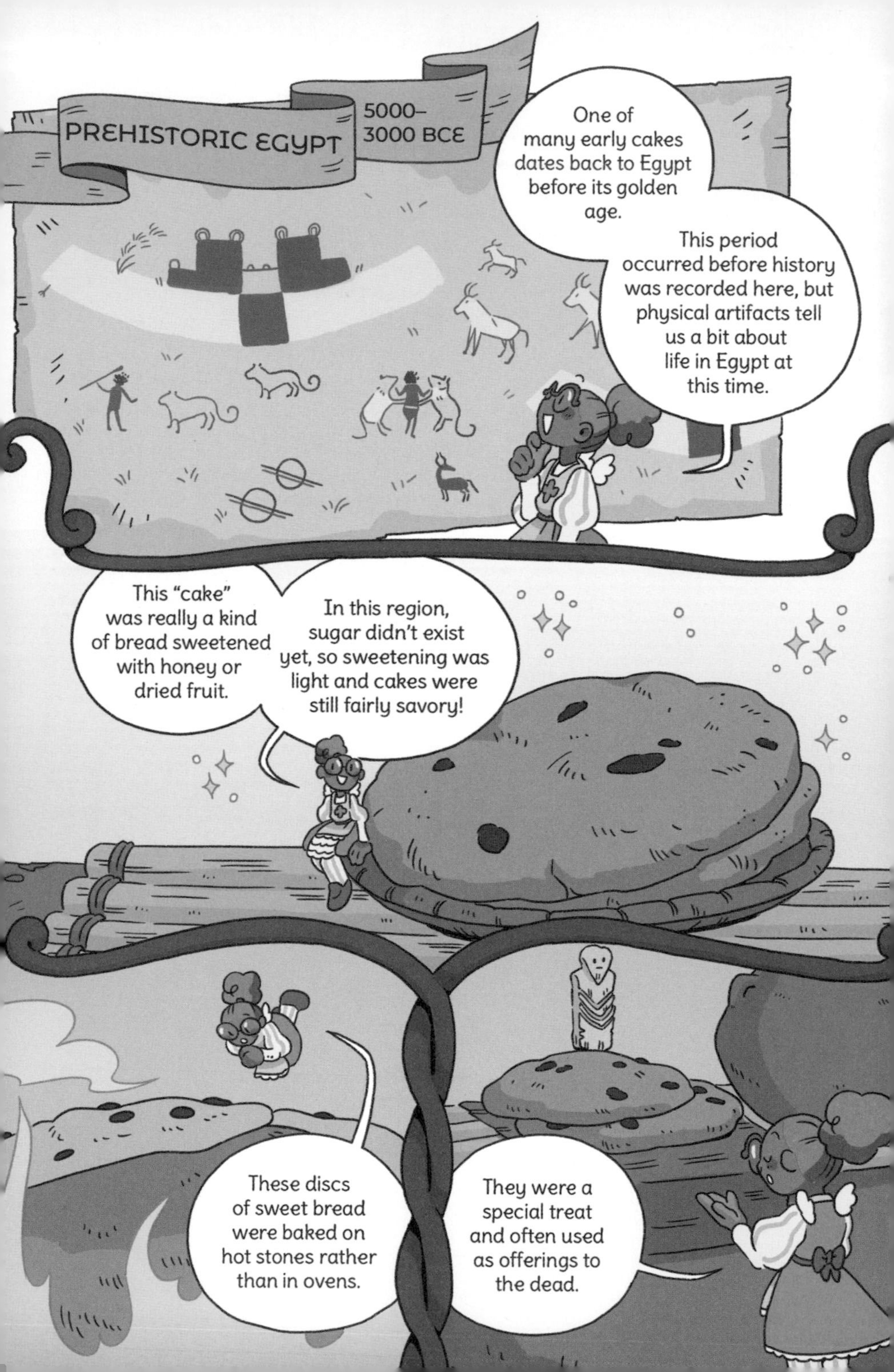
PREHISTORIC EGYPT
5000–3000 BCE
One of many early cakes dates back to Egypt before its golden age.
This period occurred before history was recorded here, but physical artifacts tell us a bit about life in Egypt at this time.
This "cake" was really a kind of bread sweetened with honey or dried fruit.
In this region, sugar didn't exist yet, so sweetening was light and cakes were still fairly savory!
These discs of sweet bread were baked on hot stones rather than in ovens.
They were a special treat and often used as offerings to the dead.

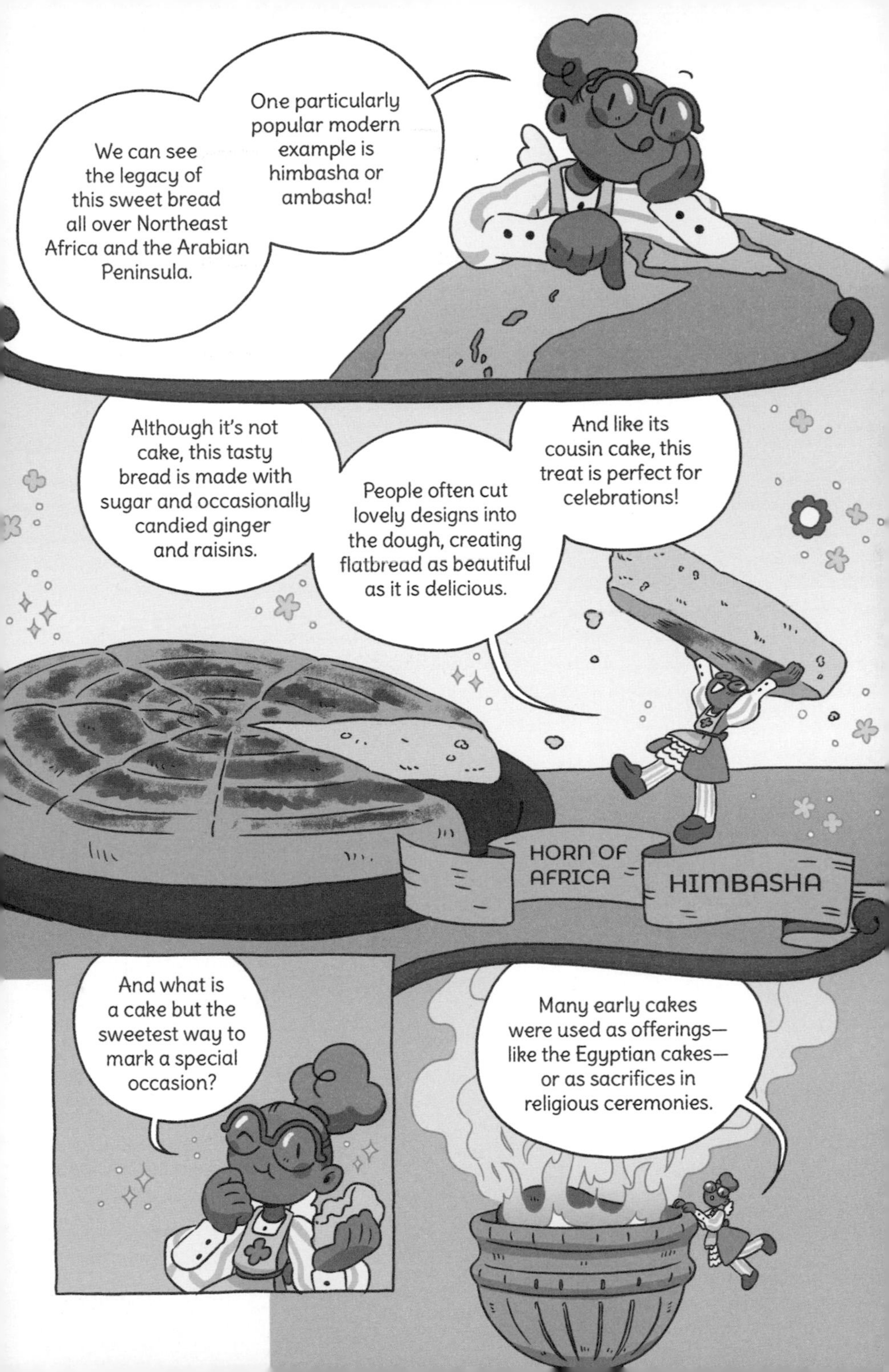

We can see the legacy of this sweet bread all over Northeast Africa and the Arabian Peninsula.
One particularly popular modern example is himbasha or ambasha!
Although it's not cake, this tasty bread is made with sugar and occasionally candied ginger and raisins.
People often cut lovely designs into the dough, creating flatbread as beautiful as it is delicious.
And like its cousin cake, this treat is perfect for celebrations!
HORN OF AFRICA
HIMBASHA
And what is a cake but the sweetest way to mark a special occasion?
Many early cakes were used as offerings—like the Egyptian cakes—or as sacrifices in religious ceremonies.

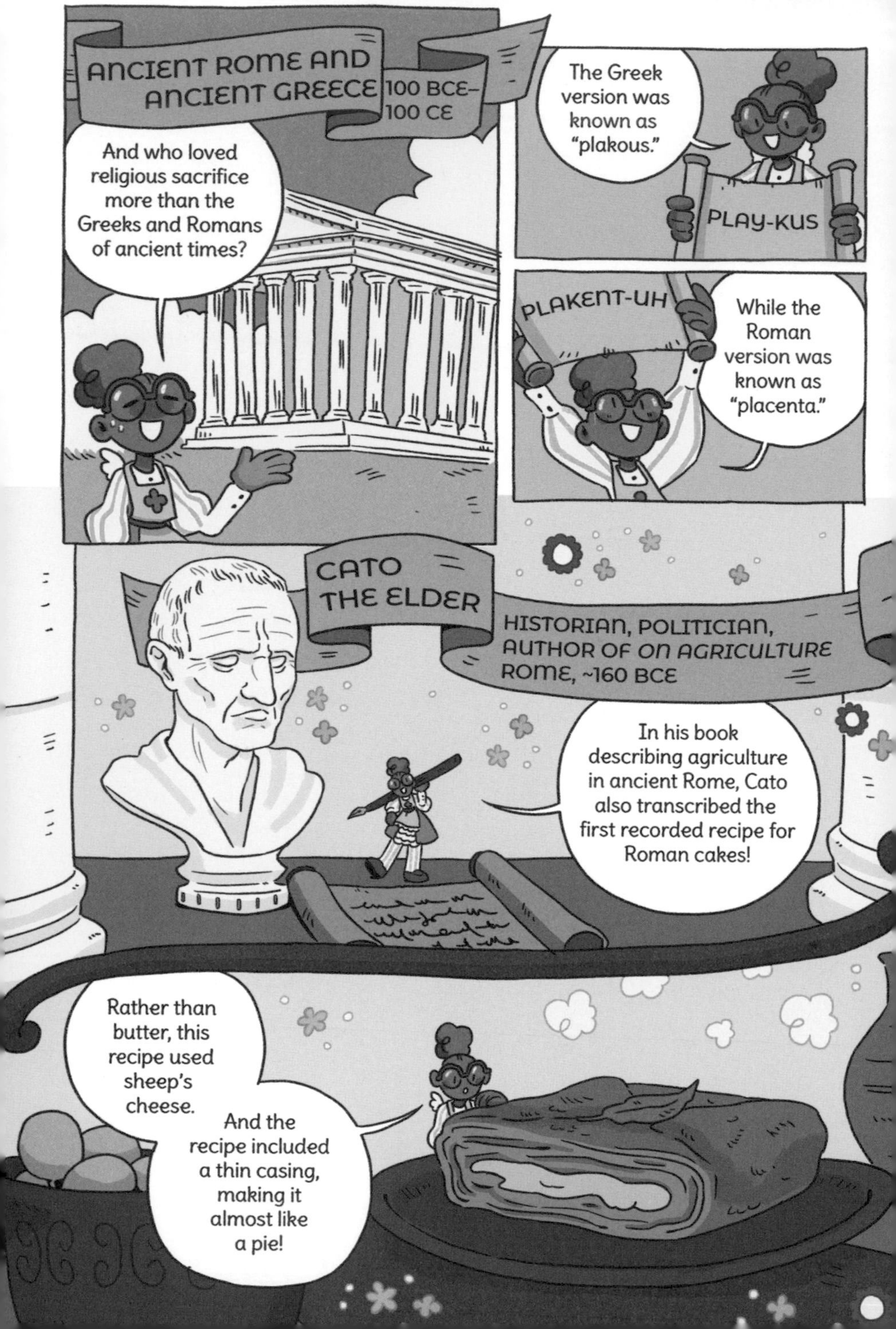
ANCIENT ROME AND ANCIENT GREECE 100 BCE–100 CE
And who loved religious sacrifice more than the Greeks and Romans of ancient times?
The Greek version was known as "plakous."
PLAY-KUS
PLAKENT-UH
While the Roman version was known as "placenta."
CATO THE ELDER
HISTORIAN, POLITICIAN, AUTHOR OF *ON AGRICULTURE* ROME, ~160 BCE
In his book describing agriculture in ancient Rome, Cato also transcribed the first recorded recipe for Roman cakes!
Rather than butter, this recipe used sheep's cheese.
And the recipe included a thin casing, making it almost like a pie!

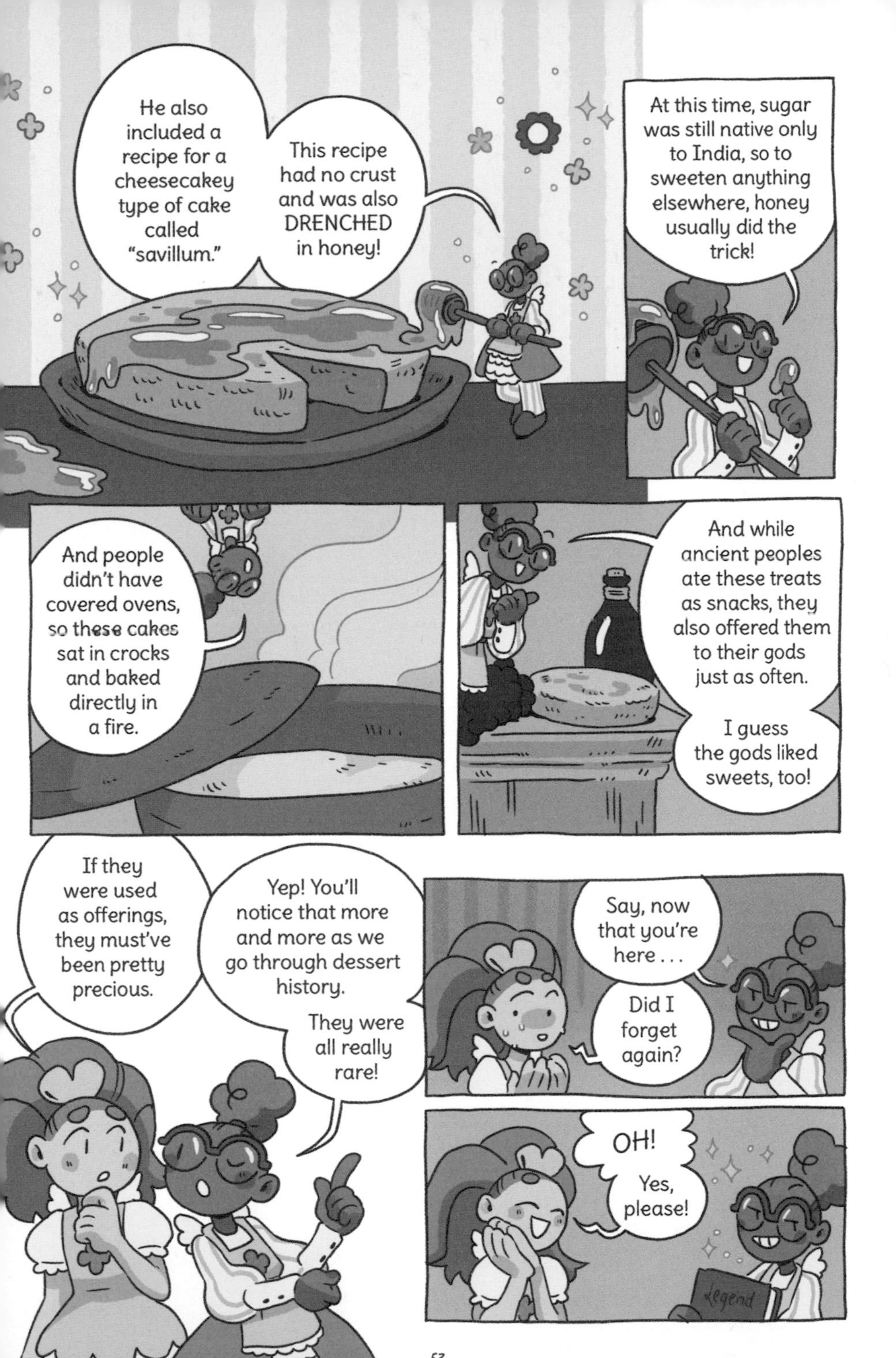
He also included a recipe for a cheesecakey type of cake called "savillum."
This recipe had no crust and was also DRENCHED in honey!
At this time, sugar was still native only to India, so to sweeten anything elsewhere, honey usually did the trick!
And people didn't have covered ovens, so these cakes sat in crocks and baked directly in a fire.
And while ancient peoples ate these treats as snacks, they also offered them to their gods just as often.
I guess the gods liked sweets, too!
If they were used as offerings, they must've been pretty precious.
Yep! You'll notice that more and more as we go through dessert history.
They were all really rare!
Say, now that you're here . . .
Did I forget again?
OH!
Yes, please!
Legend

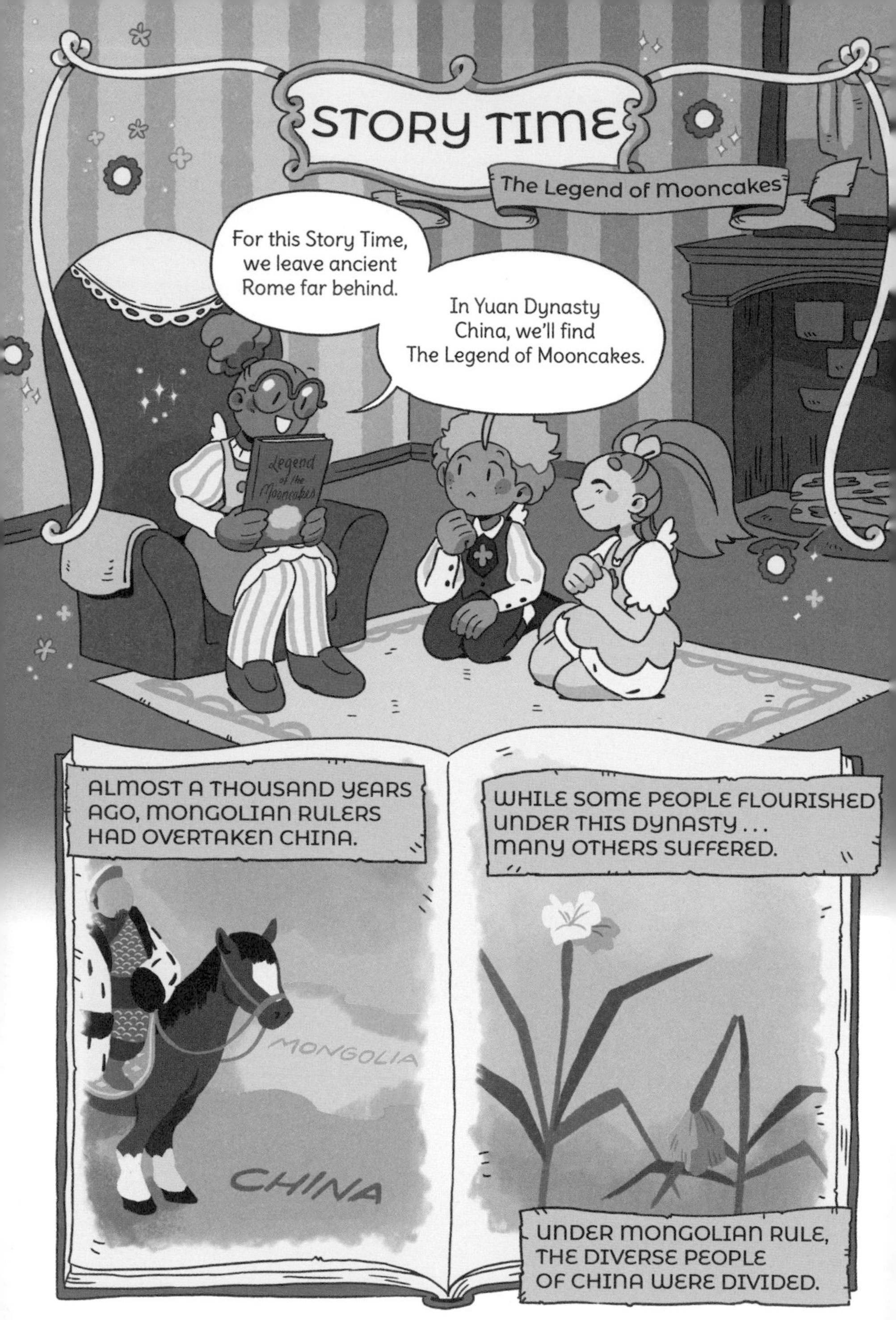
STORY TIME
The Legend of Mooncakes
For this Story Time, we leave ancient Rome far behind.
In Yuan Dynasty China, we'll find The Legend of Mooncakes.
Legend of the Mooncakes
ALMOST A THOUSAND YEARS AGO, MONGOLIAN RULERS HAD OVERTAKEN CHINA.
MONGOLIA
CHINA
WHILE SOME PEOPLE FLOURISHED UNDER THIS DYNASTY . . . MANY OTHERS SUFFERED.
UNDER MONGOLIAN RULE, THE DIVERSE PEOPLE OF CHINA WERE DIVIDED.

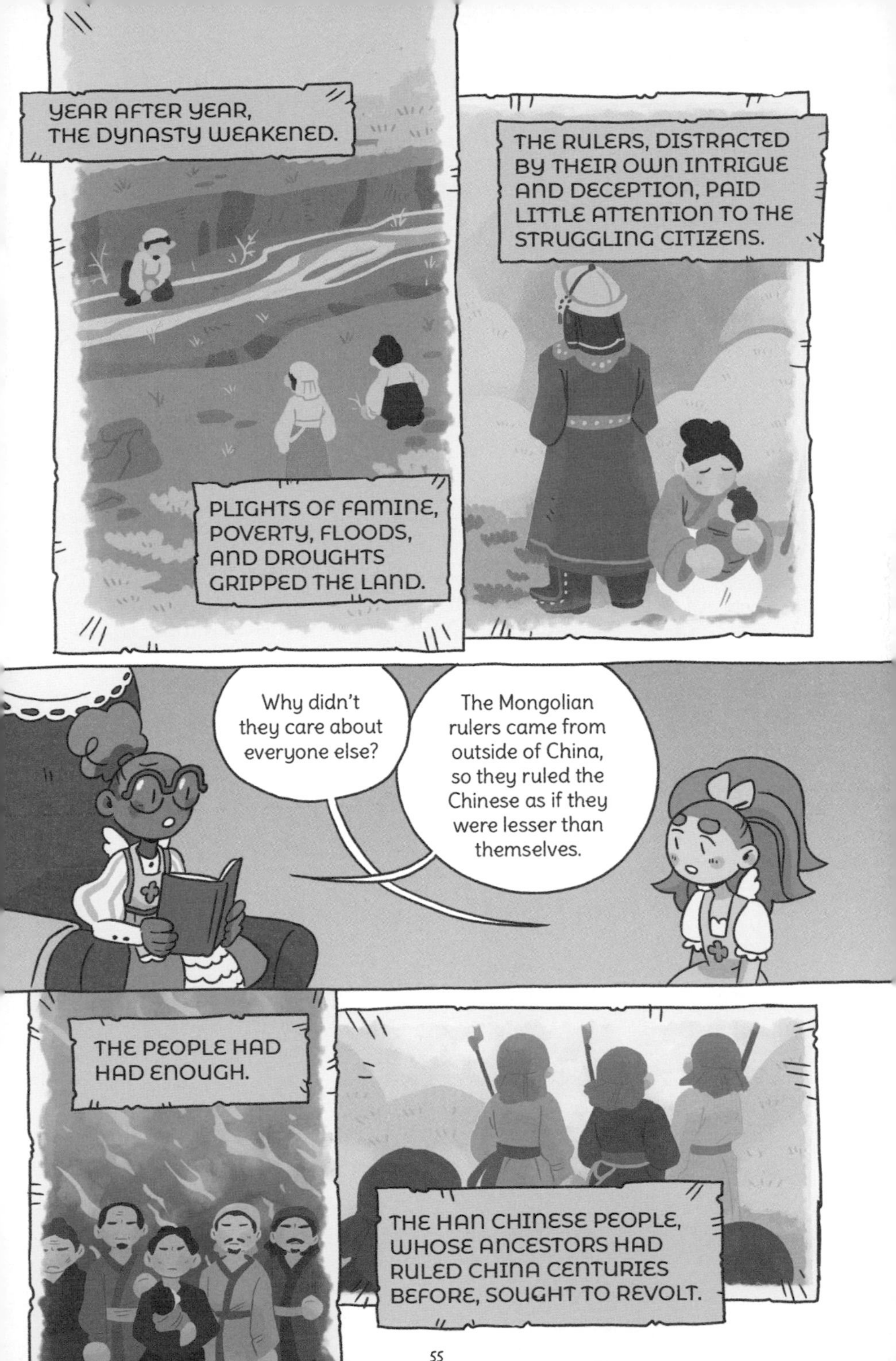
YEAR AFTER YEAR, THE DYNASTY WEAKENED.
PLIGHTS OF FAMINE, POVERTY, FLOODS, AND DROUGHTS GRIPPED THE LAND.
THE RULERS, DISTRACTED BY THEIR OWN INTRIGUE AND DECEPTION, PAID LITTLE ATTENTION TO THE STRUGGLING CITIZENS.
Why didn't they care about everyone else?
The Mongolian rulers came from outside of China, so they ruled the Chinese as if they were lesser than themselves.
THE PEOPLE HAD HAD ENOUGH.
THE HAN CHINESE PEOPLE, WHOSE ANCESTORS HAD RULED CHINA CENTURIES BEFORE, SOUGHT TO REVOLT.

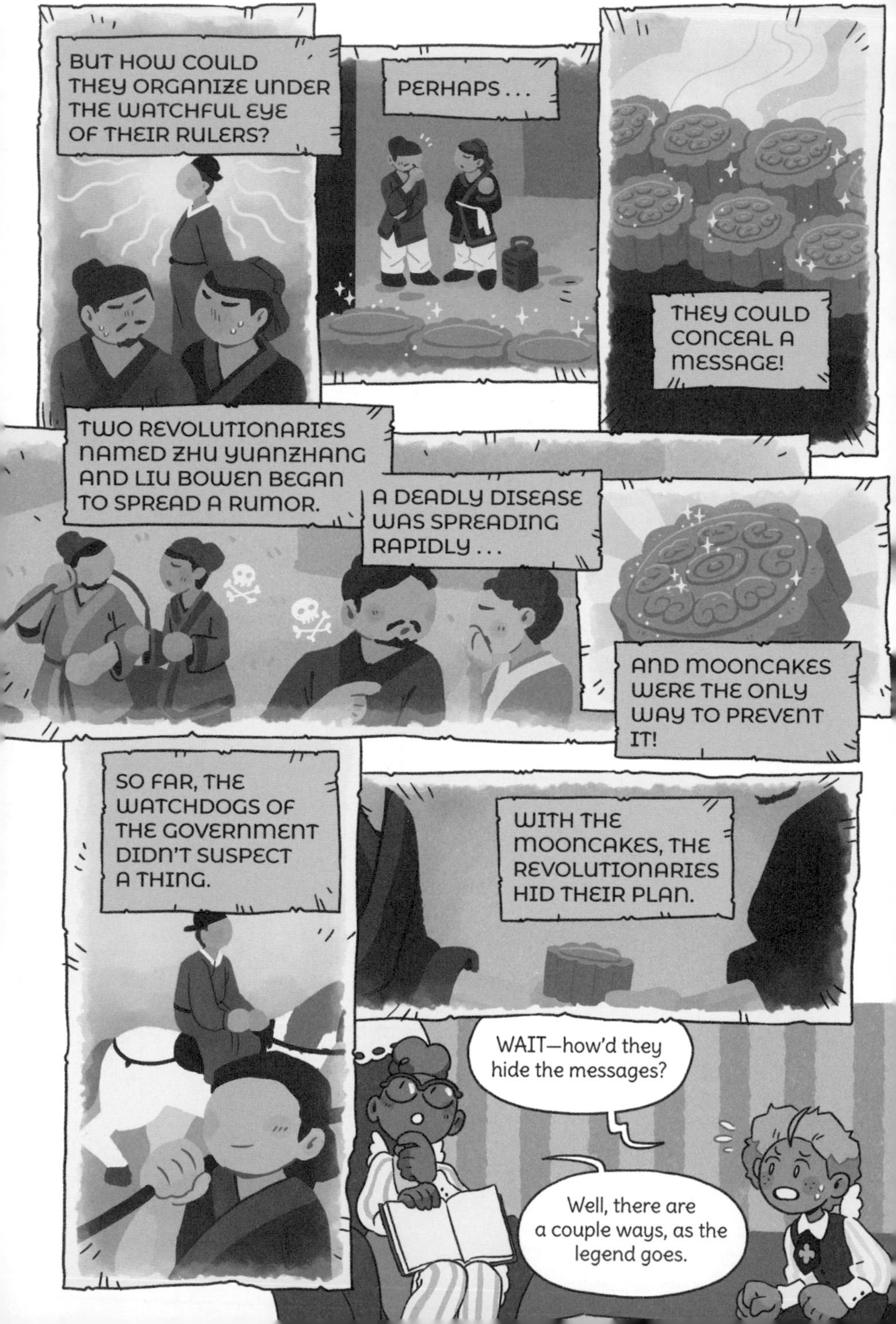
BUT HOW COULD THEY ORGANIZE UNDER THE WATCHFUL EYE OF THEIR RULERS?
PERHAPS . . .
THEY COULD CONCEAL A MESSAGE!
TWO REVOLUTIONARIES NAMED ZHU YUANZHANG AND LIU BOWEN BEGAN TO SPREAD A RUMOR.
A DEADLY DISEASE WAS SPREADING RAPIDLY . . .
AND MOONCAKES WERE THE ONLY WAY TO PREVENT IT!
SO FAR, THE WATCHDOGS OF THE GOVERNMENT DIDN'T SUSPECT A THING.
WITH THE MOONCAKES, THE REVOLUTIONARIES HID THEIR PLAN.
WAIT—how'd they hide the messages?
Well, there are a couple ways, as the legend goes.

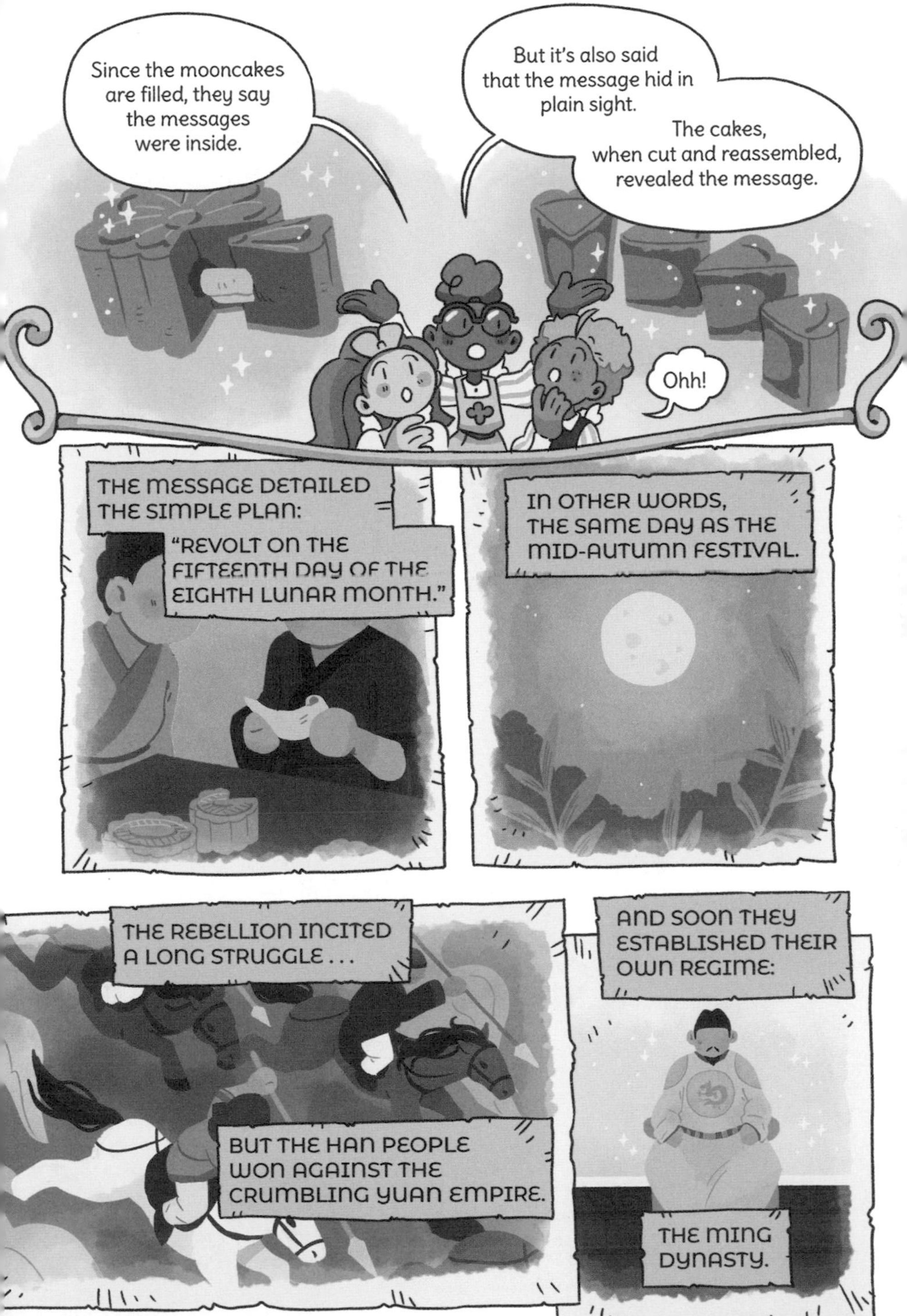

Since the mooncakes are filled, they say the messages were inside.
But it's also said that the message hid in plain sight.
The cakes, when cut and reassembled, revealed the message.
Ohh!
THE MESSAGE DETAILED THE SIMPLE PLAN:
"REVOLT ON THE FIFTEENTH DAY OF THE EIGHTH LUNAR MONTH."
IN OTHER WORDS, THE SAME DAY AS THE MID-AUTUMN FESTIVAL.
THE REBELLION INCITED A LONG STRUGGLE . . .
BUT THE HAN PEOPLE WON AGAINST THE CRUMBLING YUAN EMPIRE.
AND SOON THEY ESTABLISHED THEIR OWN REGIME:
THE MING DYNASTY.

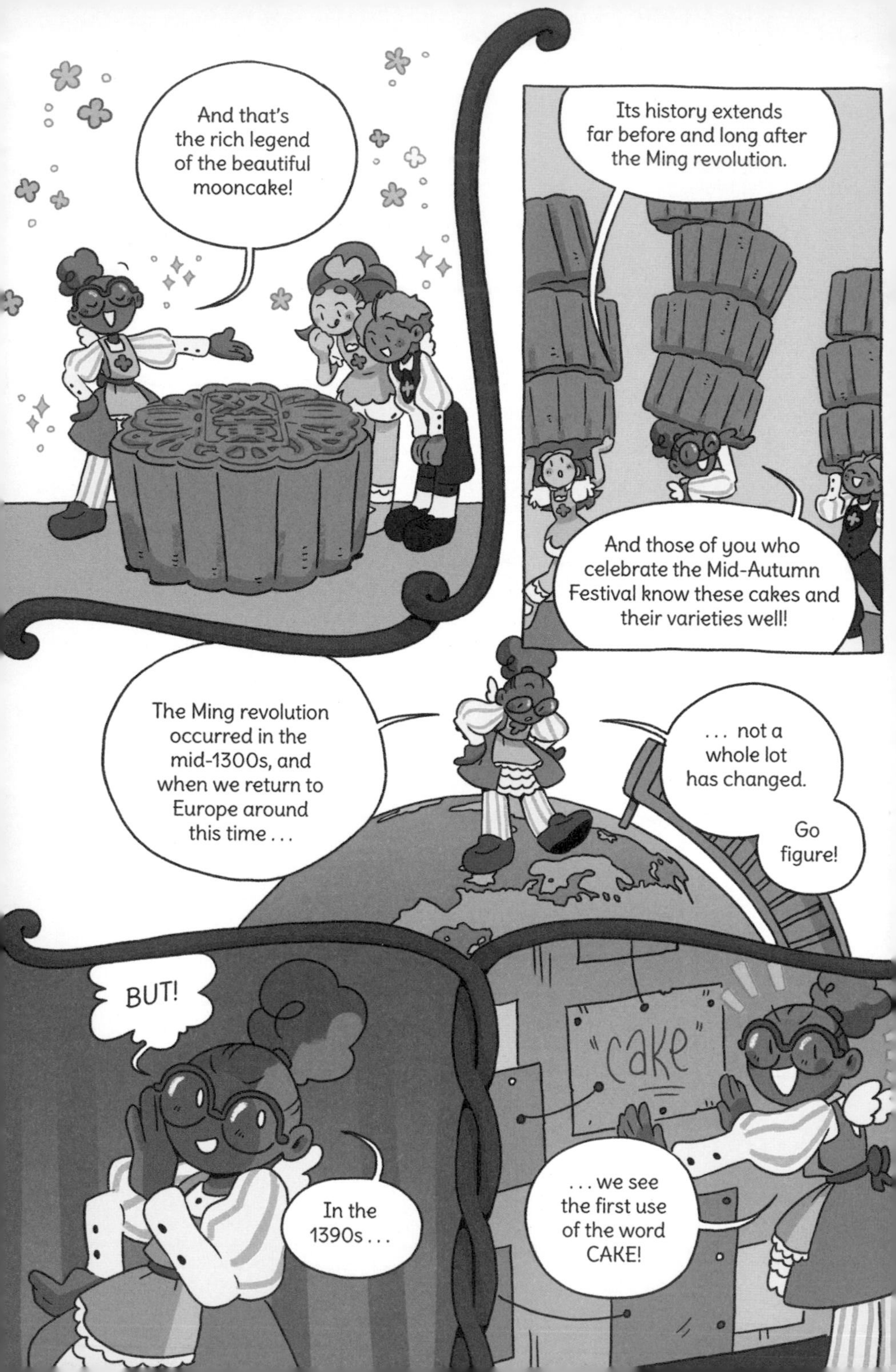
And that's the rich legend of the beautiful mooncake!
Its history extends far before and long after the Ming revolution.
And those of you who celebrate the Mid-Autumn Festival know these cakes and their varieties well!
The Ming revolution occurred in the mid-1300s, and when we return to Europe around this time . . .
. . . not a whole lot has changed.
Go figure!
BUT!
In the 1390s . . .
"cake"
. . . we see the first use of the word CAKE!

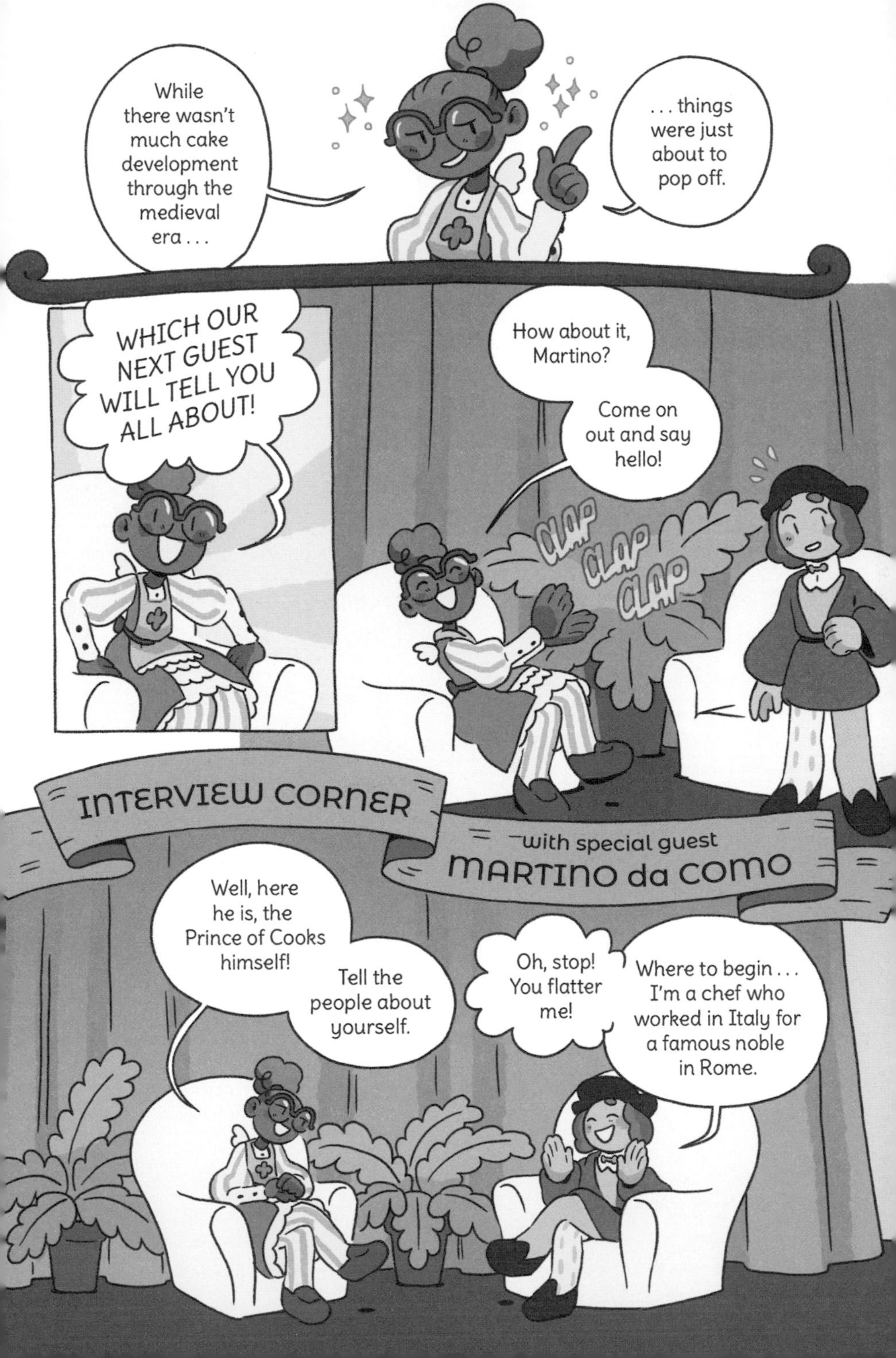
While there wasn't much cake development through the medieval era . . .
. . . things were just about to pop off.
WHICH OUR NEXT GUEST WILL TELL YOU ALL ABOUT!
How about it, Martino?
Come on out and say hello!
CLAP CLAP CLAP
INTERVIEW CORNER
with special guest
MARTINO da COMO
Well, here he is, the Prince of Cooks himself!
Tell the people about yourself.
Oh, stop! You flatter me!
Where to begin . . . I'm a chef who worked in Italy for a famous noble in Rome.

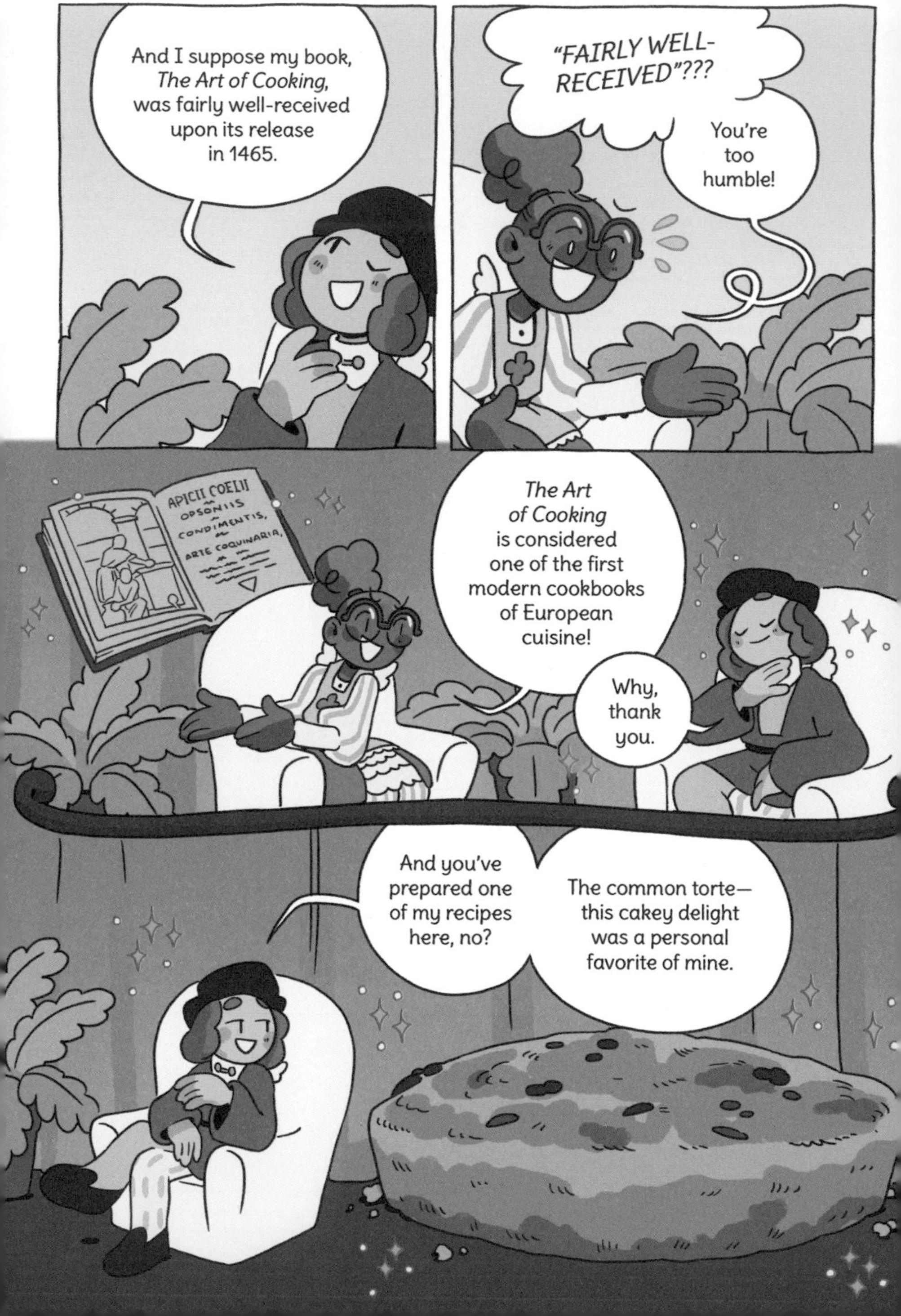
And I suppose my book, *The Art of Cooking*, was fairly well-received upon its release in 1465.
"FAIRLY WELL-RECEIVED"???
You're too humble!
APICII COELII OPSONIIS CONDIMENTIS, ARTE COQUINARIA,
*The Art of Cooking* is considered one of the first modern cookbooks of European cuisine!
Why, thank you.
And you've prepared one of my recipes here, no?
The common torte—this cakey delight was a personal favorite of mine.

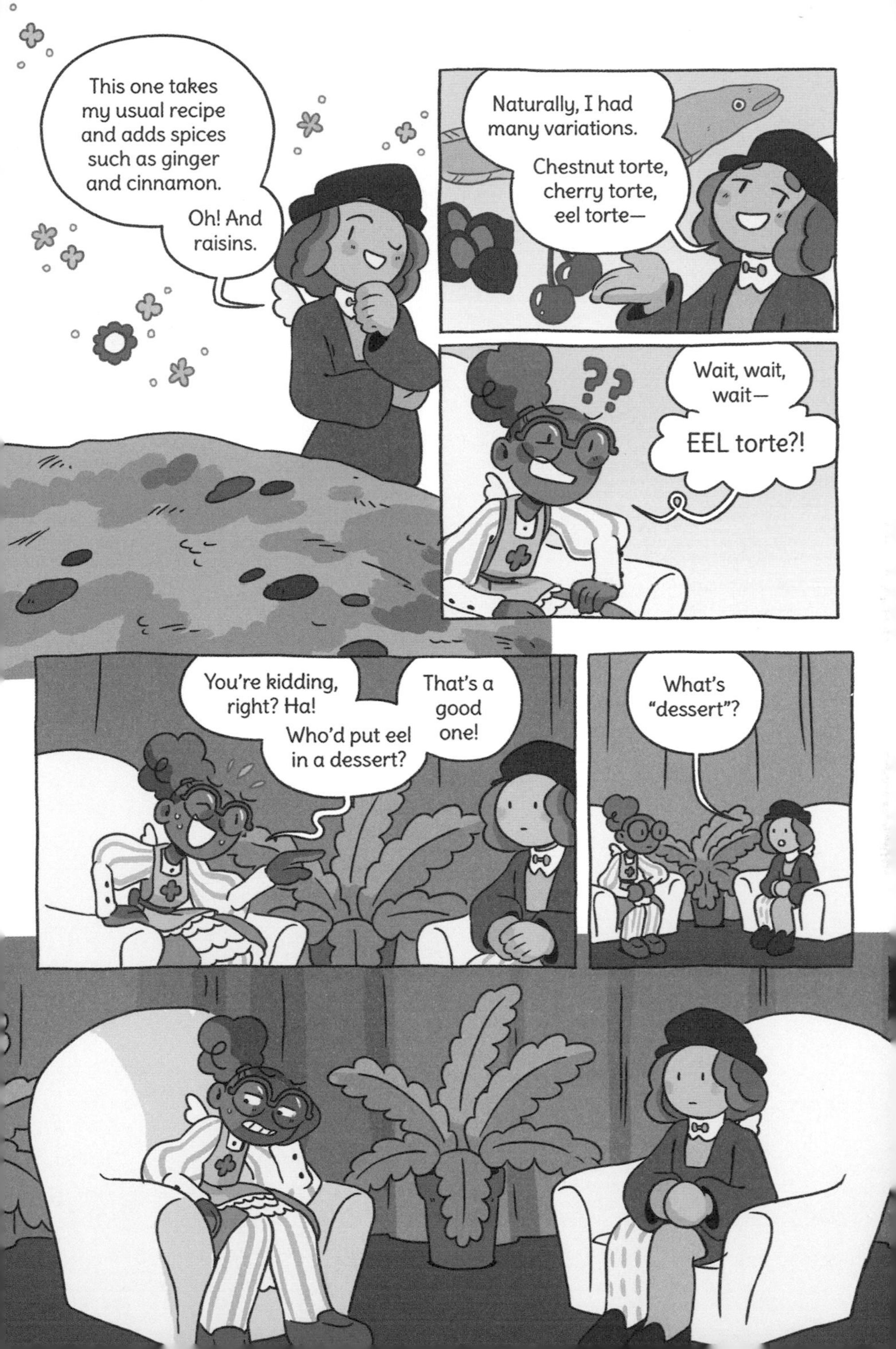
This one takes my usual recipe and adds spices such as ginger and cinnamon.
Oh! And raisins.
Naturally, I had many variations.
Chestnut torte, cherry torte, eel torte—
Wait, wait, wait—
EEL torte?!
You're kidding, right? Ha!
Who'd put eel in a dessert?
That's a good one!
What's "dessert"?

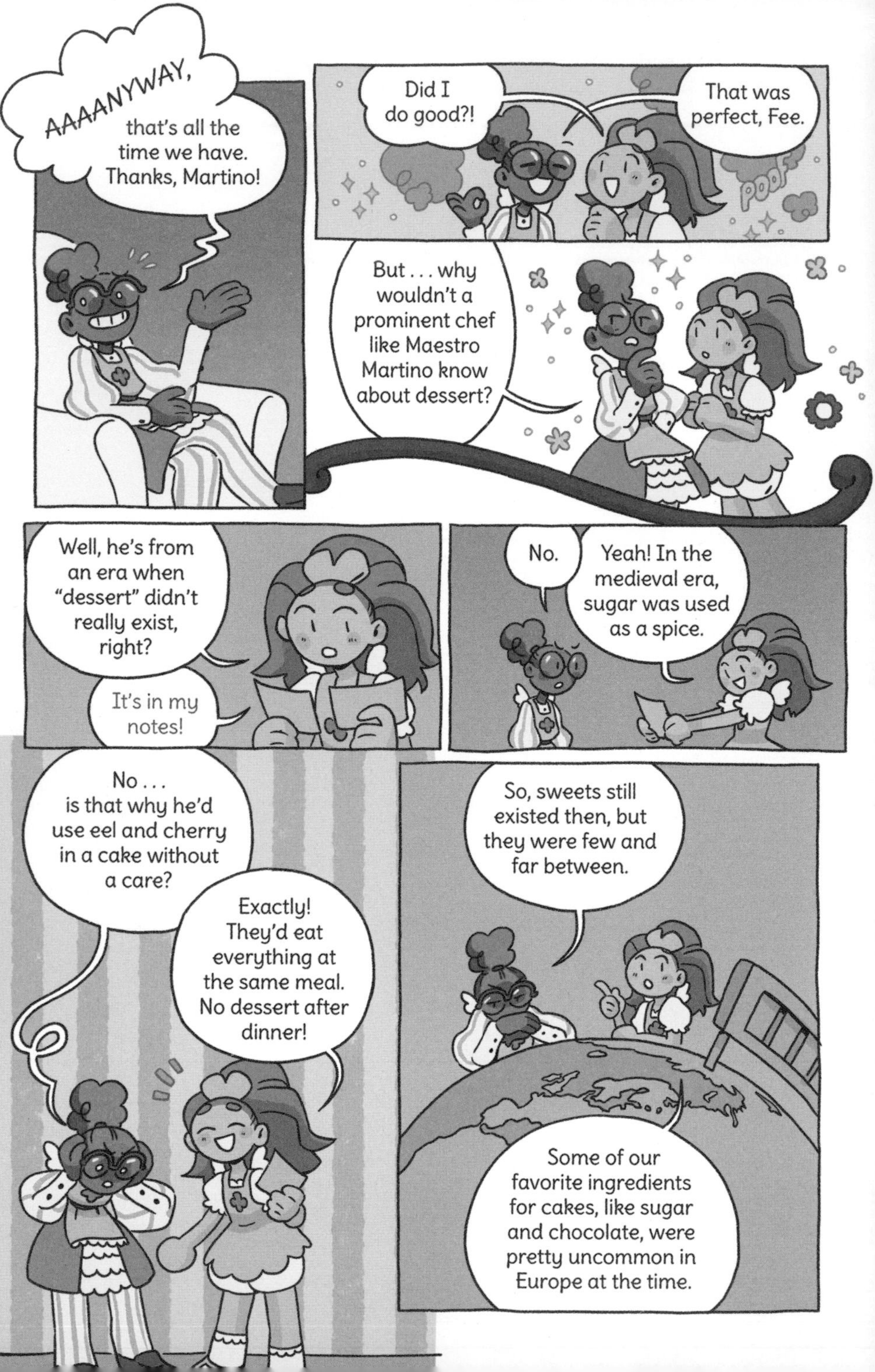
AAAANYWAY, that's all the time we have. Thanks, Martino!
Did I do good?!
That was perfect, Fee.
POOF
But . . . why wouldn't a prominent chef like Maestro Martino know about dessert?
Well, he's from an era when "dessert" didn't really exist, right?
It's in my notes!
No.
Yeah! In the medieval era, sugar was used as a spice.
No . . . is that why he'd use eel and cherry in a cake without a care?
Exactly! They'd eat everything at the same meal. No dessert after dinner!
So, sweets still existed then, but they were few and far between.
Some of our favorite ingredients for cakes, like sugar and chocolate, were pretty uncommon in Europe at the time.

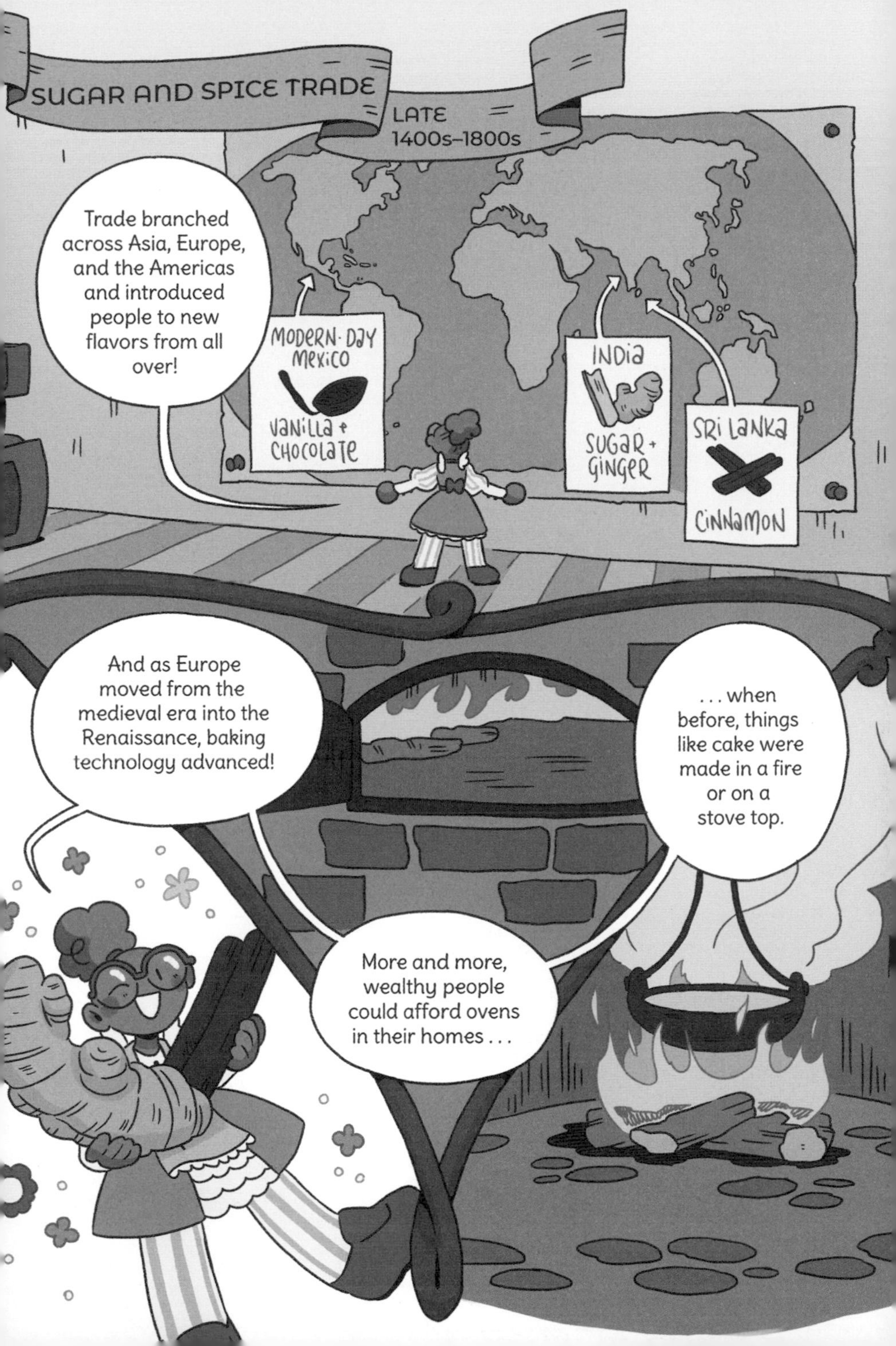
SUGAR AND SPICE TRADE
LATE 1400s–1800s
Trade branched across Asia, Europe, and the Americas and introduced people to new flavors from all over!
MODERN-DAY MEXICO
VANILLA + CHOCOLATE
INDIA
SUGAR + GINGER
SRI LANKA
CINNAMON
And as Europe moved from the medieval era into the Renaissance, baking technology advanced!
More and more, wealthy people could afford ovens in their homes . . .
. . . when before, things like cake were made in a fire or on a stove top.

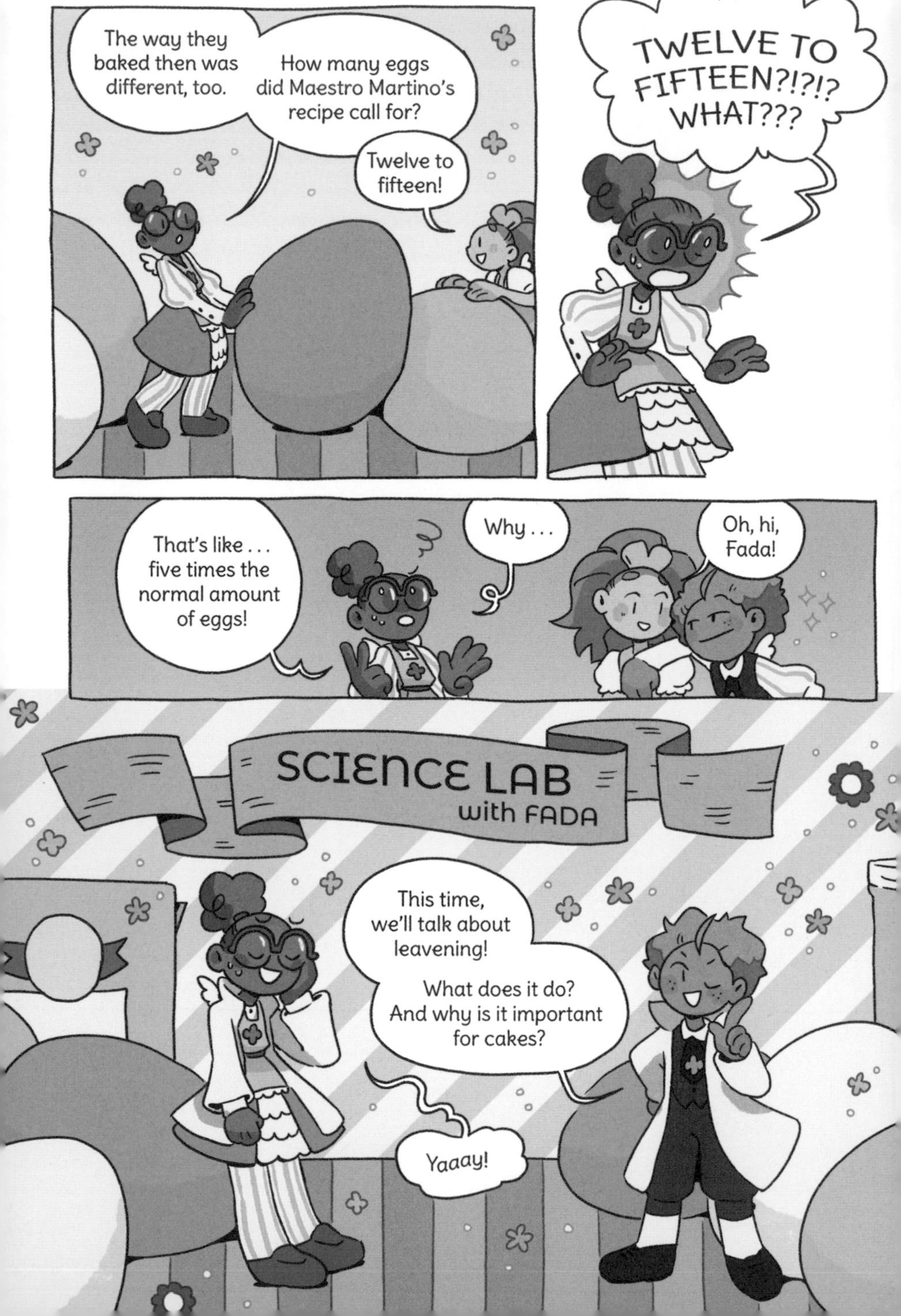

The way they baked then was different, too.
How many eggs did Maestro Martino's recipe call for?
Twelve to fifteen!
TWELVE TO FIFTEEN?!?!? WHAT???
That's like . . . five times the normal amount of eggs!
Why . . .
Oh, hi, Fada!
SCIENCE LAB with FADA
This time, we'll talk about leavening!
What does it do? And why is it important for cakes?
Yaaay!

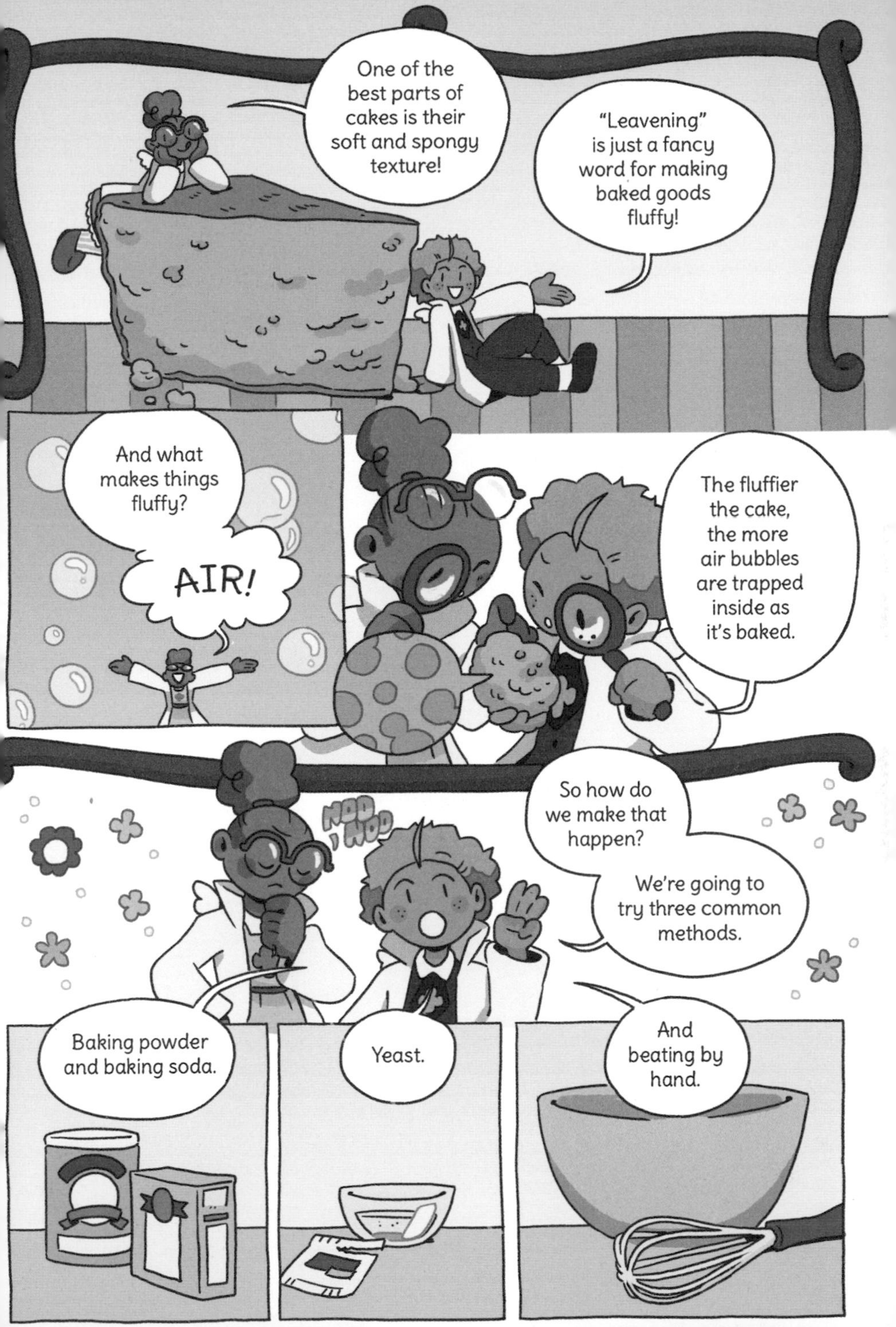
One of the best parts of cakes is their soft and spongy texture!
"Leavening" is just a fancy word for making baked goods fluffy!
And what makes things fluffy?
AIR!
The fluffier the cake, the more air bubbles are trapped inside as it's baked.
So how do we make that happen?
NOD NOD
We're going to try three common methods.
Baking powder and baking soda.
Yeast.
And beating by hand.

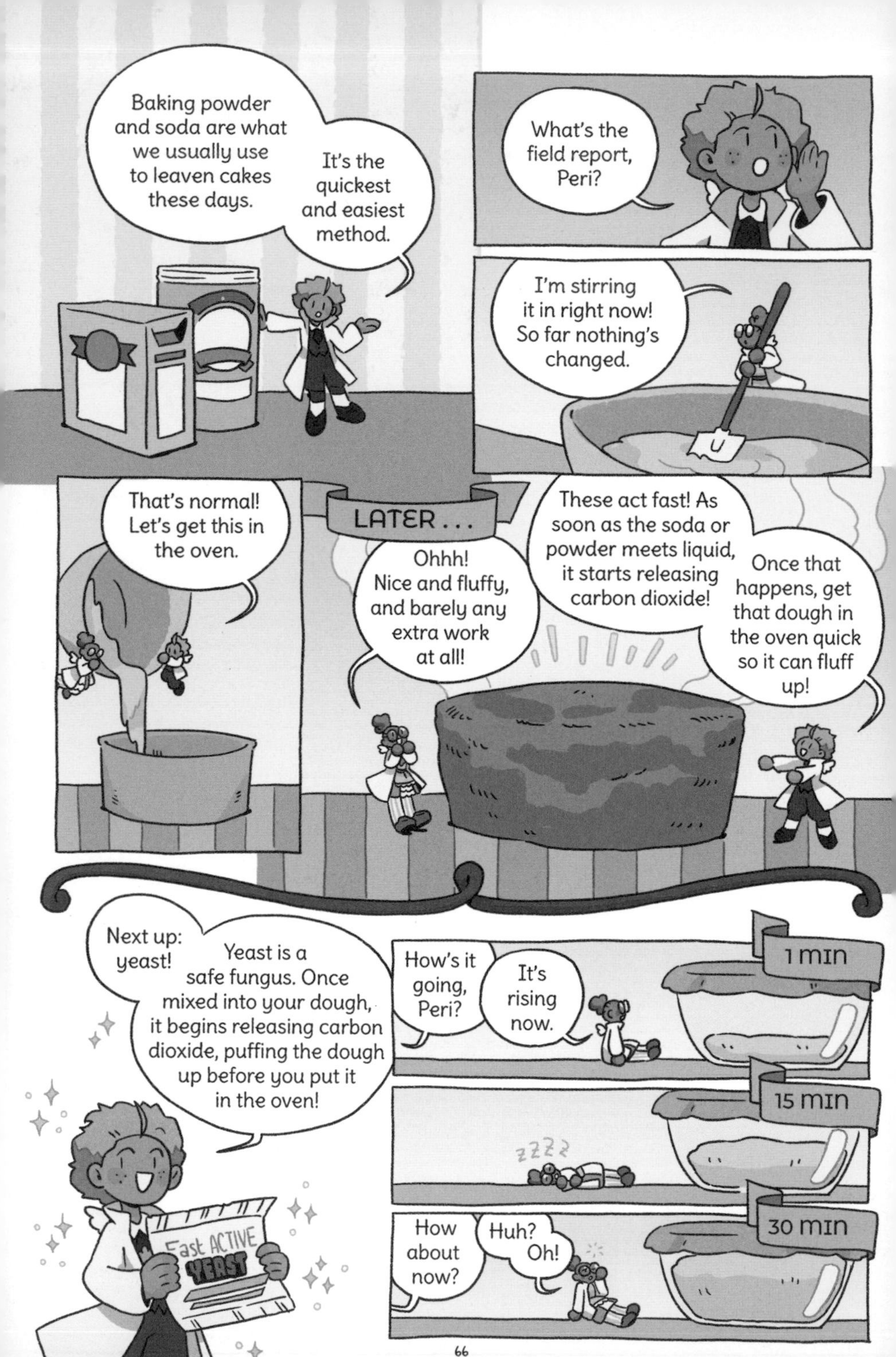

Baking powder and soda are what we usually use to leaven cakes these days.
It's the quickest and easiest method.
What's the field report, Peri?
I'm stirring it in right now! So far nothing's changed.
That's normal! Let's get this in the oven.
LATER . . .
Ohhh! Nice and fluffy, and barely any extra work at all!
These act fast! As soon as the soda or powder meets liquid, it starts releasing carbon dioxide!
Once that happens, get that dough in the oven quick so it can fluff up!
Next up: yeast!
Yeast is a safe fungus. Once mixed into your dough, it begins releasing carbon dioxide, puffing the dough up before you put it in the oven!
Fast ACTIVE YEAST
1 MIN
How's it going, Peri?
It's rising now.
15 MIN
ZZZZ
30 MIN
How about now?
Huh? Oh!

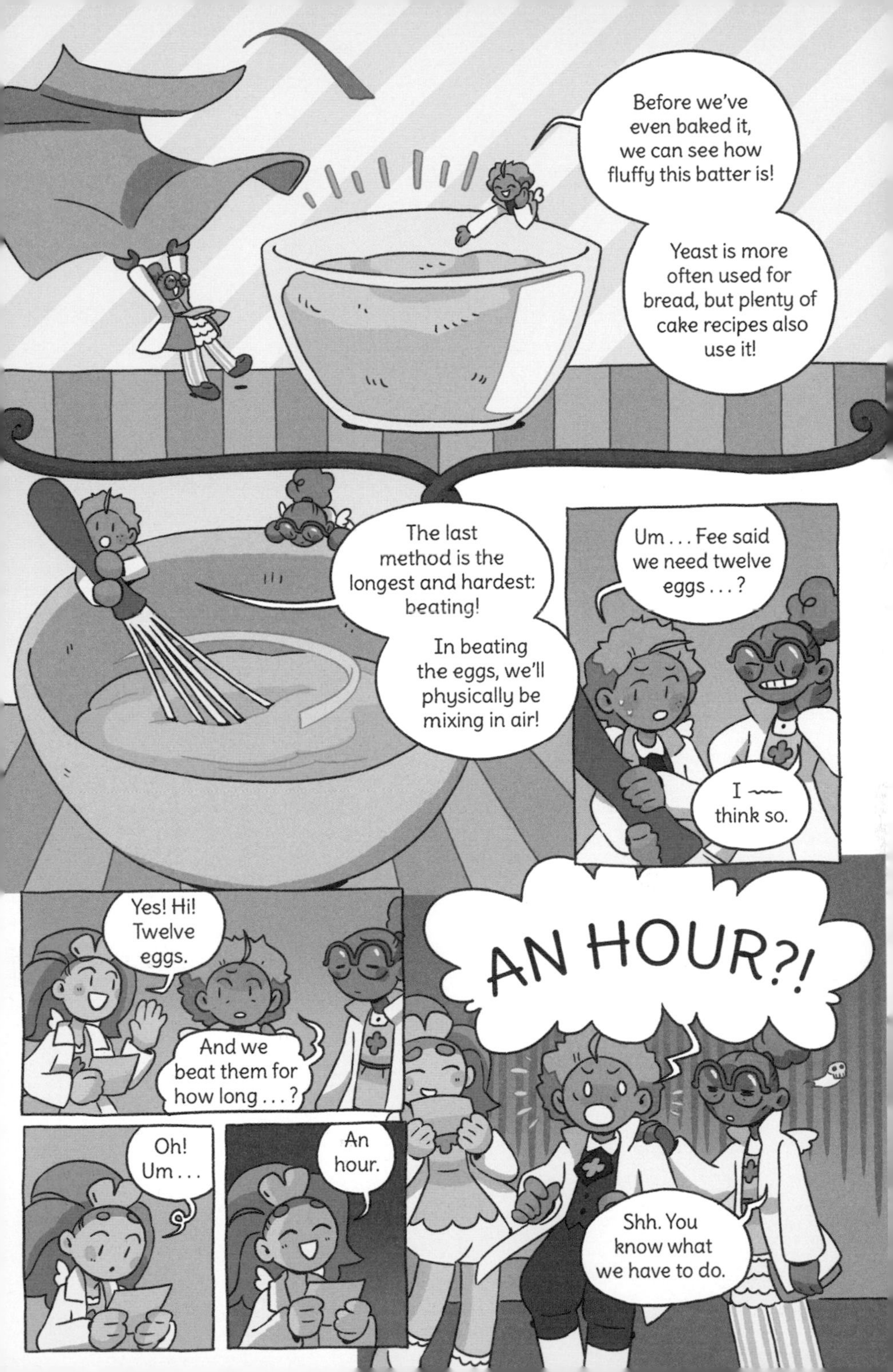

Before we've even baked it, we can see how fluffy this batter is!
Yeast is more often used for bread, but plenty of cake recipes also use it!
The last method is the longest and hardest: beating!
In beating the eggs, we'll physically be mixing in air!
Um . . . Fee said we need twelve eggs . . . ?
I — think so.
Yes! Hi! Twelve eggs.
And we beat them for how long . . . ?
Oh! Um . . .
An hour.
AN HOUR?!
Shh. You know what we have to do.

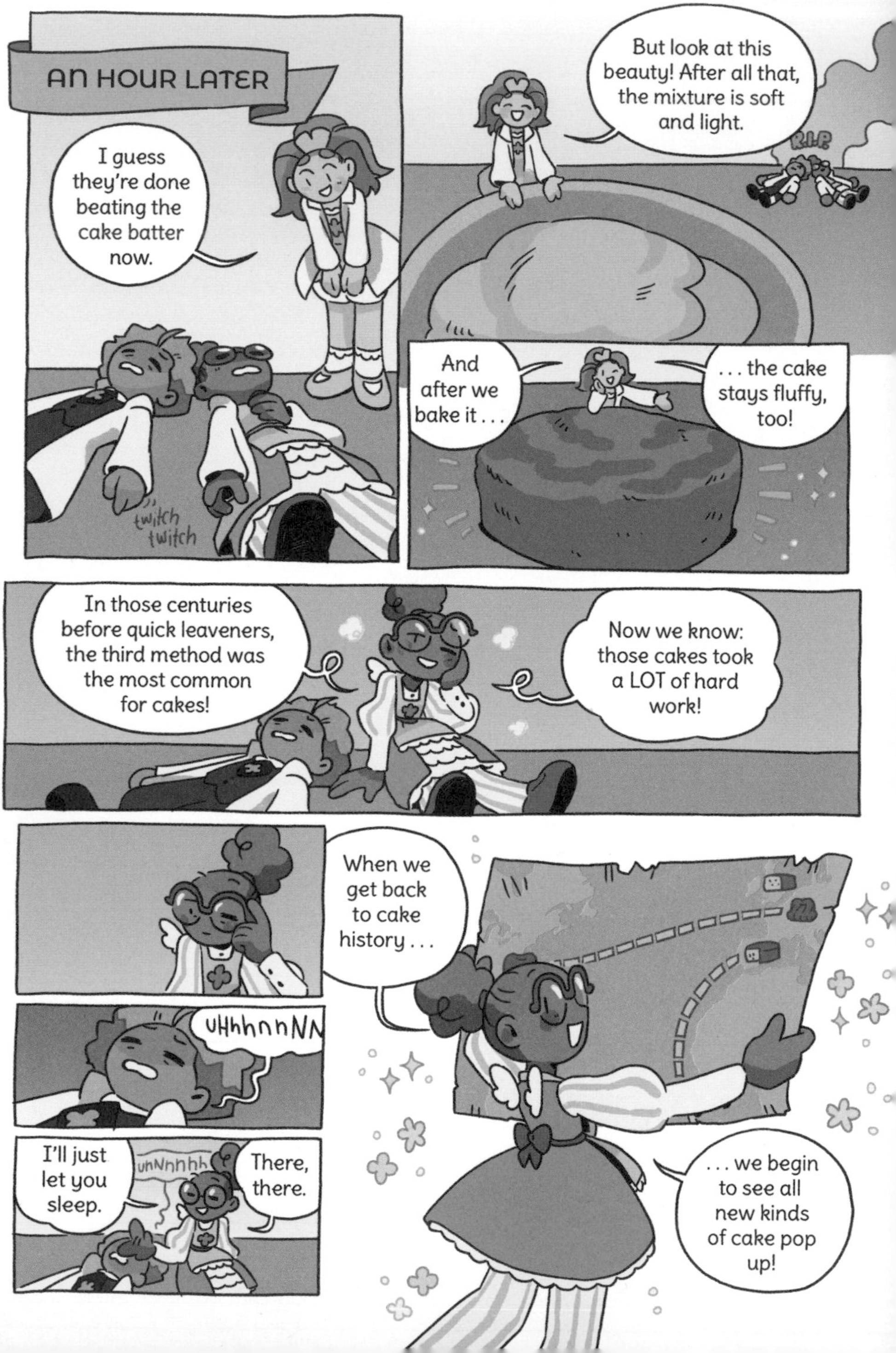
AN HOUR LATER
I guess they're done beating the cake batter now.
twitch twitch
But look at this beauty! After all that, the mixture is soft and light.
R.I.P.
And after we bake it . . .
. . . the cake stays fluffy, too!
In those centuries before quick leaveners, the third method was the most common for cakes!
Now we know: those cakes took a LOT of hard work!
UHhhnnNN
I'll just let you sleep.
uhNnhh
There, there.
When we get back to cake history . . .
. . . we begin to see all new kinds of cake pop up!

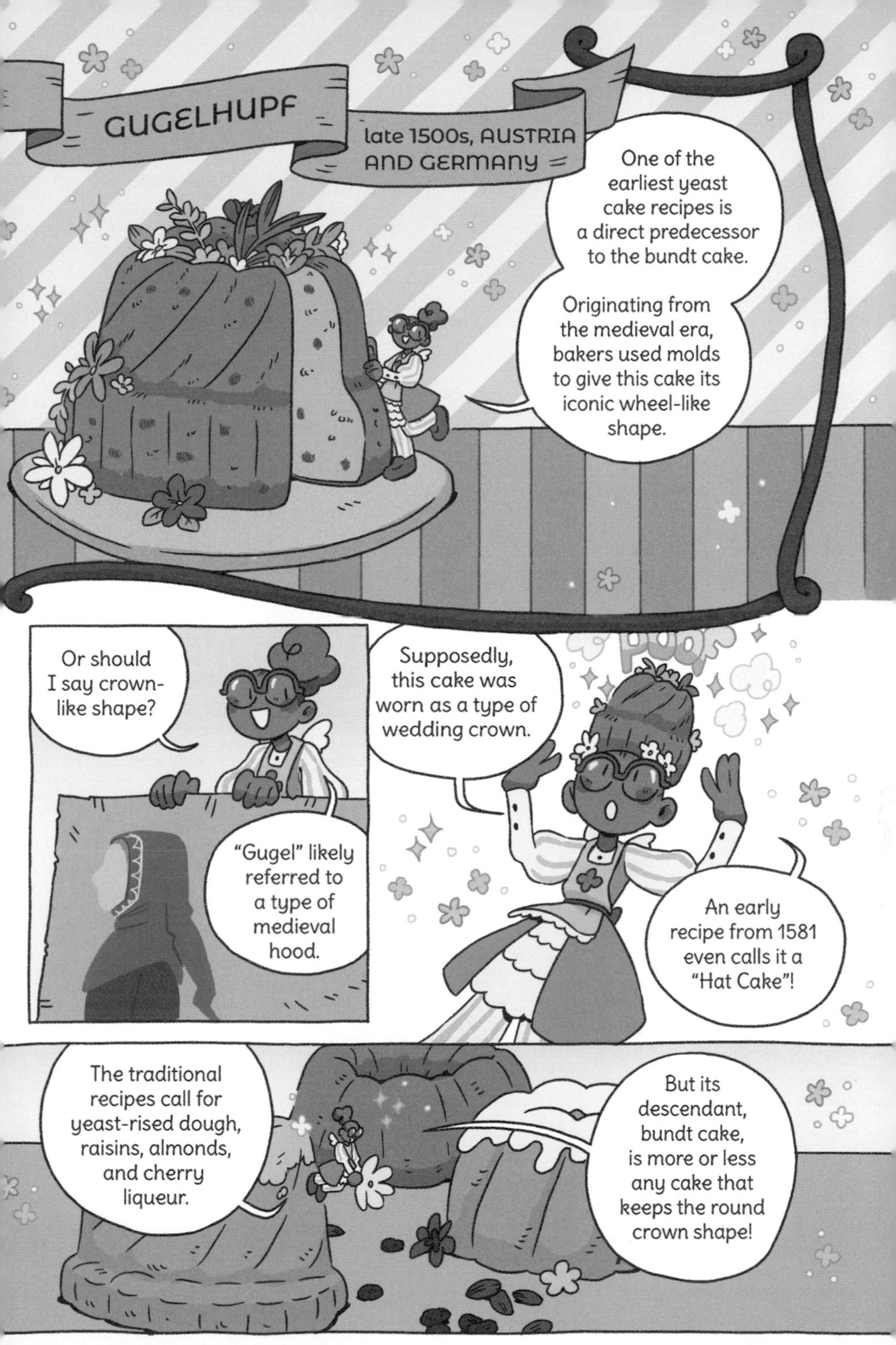
GUGELHUPF
late 1500s, AUSTRIA AND GERMANY
One of the earliest yeast cake recipes is a direct predecessor to the bundt cake.
Originating from the medieval era, bakers used molds to give this cake its iconic wheel-like shape.
Or should I say crown-like shape?
"Gugel" likely referred to a type of medieval hood.
Supposedly, this cake was worn as a type of wedding crown.
An early recipe from 1581 even calls it a "Hat Cake"!
The traditional recipes call for yeast-rised dough, raisins, almonds, and cherry liqueur.
But its descendant, bundt cake, is more or less any cake that keeps the round crown shape!

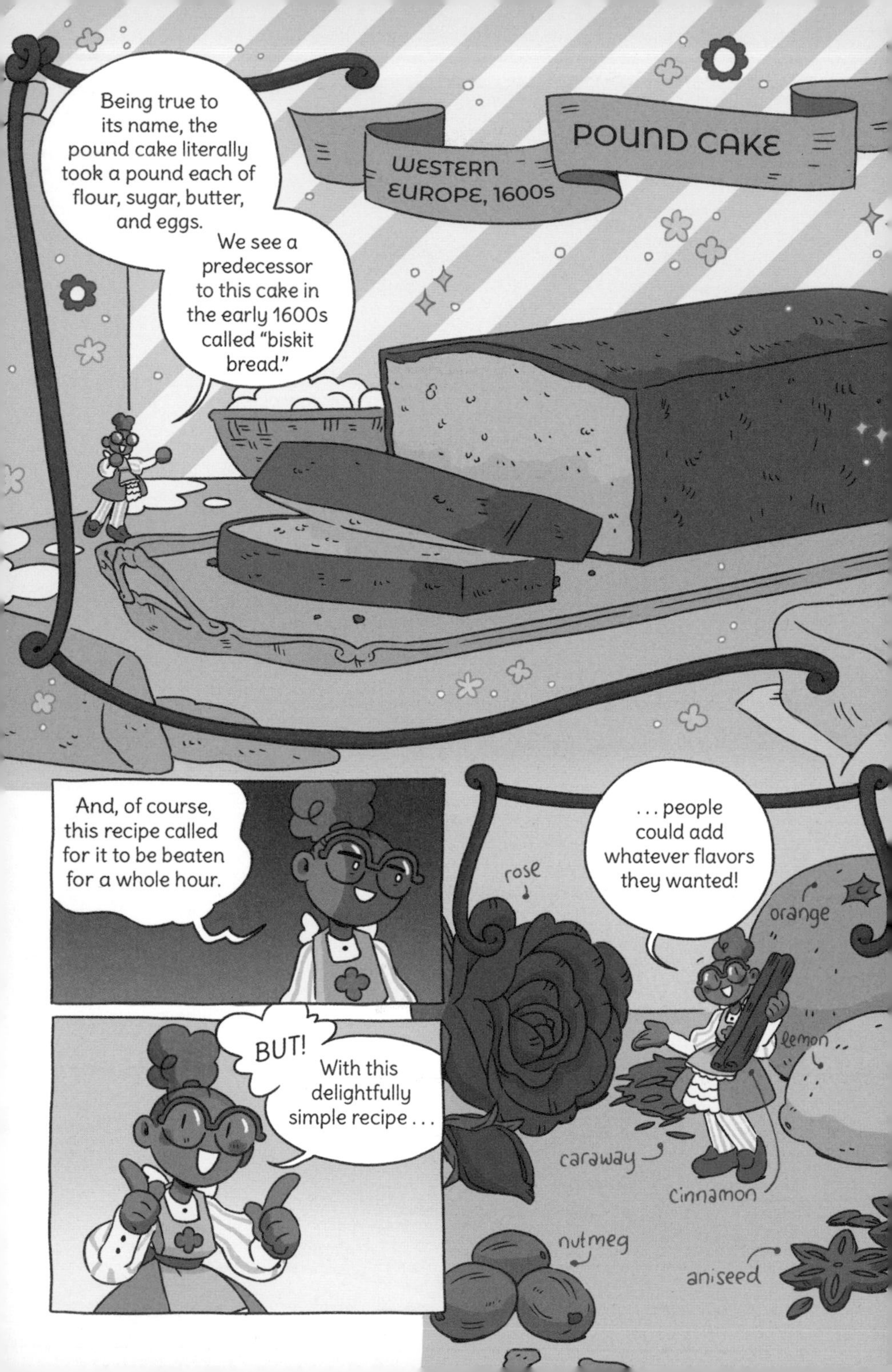
POUND CAKE
WESTERN EUROPE, 1600s
Being true to its name, the pound cake literally took a pound each of flour, sugar, butter, and eggs.
We see a predecessor to this cake in the early 1600s called "biskit bread."
And, of course, this recipe called for it to be beaten for a whole hour.
BUT!
With this delightfully simple recipe . . .
. . . people could add whatever flavors they wanted!
rose
orange
lemon
caraway
cinnamon
nutmeg
aniseed

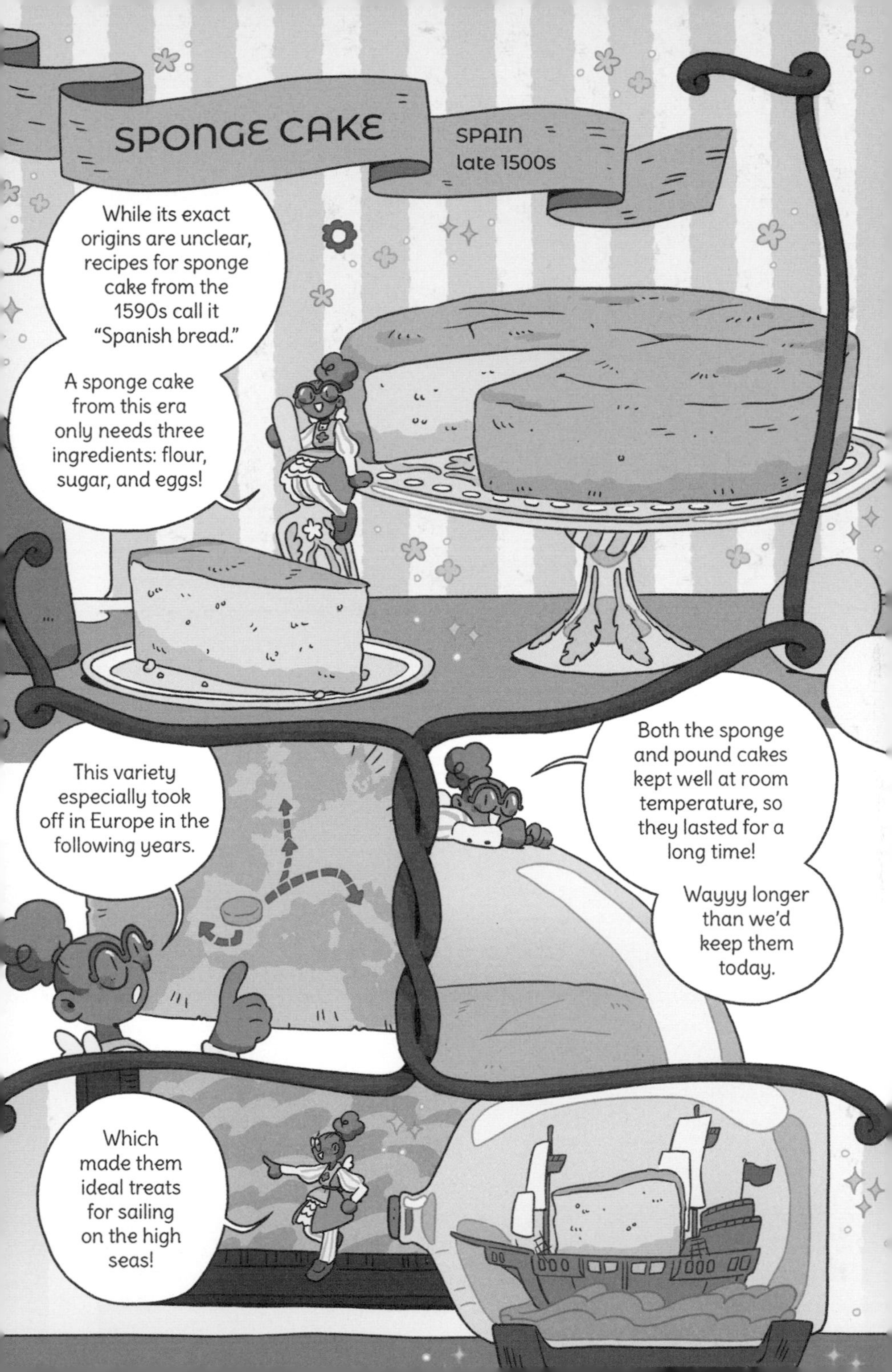
SPONGE CAKE
SPAIN late 1500s
While its exact origins are unclear, recipes for sponge cake from the 1590s call it "Spanish bread."
A sponge cake from this era only needs three ingredients: flour, sugar, and eggs!
This variety especially took off in Europe in the following years.
Both the sponge and pound cakes kept well at room temperature, so they lasted for a long time!
Wayyy longer than we'd keep them today.
Which made them ideal treats for sailing on the high seas!

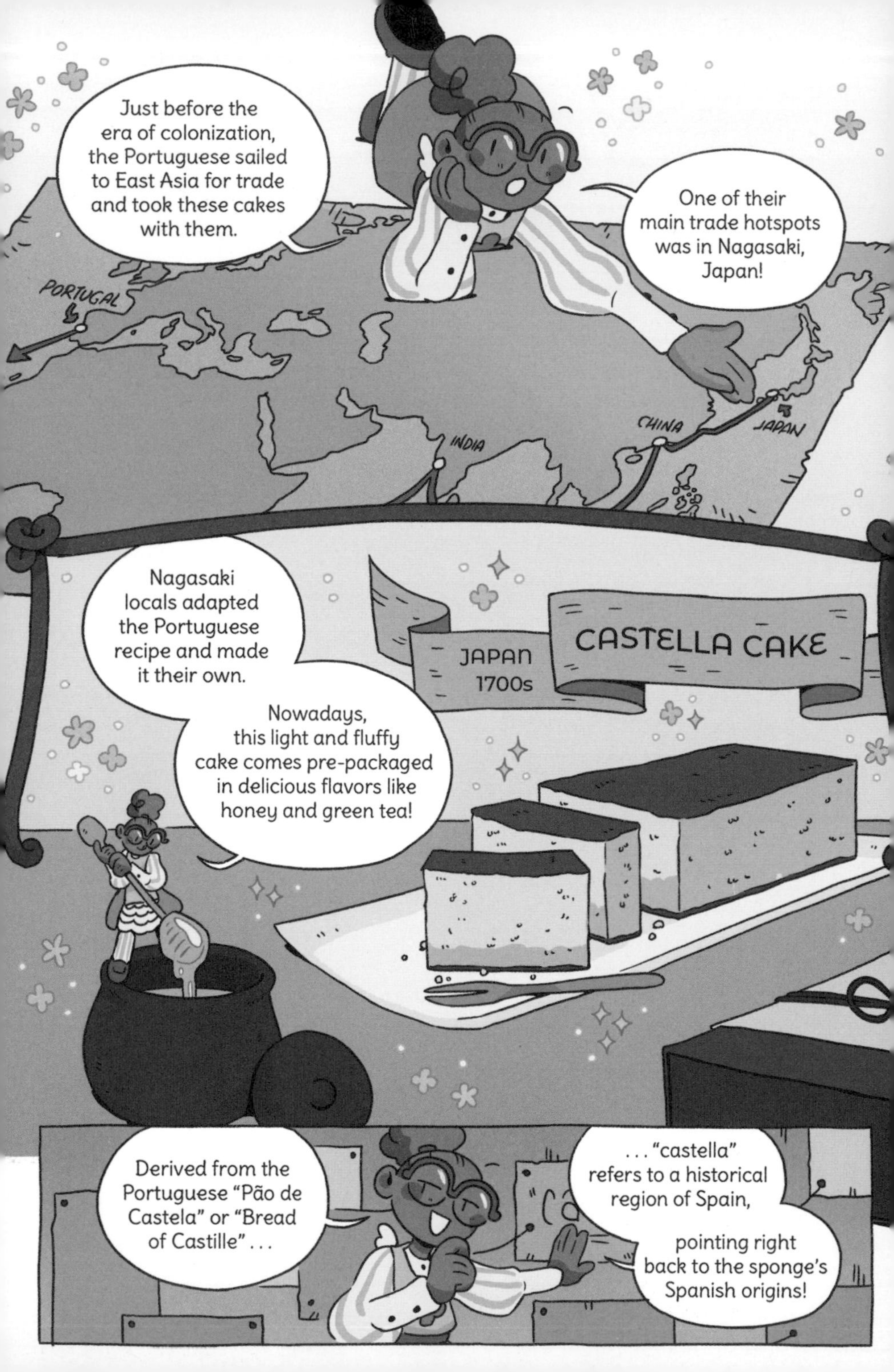
Just before the era of colonization, the Portuguese sailed to East Asia for trade and took these cakes with them.
One of their main trade hotspots was in Nagasaki, Japan!
PORTUGAL
INDIA
CHINA
JAPAN
Nagasaki locals adapted the Portuguese recipe and made it their own.
JAPAN 1700s
CASTELLA CAKE
Nowadays, this light and fluffy cake comes pre-packaged in delicious flavors like honey and green tea!
Derived from the Portuguese "Pão de Castela" or "Bread of Castille" . . .
. . . "castella" refers to a historical region of Spain,
pointing right back to the sponge's Spanish origins!

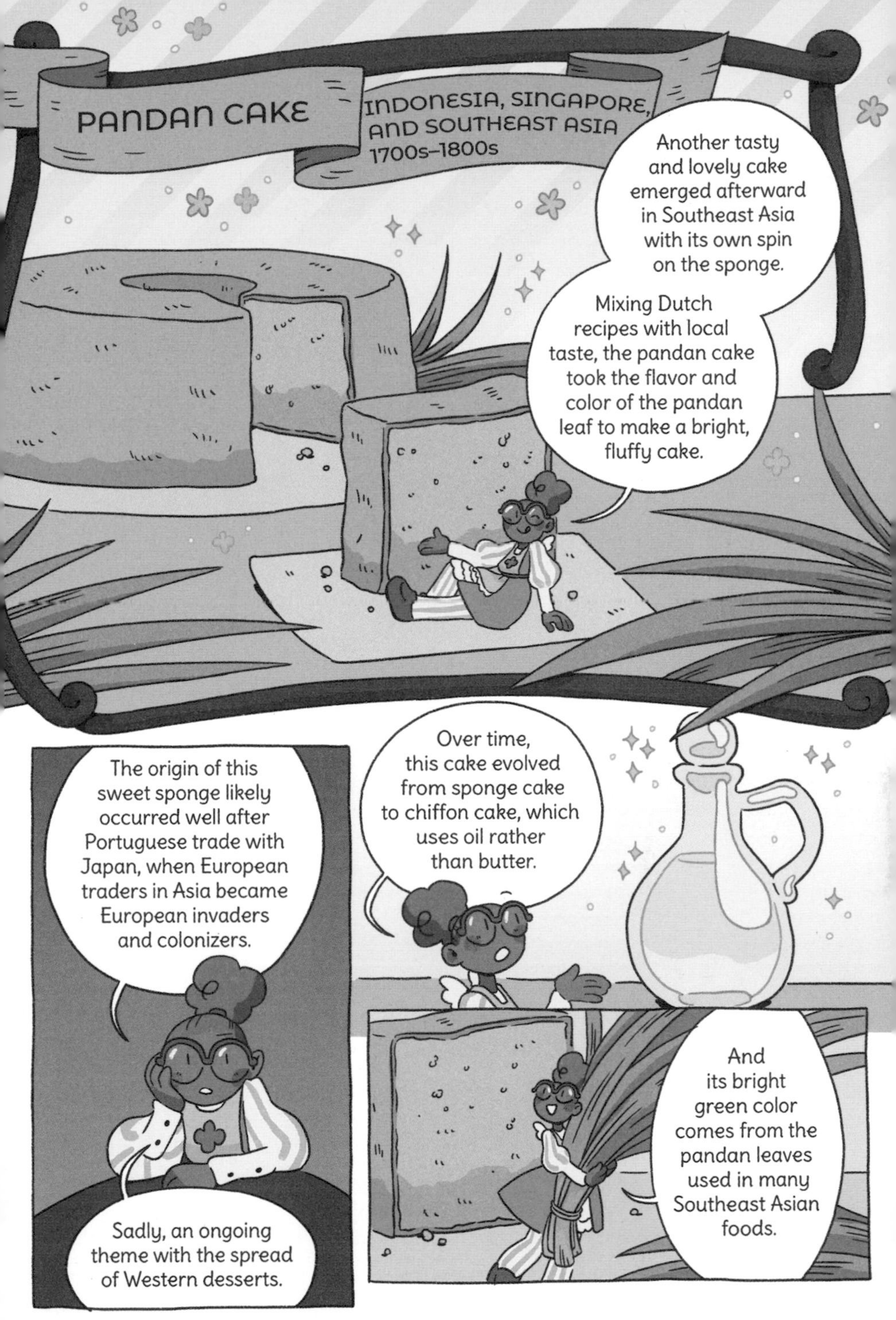
PANDAN CAKE
INDONESIA, SINGAPORE, AND SOUTHEAST ASIA 1700s–1800s
Another tasty and lovely cake emerged afterward in Southeast Asia with its own spin on the sponge.
Mixing Dutch recipes with local taste, the pandan cake took the flavor and color of the pandan leaf to make a bright, fluffy cake.
The origin of this sweet sponge likely occurred well after Portuguese trade with Japan, when European traders in Asia became European invaders and colonizers.
Sadly, an ongoing theme with the spread of Western desserts.
Over time, this cake evolved from sponge cake to chiffon cake, which uses oil rather than butter.
And its bright green color comes from the pandan leaves used in many Southeast Asian foods.

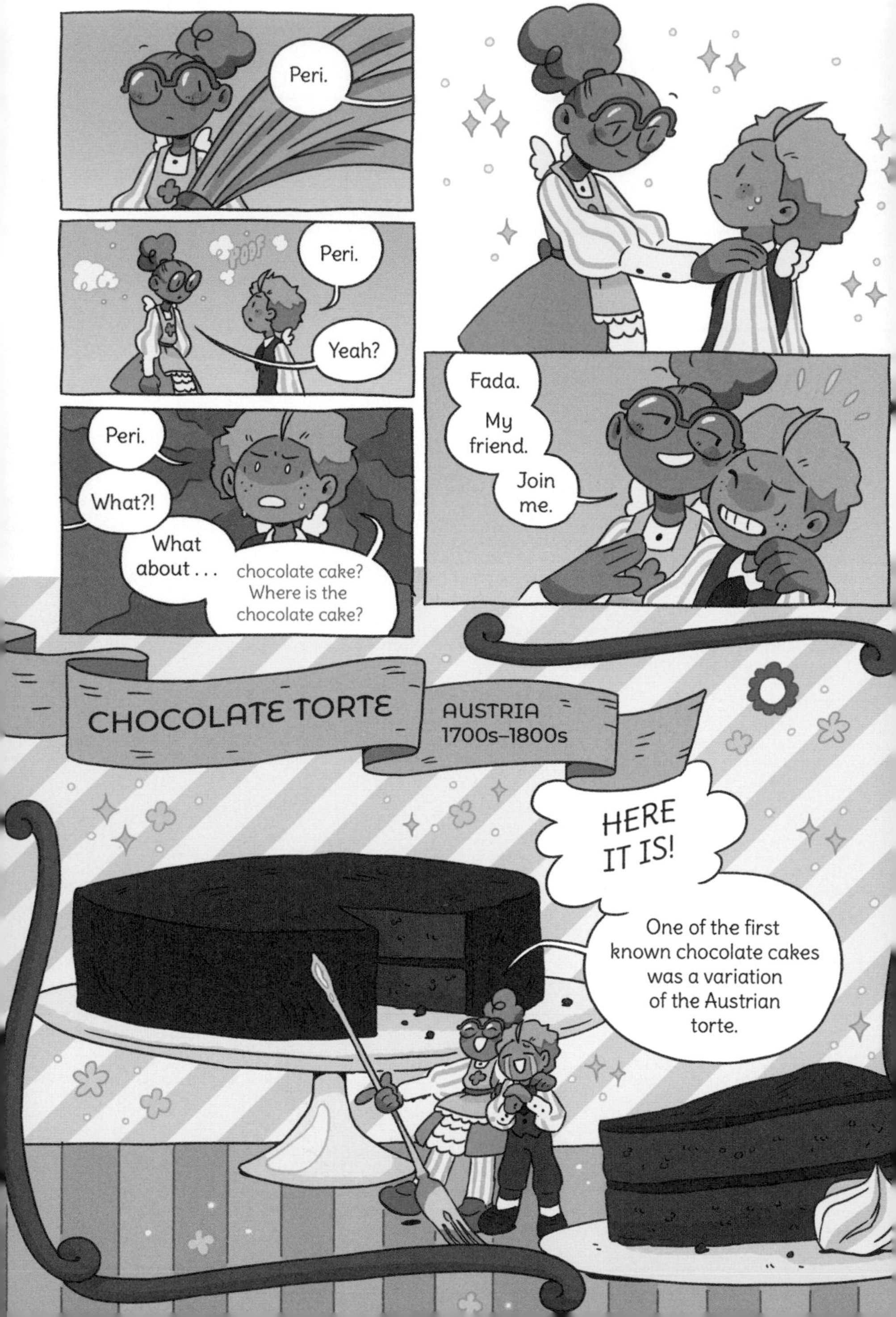

Peri.
POOF
Peri.
Yeah?
Peri.
What?!
What about . . .
chocolate cake? Where is the chocolate cake?
Fada.
My friend.
Join me.
CHOCOLATE TORTE
AUSTRIA 1700s–1800s
HERE IT IS!
One of the first known chocolate cakes was a variation of the Austrian torte.

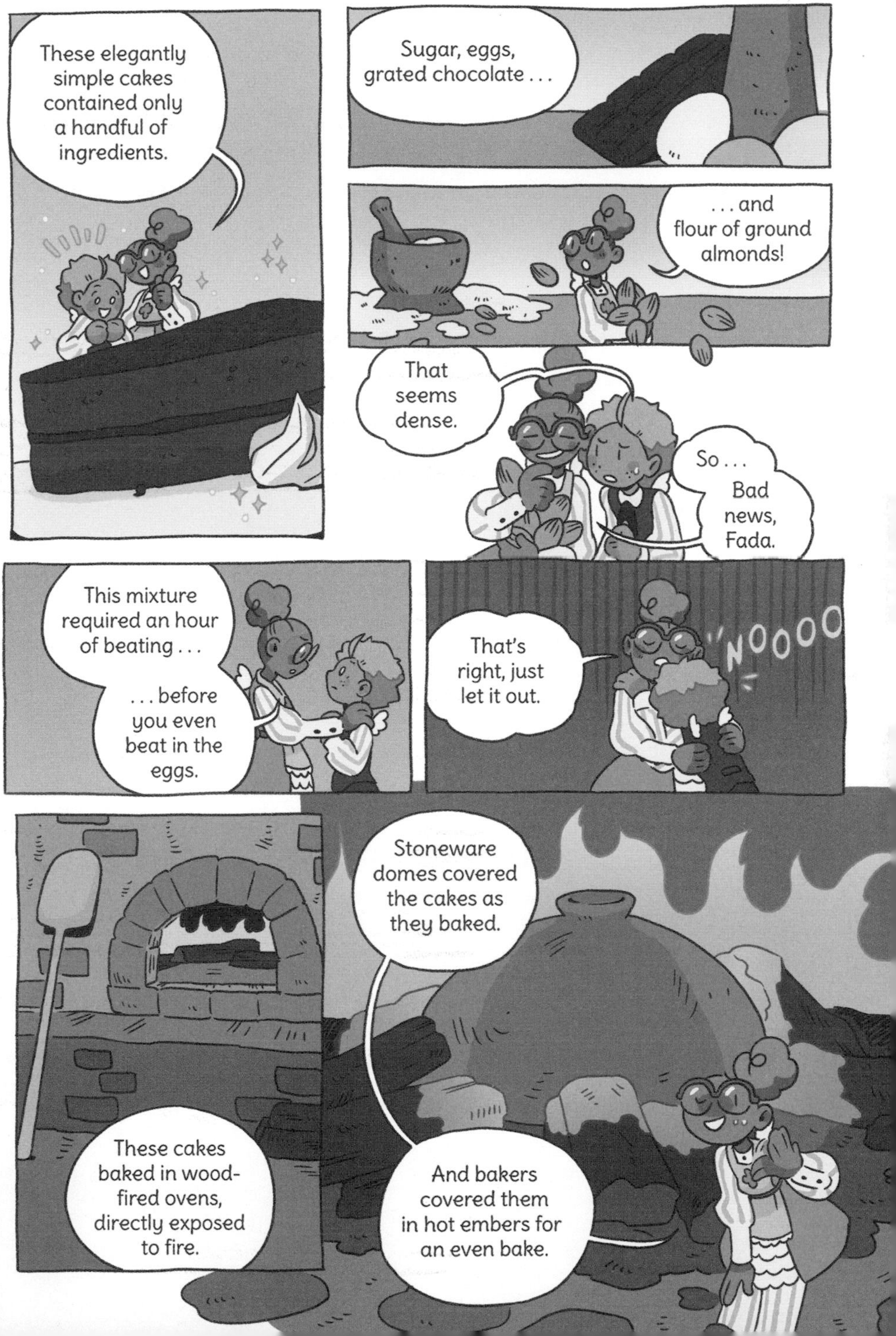
These elegantly simple cakes contained only a handful of ingredients.
Sugar, eggs, grated chocolate . . .
. . . and flour of ground almonds!
That seems dense.
So . . .
Bad news, Fada.
This mixture required an hour of beating . . .
. . . before you even beat in the eggs.
That's right, just let it out.
NOOOO
These cakes baked in wood-fired ovens, directly exposed to fire.
Stoneware domes covered the cakes as they baked.
And bakers covered them in hot embers for an even bake.

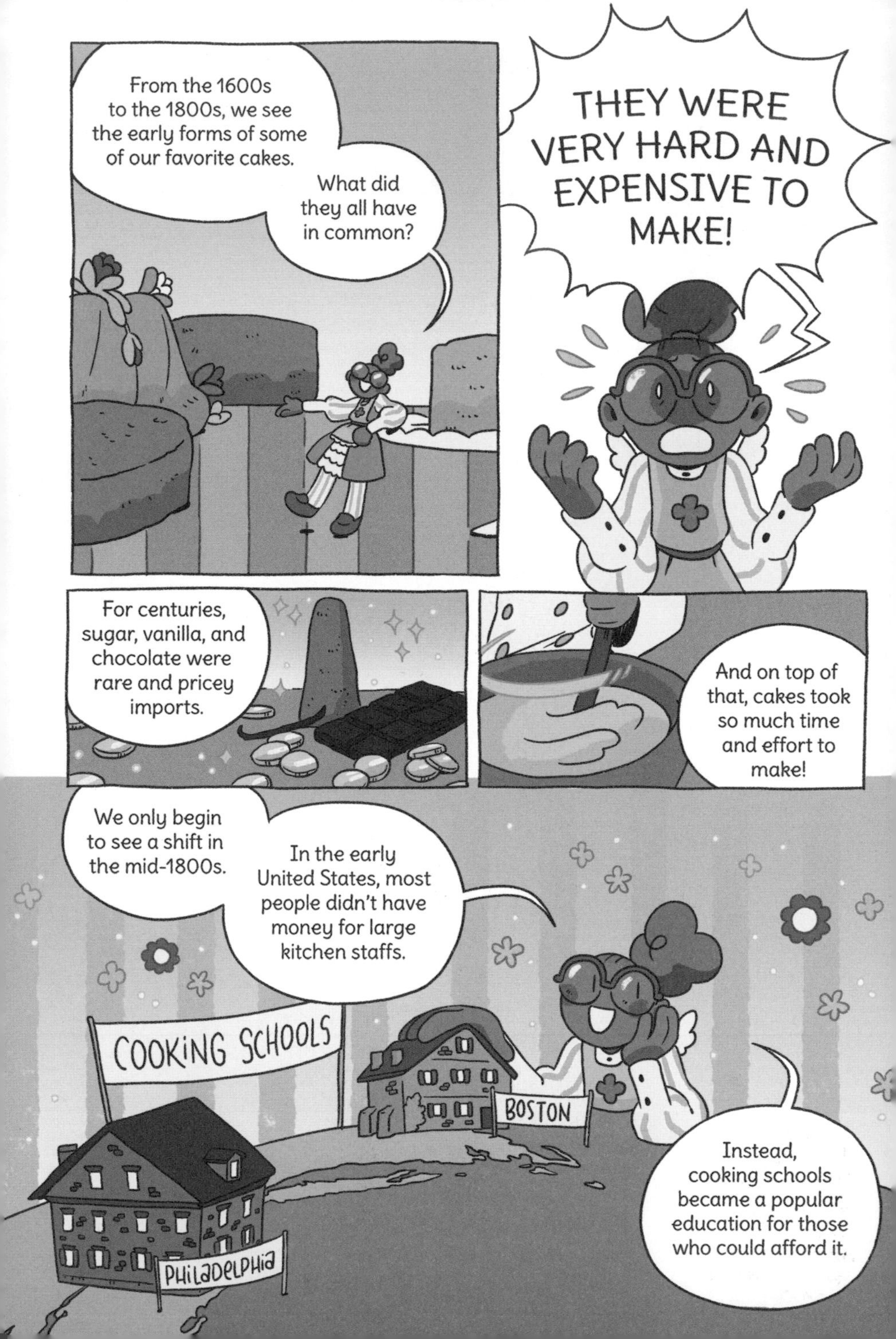
From the 1600s to the 1800s, we see the early forms of some of our favorite cakes.
What did they all have in common?
THEY WERE VERY HARD AND EXPENSIVE TO MAKE!
For centuries, sugar, vanilla, and chocolate were rare and pricey imports.
And on top of that, cakes took so much time and effort to make!
We only begin to see a shift in the mid-1800s.
In the early United States, most people didn't have money for large kitchen staffs.
COOKING SCHOOLS
BOSTON
PHILADELPHIA
Instead, cooking schools became a popular education for those who could afford it.

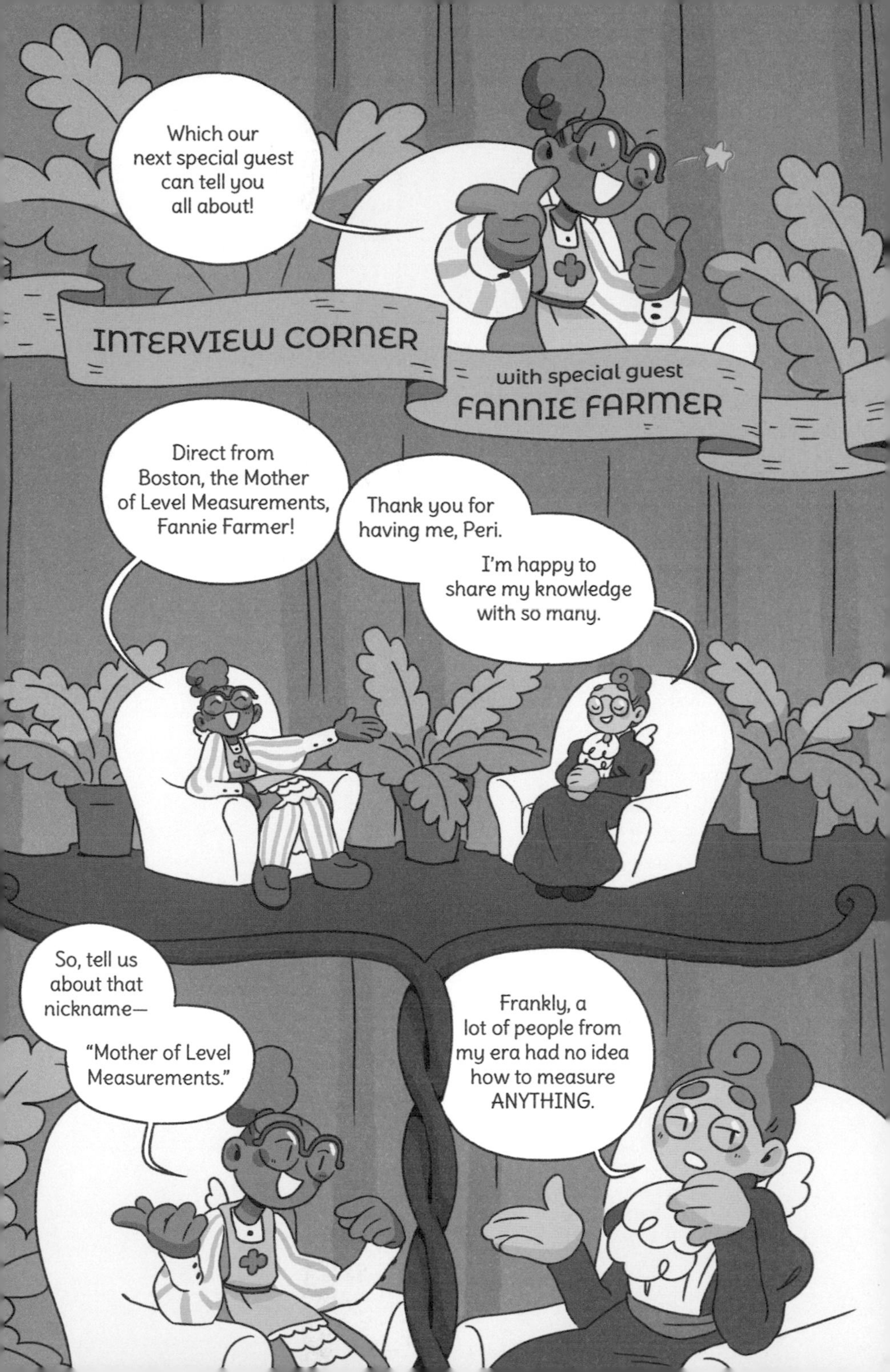
Which our next special guest can tell you all about!
INTERVIEW CORNER
with special guest
FANNIE FARMER
Direct from Boston, the Mother of Level Measurements, Fannie Farmer!
Thank you for having me, Peri.
I'm happy to share my knowledge with so many.
So, tell us about that nickname—
"Mother of Level Measurements."
Frankly, a lot of people from my era had no idea how to measure ANYTHING.

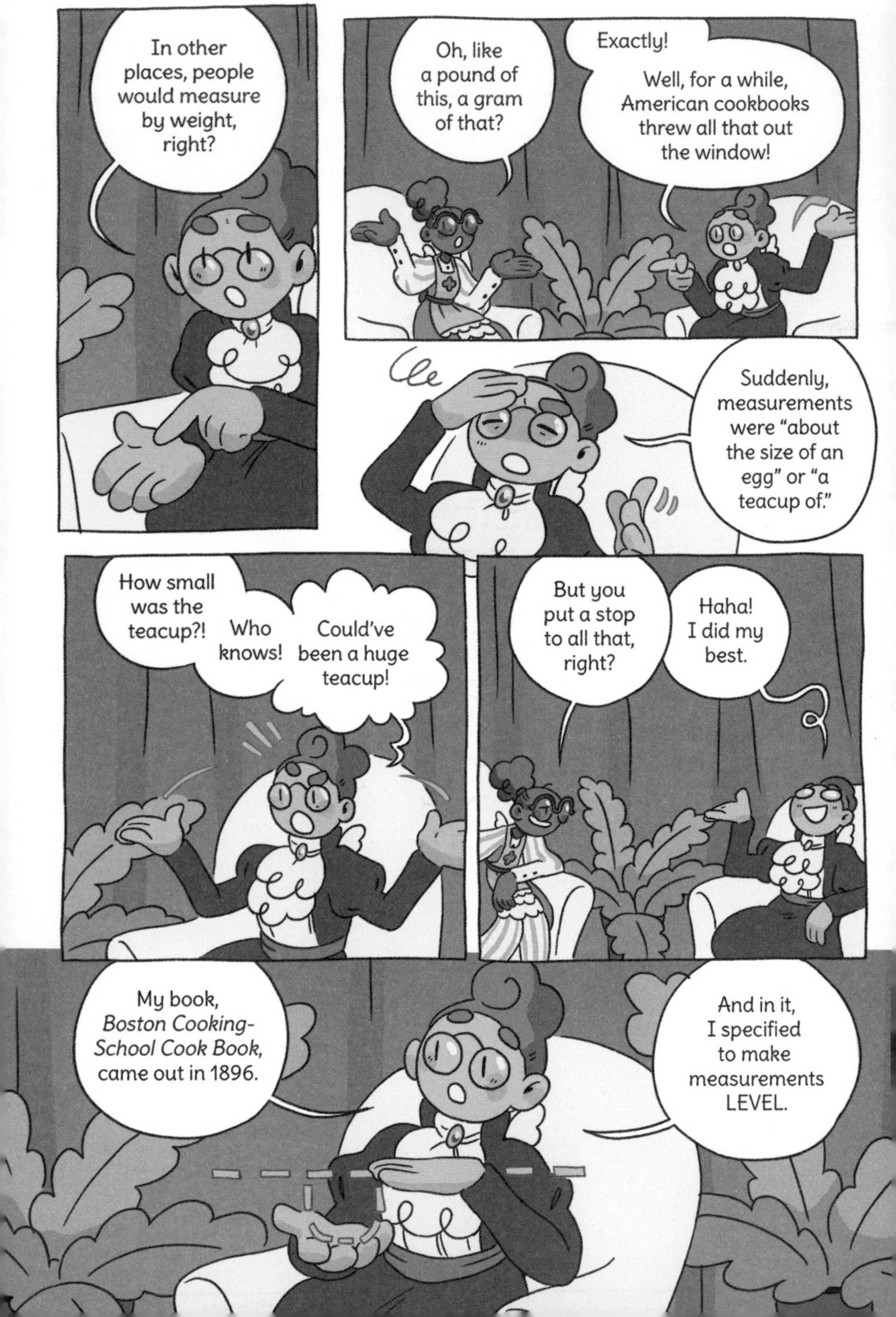

In other places, people would measure by weight, right?
Oh, like a pound of this, a gram of that?
Exactly!
Well, for a while, American cookbooks threw all that out the window!
Suddenly, measurements were "about the size of an egg" or "a teacup of."
How small was the teacup?!
Who knows!
Could've been a huge teacup!
But you put a stop to all that, right?
Haha! I did my best.
My book, *Boston Cooking-School Cook Book*, came out in 1896.
And in it, I specified to make measurements LEVEL.

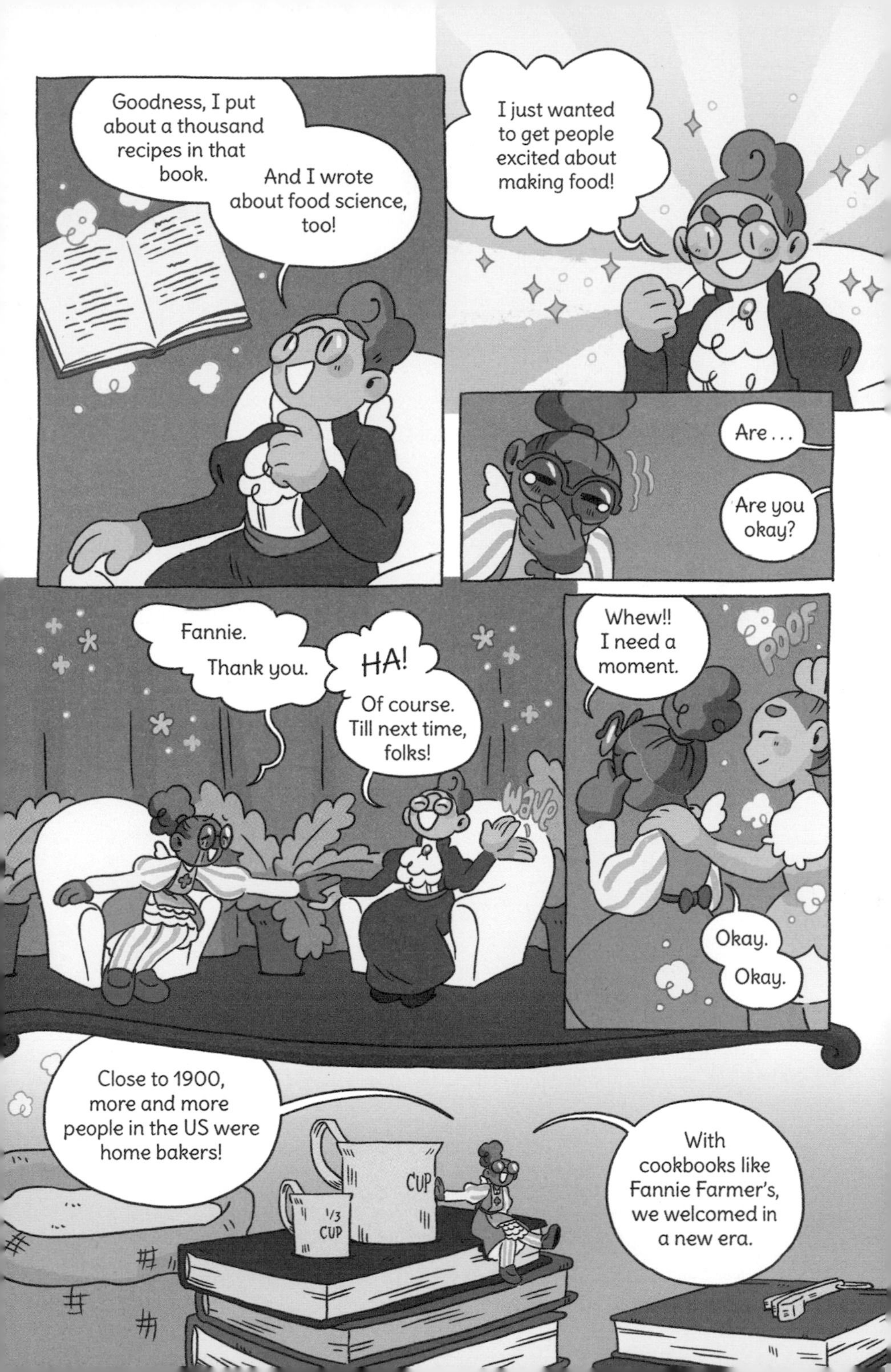
Goodness, I put about a thousand recipes in that book.
And I wrote about food science, too!
I just wanted to get people excited about making food!
Are . . .
Are you okay?
Fannie.
Thank you.
HA!
Of course. Till next time, folks!
WAVE
Whew!! I need a moment.
POOF
Okay.
Okay.
Close to 1900, more and more people in the US were home bakers!
CUP
1/3 CUP
With cookbooks like Fannie Farmer's, we welcomed in a new era.

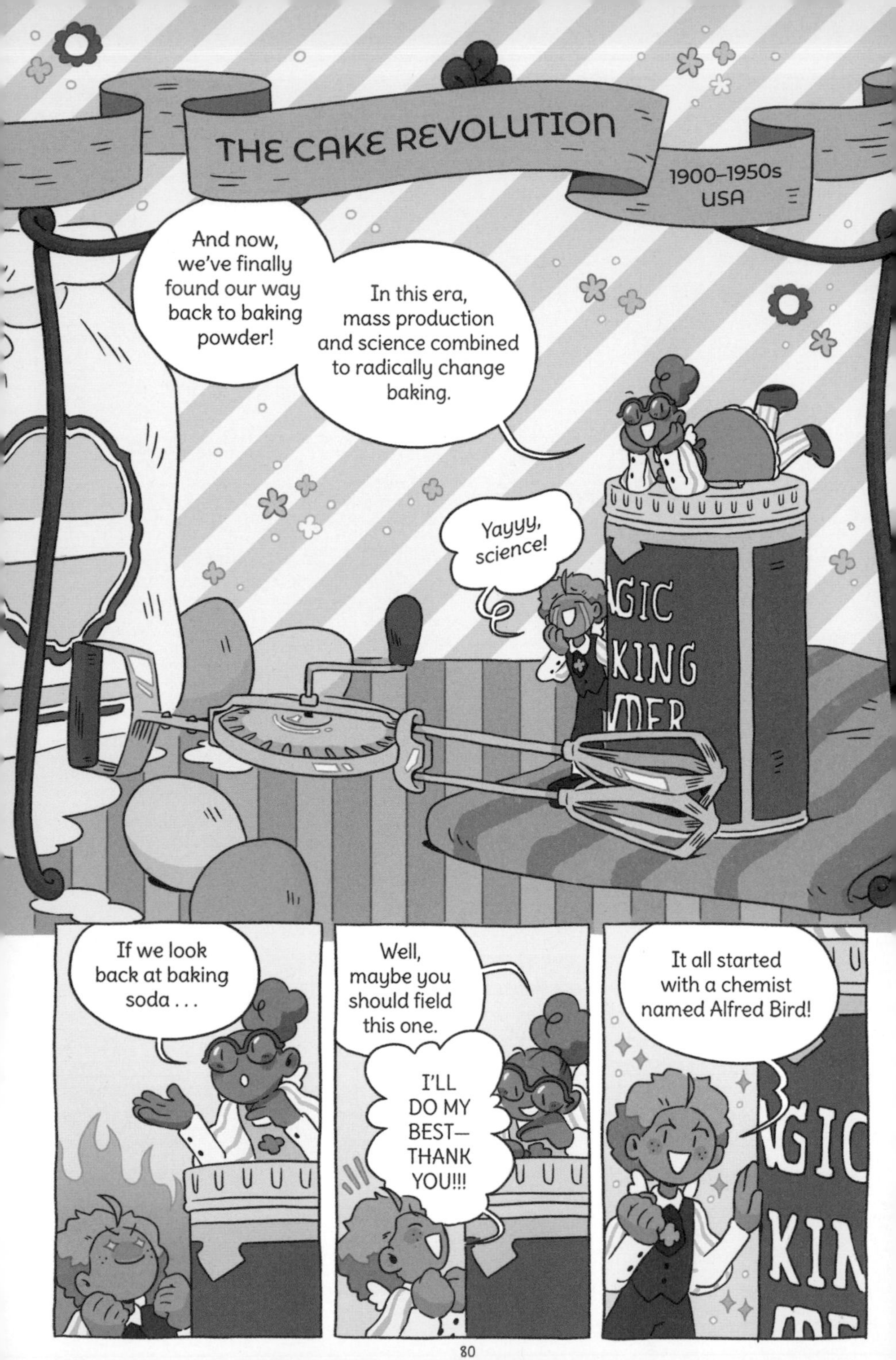
THE CAKE REVOLUTION
1900–1950s
USA
And now, we've finally found our way back to baking powder!
In this era, mass production and science combined to radically change baking.
Yayyy, science!
If we look back at baking soda . . .
Well, maybe you should field this one.
I'LL DO MY BEST— THANK YOU!!!
It all started with a chemist named Alfred Bird!

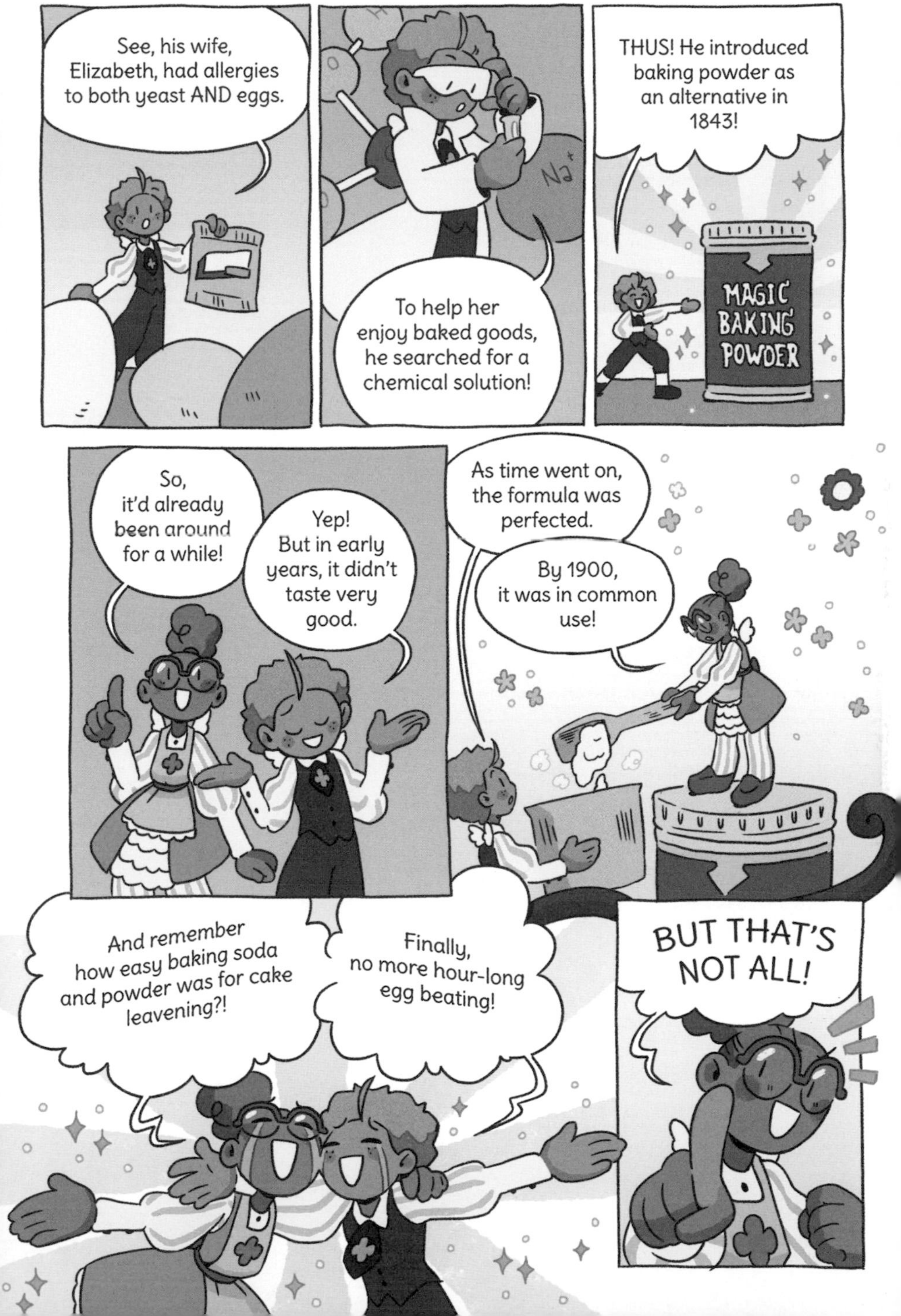
See, his wife, Elizabeth, had allergies to both yeast AND eggs.
To help her enjoy baked goods, he searched for a chemical solution!
THUS! He introduced baking powder as an alternative in 1843!
MAGIC BAKING POWDER
So, it'd already been around for a while!
Yep! But in early years, it didn't taste very good.
As time went on, the formula was perfected.
By 1900, it was in common use!
And remember how easy baking soda and powder was for cake leavening?!
Finally, no more hour-long egg beating!
BUT THAT'S NOT ALL!

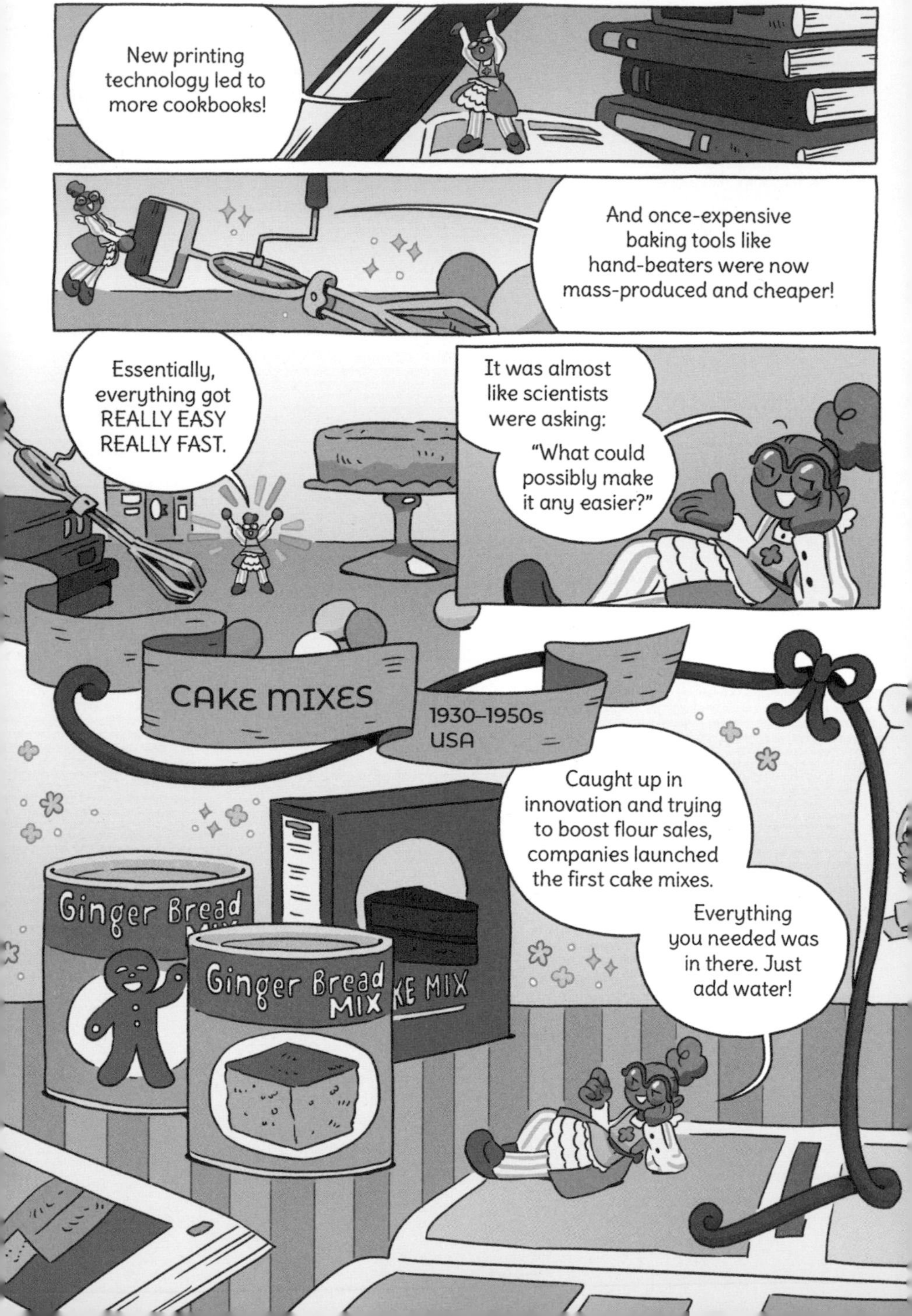
New printing technology led to more cookbooks!
And once-expensive baking tools like hand-beaters were now mass-produced and cheaper!
Essentially, everything got REALLY EASY REALLY FAST.
It was almost like scientists were asking:
"What could possibly make it any easier?"
CAKE MIXES
1930–1950s USA
Caught up in innovation and trying to boost flour sales, companies launched the first cake mixes.
Everything you needed was in there. Just add water!
Ginger Bread MIX
Ginger Bread MIX
KE MIX

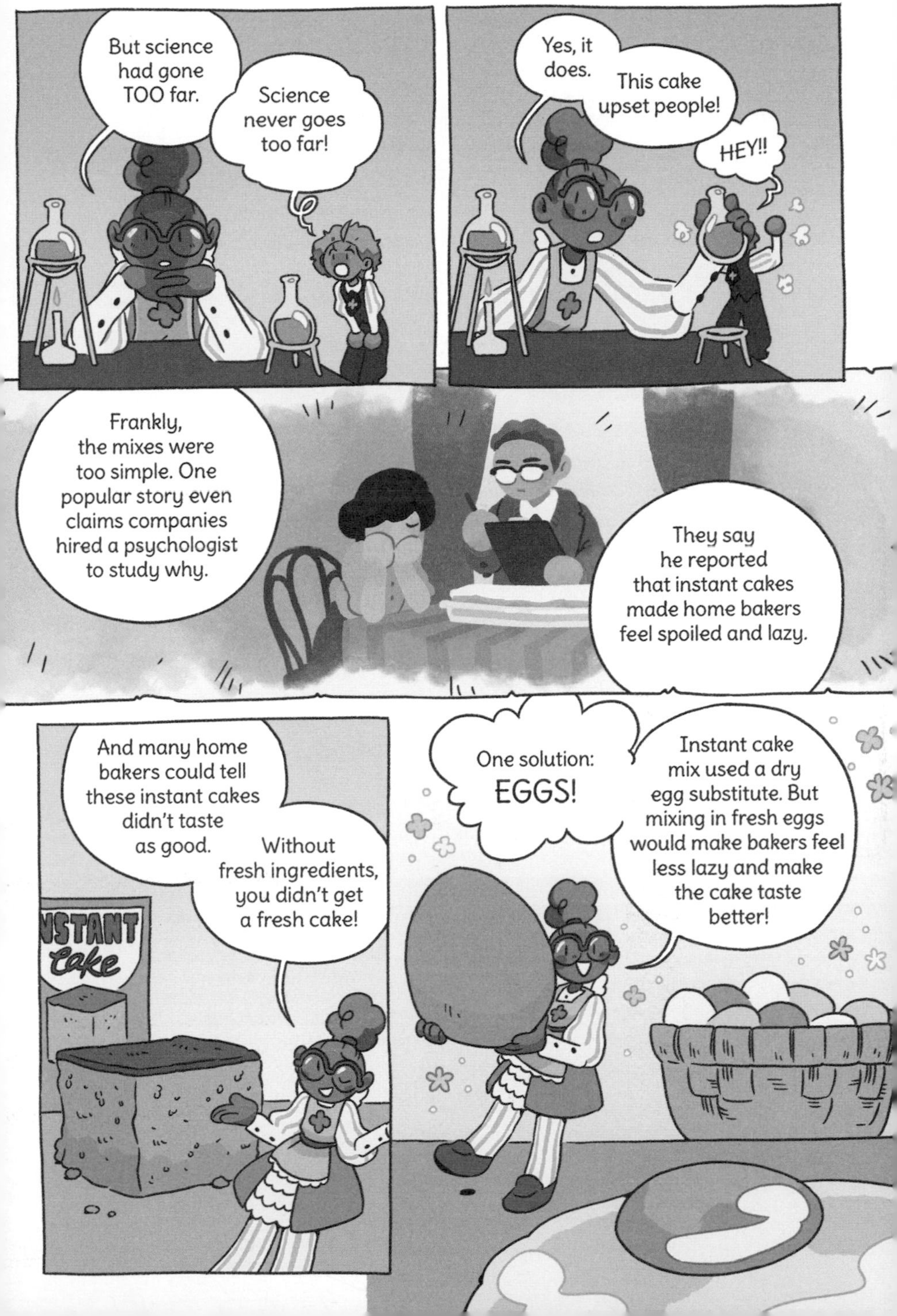

But science had gone TOO far.
Science never goes too far!
Yes, it does.
This cake upset people!
HEY!!
Frankly, the mixes were too simple. One popular story even claims companies hired a psychologist to study why.
They say he reported that instant cakes made home bakers feel spoiled and lazy.
And many home bakers could tell these instant cakes didn't taste as good.
Without fresh ingredients, you didn't get a fresh cake!
STANT
Cake
One solution: EGGS!
Instant cake mix used a dry egg substitute. But mixing in fresh eggs would make bakers feel less lazy and make the cake taste better!

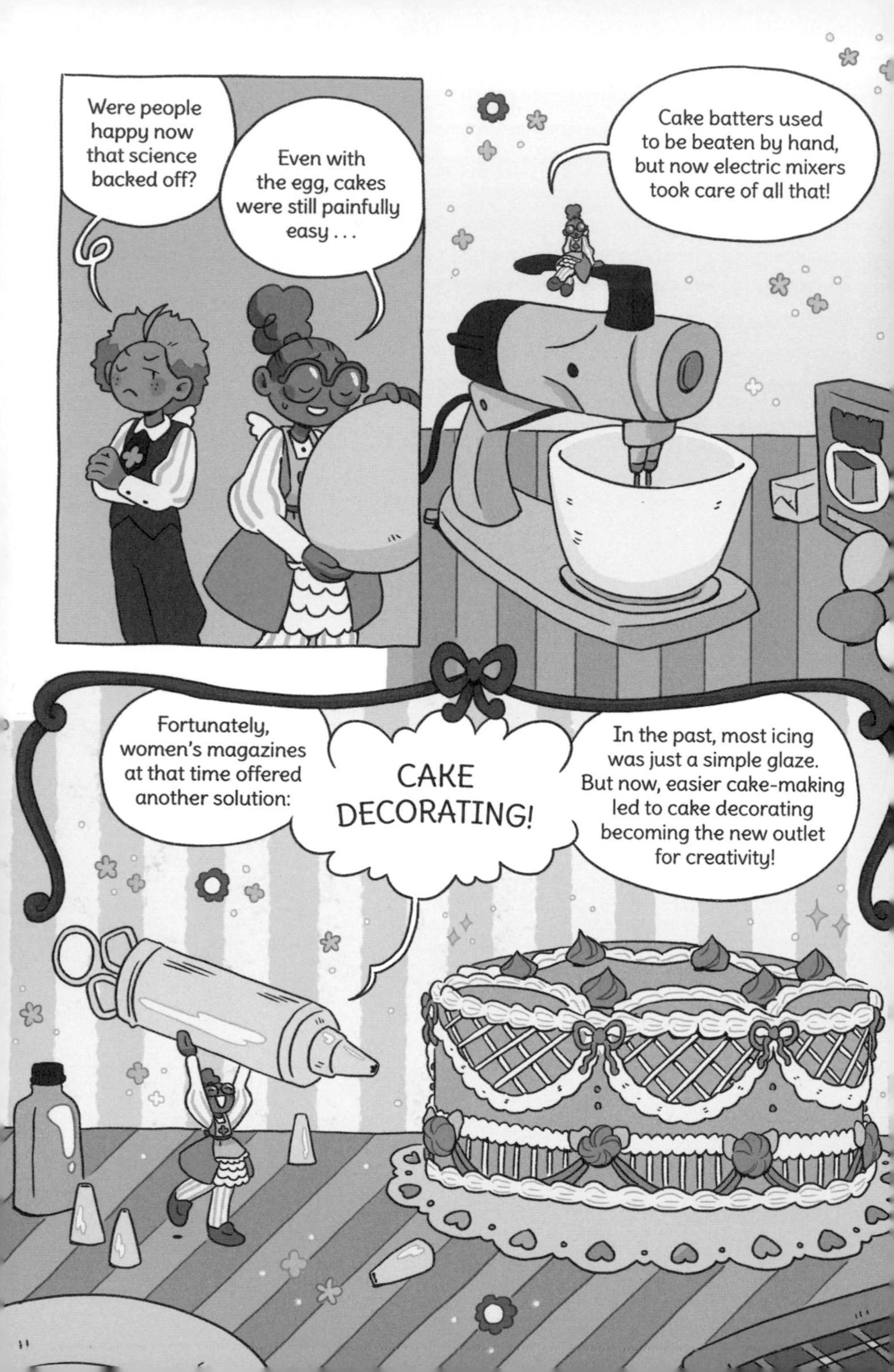
Were people happy now that science backed off?
Even with the egg, cakes were still painfully easy . . .
Cake batters used to be beaten by hand, but now electric mixers took care of all that!
Fortunately, women's magazines at that time offered another solution:
CAKE DECORATING!
In the past, most icing was just a simple glaze. But now, easier cake-making led to cake decorating becoming the new outlet for creativity!

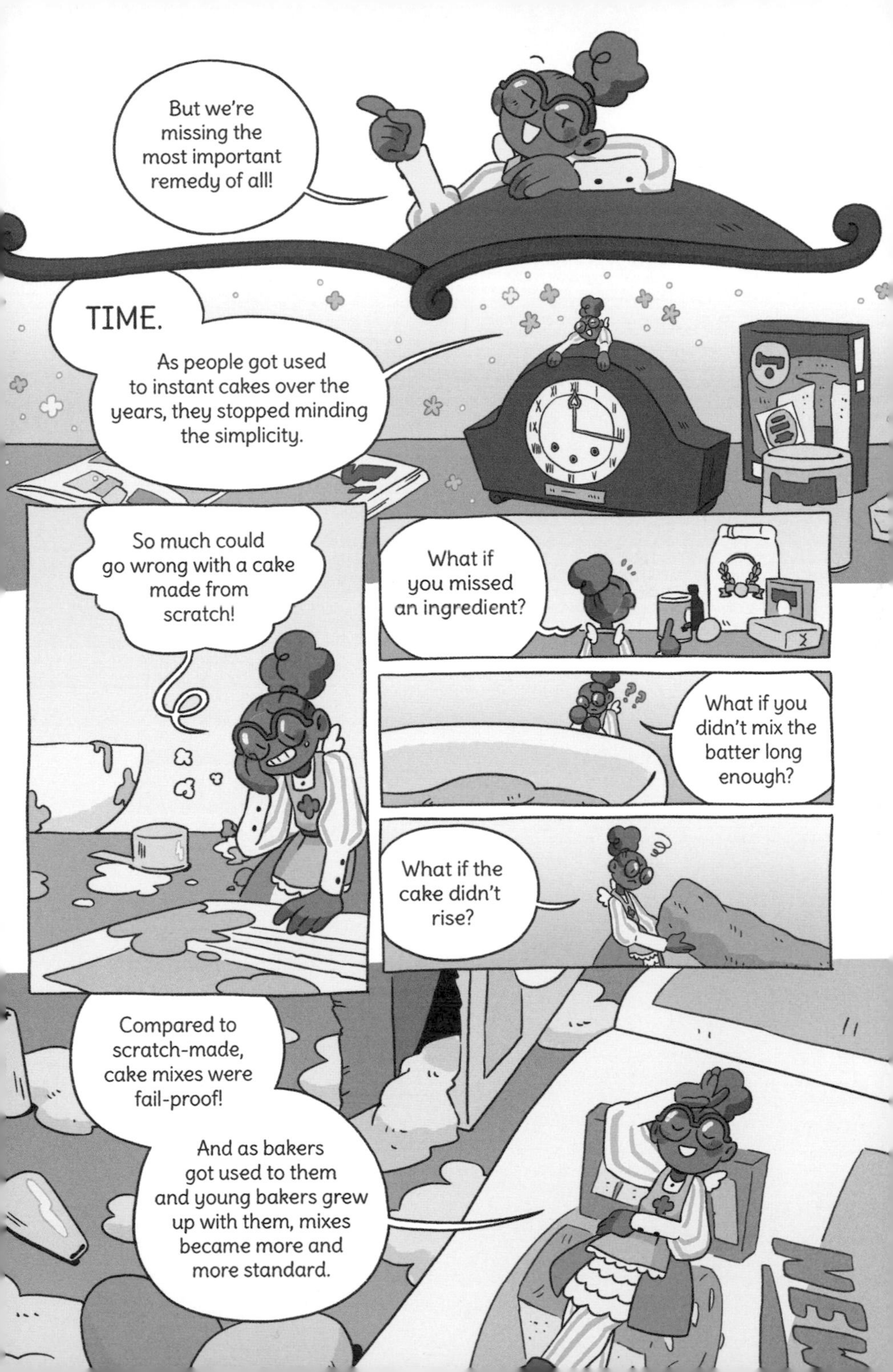

But we're missing the most important remedy of all!
TIME.
As people got used to instant cakes over the years, they stopped minding the simplicity.
So much could go wrong with a cake made from scratch!
What if you missed an ingredient?
What if you didn't mix the batter long enough?
What if the cake didn't rise?
Compared to scratch-made, cake mixes were fail-proof!
And as bakers got used to them and young bakers grew up with them, mixes became more and more standard.

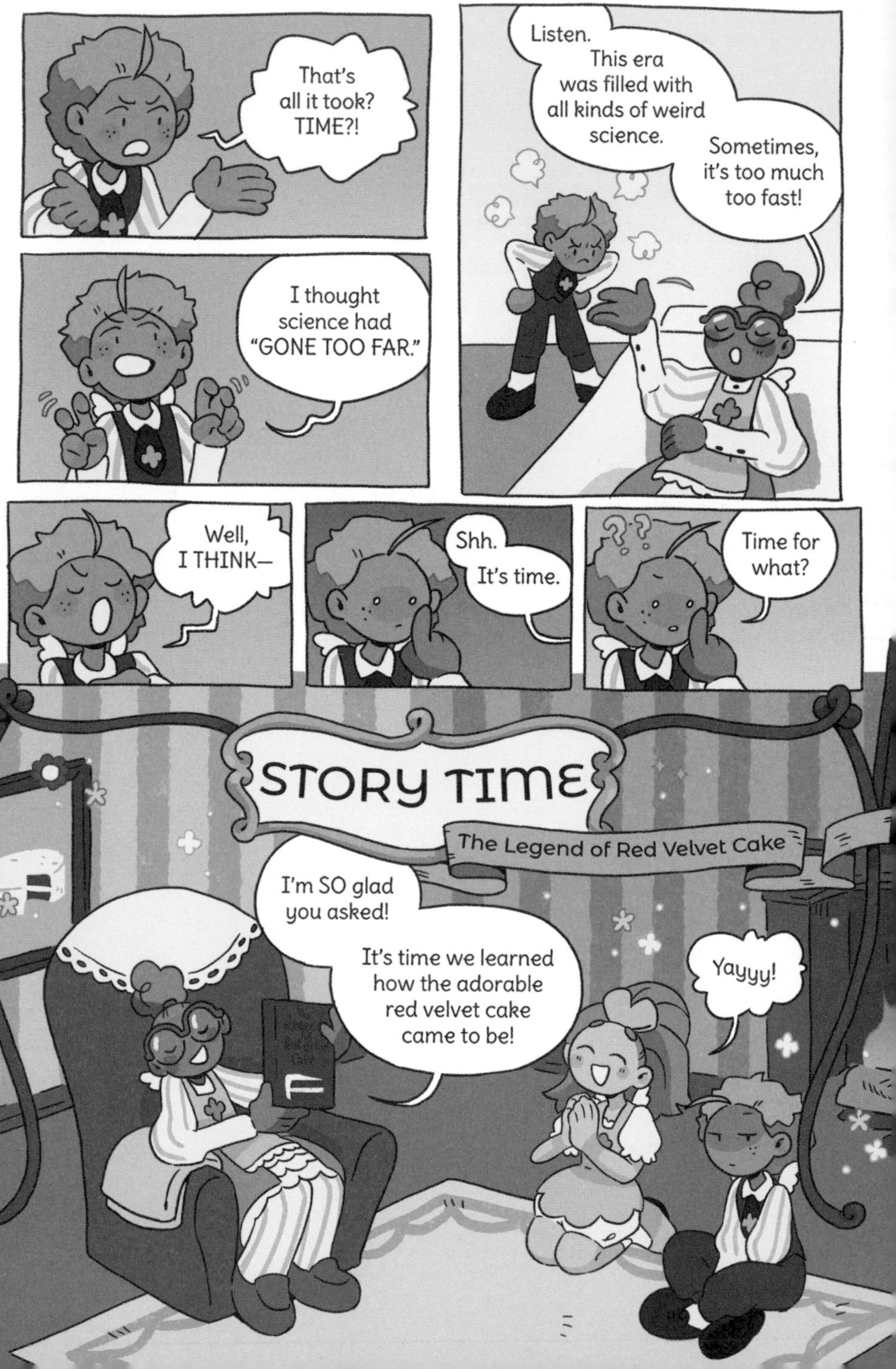
That's all it took? TIME?!
I thought science had "GONE TOO FAR."
Listen.
This era was filled with all kinds of weird science.
Sometimes, it's too much too fast!
Well, I THINK—
Shh.
It's time.
Time for what?
STORY TIME
The Legend of Red Velvet Cake
I'm SO glad you asked!
It's time we learned how the adorable red velvet cake came to be!
Yayyy!

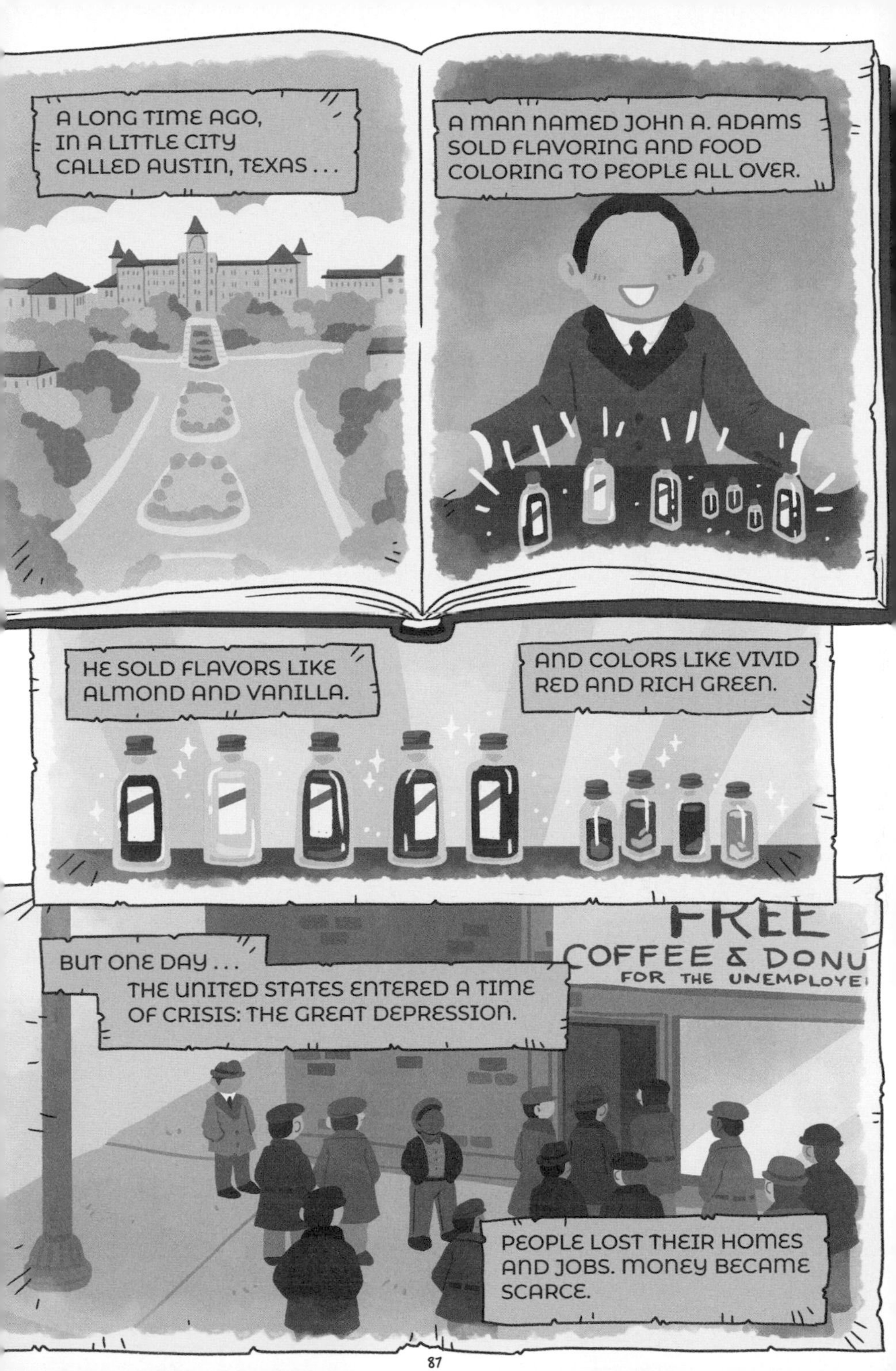
A LONG TIME AGO, IN A LITTLE CITY CALLED AUSTIN, TEXAS . . .
A MAN NAMED JOHN A. ADAMS SOLD FLAVORING AND FOOD COLORING TO PEOPLE ALL OVER.
HE SOLD FLAVORS LIKE ALMOND AND VANILLA.
AND COLORS LIKE VIVID RED AND RICH GREEN.
BUT ONE DAY . . .
THE UNITED STATES ENTERED A TIME OF CRISIS: THE GREAT DEPRESSION.
FREE
COFFEE & DONU
FOR THE UNEMPLOYE
PEOPLE LOST THEIR HOMES AND JOBS. MONEY BECAME SCARCE.

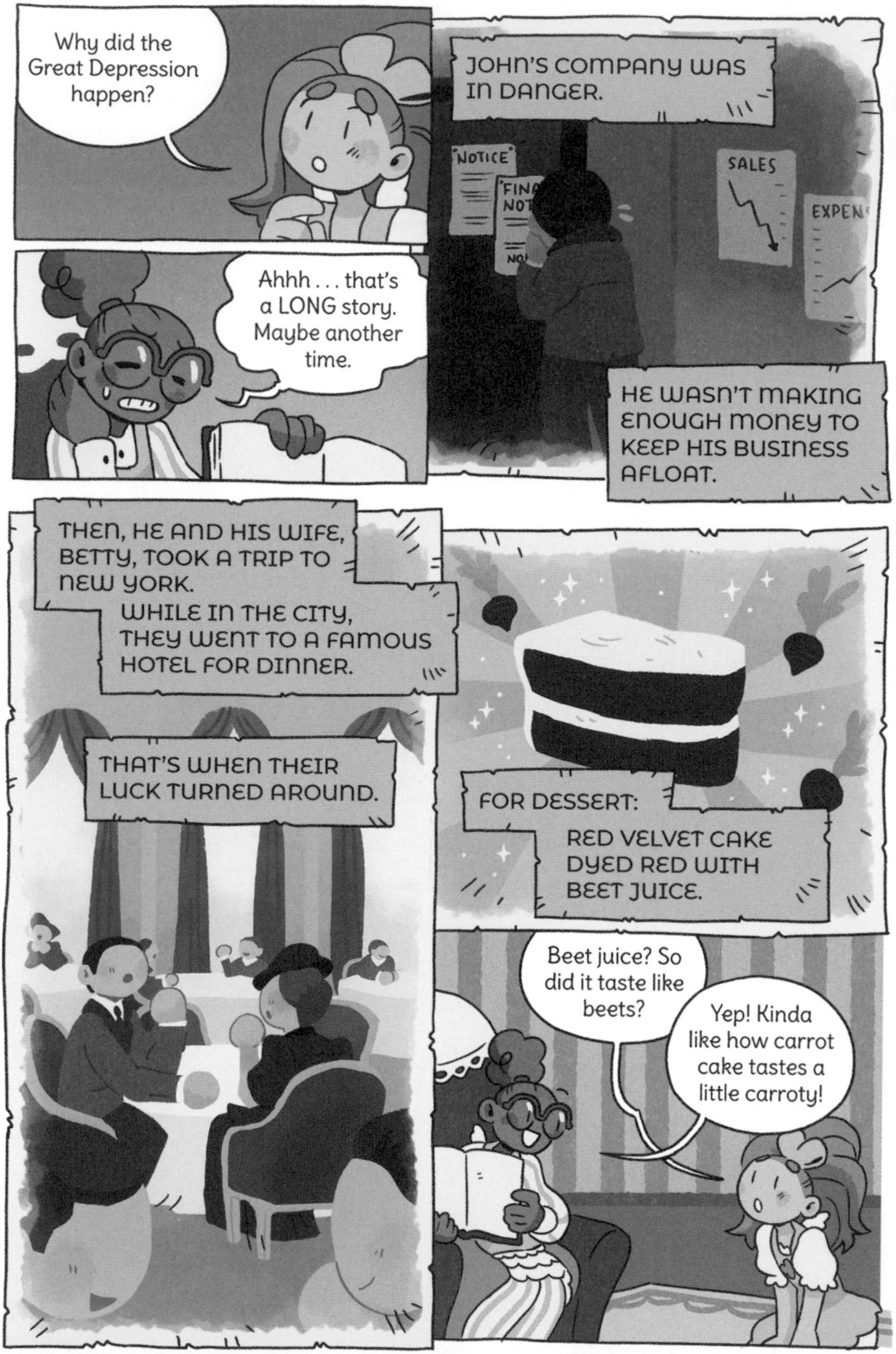
Why did the Great Depression happen?
Ahhh . . . that's a LONG story. Maybe another time.
JOHN'S COMPANY WAS IN DANGER.
NOTICE
SALES
HE WASN'T MAKING ENOUGH MONEY TO KEEP HIS BUSINESS AFLOAT.
THEN, HE AND HIS WIFE, BETTY, TOOK A TRIP TO NEW YORK.
WHILE IN THE CITY, THEY WENT TO A FAMOUS HOTEL FOR DINNER.
THAT'S WHEN THEIR LUCK TURNED AROUND.
FOR DESSERT:
RED VELVET CAKE DYED RED WITH BEET JUICE.
Beet juice? So did it taste like beets?
Yep! Kinda like how carrot cake tastes a little carroty!

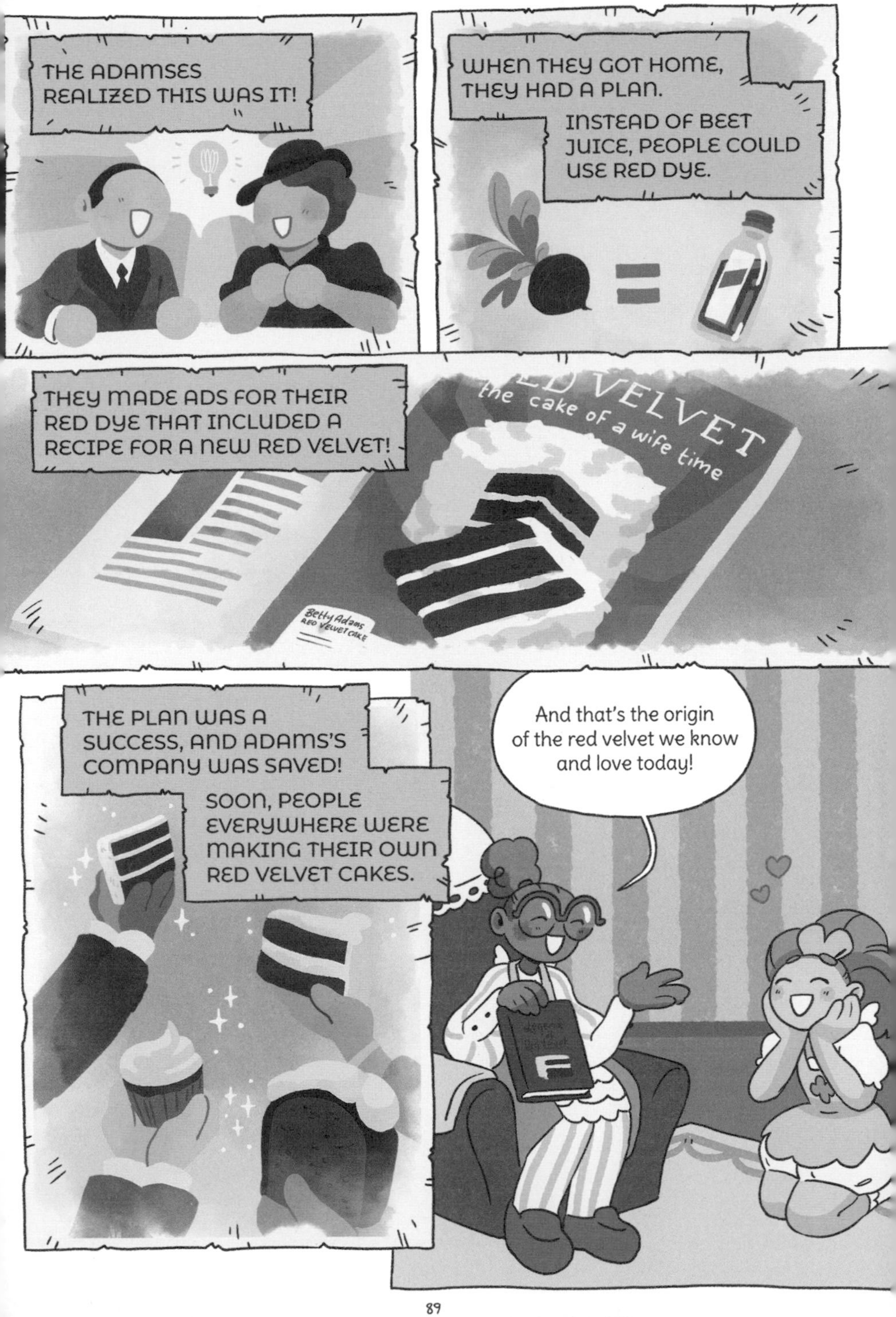
THE ADAMSES REALIZED THIS WAS IT!
WHEN THEY GOT HOME, THEY HAD A PLAN.
INSTEAD OF BEET JUICE, PEOPLE COULD USE RED DYE.
THEY MADE ADS FOR THEIR RED DYE THAT INCLUDED A RECIPE FOR A NEW RED VELVET!
ED VELVET
the cake of a wife time
Betty Adams
RED VELVET CAKE
THE PLAN WAS A SUCCESS, AND ADAMS'S COMPANY WAS SAVED!
SOON, PEOPLE EVERYWHERE WERE MAKING THEIR OWN RED VELVET CAKES.
And that's the origin of the red velvet we know and love today!

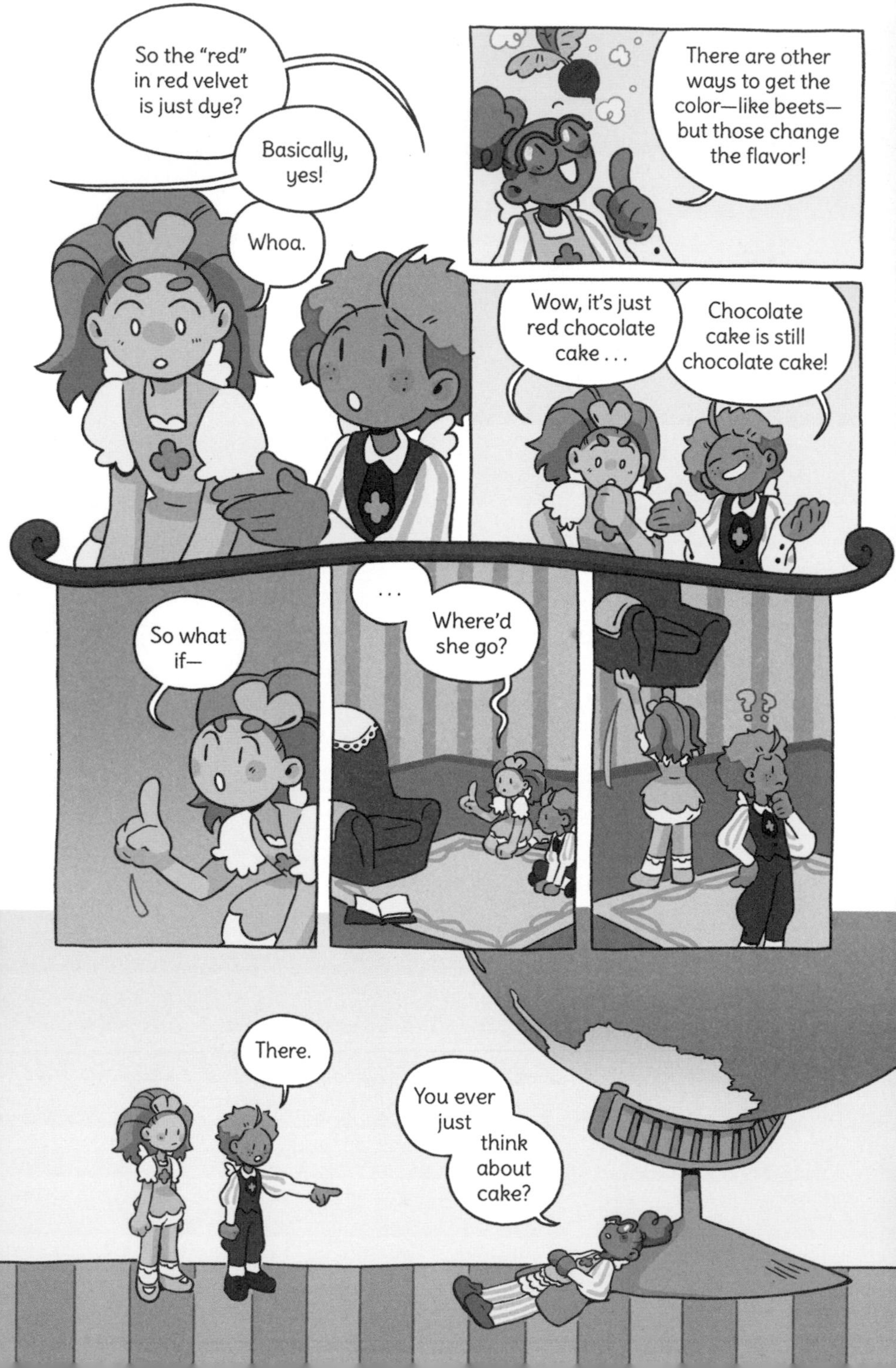
So the "red" in red velvet is just dye?
Basically, yes!
Whoa.
There are other ways to get the color—like beets—but those change the flavor!
Wow, it's just red chocolate cake . . .
Chocolate cake is still chocolate cake!
So what if—
. . .
Where'd she go?
??
There.
You ever just think about cake?

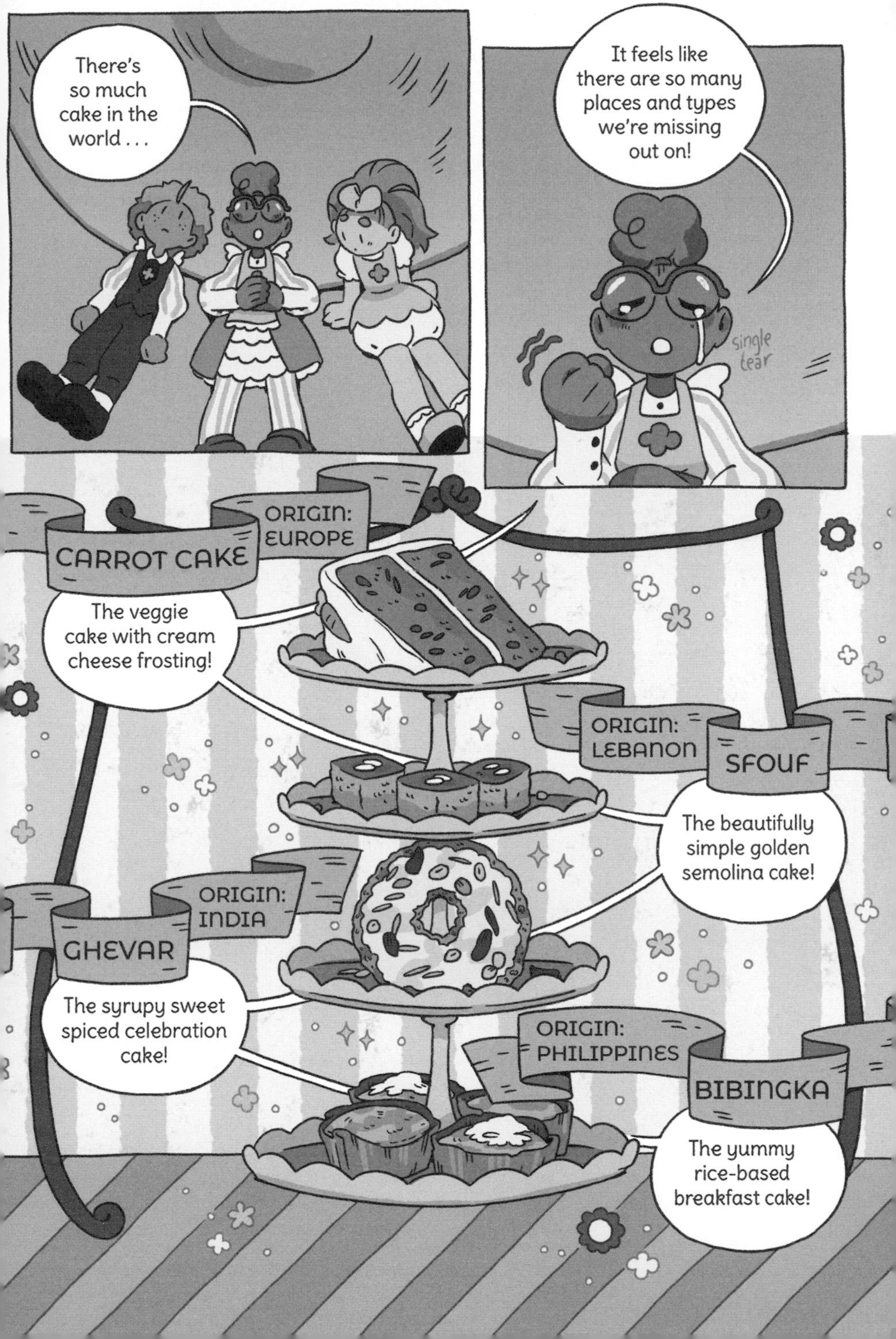
There's so much cake in the world . . .
It feels like there are so many places and types we're missing out on!
single tear
CARROT CAKE
ORIGIN: EUROPE
The veggie cake with cream cheese frosting!
ORIGIN: LEBANON
SFOUF
The beautifully simple golden semolina cake!
ORIGIN: INDIA
GHEVAR
The syrupy sweet spiced celebration cake!
ORIGIN: PHILIPPINES
BIBINGKA
The yummy rice-based breakfast cake!

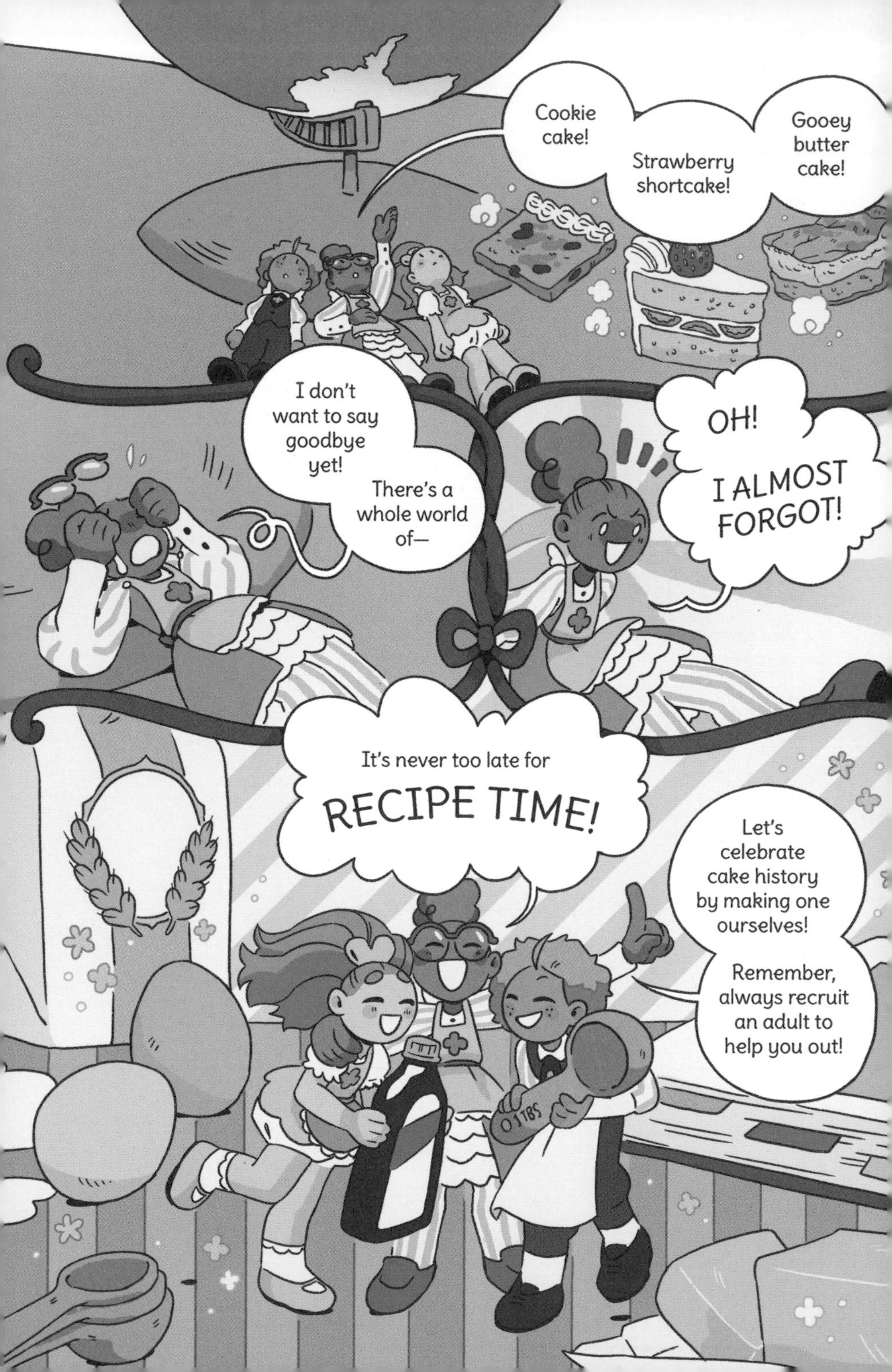
Cookie cake!
Strawberry shortcake!
Gooey butter cake!
I don't want to say goodbye yet!
There's a whole world of—
OH!
I ALMOST FORGOT!
It's never too late for
RECIPE TIME!
Let's celebrate cake history by making one ourselves!
Remember, always recruit an adult to help you out!
1 TBS

# FUNFETTI CAKE

## YOU WILL NEED:

- 1 cup sugar
- ½ cup butter
- ¼ cup sour cream
- 2 eggs
- 2 teaspoons vanilla extract
- 1 ½ cups flour
- 2 teaspoons baking powder
- 1 cup milk
- ½ teaspoon salt
- ½ cup sprinkles
- 1 can of your favorite frosting!

AND MORE SPRINKLES!

- 8x8-inch cake pan or 1 cupcake tin
- mixer with beater attachment
- whisk and spatula
- 2 large mixing bowls

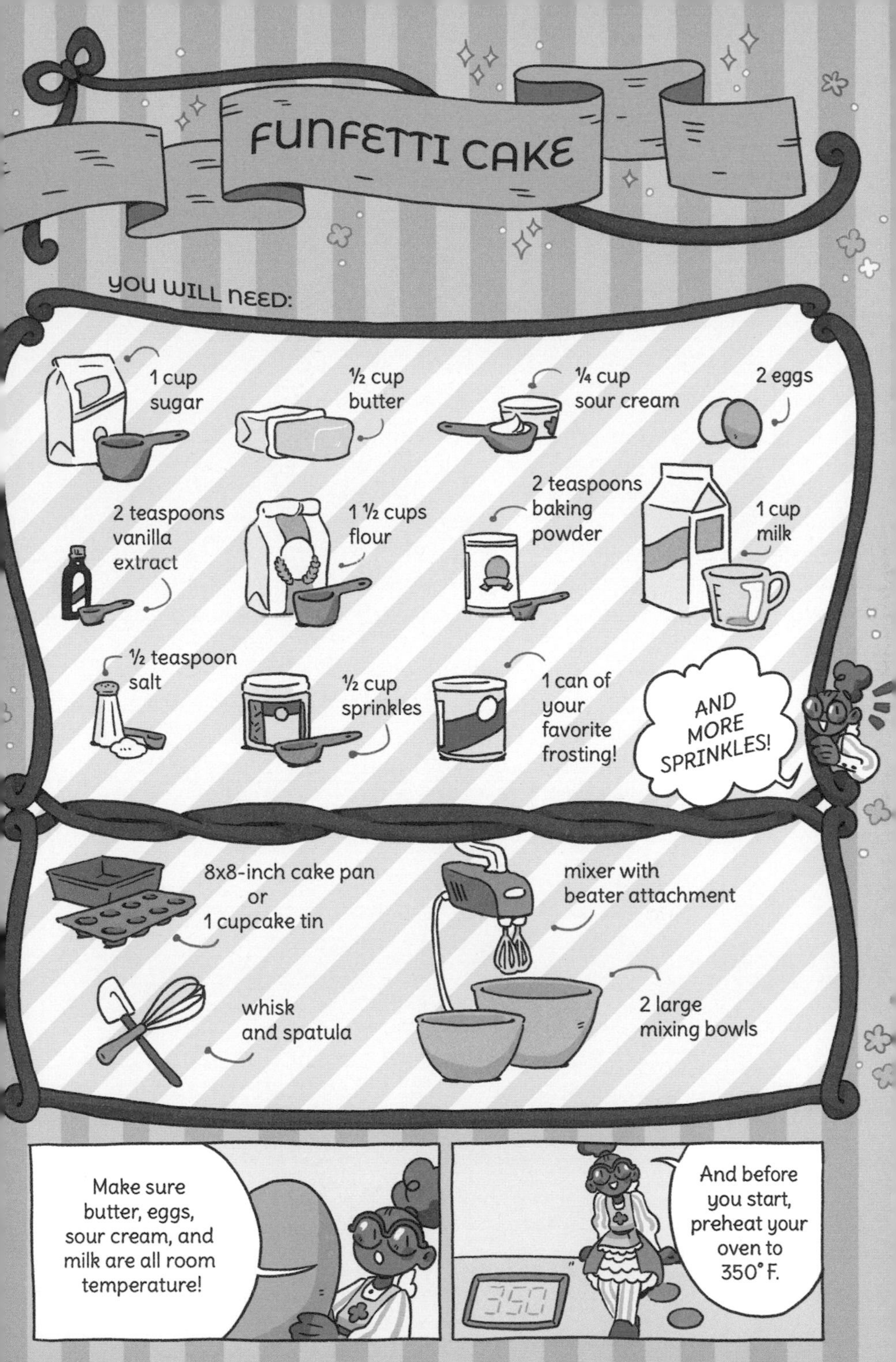
Make sure butter, eggs, sour cream, and milk are all room temperature!
350
And before you start, preheat your oven to 350° F.

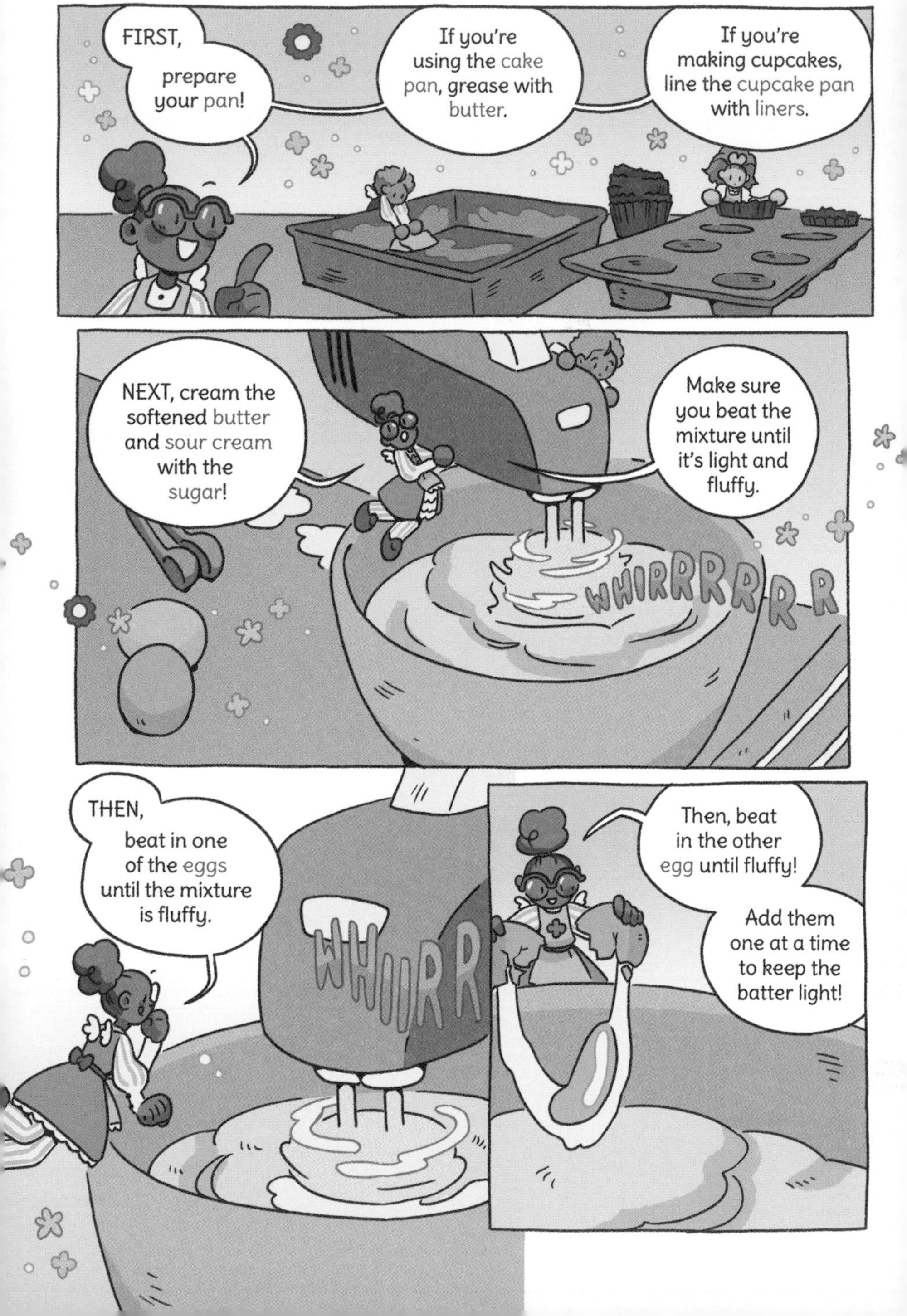
FIRST, prepare your pan!
If you're using the cake pan, grease with butter.
If you're making cupcakes, line the cupcake pan with liners.
NEXT, cream the softened butter and sour cream with the sugar!
Make sure you beat the mixture until it's light and fluffy.
WHIRRRRRR
THEN, beat in one of the eggs until the mixture is fluffy.
WHIIRR
Then, beat in the other egg until fluffy!
Add them one at a time to keep the batter light!

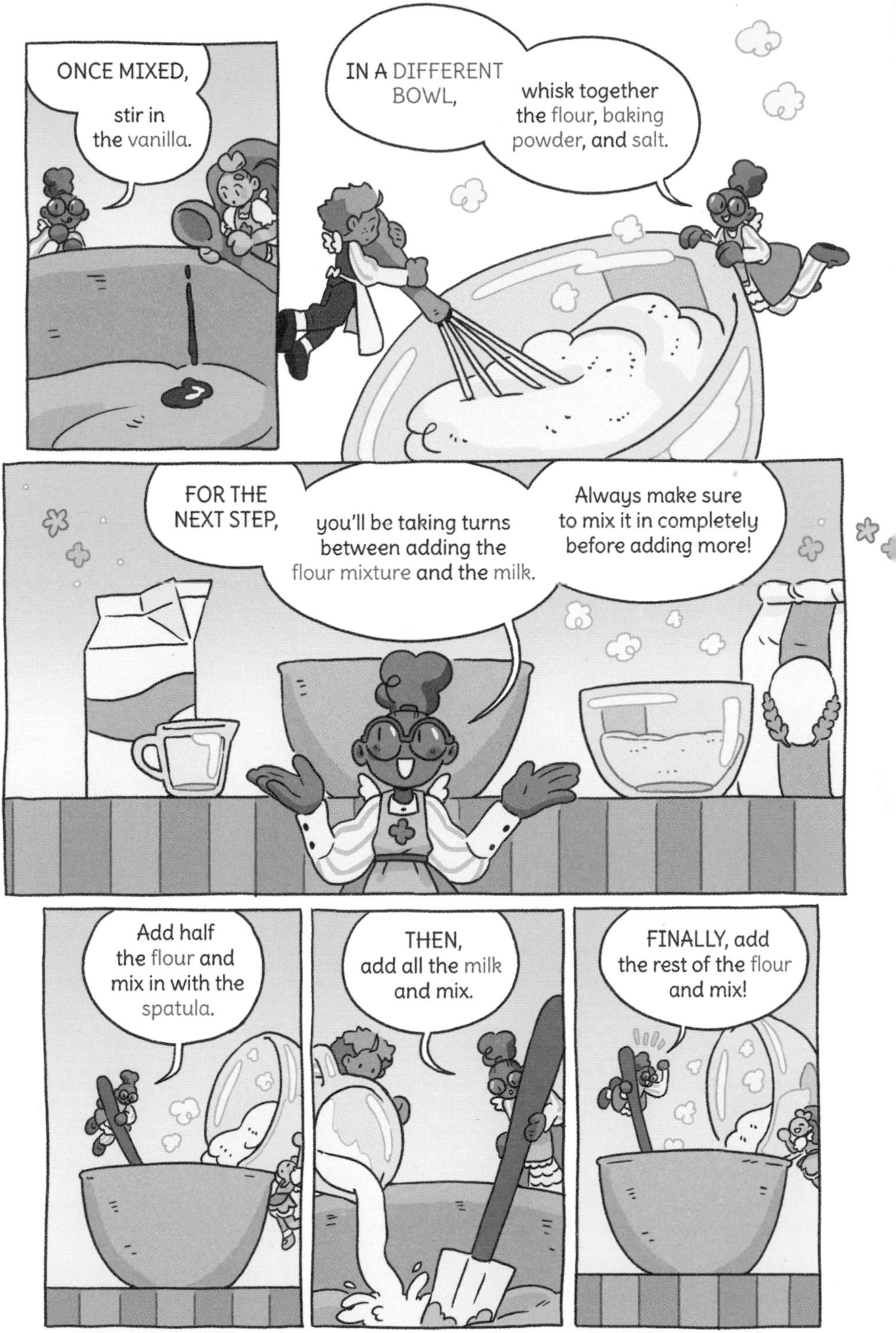
ONCE MIXED,
stir in the vanilla.
IN A DIFFERENT BOWL,
whisk together the flour, baking powder, and salt.
FOR THE NEXT STEP,
you'll be taking turns between adding the flour mixture and the milk.
Always make sure to mix it in completely before adding more!
Add half the flour and mix in with the spatula.
THEN, add all the milk and mix.
FINALLY, add the rest of the flour and mix!

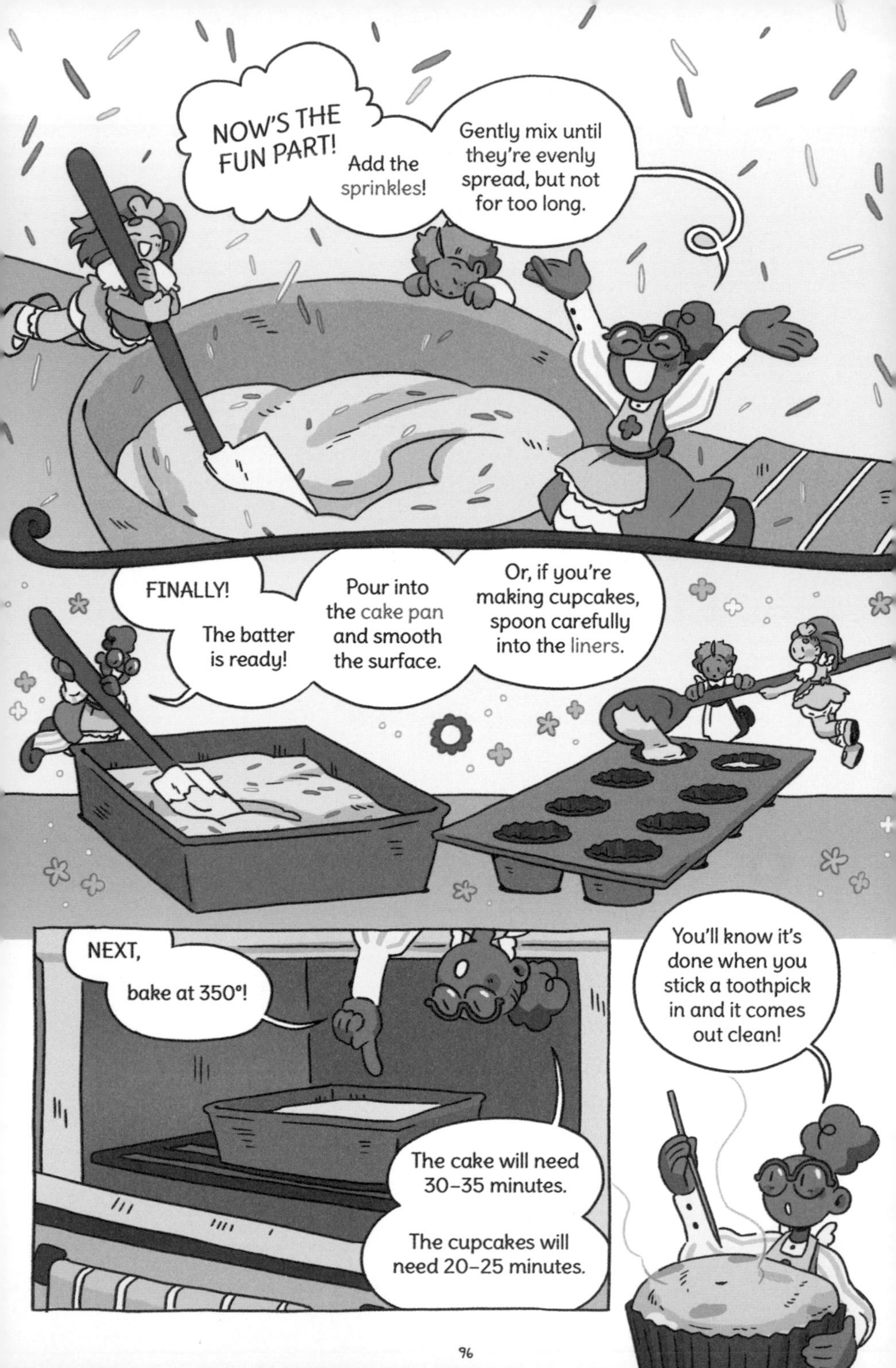
NOW'S THE FUN PART!
Add the sprinkles!
Gently mix until they're evenly spread, but not for too long.
FINALLY!
The batter is ready!
Pour into the cake pan and smooth the surface.
Or, if you're making cupcakes, spoon carefully into the liners.
NEXT,
bake at 350°!
The cake will need 30–35 minutes.
The cupcakes will need 20–25 minutes.
You'll know it's done when you stick a toothpick in and it comes out clean!

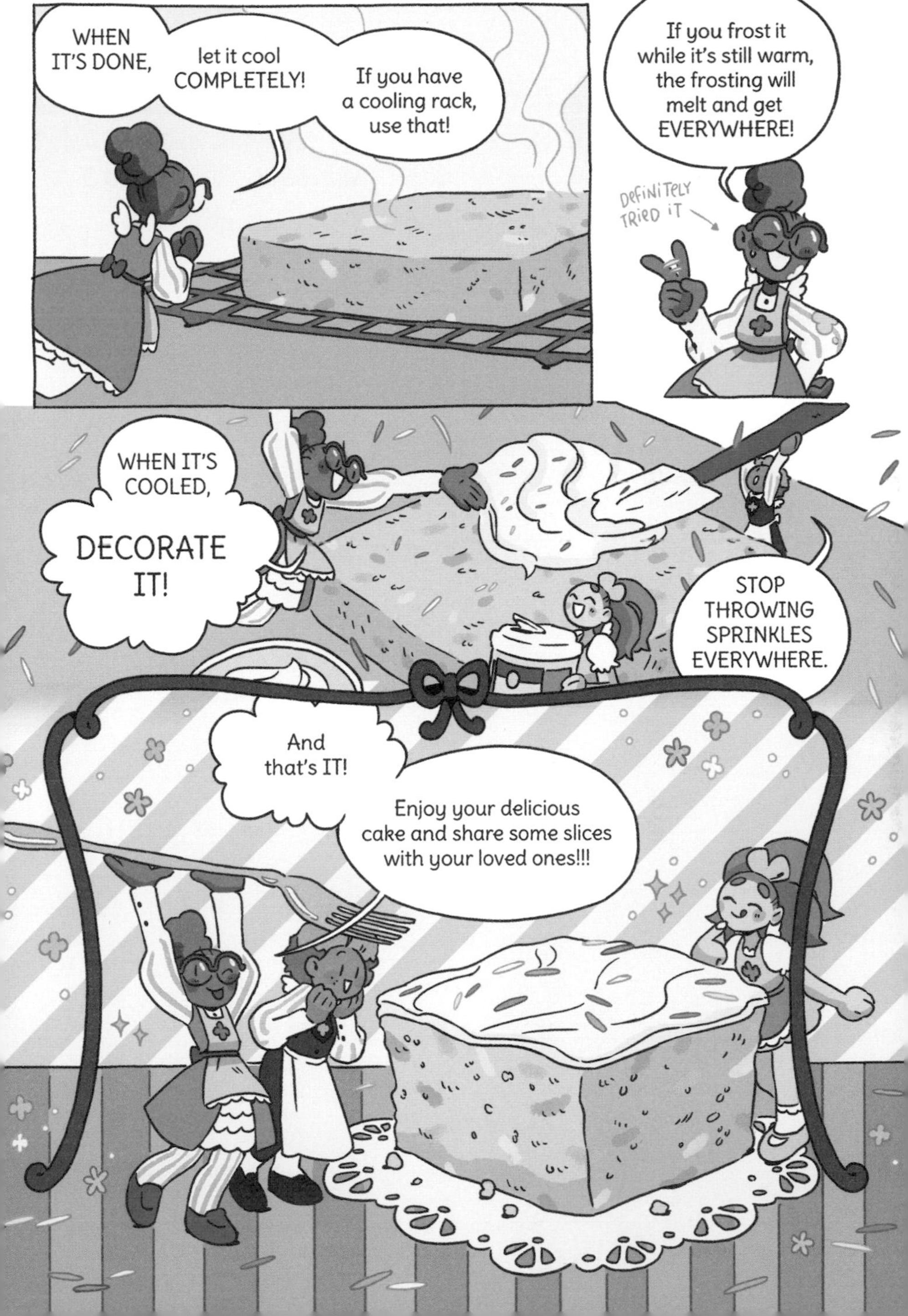
WHEN IT'S DONE,
let it cool COMPLETELY!
If you have a cooling rack, use that!
If you frost it while it's still warm, the frosting will melt and get EVERYWHERE!
DEFINITELY TRIED IT
WHEN IT'S COOLED,
DECORATE IT!
STOP THROWING SPRINKLES EVERYWHERE.
And that's IT!
Enjoy your delicious cake and share some slices with your loved ones!!!

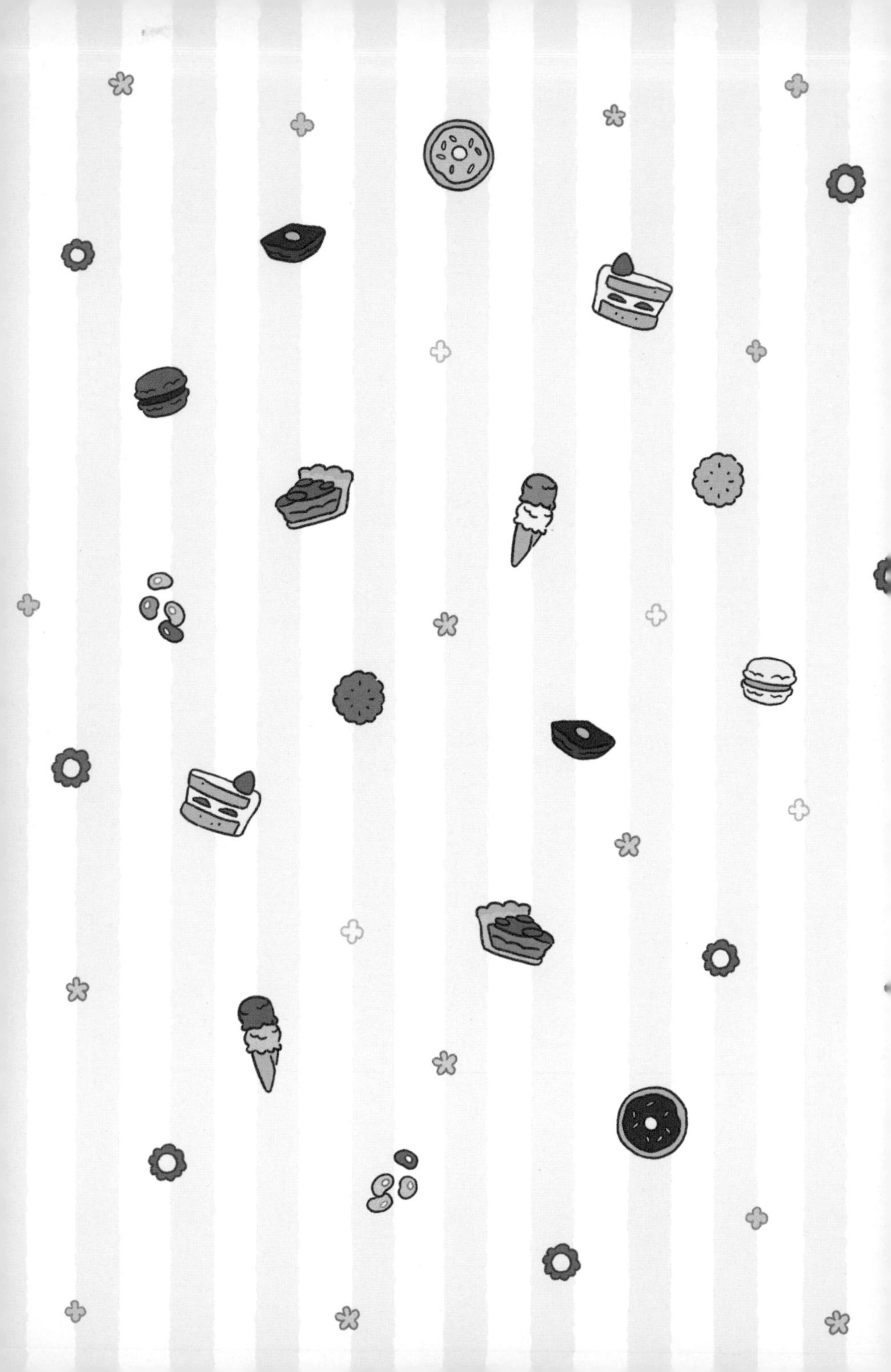

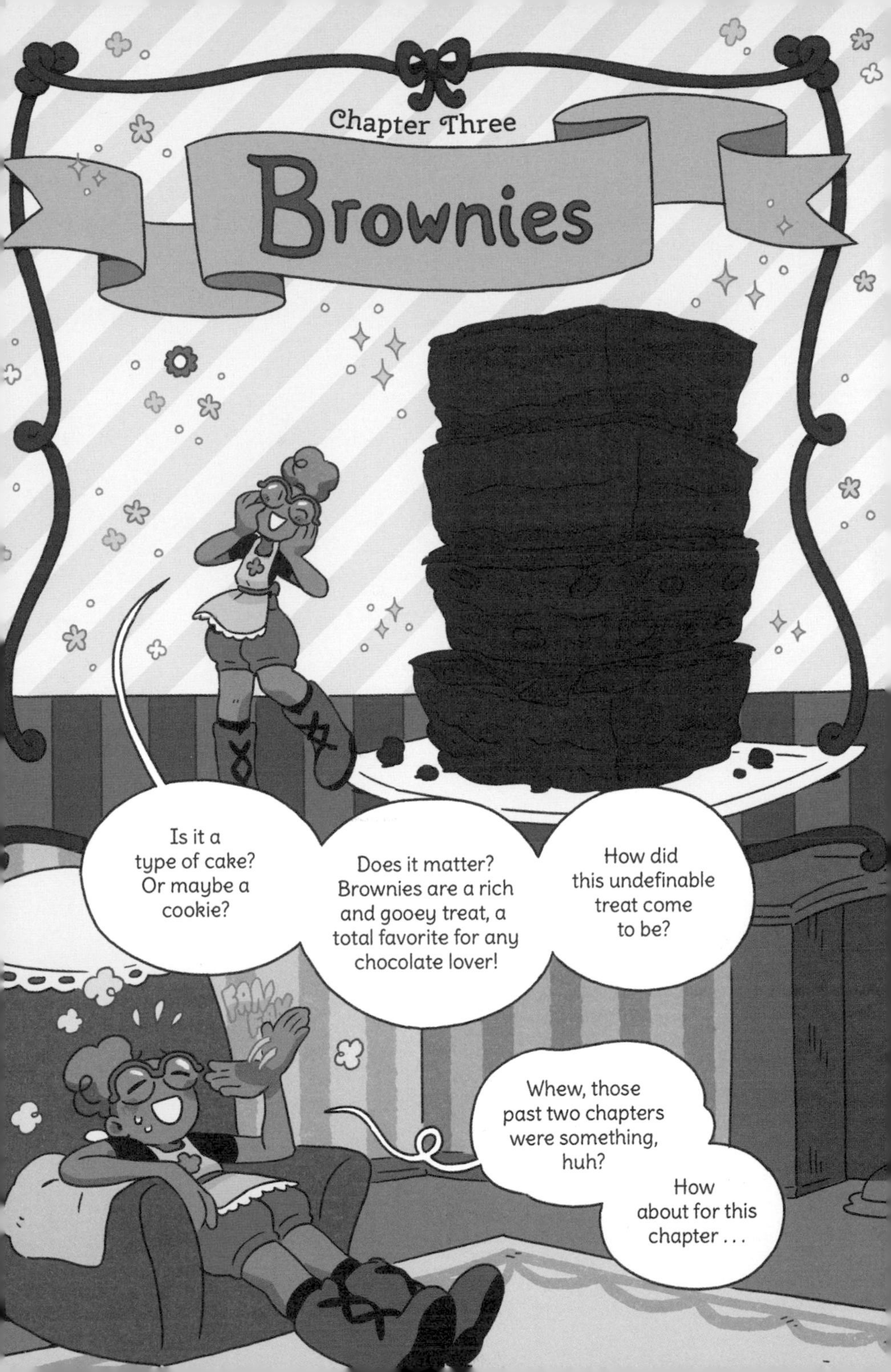
Chapter Three
Brownies
Is it a type of cake? Or maybe a cookie?
Does it matter? Brownies are a rich and gooey treat, a total favorite for any chocolate lover!
How did this undefinable treat come to be?
FAN FAN
Whew, those past two chapters were something, huh?
How about for this chapter . . .

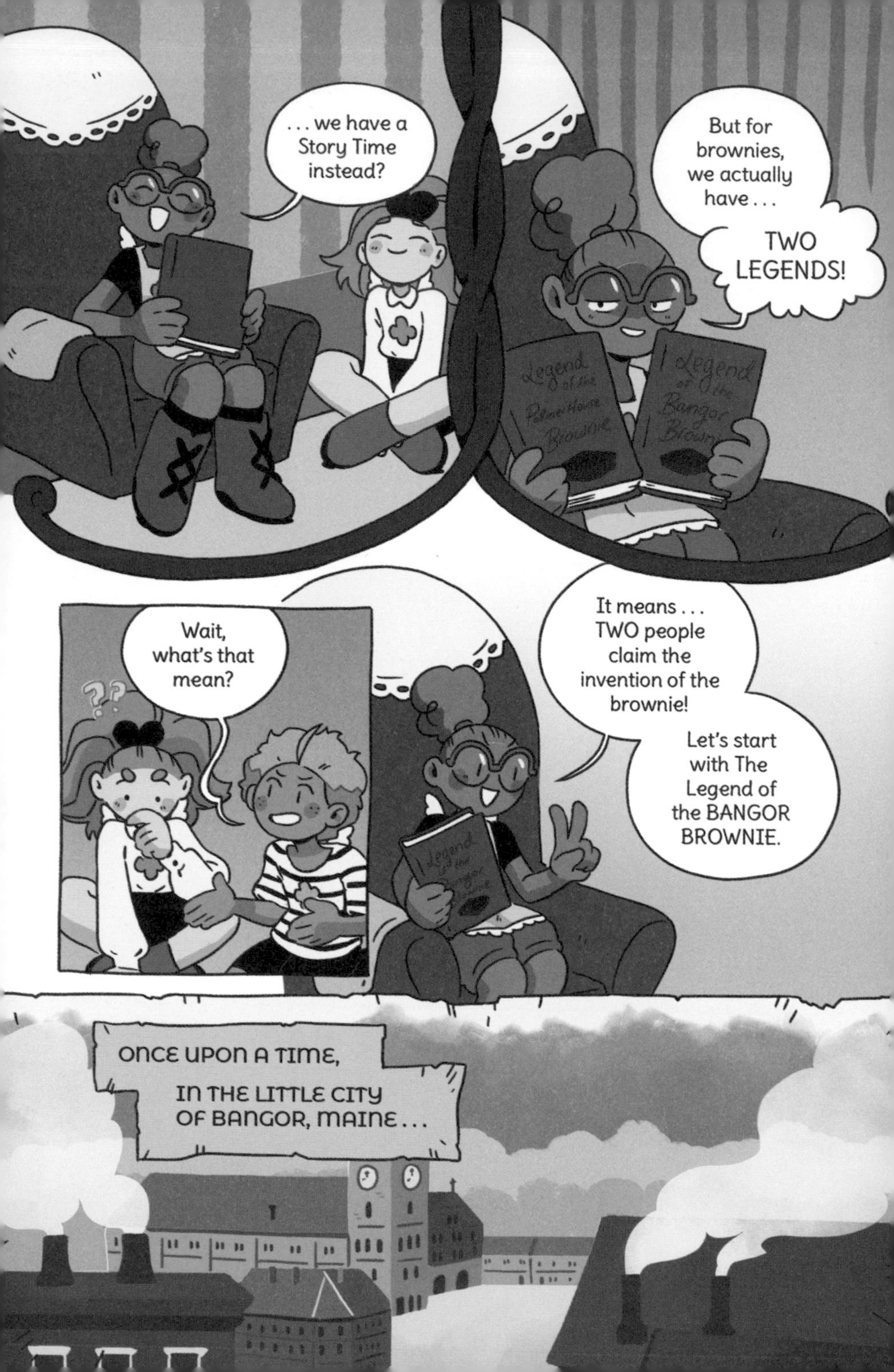

. . . we have a Story Time instead?
But for brownies, we actually have . . .
TWO LEGENDS!
Wait, what's that mean?
It means . . . TWO people claim the invention of the brownie!
Let's start with The Legend of the BANGOR BROWNIE.
ONCE UPON A TIME,
IN THE LITTLE CITY OF BANGOR, MAINE . . .

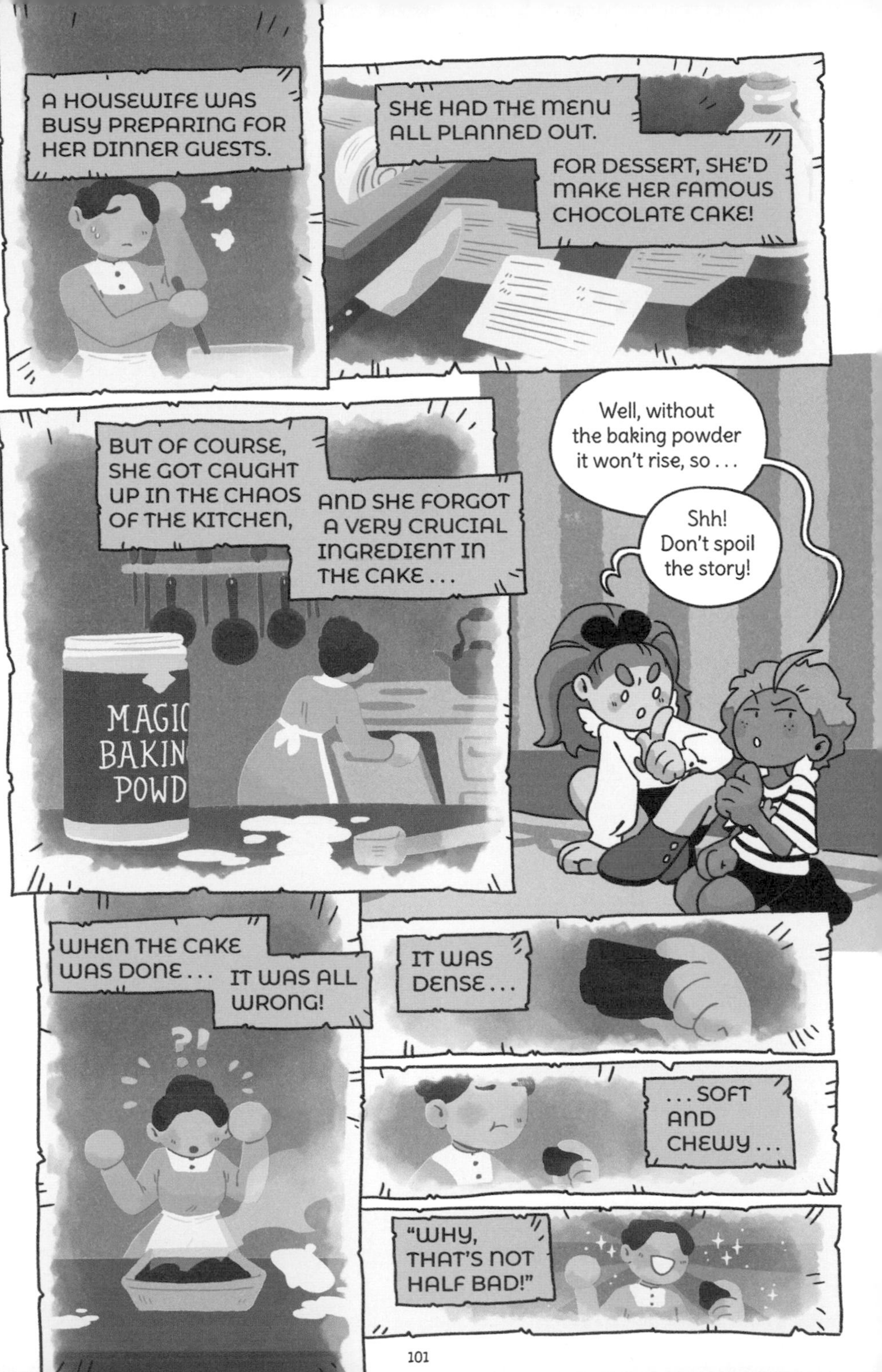
A HOUSEWIFE WAS BUSY PREPARING FOR HER DINNER GUESTS.
SHE HAD THE MENU ALL PLANNED OUT.
FOR DESSERT, SHE'D MAKE HER FAMOUS CHOCOLATE CAKE!
BUT OF COURSE, SHE GOT CAUGHT UP IN THE CHAOS OF THE KITCHEN,
AND SHE FORGOT A VERY CRUCIAL INGREDIENT IN THE CAKE . . .
MAGIC BAKING POWD
Well, without the baking powder it won't rise, so . . .
Shh! Don't spoil the story!
WHEN THE CAKE WAS DONE . . .
IT WAS ALL WRONG!
?!
IT WAS DENSE . . .
. . . SOFT AND CHEWY . . .
"WHY, THAT'S NOT HALF BAD!"

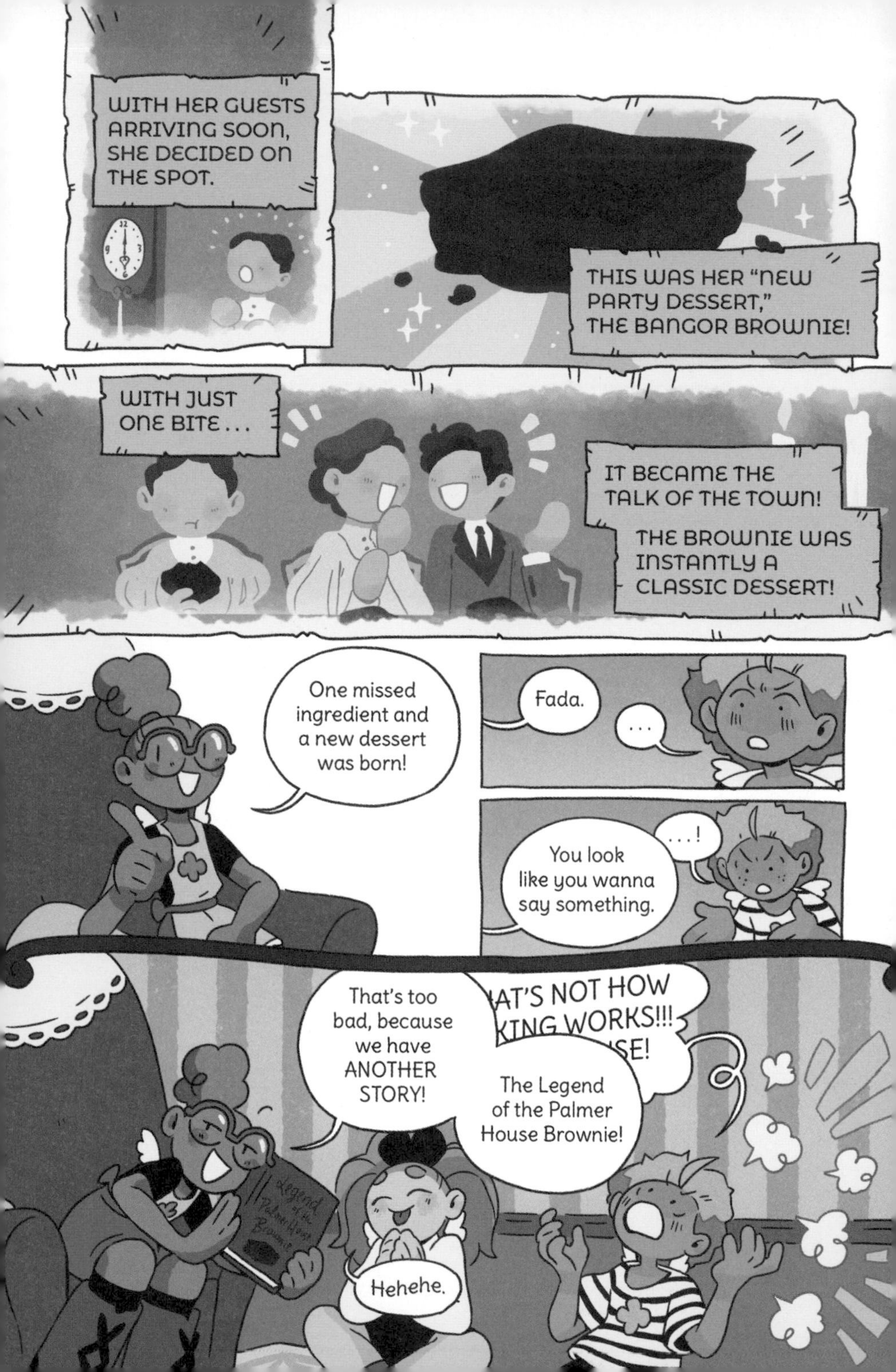
WITH HER GUESTS ARRIVING SOON, SHE DECIDED ON THE SPOT.
THIS WAS HER "NEW PARTY DESSERT," THE BANGOR BROWNIE!
WITH JUST ONE BITE . . .
IT BECAME THE TALK OF THE TOWN!
THE BROWNIE WAS INSTANTLY A CLASSIC DESSERT!
One missed ingredient and a new dessert was born!
Fada.
. . .
. . .!
You look like you wanna say something.
AT'S NOT HOW
KING WORKS!!!
SE!
That's too bad, because we have ANOTHER STORY!
The Legend of the Palmer House Brownie!
Hehehe.

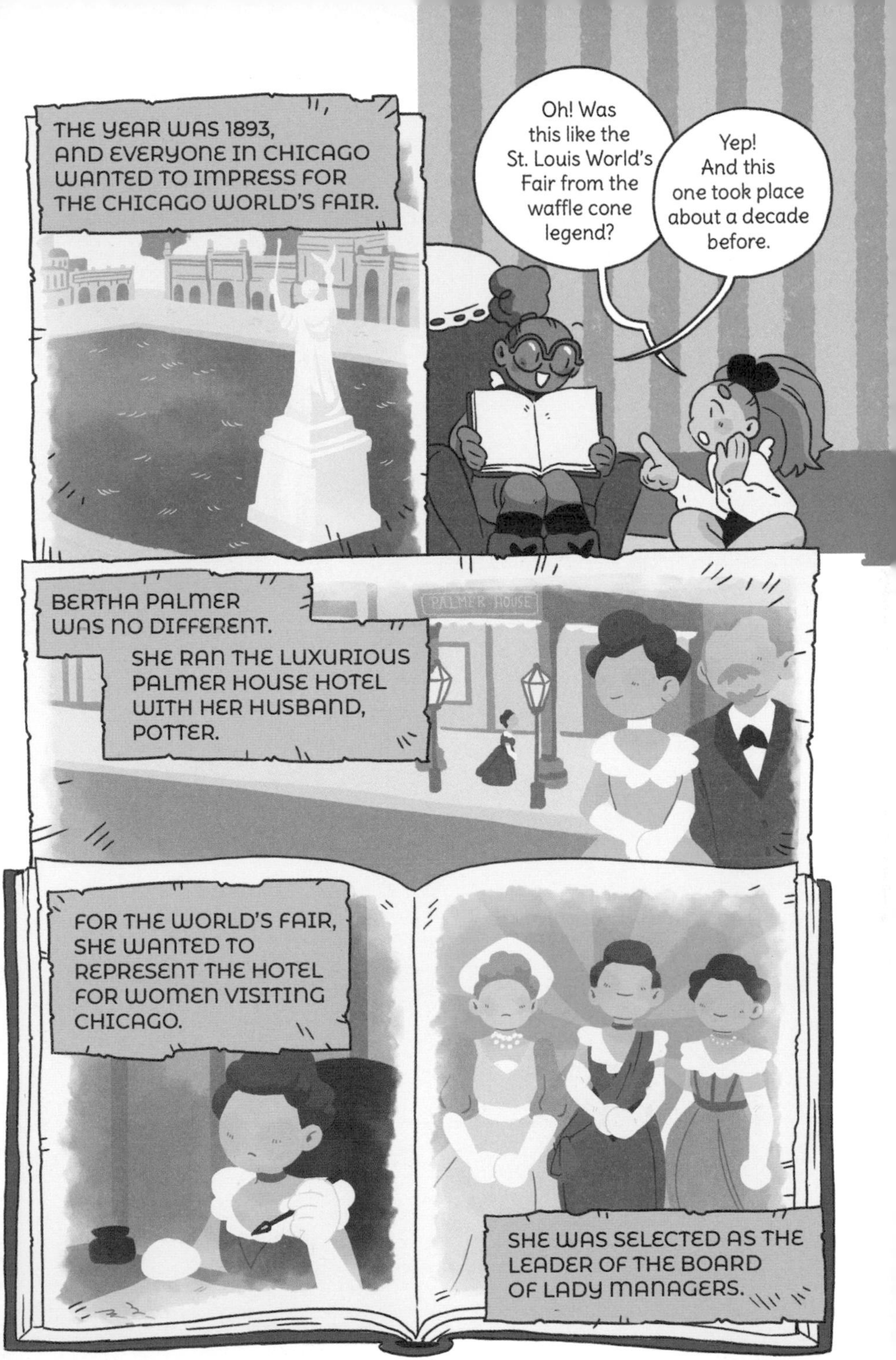
THE YEAR WAS 1893, AND EVERYONE IN CHICAGO WANTED TO IMPRESS FOR THE CHICAGO WORLD'S FAIR.
Oh! Was this like the St. Louis World's Fair from the waffle cone legend?
Yep! And this one took place about a decade before.
BERTHA PALMER WAS NO DIFFERENT.
SHE RAN THE LUXURIOUS PALMER HOUSE HOTEL WITH HER HUSBAND, POTTER.
PALMER HOUSE
FOR THE WORLD'S FAIR, SHE WANTED TO REPRESENT THE HOTEL FOR WOMEN VISITING CHICAGO.
SHE WAS SELECTED AS THE LEADER OF THE BOARD OF LADY MANAGERS.

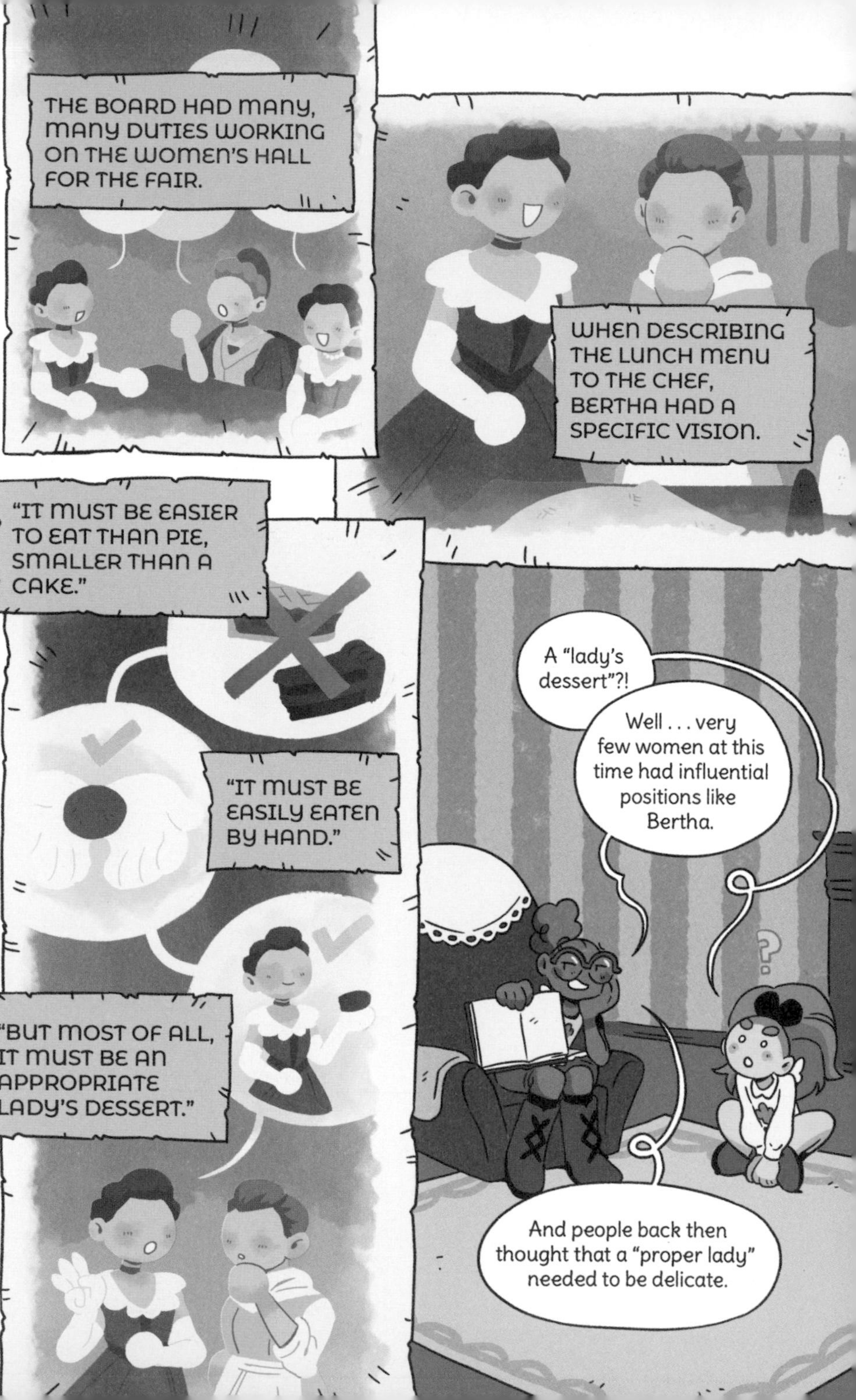
THE BOARD HAD MANY, MANY DUTIES WORKING ON THE WOMEN'S HALL FOR THE FAIR.
WHEN DESCRIBING THE LUNCH MENU TO THE CHEF, BERTHA HAD A SPECIFIC VISION.
"IT MUST BE EASIER TO EAT THAN PIE, SMALLER THAN A CAKE."
"IT MUST BE EASILY EATEN BY HAND."
"BUT MOST OF ALL, IT MUST BE AN APPROPRIATE LADY'S DESSERT."
A "lady's dessert"?!
Well . . . very few women at this time had influential positions like Bertha.
And people back then thought that a "proper lady" needed to be delicate.

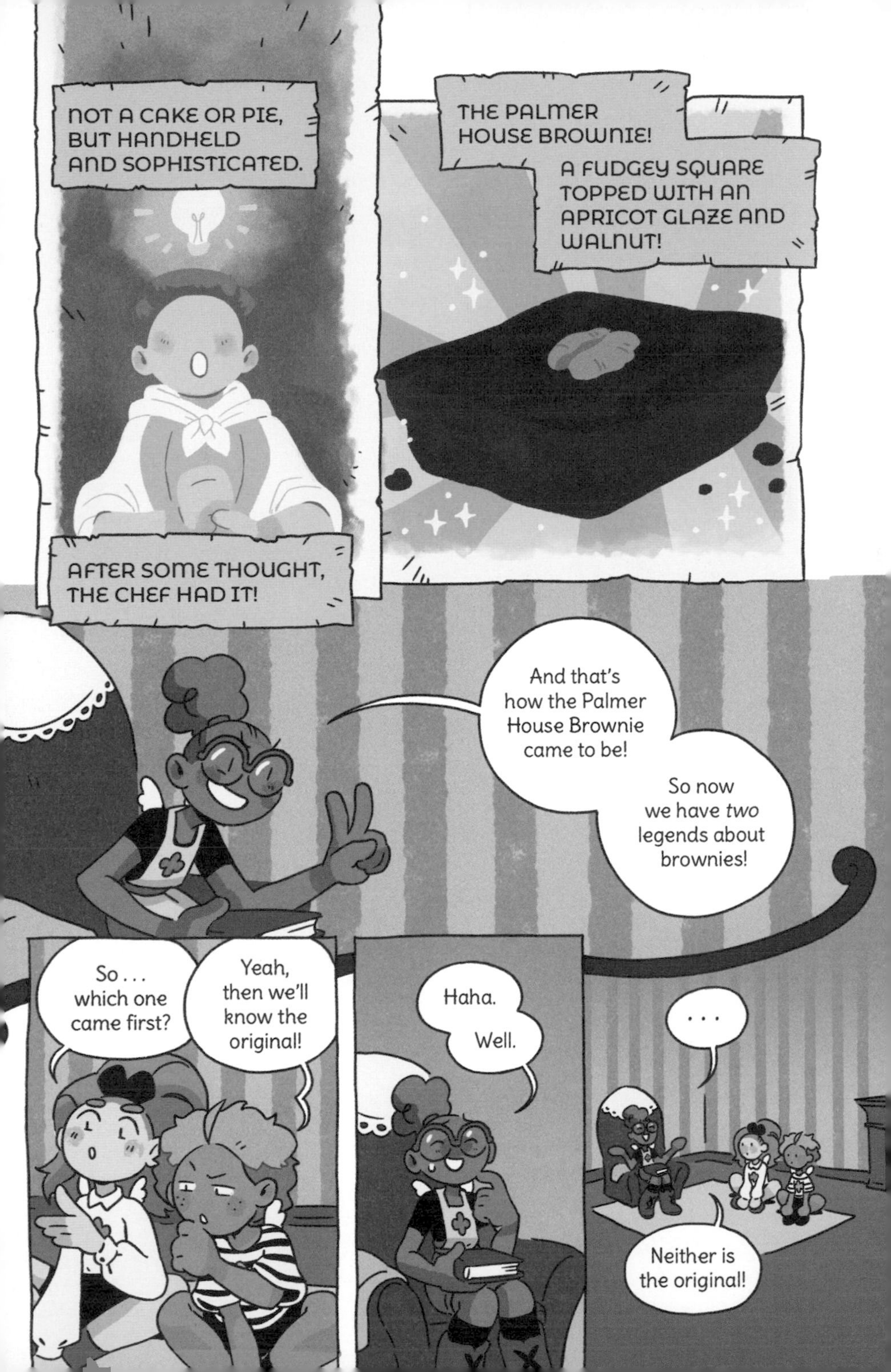
NOT A CAKE OR PIE, BUT HANDHELD AND SOPHISTICATED.
AFTER SOME THOUGHT, THE CHEF HAD IT!
THE PALMER HOUSE BROWNIE!
A FUDGEY SQUARE TOPPED WITH AN APRICOT GLAZE AND WALNUT!
And that's how the Palmer House Brownie came to be!
So now we have *two* legends about brownies!
So . . . which one came first?
Yeah, then we'll know the original!
Haha.
Well.
. . .
Neither is the original!

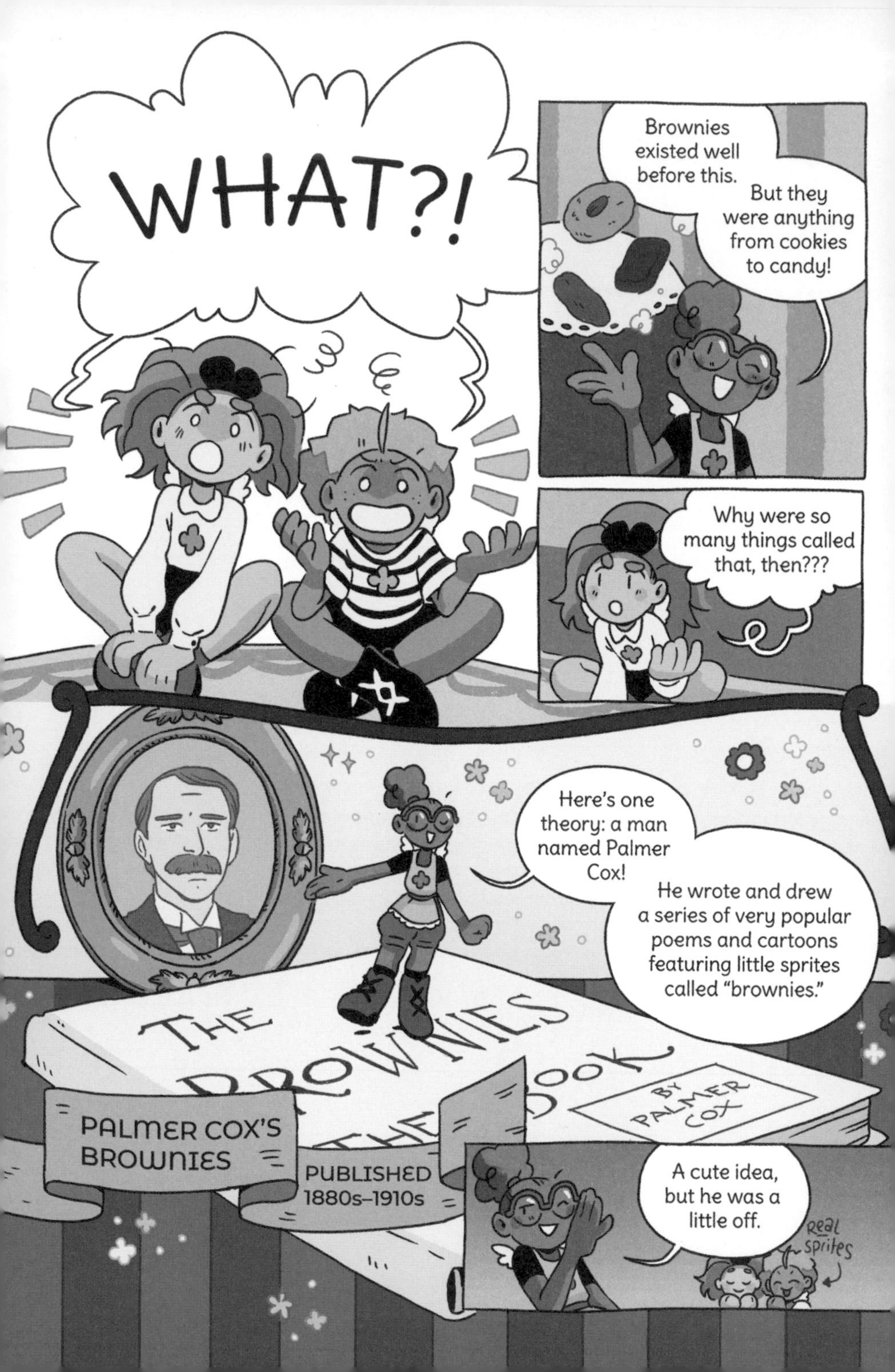

WHAT?!
Brownies existed well before this.
But they were anything from cookies to candy!
Why were so many things called that, then???
Here's one theory: a man named Palmer Cox!
He wrote and drew a series of very popular poems and cartoons featuring little sprites called "brownies."
THE BROWNIES BOOK
BY PALMER COX
PALMER COX'S BROWNIES
PUBLISHED 1880s–1910s
A cute idea, but he was a little off.
Real sprites

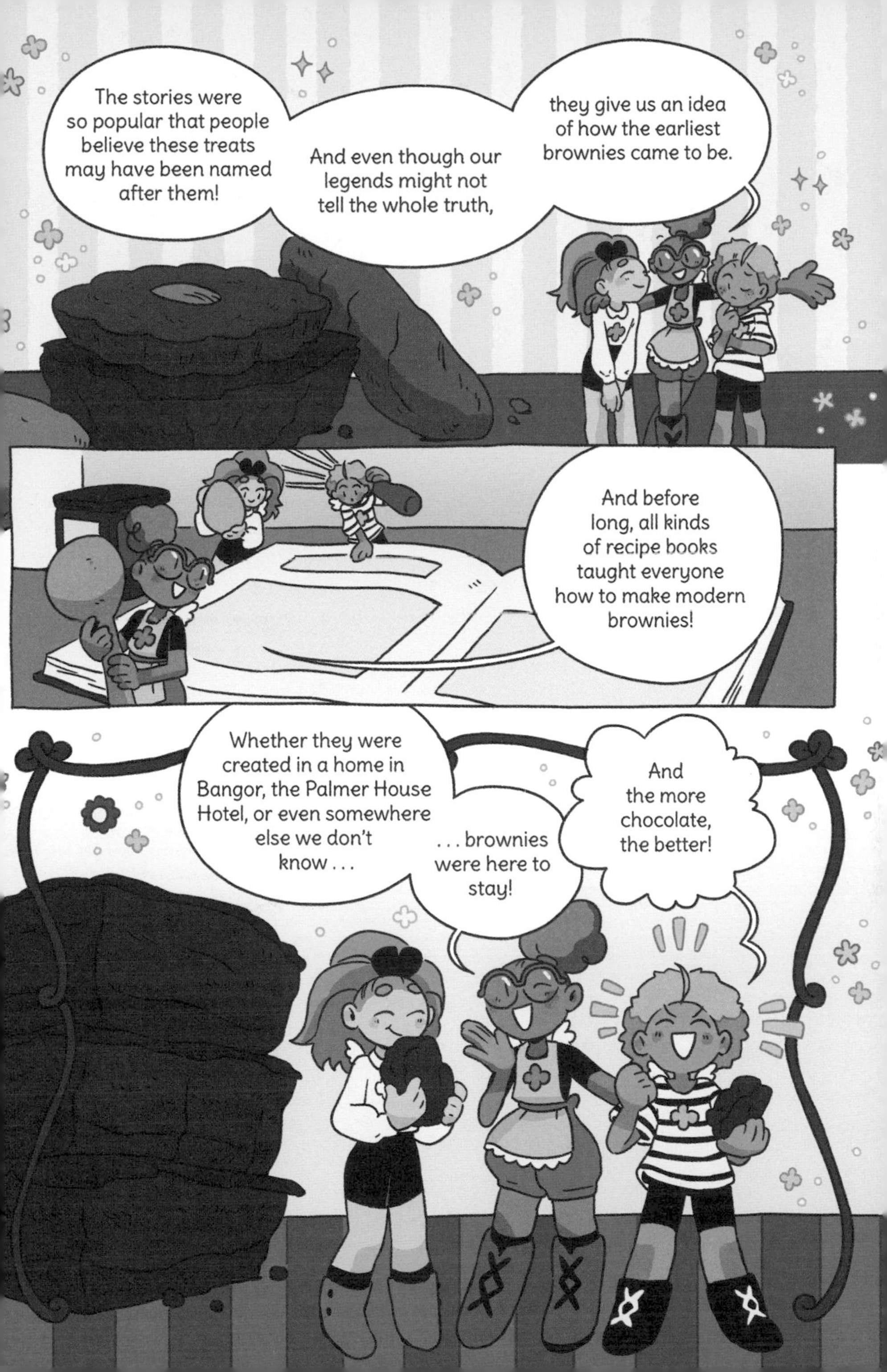
The stories were so popular that people believe these treats may have been named after them!
And even though our legends might not tell the whole truth,
they give us an idea of how the earliest brownies came to be.
And before long, all kinds of recipe books taught everyone how to make modern brownies!
Whether they were created in a home in Bangor, the Palmer House Hotel, or even somewhere else we don't know . . .
. . . brownies were here to stay!
And the more chocolate, the better!

# The Abridged
# Atlas of Donut History

1  Ancient Egyptian Proto-Donuts

2  Ancient Greek Enkris

3  Ancient Roman Globus

4  Middle Eastern Lokma

5  Indian Gulab Jamun

6  African Great Lakes Mandazi

7  French Nun's Farts

8  Islamic World Jalebi

9  German Fastnachts

10  Polish Paçzki

11  Portuguese Malasada

12  Jewish Diaspora Sufganiyot

13  Spanish, Portuguese, Mexican, and Filipino Churros

14  West African, French, and New Orleans Calas and Beignets

15  Chilean Calzones Rotos

16  Chilean and Peruvian Picarones

17  Captain Hanson Gregory

18  Dutch Olie Koeken

19  Adolph Levitt's Donut Machine

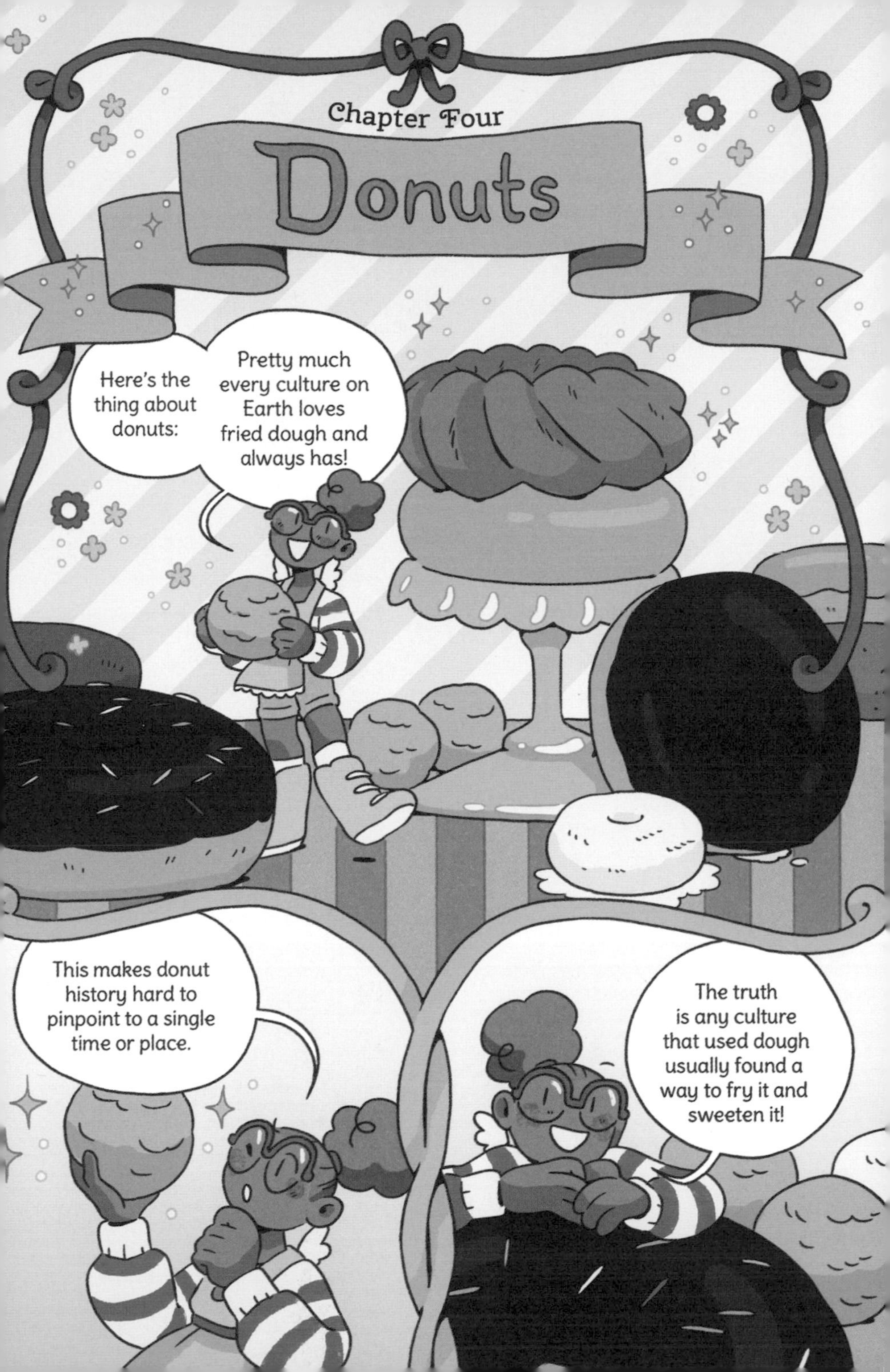
Chapter Four
Donuts
Here's the thing about donuts:
Pretty much every culture on Earth loves fried dough and always has!
This makes donut history hard to pinpoint to a single time or place.
The truth is any culture that used dough usually found a way to fry it and sweeten it!

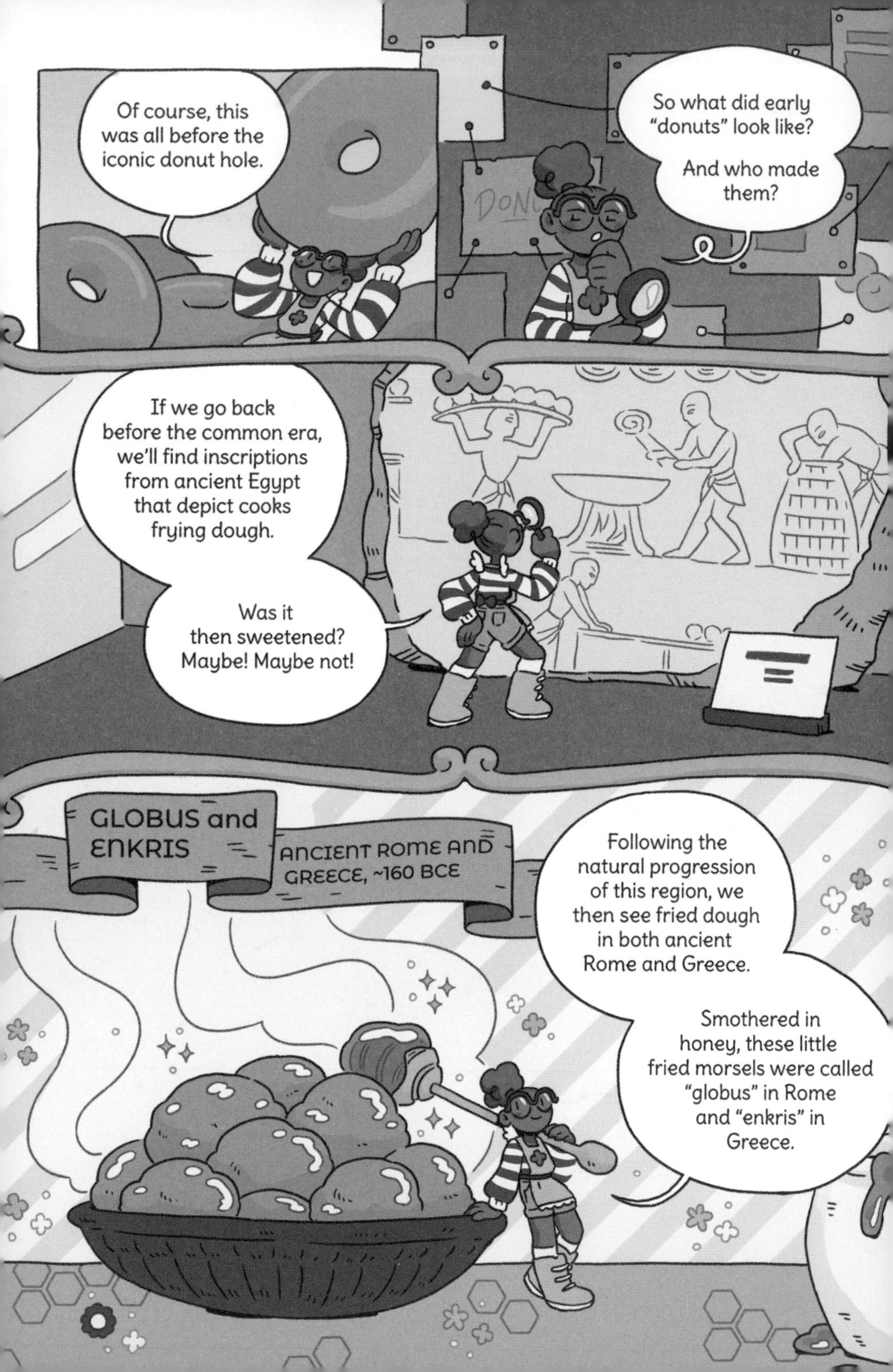
Of course, this was all before the iconic donut hole.
So what did early "donuts" look like?
And who made them?
DONU
If we go back before the common era, we'll find inscriptions from ancient Egypt that depict cooks frying dough.
Was it then sweetened? Maybe! Maybe not!
GLOBUS and ENKRIS
ANCIENT ROME AND GREECE, ~160 BCE
Following the natural progression of this region, we then see fried dough in both ancient Rome and Greece.
Smothered in honey, these little fried morsels were called "globus" in Rome and "enkris" in Greece.

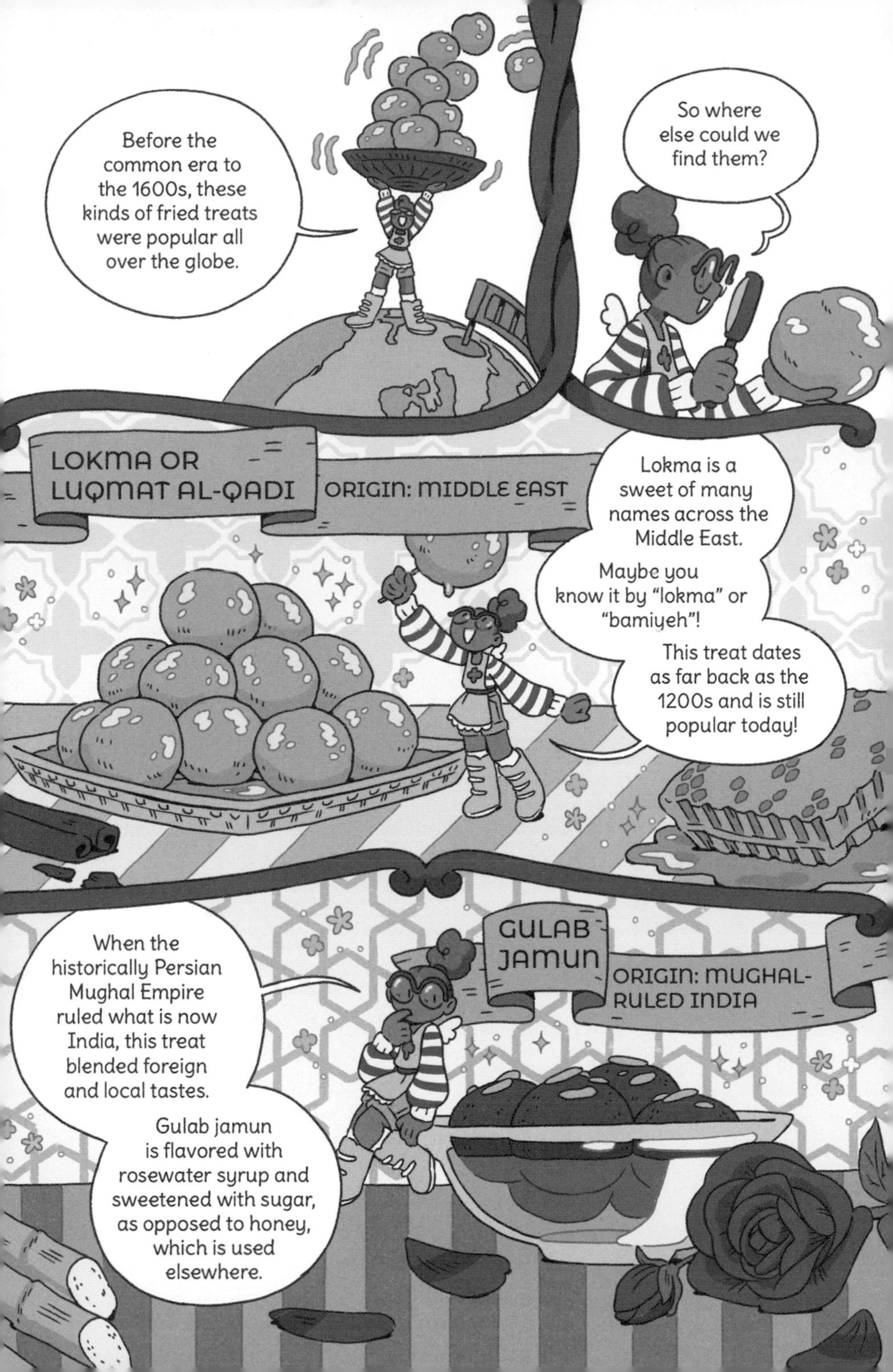

Before the common era to the 1600s, these kinds of fried treats were popular all over the globe.
So where else could we find them?
LOKMA OR LUQMAT AL-QADI
ORIGIN: MIDDLE EAST
Lokma is a sweet of many names across the Middle East.
Maybe you know it by "lokma" or "bamiyeh"!
This treat dates as far back as the 1200s and is still popular today!
GULAB JAMUN
ORIGIN: MUGHAL-RULED INDIA
When the historically Persian Mughal Empire ruled what is now India, this treat blended foreign and local tastes.
Gulab jamun is flavored with rosewater syrup and sweetened with sugar, as opposed to honey, which is used elsewhere.

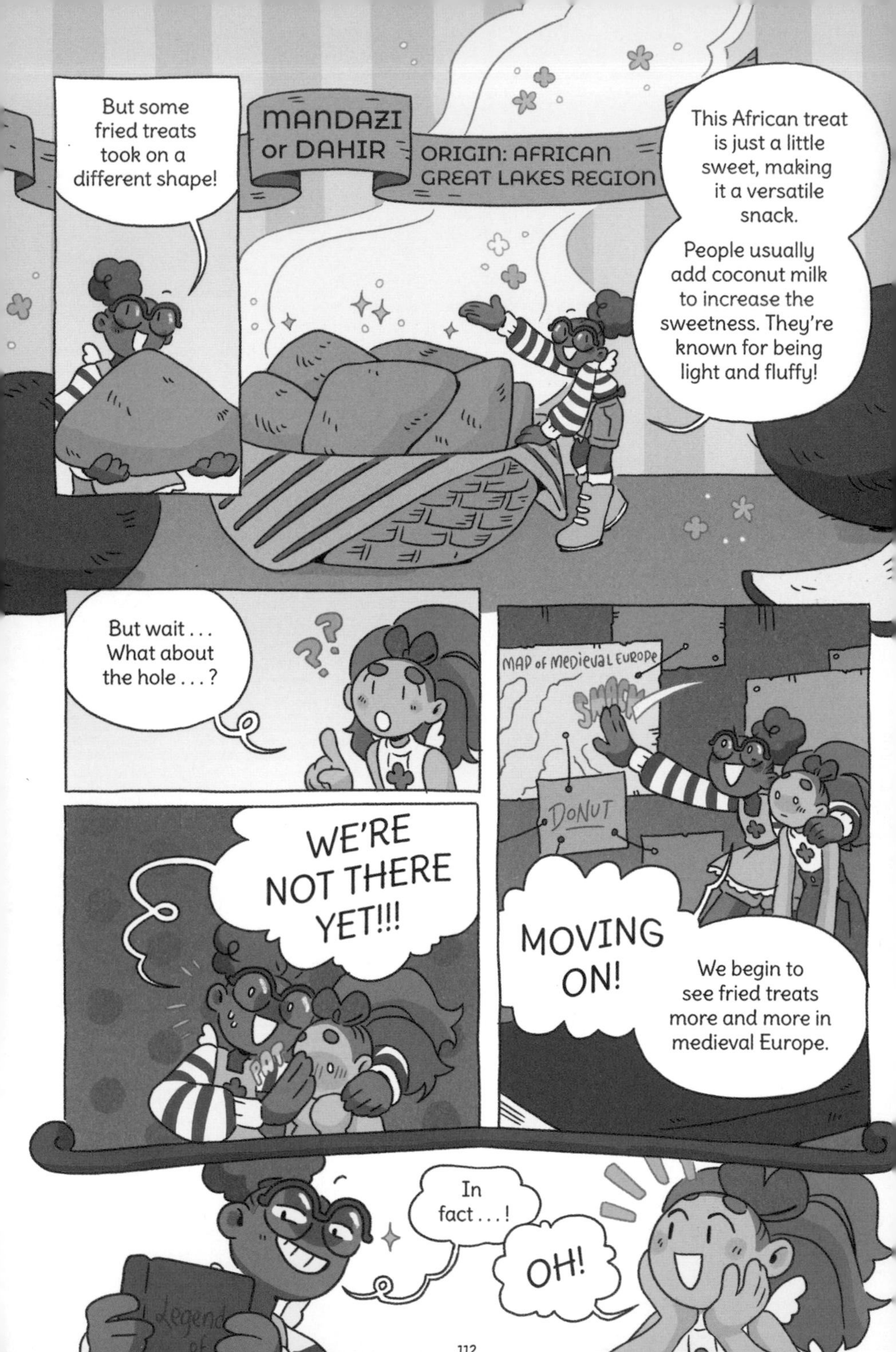
But some fried treats took on a different shape!
MANDAZI or DAHIR
ORIGIN: AFRICAN GREAT LAKES REGION
This African treat is just a little sweet, making it a versatile snack.
People usually add coconut milk to increase the sweetness. They're known for being light and fluffy!
But wait . . . What about the hole . . . ?
MAP of MEDIEVAL EUROPE
SMACK
DONUT
WE'RE NOT THERE YET!!!
PAT
MOVING ON!
We begin to see fried treats more and more in medieval Europe.
In fact . . . !
OH!

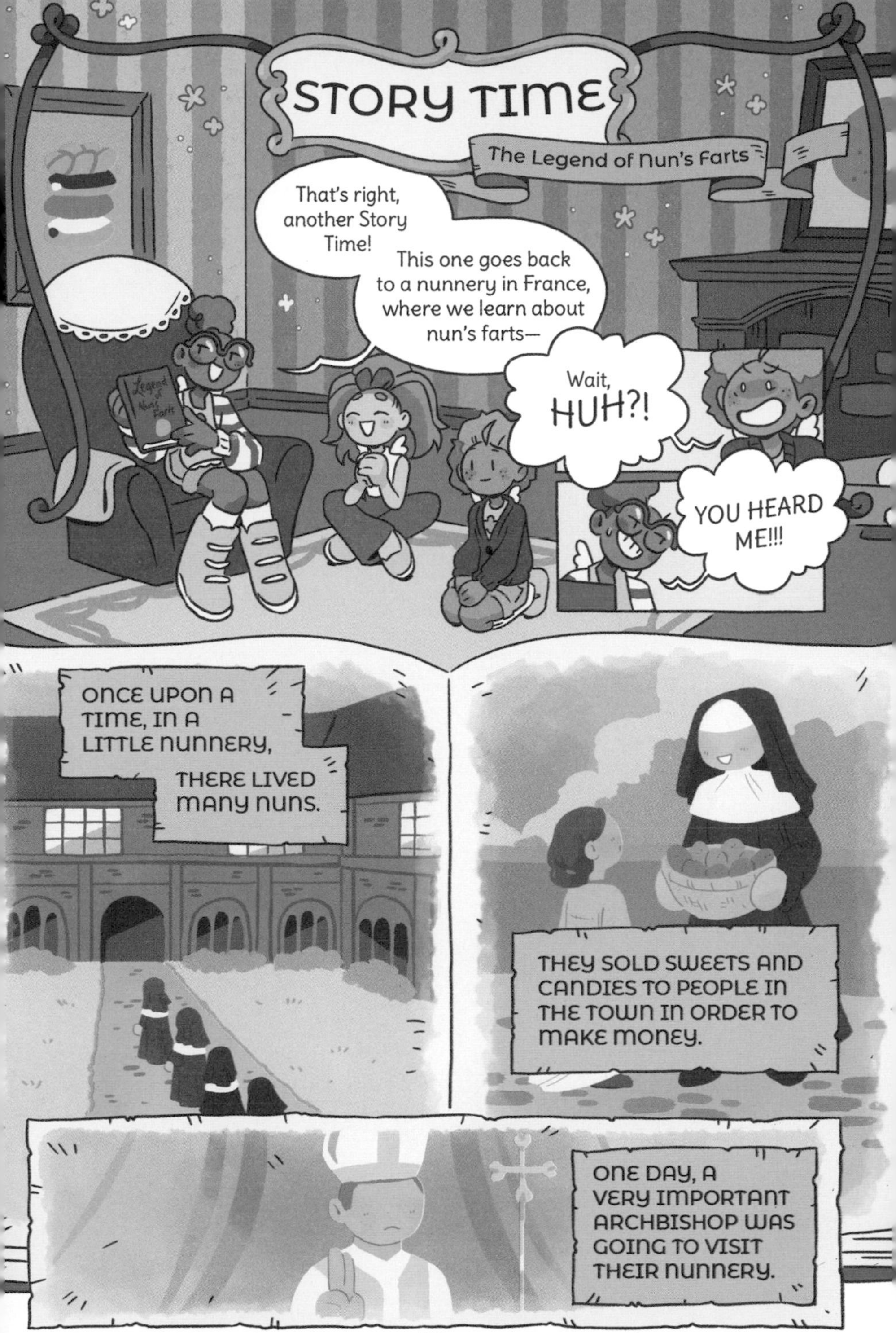
STORY TIME
The Legend of Nun's Farts
That's right, another Story Time!
This one goes back to a nunnery in France, where we learn about nun's farts—
Wait, HUH?!
YOU HEARD ME!!!
ONCE UPON A TIME, IN A LITTLE NUNNERY,
THERE LIVED MANY NUNS.
THEY SOLD SWEETS AND CANDIES TO PEOPLE IN THE TOWN IN ORDER TO MAKE MONEY.
ONE DAY, A VERY IMPORTANT ARCHBISHOP WAS GOING TO VISIT THEIR NUNNERY.

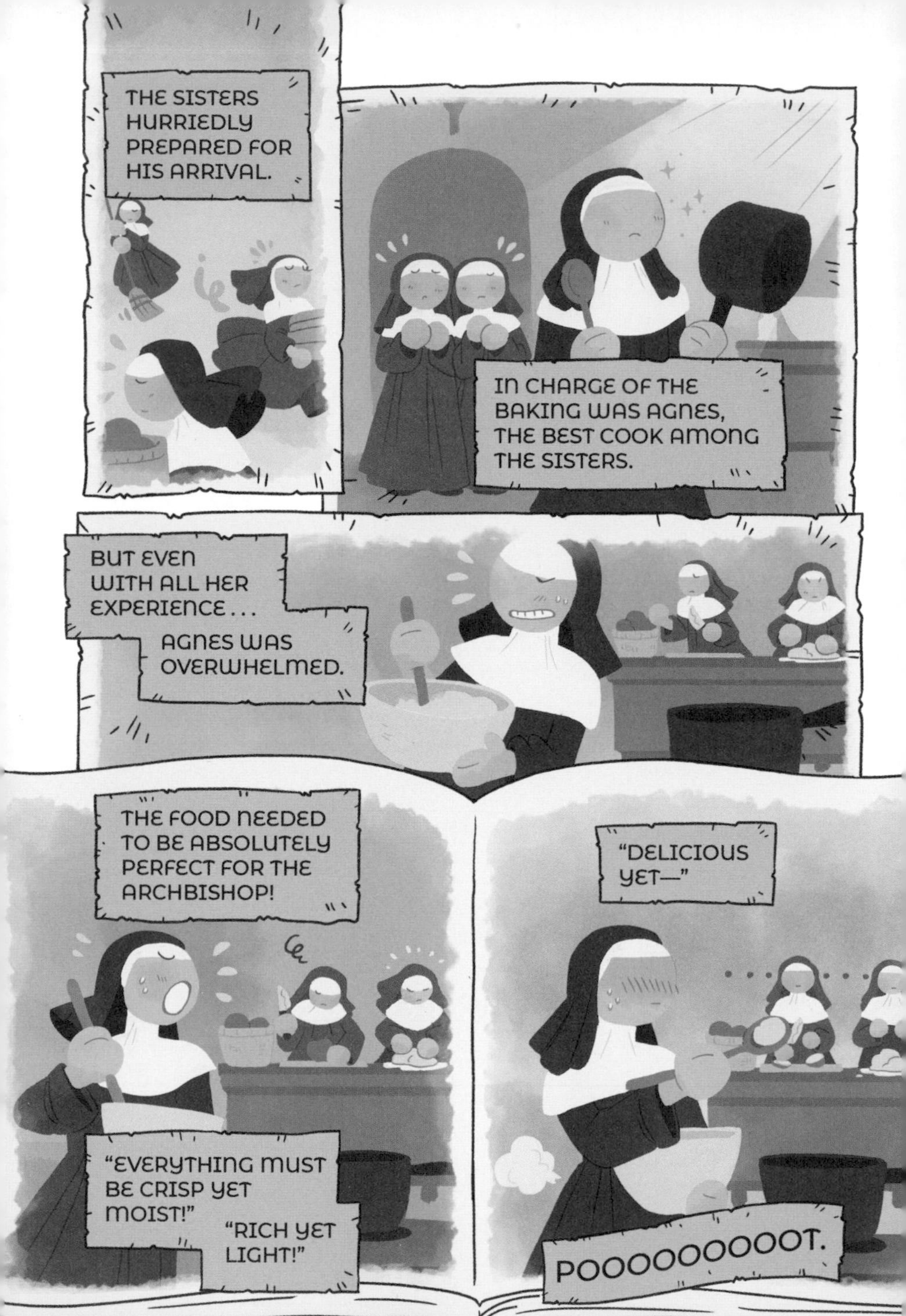
THE SISTERS HURRIEDLY PREPARED FOR HIS ARRIVAL.
IN CHARGE OF THE BAKING WAS AGNES, THE BEST COOK AMONG THE SISTERS.
BUT EVEN WITH ALL HER EXPERIENCE . . .
AGNES WAS OVERWHELMED.
THE FOOD NEEDED TO BE ABSOLUTELY PERFECT FOR THE ARCHBISHOP!
"EVERYTHING MUST BE CRISP YET MOIST!"
"RICH YET LIGHT!"
"DELICIOUS YET—"
POOOOOOOOOT.

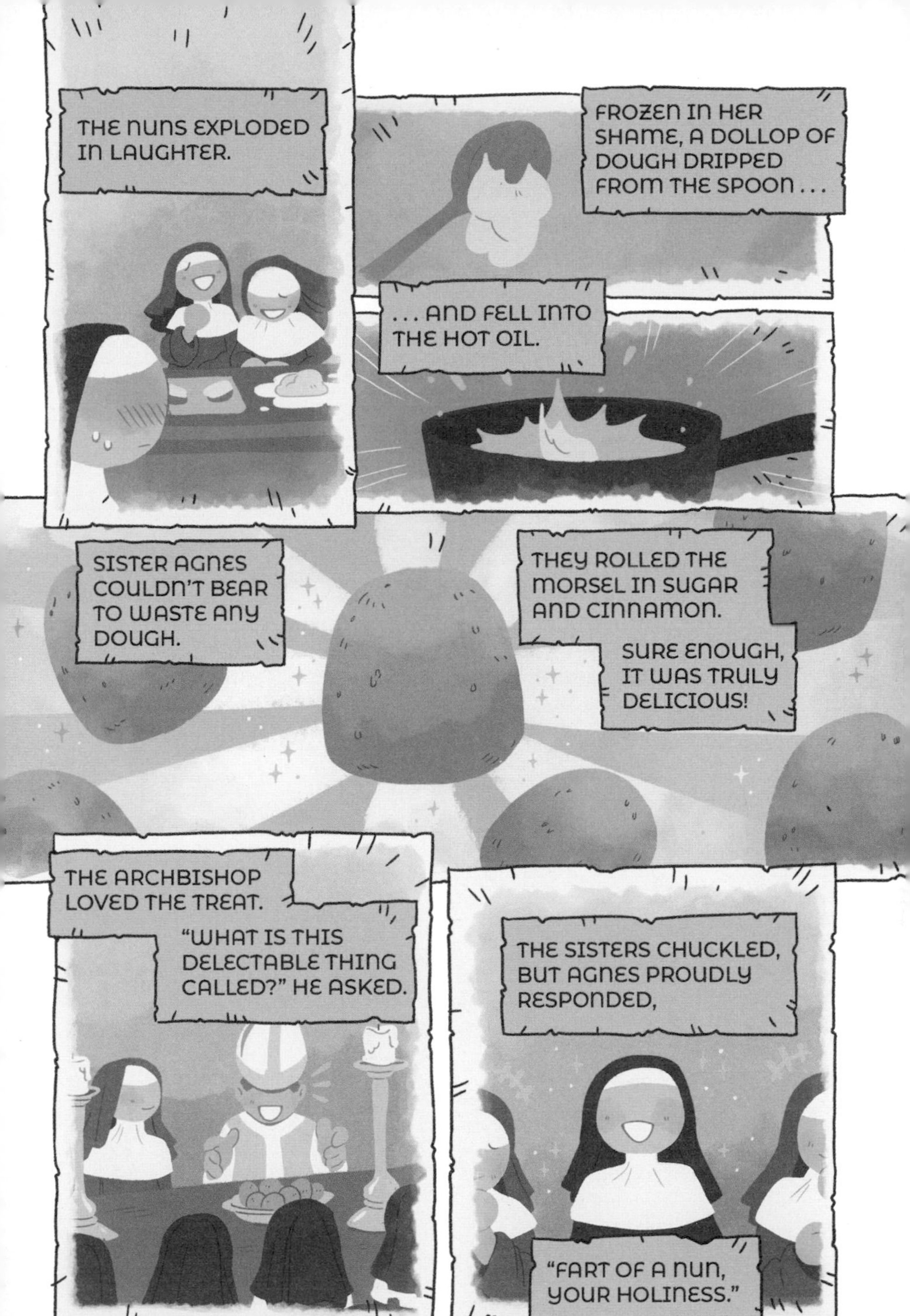
THE NUNS EXPLODED IN LAUGHTER.
FROZEN IN HER SHAME, A DOLLOP OF DOUGH DRIPPED FROM THE SPOON . . .
. . . AND FELL INTO THE HOT OIL.
SISTER AGNES COULDN'T BEAR TO WASTE ANY DOUGH.
THEY ROLLED THE MORSEL IN SUGAR AND CINNAMON.
SURE ENOUGH, IT WAS TRULY DELICIOUS!
THE ARCHBISHOP LOVED THE TREAT.
"WHAT IS THIS DELECTABLE THING CALLED?" HE ASKED.
THE SISTERS CHUCKLED, BUT AGNES PROUDLY RESPONDED,
"FART OF A NUN, YOUR HOLINESS."

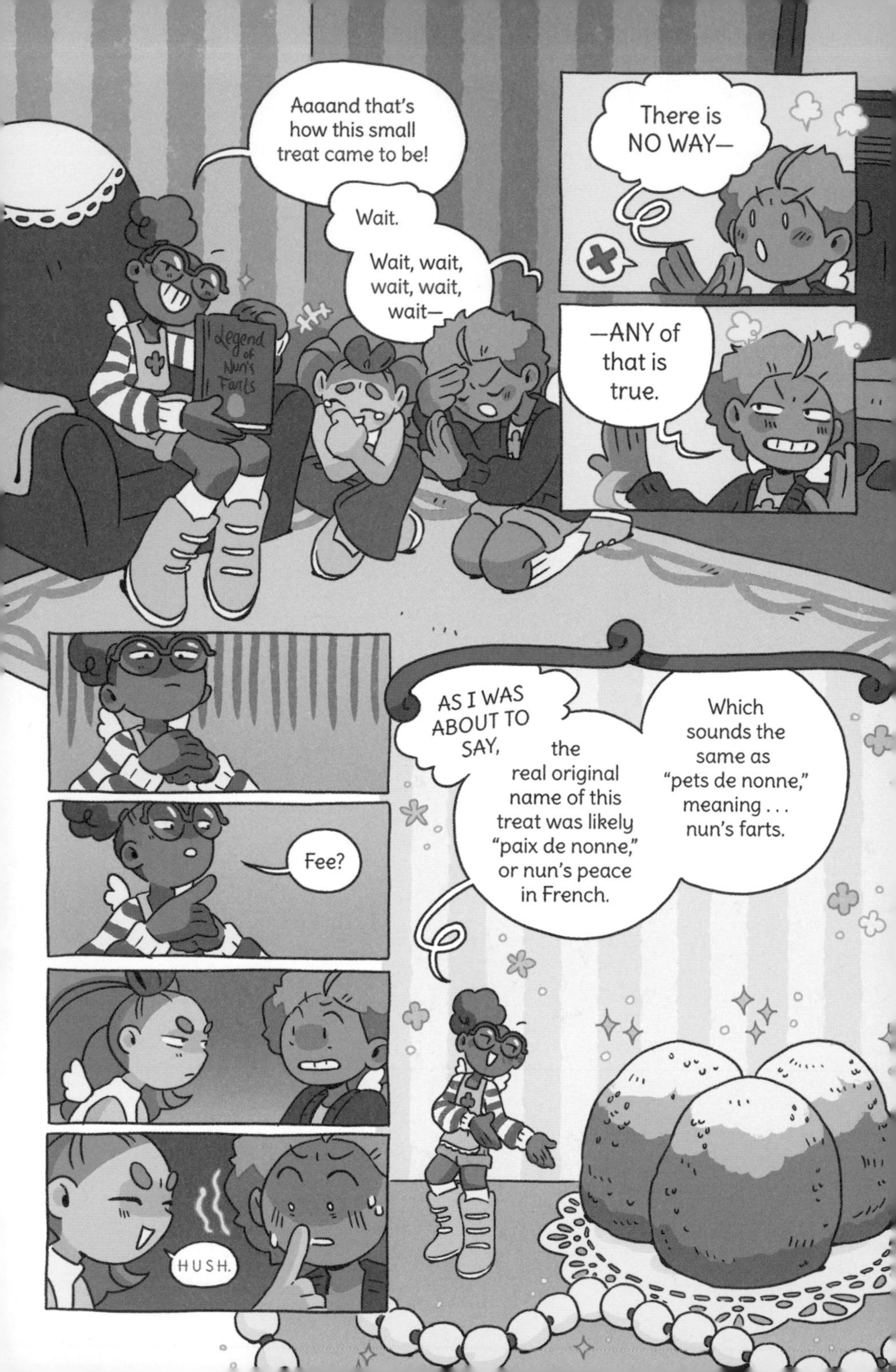
Aaaand that's how this small treat came to be!
Wait.
Wait, wait, wait, wait, wait—
Legend of Nun's Farts
There is NO WAY—
—ANY of that is true.
Fee?
HUSH.
AS I WAS ABOUT TO SAY, the real original name of this treat was likely "paix de nonne," or nun's peace in French.
Which sounds the same as "pets de nonne," meaning . . . nun's farts.

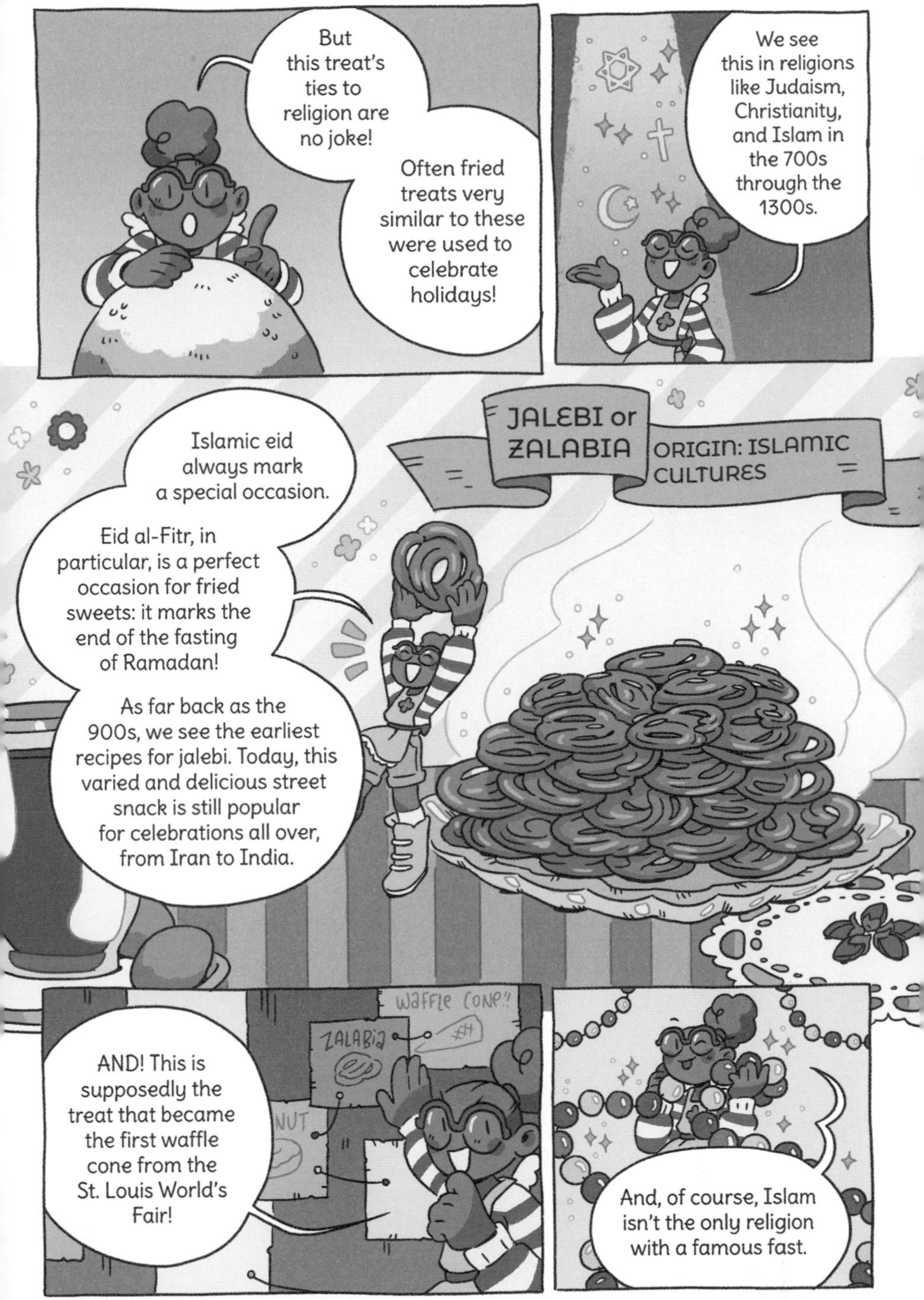

But this treat's ties to religion are no joke!
Often fried treats very similar to these were used to celebrate holidays!
We see this in religions like Judaism, Christianity, and Islam in the 700s through the 1300s.
JALEBI or ZALABIA
ORIGIN: ISLAMIC CULTURES
Islamic eid always mark a special occasion.
Eid al-Fitr, in particular, is a perfect occasion for fried sweets: it marks the end of the fasting of Ramadan!
As far back as the 900s, we see the earliest recipes for jalebi. Today, this varied and delicious street snack is still popular for celebrations all over, from Iran to India.
ZALABia
Waffle cone!!
NUT
AND! This is supposedly the treat that became the first waffle cone from the St. Louis World's Fair!
And, of course, Islam isn't the only religion with a famous fast.

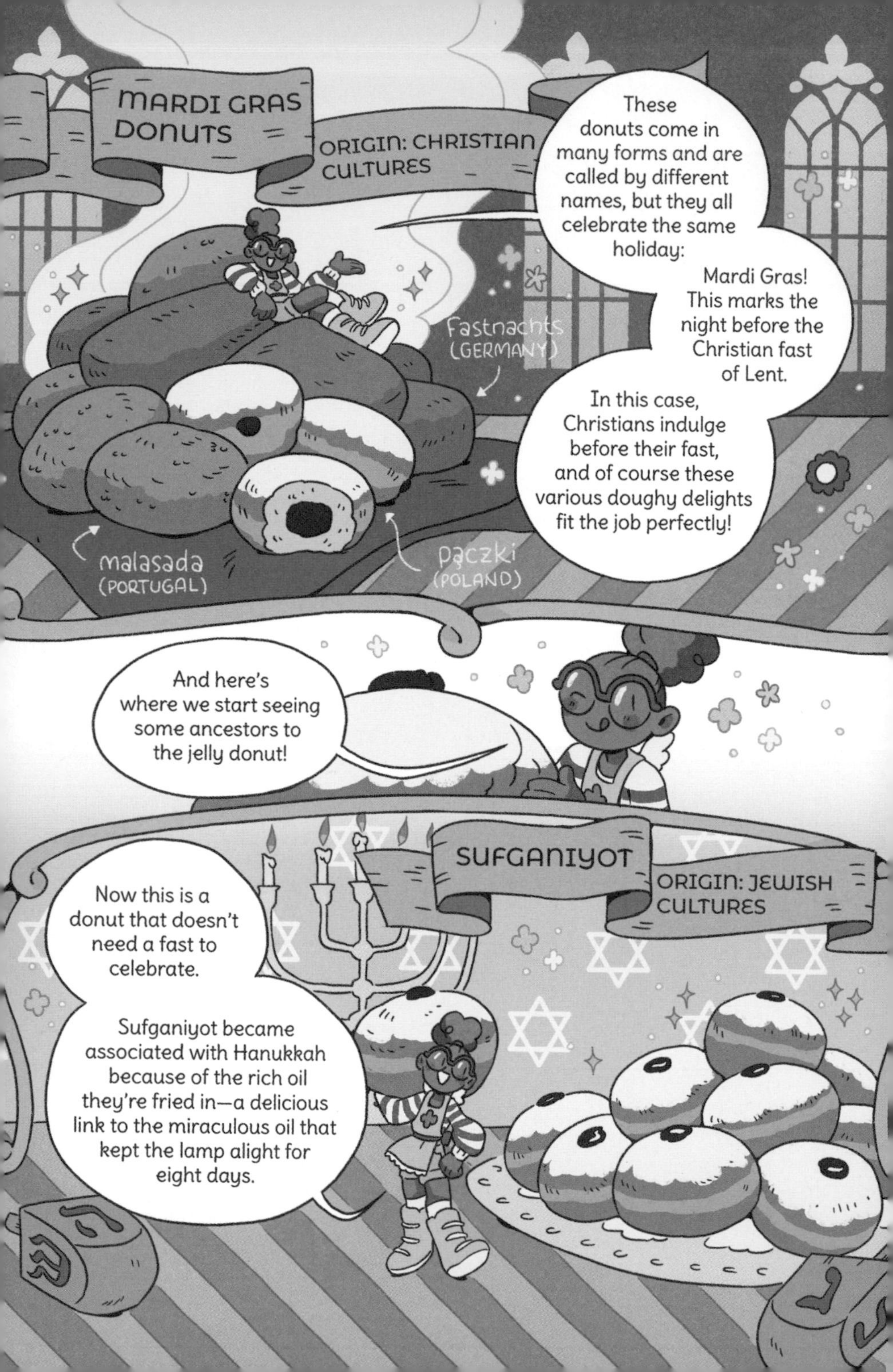
MARDI GRAS DONUTS
ORIGIN: CHRISTIAN CULTURES
These donuts come in many forms and are called by different names, but they all celebrate the same holiday:
Mardi Gras! This marks the night before the Christian fast of Lent.
In this case, Christians indulge before their fast, and of course these various doughy delights fit the job perfectly!
Fastnachts (GERMANY)
malasada (PORTUGAL)
pączki (POLAND)
And here's where we start seeing some ancestors to the jelly donut!
SUFGANIYOT
ORIGIN: JEWISH CULTURES
Now this is a donut that doesn't need a fast to celebrate.
Sufganiyot became associated with Hanukkah because of the rich oil they're fried in—a delicious link to the miraculous oil that kept the lamp alight for eight days.

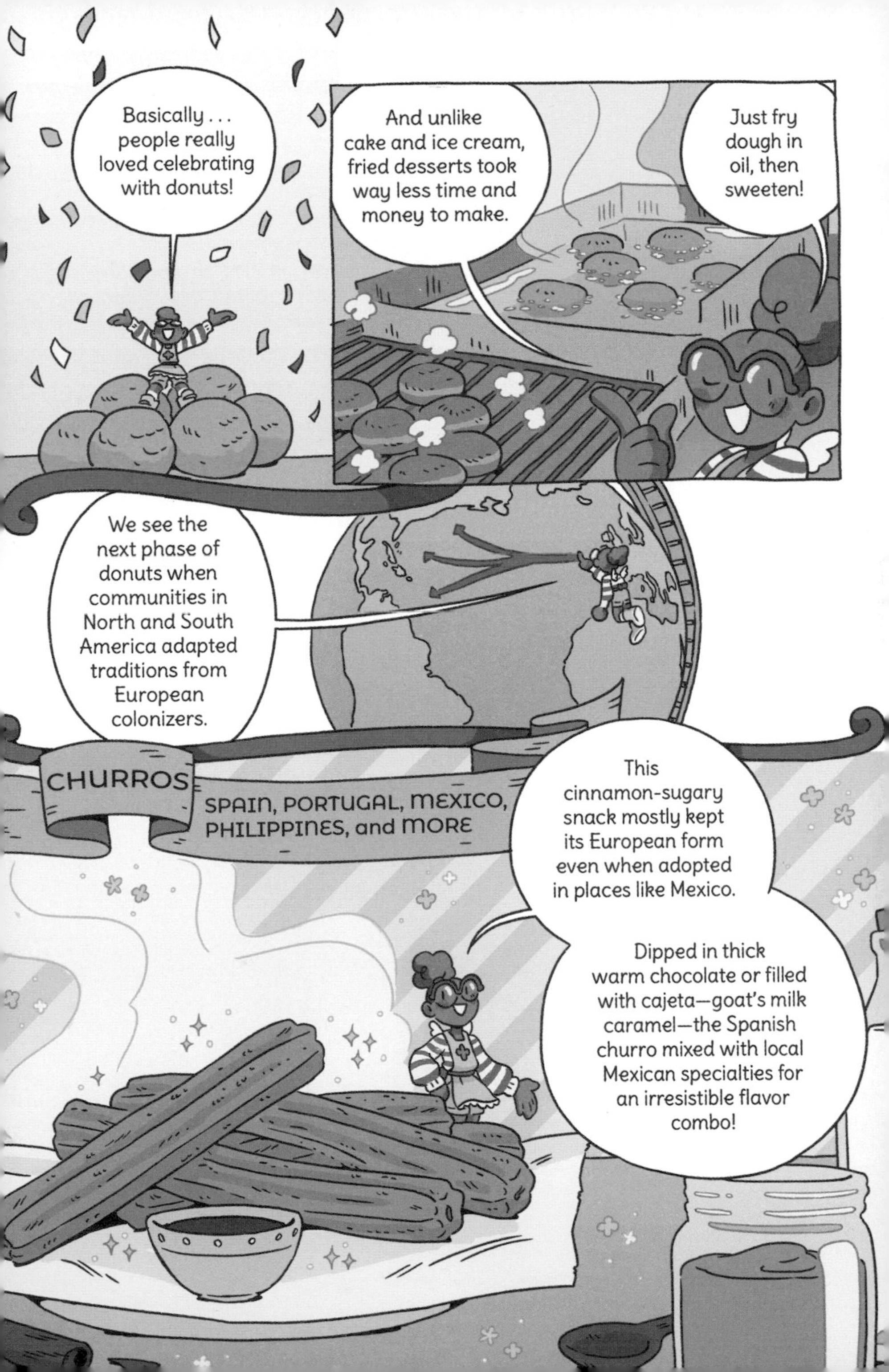

Basically . . . people really loved celebrating with donuts!
And unlike cake and ice cream, fried desserts took way less time and money to make.
Just fry dough in oil, then sweeten!
We see the next phase of donuts when communities in North and South America adapted traditions from European colonizers.
CHURROS
SPAIN, PORTUGAL, MEXICO, PHILIPPINES, and MORE
This cinnamon-sugary snack mostly kept its European form even when adopted in places like Mexico.
Dipped in thick warm chocolate or filled with cajeta—goat's milk caramel—the Spanish churro mixed with local Mexican specialties for an irresistible flavor combo!

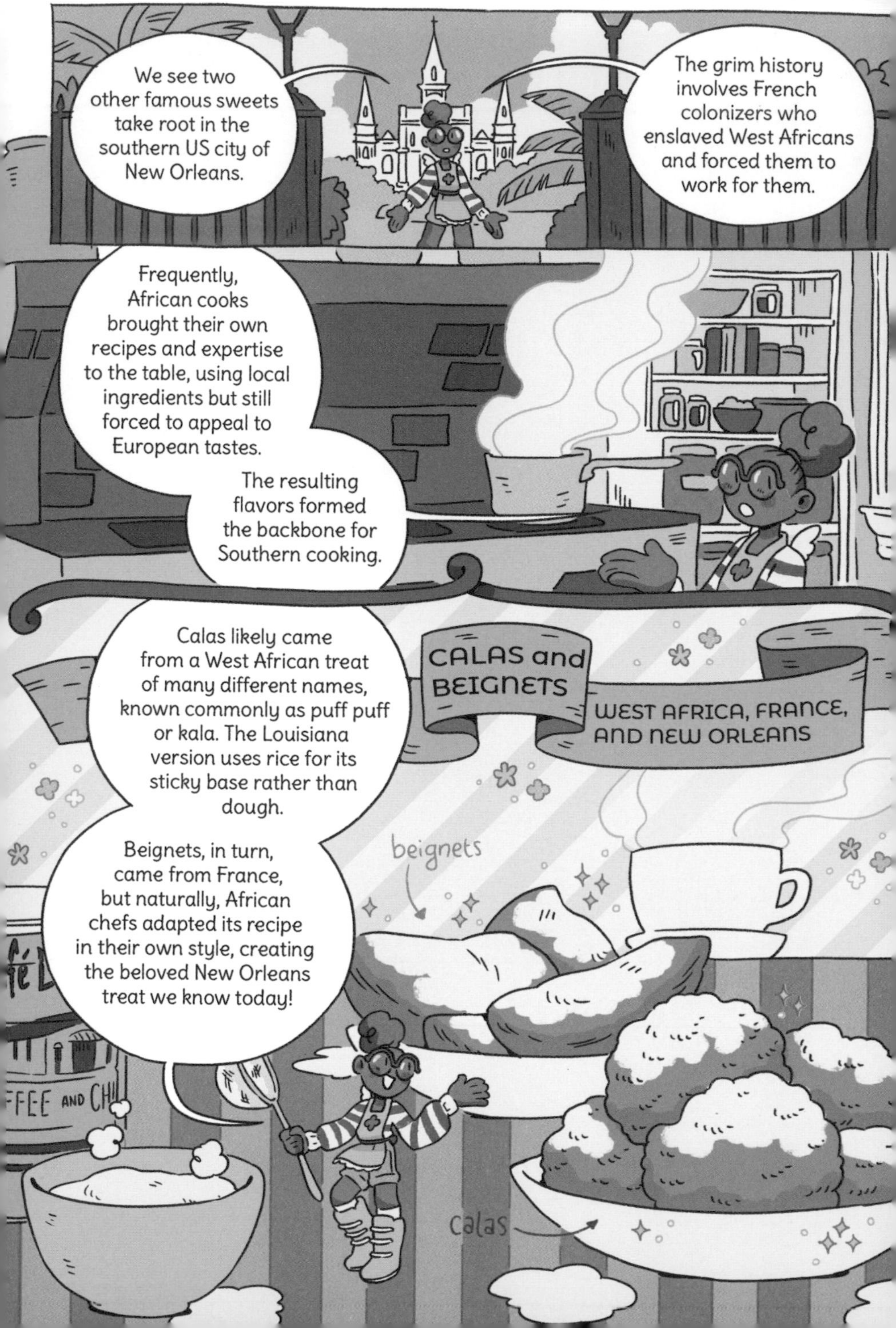

We see two other famous sweets take root in the southern US city of New Orleans.
The grim history involves French colonizers who enslaved West Africans and forced them to work for them.
Frequently, African cooks brought their own recipes and expertise to the table, using local ingredients but still forced to appeal to European tastes.
The resulting flavors formed the backbone for Southern cooking.
Calas likely came from a West African treat of many different names, known commonly as puff puff or kala. The Louisiana version uses rice for its sticky base rather than dough.
CALAS and BEIGNETS
WEST AFRICA, FRANCE, AND NEW ORLEANS
Beignets, in turn, came from France, but naturally, African chefs adapted its recipe in their own style, creating the beloved New Orleans treat we know today!
beignets
calas

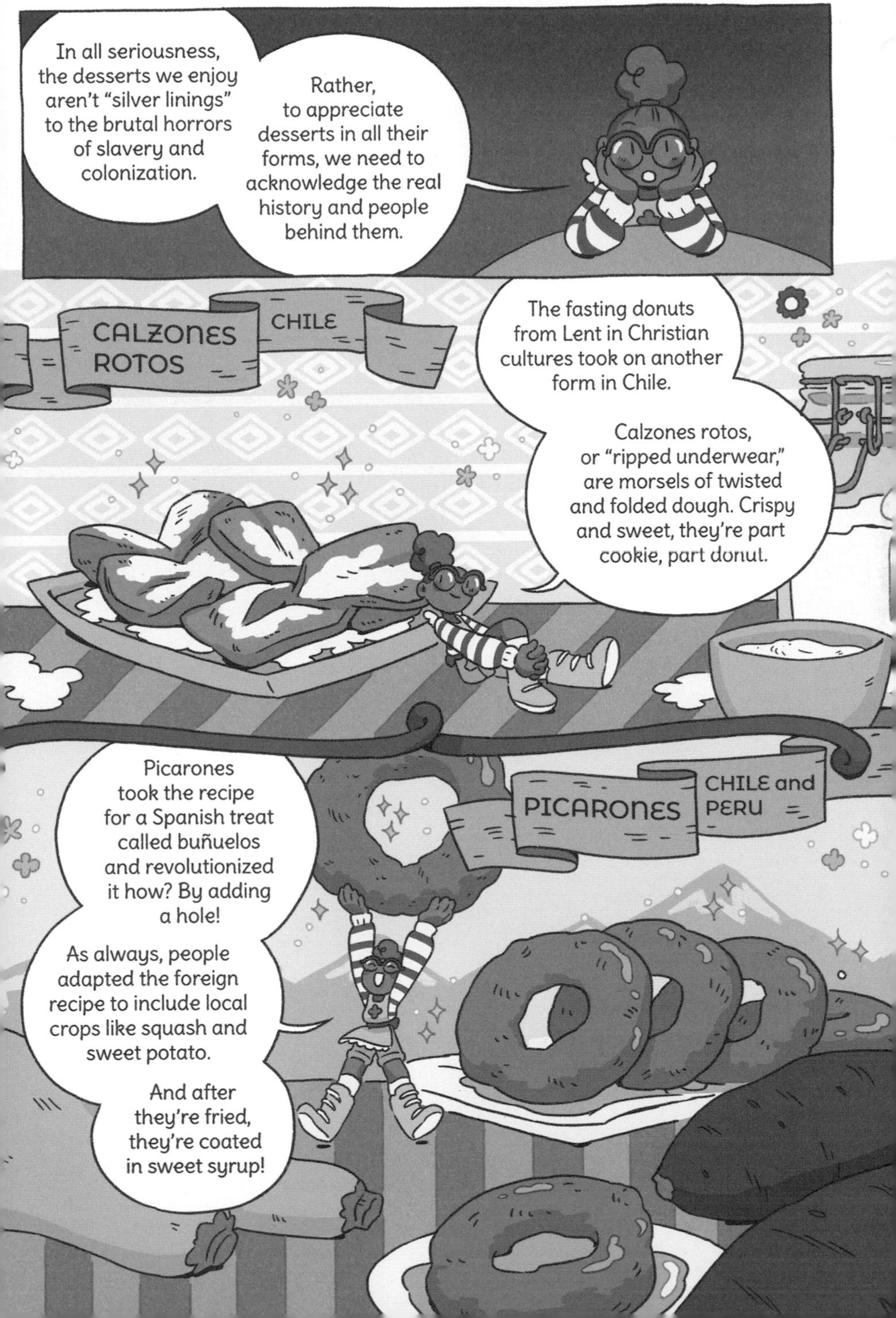
In all seriousness, the desserts we enjoy aren't "silver linings" to the brutal horrors of slavery and colonization.
Rather, to appreciate desserts in all their forms, we need to acknowledge the real history and people behind them.
CALZONES ROTOS
CHILE
The fasting donuts from Lent in Christian cultures took on another form in Chile.
Calzones rotos, or "ripped underwear," are morsels of twisted and folded dough. Crispy and sweet, they're part cookie, part donut.
PICARONES
CHILE and PERU
Picarones took the recipe for a Spanish treat called buñuelos and revolutionized it how? By adding a hole!
As always, people adapted the foreign recipe to include local crops like squash and sweet potato.
And after they're fried, they're coated in sweet syrup!

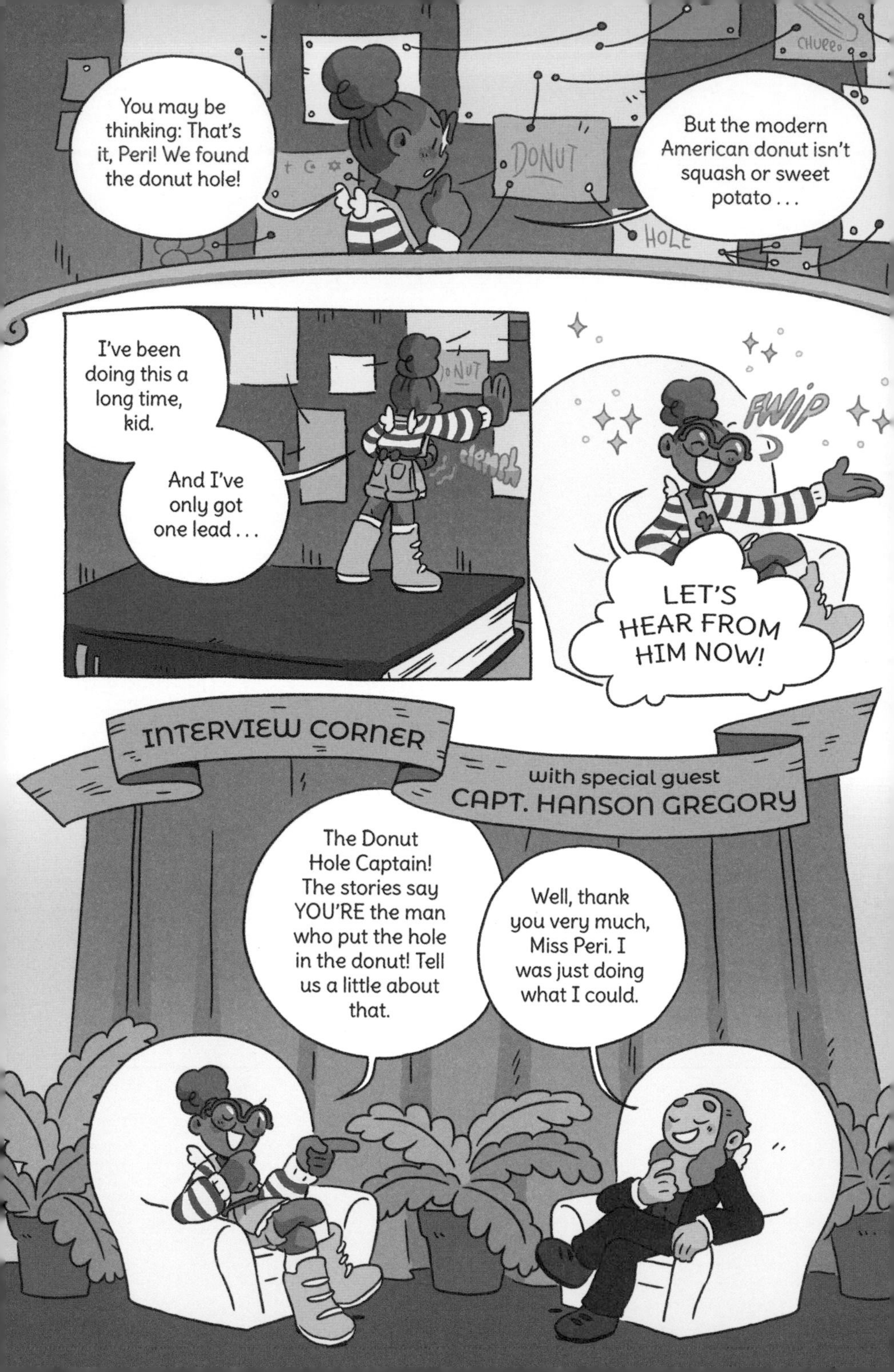
CHURRO
You may be thinking: That's it, Peri! We found the donut hole!
DONUT
HOLE
But the modern American donut isn't squash or sweet potato . . .
I've been doing this a long time, kid.
And I've only got one lead . . .
DONUT
FWIP
LET'S HEAR FROM HIM NOW!
INTERVIEW CORNER
with special guest
CAPT. HANSON GREGORY
The Donut Hole Captain! The stories say YOU'RE the man who put the hole in the donut! Tell us a little about that.
Well, thank you very much, Miss Peri. I was just doing what I could.

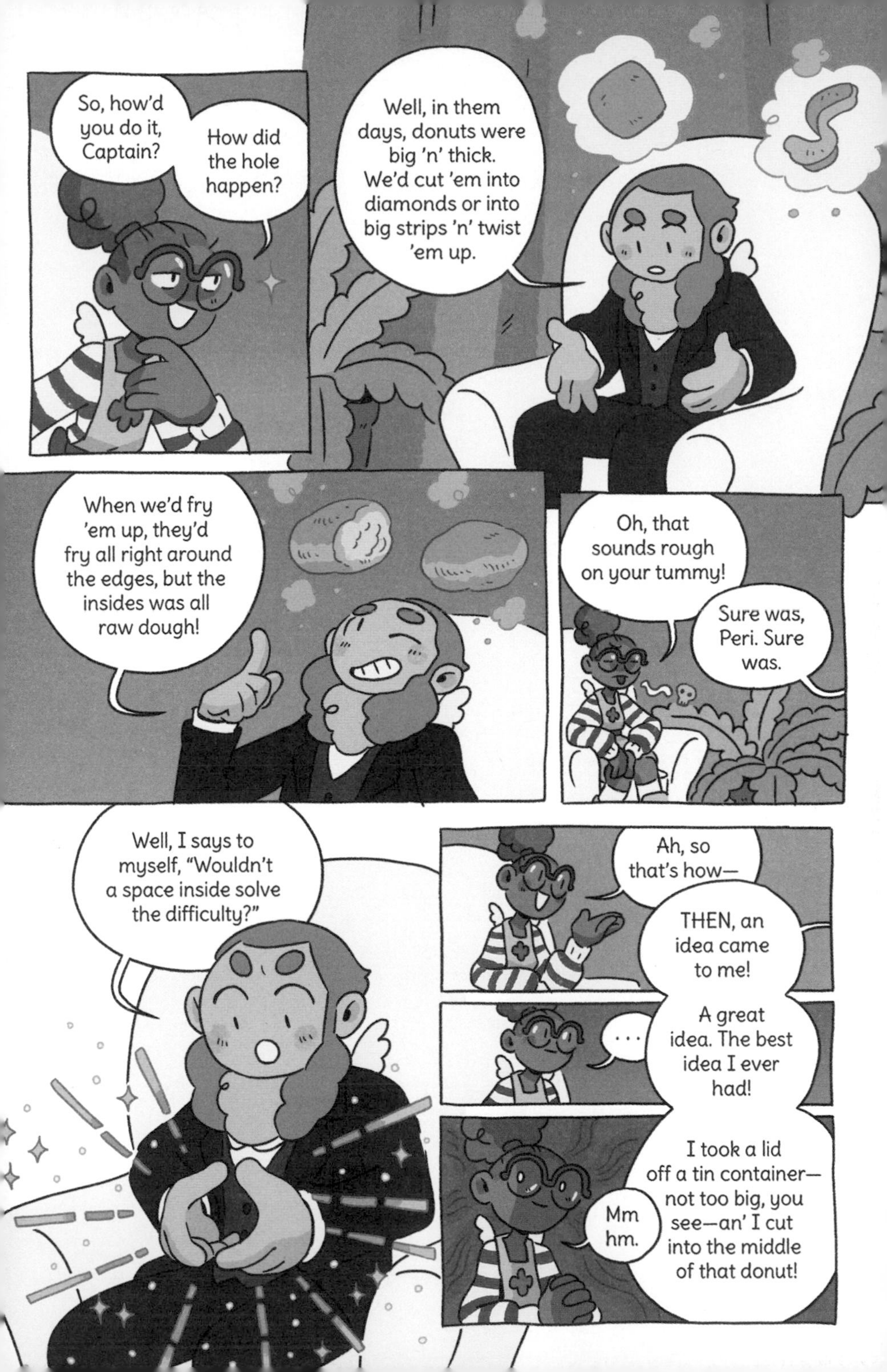

So, how'd you do it, Captain?
How did the hole happen?
Well, in them days, donuts were big 'n' thick. We'd cut 'em into diamonds or into big strips 'n' twist 'em up.
When we'd fry 'em up, they'd fry all right around the edges, but the insides was all raw dough!
Oh, that sounds rough on your tummy!
Sure was, Peri. Sure was.
Well, I says to myself, "Wouldn't a space inside solve the difficulty?"
Ah, so that's how—
THEN, an idea came to me!
...
A great idea. The best idea I ever had!
I took a lid off a tin container—not too big, you see—an' I cut into the middle of that donut!
Mm hm.

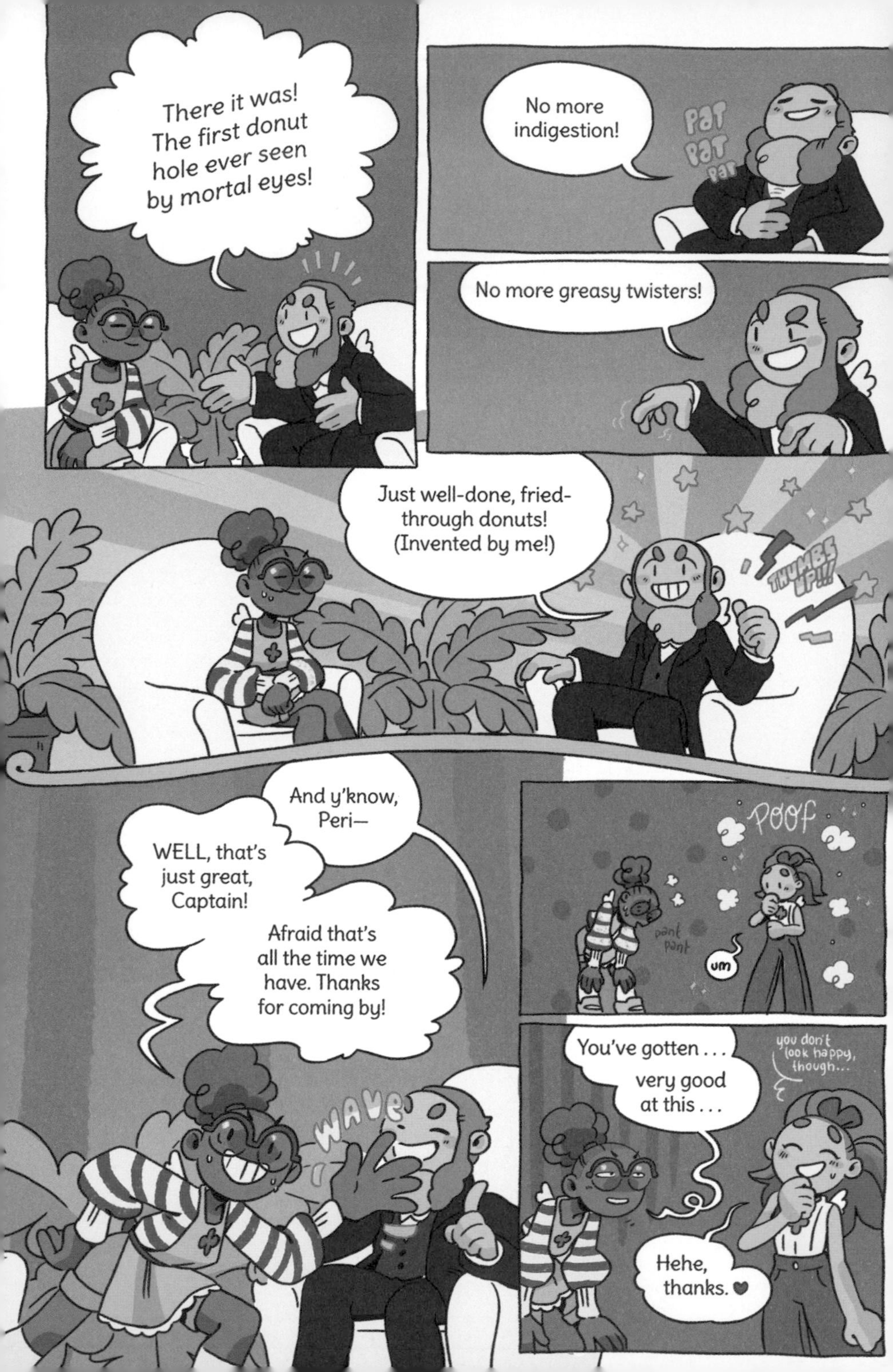
There it was! The first donut hole ever seen by mortal eyes!
No more indigestion!
PAT PAT PAT
No more greasy twisters!
Just well-done, fried-through donuts! (Invented by me!)
THUMBS UP!!!
And y'know, Peri—
WELL, that's just great, Captain!
Afraid that's all the time we have. Thanks for coming by!
WAVE
POOF
pant pant
um
You've gotten . . .
very good at this . . .
you don't look happy, though...
Hehe, thanks.

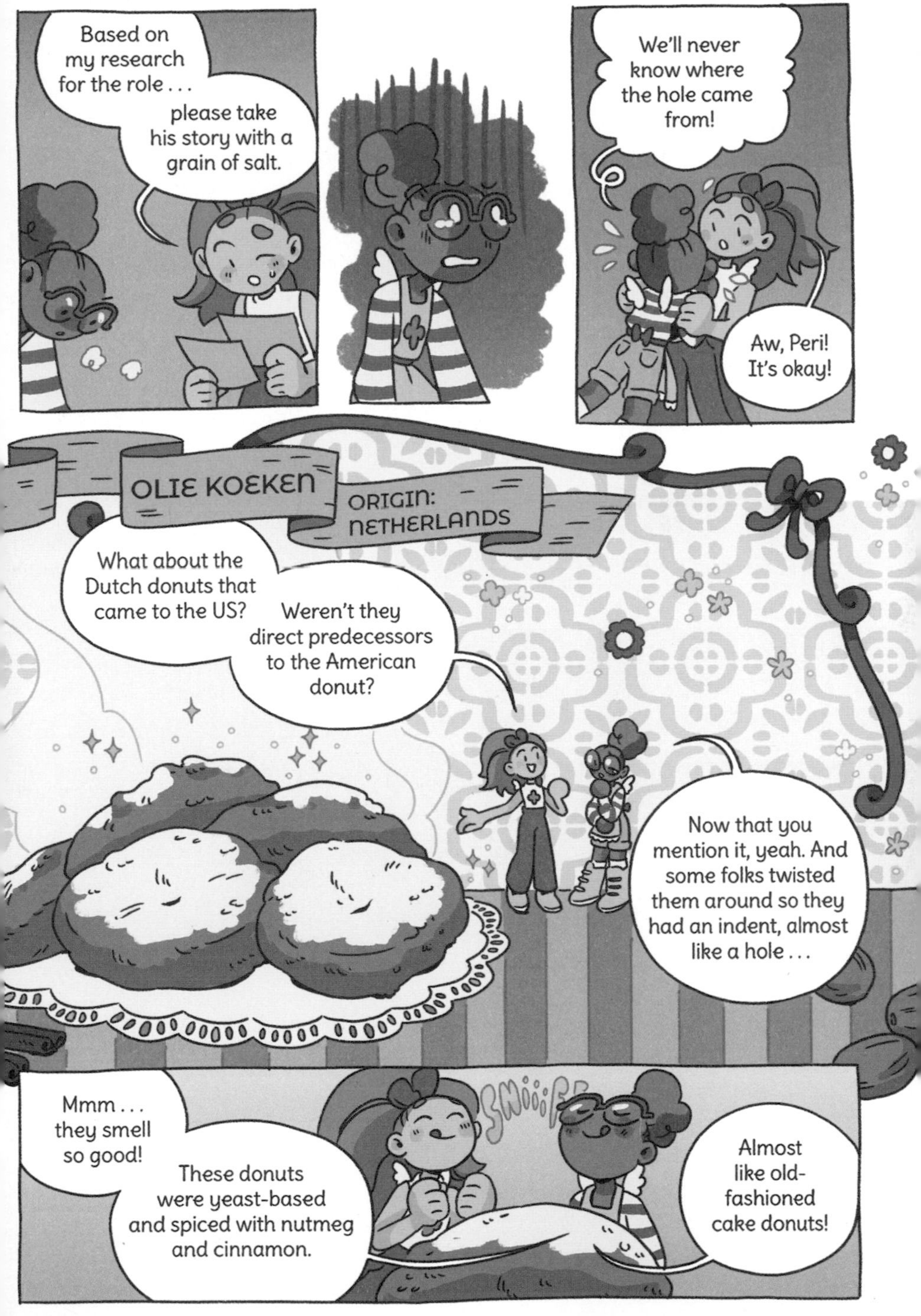
Based on my research for the role . . .
please take his story with a grain of salt.
We'll never know where the hole came from!
Aw, Peri! It's okay!
OLIE KOEKEN
ORIGIN: NETHERLANDS
What about the Dutch donuts that came to the US?
Weren't they direct predecessors to the American donut?
Now that you mention it, yeah. And some folks twisted them around so they had an indent, almost like a hole . . .
Mmm . . . they smell so good!
These donuts were yeast-based and spiced with nutmeg and cinnamon.
Almost like old-fashioned cake donuts!

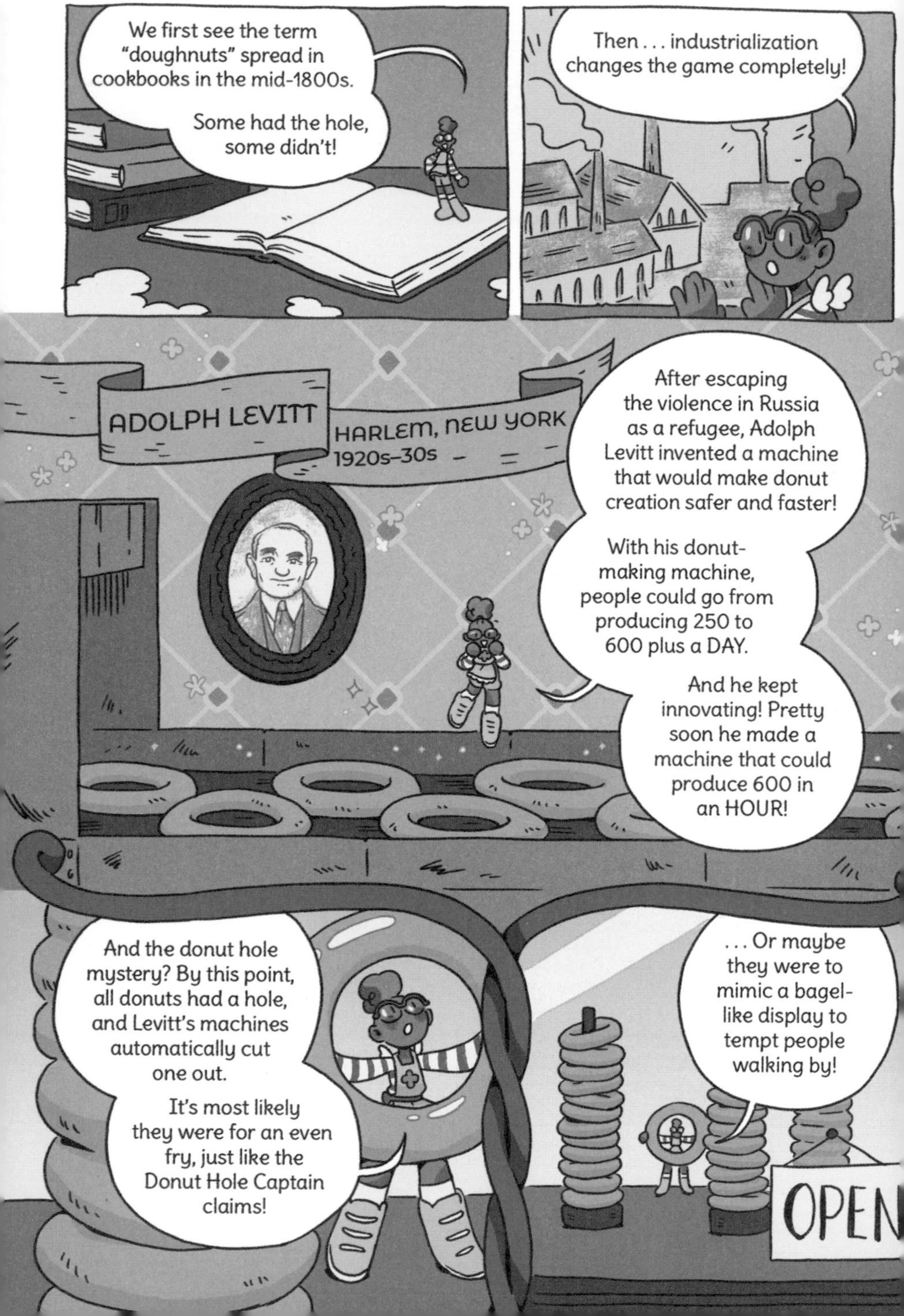

We first see the term "doughnuts" spread in cookbooks in the mid-1800s.
Some had the hole, some didn't!
Then . . . industrialization changes the game completely!
ADOLPH LEVITT
HARLEM, NEW YORK 1920s–30s
After escaping the violence in Russia as a refugee, Adolph Levitt invented a machine that would make donut creation safer and faster!
With his donut-making machine, people could go from producing 250 to 600 plus a DAY.
And he kept innovating! Pretty soon he made a machine that could produce 600 in an HOUR!
And the donut hole mystery? By this point, all donuts had a hole, and Levitt's machines automatically cut one out.
It's most likely they were for an even fry, just like the Donut Hole Captain claims!
. . . Or maybe they were to mimic a bagel-like display to tempt people walking by!
OPEN

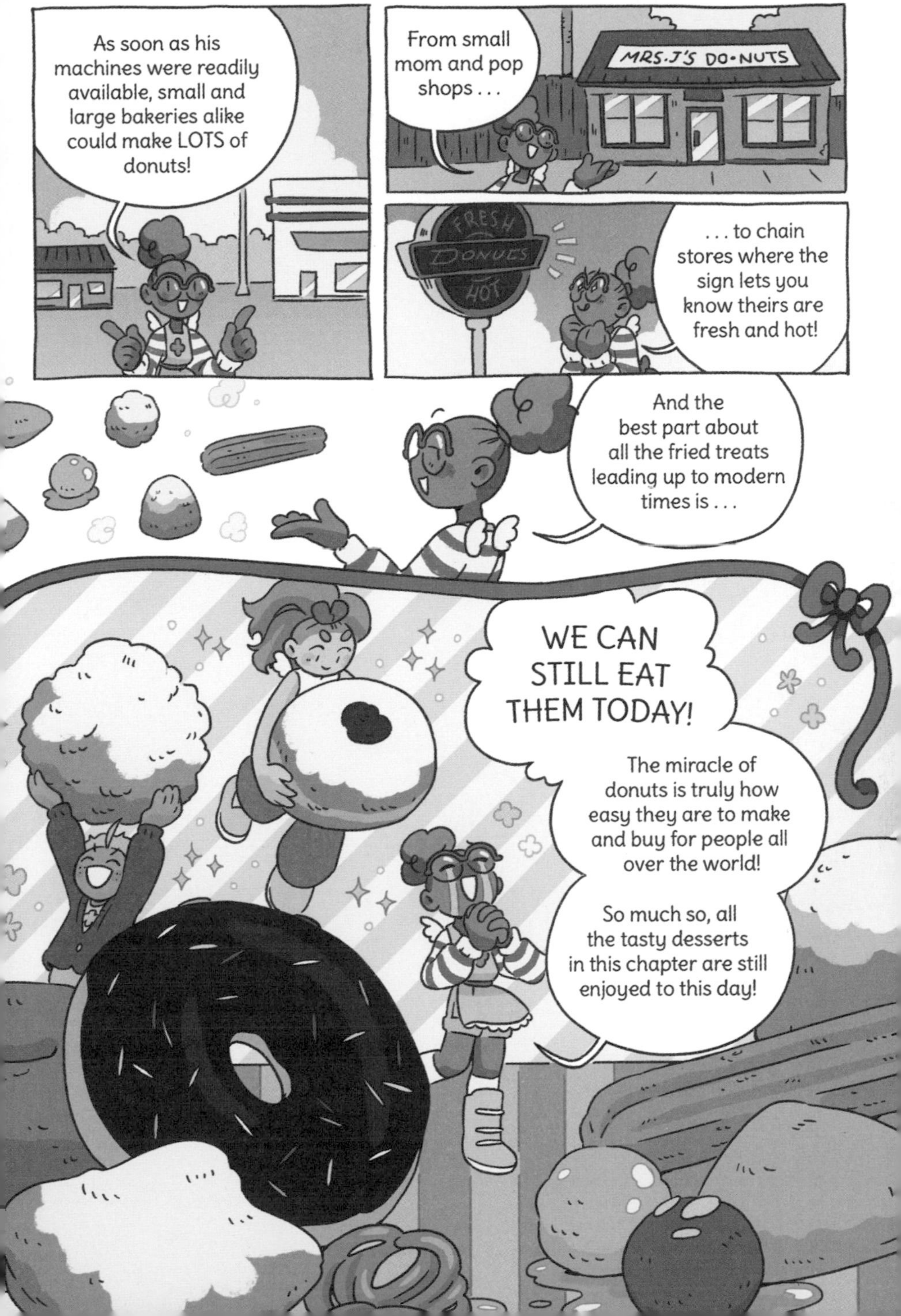
As soon as his machines were readily available, small and large bakeries alike could make LOTS of donuts!
From small mom and pop shops . . .
MRS. J'S DO•NUTS
FRESH DONUTS HOT
. . . to chain stores where the sign lets you know theirs are fresh and hot!
And the best part about all the fried treats leading up to modern times is . . .
WE CAN STILL EAT THEM TODAY!
The miracle of donuts is truly how easy they are to make and buy for people all over the world!
So much so, all the tasty desserts in this chapter are still enjoyed to this day!

# The Abridged

## Atlas of Pie History

1. Arabic Peninsula Pastry Dough
2. Greek Phyllo Dough
3. European Coffyns
4. Tartys in Applys and *Forme of Cury*
5. Dutch Appeltaarten
6. German Apfeltorte and Apfelstrudel
7. French Tarte Tatin
8. American Blackberry and Blueberry Pie
9. Hannah Glasse's *The Art of Cookery Made Plain and Easy*
10. Areas of Pumpkin and Sweet Potato Pie Traditions
11. Portuguese Pastel de Nata
12. Chinese Egg Tart
13. South African Melktert
14. American Buttermilk Pie
15. American Pecan Pie
16. Filipino Buko Pie
17. American Key Lime Pie
18. Areas of Empanada Traditions

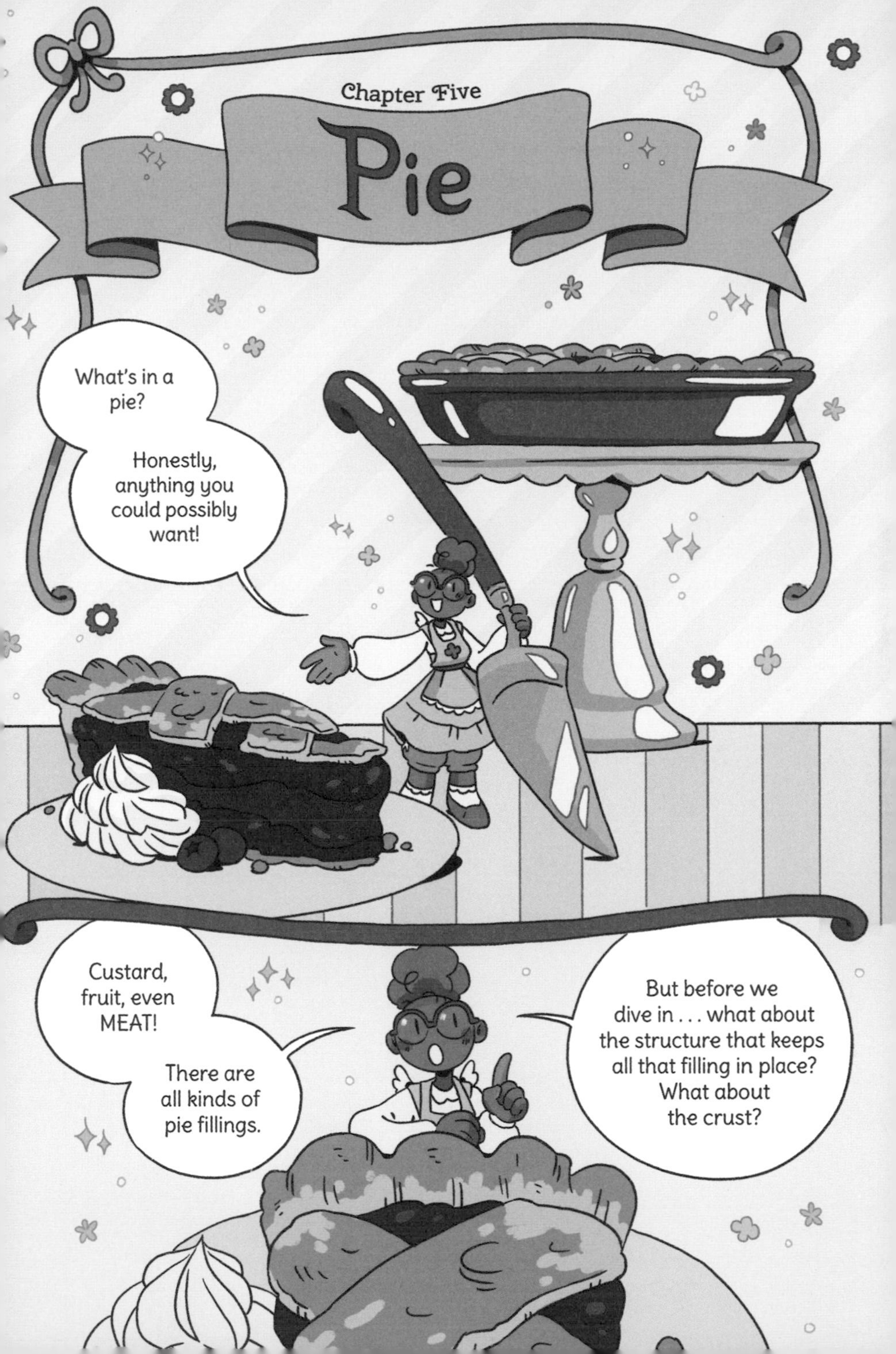
Chapter Five
Pie
What's in a pie?
Honestly, anything you could possibly want!
Custard, fruit, even MEAT!
There are all kinds of pie fillings.
But before we dive in . . . what about the structure that keeps all that filling in place? What about the crust?

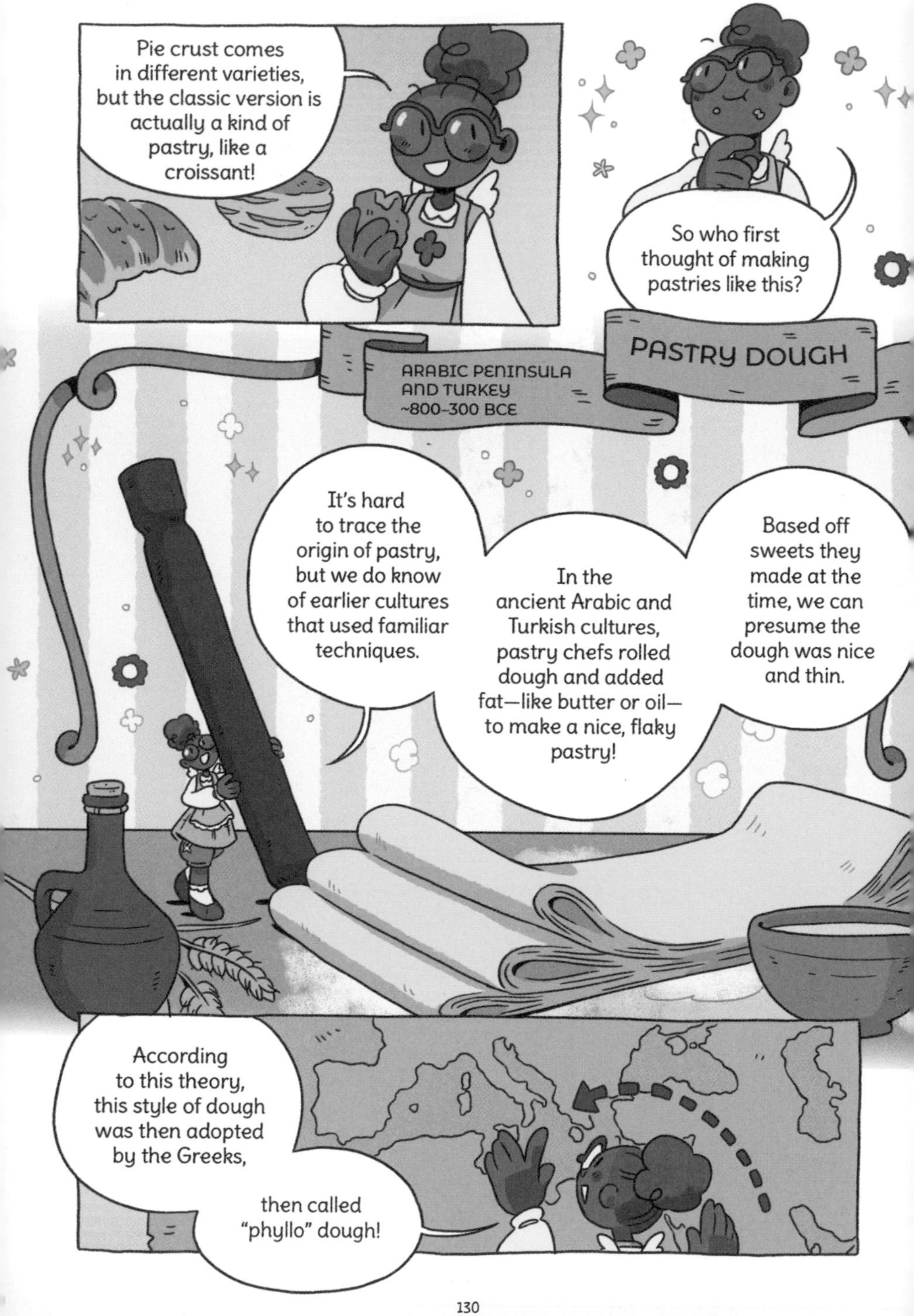

Pie crust comes in different varieties, but the classic version is actually a kind of pastry, like a croissant!
So who first thought of making pastries like this?
PASTRY DOUGH
ARABIC PENINSULA AND TURKEY ~800–300 BCE
It's hard to trace the origin of pastry, but we do know of earlier cultures that used familiar techniques.
In the ancient Arabic and Turkish cultures, pastry chefs rolled dough and added fat—like butter or oil—to make a nice, flaky pastry!
Based off sweets they made at the time, we can presume the dough was nice and thin.
According to this theory, this style of dough was then adopted by the Greeks,
then called "phyllo" dough!

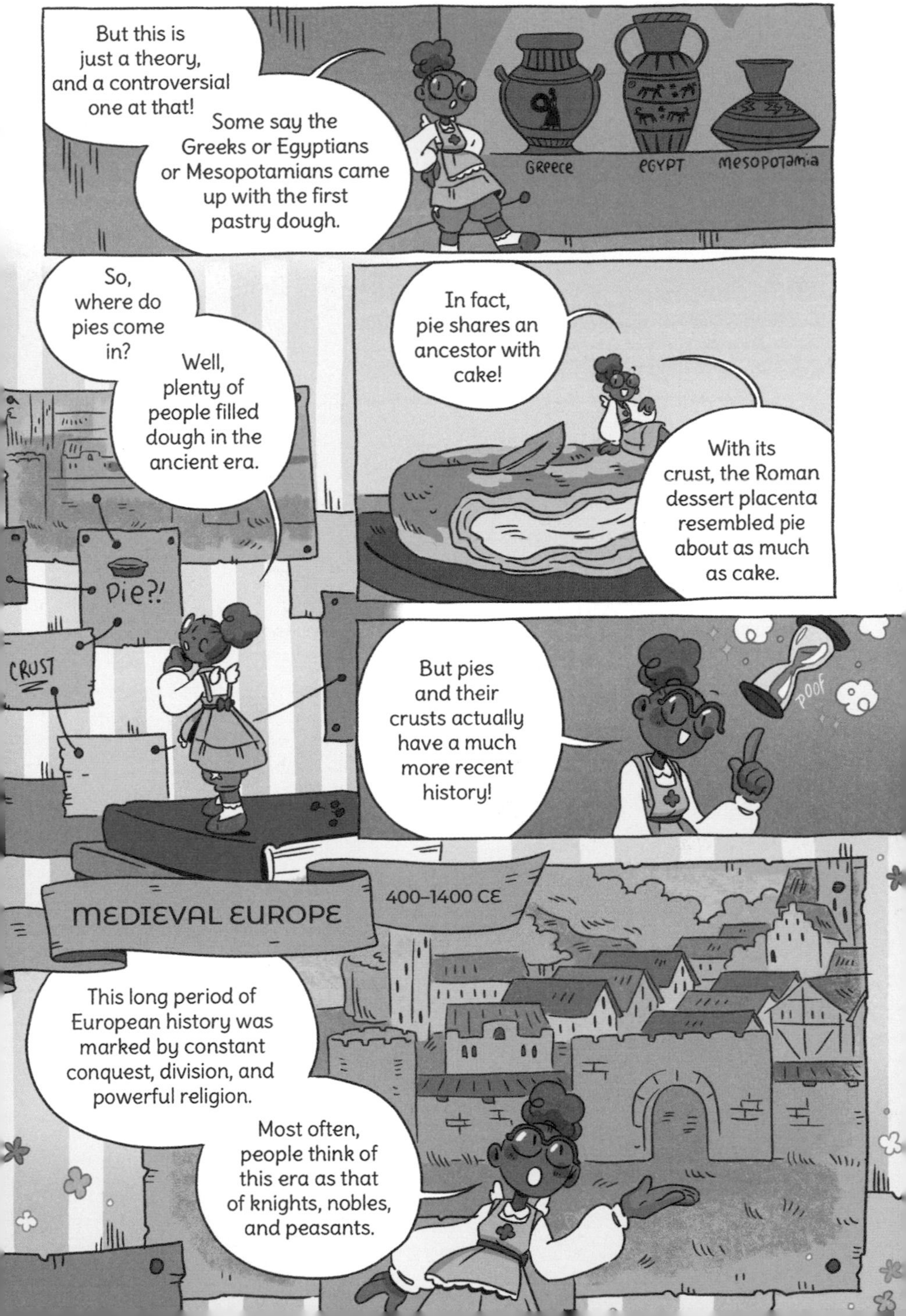
But this is just a theory, and a controversial one at that!
Some say the Greeks or Egyptians or Mesopotamians came up with the first pastry dough.
GREECE
EGYPT
MESOPOTAMIA
So, where do pies come in?
Well, plenty of people filled dough in the ancient era.
PIE?!
CRUST
In fact, pie shares an ancestor with cake!
With its crust, the Roman dessert placenta resembled pie about as much as cake.
But pies and their crusts actually have a much more recent history!
POOF
MEDIEVAL EUROPE
400–1400 CE
This long period of European history was marked by constant conquest, division, and powerful religion.
Most often, people think of this era as that of knights, nobles, and peasants.

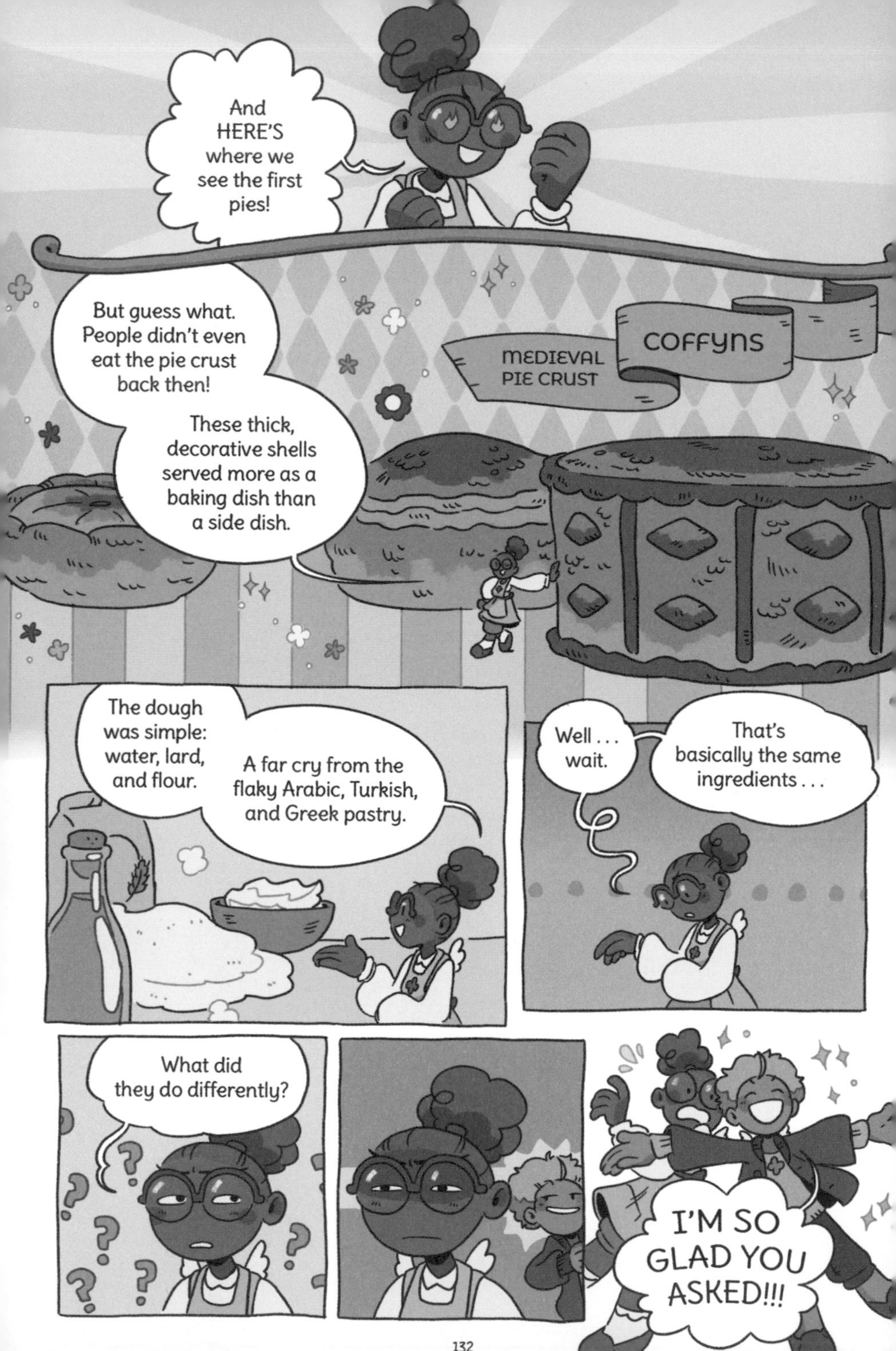
And HERE'S where we see the first pies!
But guess what. People didn't even eat the pie crust back then!
These thick, decorative shells served more as a baking dish than a side dish.
MEDIEVAL PIE CRUST
COFFYNS
The dough was simple: water, lard, and flour.
A far cry from the flaky Arabic, Turkish, and Greek pastry.
Well . . . wait.
That's basically the same ingredients . . .
What did they do differently?
I'M SO GLAD YOU ASKED!!!

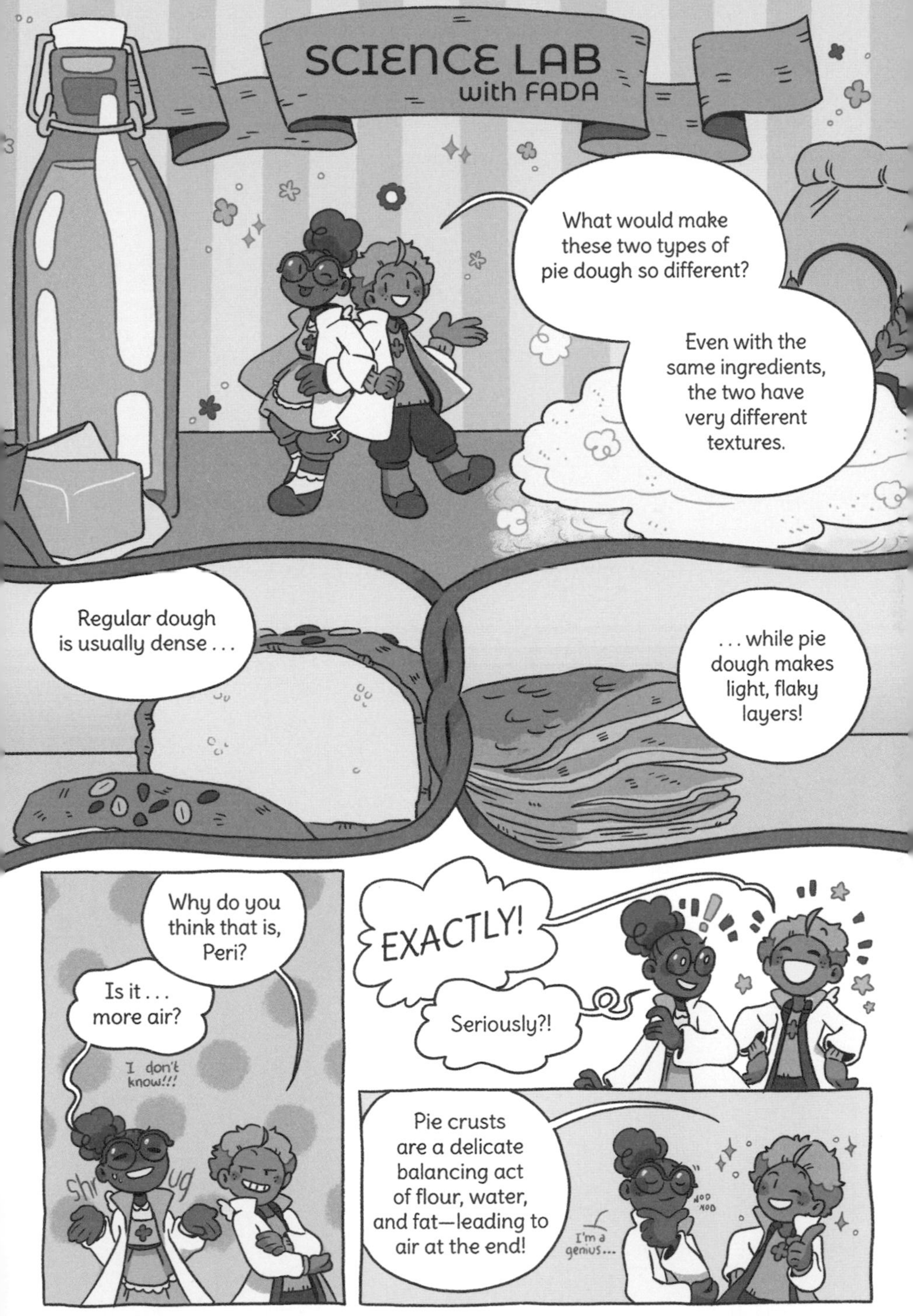
SCIENCE LAB
with FADA
What would make these two types of pie dough so different?
Even with the same ingredients, the two have very different textures.
Regular dough is usually dense . . .
. . . while pie dough makes light, flaky layers!
Why do you think that is, Peri?
Is it . . . more air?
I don't know!!!
shrug
EXACTLY!
Seriously?!
Pie crusts are a delicate balancing act of flour, water, and fat—leading to air at the end!
NOD NOD
I'm a genius...

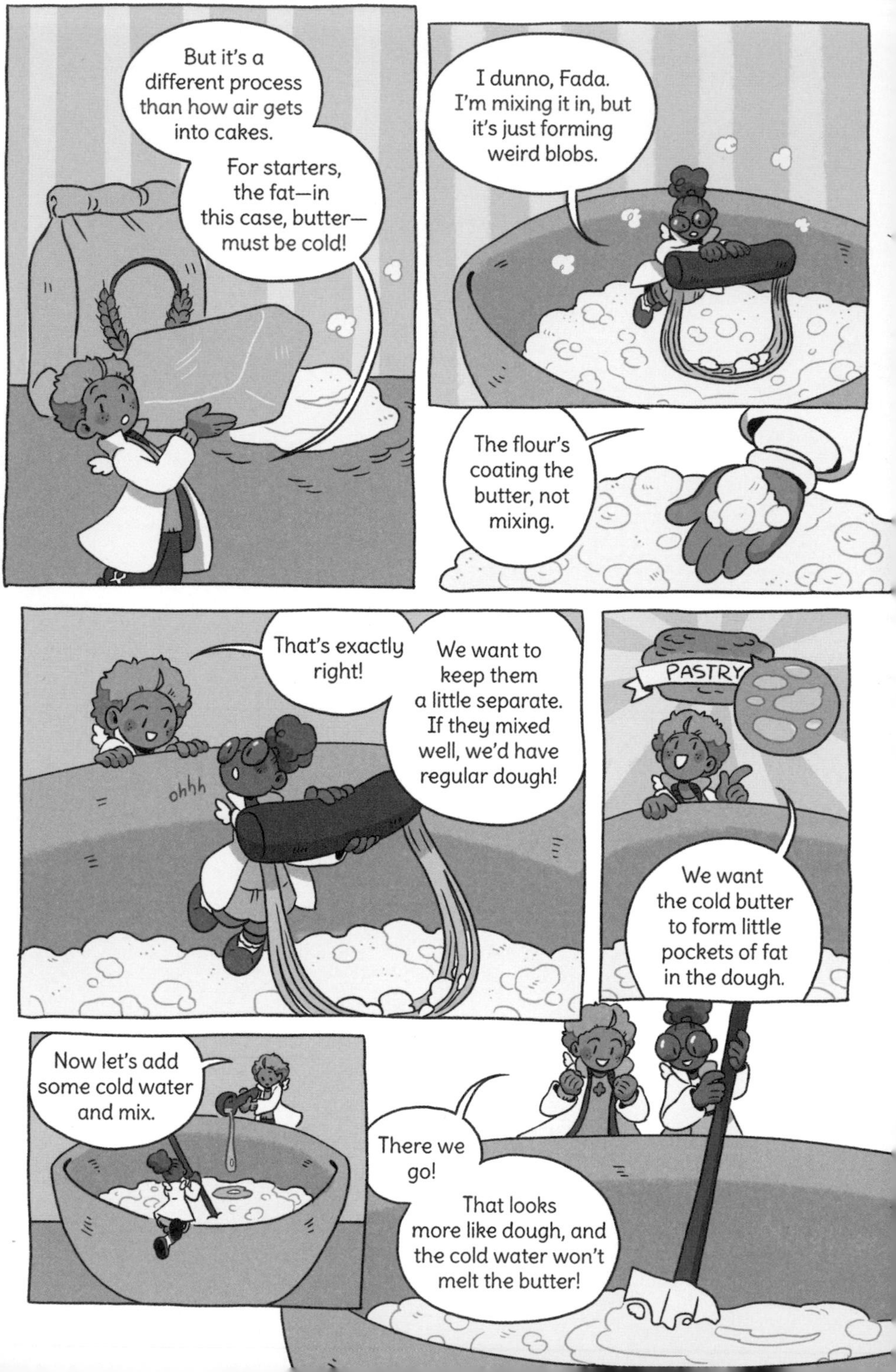
But it's a different process than how air gets into cakes.
For starters, the fat—in this case, butter—must be cold!
I dunno, Fada. I'm mixing it in, but it's just forming weird blobs.
The flour's coating the butter, not mixing.
That's exactly right!
We want to keep them a little separate. If they mixed well, we'd have regular dough!
ohhh
PASTRY
We want the cold butter to form little pockets of fat in the dough.
Now let's add some cold water and mix.
There we go!
That looks more like dough, and the cold water won't melt the butter!

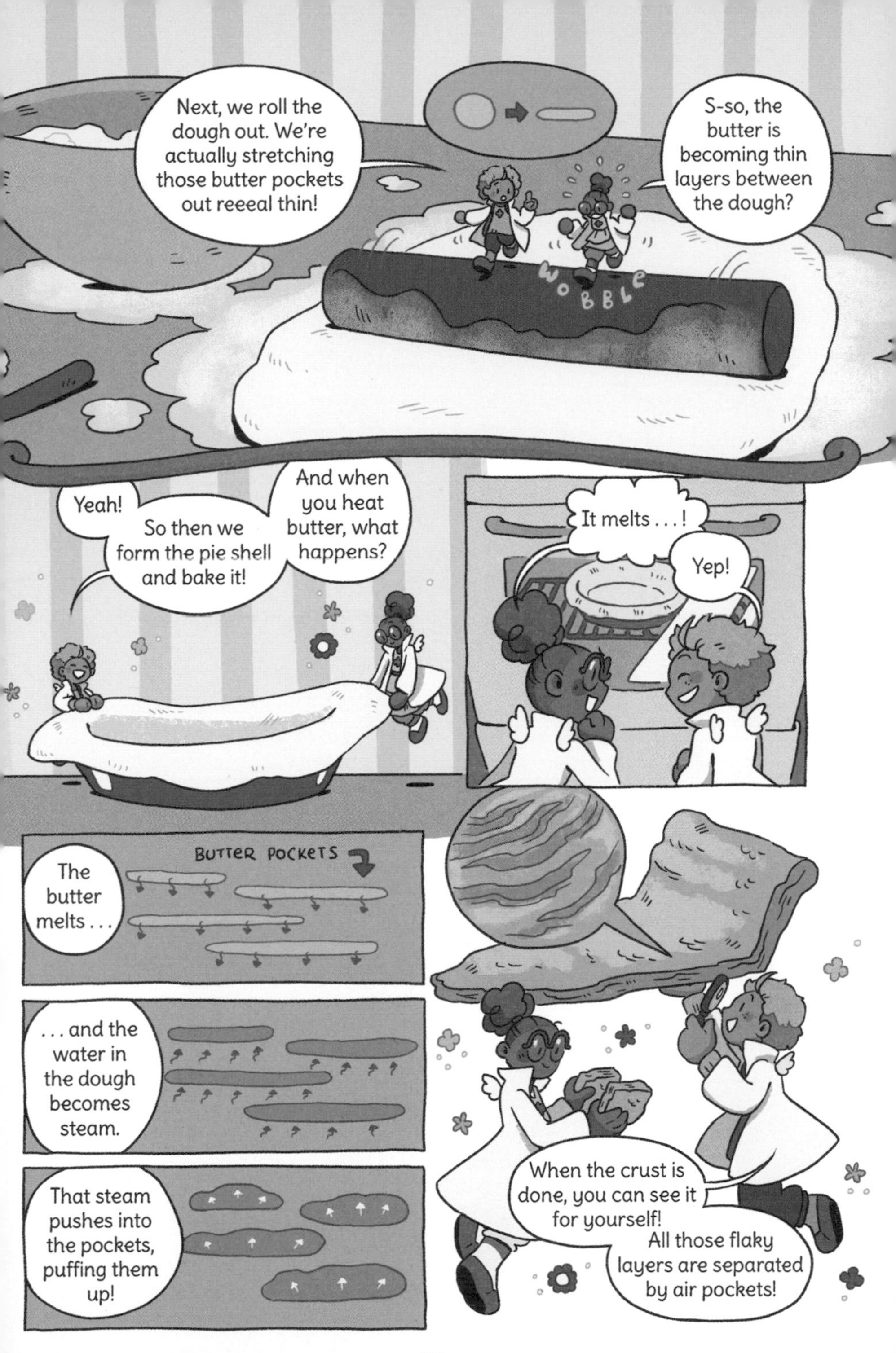
Next, we roll the dough out. We're actually stretching those butter pockets out reeeal thin!
S-so, the butter is becoming thin layers between the dough?
WOBBLE
Yeah!
So then we form the pie shell and bake it!
And when you heat butter, what happens?
It melts . . . !
Yep!
BUTTER POCKETS
The butter melts . . .
. . . and the water in the dough becomes steam.
That steam pushes into the pockets, puffing them up!
When the crust is done, you can see it for yourself!
All those flaky layers are separated by air pockets!

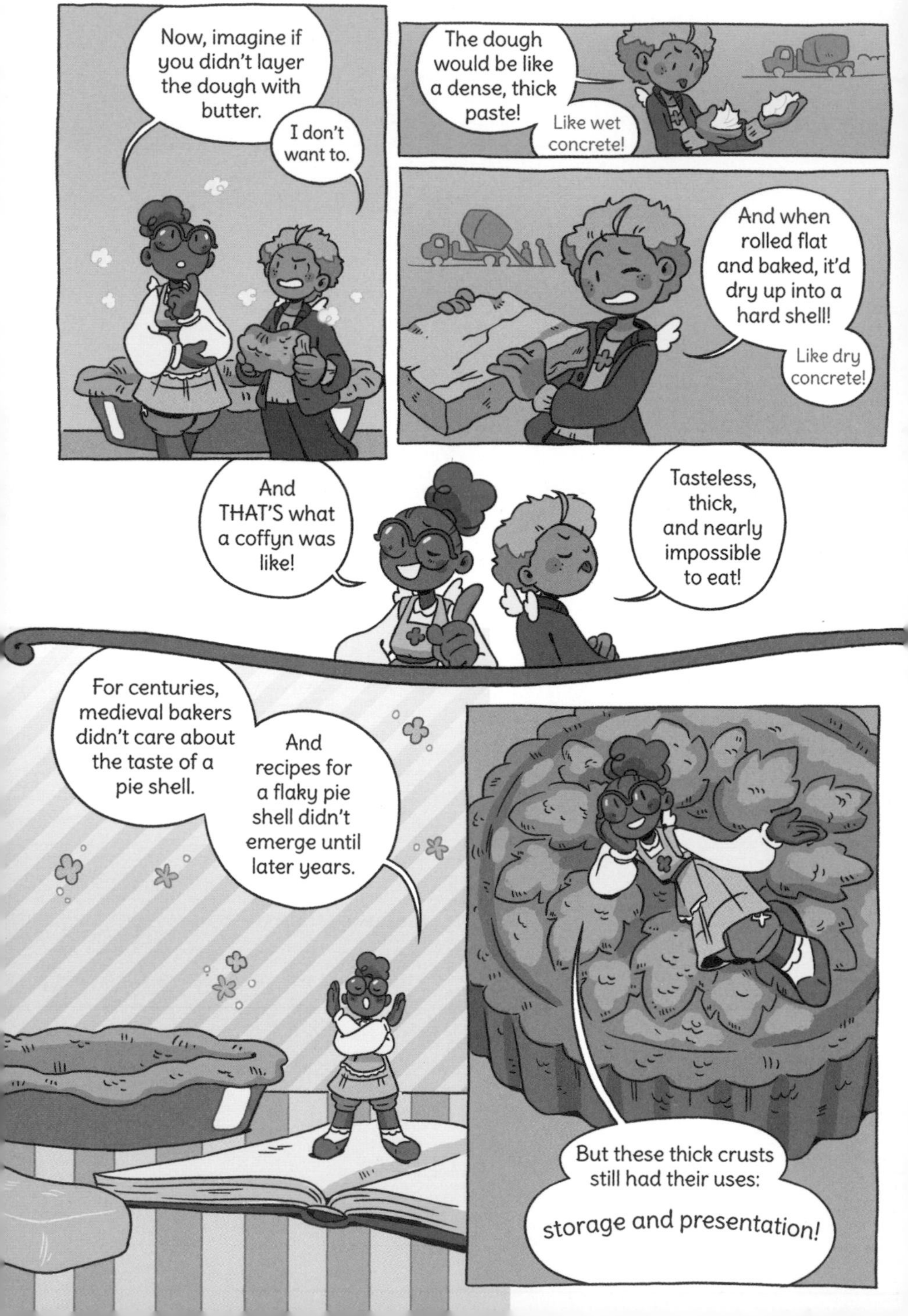

Now, imagine if you didn't layer the dough with butter.
I don't want to.
The dough would be like a dense, thick paste!
Like wet concrete!
And when rolled flat and baked, it'd dry up into a hard shell!
Like dry concrete!
And THAT'S what a coffyn was like!
Tasteless, thick, and nearly impossible to eat!
For centuries, medieval bakers didn't care about the taste of a pie shell.
And recipes for a flaky pie shell didn't emerge until later years.
But these thick crusts still had their uses:
storage and presentation!

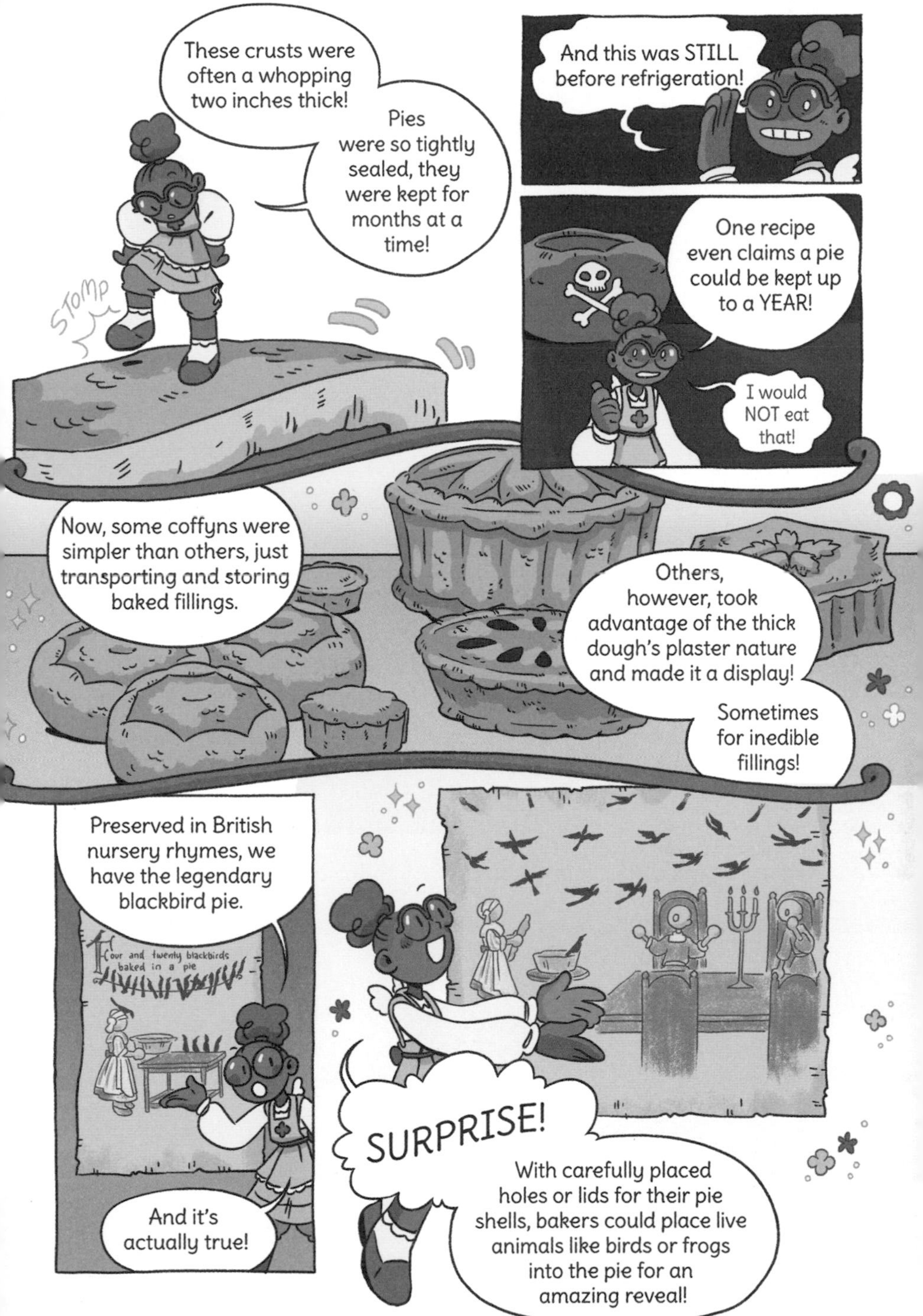
These crusts were often a whopping two inches thick!
Pies were so tightly sealed, they were kept for months at a time!
STOMP
And this was STILL before refrigeration!
One recipe even claims a pie could be kept up to a YEAR!
I would NOT eat that!
Now, some coffyns were simpler than others, just transporting and storing baked fillings.
Others, however, took advantage of the thick dough's plaster nature and made it a display!
Sometimes for inedible fillings!
Preserved in British nursery rhymes, we have the legendary blackbird pie.
Four and twenty blackbirds baked in a pie
And it's actually true!
SURPRISE!
With carefully placed holes or lids for their pie shells, bakers could place live animals like birds or frogs into the pie for an amazing reveal!

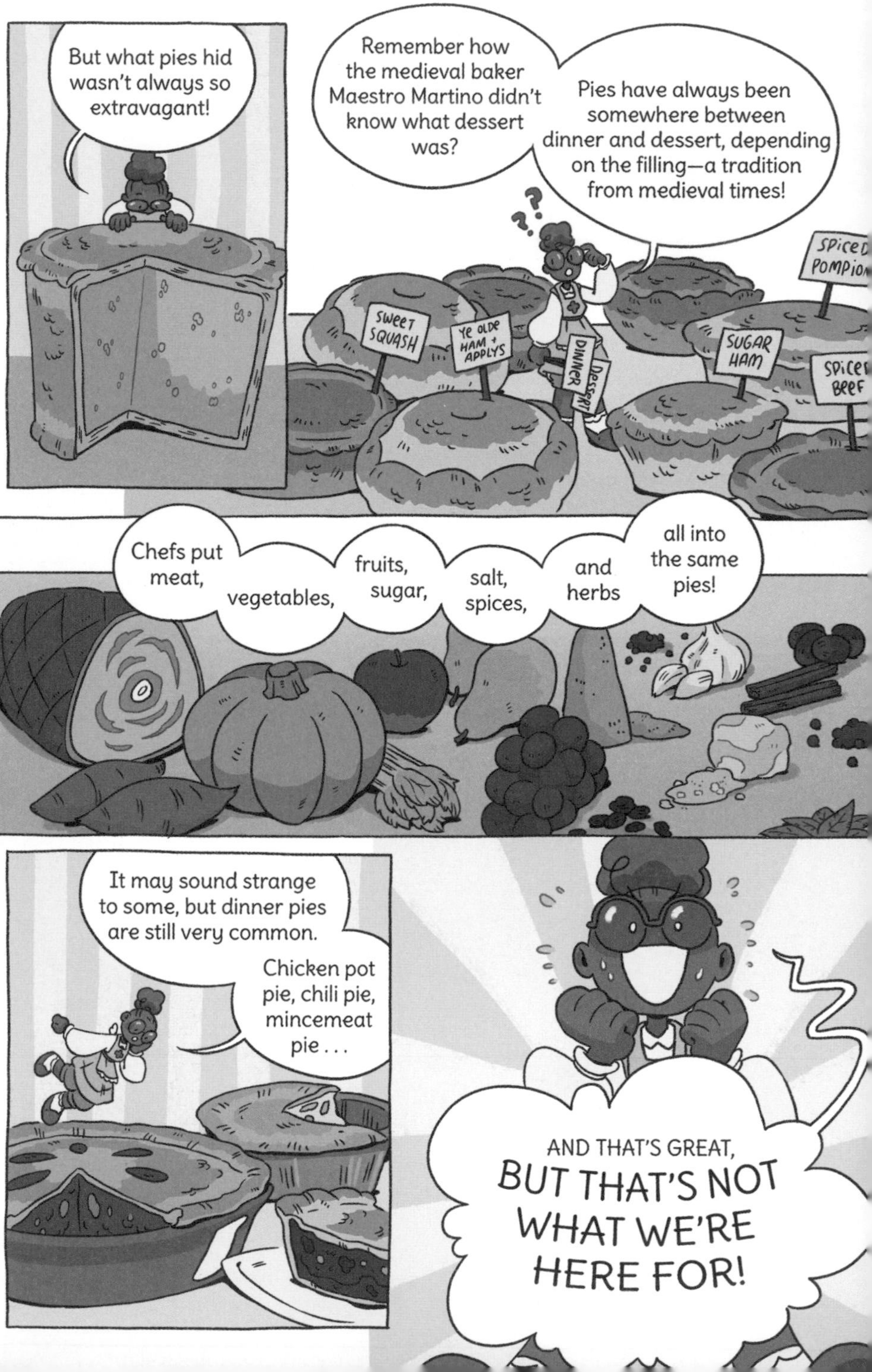
But what pies hid wasn't always so extravagant!
Remember how the medieval baker Maestro Martino didn't know what dessert was?
Pies have always been somewhere between dinner and dessert, depending on the filling—a tradition from medieval times!
SWEET SQUASH
YE OLDE HAM + APPLYS
DINNER
DESSERT
SPICED POMPION
SUGAR HAM
SPICED BEEF
Chefs put meat,
vegetables,
fruits, sugar,
salt, spices,
and herbs
all into the same pies!
It may sound strange to some, but dinner pies are still very common.
Chicken pot pie, chili pie, mincemeat pie . . .
AND THAT'S GREAT, BUT THAT'S NOT WHAT WE'RE HERE FOR!

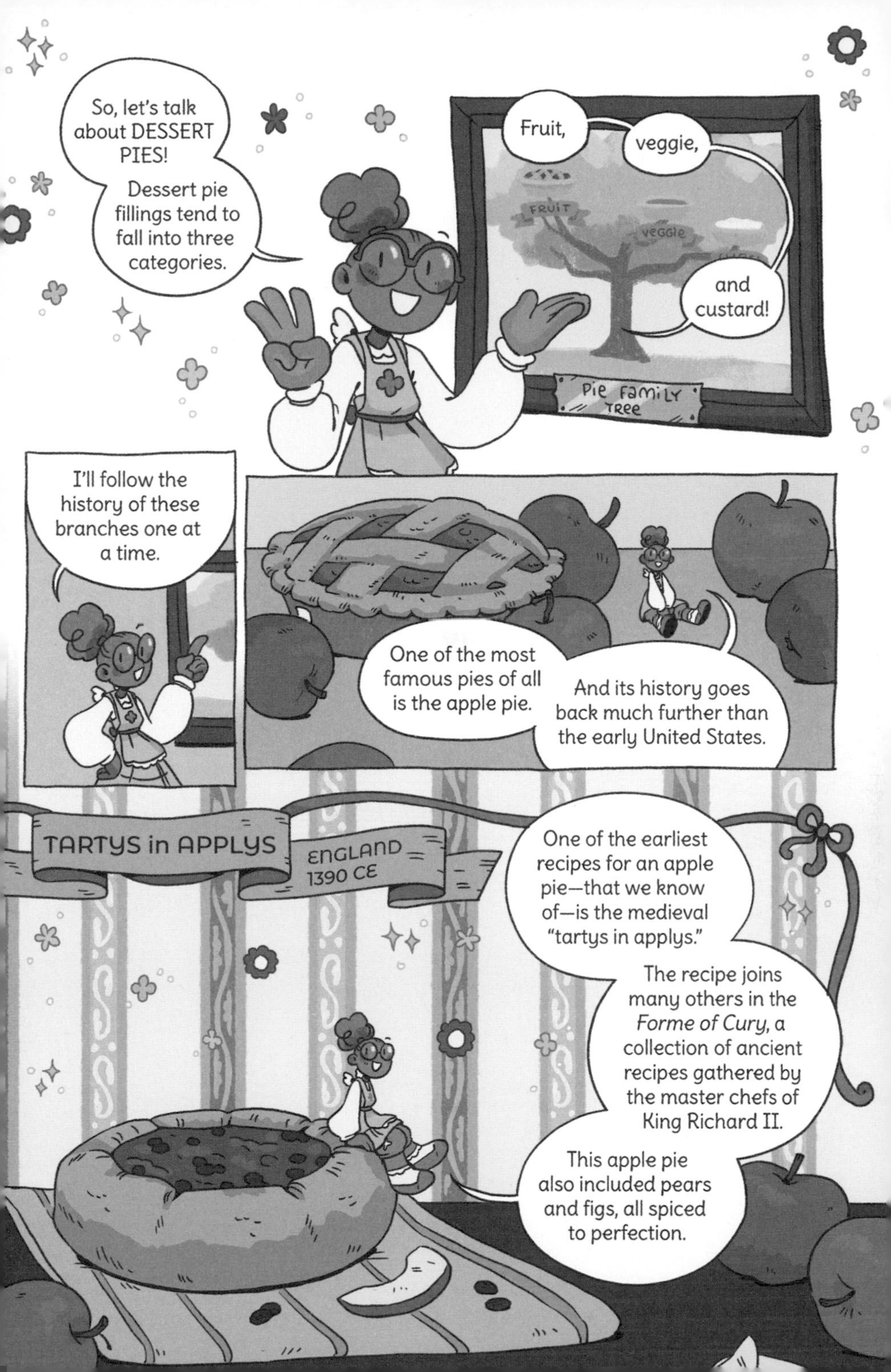
So, let's talk about DESSERT PIES!
Dessert pie fillings tend to fall into three categories.
Fruit,
veggie,
and custard!
FRUIT
VEGGIE
PIE FAMILY TREE
I'll follow the history of these branches one at a time.
One of the most famous pies of all is the apple pie.
And its history goes back much further than the early United States.
TARTYS in APPLYS
ENGLAND 1390 CE
One of the earliest recipes for an apple pie—that we know of—is the medieval "tartys in applys."
The recipe joins many others in the *Forme of Cury*, a collection of ancient recipes gathered by the master chefs of King Richard II.
This apple pie also included pears and figs, all spiced to perfection.

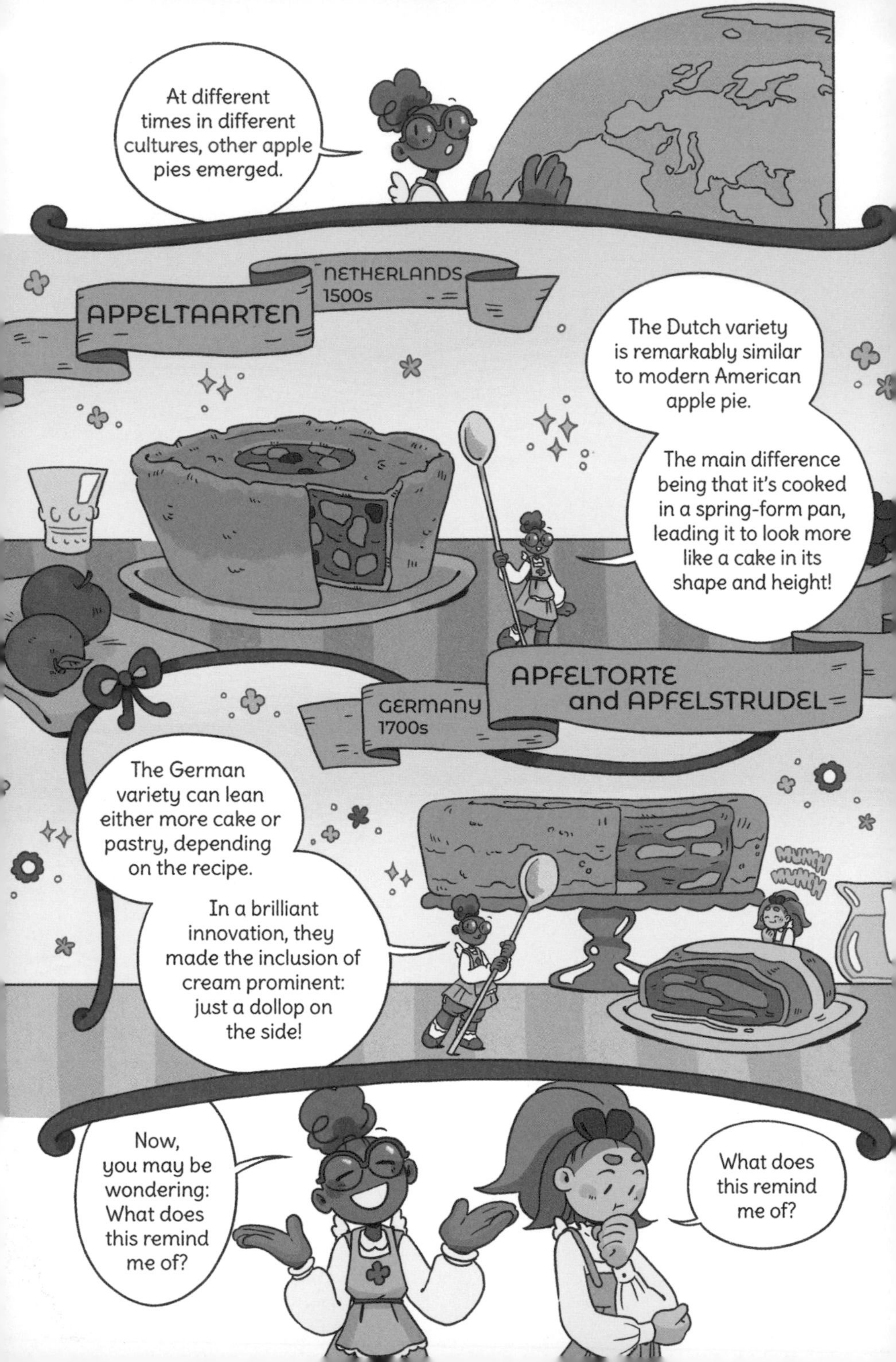

At different times in different cultures, other apple pies emerged.
NETHERLANDS 1500s
APPELTAARTEN
The Dutch variety is remarkably similar to modern American apple pie.
The main difference being that it's cooked in a spring-form pan, leading it to look more like a cake in its shape and height!
GERMANY 1700s
APFELTORTE and APFELSTRUDEL
The German variety can lean either more cake or pastry, depending on the recipe.
In a brilliant innovation, they made the inclusion of cream prominent: just a dollop on the side!
MUNCH MUNCH
Now, you may be wondering: What does this remind me of?
What does this remind me of?

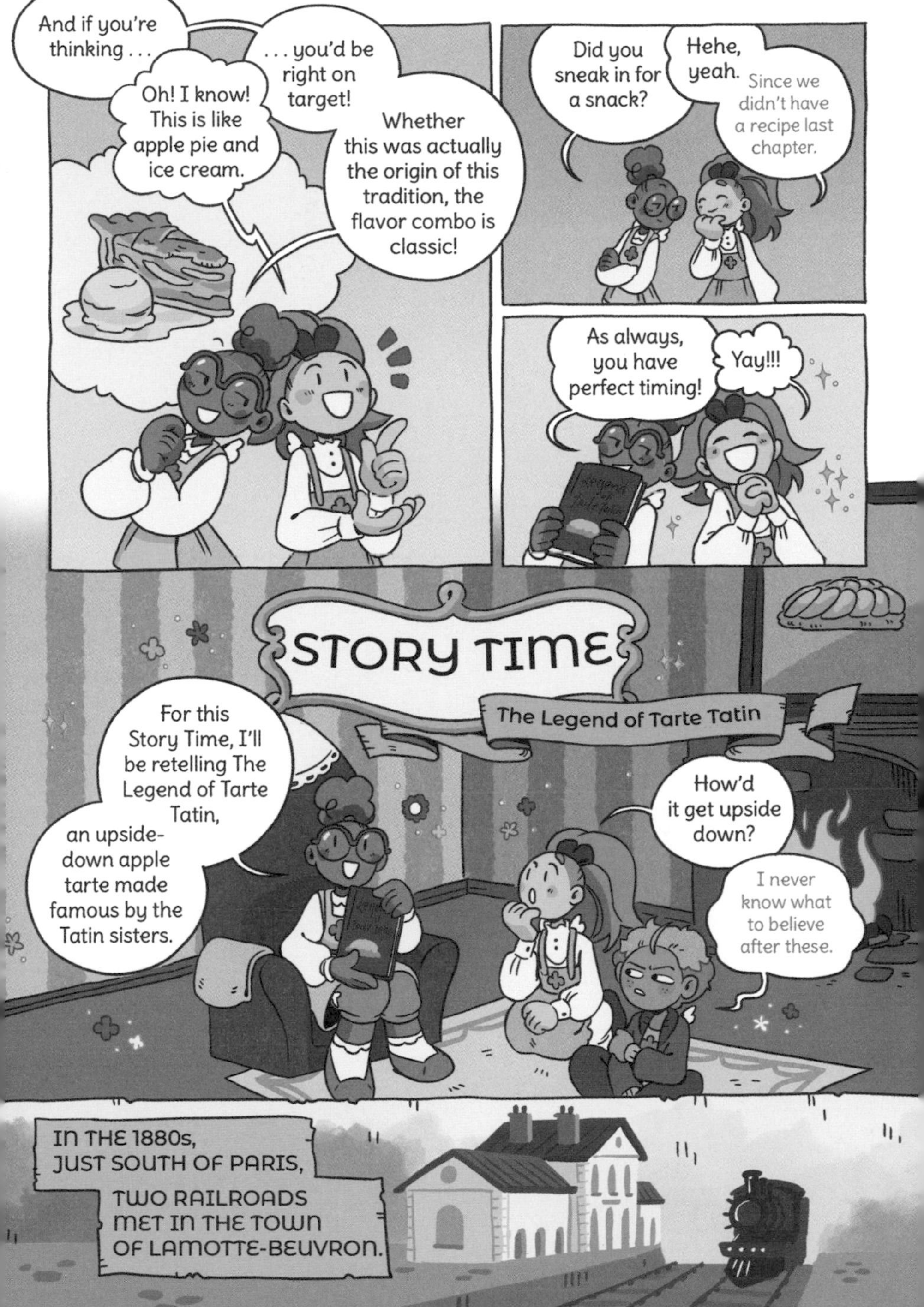

And if you're thinking . . .
Oh! I know! This is like apple pie and ice cream.
. . . you'd be right on target!
Whether this was actually the origin of this tradition, the flavor combo is classic!
Did you sneak in for a snack?
Hehe, yeah.
Since we didn't have a recipe last chapter.
As always, you have perfect timing!
Yay!!!
STORY TIME
The Legend of Tarte Tatin
For this Story Time, I'll be retelling The Legend of Tarte Tatin,
an upside-down apple tarte made famous by the Tatin sisters.
How'd it get upside down?
I never know what to believe after these.
IN THE 1880s, JUST SOUTH OF PARIS,
TWO RAILROADS MET IN THE TOWN OF LAMOTTE-BEUVRON.

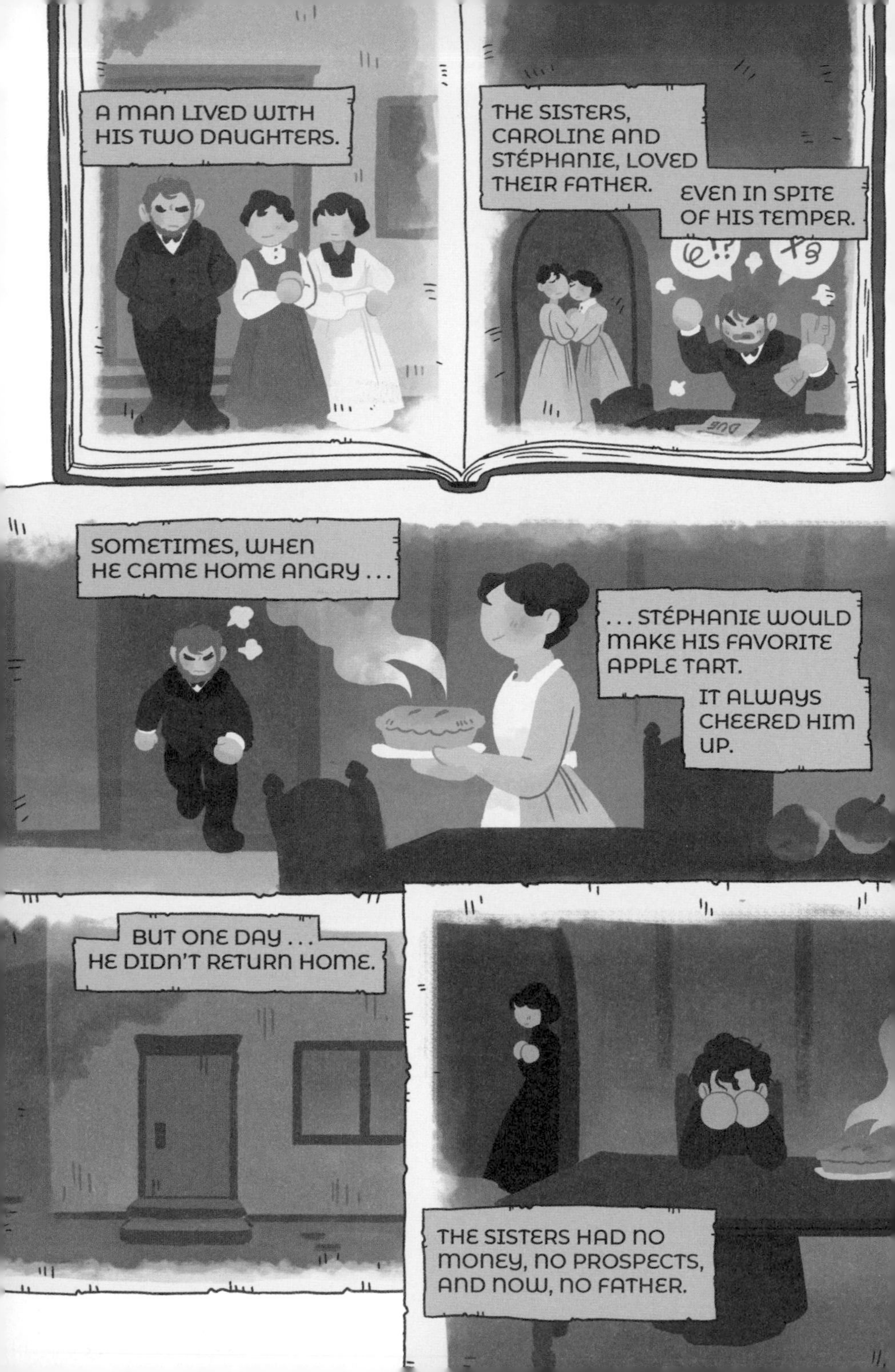
A MAN LIVED WITH HIS TWO DAUGHTERS.
THE SISTERS, CAROLINE AND STÉPHANIE, LOVED THEIR FATHER.
EVEN IN SPITE OF HIS TEMPER.
DUE
SOMETIMES, WHEN HE CAME HOME ANGRY . . .
. . . STÉPHANIE WOULD MAKE HIS FAVORITE APPLE TART.
IT ALWAYS CHEERED HIM UP.
BUT ONE DAY . . . HE DIDN'T RETURN HOME.
THE SISTERS HAD NO MONEY, NO PROSPECTS, AND NOW, NO FATHER.

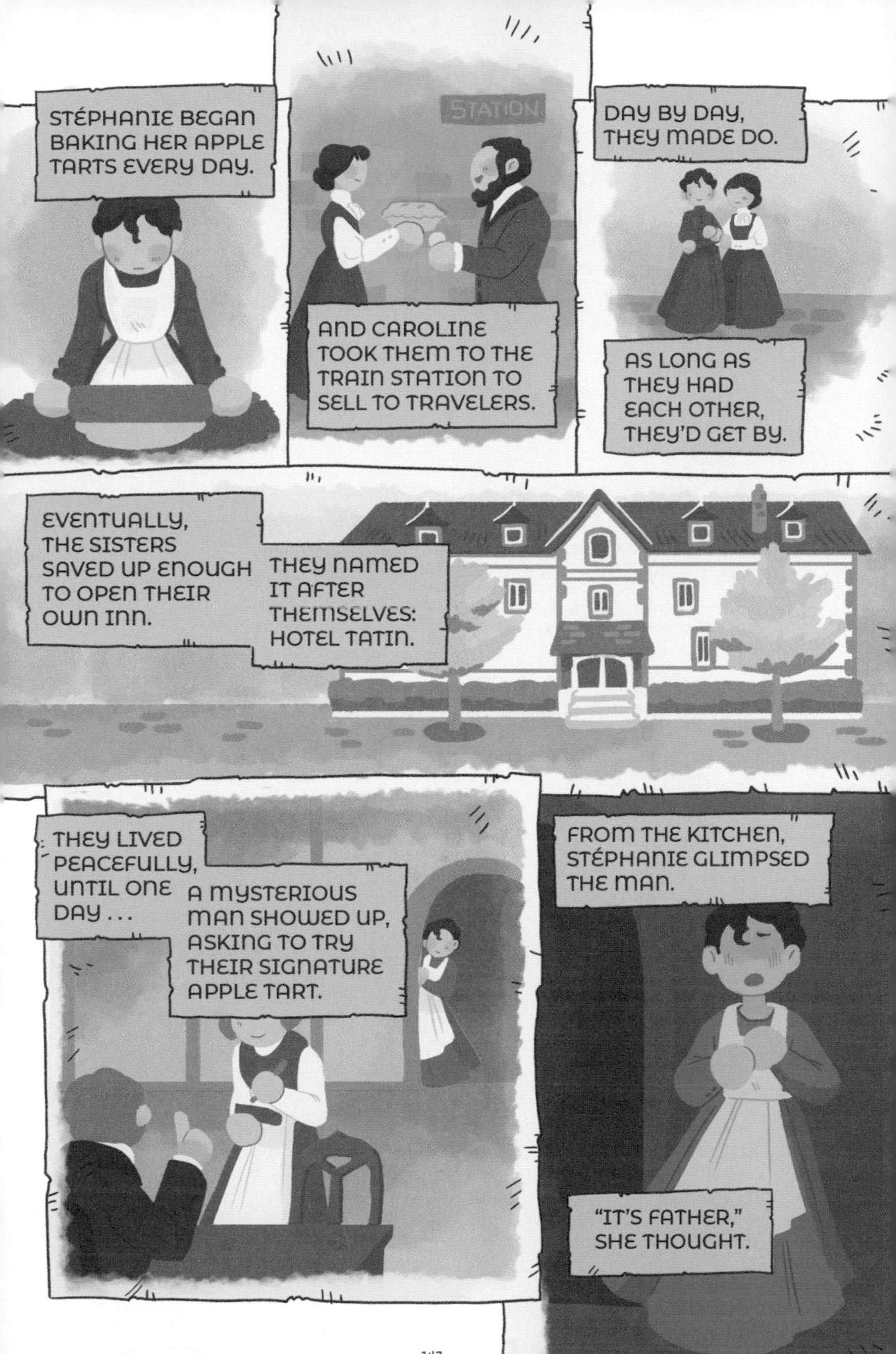
STÉPHANIE BEGAN BAKING HER APPLE TARTS EVERY DAY.
STATION
AND CAROLINE TOOK THEM TO THE TRAIN STATION TO SELL TO TRAVELERS.
DAY BY DAY, THEY MADE DO.
AS LONG AS THEY HAD EACH OTHER, THEY'D GET BY.
EVENTUALLY, THE SISTERS SAVED UP ENOUGH TO OPEN THEIR OWN INN.
THEY NAMED IT AFTER THEMSELVES: HOTEL TATIN.
THEY LIVED PEACEFULLY, UNTIL ONE DAY . . .
A MYSTERIOUS MAN SHOWED UP, ASKING TO TRY THEIR SIGNATURE APPLE TART.
FROM THE KITCHEN, STÉPHANIE GLIMPSED THE MAN.
"IT'S FATHER," SHE THOUGHT.

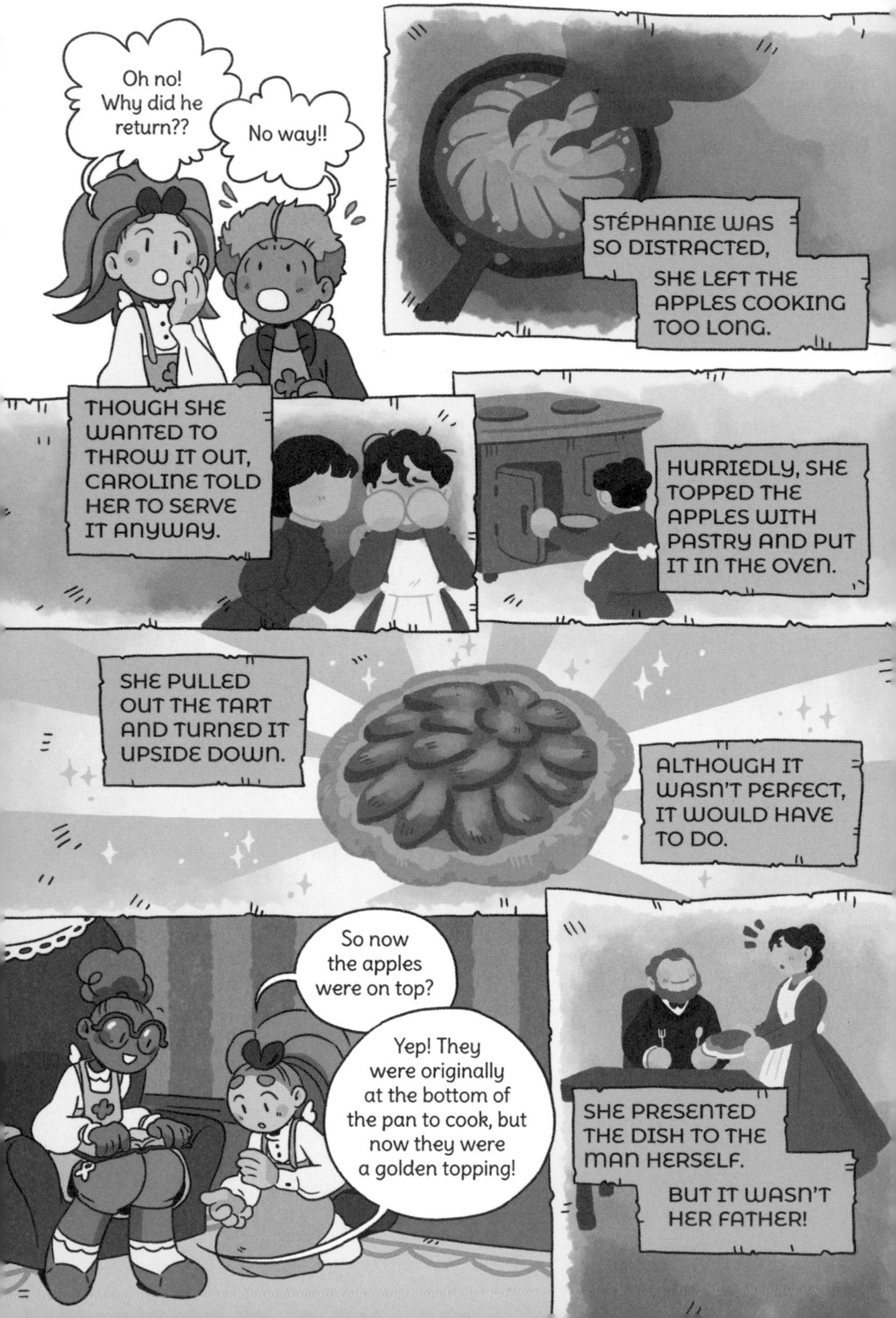
Oh no! Why did he return??
No way!!
STÉPHANIE WAS SO DISTRACTED,
SHE LEFT THE APPLES COOKING TOO LONG.
THOUGH SHE WANTED TO THROW IT OUT, CAROLINE TOLD HER TO SERVE IT ANYWAY.
HURRIEDLY, SHE TOPPED THE APPLES WITH PASTRY AND PUT IT IN THE OVEN.
SHE PULLED OUT THE TART AND TURNED IT UPSIDE DOWN.
ALTHOUGH IT WASN'T PERFECT, IT WOULD HAVE TO DO.
So now the apples were on top?
Yep! They were originally at the bottom of the pan to cook, but now they were a golden topping!
SHE PRESENTED THE DISH TO THE MAN HERSELF.
BUT IT WASN'T HER FATHER!

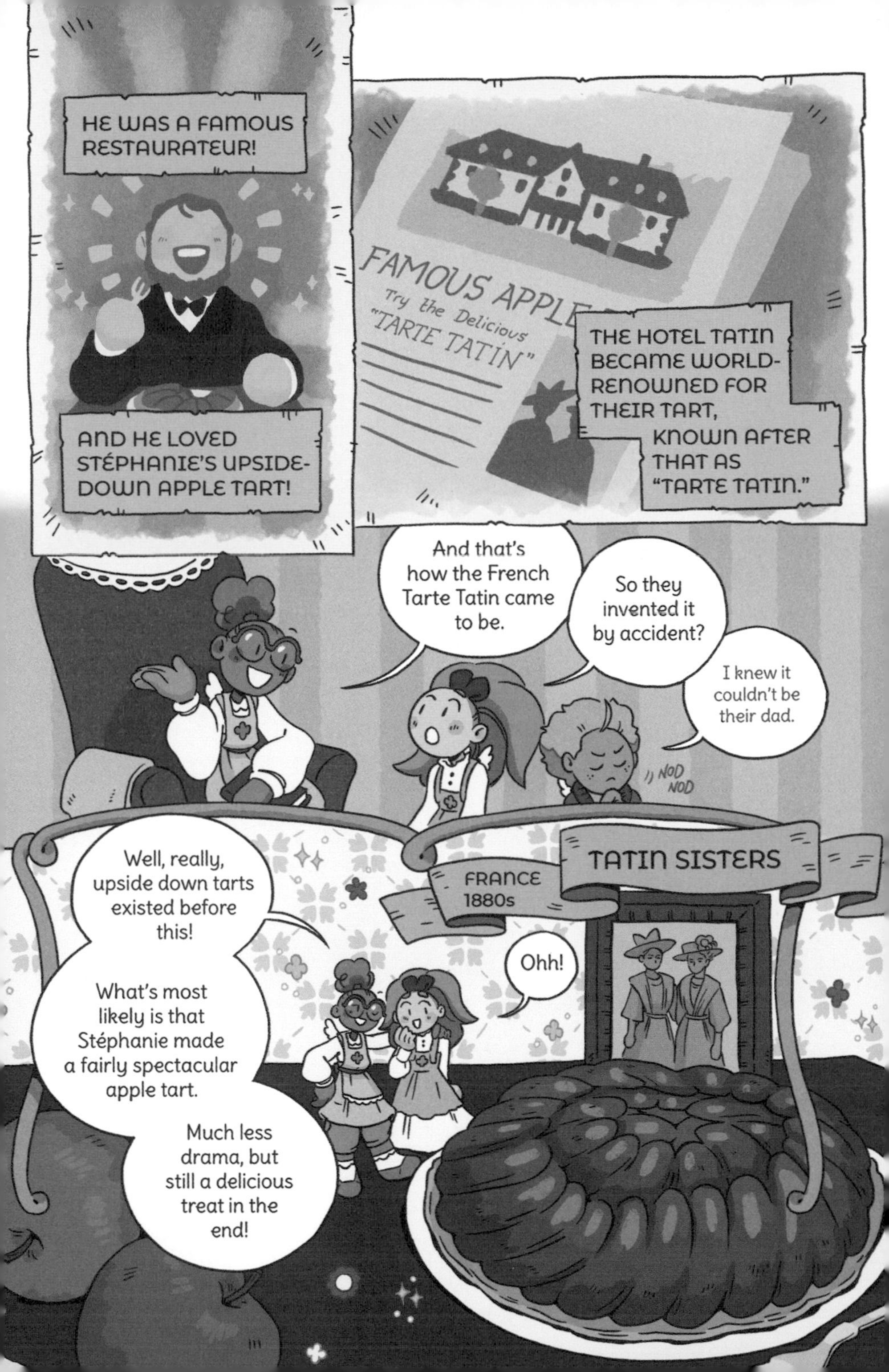

HE WAS A FAMOUS RESTAURATEUR!
AND HE LOVED STÉPHANIE'S UPSIDE-DOWN APPLE TART!
FAMOUS APPLE
Try the Delicious "TARTE TATIN"
THE HOTEL TATIN BECAME WORLD-RENOWNED FOR THEIR TART,
KNOWN AFTER THAT AS "TARTE TATIN."
And that's how the French Tarte Tatin came to be.
So they invented it by accident?
I knew it couldn't be their dad.
NOD NOD
TATIN SISTERS
FRANCE 1880s
Well, really, upside down tarts existed before this!
What's most likely is that Stéphanie made a fairly spectacular apple tart.
Much less drama, but still a delicious treat in the end!
Ohh!

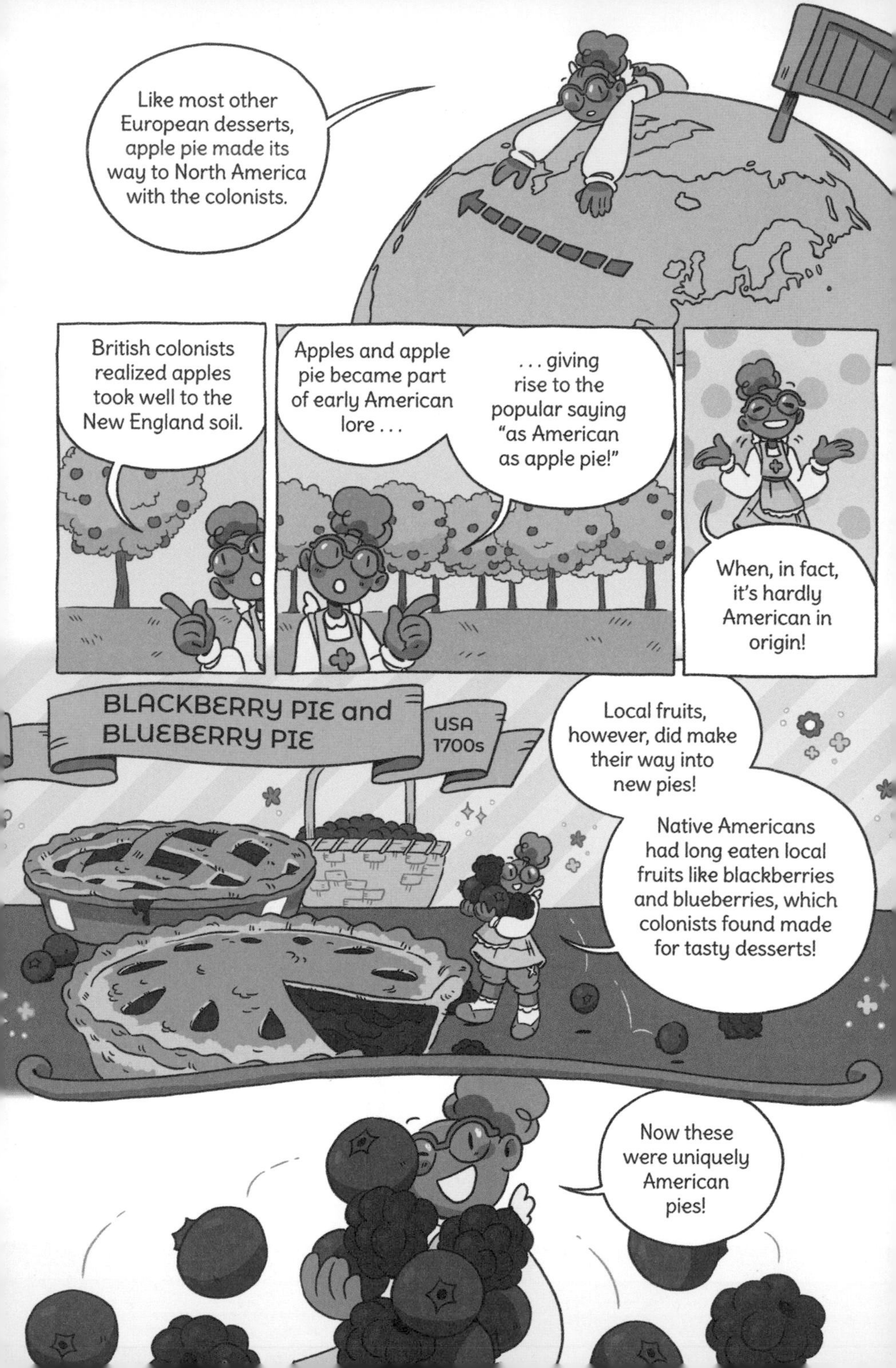
Like most other European desserts, apple pie made its way to North America with the colonists.
British colonists realized apples took well to the New England soil.
Apples and apple pie became part of early American lore . . .
. . . giving rise to the popular saying "as American as apple pie!"
When, in fact, it's hardly American in origin!
BLACKBERRY PIE and BLUEBERRY PIE
USA 1700s
Local fruits, however, did make their way into new pies!
Native Americans had long eaten local fruits like blackberries and blueberries, which colonists found made for tasty desserts!
Now these were uniquely American pies!

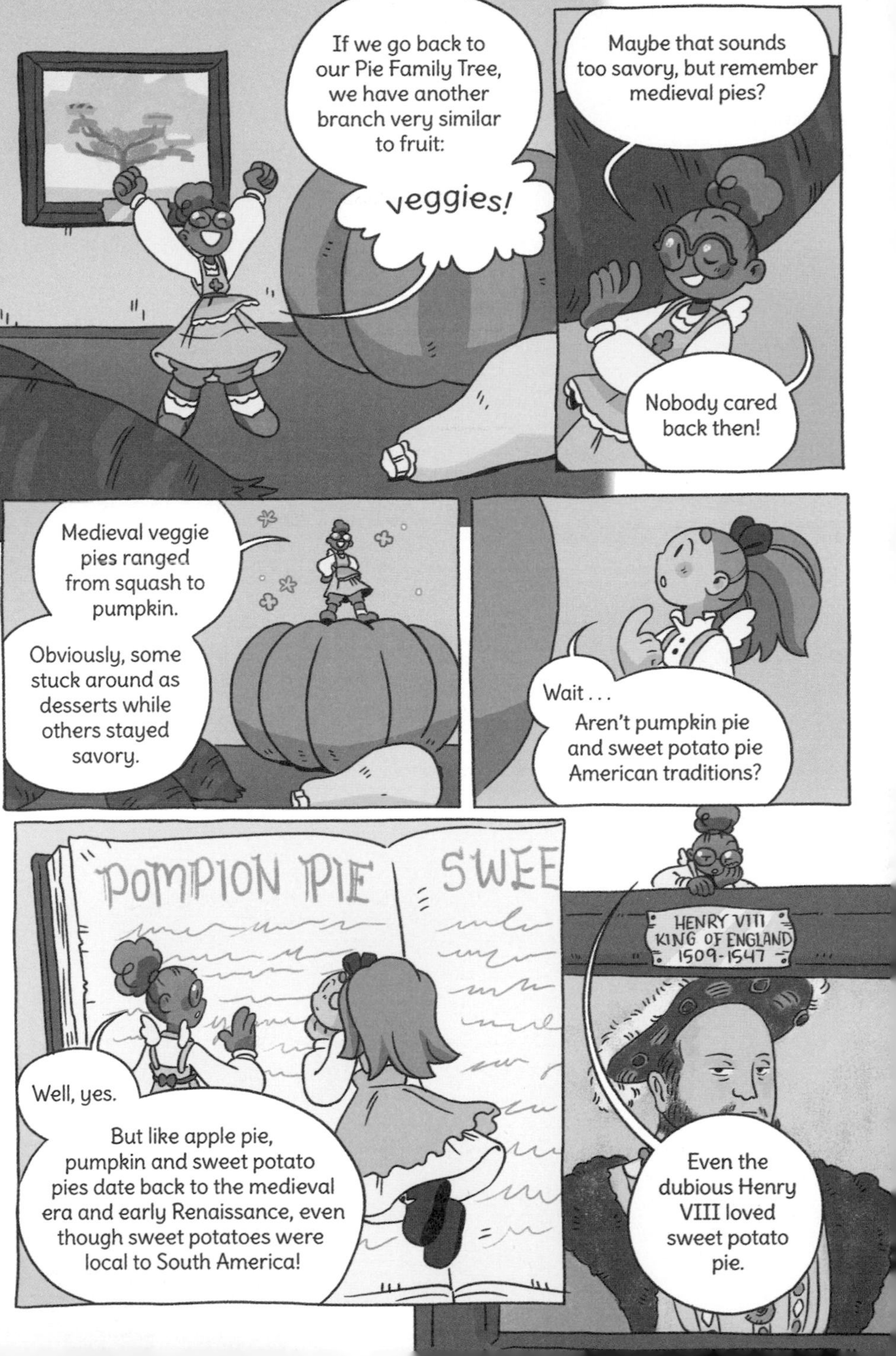
If we go back to our Pie Family Tree, we have another branch very similar to fruit:
veggies!
Maybe that sounds too savory, but remember medieval pies?
Nobody cared back then!
Medieval veggie pies ranged from squash to pumpkin.
Obviously, some stuck around as desserts while others stayed savory.
Wait . . .
Aren't pumpkin pie and sweet potato pie American traditions?
POMPION PIE
SWEE
HENRY VIII
KING OF ENGLAND
1509-1547
Well, yes.
But like apple pie, pumpkin and sweet potato pies date back to the medieval era and early Renaissance, even though sweet potatoes were local to South America!
Even the dubious Henry VIII loved sweet potato pie.

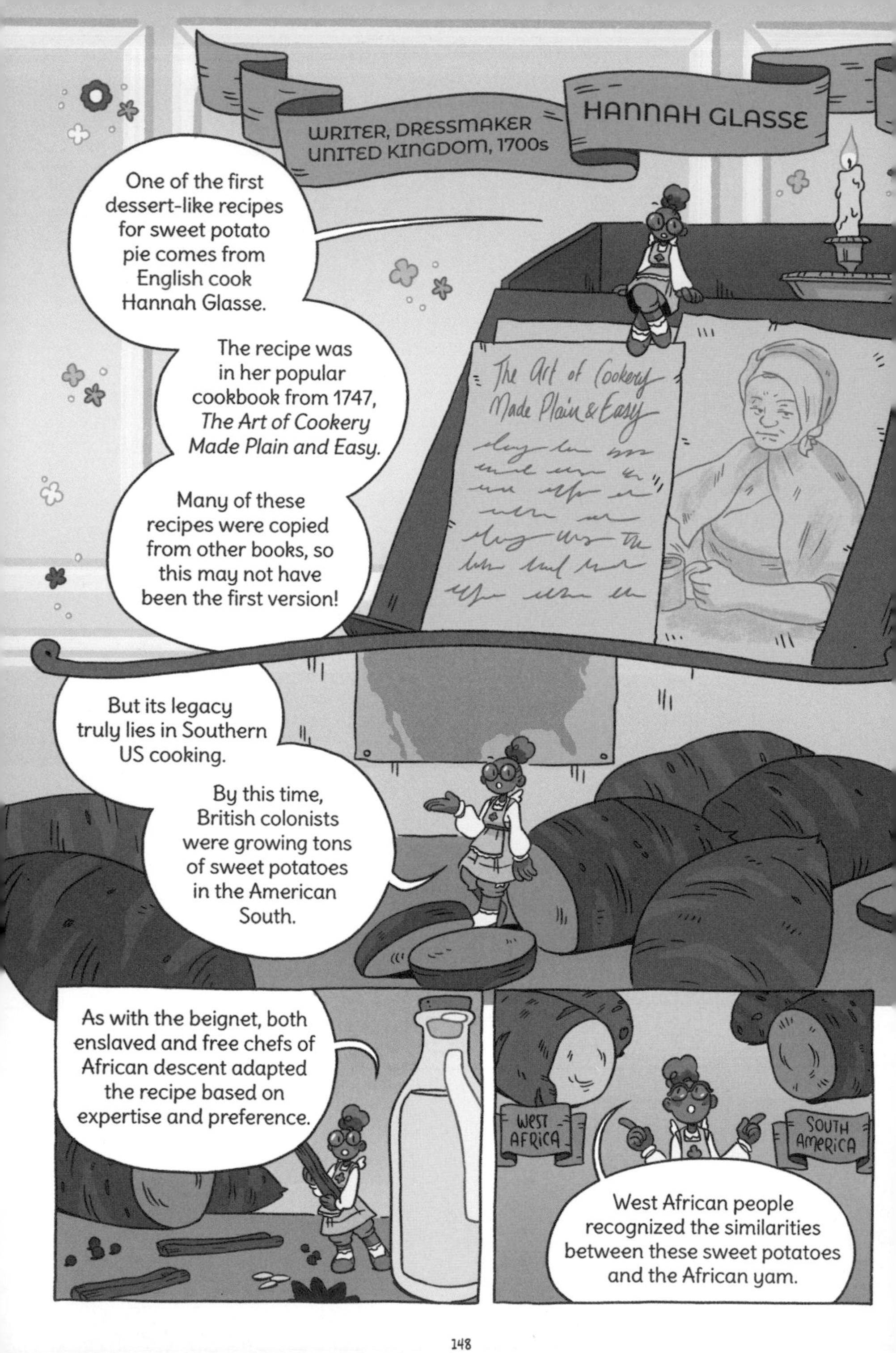
HANNAH GLASSE
WRITER, DRESSMAKER
UNITED KINGDOM, 1700s
One of the first dessert-like recipes for sweet potato pie comes from English cook Hannah Glasse.
The recipe was in her popular cookbook from 1747, *The Art of Cookery Made Plain and Easy.*
Many of these recipes were copied from other books, so this may not have been the first version!
The Art of Cookery Made Plain & Easy
But its legacy truly lies in Southern US cooking.
By this time, British colonists were growing tons of sweet potatoes in the American South.
As with the beignet, both enslaved and free chefs of African descent adapted the recipe based on expertise and preference.
WEST AFRICA
SOUTH AMERICA
West African people recognized the similarities between these sweet potatoes and the African yam.

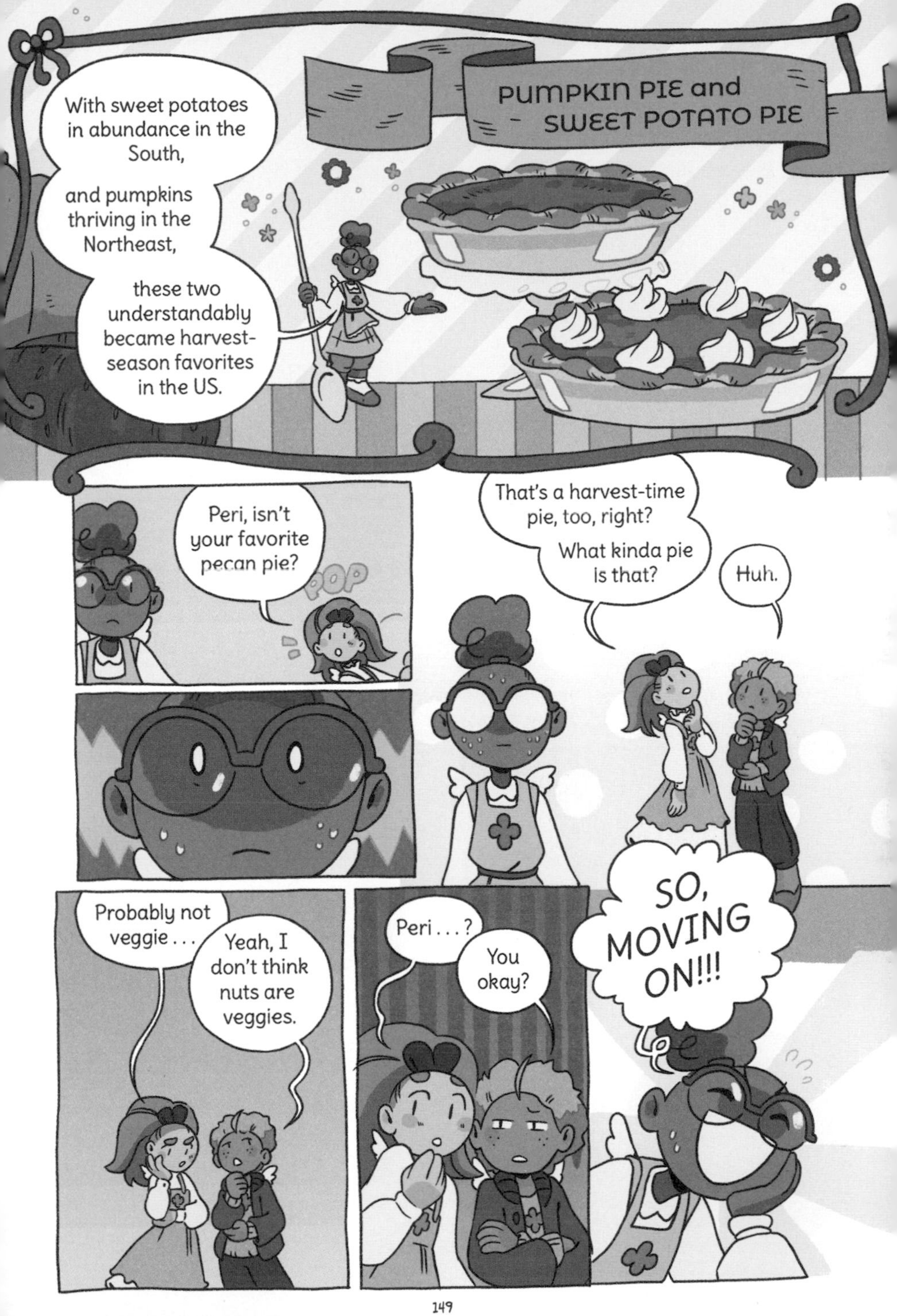
PUMPKIN PIE and SWEET POTATO PIE
With sweet potatoes in abundance in the South,
and pumpkins thriving in the Northeast,
these two understandably became harvest-season favorites in the US.
Peri, isn't your favorite pecan pie?
POP
That's a harvest-time pie, too, right?
What kinda pie is that?
Huh.
Probably not veggie . . .
Yeah, I don't think nuts are veggies.
Peri . . . ?
You okay?
SO, MOVING ON!!!

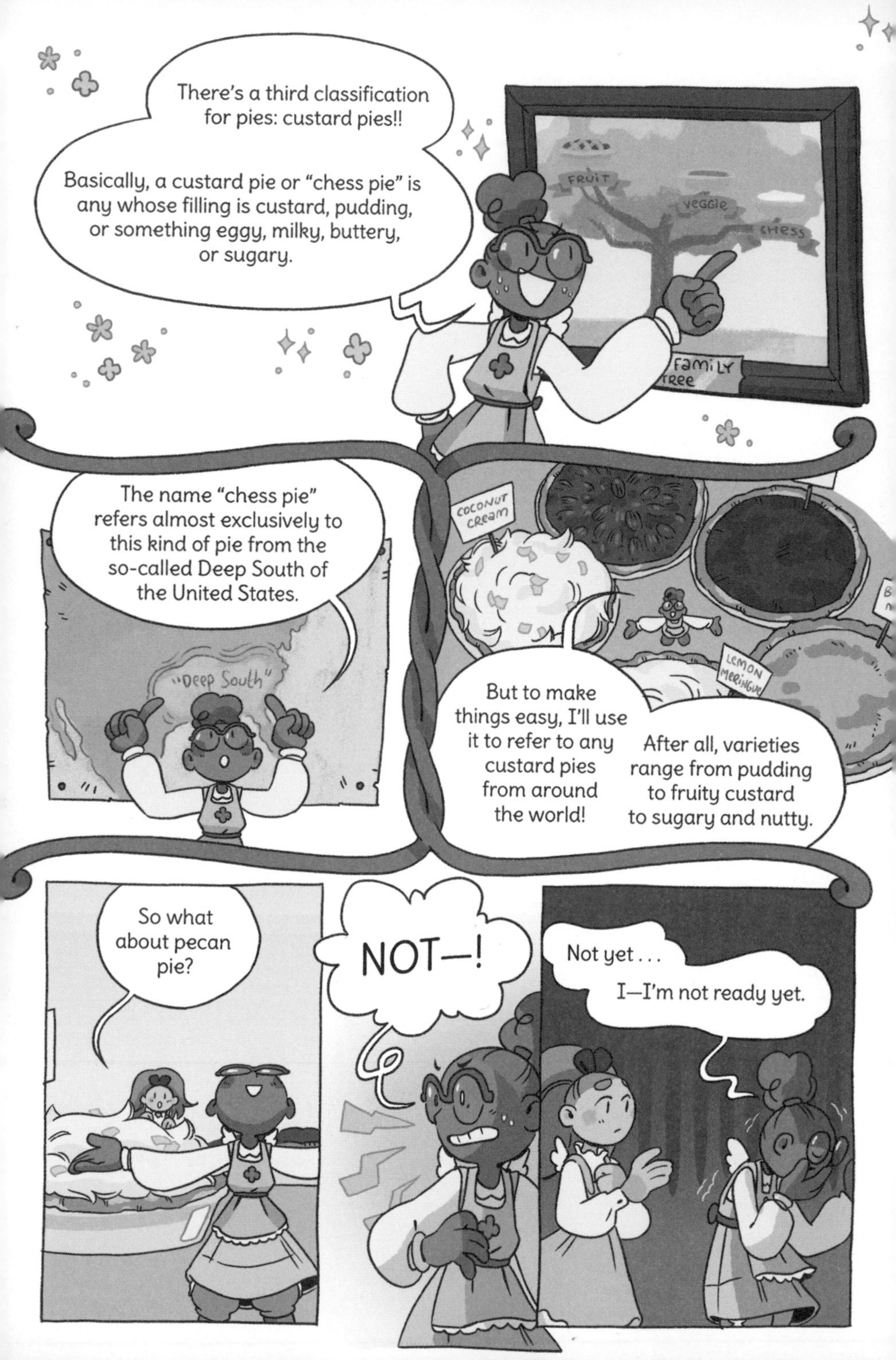
There's a third classification for pies: custard pies!!
Basically, a custard pie or "chess pie" is any whose filling is custard, pudding, or something eggy, milky, buttery, or sugary.
FRUIT
VEGGIE
CHESS
FAMILY TREE
The name "chess pie" refers almost exclusively to this kind of pie from the so-called Deep South of the United States.
"Deep South"
COCONUT CREAM
LEMON MERINGUE
But to make things easy, I'll use it to refer to any custard pies from around the world!
After all, varieties range from pudding to fruity custard to sugary and nutty.
So what about pecan pie?
NOT—!
Not yet . . .
I—I'm not ready yet.

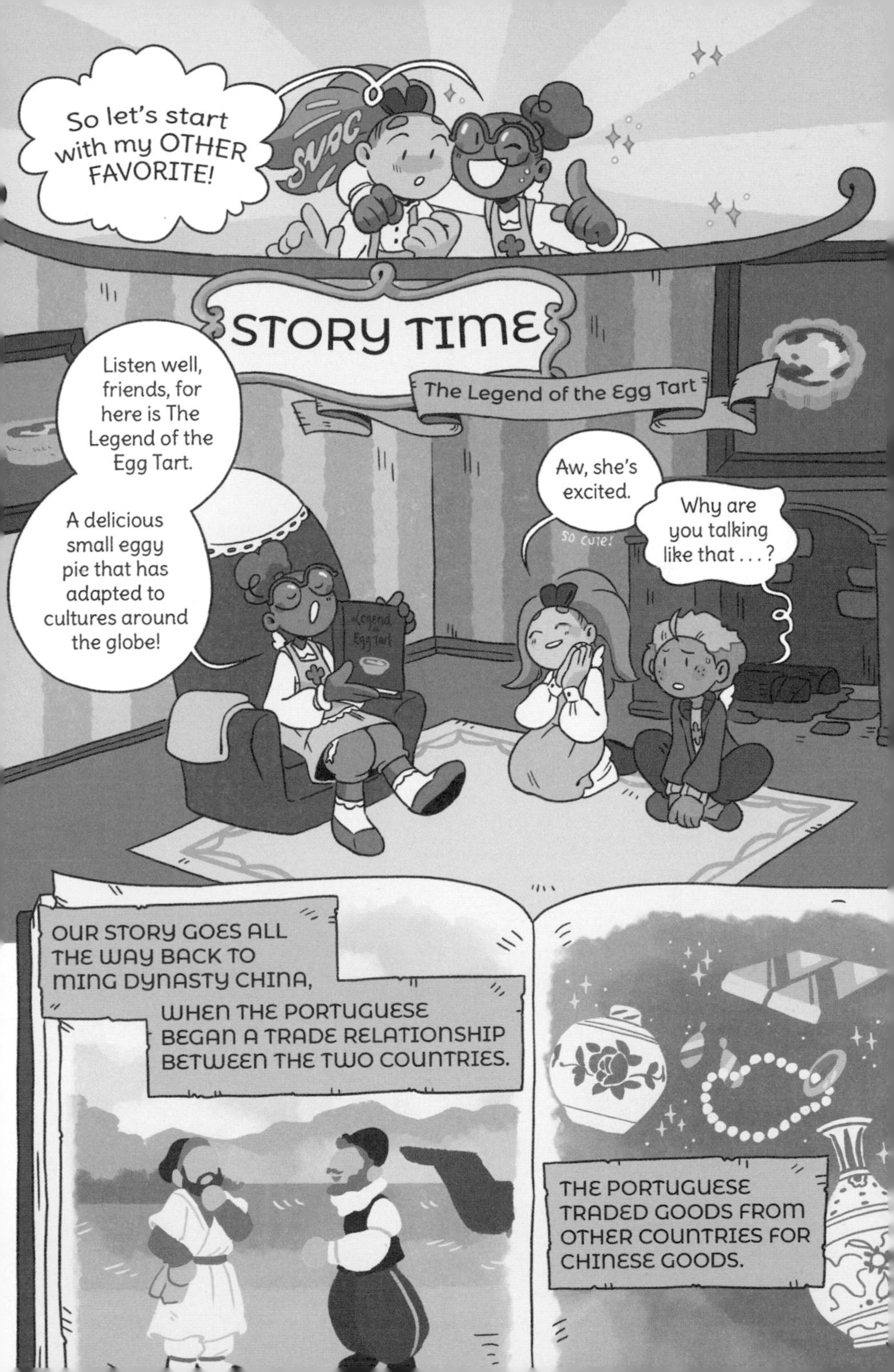
So let's start with my OTHER FAVORITE!
STORY TIME
The Legend of the Egg Tart
Listen well, friends, for here is The Legend of the Egg Tart.
A delicious small eggy pie that has adapted to cultures around the globe!
Aw, she's excited.
SO CUTE!
Why are you talking like that . . . ?
OUR STORY GOES ALL THE WAY BACK TO MING DYNASTY CHINA,
WHEN THE PORTUGUESE BEGAN A TRADE RELATIONSHIP BETWEEN THE TWO COUNTRIES.
THE PORTUGUESE TRADED GOODS FROM OTHER COUNTRIES FOR CHINESE GOODS.

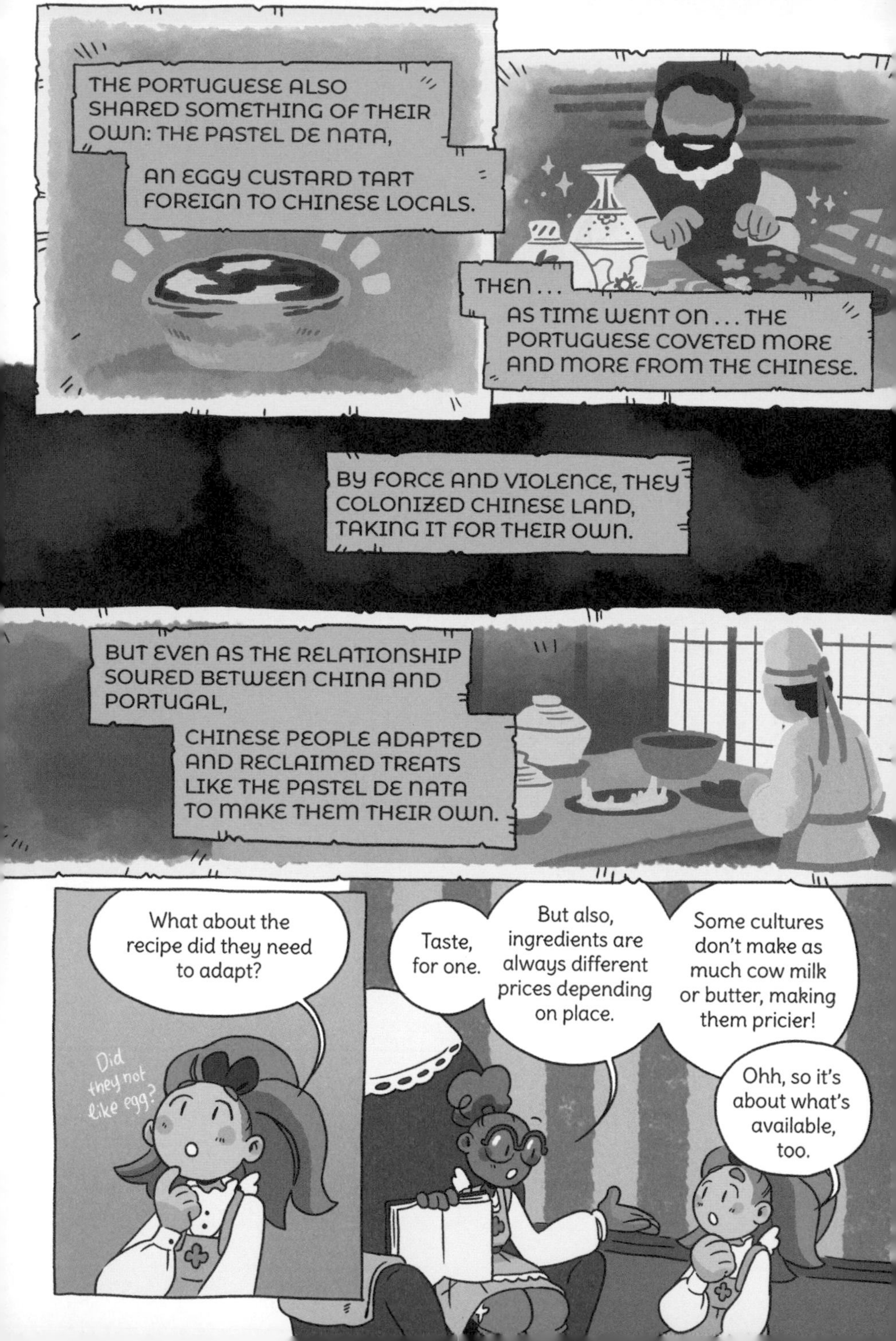
THE PORTUGUESE ALSO SHARED SOMETHING OF THEIR OWN: THE PASTEL DE NATA,
AN EGGY CUSTARD TART FOREIGN TO CHINESE LOCALS.
THEN . . .
AS TIME WENT ON . . . THE PORTUGUESE COVETED MORE AND MORE FROM THE CHINESE.
BY FORCE AND VIOLENCE, THEY COLONIZED CHINESE LAND, TAKING IT FOR THEIR OWN.
BUT EVEN AS THE RELATIONSHIP SOURED BETWEEN CHINA AND PORTUGAL,
CHINESE PEOPLE ADAPTED AND RECLAIMED TREATS LIKE THE PASTEL DE NATA TO MAKE THEM THEIR OWN.
What about the recipe did they need to adapt?
Did they not like egg?
Taste, for one.
But also, ingredients are always different prices depending on place.
Some cultures don't make as much cow milk or butter, making them pricier!
Ohh, so it's about what's available, too.

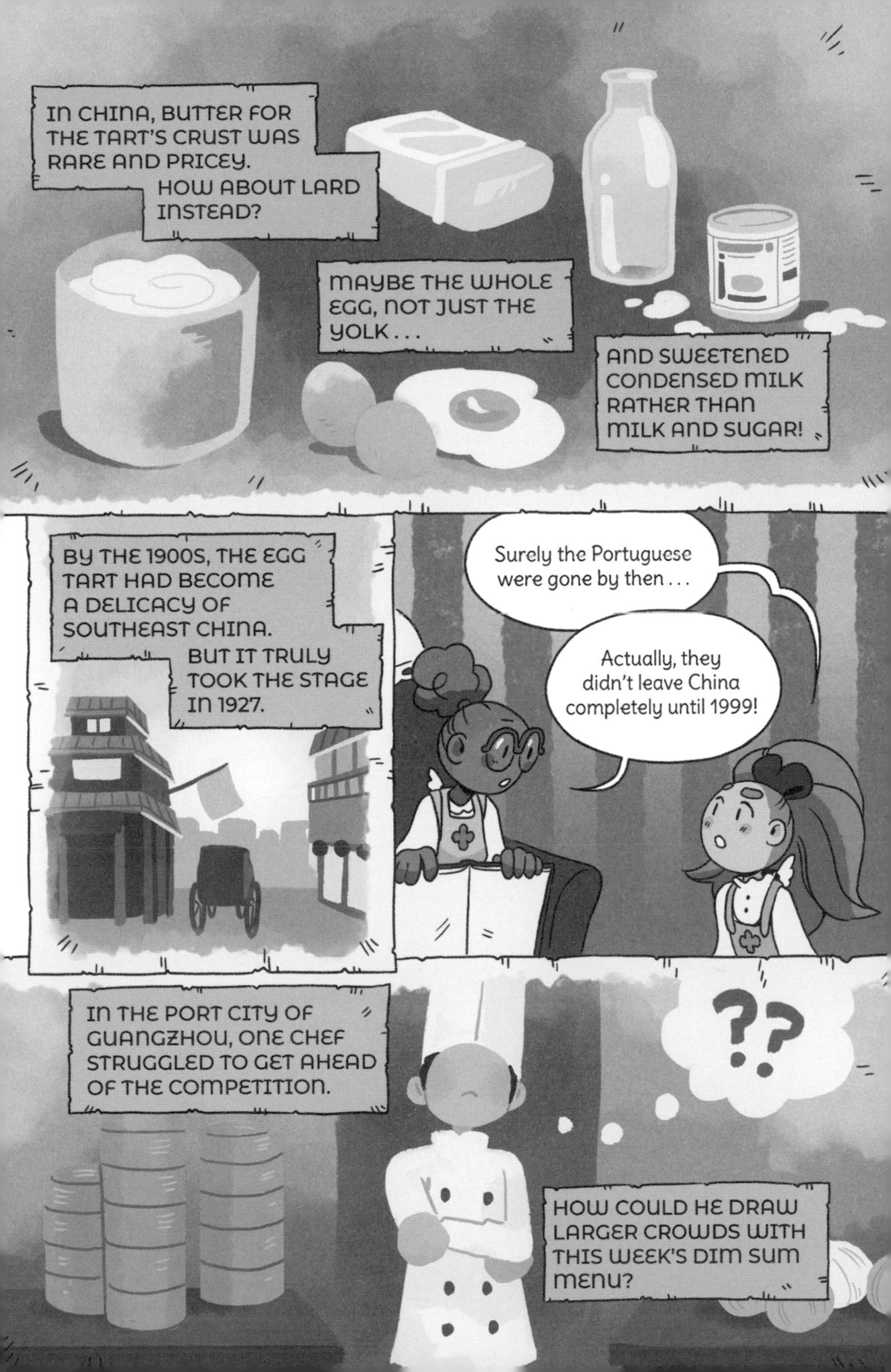
IN CHINA, BUTTER FOR THE TART'S CRUST WAS RARE AND PRICEY.
HOW ABOUT LARD INSTEAD?
MAYBE THE WHOLE EGG, NOT JUST THE YOLK . . .
AND SWEETENED CONDENSED MILK RATHER THAN MILK AND SUGAR!
BY THE 1900S, THE EGG TART HAD BECOME A DELICACY OF SOUTHEAST CHINA.
BUT IT TRULY TOOK THE STAGE IN 1927.
Surely the Portuguese were gone by then . . .
Actually, they didn't leave China completely until 1999!
IN THE PORT CITY OF GUANGZHOU, ONE CHEF STRUGGLED TO GET AHEAD OF THE COMPETITION.
??
HOW COULD HE DRAW LARGER CROWDS WITH THIS WEEK'S DIM SUM MENU?

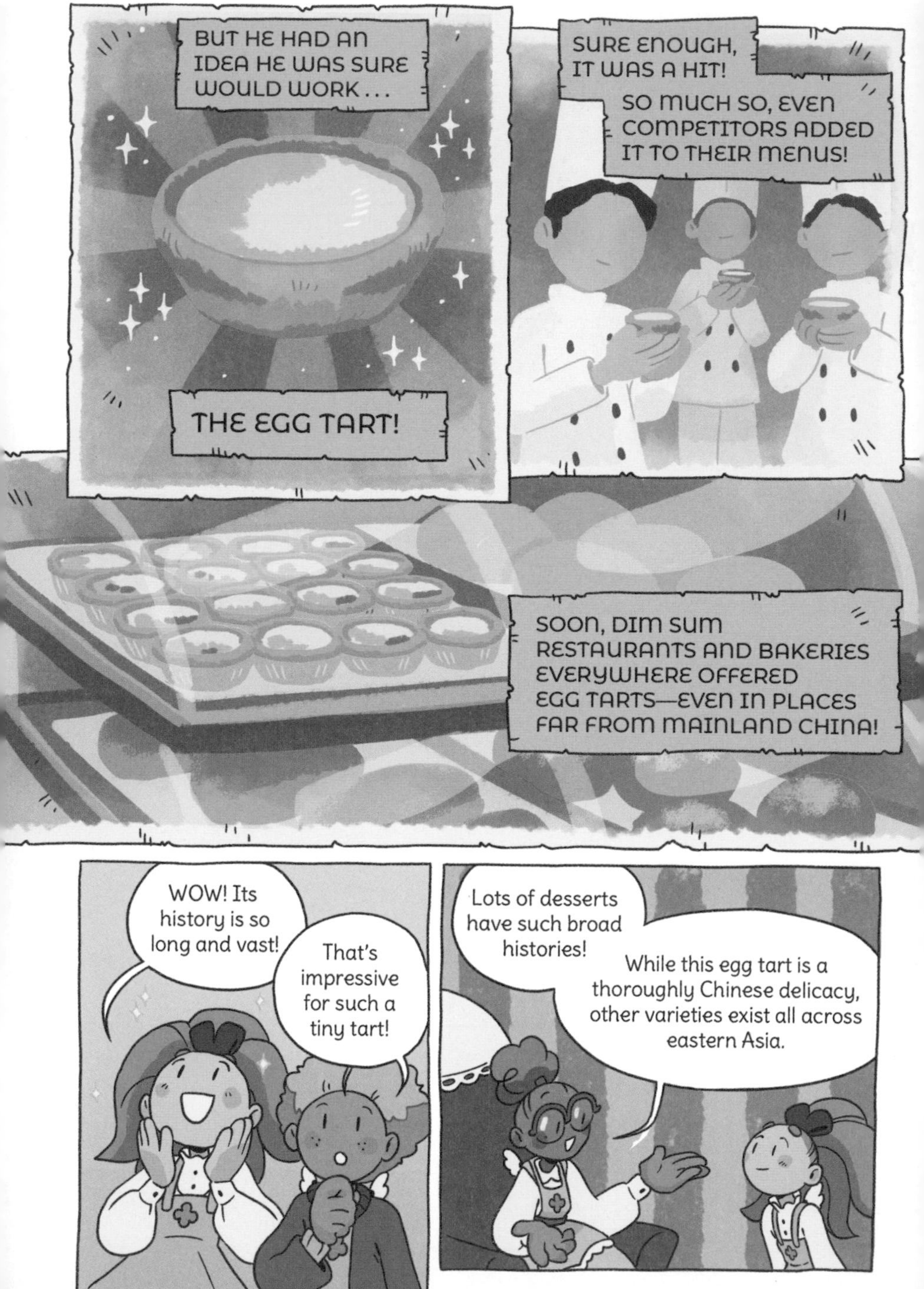
BUT HE HAD AN IDEA HE WAS SURE WOULD WORK . . .
THE EGG TART!
SURE ENOUGH, IT WAS A HIT!
SO MUCH SO, EVEN COMPETITORS ADDED IT TO THEIR MENUS!
SOON, DIM SUM RESTAURANTS AND BAKERIES EVERYWHERE OFFERED EGG TARTS—EVEN IN PLACES FAR FROM MAINLAND CHINA!
WOW! Its history is so long and vast!
That's impressive for such a tiny tart!
Lots of desserts have such broad histories!
While this egg tart is a thoroughly Chinese delicacy, other varieties exist all across eastern Asia.

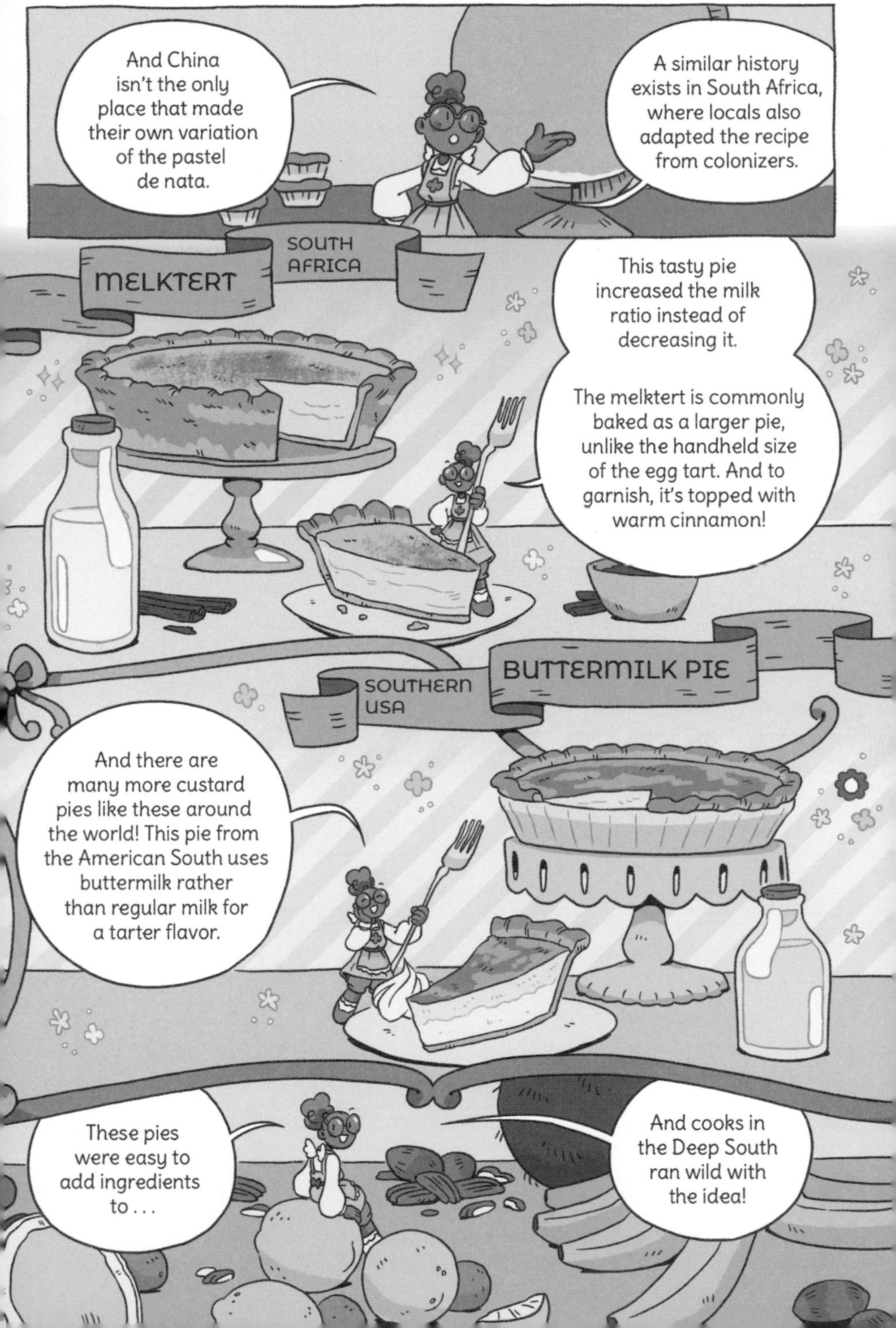
And China isn't the only place that made their own variation of the pastel de nata.
A similar history exists in South Africa, where locals also adapted the recipe from colonizers.
MELKTERT
SOUTH AFRICA
This tasty pie increased the milk ratio instead of decreasing it.
The melktert is commonly baked as a larger pie, unlike the handheld size of the egg tart. And to garnish, it's topped with warm cinnamon!
BUTTERMILK PIE
SOUTHERN USA
And there are many more custard pies like these around the world! This pie from the American South uses buttermilk rather than regular milk for a tarter flavor.
These pies were easy to add ingredients to . . .
And cooks in the Deep South ran wild with the idea!

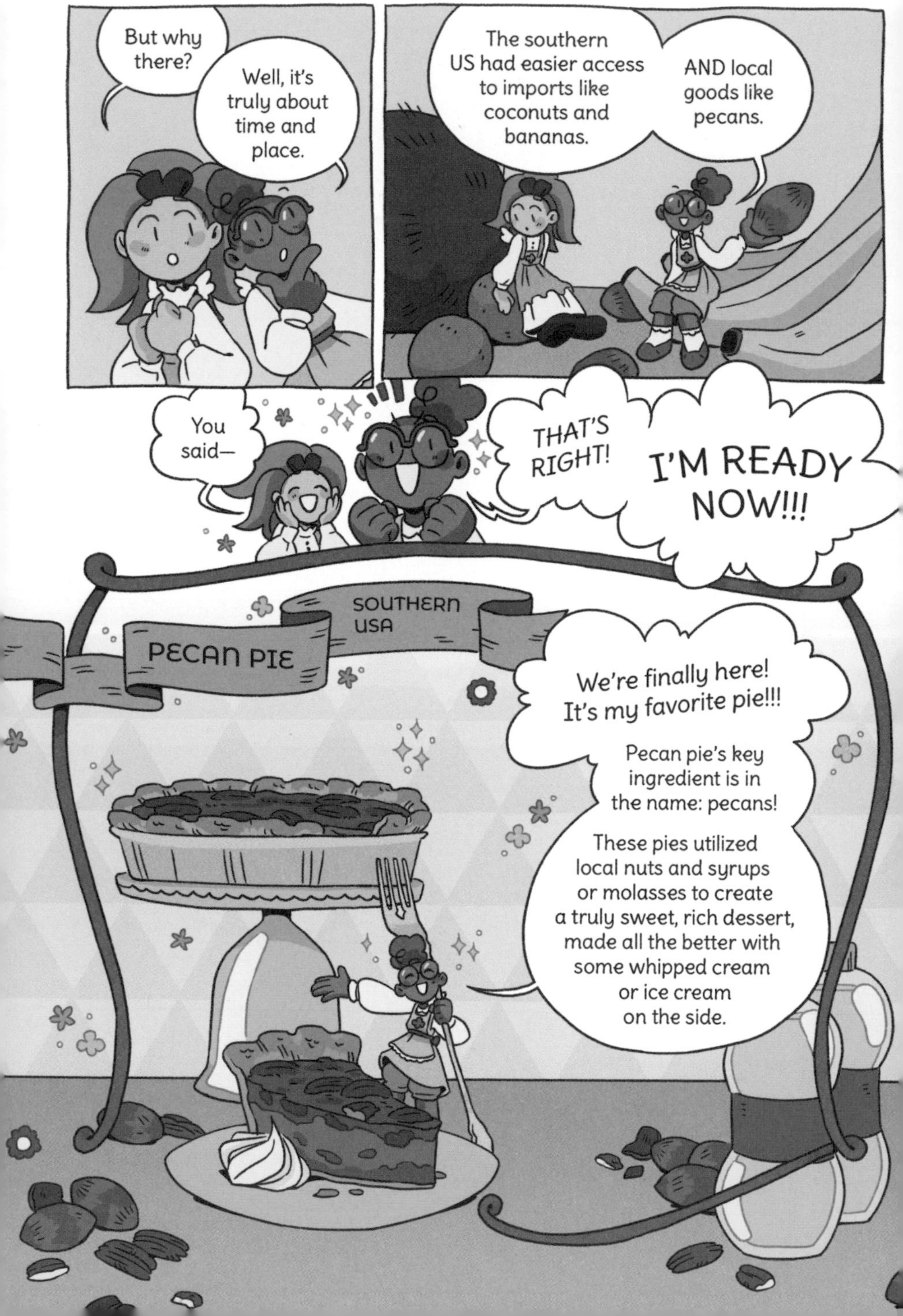

But why there?
Well, it's truly about time and place.
The southern US had easier access to imports like coconuts and bananas.
AND local goods like pecans.
You said—
THAT'S RIGHT!
I'M READY NOW!!!
PECAN PIE
SOUTHERN USA
We're finally here! It's my favorite pie!!!
Pecan pie's key ingredient is in the name: pecans!
These pies utilized local nuts and syrups or molasses to create a truly sweet, rich dessert, made all the better with some whipped cream or ice cream on the side.

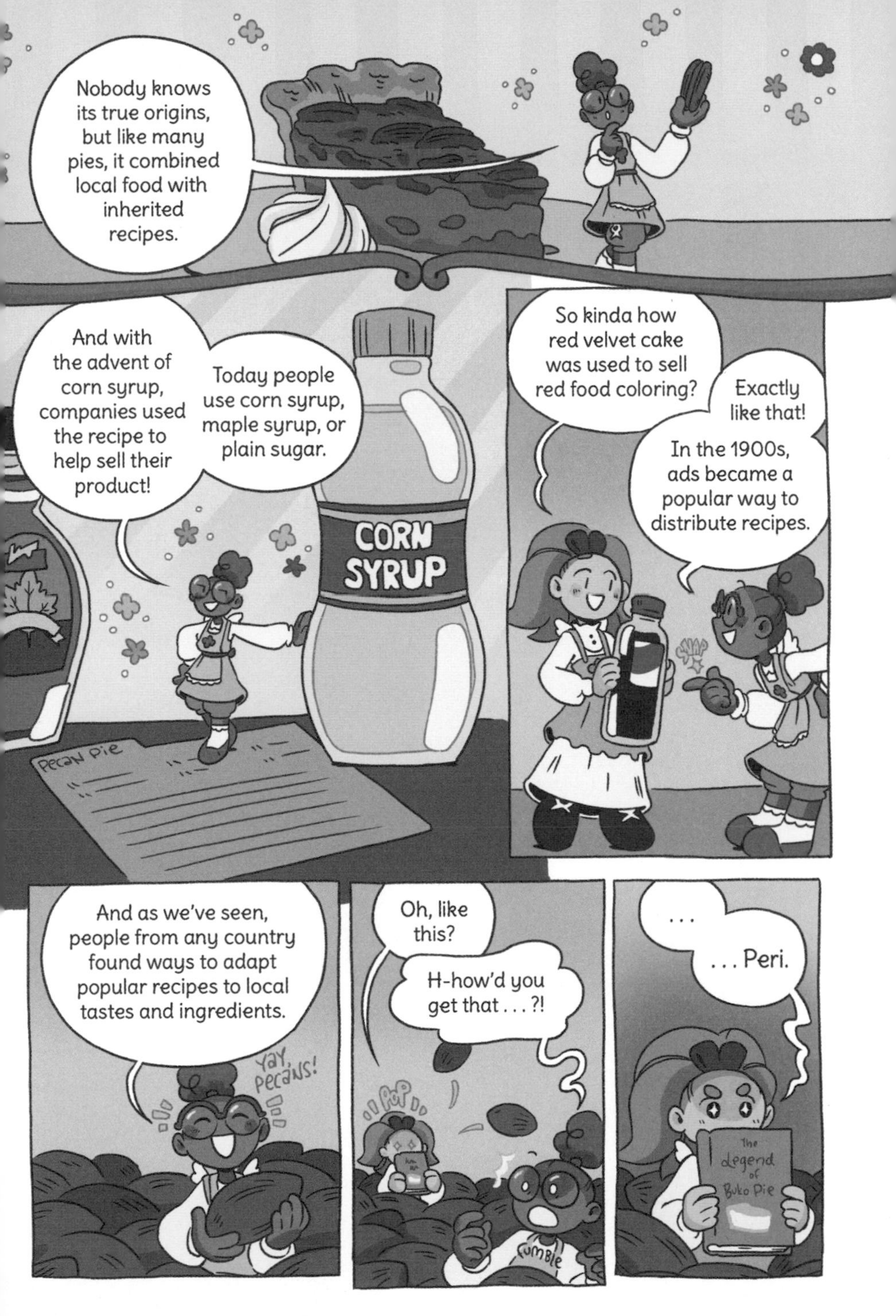
Nobody knows its true origins, but like many pies, it combined local food with inherited recipes.
And with the advent of corn syrup, companies used the recipe to help sell their product!
Today people use corn syrup, maple syrup, or plain sugar.
CORN SYRUP
PECAN PIE
So kinda how red velvet cake was used to sell red food coloring?
Exactly like that!
In the 1900s, ads became a popular way to distribute recipes.
SNAP
And as we've seen, people from any country found ways to adapt popular recipes to local tastes and ingredients.
YAY, PECANS!
Oh, like this?
H-how'd you get that . . . ?!
POP
FUMBLE
. . .
. . . Peri.
The Legend of Buko Pie

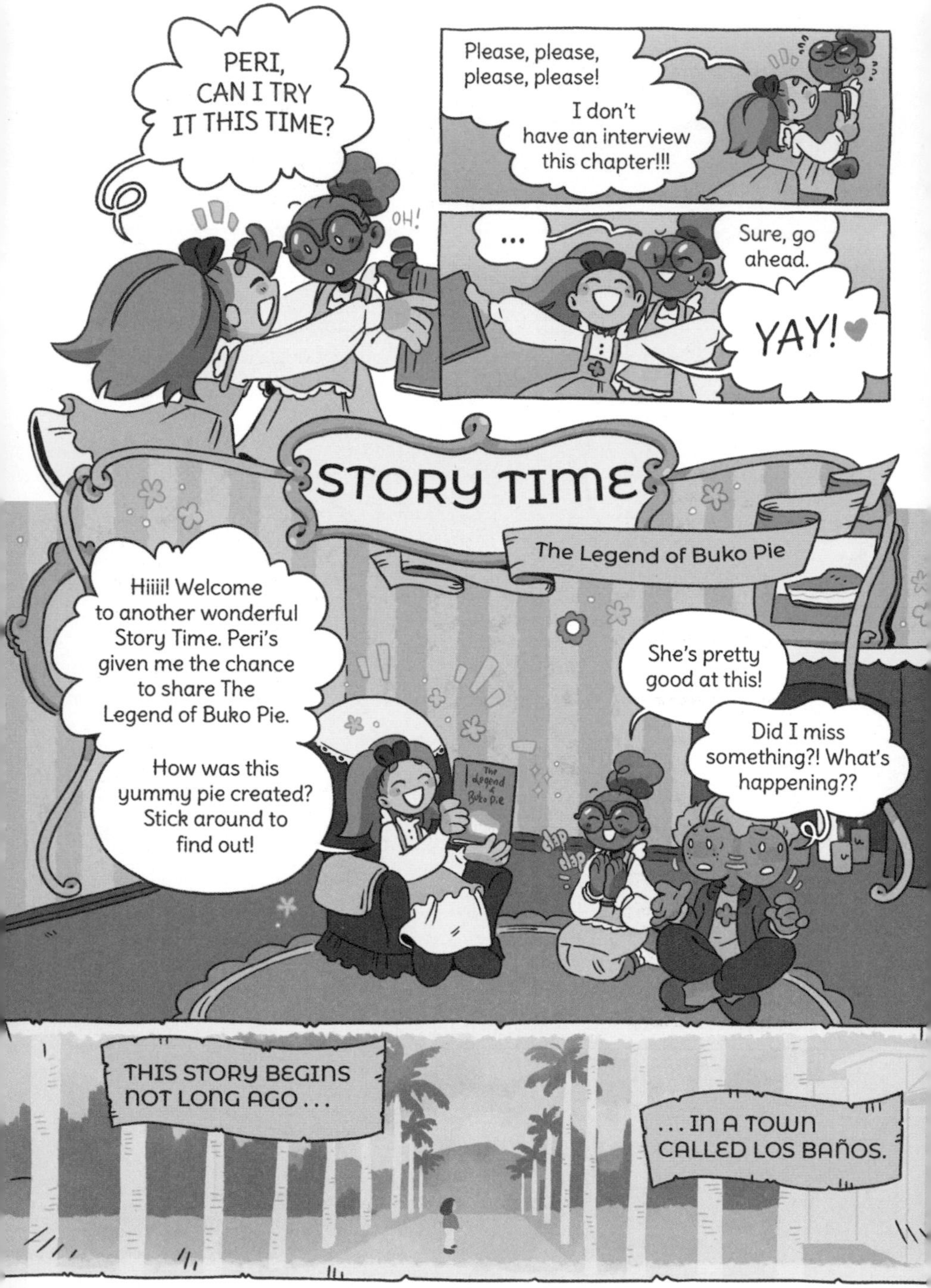
PERI, CAN I TRY IT THIS TIME?
OH!
Please, please, please, please!
I don't have an interview this chapter!!!
...
Sure, go ahead.
YAY!
STORY TIME
The Legend of Buko Pie
Hiiii! Welcome to another wonderful Story Time. Peri's given me the chance to share The Legend of Buko Pie.
How was this yummy pie created? Stick around to find out!
She's pretty good at this!
Did I miss something?! What's happening??
THIS STORY BEGINS NOT LONG AGO . . .
. . . IN A TOWN CALLED LOS BAÑOS.

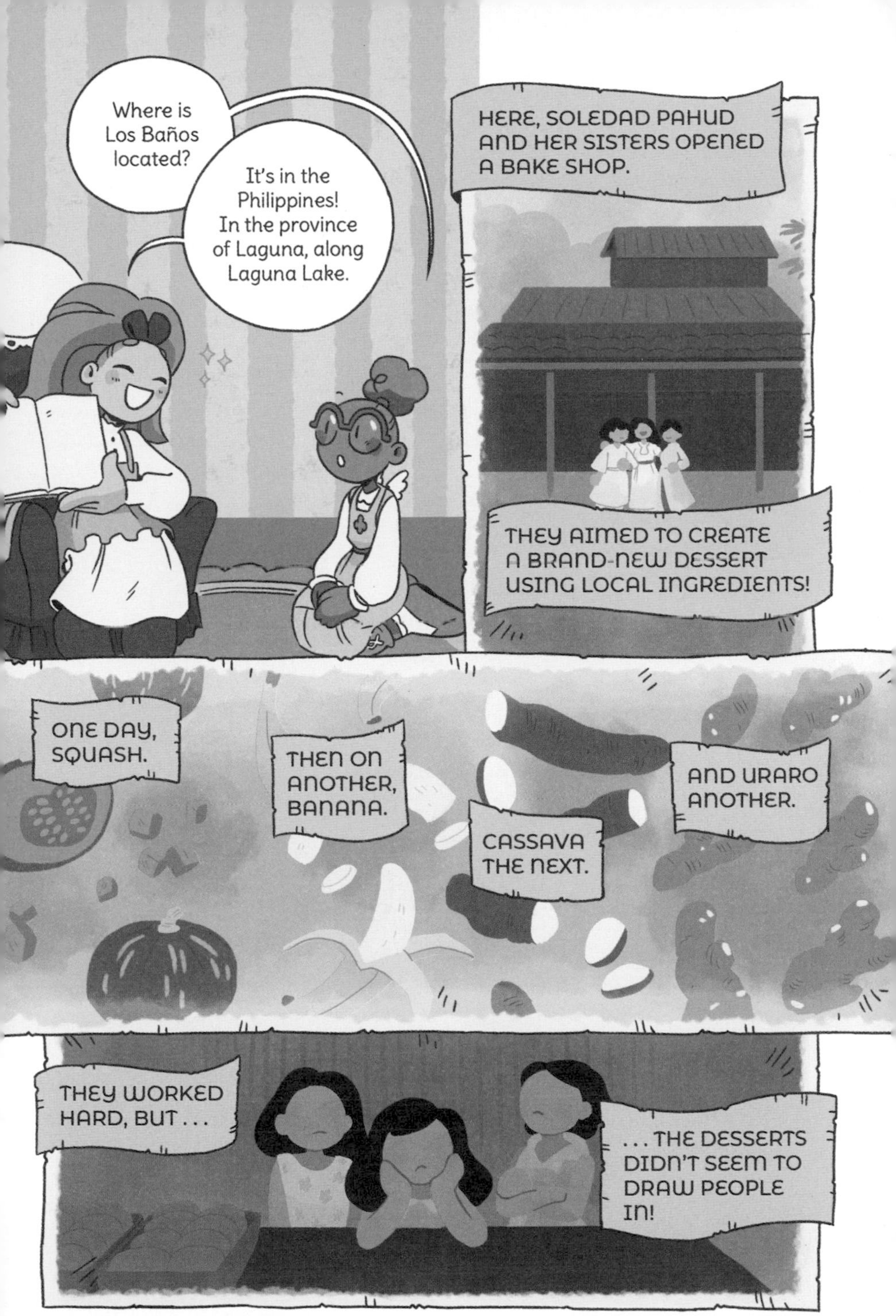

Where is Los Baños located?
It's in the Philippines! In the province of Laguna, along Laguna Lake.
HERE, SOLEDAD PAHUD AND HER SISTERS OPENED A BAKE SHOP.
THEY AIMED TO CREATE A BRAND-NEW DESSERT USING LOCAL INGREDIENTS!
ONE DAY, SQUASH.
THEN ON ANOTHER, BANANA.
CASSAVA THE NEXT.
AND URARO ANOTHER.
THEY WORKED HARD, BUT . . .
. . . THE DESSERTS DIDN'T SEEM TO DRAW PEOPLE IN!

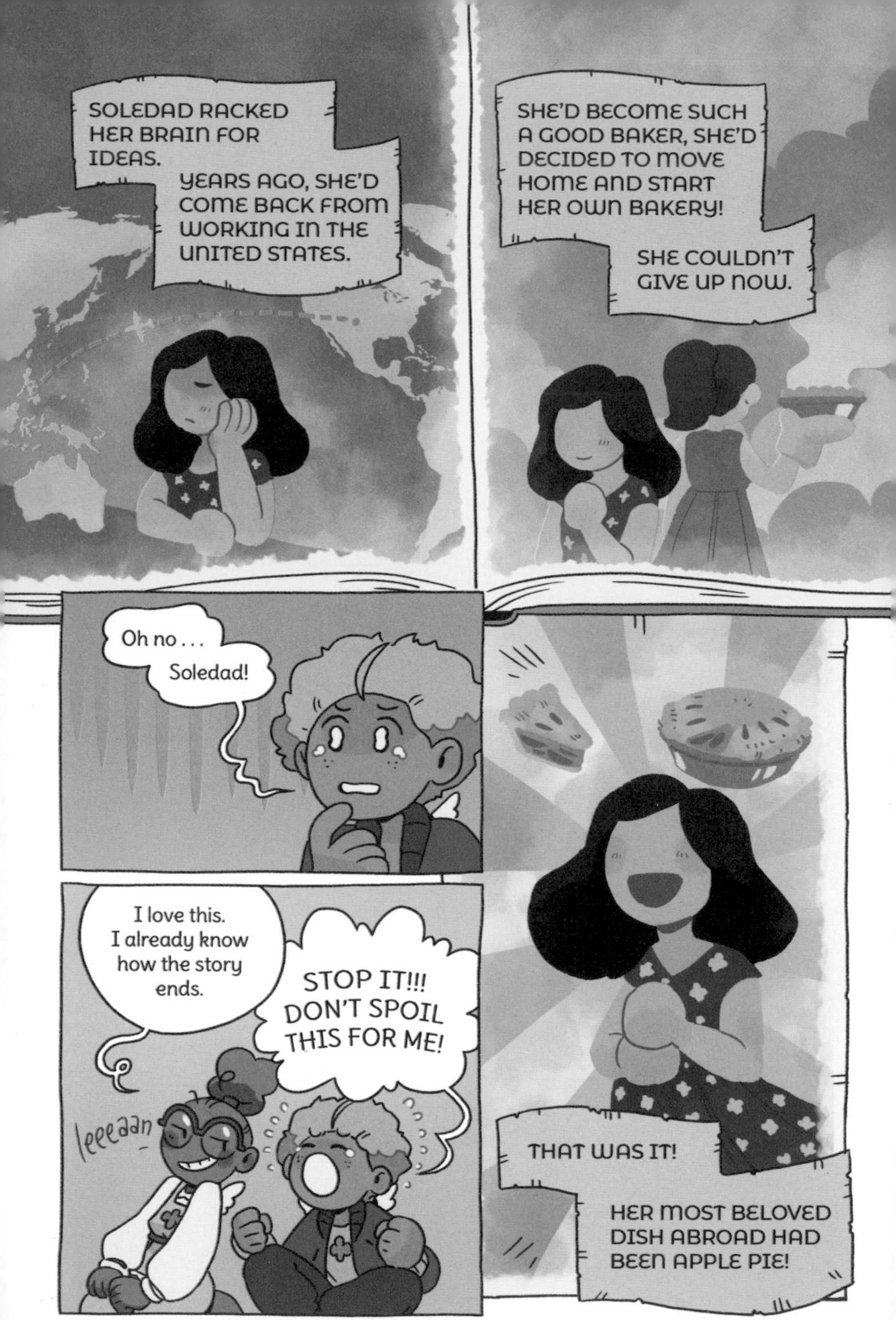
SOLEDAD RACKED HER BRAIN FOR IDEAS.
YEARS AGO, SHE'D COME BACK FROM WORKING IN THE UNITED STATES.
SHE'D BECOME SUCH A GOOD BAKER, SHE'D DECIDED TO MOVE HOME AND START HER OWN BAKERY!
SHE COULDN'T GIVE UP NOW.
Oh no . . .
Soledad!
I love this. I already know how the story ends.
STOP IT!!! DON'T SPOIL THIS FOR ME!
leeeaan
THAT WAS IT!
HER MOST BELOVED DISH ABROAD HAD BEEN APPLE PIE!

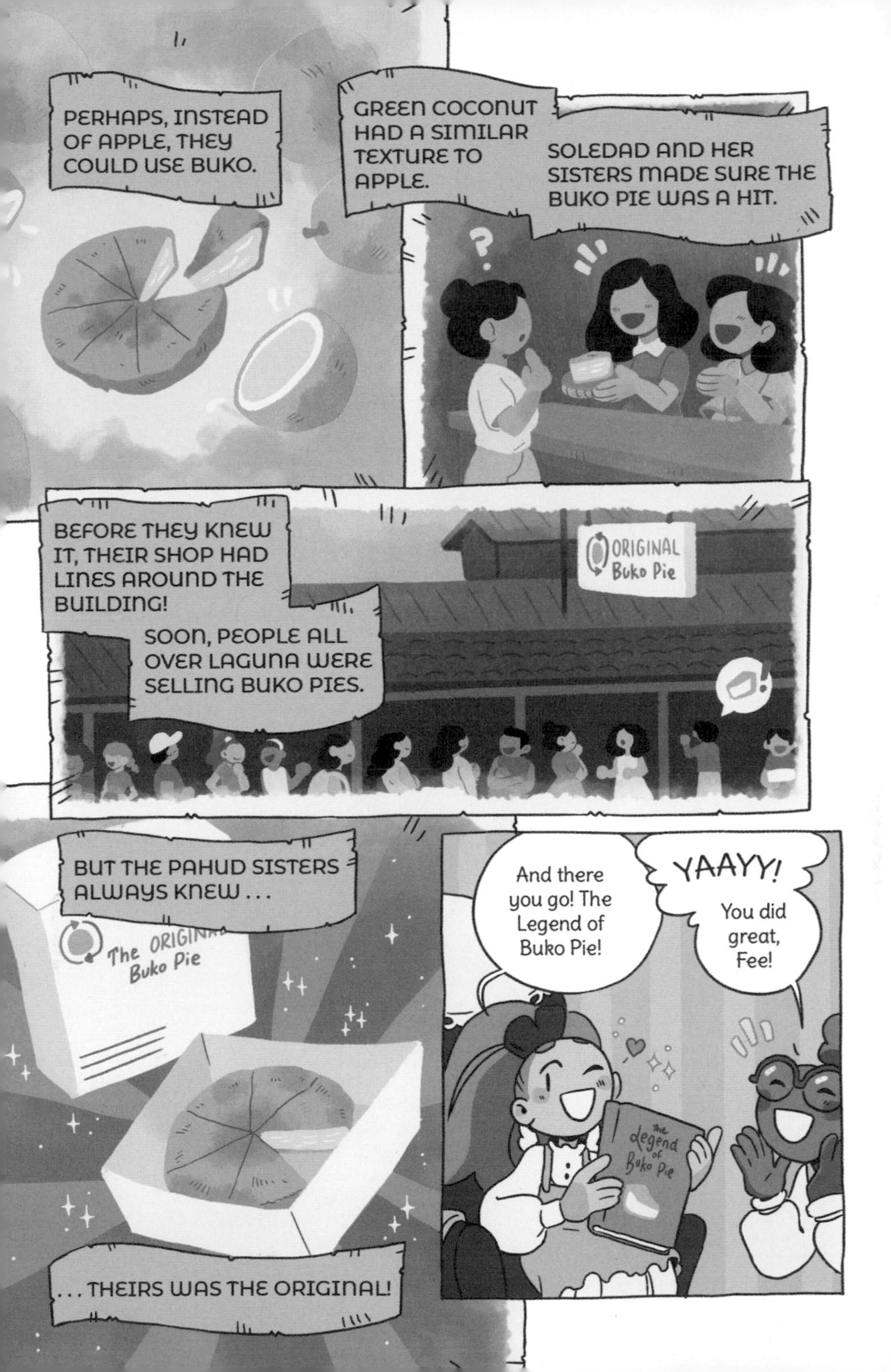
PERHAPS, INSTEAD OF APPLE, THEY COULD USE BUKO.
GREEN COCONUT HAD A SIMILAR TEXTURE TO APPLE.
SOLEDAD AND HER SISTERS MADE SURE THE BUKO PIE WAS A HIT.
BEFORE THEY KNEW IT, THEIR SHOP HAD LINES AROUND THE BUILDING!
ORIGINAL Buko Pie
SOON, PEOPLE ALL OVER LAGUNA WERE SELLING BUKO PIES.
BUT THE PAHUD SISTERS ALWAYS KNEW . . .
. . . THEIRS WAS THE ORIGINAL!
And there you go! The Legend of Buko Pie!
YAAYY!
You did great, Fee!
The Legend of Buko Pie

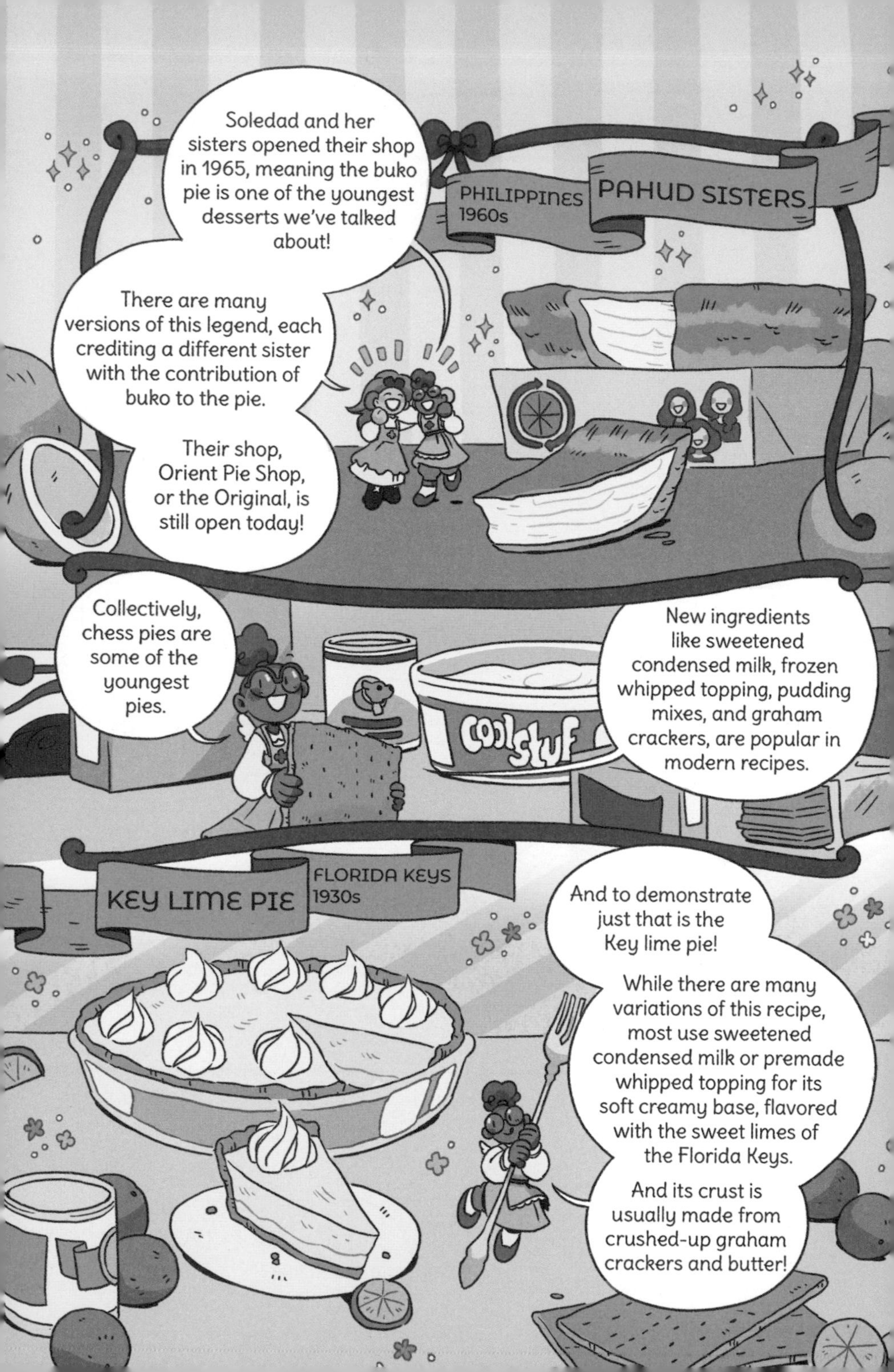
PHILIPPINES 1960s
PAHUD SISTERS
Soledad and her sisters opened their shop in 1965, meaning the buko pie is one of the youngest desserts we've talked about!
There are many versions of this legend, each crediting a different sister with the contribution of buko to the pie.
Their shop, Orient Pie Shop, or the Original, is still open today!
Collectively, chess pies are some of the youngest pies.
New ingredients like sweetened condensed milk, frozen whipped topping, pudding mixes, and graham crackers, are popular in modern recipes.
Coolstuf
KEY LIME PIE
FLORIDA KEYS 1930s
And to demonstrate just that is the Key lime pie!
While there are many variations of this recipe, most use sweetened condensed milk or premade whipped topping for its soft creamy base, flavored with the sweet limes of the Florida Keys.
And its crust is usually made from crushed-up graham crackers and butter!

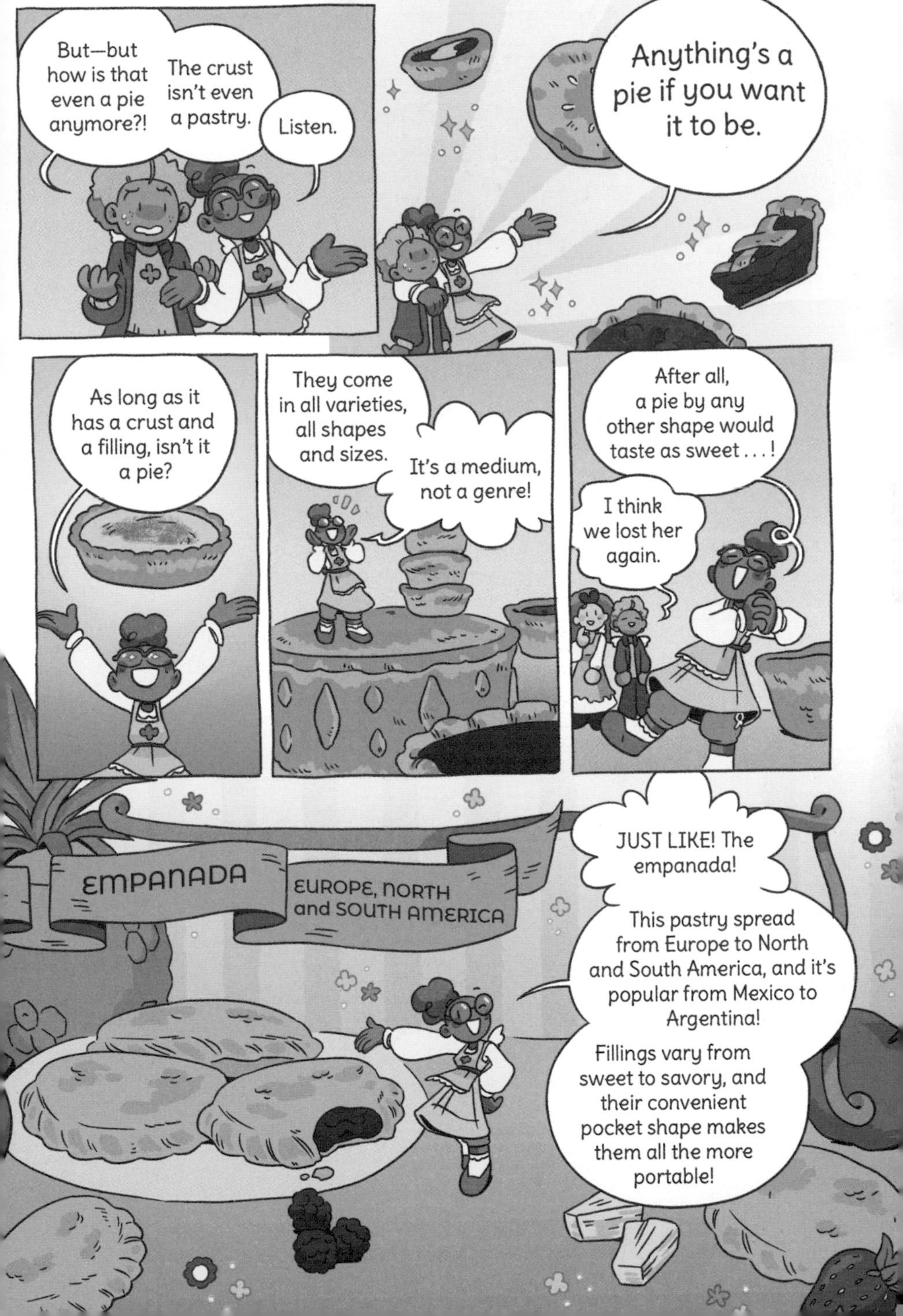
But—but how is that even a pie anymore?!
The crust isn't even a pastry.
Listen.
Anything's a pie if you want it to be.
As long as it has a crust and a filling, isn't it a pie?
They come in all varieties, all shapes and sizes.
It's a medium, not a genre!
After all, a pie by any other shape would taste as sweet . . . !
I think we lost her again.
EMPANADA
EUROPE, NORTH and SOUTH AMERICA
JUST LIKE! The empanada!
This pastry spread from Europe to North and South America, and it's popular from Mexico to Argentina!
Fillings vary from sweet to savory, and their convenient pocket shape makes them all the more portable!

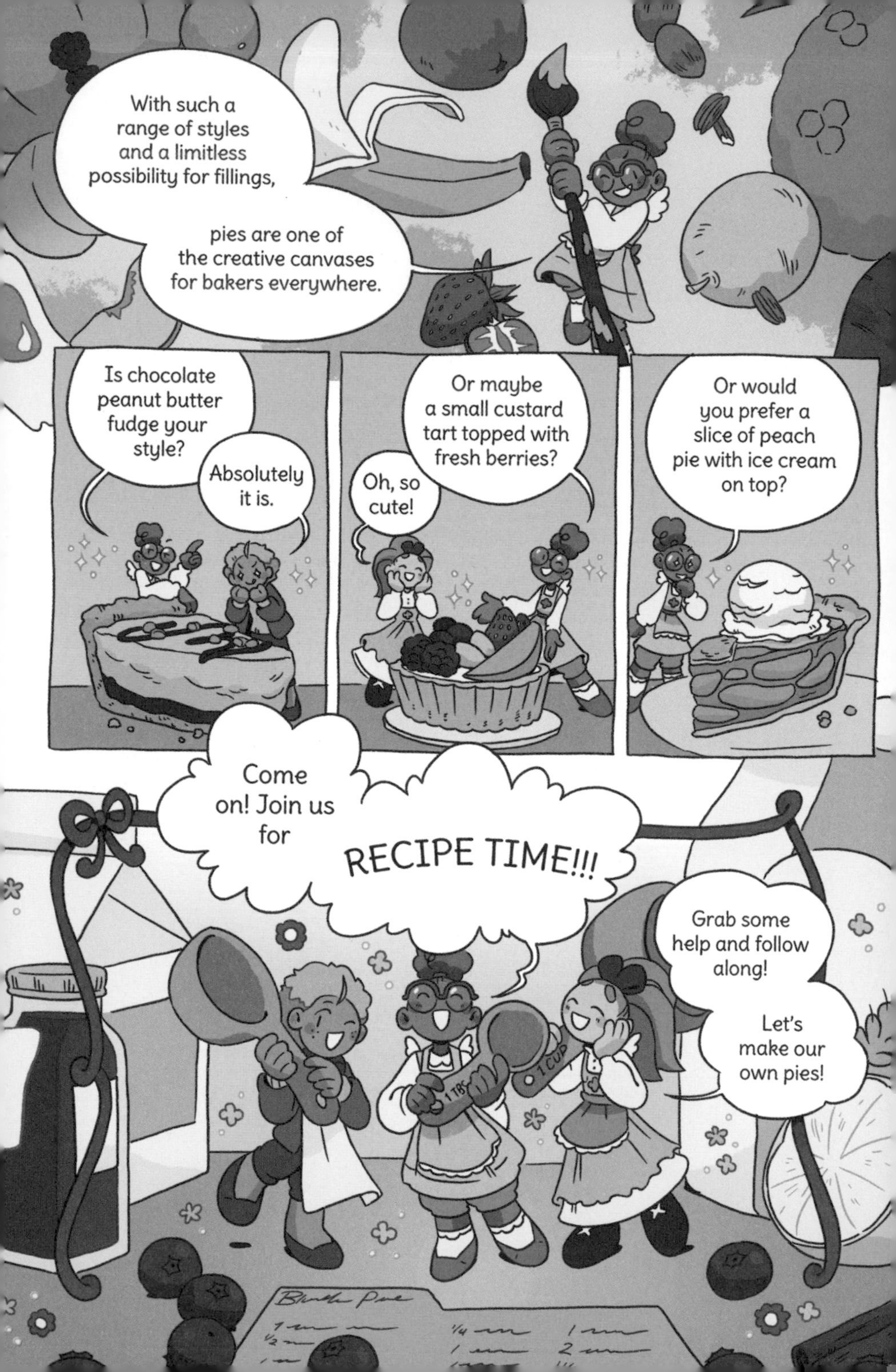
With such a range of styles and a limitless possibility for fillings,
pies are one of the creative canvases for bakers everywhere.
Is chocolate peanut butter fudge your style?
Absolutely it is.
Or maybe a small custard tart topped with fresh berries?
Oh, so cute!
Or would you prefer a slice of peach pie with ice cream on top?
Come on! Join us for
RECIPE TIME!!!
Grab some help and follow along!
Let's make our own pies!
1 TBS
1 CUP

# BLUEBERRY PIE

## YOU WILL NEED:

5 cups fresh blueberries

juice from ½ lemon

2 tablespoons milk or cream

4 tablespoons flour

½ cup brown sugar

¼ teaspoon ground cinnamon

9-inch pie dish

mixing bowl, spatula, and whisk

## FOR THE CRUST:

2 ½ cups flour

1 teaspoon salt

¾ cup cold water

1 cup butter, chilled and cubed

1 egg for egg wash

1 teaspoon sugar

mixing bowl

pastry brush

OPTIONAL: cookie cutters

pastry cutter, knives, or forks

plastic wrap

rolling pin and spatula

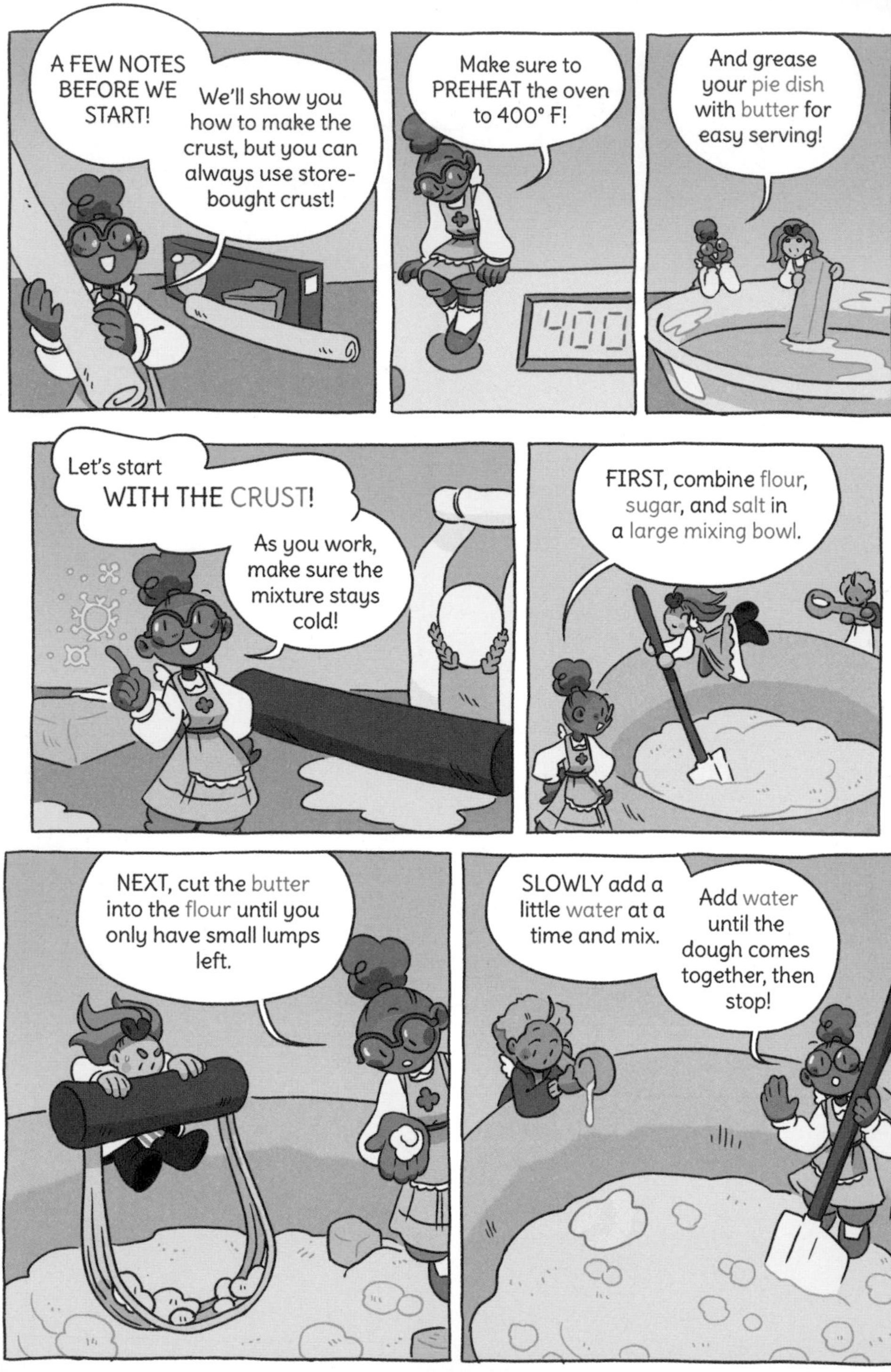
A FEW NOTES BEFORE WE START!
We'll show you how to make the crust, but you can always use store-bought crust!
Make sure to PREHEAT the oven to 400° F!
400
And grease your pie dish with butter for easy serving!
Let's start WITH THE CRUST!
As you work, make sure the mixture stays cold!
FIRST, combine flour, sugar, and salt in a large mixing bowl.
NEXT, cut the butter into the flour until you only have small lumps left.
SLOWLY add a little water at a time and mix.
Add water until the dough comes together, then stop!

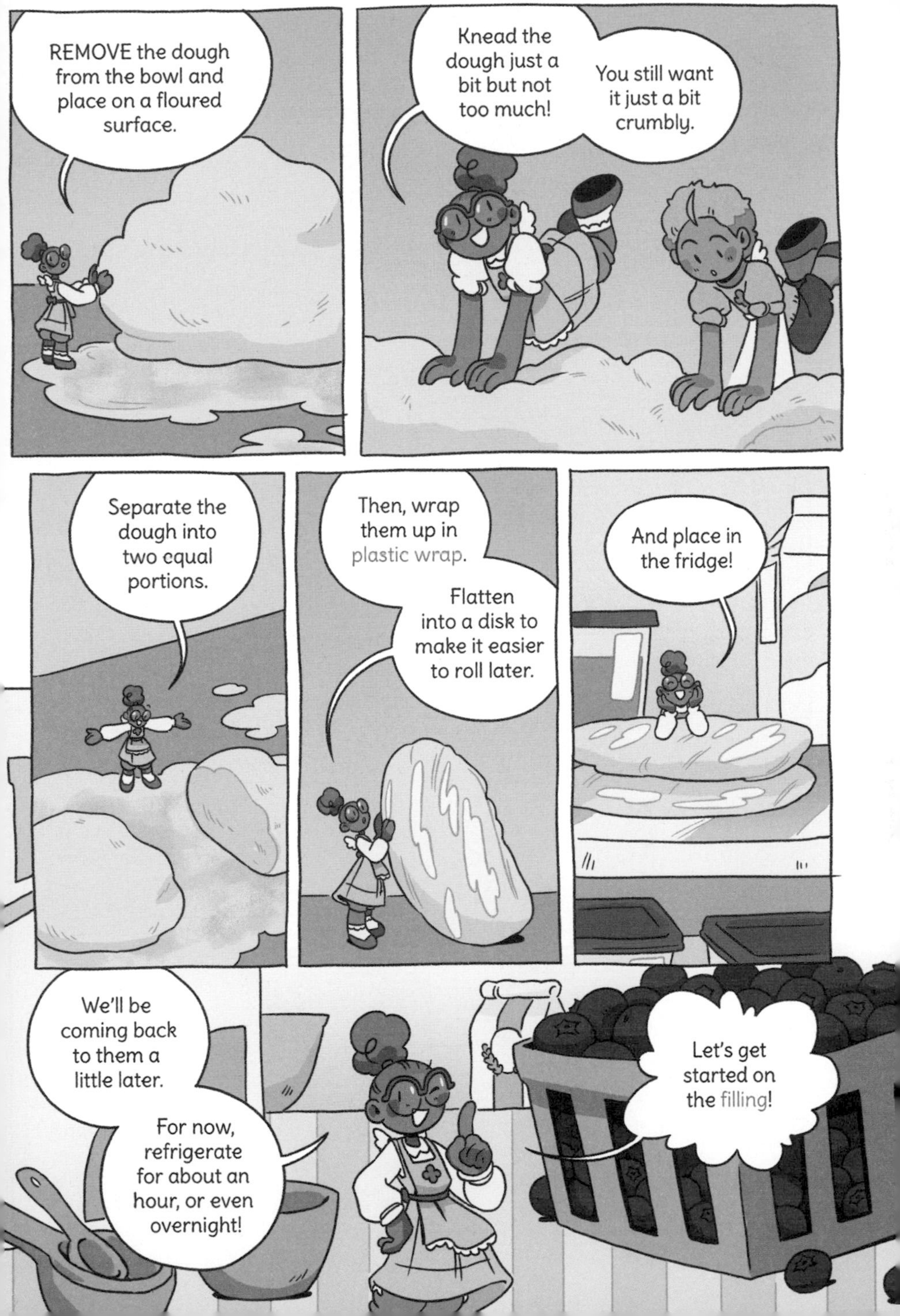
REMOVE the dough from the bowl and place on a floured surface.
Knead the dough just a bit but not too much!
You still want it just a bit crumbly.
Separate the dough into two equal portions.
Then, wrap them up in plastic wrap.
Flatten into a disk to make it easier to roll later.
And place in the fridge!
We'll be coming back to them a little later.
For now, refrigerate for about an hour, or even overnight!
Let's get started on the filling!

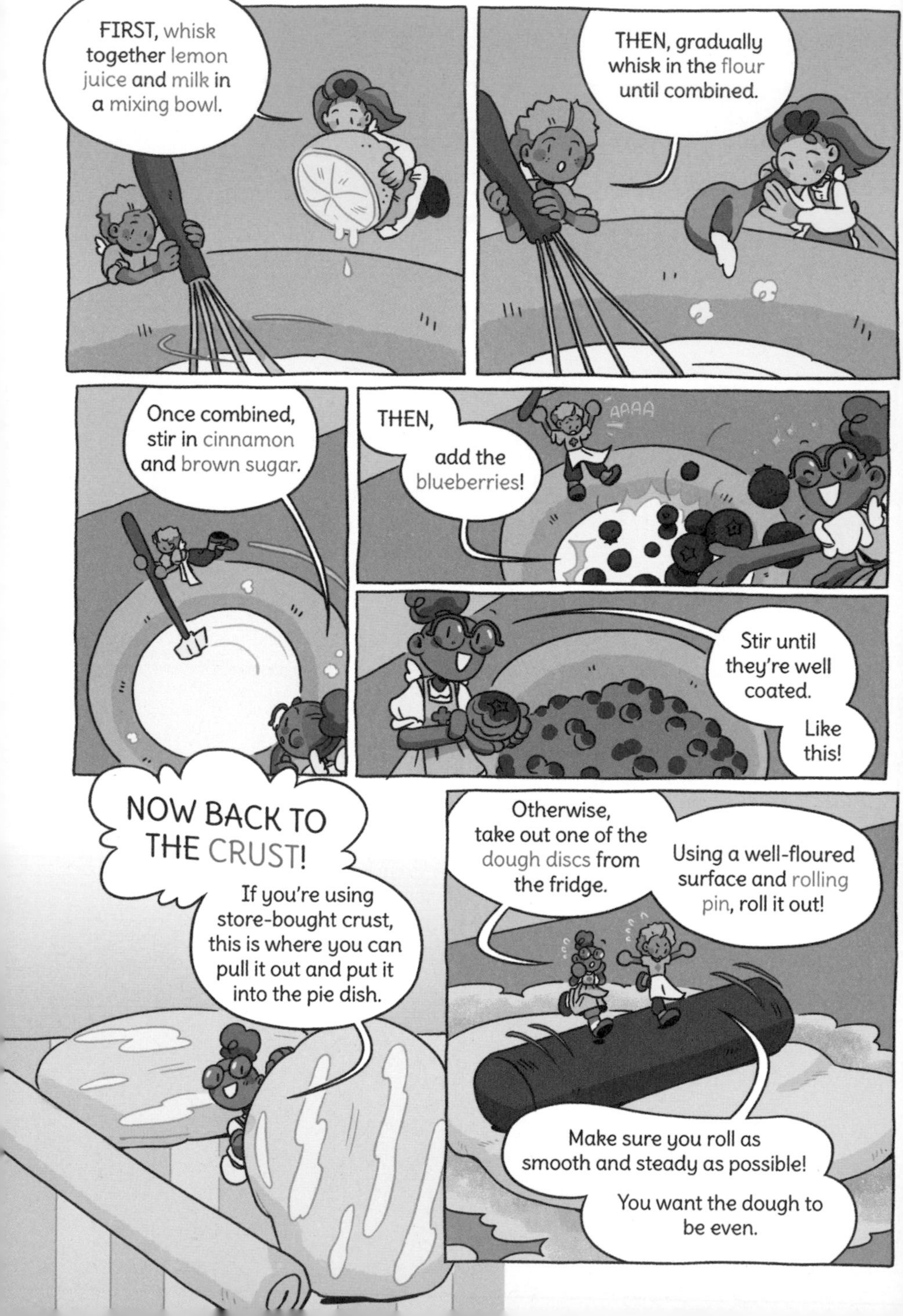
FIRST, whisk together lemon juice and milk in a mixing bowl.
THEN, gradually whisk in the flour until combined.
Once combined, stir in cinnamon and brown sugar.
THEN,
add the blueberries!
AAAA
Stir until they're well coated.
Like this!
NOW BACK TO THE CRUST!
If you're using store-bought crust, this is where you can pull it out and put it into the pie dish.
Otherwise, take out one of the dough discs from the fridge.
Using a well-floured surface and rolling pin, roll it out!
Make sure you roll as smooth and steady as possible!
You want the dough to be even.

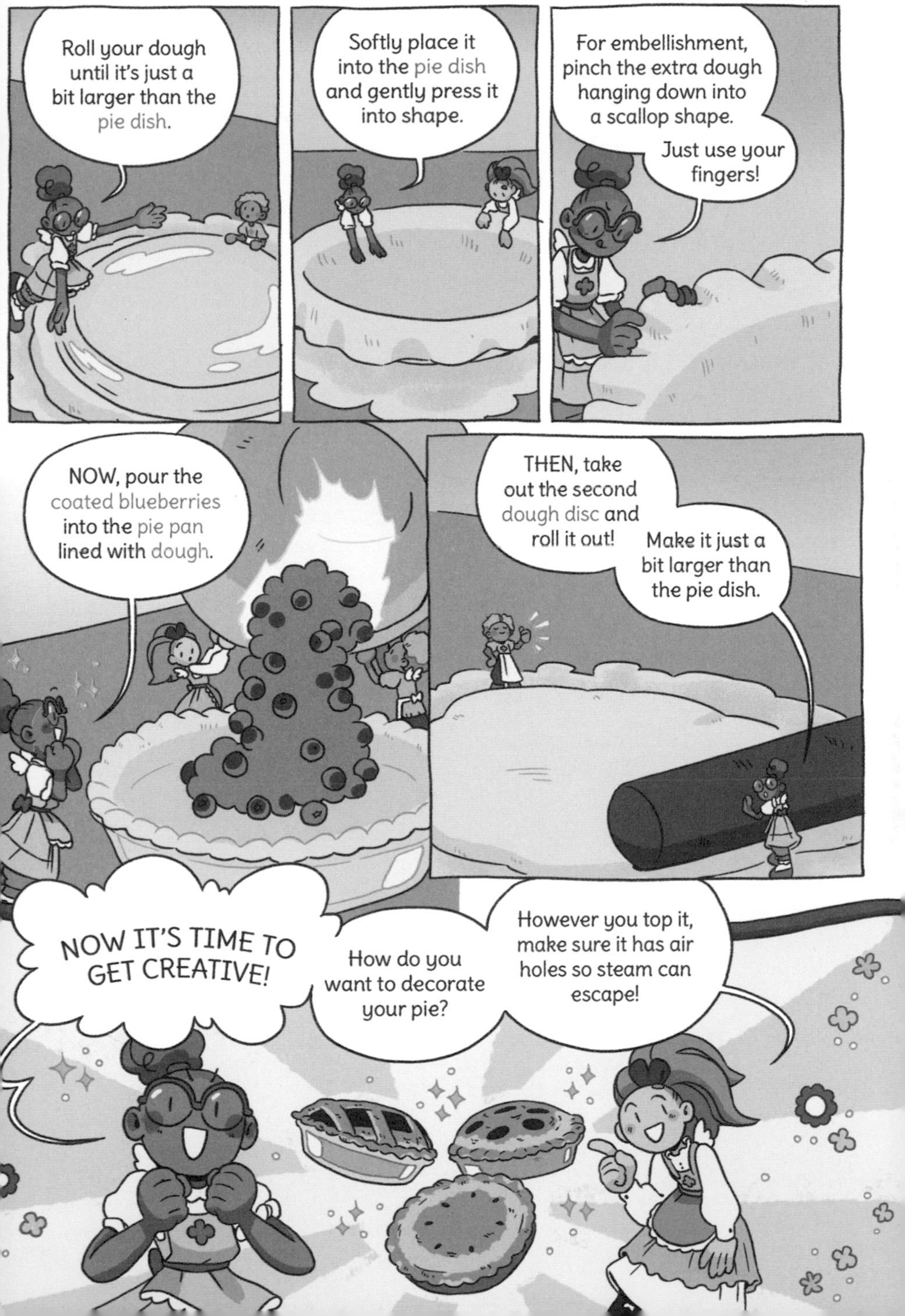
Roll your dough until it's just a bit larger than the pie dish.
Softly place it into the pie dish and gently press it into shape.
For embellishment, pinch the extra dough hanging down into a scallop shape.
Just use your fingers!
NOW, pour the coated blueberries into the pie pan lined with dough.
THEN, take out the second dough disc and roll it out!
Make it just a bit larger than the pie dish.
NOW IT'S TIME TO GET CREATIVE!
How do you want to decorate your pie?
However you top it, make sure it has air holes so steam can escape!

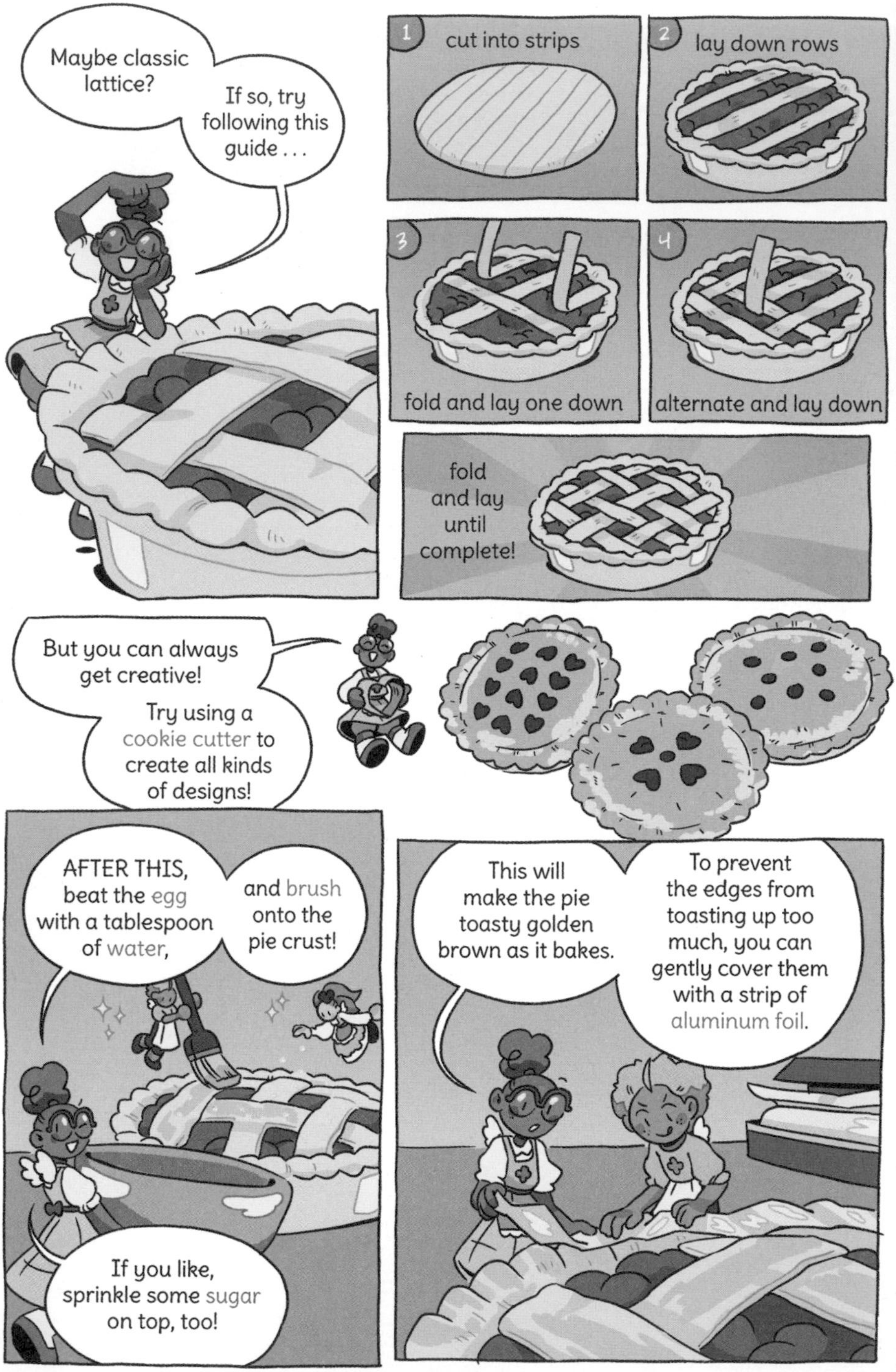

Maybe classic lattice?
If so, try following this guide . . .
1 cut into strips
2 lay down rows
3 fold and lay one down
4 alternate and lay down
fold and lay until complete!
But you can always get creative!
Try using a cookie cutter to create all kinds of designs!
AFTER THIS, beat the egg with a tablespoon of water,
and brush onto the pie crust!
If you like, sprinkle some sugar on top, too!
This will make the pie toasty golden brown as it bakes.
To prevent the edges from toasting up too much, you can gently cover them with a strip of aluminum foil.

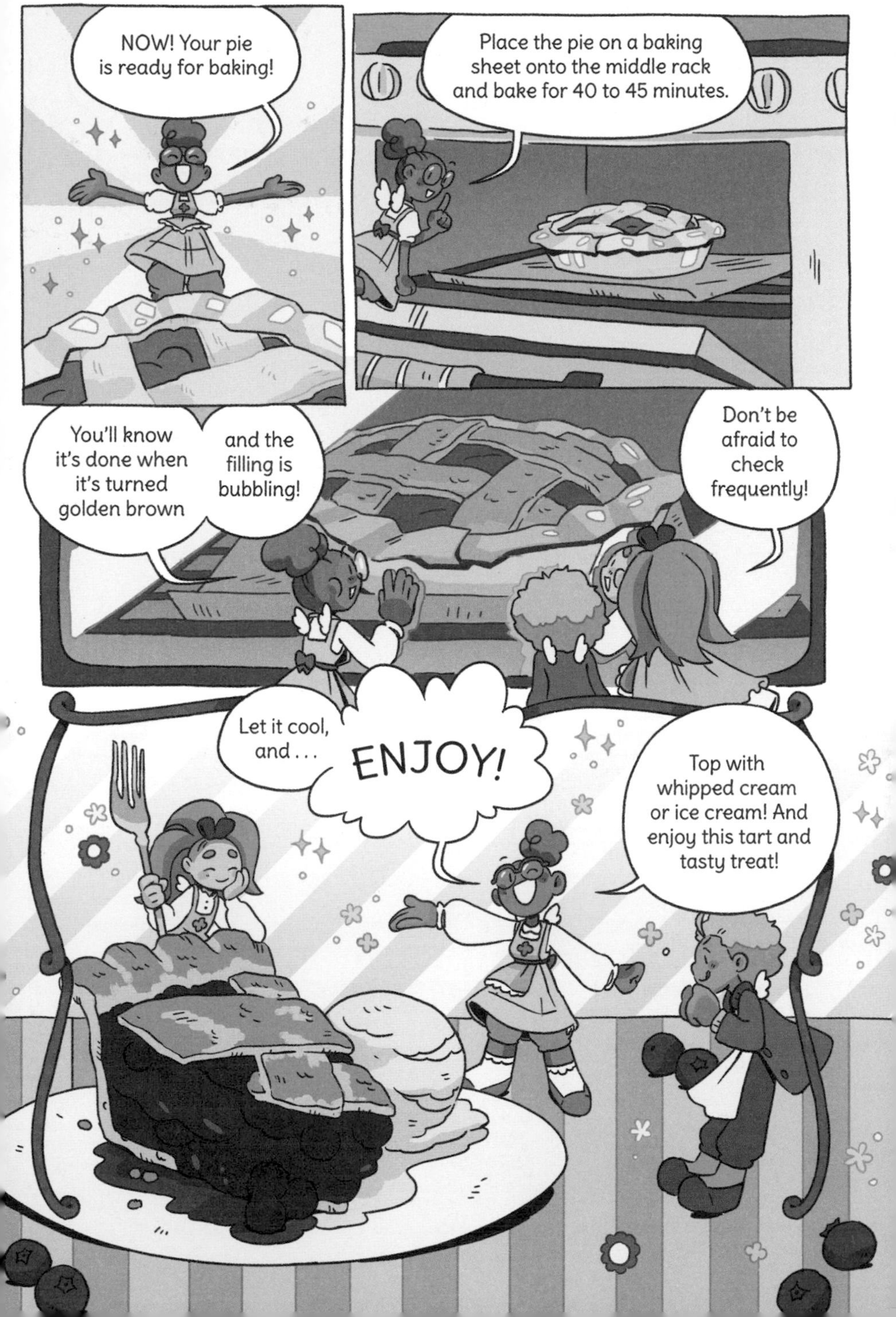
NOW! Your pie is ready for baking!
Place the pie on a baking sheet onto the middle rack and bake for 40 to 45 minutes.
You'll know it's done when it's turned golden brown
and the filling is bubbling!
Don't be afraid to check frequently!
Let it cool, and . . .
ENJOY!
Top with whipped cream or ice cream! And enjoy this tart and tasty treat!

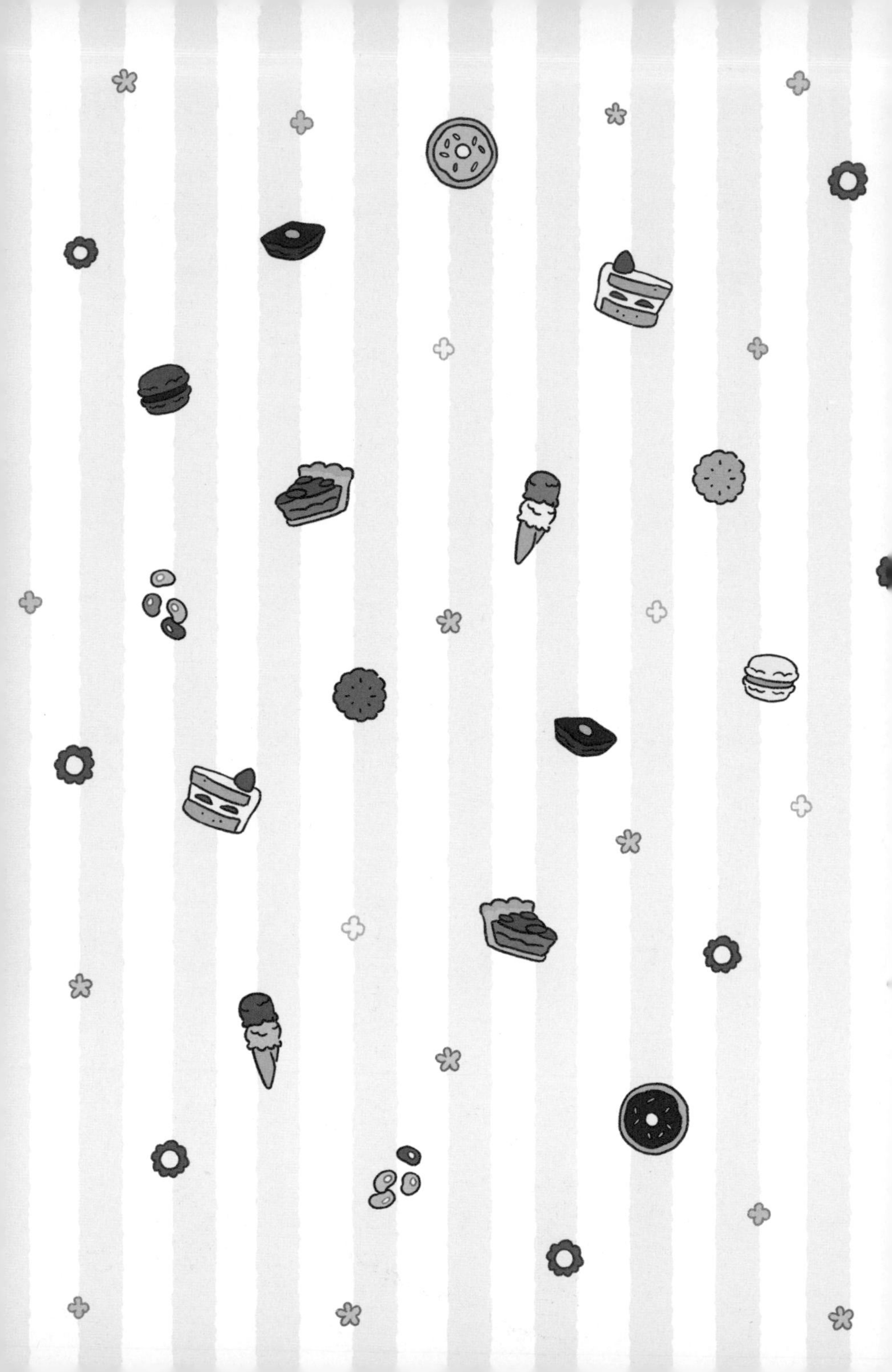

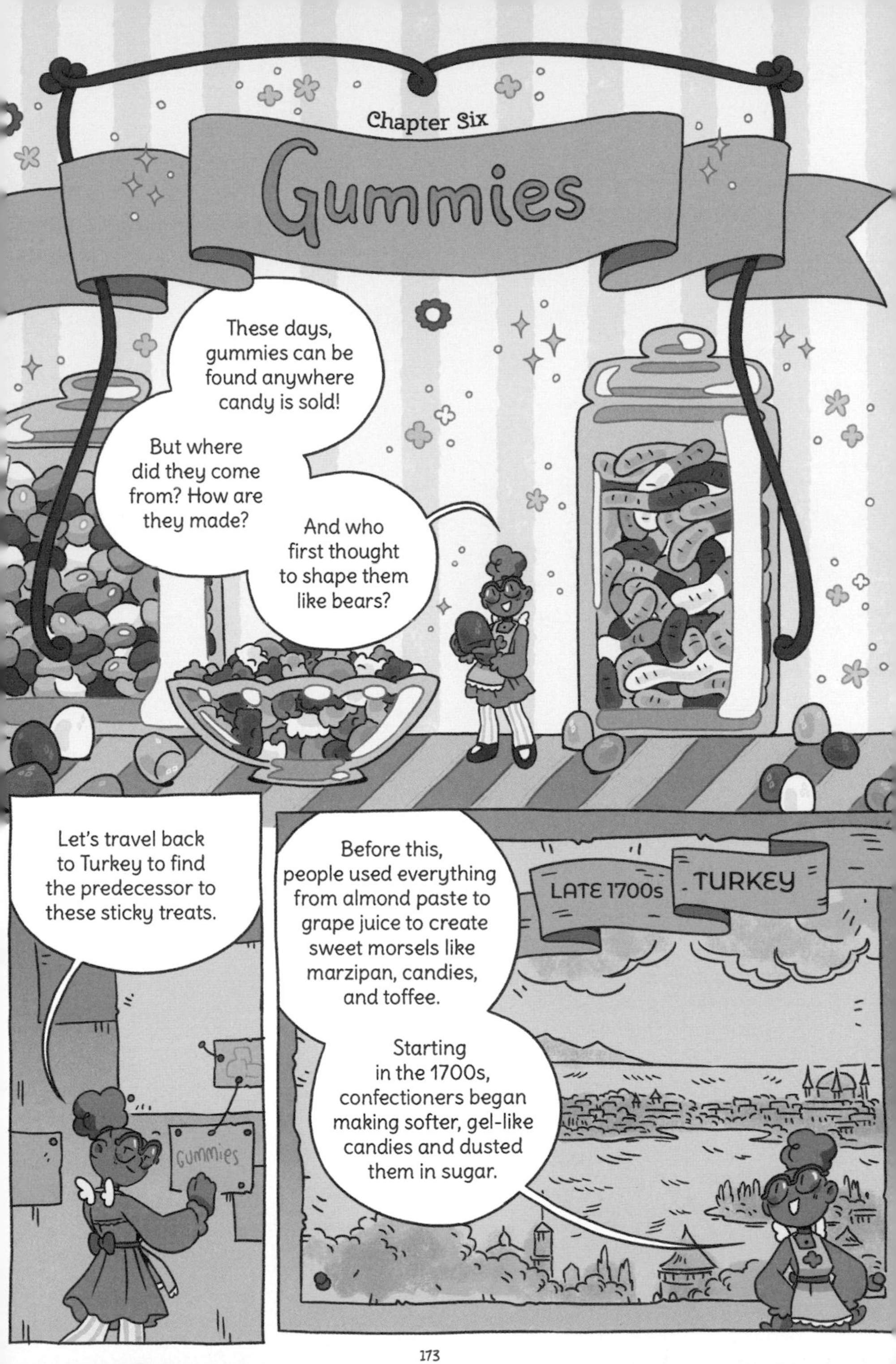
Chapter Six
Gummies
These days, gummies can be found anywhere candy is sold!
But where did they come from? How are they made?
And who first thought to shape them like bears?
Let's travel back to Turkey to find the predecessor to these sticky treats.
GUMMIES
LATE 1700s
TURKEY
Before this, people used everything from almond paste to grape juice to create sweet morsels like marzipan, candies, and toffee.
Starting in the 1700s, confectioners began making softer, gel-like candies and dusted them in sugar.

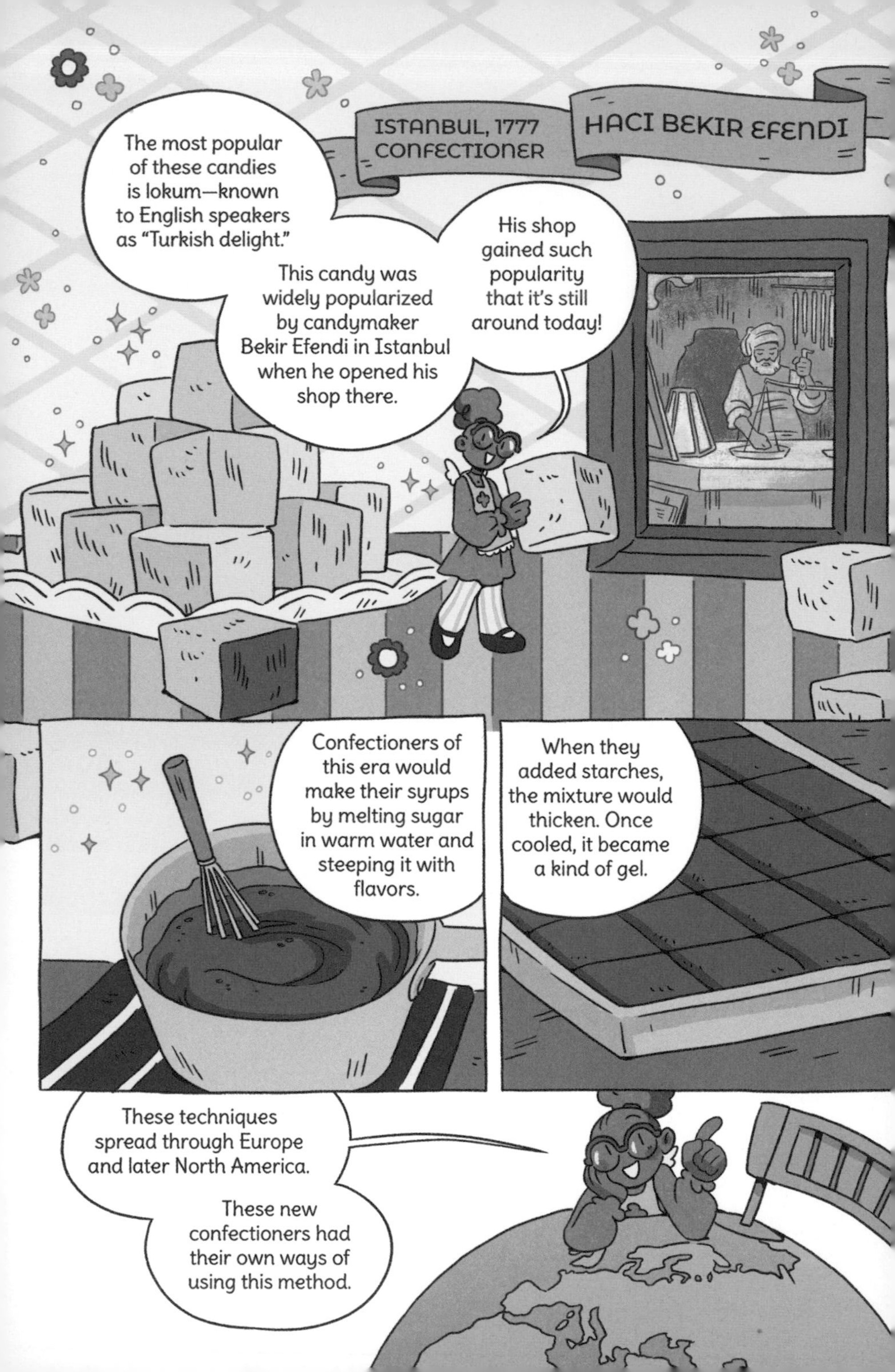
ISTANBUL, 1777 CONFECTIONER
HACI BEKIR EFENDI
The most popular of these candies is lokum—known to English speakers as "Turkish delight."
This candy was widely popularized by candymaker Bekir Efendi in Istanbul when he opened his shop there.
His shop gained such popularity that it's still around today!
Confectioners of this era would make their syrups by melting sugar in warm water and steeping it with flavors.
When they added starches, the mixture would thicken. Once cooled, it became a kind of gel.
These techniques spread through Europe and later North America.
These new confectioners had their own ways of using this method.

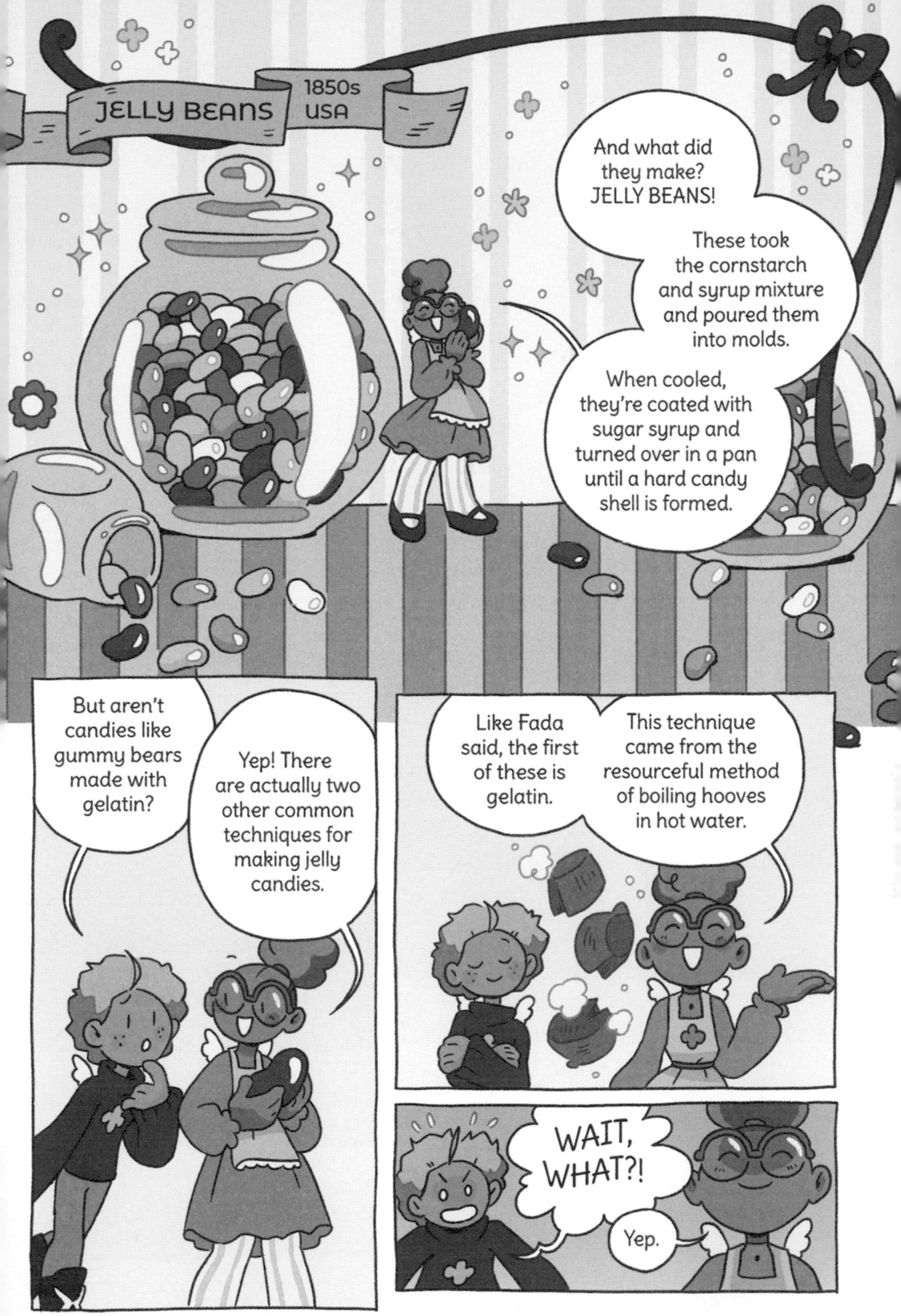
JELLY BEANS
1850s USA
And what did they make? JELLY BEANS!
These took the cornstarch and syrup mixture and poured them into molds.
When cooled, they're coated with sugar syrup and turned over in a pan until a hard candy shell is formed.
But aren't candies like gummy bears made with gelatin?
Yep! There are actually two other common techniques for making jelly candies.
Like Fada said, the first of these is gelatin.
This technique came from the resourceful method of boiling hooves in hot water.
WAIT, WHAT?!
Yep.

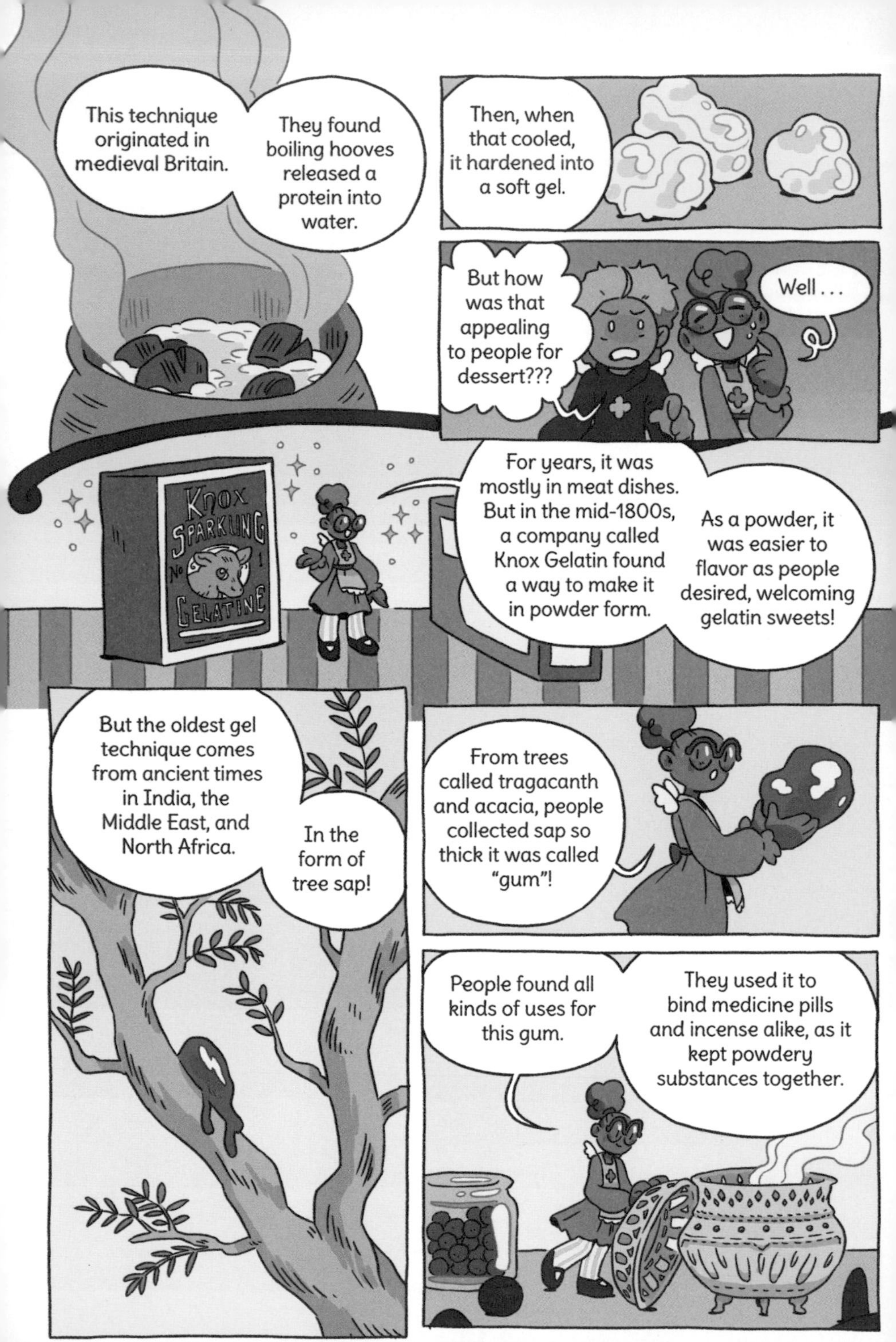
This technique originated in medieval Britain.
They found boiling hooves released a protein into water.
Then, when that cooled, it hardened into a soft gel.
But how was that appealing to people for dessert???
Well . . .
KNOX SPARKLING No 1 GELATINE
For years, it was mostly in meat dishes. But in the mid-1800s, a company called Knox Gelatin found a way to make it in powder form.
As a powder, it was easier to flavor as people desired, welcoming gelatin sweets!
But the oldest gel technique comes from ancient times in India, the Middle East, and North Africa.
In the form of tree sap!
From trees called tragacanth and acacia, people collected sap so thick it was called "gum"!
People found all kinds of uses for this gum.
They used it to bind medicine pills and incense alike, as it kept powdery substances together.

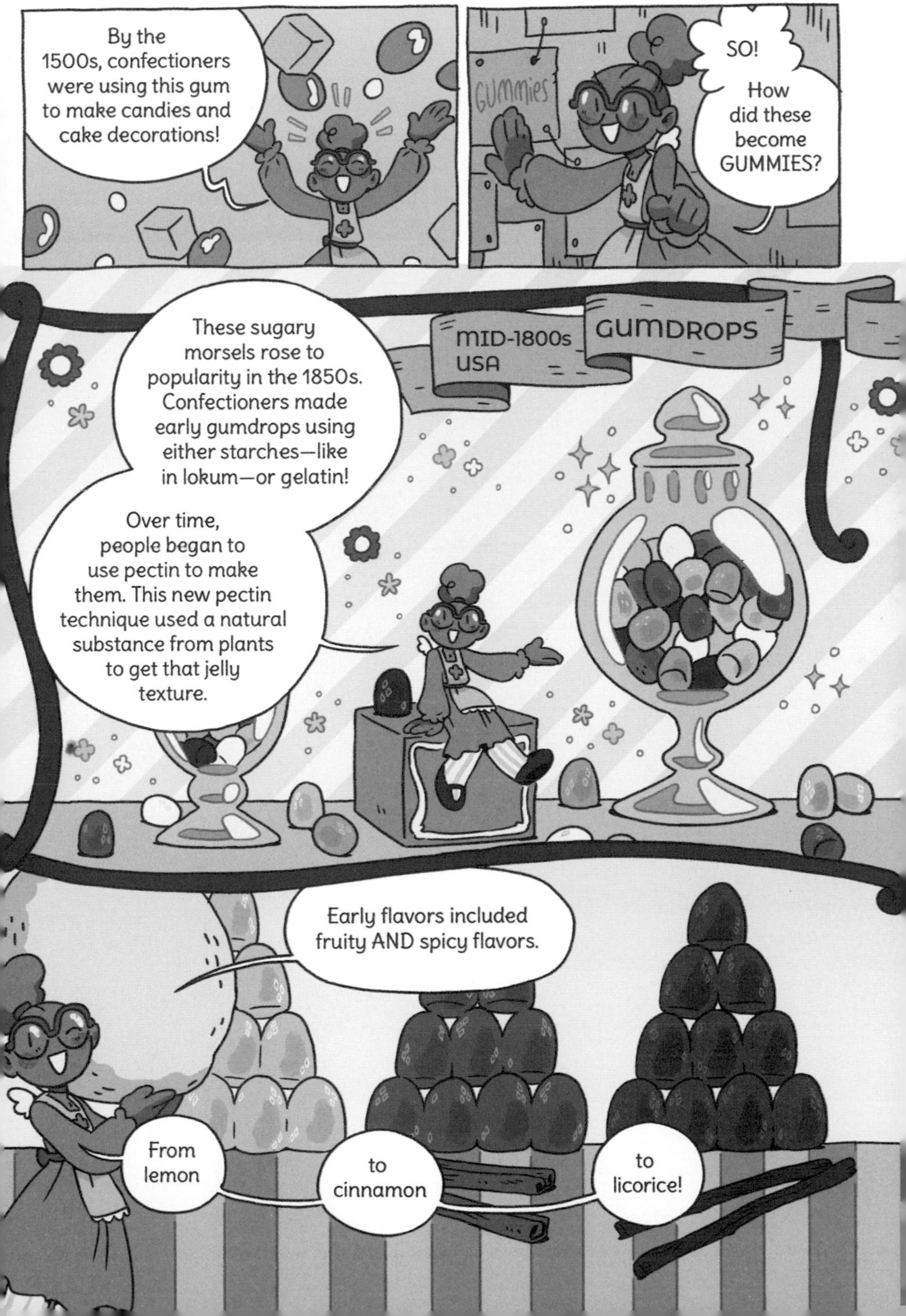
By the 1500s, confectioners were using this gum to make candies and cake decorations!
GUMMIES
SO!
How did these become GUMMIES?
MID-1800s USA
GUMDROPS
These sugary morsels rose to popularity in the 1850s. Confectioners made early gumdrops using either starches—like in lokum—or gelatin!
Over time, people began to use pectin to make them. This new pectin technique used a natural substance from plants to get that jelly texture.
Early flavors included fruity AND spicy flavors.
From lemon
to cinnamon
to licorice!

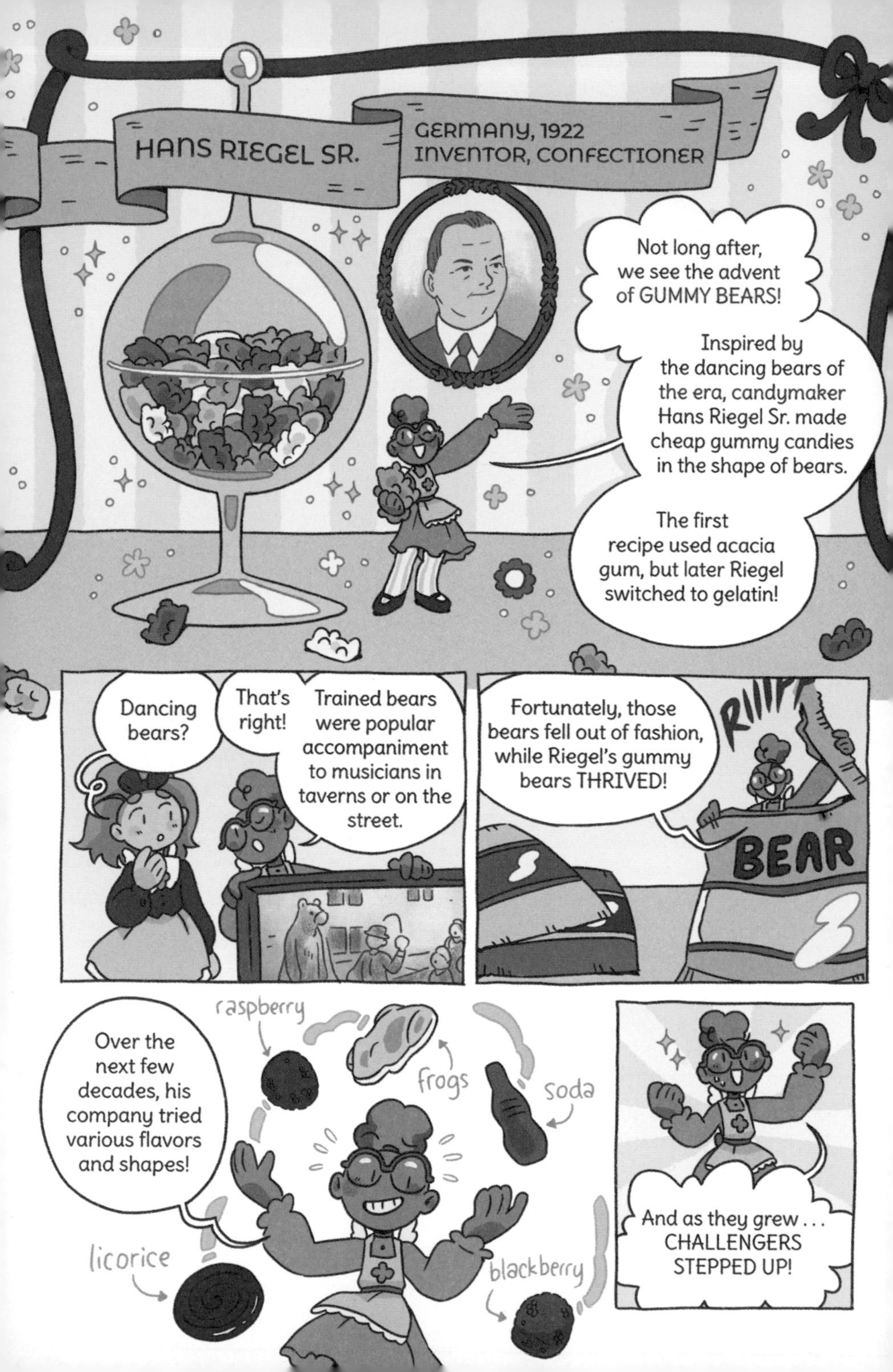
HANS RIEGEL SR.
GERMANY, 1922
INVENTOR, CONFECTIONER
Not long after, we see the advent of GUMMY BEARS!
Inspired by the dancing bears of the era, candymaker Hans Riegel Sr. made cheap gummy candies in the shape of bears.
The first recipe used acacia gum, but later Riegel switched to gelatin!
Dancing bears?
That's right!
Trained bears were popular accompaniment to musicians in taverns or on the street.
Fortunately, those bears fell out of fashion, while Riegel's gummy bears THRIVED!
RIIIPP
BEAR
Over the next few decades, his company tried various flavors and shapes!
raspberry
frogs
soda
licorice
blackberry
And as they grew . . . CHALLENGERS STEPPED UP!

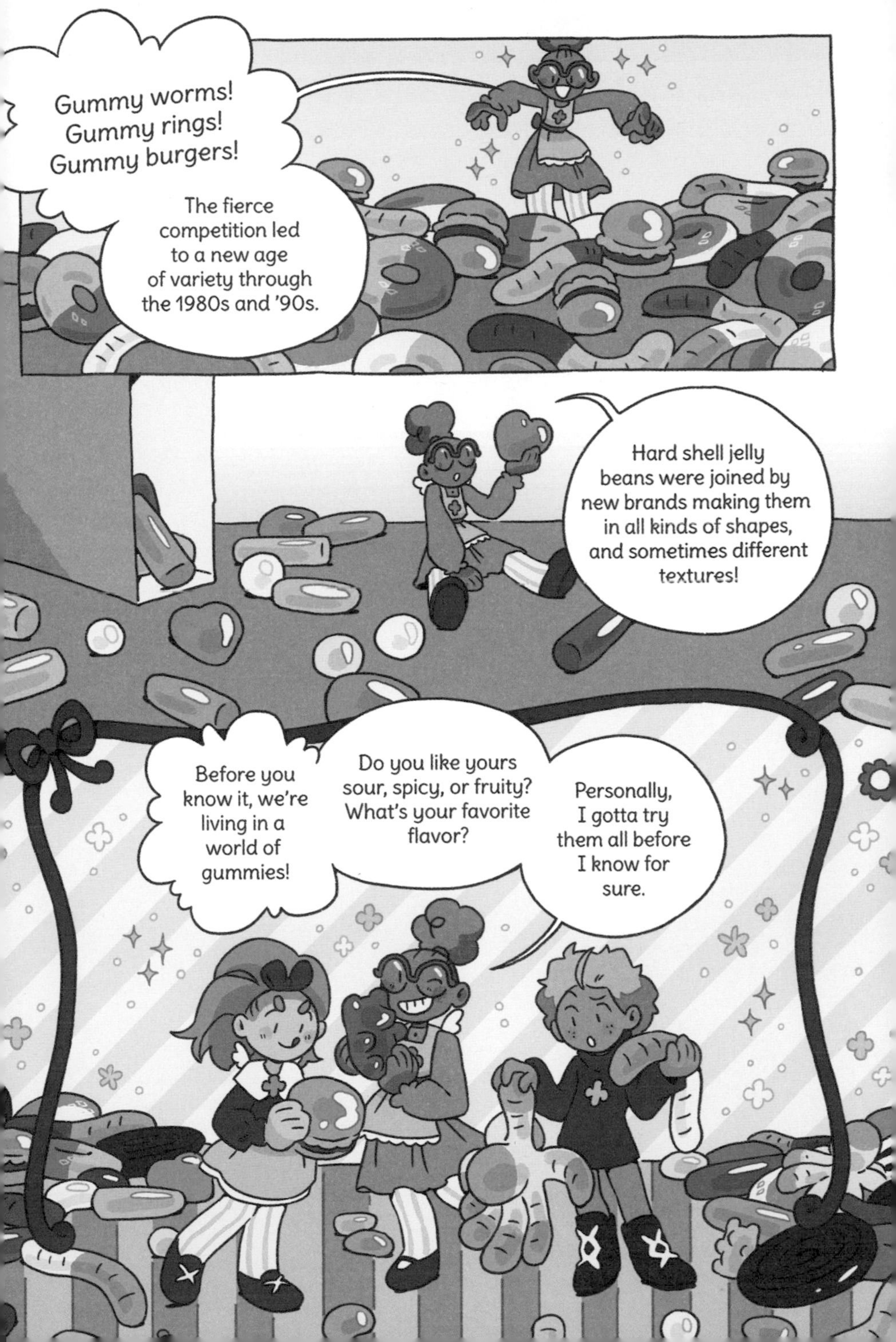
Gummy worms! Gummy rings! Gummy burgers!
The fierce competition led to a new age of variety through the 1980s and '90s.
Hard shell jelly beans were joined by new brands making them in all kinds of shapes, and sometimes different textures!
Before you know it, we're living in a world of gummies!
Do you like yours sour, spicy, or fruity? What's your favorite flavor?
Personally, I gotta try them all before I know for sure.

# The Abridged Atlas of Cookie History

1 Ancient Roman Biscotus

2 Spread of Almond Flour Use from Islamic Cultures to Sicily

3 Persian and Arabic Qurabiya

4 Italian Biscotti

5 Egyptian Kahk

6 Levantine Ma'amoul

7 European Gingerbread

8 Indian and Pakistani Nankhatai

9 European Molded Spice Cookies

10 French Madeleines

11 Scottish Shortbread

12 Maria Sanders van Rensselaer's Handwritten Cook Book

13 British and Dutch Industrial Cookie Culture

14 Regions of Maria Cookie Traditions

15 American Drop Cookies

16 Ruth Graves Wakefield's *Toll House Tried and True Recipes*

17 Southeast Asian Kuih Cookie Traditions

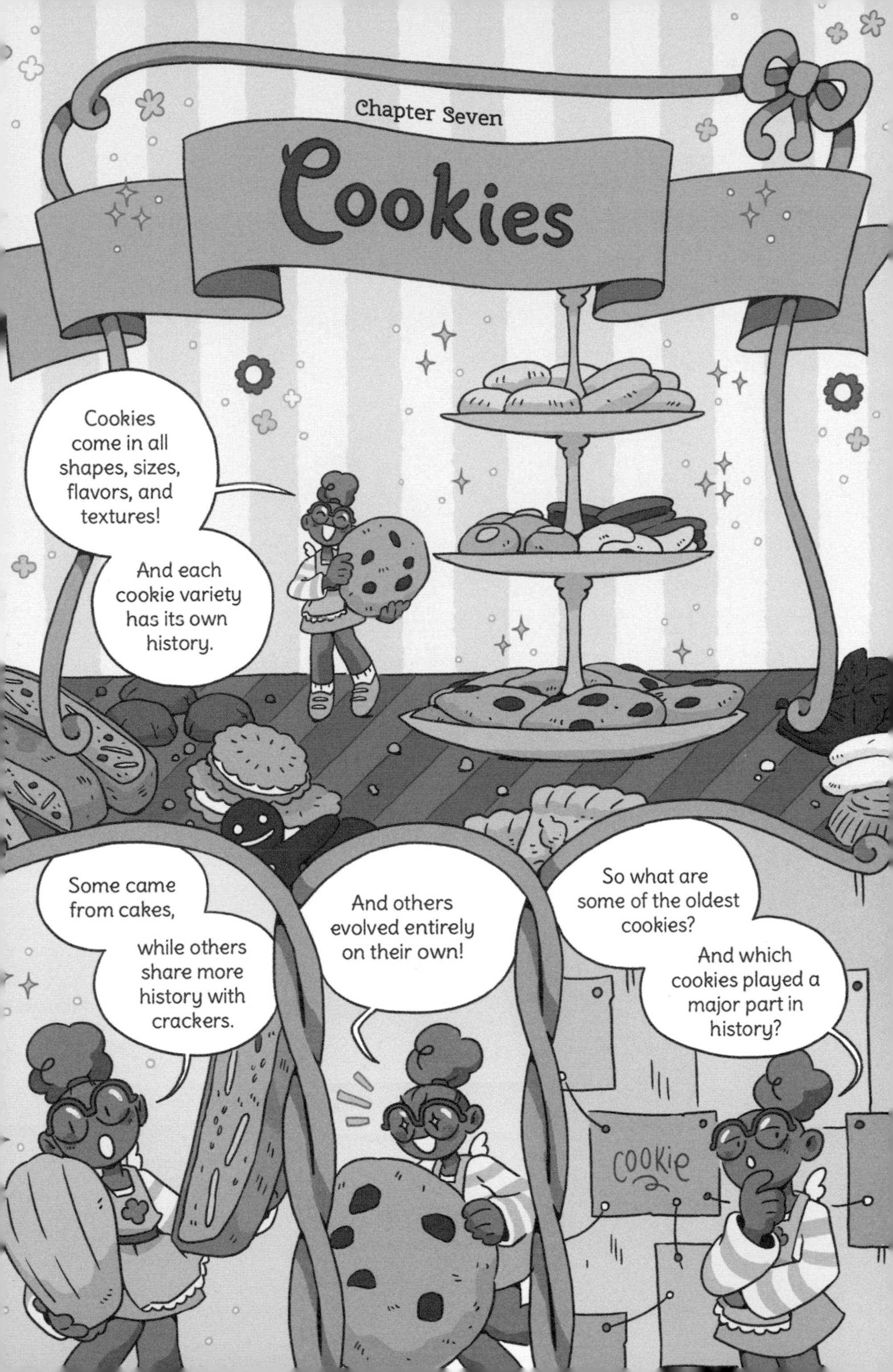

Chapter Seven
Cookies
Cookies come in all shapes, sizes, flavors, and textures!
And each cookie variety has its own history.
Some came from cakes,
while others share more history with crackers.
And others evolved entirely on their own!
So what are some of the oldest cookies?
And which cookies played a major part in history?
COOKIE

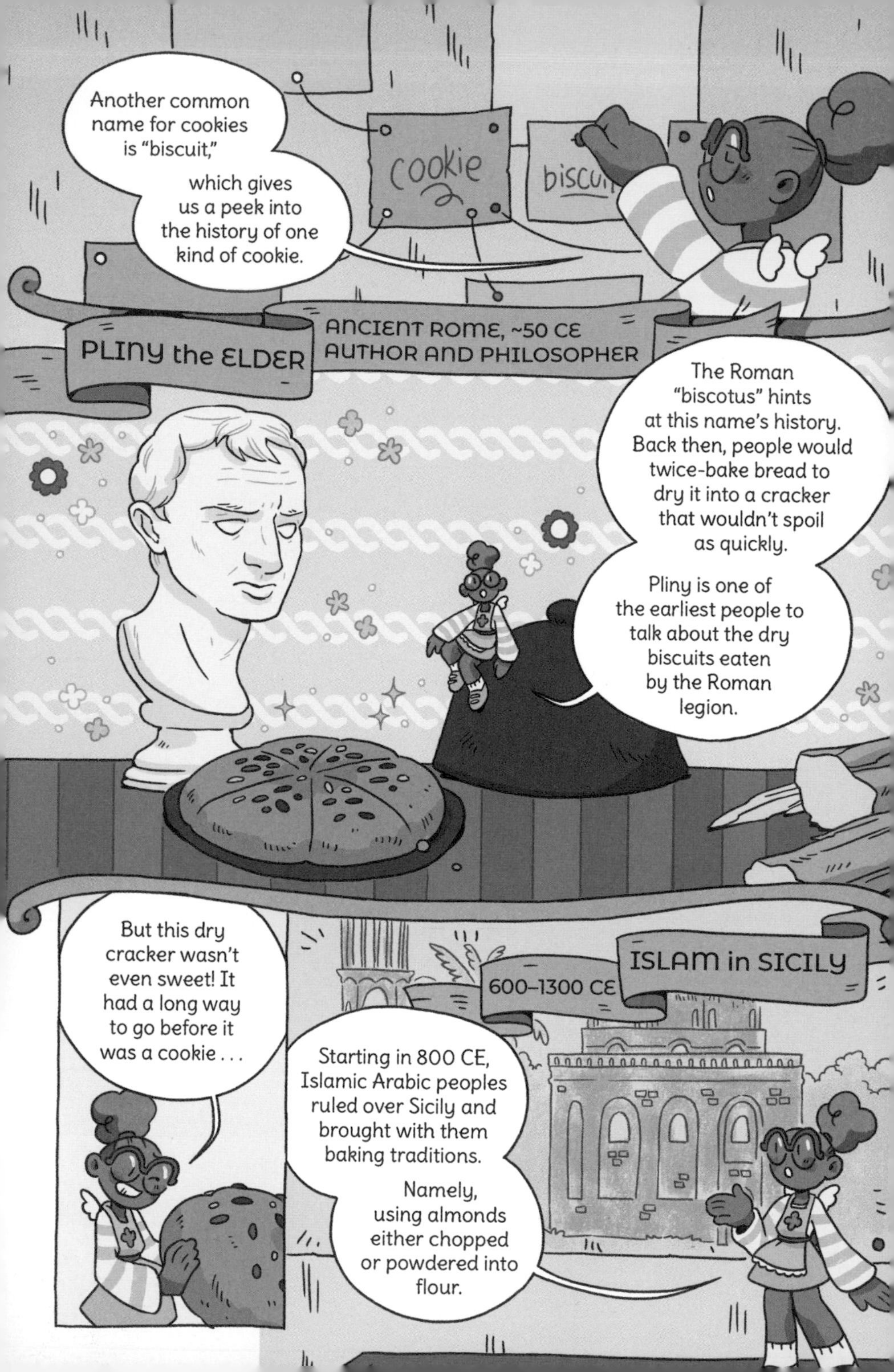
Another common name for cookies is "biscuit,"
which gives us a peek into the history of one kind of cookie.
cookie
biscu
PLINY the ELDER
ANCIENT ROME, ~50 CE
AUTHOR AND PHILOSOPHER
The Roman "biscotus" hints at this name's history. Back then, people would twice-bake bread to dry it into a cracker that wouldn't spoil as quickly.
Pliny is one of the earliest people to talk about the dry biscuits eaten by the Roman legion.
But this dry cracker wasn't even sweet! It had a long way to go before it was a cookie . . .
ISLAM in SICILY
600–1300 CE
Starting in 800 CE, Islamic Arabic peoples ruled over Sicily and brought with them baking traditions.
Namely, using almonds either chopped or powdered into flour.

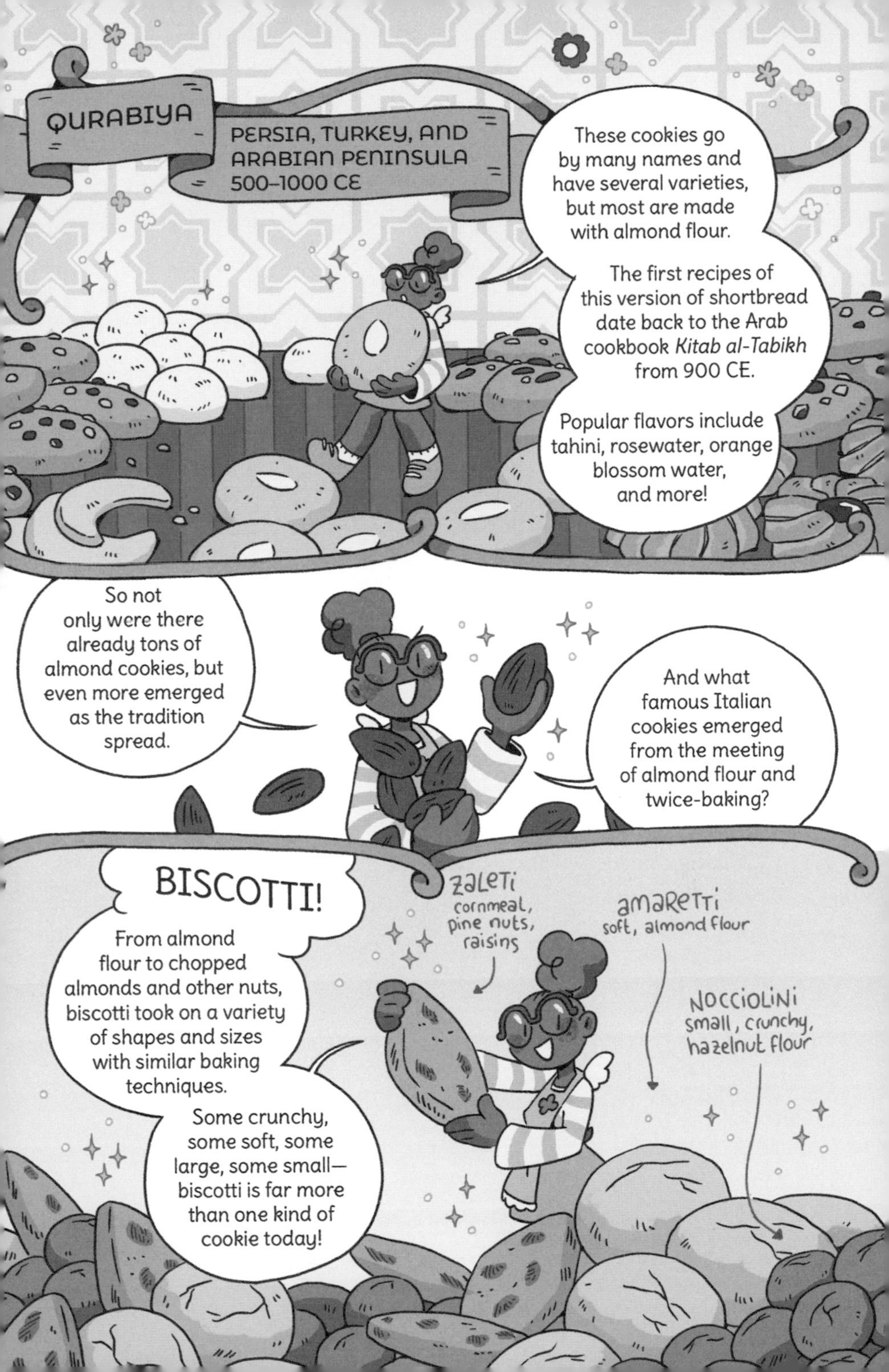
QURABIYA
PERSIA, TURKEY, AND ARABIAN PENINSULA 500–1000 CE
These cookies go by many names and have several varieties, but most are made with almond flour.
The first recipes of this version of shortbread date back to the Arab cookbook *Kitab al-Tabikh* from 900 CE.
Popular flavors include tahini, rosewater, orange blossom water, and more!
So not only were there already tons of almond cookies, but even more emerged as the tradition spread.
And what famous Italian cookies emerged from the meeting of almond flour and twice-baking?
BISCOTTI!
From almond flour to chopped almonds and other nuts, biscotti took on a variety of shapes and sizes with similar baking techniques.
Some crunchy, some soft, some large, some small—biscotti is far more than one kind of cookie today!
ZALETI cornmeal, pine nuts, raisins
AMARETTI soft, almond flour
NOCCIOLINI small, crunchy, hazelnut flour

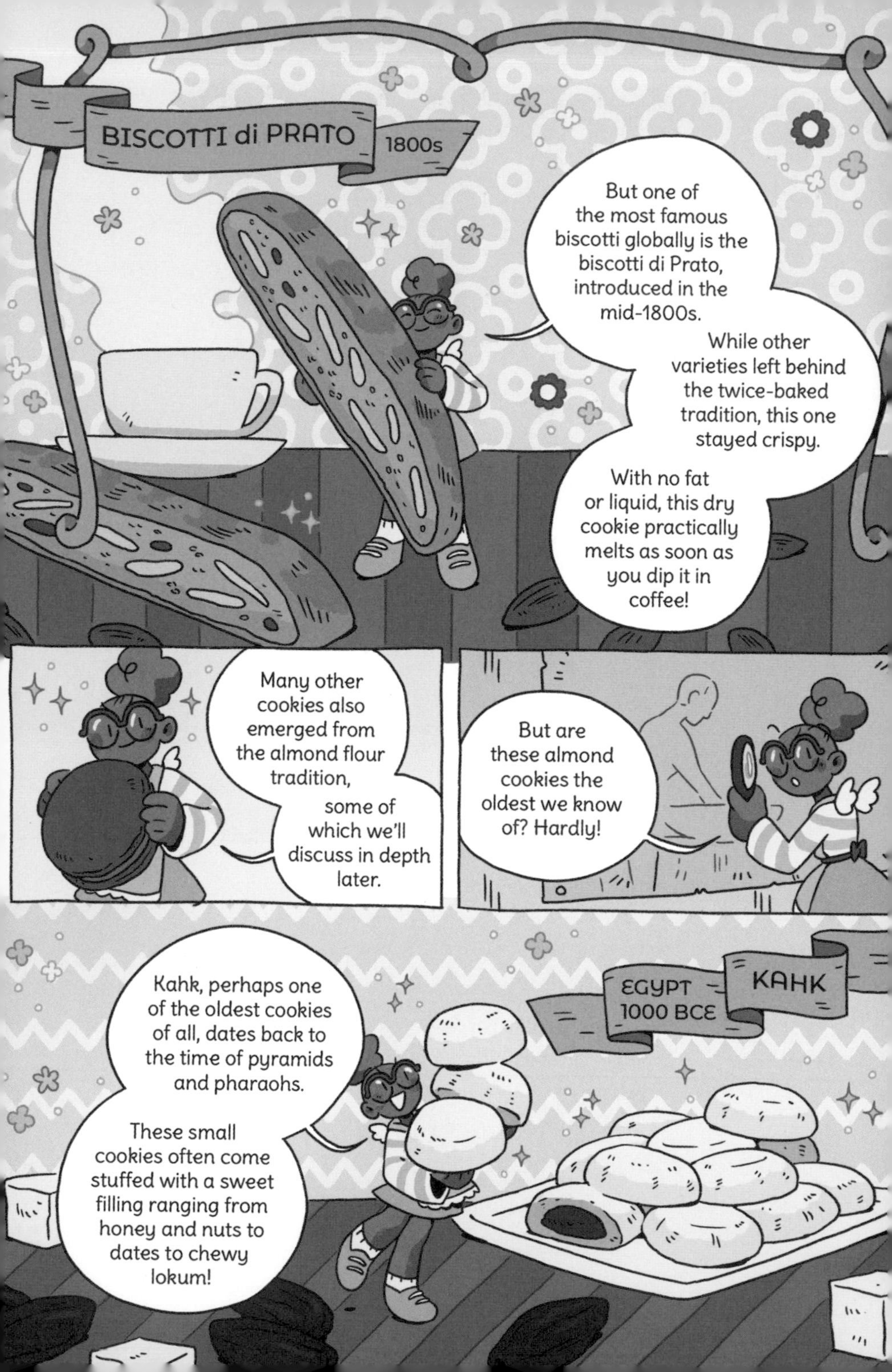

BISCOTTI di PRATO
1800s
But one of the most famous biscotti globally is the biscotti di Prato, introduced in the mid-1800s.
While other varieties left behind the twice-baked tradition, this one stayed crispy.
With no fat or liquid, this dry cookie practically melts as soon as you dip it in coffee!
Many other cookies also emerged from the almond flour tradition,
some of which we'll discuss in depth later.
But are these almond cookies the oldest we know of? Hardly!
KAHK
EGYPT 1000 BCE
Kahk, perhaps one of the oldest cookies of all, dates back to the time of pyramids and pharaohs.
These small cookies often come stuffed with a sweet filling ranging from honey and nuts to dates to chewy lokum!

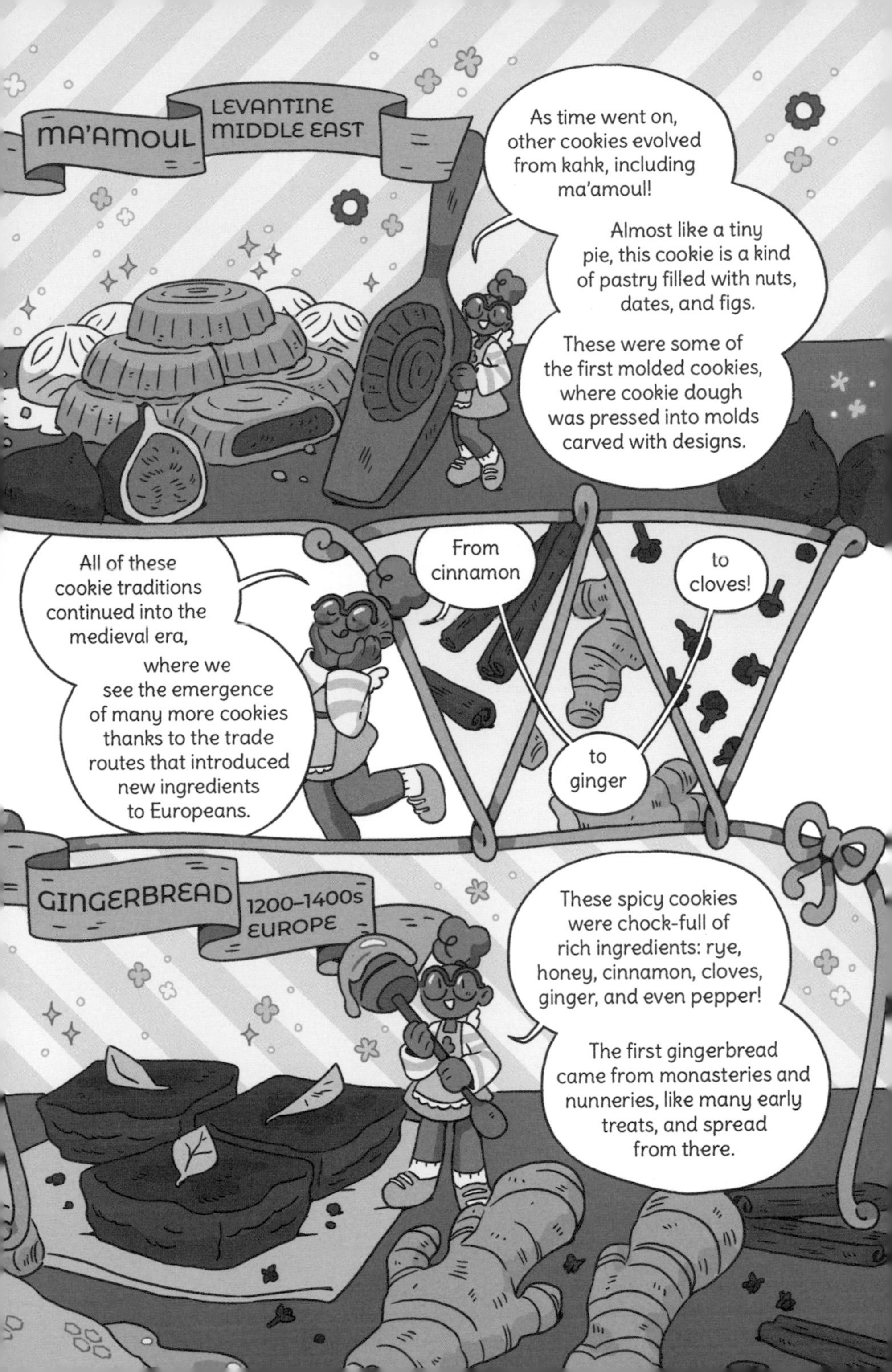
MA'AMOUL
LEVANTINE MIDDLE EAST
As time went on, other cookies evolved from kahk, including ma'amoul!
Almost like a tiny pie, this cookie is a kind of pastry filled with nuts, dates, and figs.
These were some of the first molded cookies, where cookie dough was pressed into molds carved with designs.
All of these cookie traditions continued into the medieval era,
where we see the emergence of many more cookies thanks to the trade routes that introduced new ingredients to Europeans.
From cinnamon
to ginger
to cloves!
GINGERBREAD
1200–1400s EUROPE
These spicy cookies were chock-full of rich ingredients: rye, honey, cinnamon, cloves, ginger, and even pepper!
The first gingerbread came from monasteries and nunneries, like many early treats, and spread from there.

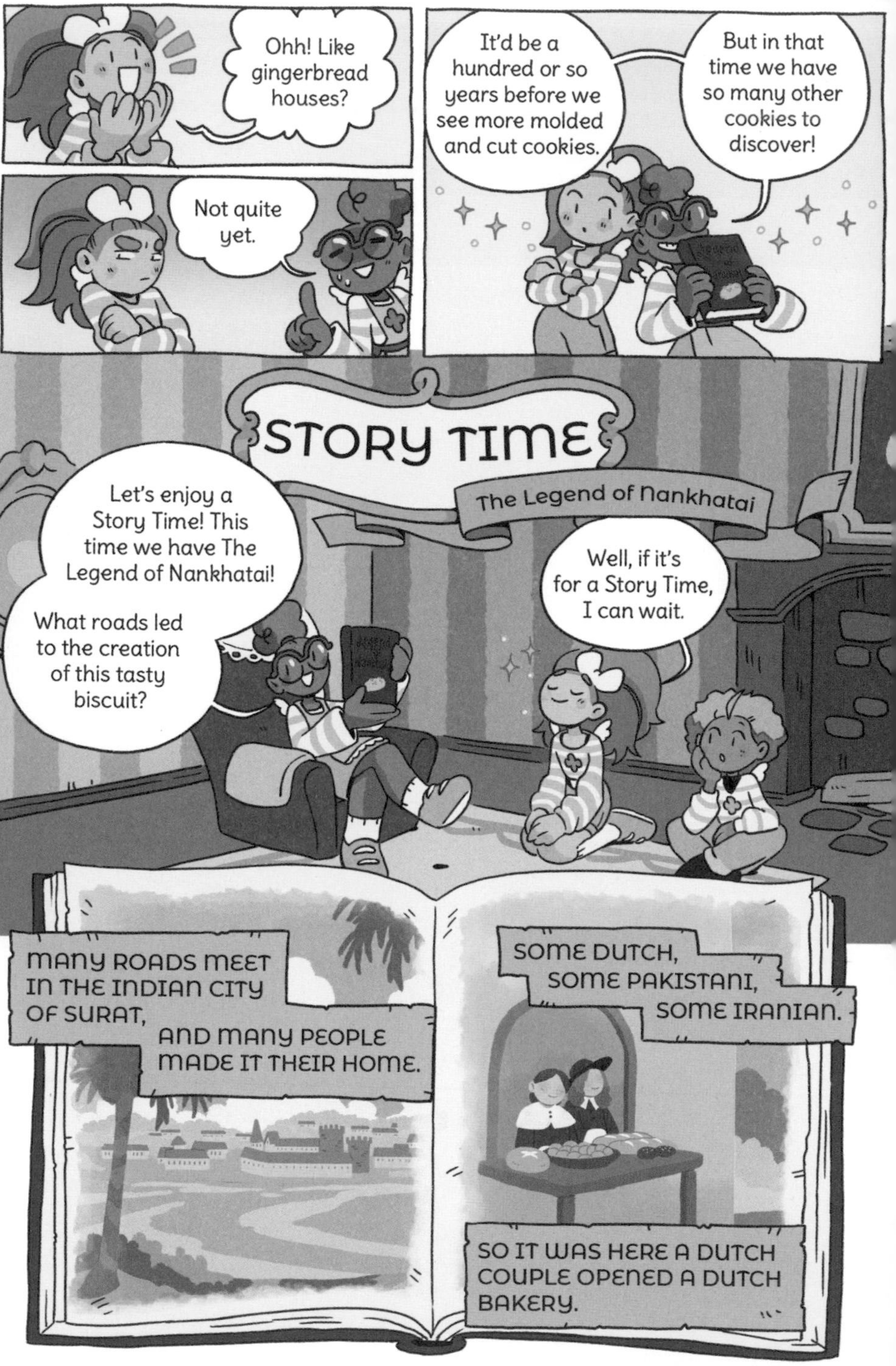

Ohh! Like gingerbread houses?
Not quite yet.
It'd be a hundred or so years before we see more molded and cut cookies.
But in that time we have so many other cookies to discover!
STORY TIME
The Legend of Nankhatai
Let's enjoy a Story Time! This time we have The Legend of Nankhatai!
What roads led to the creation of this tasty biscuit?
Well, if it's for a Story Time, I can wait.
MANY ROADS MEET IN THE INDIAN CITY OF SURAT,
AND MANY PEOPLE MADE IT THEIR HOME.
SOME DUTCH,
SOME PAKISTANI,
SOME IRANIAN.
SO IT WAS HERE A DUTCH COUPLE OPENED A DUTCH BAKERY.

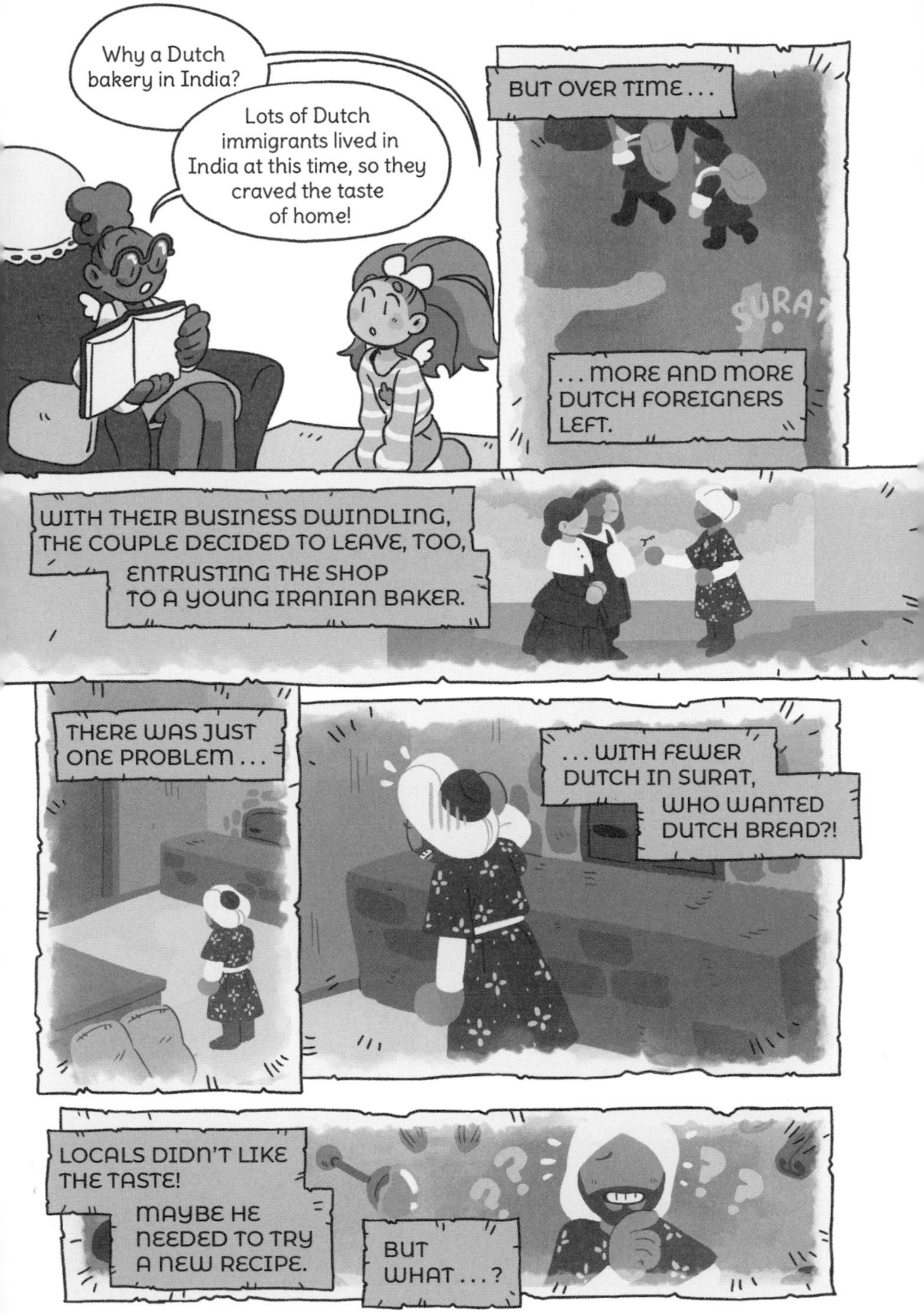
Why a Dutch bakery in India?
Lots of Dutch immigrants lived in India at this time, so they craved the taste of home!
BUT OVER TIME . . .
SURAT
. . . MORE AND MORE DUTCH FOREIGNERS LEFT.
WITH THEIR BUSINESS DWINDLING, THE COUPLE DECIDED TO LEAVE, TOO, ENTRUSTING THE SHOP TO A YOUNG IRANIAN BAKER.
THERE WAS JUST ONE PROBLEM . . .
. . . WITH FEWER DUTCH IN SURAT, WHO WANTED DUTCH BREAD?!
LOCALS DIDN'T LIKE THE TASTE!
MAYBE HE NEEDED TO TRY A NEW RECIPE.
BUT WHAT . . . ?

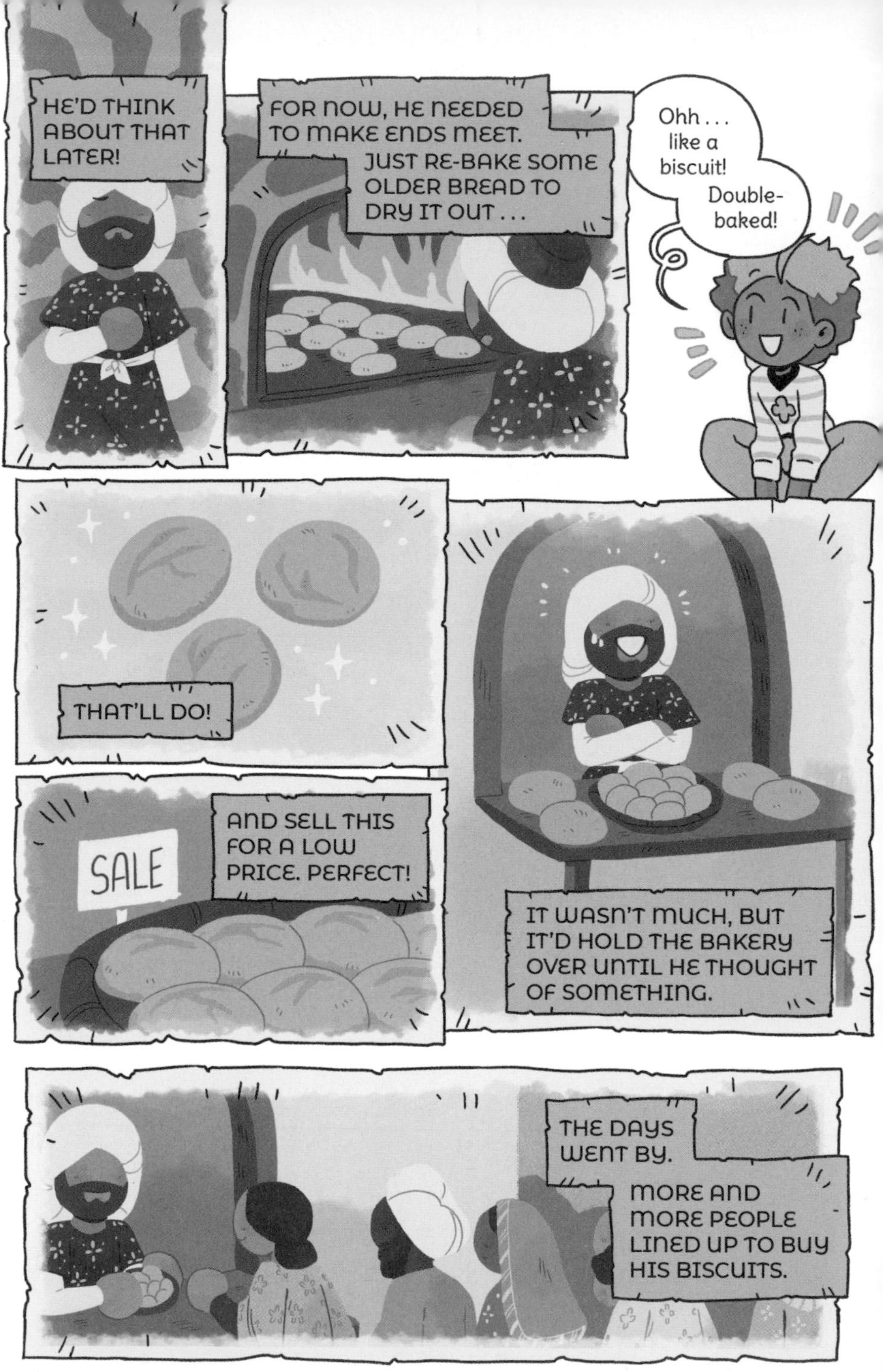

HE'D THINK ABOUT THAT LATER!
FOR NOW, HE NEEDED TO MAKE ENDS MEET.
JUST RE-BAKE SOME OLDER BREAD TO DRY IT OUT . . .
Ohh . . . like a biscuit!
Double-baked!
THAT'LL DO!
AND SELL THIS FOR A LOW PRICE. PERFECT!
SALE
IT WASN'T MUCH, BUT IT'D HOLD THE BAKERY OVER UNTIL HE THOUGHT OF SOMETHING.
THE DAYS WENT BY.
MORE AND MORE PEOPLE LINED UP TO BUY HIS BISCUITS.

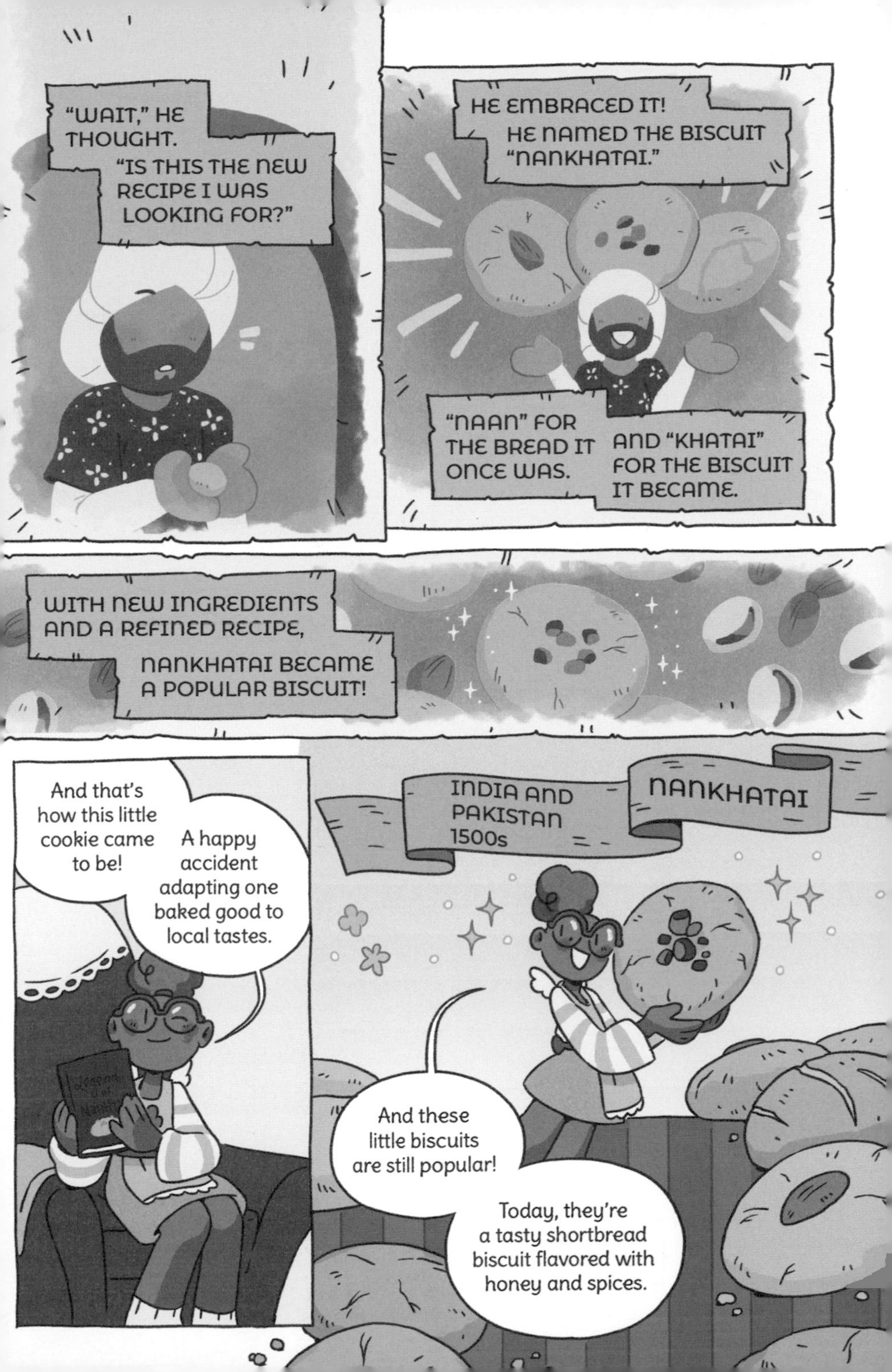
"WAIT," HE THOUGHT.
"IS THIS THE NEW RECIPE I WAS LOOKING FOR?"
HE EMBRACED IT!
HE NAMED THE BISCUIT "NANKHATAI."
"NAAN" FOR THE BREAD IT ONCE WAS.
AND "KHATAI" FOR THE BISCUIT IT BECAME.
WITH NEW INGREDIENTS AND A REFINED RECIPE,
NANKHATAI BECAME A POPULAR BISCUIT!
And that's how this little cookie came to be!
A happy accident adapting one baked good to local tastes.
INDIA AND PAKISTAN 1500s
NANKHATAI
And these little biscuits are still popular!
Today, they're a tasty shortbread biscuit flavored with honey and spices.

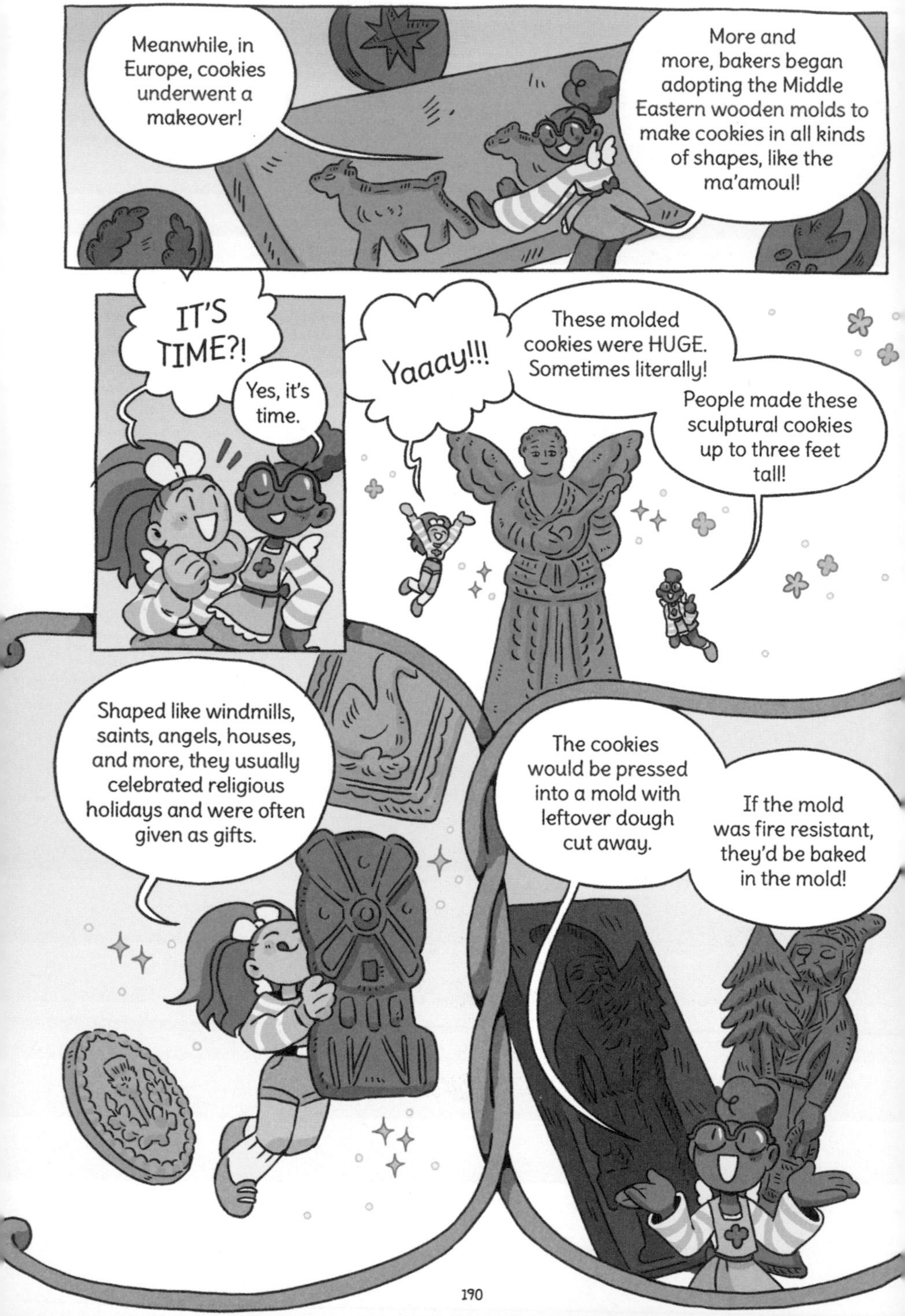
Meanwhile, in Europe, cookies underwent a makeover!
More and more, bakers began adopting the Middle Eastern wooden molds to make cookies in all kinds of shapes, like the ma'amoul!
IT'S TIME?!
Yes, it's time.
Yaaay!!!
These molded cookies were HUGE. Sometimes literally!
People made these sculptural cookies up to three feet tall!
Shaped like windmills, saints, angels, houses, and more, they usually celebrated religious holidays and were often given as gifts.
The cookies would be pressed into a mold with leftover dough cut away.
If the mold was fire resistant, they'd be baked in the mold!

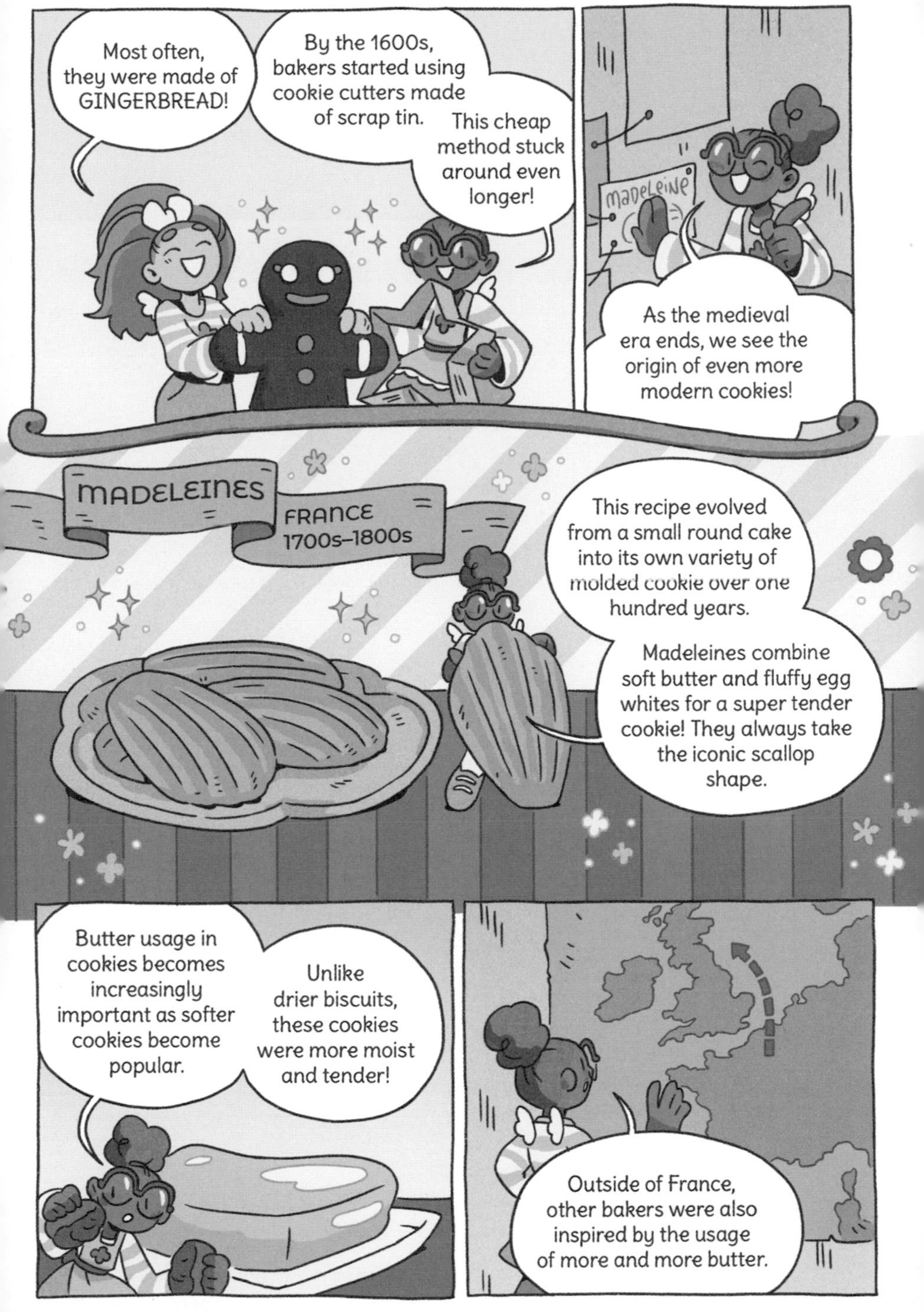
Most often, they were made of GINGERBREAD!
By the 1600s, bakers started using cookie cutters made of scrap tin.
This cheap method stuck around even longer!
MADELEINE
As the medieval era ends, we see the origin of even more modern cookies!
MADELEINES
FRANCE 1700s–1800s
This recipe evolved from a small round cake into its own variety of molded cookie over one hundred years.
Madeleines combine soft butter and fluffy egg whites for a super tender cookie! They always take the iconic scallop shape.
Butter usage in cookies becomes increasingly important as softer cookies become popular.
Unlike drier biscuits, these cookies were more moist and tender!
Outside of France, other bakers were also inspired by the usage of more and more butter.

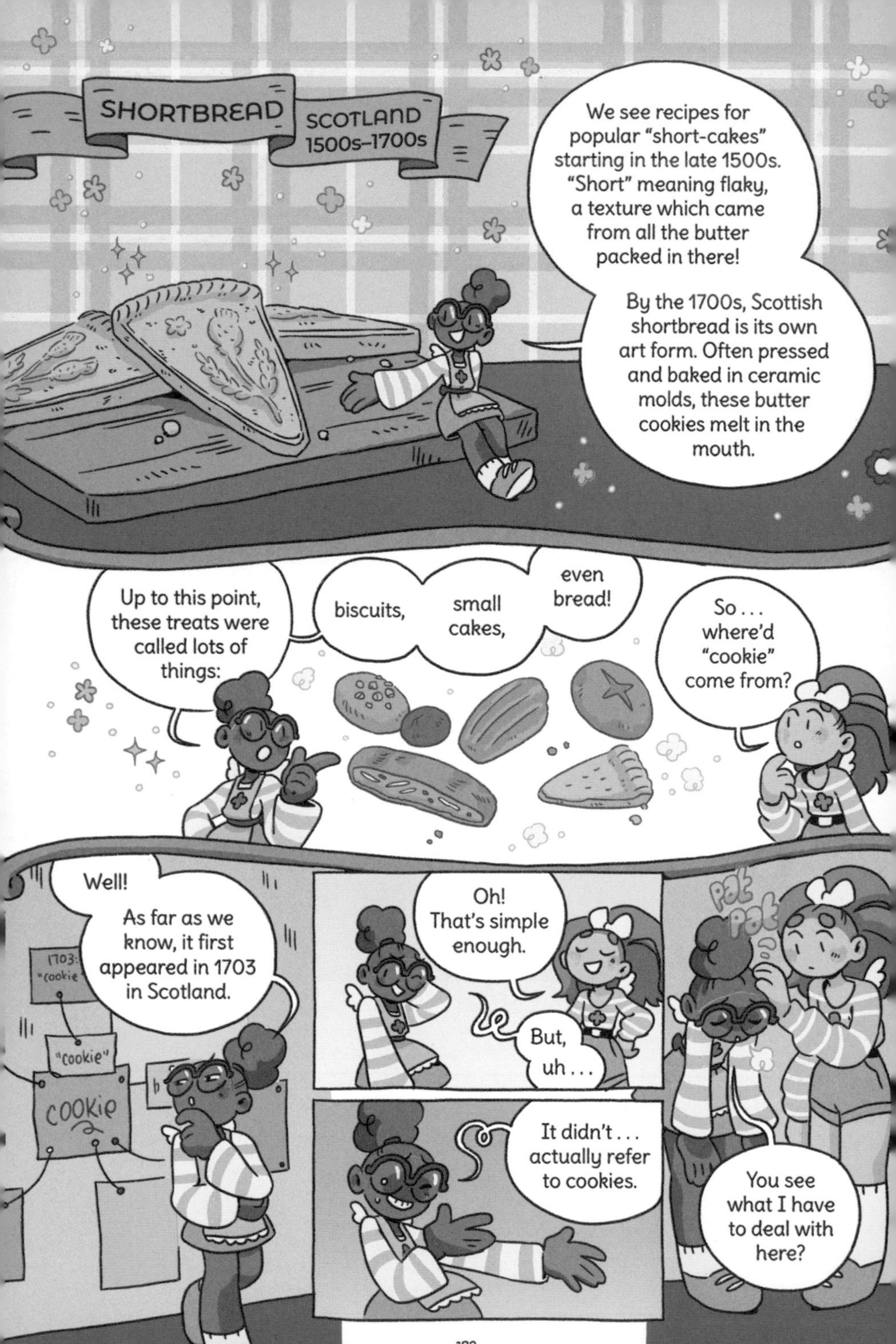
SHORTBREAD
SCOTLAND 1500s–1700s
We see recipes for popular "short-cakes" starting in the late 1500s. "Short" meaning flaky, a texture which came from all the butter packed in there!
By the 1700s, Scottish shortbread is its own art form. Often pressed and baked in ceramic molds, these butter cookies melt in the mouth.
Up to this point, these treats were called lots of things:
biscuits,
small cakes,
even bread!
So . . . where'd "cookie" come from?
Well!
As far as we know, it first appeared in 1703 in Scotland.
1703: "cookie"
"cookie"
COOKIE
Oh! That's simple enough.
But, uh . . .
It didn't . . . actually refer to cookies.
pat pat
You see what I have to deal with here?

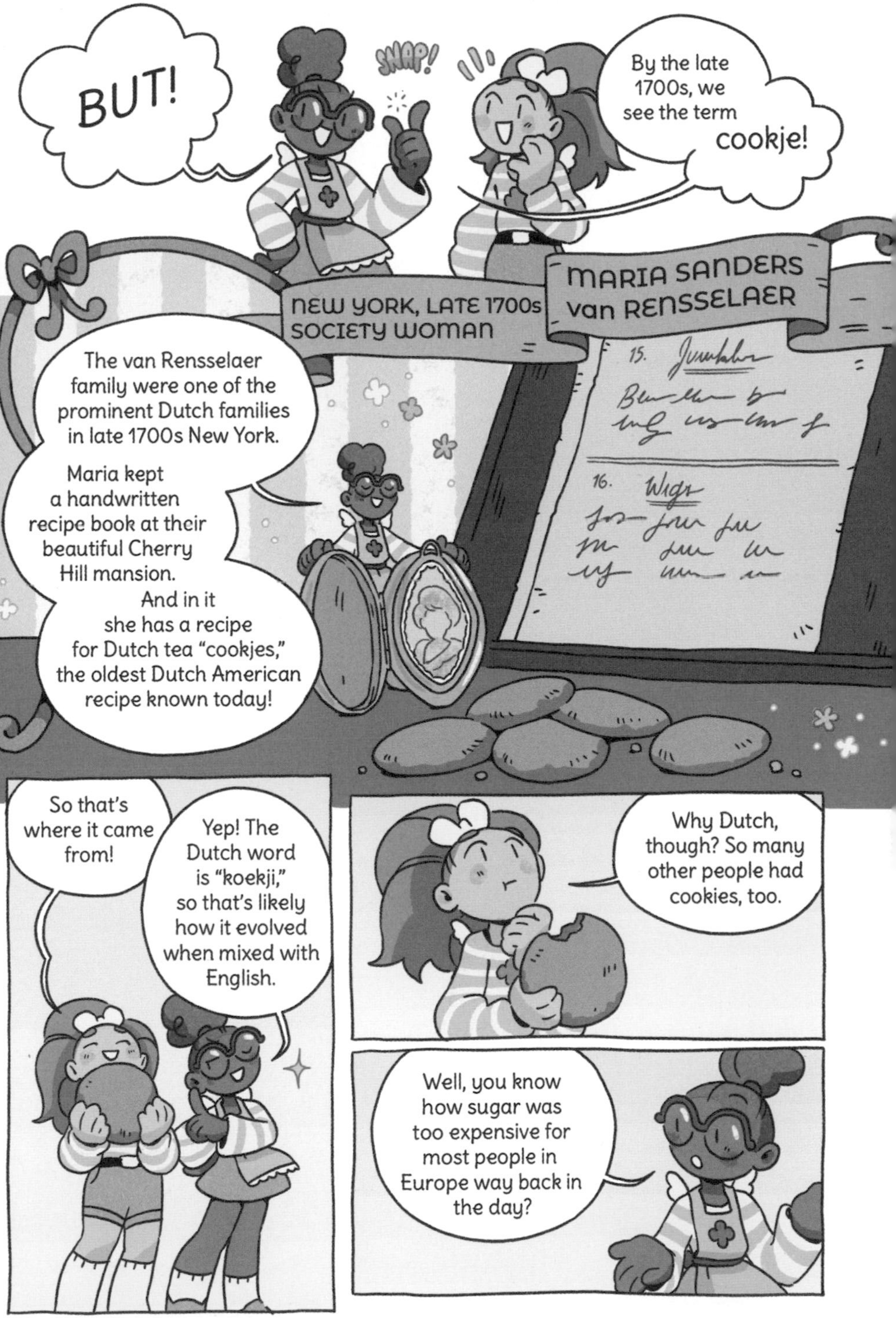
BUT!
SNAP!
By the late 1700s, we see the term cookje!
NEW YORK, LATE 1700s SOCIETY WOMAN
MARIA SANDERS van RENSSELAER
The van Rensselaer family were one of the prominent Dutch families in late 1700s New York.
Maria kept a handwritten recipe book at their beautiful Cherry Hill mansion.
And in it she has a recipe for Dutch tea "cookjes," the oldest Dutch American recipe known today!
So that's where it came from!
Yep! The Dutch word is "koekji," so that's likely how it evolved when mixed with English.
Why Dutch, though? So many other people had cookies, too.
Well, you know how sugar was too expensive for most people in Europe way back in the day?

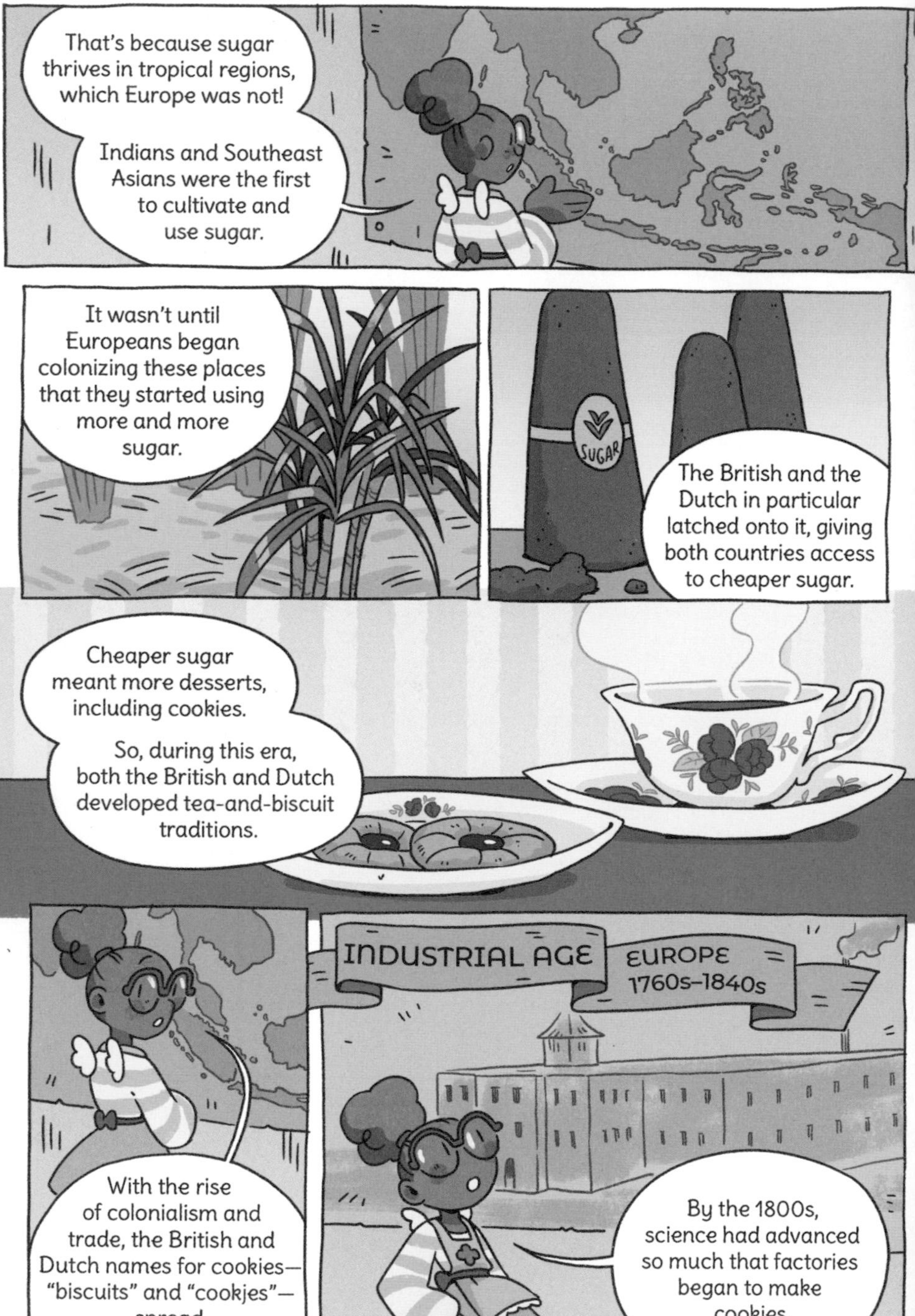
That's because sugar thrives in tropical regions, which Europe was not!
Indians and Southeast Asians were the first to cultivate and use sugar.
It wasn't until Europeans began colonizing these places that they started using more and more sugar.
SUGAR
The British and the Dutch in particular latched onto it, giving both countries access to cheaper sugar.
Cheaper sugar meant more desserts, including cookies.
So, during this era, both the British and Dutch developed tea-and-biscuit traditions.
With the rise of colonialism and trade, the British and Dutch names for cookies—"biscuits" and "cookjes"—spread.
INDUSTRIAL AGE
EUROPE 1760s–1840s
By the 1800s, science had advanced so much that factories began to make cookies.

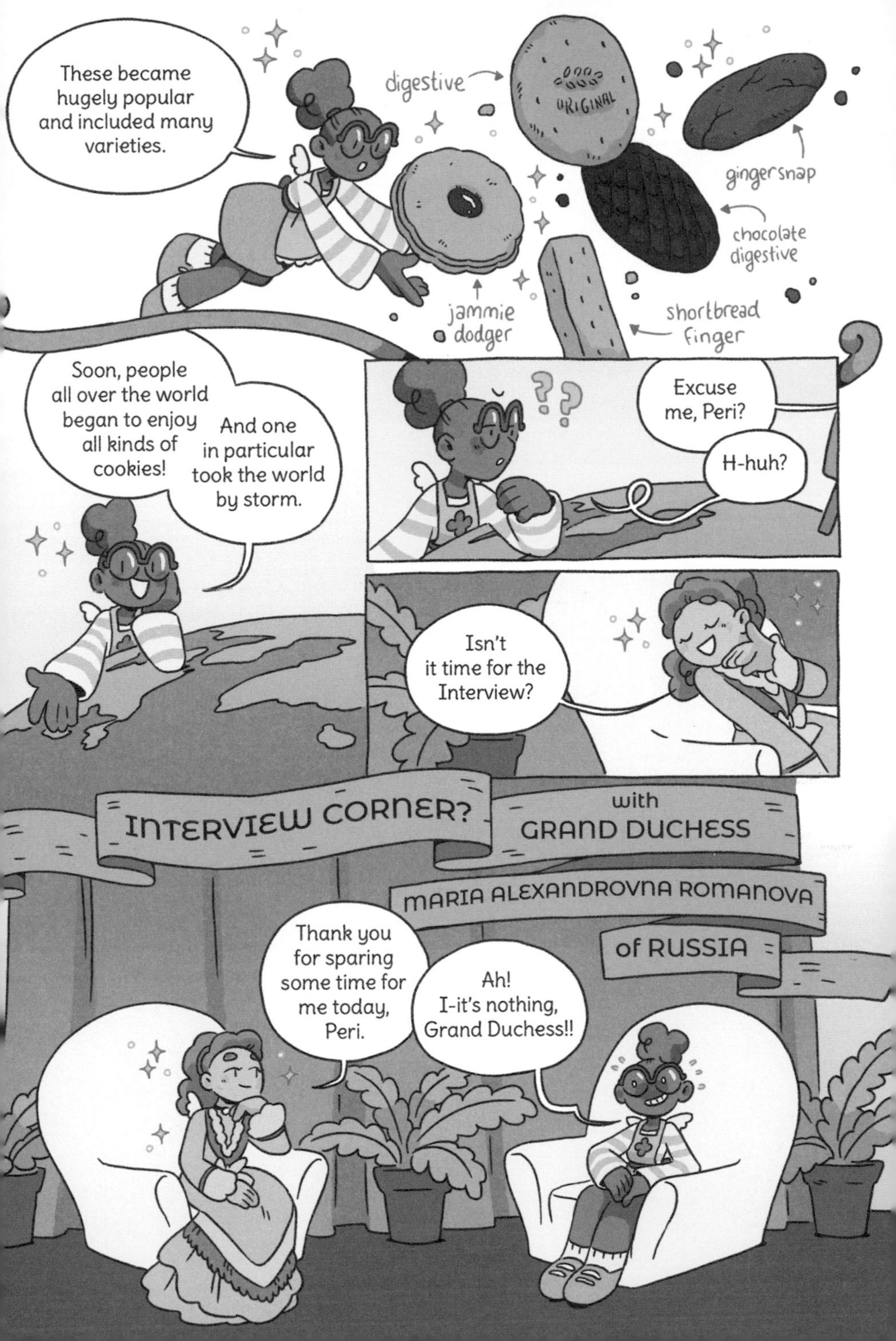
These became hugely popular and included many varieties.
digestive
ORIGINAL
gingersnap
chocolate digestive
jammie dodger
shortbread finger
Soon, people all over the world began to enjoy all kinds of cookies!
And one in particular took the world by storm.
Excuse me, Peri?
H-huh?
Isn't it time for the Interview?
INTERVIEW CORNER?
with GRAND DUCHESS
MARIA ALEXANDROVNA ROMANOVA
of RUSSIA
Thank you for sparing some time for me today, Peri.
Ah! I-it's nothing, Grand Duchess!!

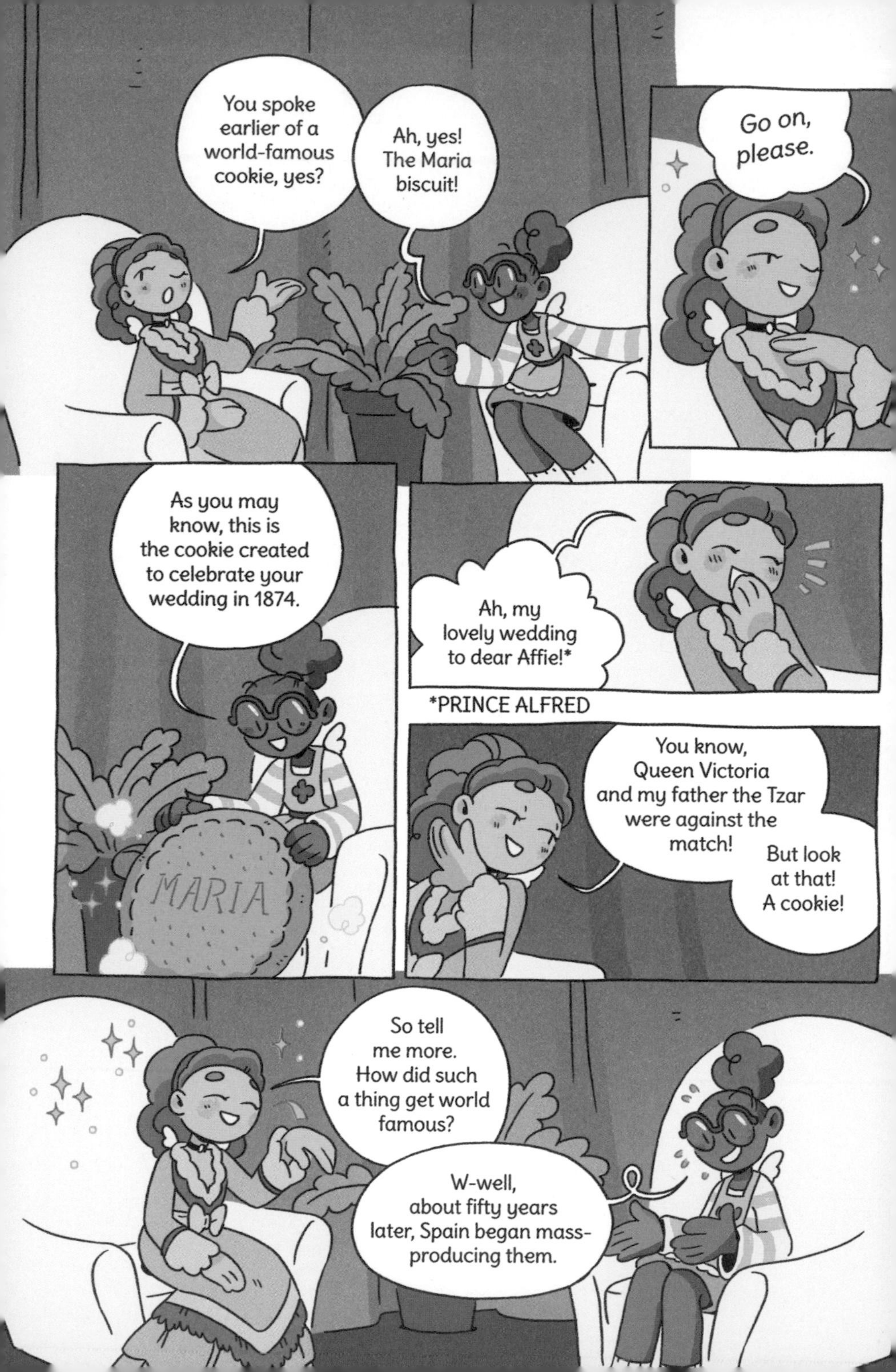

You spoke earlier of a world-famous cookie, yes?
Ah, yes! The Maria biscuit!
Go on, please.
As you may know, this is the cookie created to celebrate your wedding in 1874.
MARIA
Ah, my lovely wedding to dear Affie!*
*PRINCE ALFRED
You know, Queen Victoria and my father the Tzar were against the match!
But look at that! A cookie!
So tell me more. How did such a thing get world famous?
W-well, about fifty years later, Spain began mass-producing them.

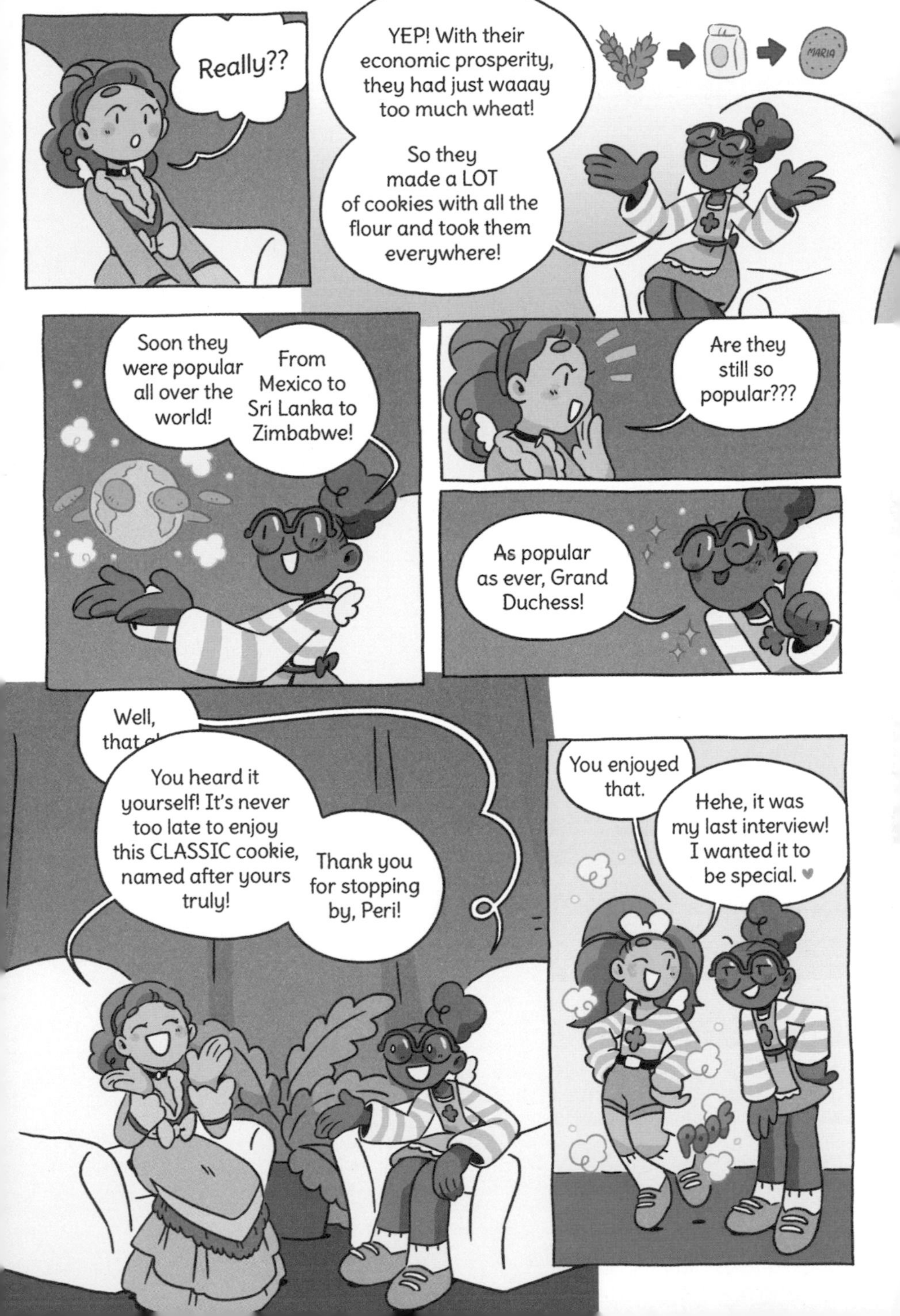

Really??
YEP! With their economic prosperity, they had just waaay too much wheat!
So they made a LOT of cookies with all the flour and took them everywhere!
MARIA
Soon they were popular all over the world!
From Mexico to Sri Lanka to Zimbabwe!
Are they still so popular???
As popular as ever, Grand Duchess!
Well, that
You heard it yourself! It's never too late to enjoy this CLASSIC cookie, named after yours truly!
Thank you for stopping by, Peri!
You enjoyed that.
Hehe, it was my last interview! I wanted it to be special.
POOF

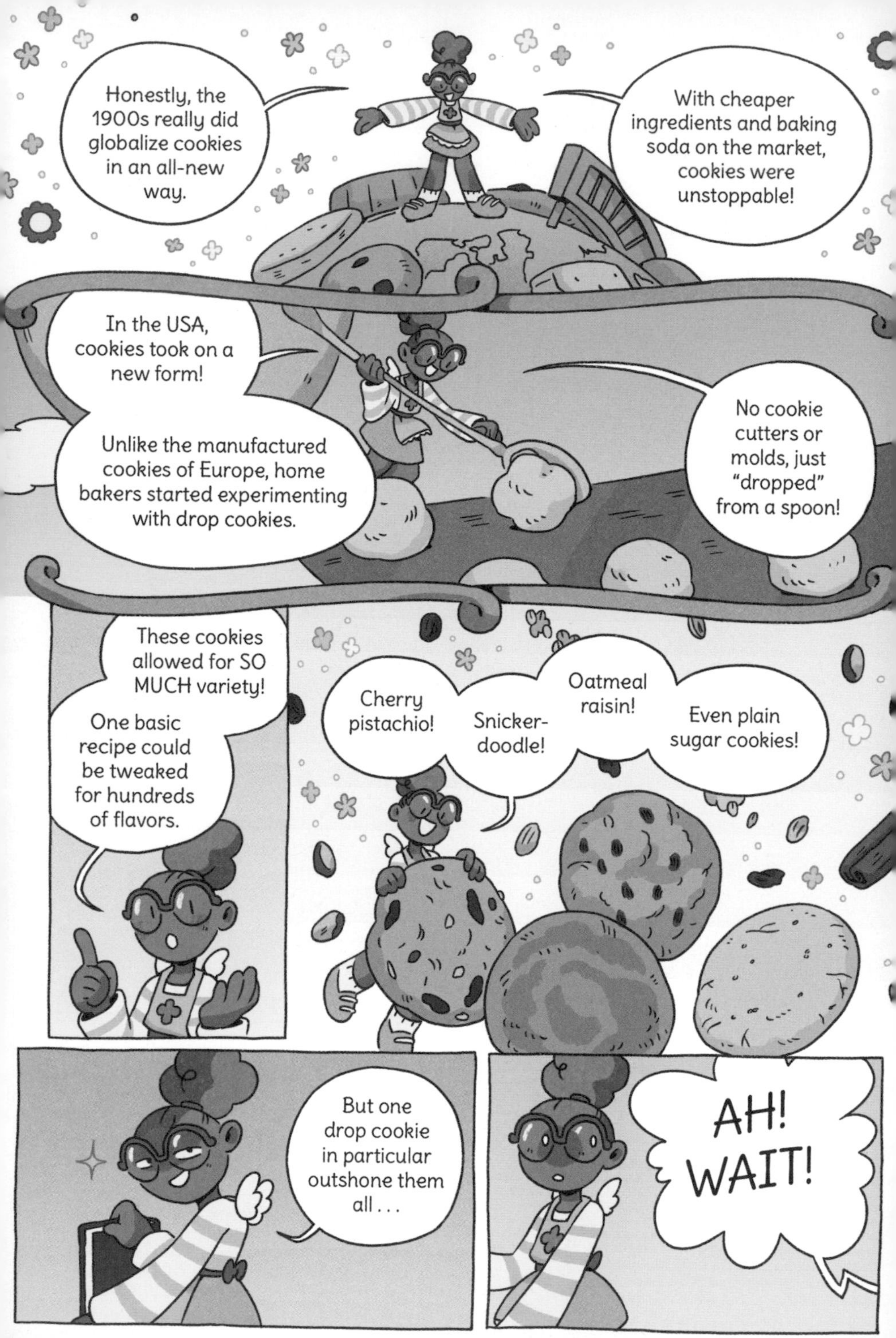

Honestly, the 1900s really did globalize cookies in an all-new way.
With cheaper ingredients and baking soda on the market, cookies were unstoppable!
In the USA, cookies took on a new form!
Unlike the manufactured cookies of Europe, home bakers started experimenting with drop cookies.
No cookie cutters or molds, just "dropped" from a spoon!
These cookies allowed for SO MUCH variety!
One basic recipe could be tweaked for hundreds of flavors.
Cherry pistachio!
Snicker-doodle!
Oatmeal raisin!
Even plain sugar cookies!
But one drop cookie in particular outshone them all . . .
AH! WAIT!

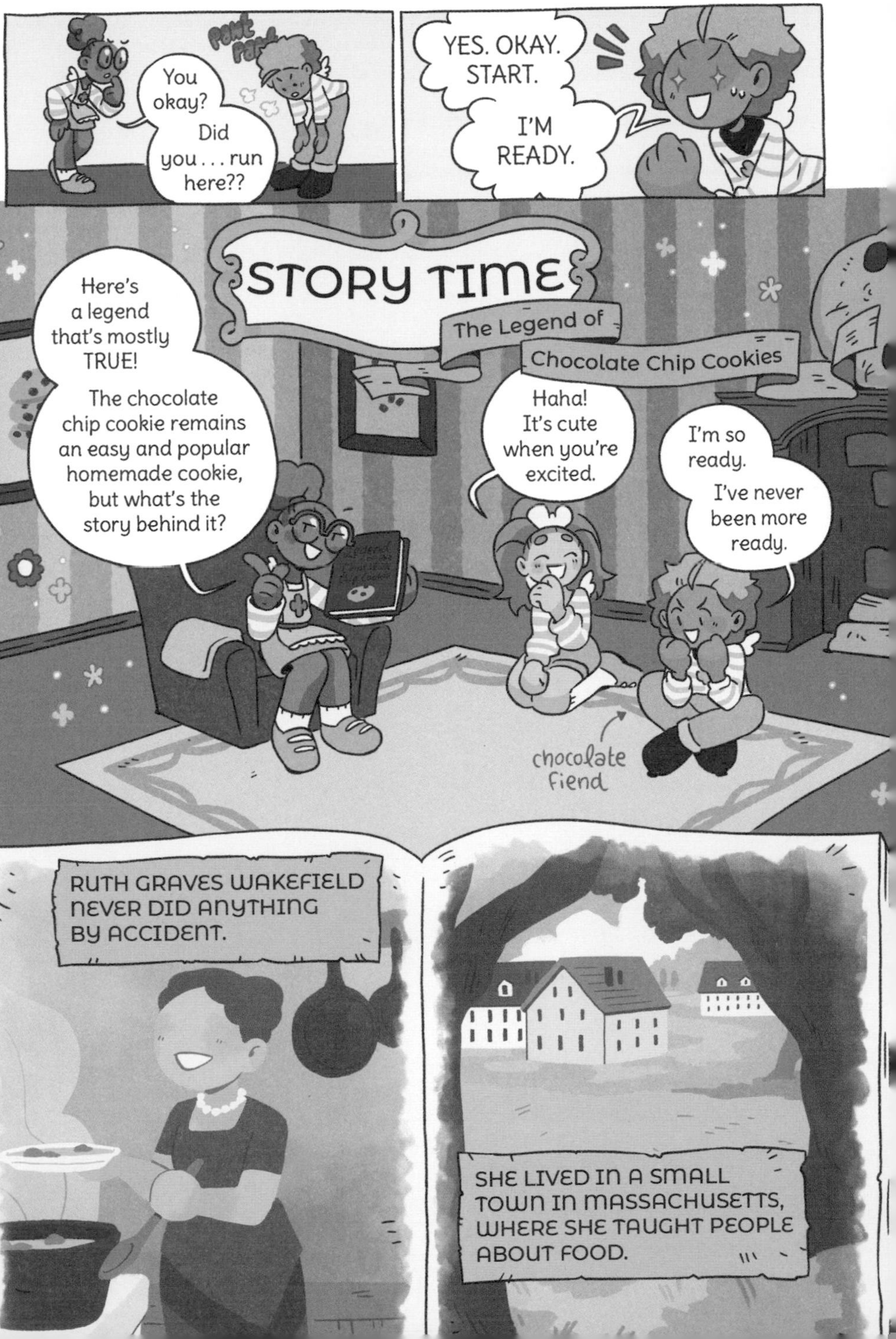
You okay?
Did you . . . run here??
YES. OKAY. START.
I'M READY.
STORY TIME
The Legend of Chocolate Chip Cookies
Here's a legend that's mostly TRUE!
The chocolate chip cookie remains an easy and popular homemade cookie, but what's the story behind it?
Haha! It's cute when you're excited.
I'm so ready.
I've never been more ready.
chocolate fiend
RUTH GRAVES WAKEFIELD NEVER DID ANYTHING BY ACCIDENT.
SHE LIVED IN A SMALL TOWN IN MASSACHUSETTS, WHERE SHE TAUGHT PEOPLE ABOUT FOOD.

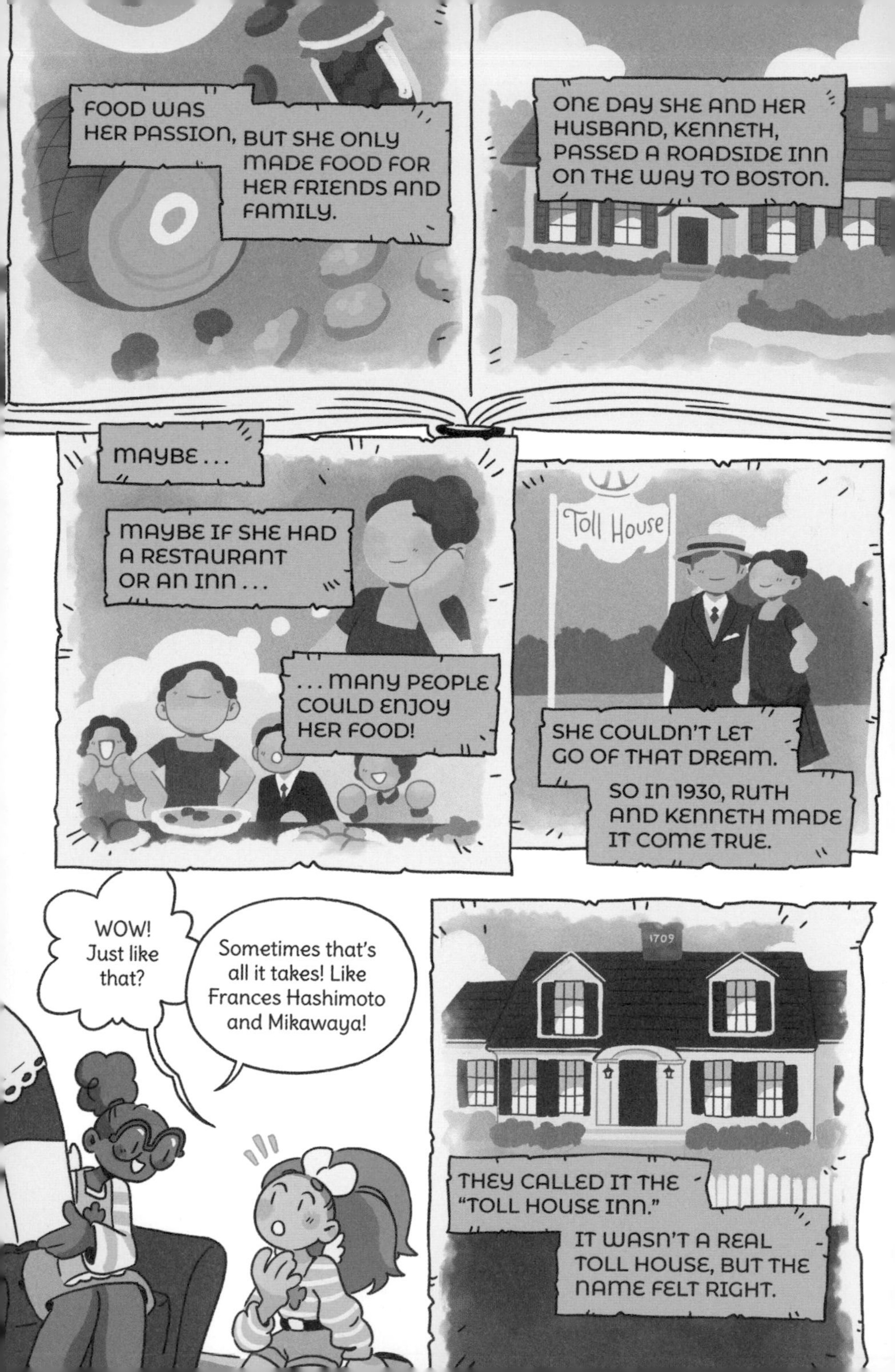
FOOD WAS HER PASSION, BUT SHE ONLY MADE FOOD FOR HER FRIENDS AND FAMILY.
ONE DAY SHE AND HER HUSBAND, KENNETH, PASSED A ROADSIDE INN ON THE WAY TO BOSTON.
MAYBE . . .
MAYBE IF SHE HAD A RESTAURANT OR AN INN . . .
. . . MANY PEOPLE COULD ENJOY HER FOOD!
Toll House
SHE COULDN'T LET GO OF THAT DREAM.
SO IN 1930, RUTH AND KENNETH MADE IT COME TRUE.
WOW! Just like that?
Sometimes that's all it takes! Like Frances Hashimoto and Mikawaya!
1709
THEY CALLED IT THE "TOLL HOUSE INN."
IT WASN'T A REAL TOLL HOUSE, BUT THE NAME FELT RIGHT.

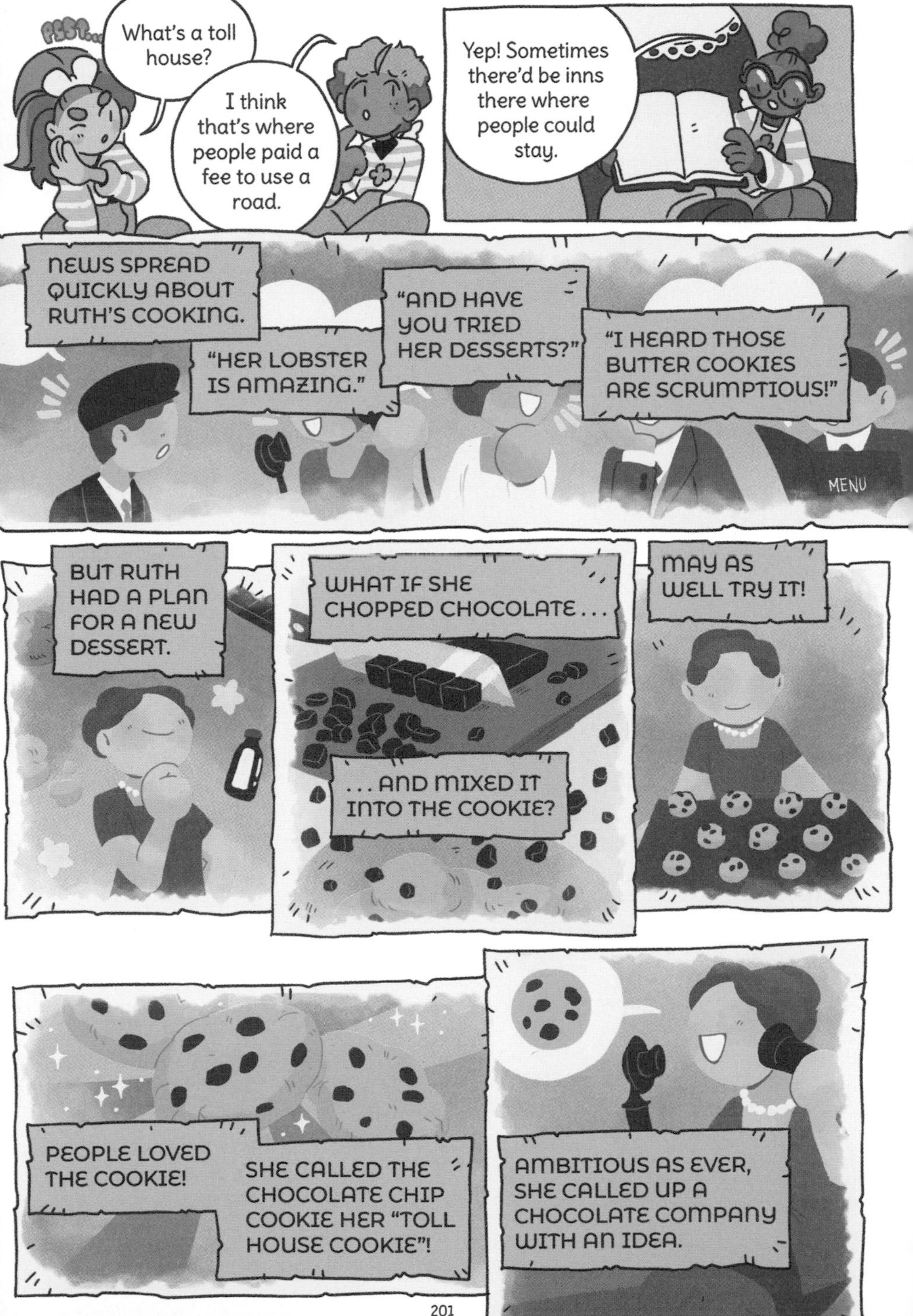
PSST...
What's a toll house?
I think that's where people paid a fee to use a road.
Yep! Sometimes there'd be inns there where people could stay.
NEWS SPREAD QUICKLY ABOUT RUTH'S COOKING.
"HER LOBSTER IS AMAZING."
"AND HAVE YOU TRIED HER DESSERTS?"
"I HEARD THOSE BUTTER COOKIES ARE SCRUMPTIOUS!"
MENU
BUT RUTH HAD A PLAN FOR A NEW DESSERT.
WHAT IF SHE CHOPPED CHOCOLATE . . .
. . . AND MIXED IT INTO THE COOKIE?
MAY AS WELL TRY IT!
PEOPLE LOVED THE COOKIE!
SHE CALLED THE CHOCOLATE CHIP COOKIE HER "TOLL HOUSE COOKIE"!
AMBITIOUS AS EVER, SHE CALLED UP A CHOCOLATE COMPANY WITH AN IDEA.

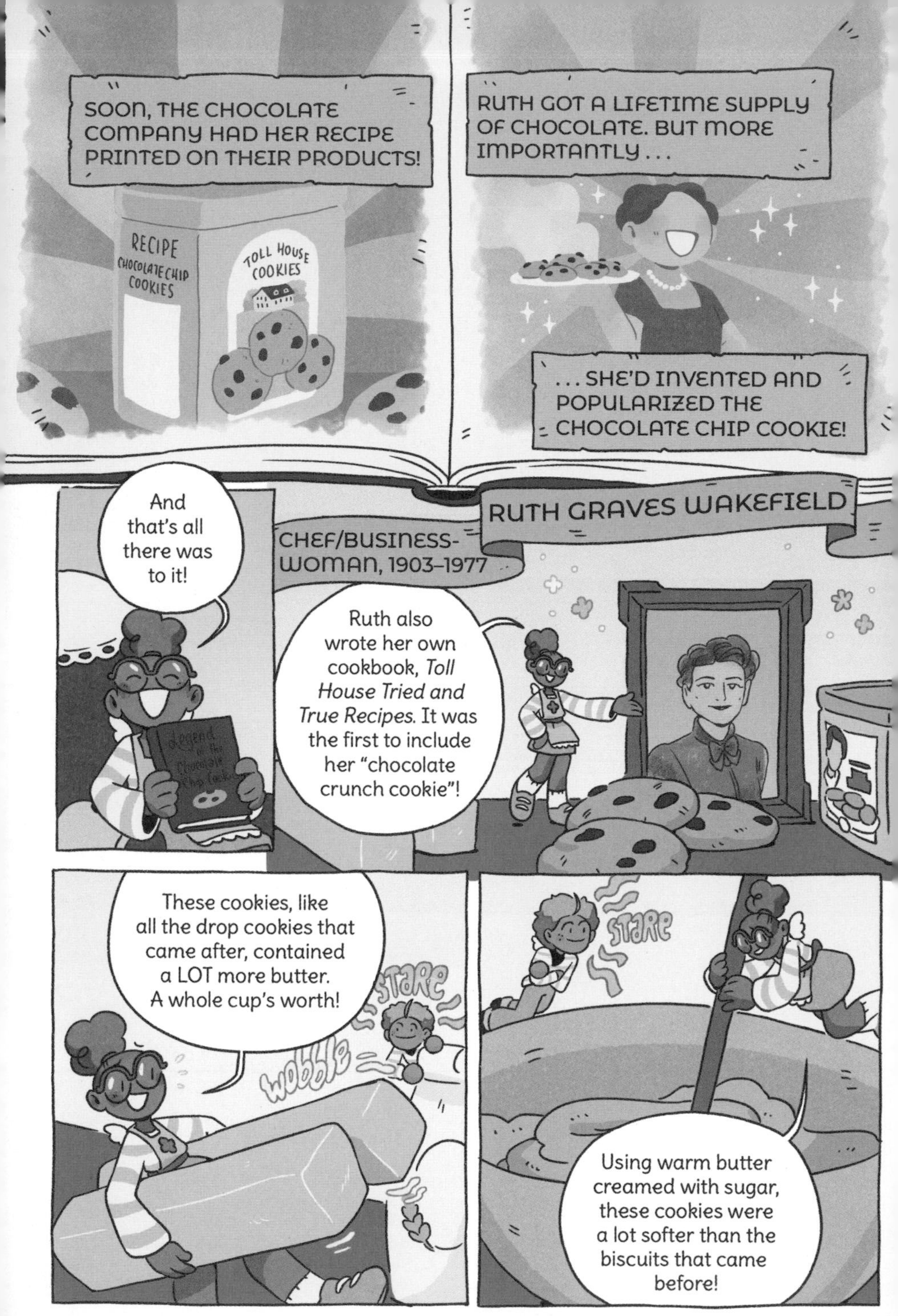
SOON, THE CHOCOLATE COMPANY HAD HER RECIPE PRINTED ON THEIR PRODUCTS!
RECIPE CHOCOLATE CHIP COOKIES
TOLL HOUSE COOKIES
RUTH GOT A LIFETIME SUPPLY OF CHOCOLATE. BUT MORE IMPORTANTLY . . .
. . . SHE'D INVENTED AND POPULARIZED THE CHOCOLATE CHIP COOKIE!
And that's all there was to it!
RUTH GRAVES WAKEFIELD
CHEF/BUSINESS-WOMAN, 1903–1977
Ruth also wrote her own cookbook, *Toll House Tried and True Recipes*. It was the first to include her "chocolate crunch cookie"!
These cookies, like all the drop cookies that came after, contained a LOT more butter. A whole cup's worth!
STARE
wobble
STARE
Using warm butter creamed with sugar, these cookies were a lot softer than the biscuits that came before!

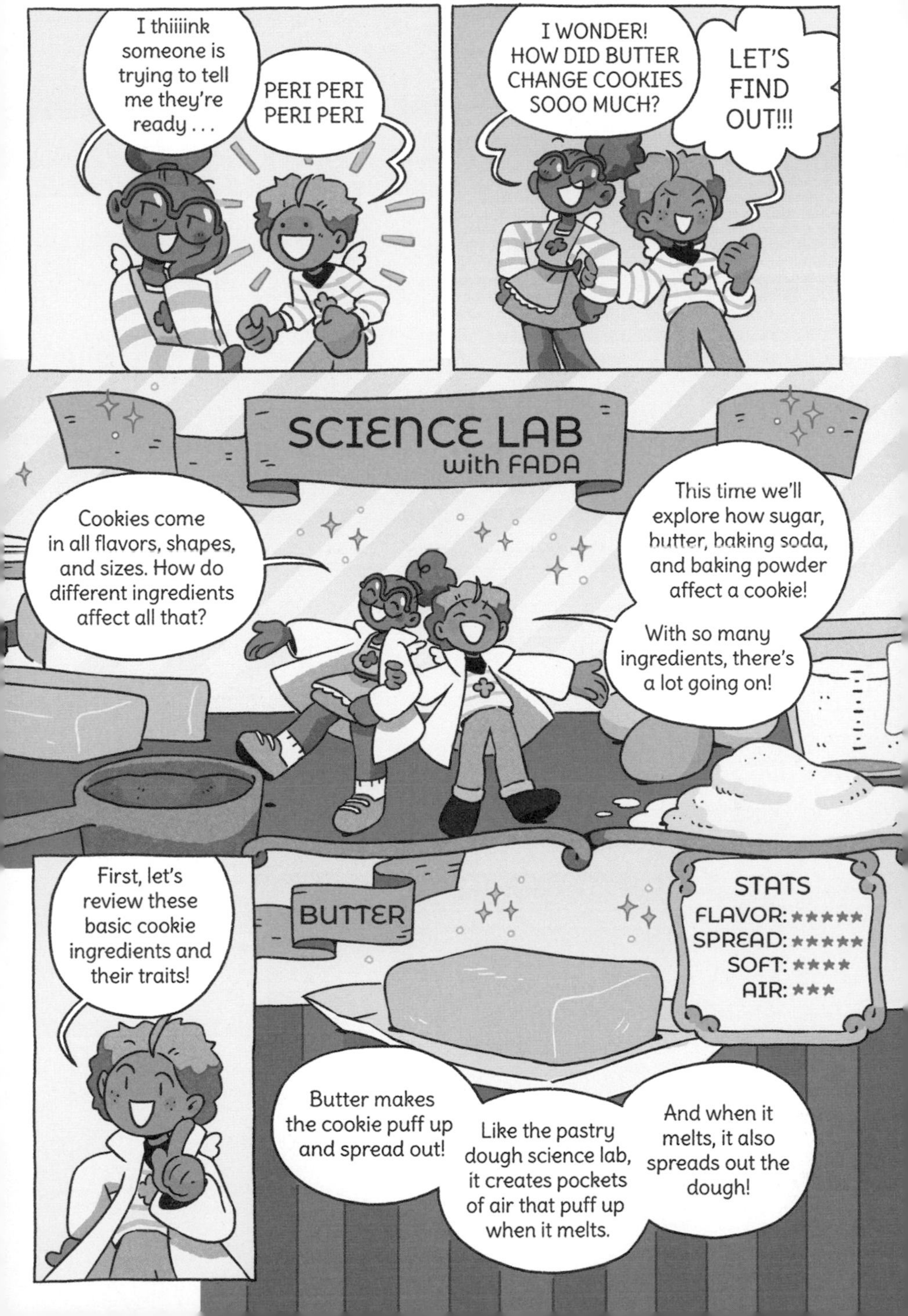
I thiiiink someone is trying to tell me they're ready . . .
PERI PERI PERI PERI
I WONDER! HOW DID BUTTER CHANGE COOKIES SOOO MUCH?
LET'S FIND OUT!!!
SCIENCE LAB with FADA
Cookies come in all flavors, shapes, and sizes. How do different ingredients affect all that?
This time we'll explore how sugar, butter, baking soda, and baking powder affect a cookie!
With so many ingredients, there's a lot going on!
First, let's review these basic cookie ingredients and their traits!
BUTTER
STATS
FLAVOR: ★★★★★
SPREAD: ★★★★★
SOFT: ★★★★
AIR: ★★★
Butter makes the cookie puff up and spread out!
Like the pastry dough science lab, it creates pockets of air that puff up when it melts.
And when it melts, it also spreads out the dough!

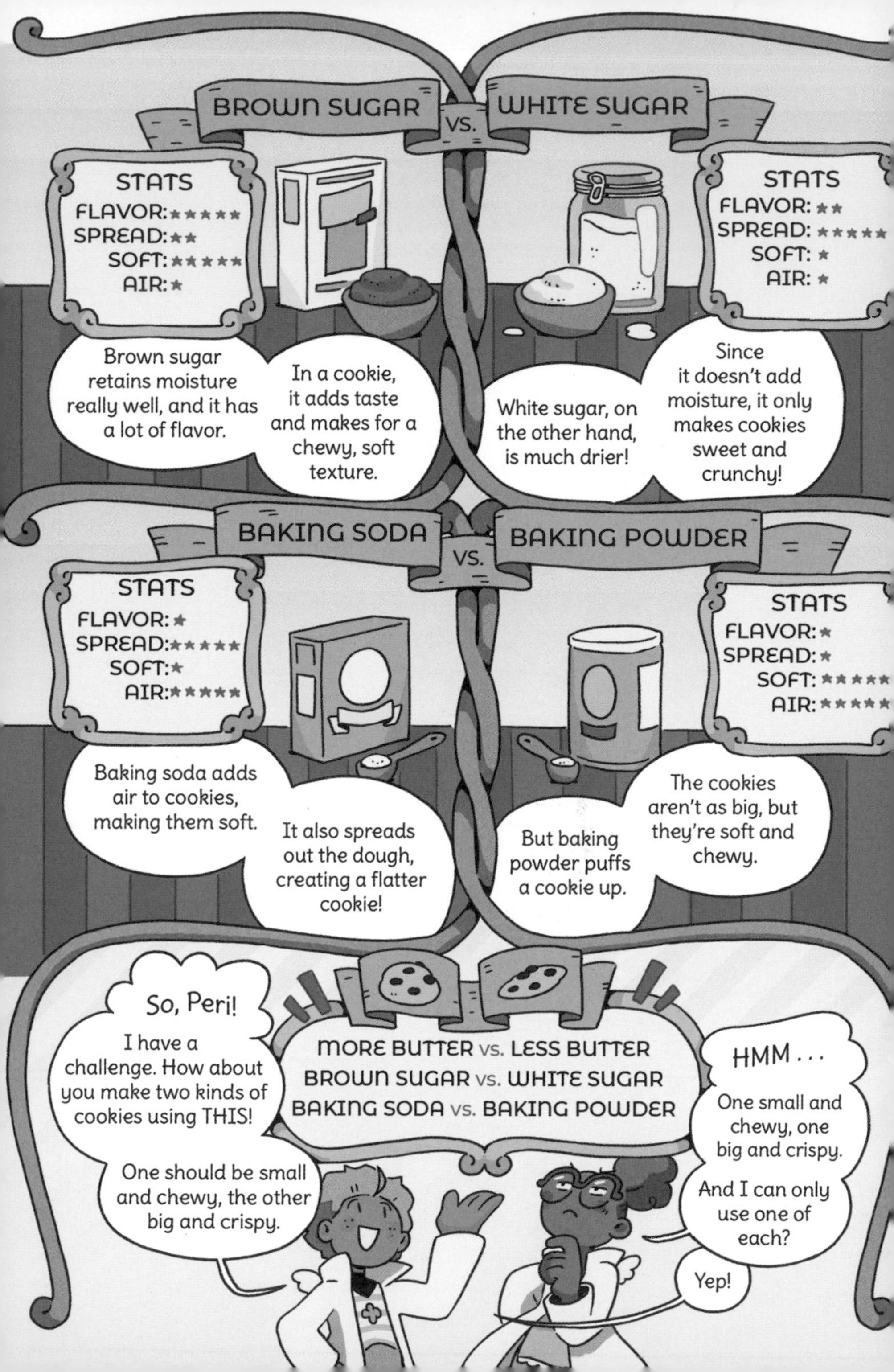
BROWN SUGAR
VS.
WHITE SUGAR
STATS
FLAVOR: ★★★★★
SPREAD: ★★
SOFT: ★★★★★
AIR: ★
STATS
FLAVOR: ★★
SPREAD: ★★★★★
SOFT: ★
AIR: ★
Brown sugar retains moisture really well, and it has a lot of flavor.
In a cookie, it adds taste and makes for a chewy, soft texture.
White sugar, on the other hand, is much drier!
Since it doesn't add moisture, it only makes cookies sweet and crunchy!
BAKING SODA
VS.
BAKING POWDER
STATS
FLAVOR: ★
SPREAD: ★★★★★
SOFT: ★
AIR: ★★★★★
STATS
FLAVOR: ★
SPREAD: ★
SOFT: ★★★★★
AIR: ★★★★★
Baking soda adds air to cookies, making them soft.
It also spreads out the dough, creating a flatter cookie!
But baking powder puffs a cookie up.
The cookies aren't as big, but they're soft and chewy.
So, Peri!
I have a challenge. How about you make two kinds of cookies using THIS!
MORE BUTTER VS. LESS BUTTER
BROWN SUGAR VS. WHITE SUGAR
BAKING SODA VS. BAKING POWDER
One should be small and chewy, the other big and crispy.
HMM . . .
One small and chewy, one big and crispy.
And I can only use one of each?
Yep!

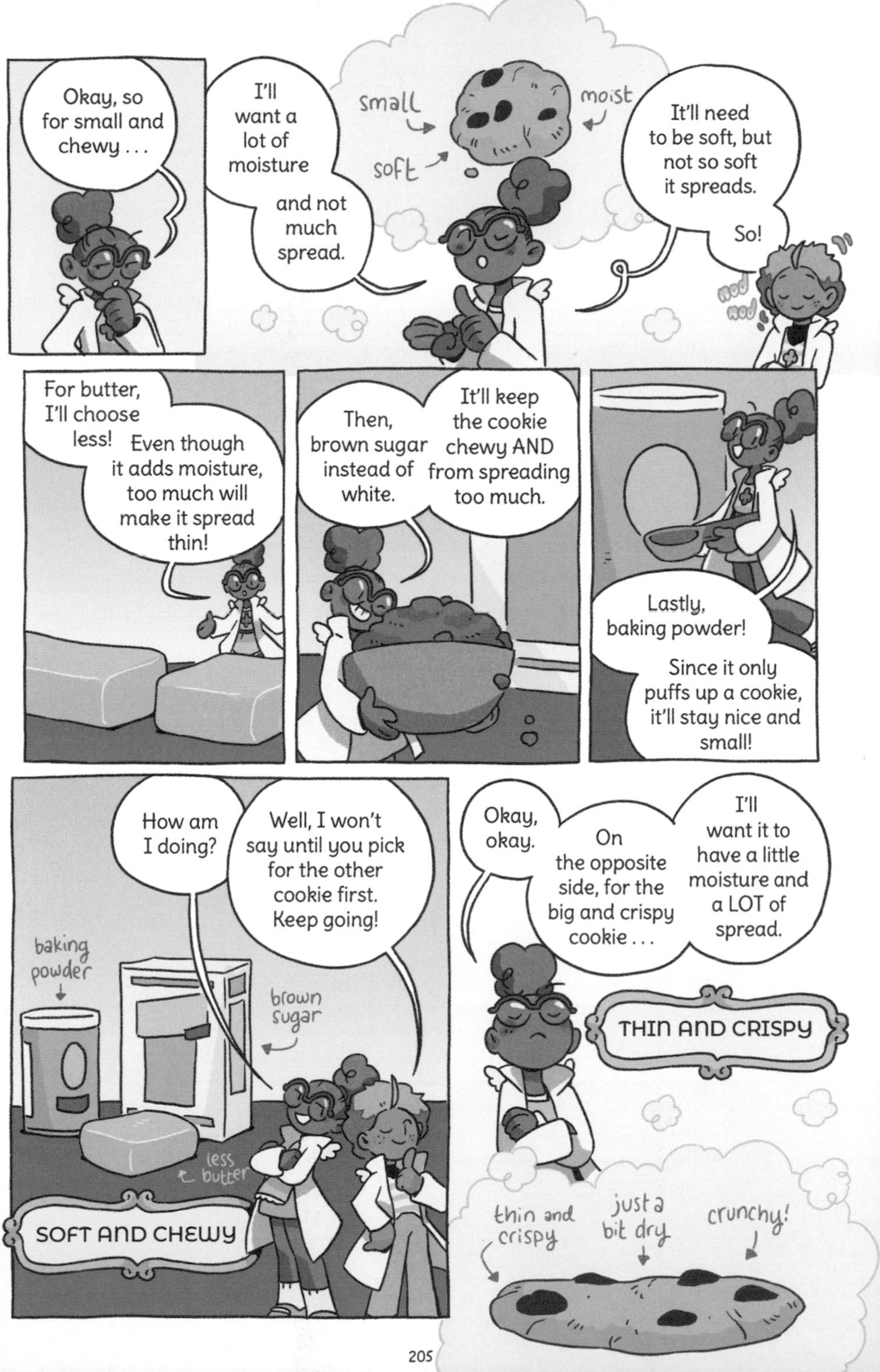

Okay, so for small and chewy . . .
I'll want a lot of moisture
and not much spread.
small
moist
soft
It'll need to be soft, but not so soft it spreads.
So!
nod nod
For butter, I'll choose less!
Even though it adds moisture, too much will make it spread thin!
Then, brown sugar instead of white.
It'll keep the cookie chewy AND from spreading too much.
Lastly, baking powder!
Since it only puffs up a cookie, it'll stay nice and small!
How am I doing?
Well, I won't say until you pick for the other cookie first. Keep going!
baking powder
brown sugar
less butter
SOFT AND CHEWY
Okay, okay.
On the opposite side, for the big and crispy cookie . . .
I'll want it to have a little moisture and a LOT of spread.
THIN AND CRISPY
thin and crispy
just a bit dry
crunchy!

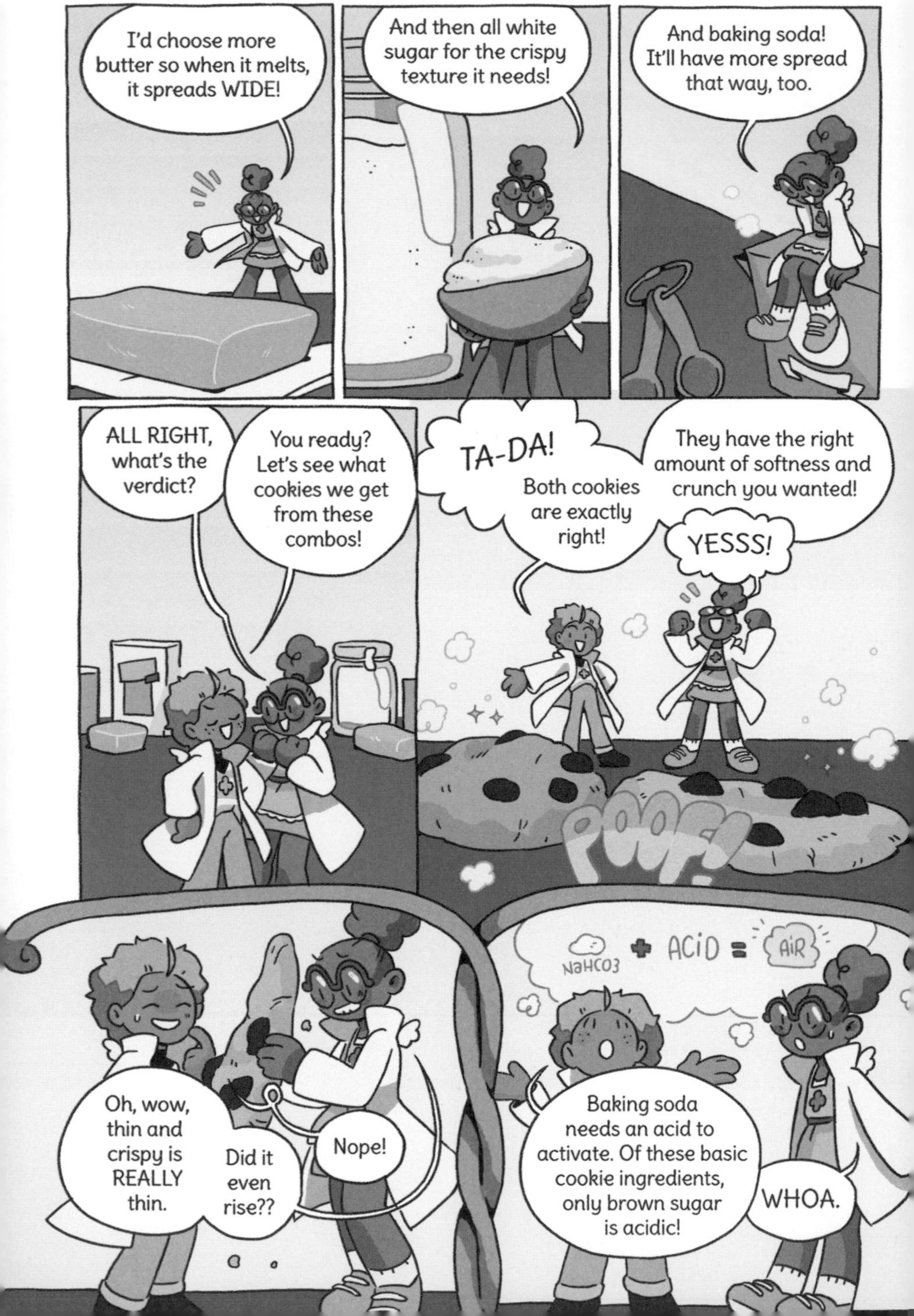
I'd choose more butter so when it melts, it spreads WIDE!
And then all white sugar for the crispy texture it needs!
And baking soda! It'll have more spread that way, too.
ALL RIGHT, what's the verdict?
You ready? Let's see what cookies we get from these combos!
TA-DA!
Both cookies are exactly right!
They have the right amount of softness and crunch you wanted!
YESSS!
POOF!
NaHCO3 + ACID = AIR
Oh, wow, thin and crispy is REALLY thin.
Did it even rise??
Nope!
Baking soda needs an acid to activate. Of these basic cookie ingredients, only brown sugar is acidic!
WHOA.

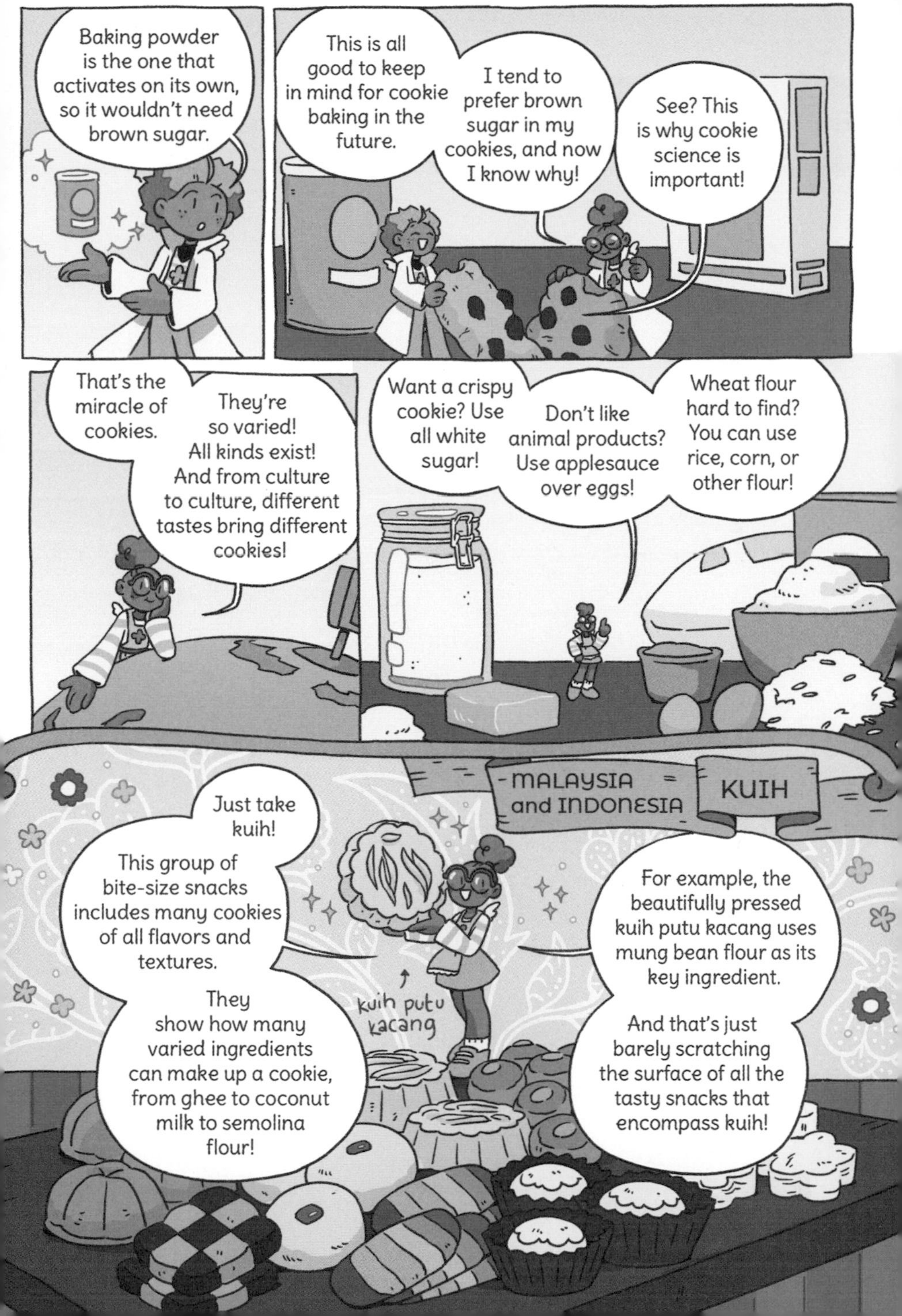

Baking powder is the one that activates on its own, so it wouldn't need brown sugar.
This is all good to keep in mind for cookie baking in the future.
I tend to prefer brown sugar in my cookies, and now I know why!
See? This is why cookie science is important!
That's the miracle of cookies.
They're so varied! All kinds exist! And from culture to culture, different tastes bring different cookies!
Want a crispy cookie? Use all white sugar!
Don't like animal products? Use applesauce over eggs!
Wheat flour hard to find? You can use rice, corn, or other flour!
MALAYSIA and INDONESIA
KUIH
Just take kuih!
This group of bite-size snacks includes many cookies of all flavors and textures.
They show how many varied ingredients can make up a cookie, from ghee to coconut milk to semolina flour!
kuih putu kacang
For example, the beautifully pressed kuih putu kacang uses mung bean flour as its key ingredient.
And that's just barely scratching the surface of all the tasty snacks that encompass kuih!

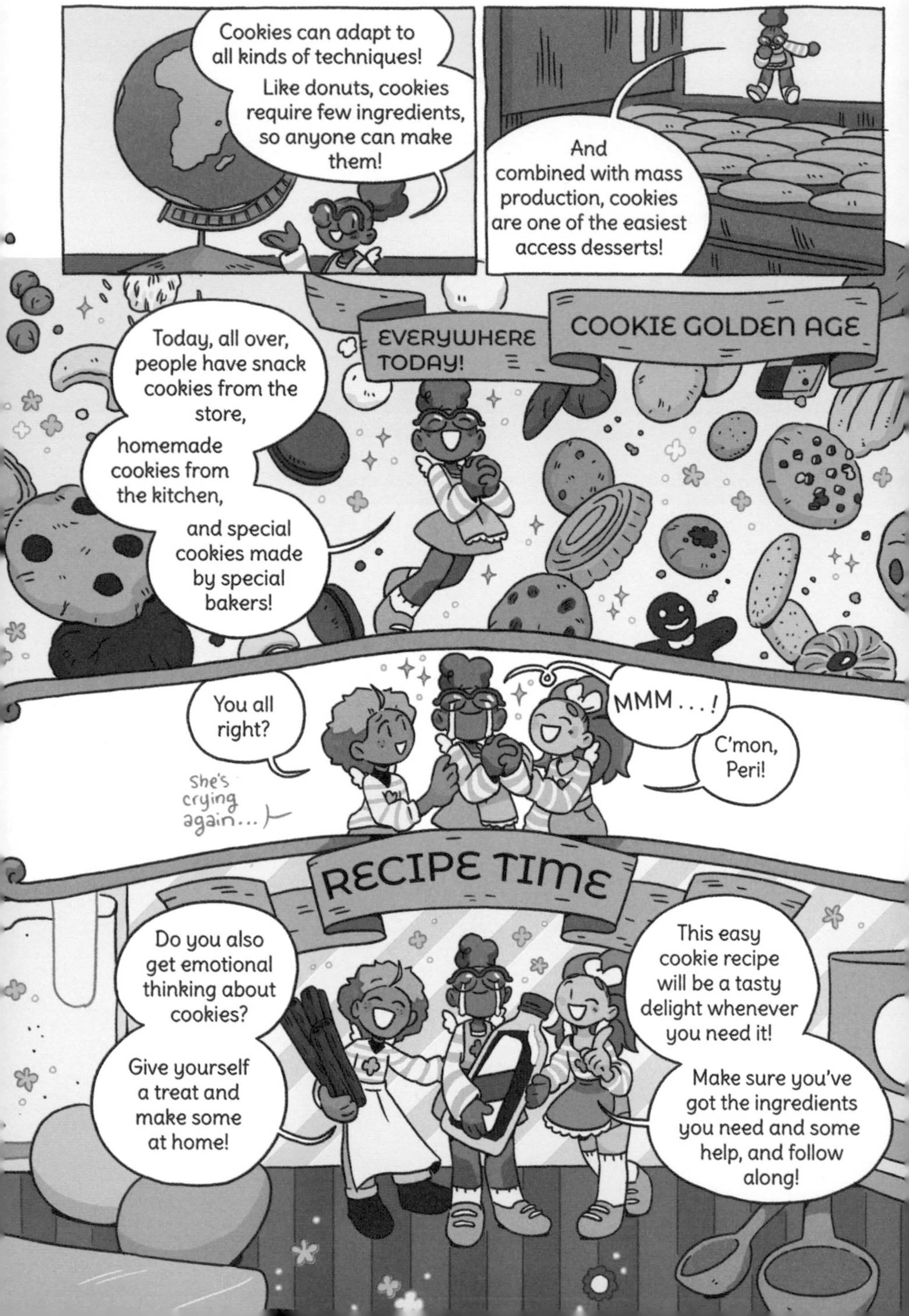
Cookies can adapt to all kinds of techniques!
Like donuts, cookies require few ingredients, so anyone can make them!
And combined with mass production, cookies are one of the easiest access desserts!
EVERYWHERE TODAY!
COOKIE GOLDEN AGE
Today, all over, people have snack cookies from the store,
homemade cookies from the kitchen,
and special cookies made by special bakers!
You all right?
She's crying again...
MMM...!
C'mon, Peri!
RECIPE TIME
Do you also get emotional thinking about cookies?
Give yourself a treat and make some at home!
This easy cookie recipe will be a tasty delight whenever you need it!
Make sure you've got the ingredients you need and some help, and follow along!

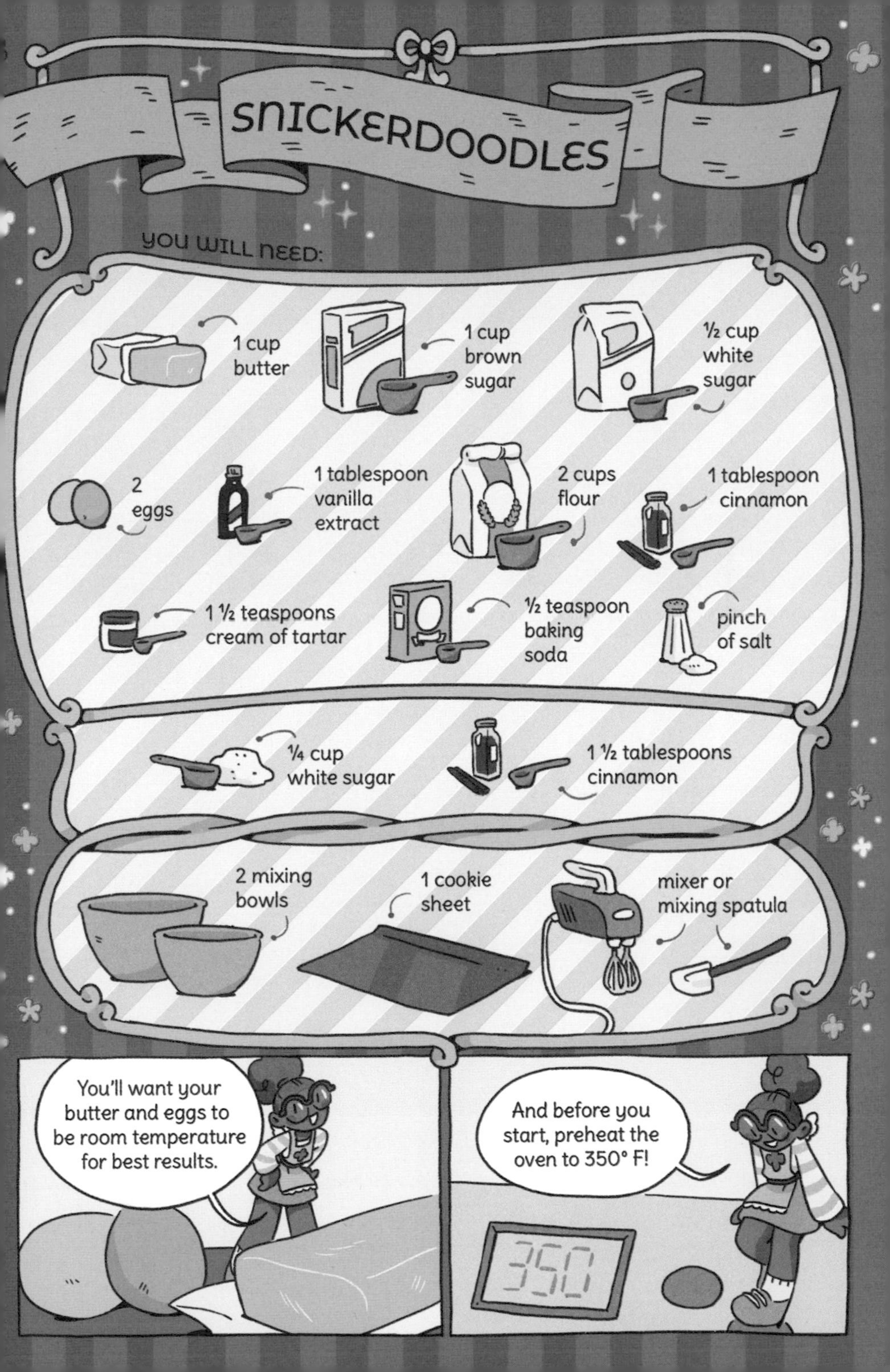
SNICKERDOODLES
YOU WILL NEED:
1 cup butter
1 cup brown sugar
½ cup white sugar
2 eggs
1 tablespoon vanilla extract
2 cups flour
1 tablespoon cinnamon
1 ½ teaspoons cream of tartar
½ teaspoon baking soda
pinch of salt
¼ cup white sugar
1 ½ tablespoons cinnamon
2 mixing bowls
1 cookie sheet
mixer or mixing spatula
You'll want your butter and eggs to be room temperature for best results.
And before you start, preheat the oven to 350° F!
350

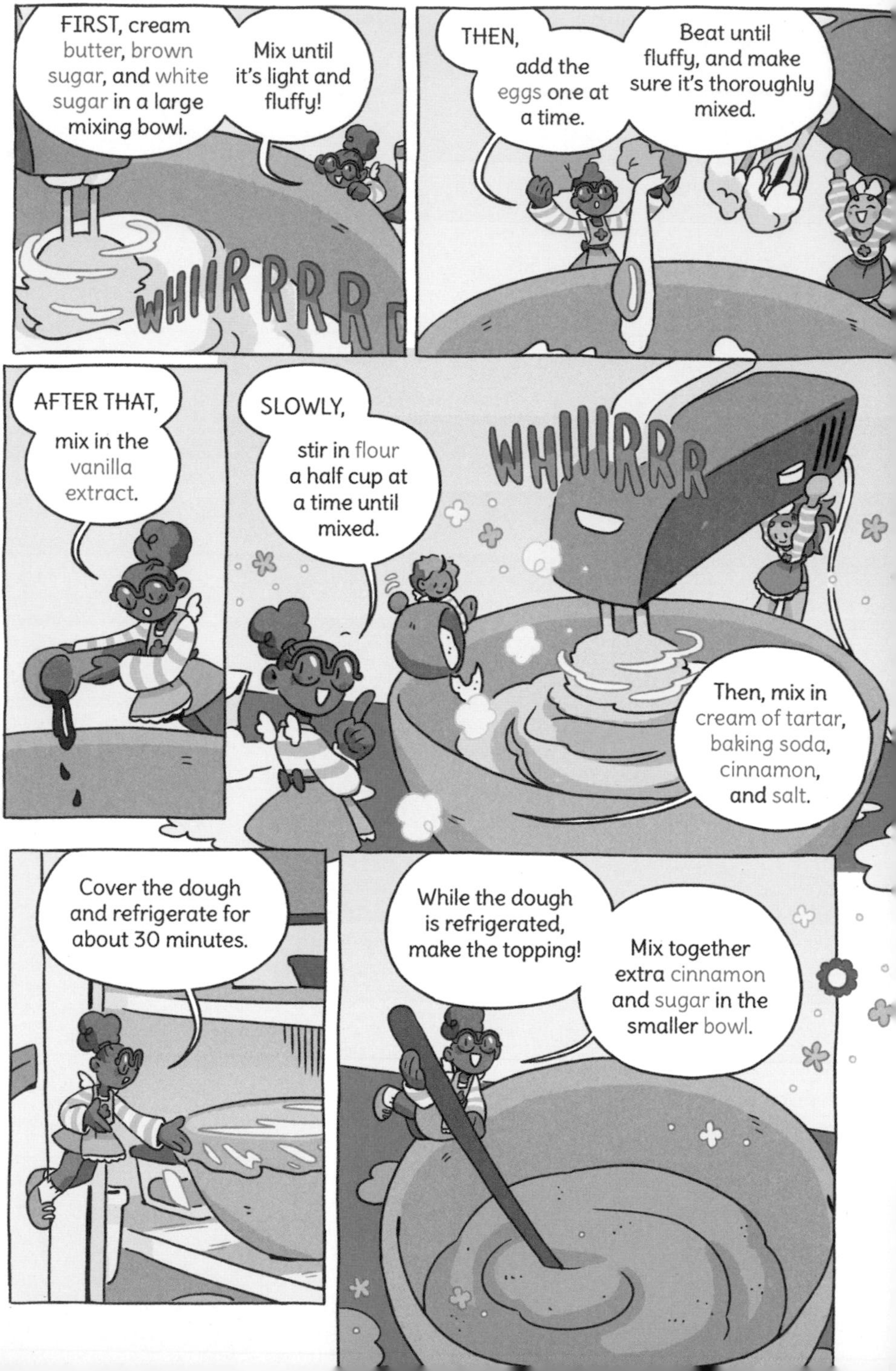

FIRST, cream butter, brown sugar, and white sugar in a large mixing bowl.
Mix until it's light and fluffy!
WHIIRRRR
THEN,
add the eggs one at a time.
Beat until fluffy, and make sure it's thoroughly mixed.
AFTER THAT,
mix in the vanilla extract.
SLOWLY,
stir in flour a half cup at a time until mixed.
WHIIIRRR
Then, mix in cream of tartar, baking soda, cinnamon, and salt.
Cover the dough and refrigerate for about 30 minutes.
While the dough is refrigerated, make the topping!
Mix together extra cinnamon and sugar in the smaller bowl.

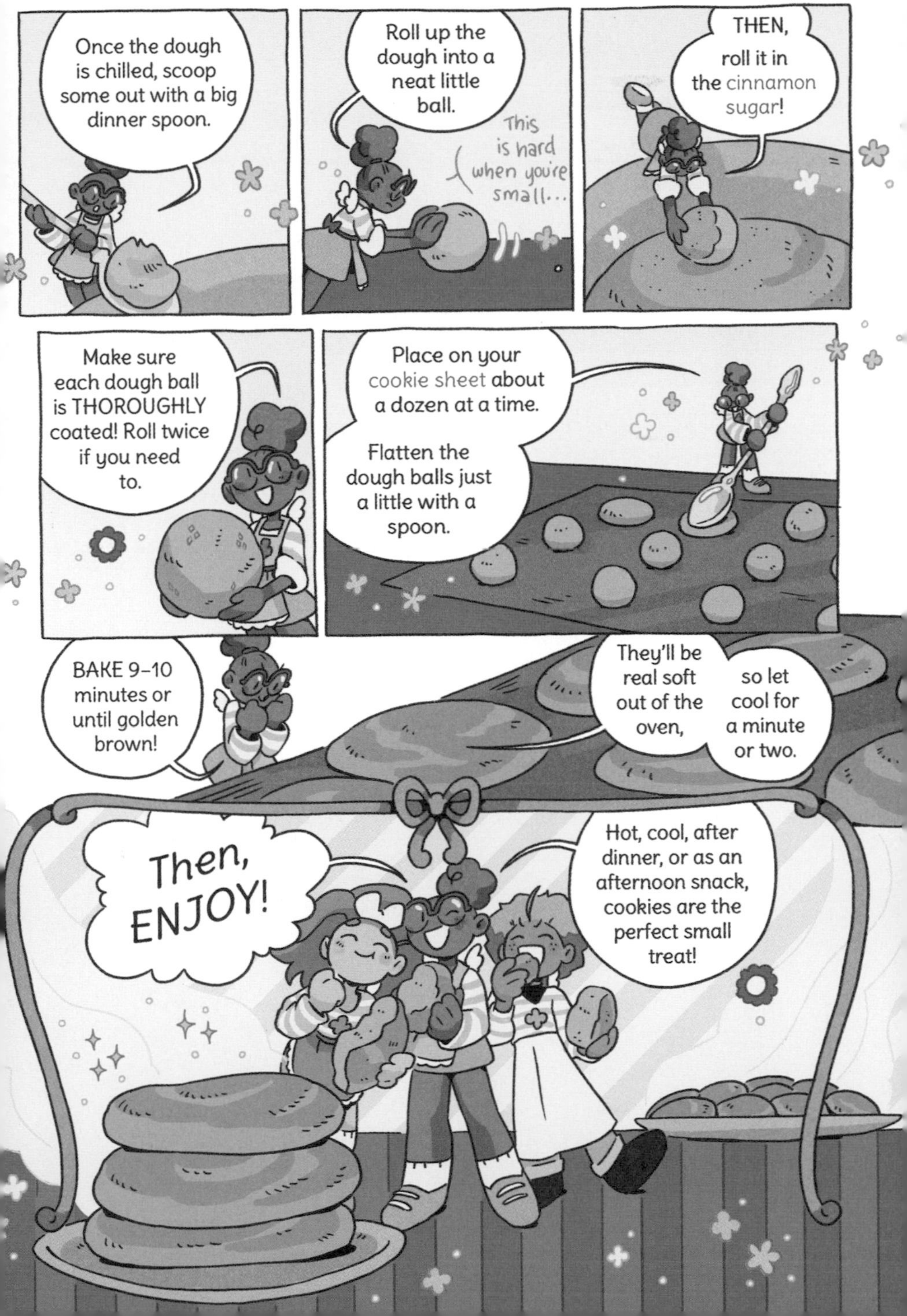

Once the dough is chilled, scoop some out with a big dinner spoon.
Roll up the dough into a neat little ball.
This is hard when you're small...
THEN,
roll it in the cinnamon sugar!
Make sure each dough ball is THOROUGHLY coated! Roll twice if you need to.
Place on your cookie sheet about a dozen at a time.
Flatten the dough balls just a little with a spoon.
BAKE 9–10 minutes or until golden brown!
They'll be real soft out of the oven,
so let cool for a minute or two.
Then, ENJOY!
Hot, cool, after dinner, or as an afternoon snack, cookies are the perfect small treat!

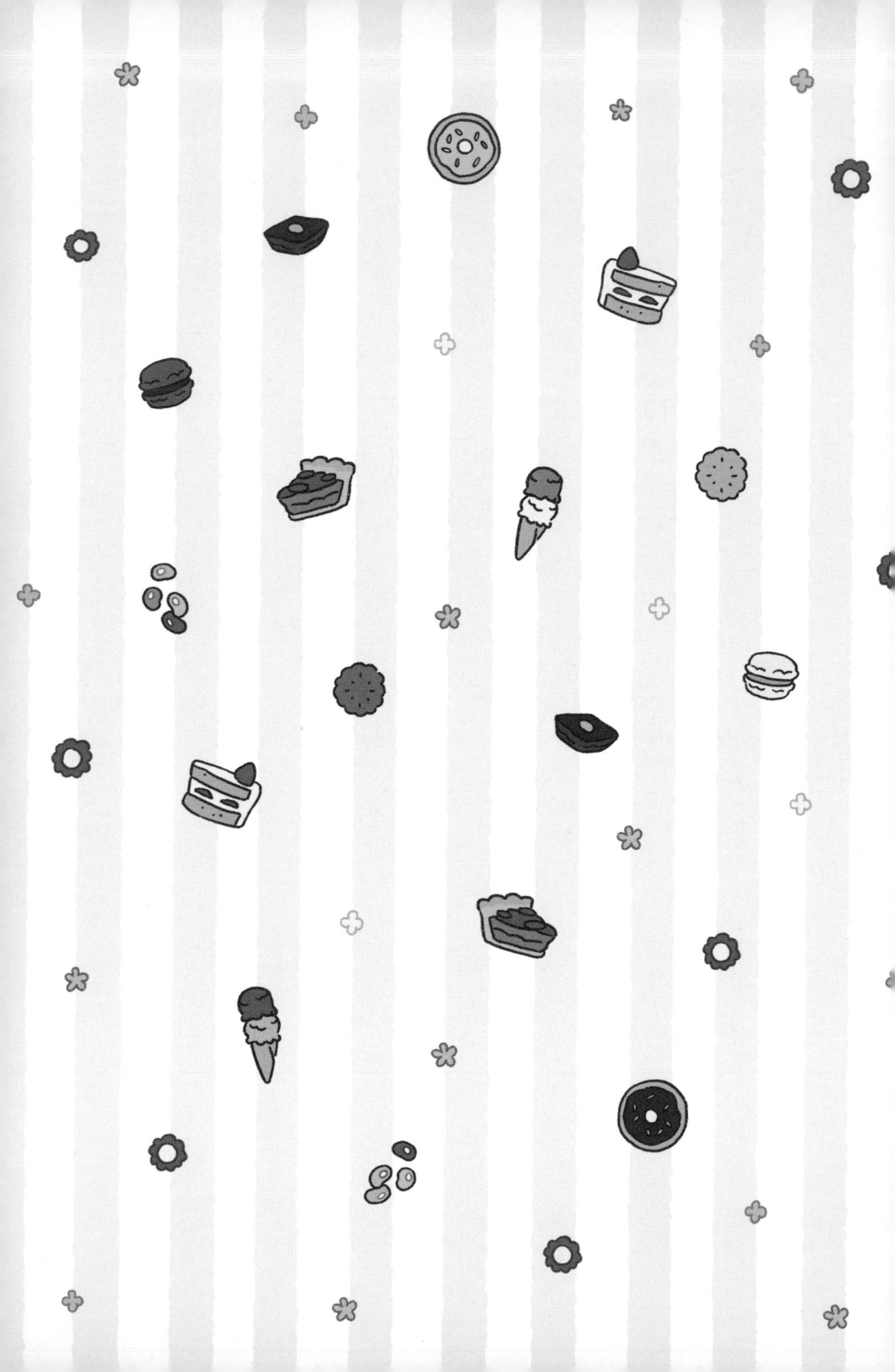

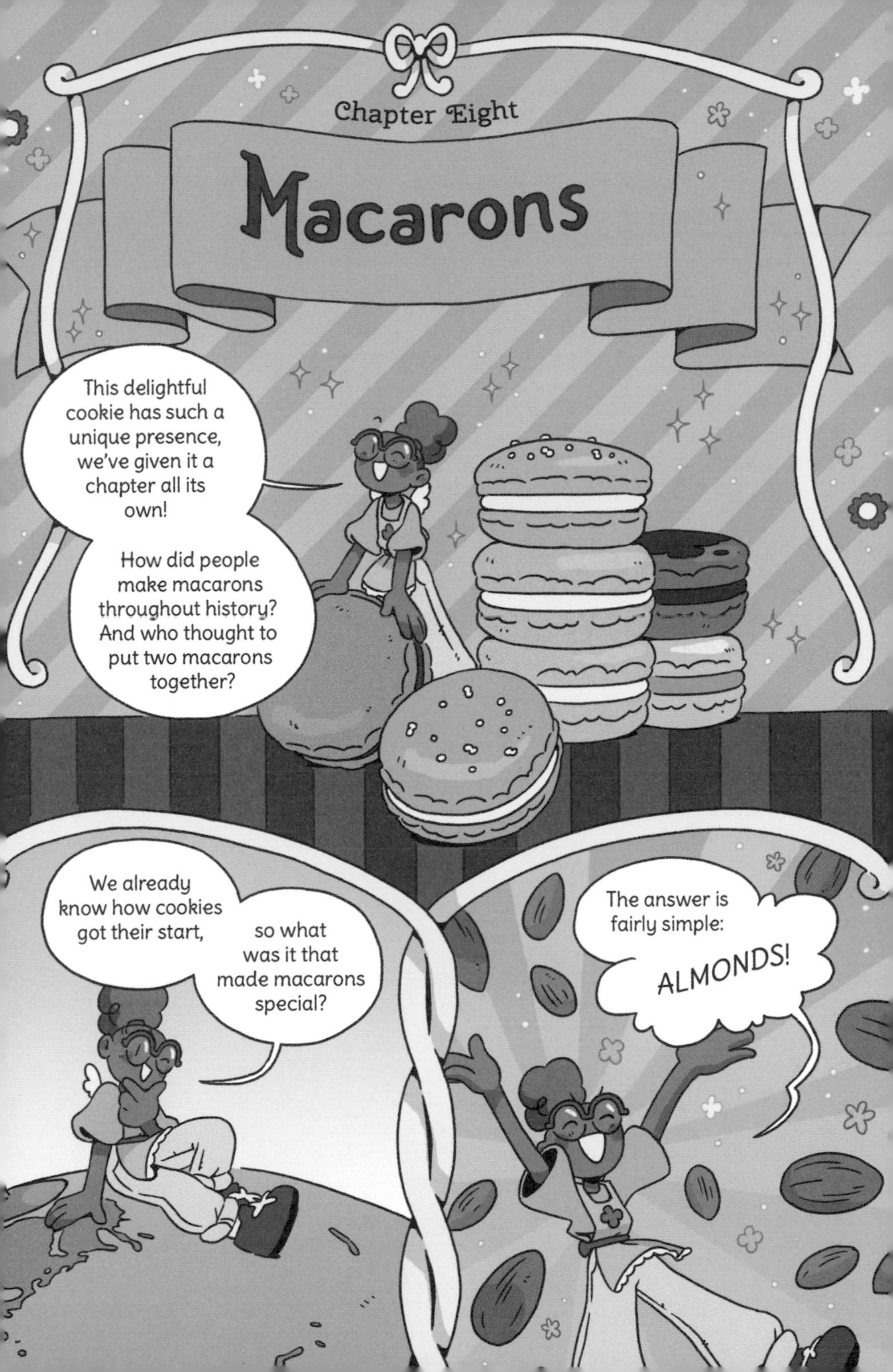
Chapter Eight
Macarons
This delightful cookie has such a unique presence, we've given it a chapter all its own!
How did people make macarons throughout history? And who thought to put two macarons together?
We already know how cookies got their start,
so what was it that made macarons special?
The answer is fairly simple:
ALMONDS!

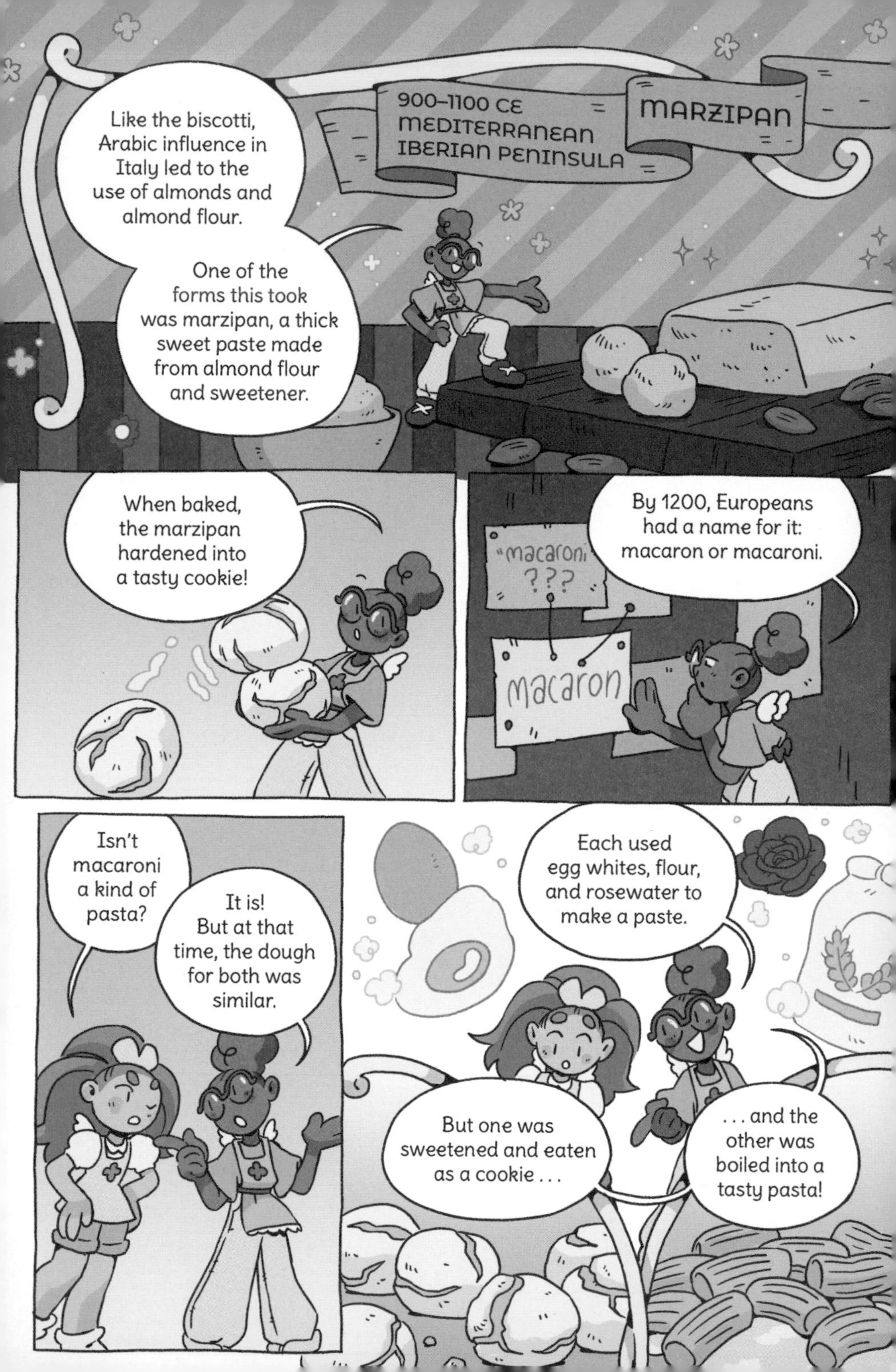
900–1100 CE
MEDITERRANEAN
IBERIAN PENINSULA
MARZIPAN
Like the biscotti, Arabic influence in Italy led to the use of almonds and almond flour.
One of the forms this took was marzipan, a thick sweet paste made from almond flour and sweetener.
When baked, the marzipan hardened into a tasty cookie!
"macaroni" ???
macaron
By 1200, Europeans had a name for it: macaron or macaroni.
Isn't macaroni a kind of pasta?
It is! But at that time, the dough for both was similar.
Each used egg whites, flour, and rosewater to make a paste.
But one was sweetened and eaten as a cookie . . .
. . . and the other was boiled into a tasty pasta!

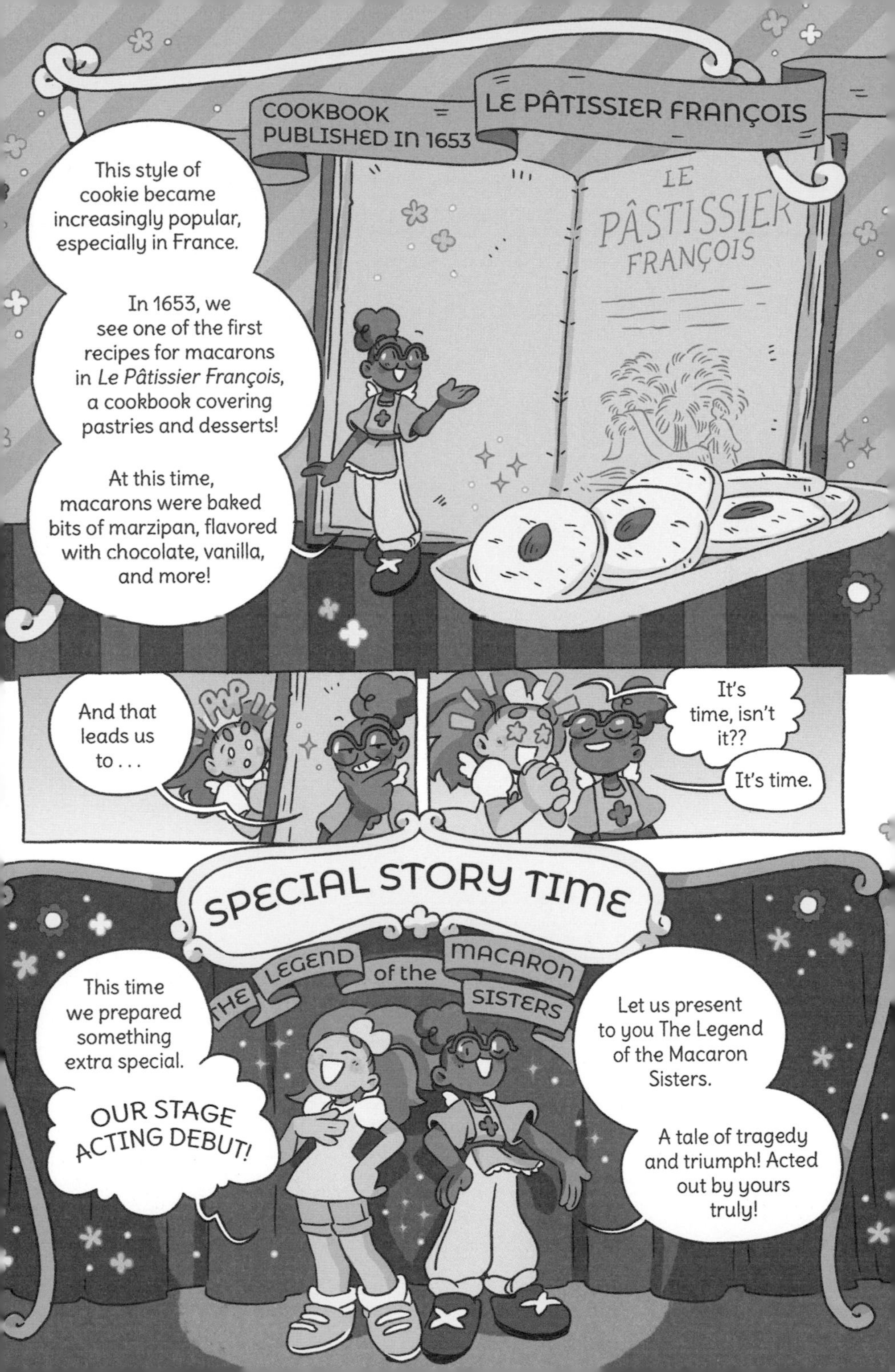
COOKBOOK PUBLISHED IN 1653
LE PÂTISSIER FRANÇOIS
This style of cookie became increasingly popular, especially in France.
In 1653, we see one of the first recipes for macarons in *Le Pâtissier François*, a cookbook covering pastries and desserts!
At this time, macarons were baked bits of marzipan, flavored with chocolate, vanilla, and more!
LE PÂSTISSIER FRANÇOIS
And that leads us to . . .
POP
It's time, isn't it??
It's time.
SPECIAL STORY TIME
THE LEGEND of the MACARON SISTERS
This time we prepared something extra special.
OUR STAGE ACTING DEBUT!
Let us present to you The Legend of the Macaron Sisters.
A tale of tragedy and triumph! Acted out by yours truly!

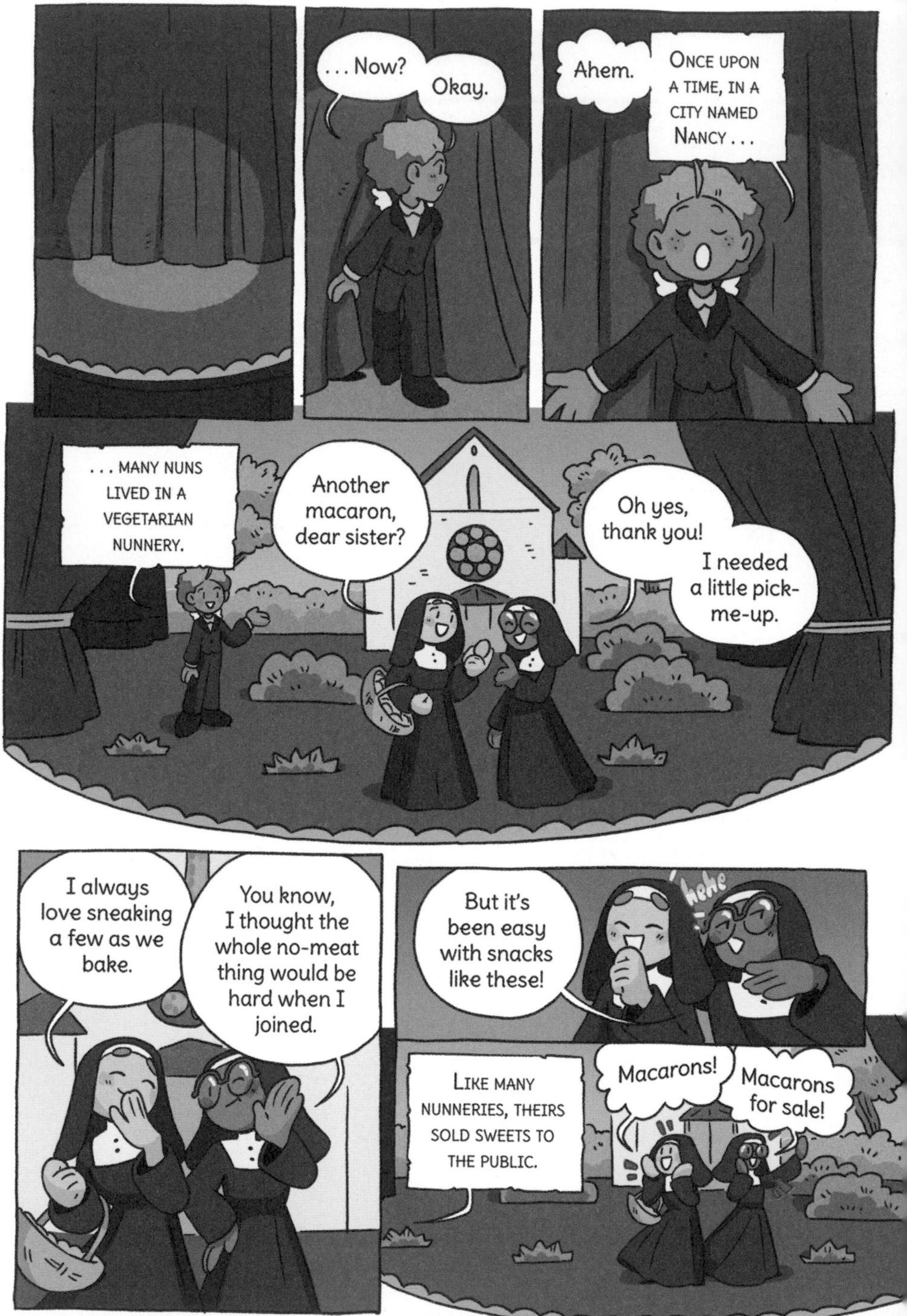
. . . Now?
Okay.
Ahem.
ONCE UPON A TIME, IN A CITY NAMED NANCY . . .
. . . MANY NUNS LIVED IN A VEGETARIAN NUNNERY.
Another macaron, dear sister?
Oh yes, thank you!
I needed a little pick-me-up.
I always love sneaking a few as we bake.
You know, I thought the whole no-meat thing would be hard when I joined.
But it's been easy with snacks like these!
hehe
LIKE MANY NUNNERIES, THEIRS SOLD SWEETS TO THE PUBLIC.
Macarons!
Macarons for sale!

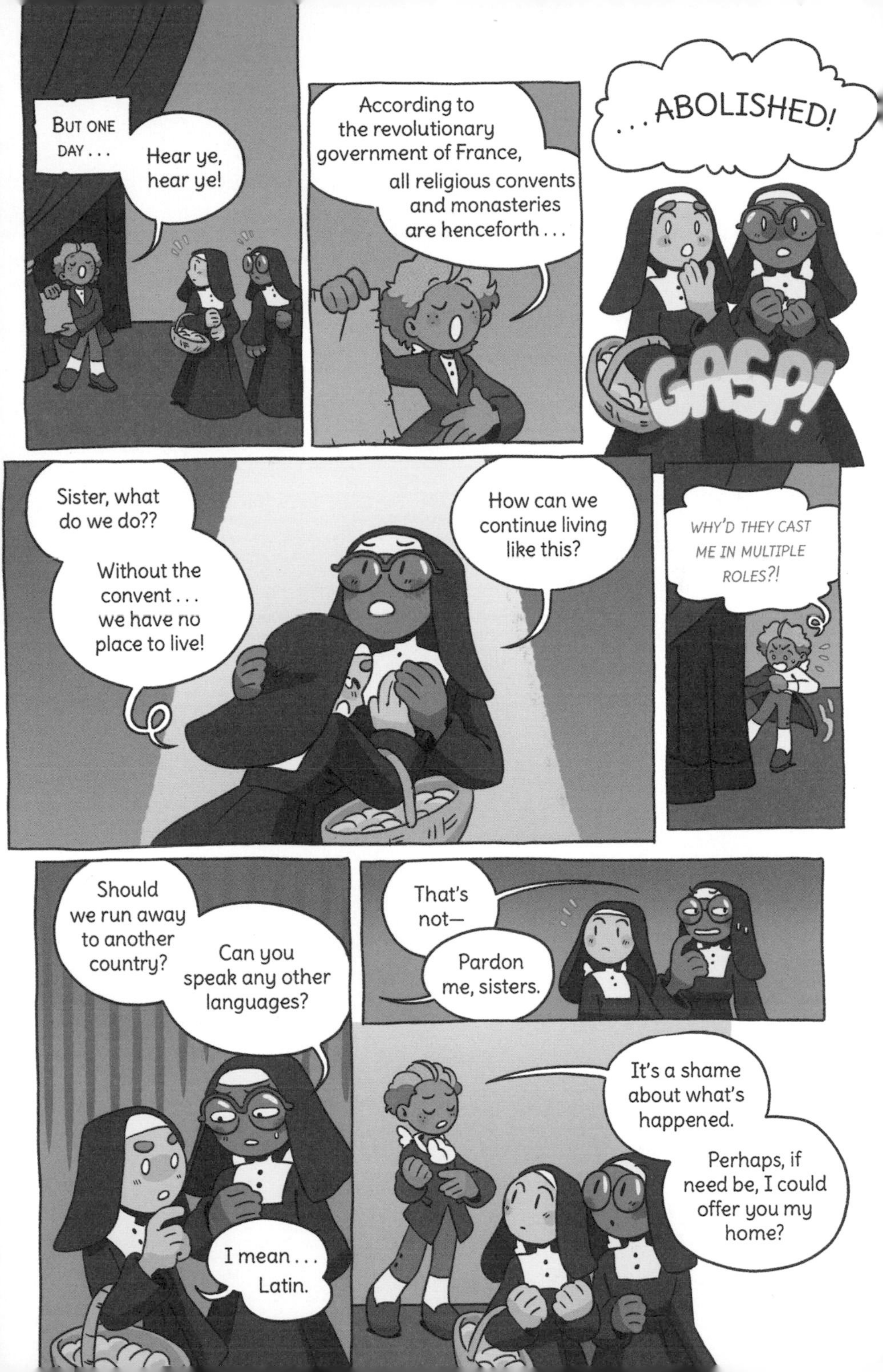
But one day . . .
Hear ye, hear ye!
According to the revolutionary government of France,
all religious convents and monasteries are henceforth . . .
. . . ABOLISHED!
GASP!
Sister, what do we do??
Without the convent . . . we have no place to live!
How can we continue living like this?
WHY'D THEY CAST ME IN MULTIPLE ROLES?!
Should we run away to another country?
Can you speak any other languages?
I mean . . .
Latin.
That's not—
Pardon me, sisters.
It's a shame about what's happened.
Perhaps, if need be, I could offer you my home?

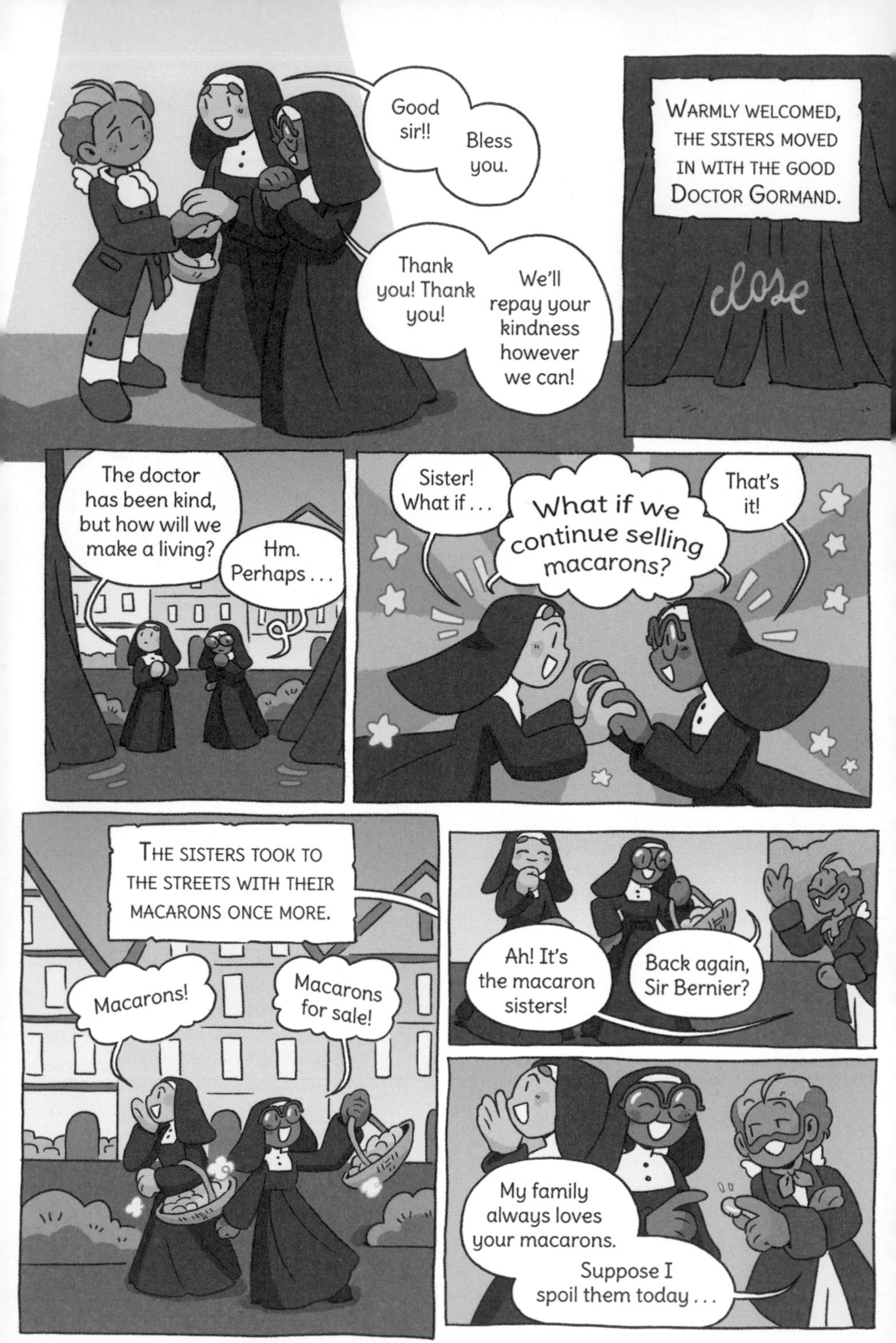
Good sir!!
Bless you.
Thank you! Thank you!
We'll repay your kindness however we can!
WARMLY WELCOMED, THE SISTERS MOVED IN WITH THE GOOD DOCTOR GORMAND.
close
The doctor has been kind, but how will we make a living?
Hm. Perhaps . . .
Sister! What if . . .
What if we continue selling macarons?
That's it!
THE SISTERS TOOK TO THE STREETS WITH THEIR MACARONS ONCE MORE.
Macarons!
Macarons for sale!
Ah! It's the macaron sisters!
Back again, Sir Bernier?
My family always loves your macarons.
Suppose I spoil them today . . .

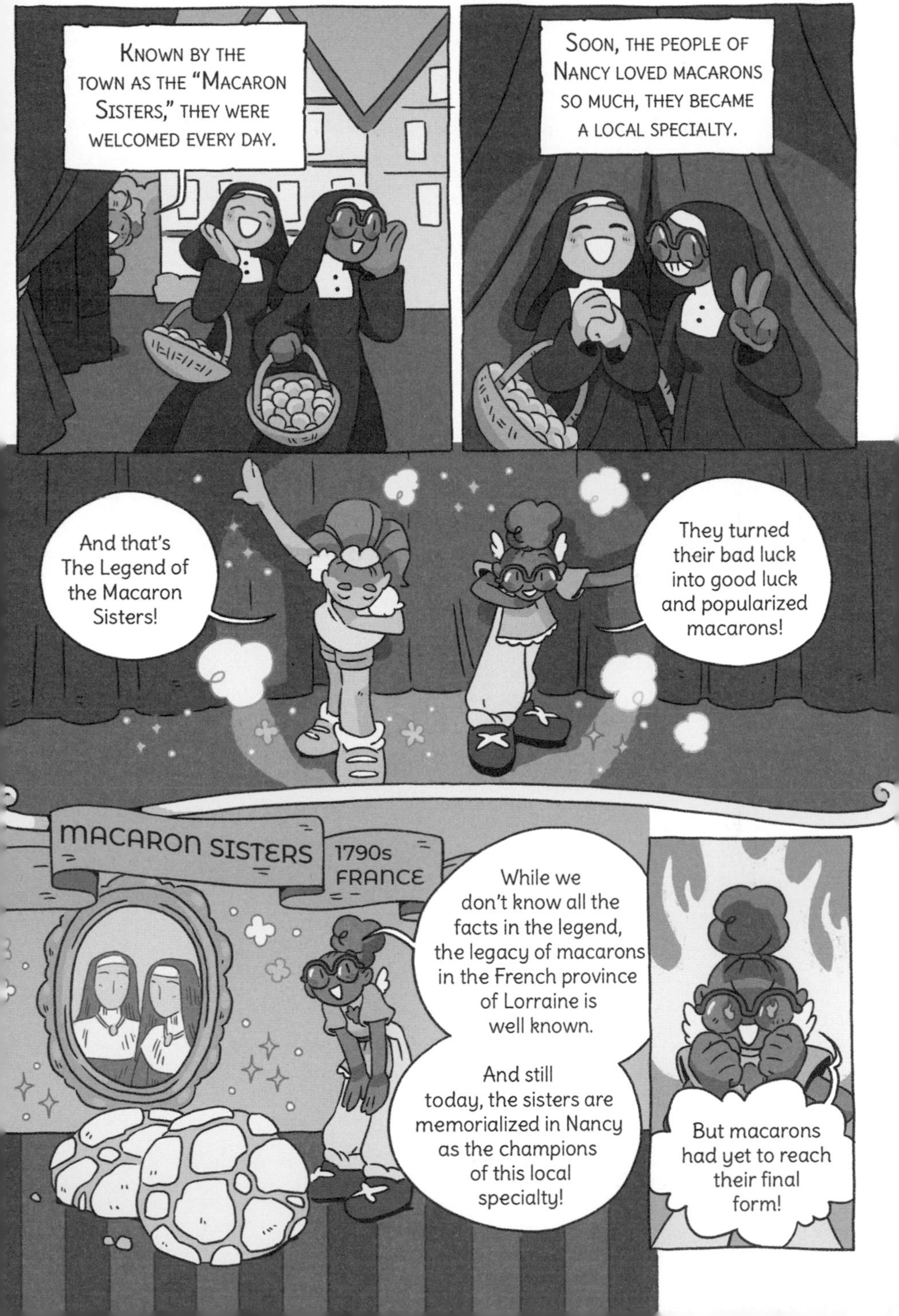

KNOWN BY THE TOWN AS THE "MACARON SISTERS," THEY WERE WELCOMED EVERY DAY.
SOON, THE PEOPLE OF NANCY LOVED MACARONS SO MUCH, THEY BECAME A LOCAL SPECIALTY.
And that's The Legend of the Macaron Sisters!
They turned their bad luck into good luck and popularized macarons!
MACARON SISTERS
1790s FRANCE
While we don't know all the facts in the legend, the legacy of macarons in the French province of Lorraine is well known.
And still today, the sisters are memorialized in Nancy as the champions of this local specialty!
But macarons had yet to reach their final form!

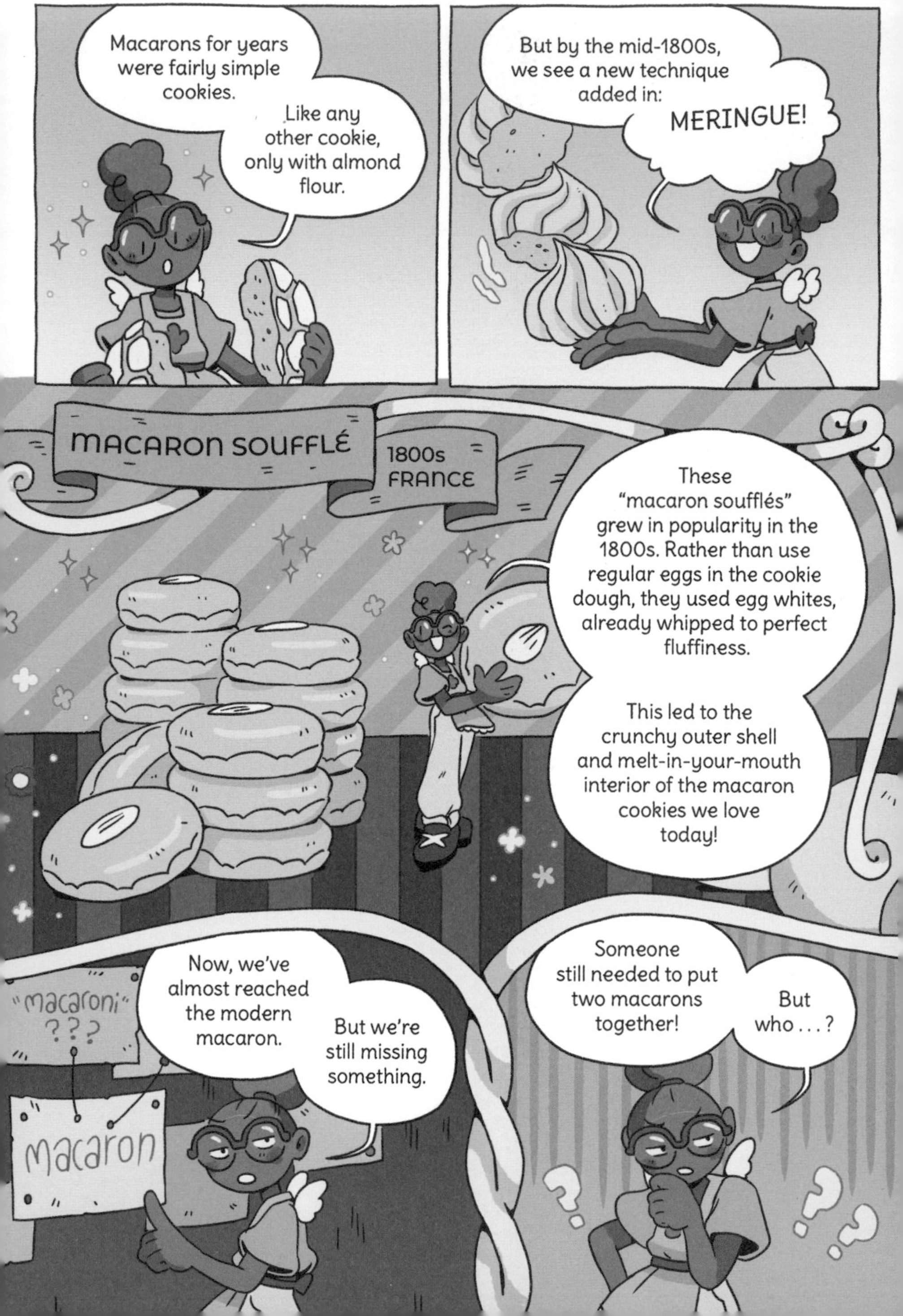
Macarons for years were fairly simple cookies.
Like any other cookie, only with almond flour.
But by the mid-1800s, we see a new technique added in:
MERINGUE!
MACARON SOUFFLÉ
1800s FRANCE
These "macaron soufflés" grew in popularity in the 1800s. Rather than use regular eggs in the cookie dough, they used egg whites, already whipped to perfect fluffiness.
This led to the crunchy outer shell and melt-in-your-mouth interior of the macaron cookies we love today!
"macaroni" ???
macaron
Now, we've almost reached the modern macaron.
But we're still missing something.
Someone still needed to put two macarons together!
But who . . . ?

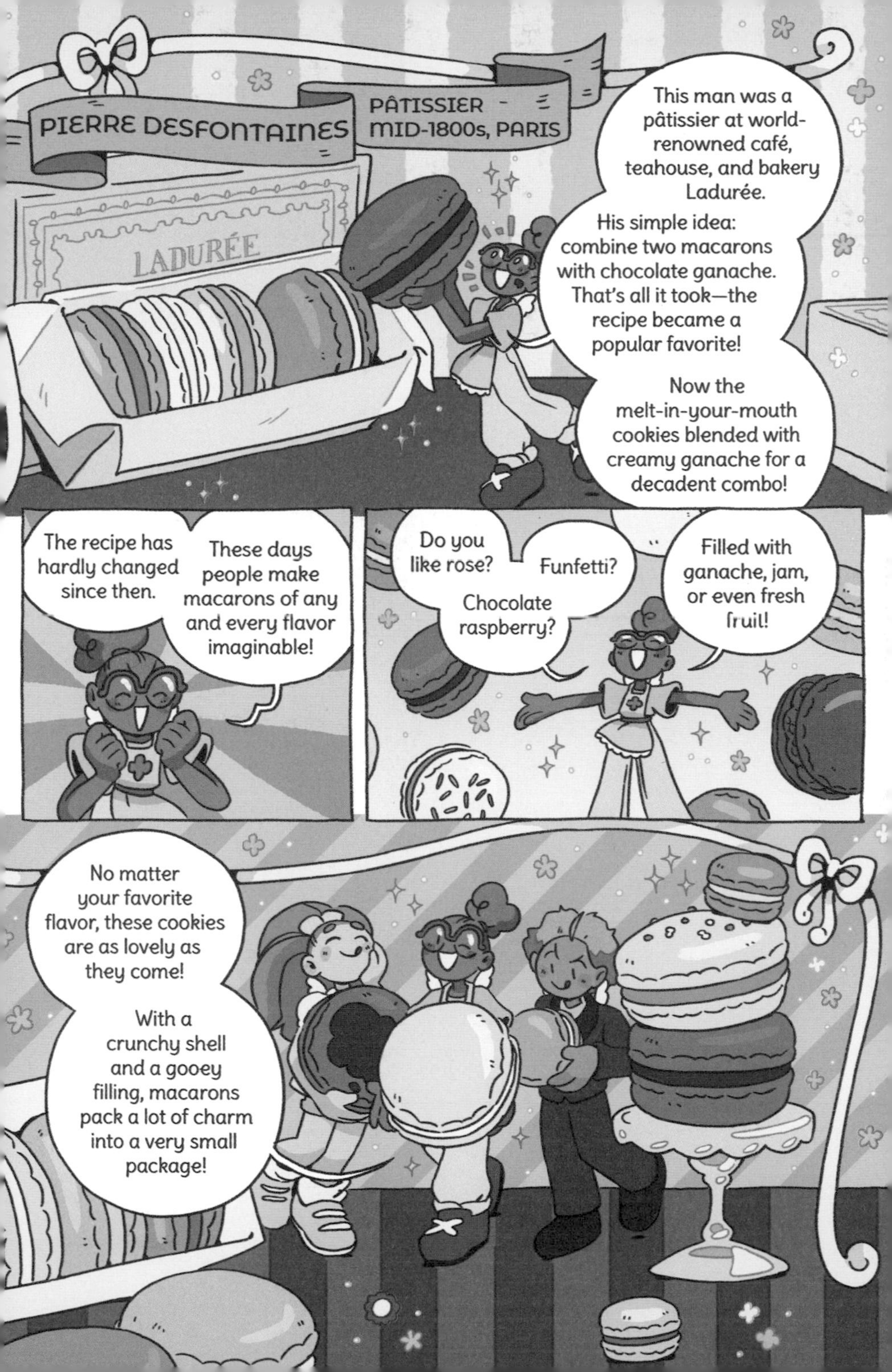
PIERRE DESFONTAINES
PÂTISSIER
MID-1800s, PARIS
LADURÉE
This man was a pâtissier at world-renowned café, teahouse, and bakery Ladurée.
His simple idea: combine two macarons with chocolate ganache. That's all it took—the recipe became a popular favorite!
Now the melt-in-your-mouth cookies blended with creamy ganache for a decadent combo!
The recipe has hardly changed since then.
These days people make macarons of any and every flavor imaginable!
Do you like rose?
Funfetti?
Chocolate raspberry?
Filled with ganache, jam, or even fresh fruit!
No matter your favorite flavor, these cookies are as lovely as they come!
With a crunchy shell and a gooey filling, macarons pack a lot of charm into a very small package!

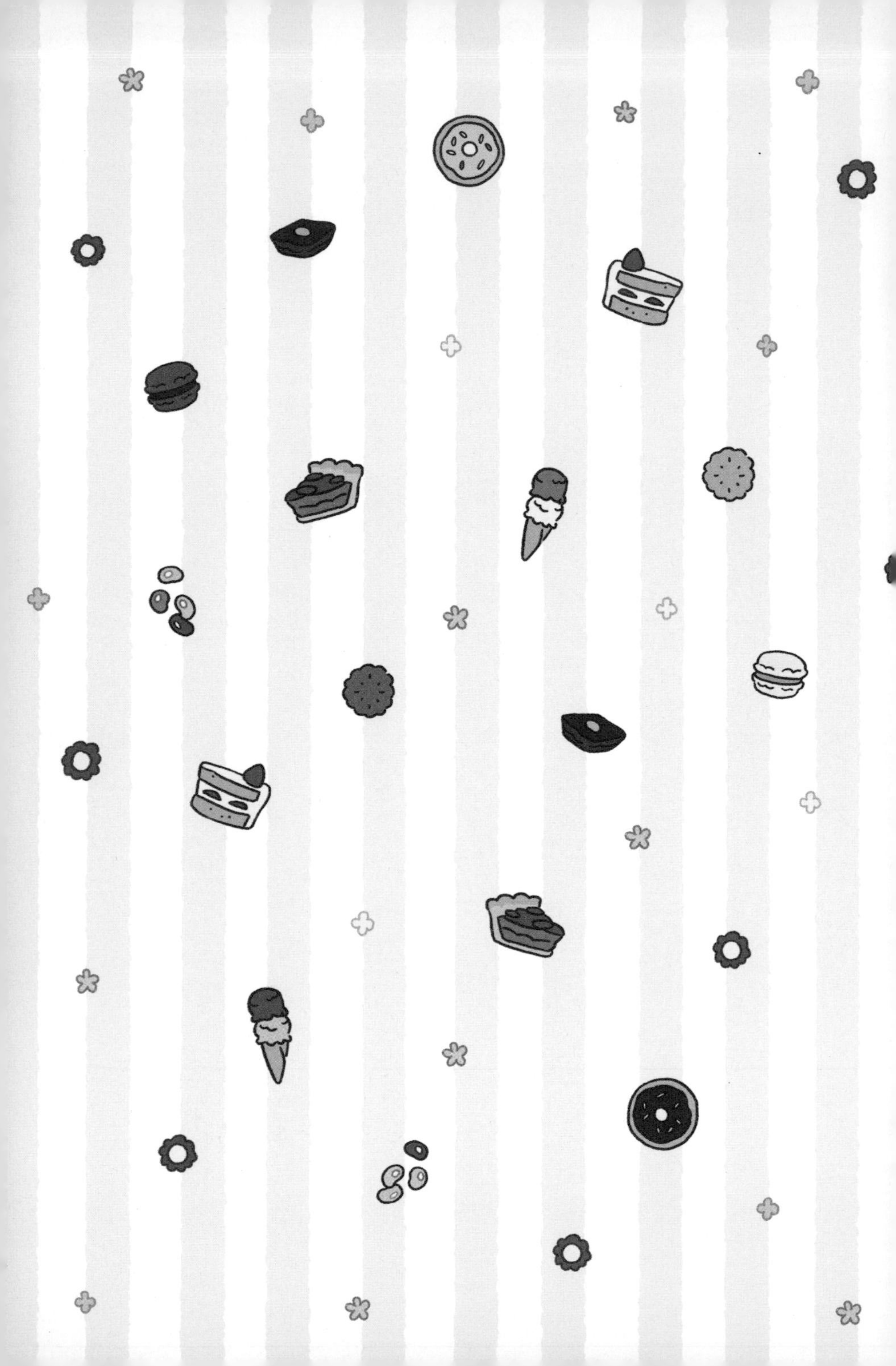

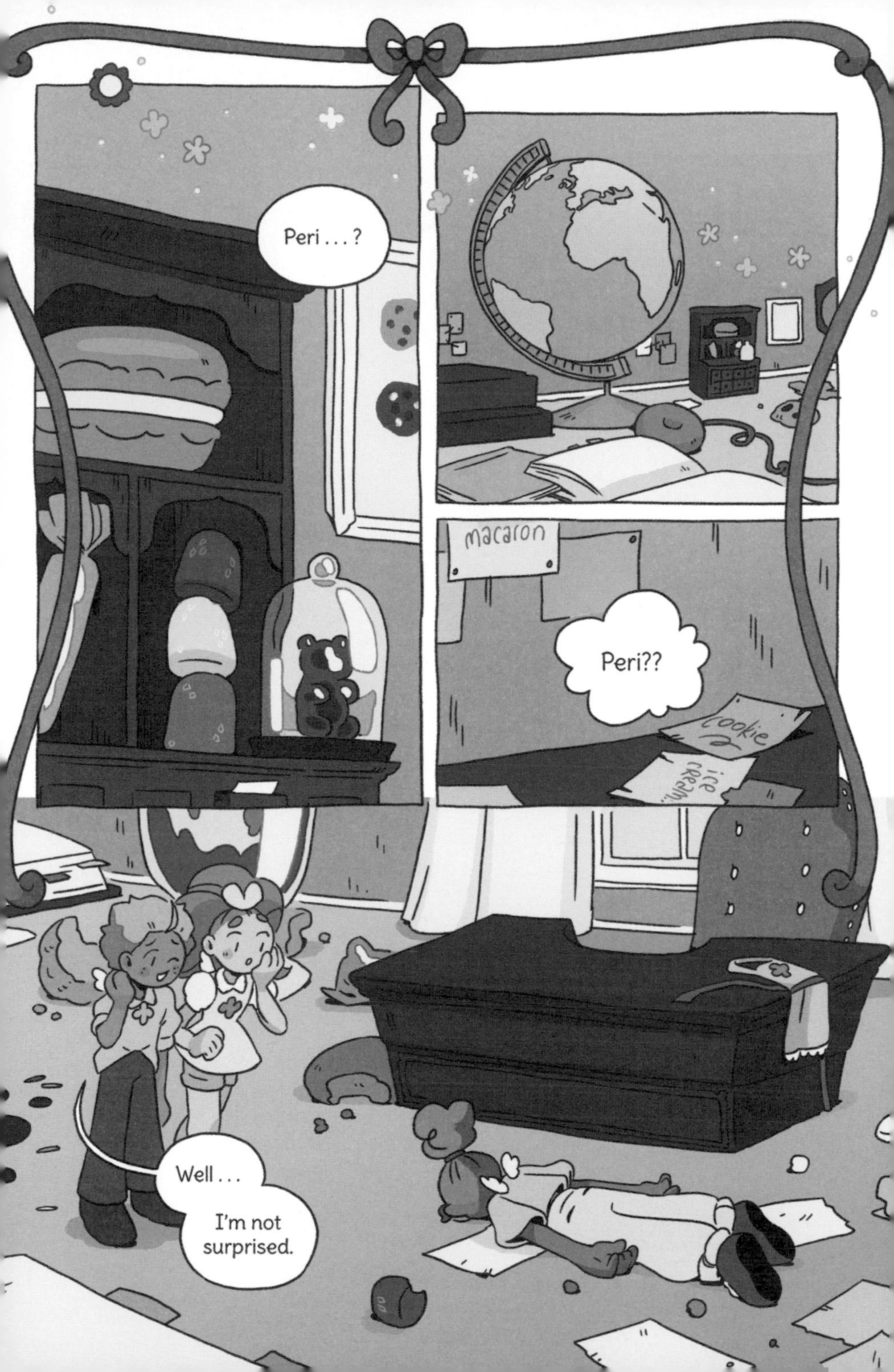
Peri . . . ?
Peri??
macaron
cookie
ice cream..
Well . . .
I'm not surprised.

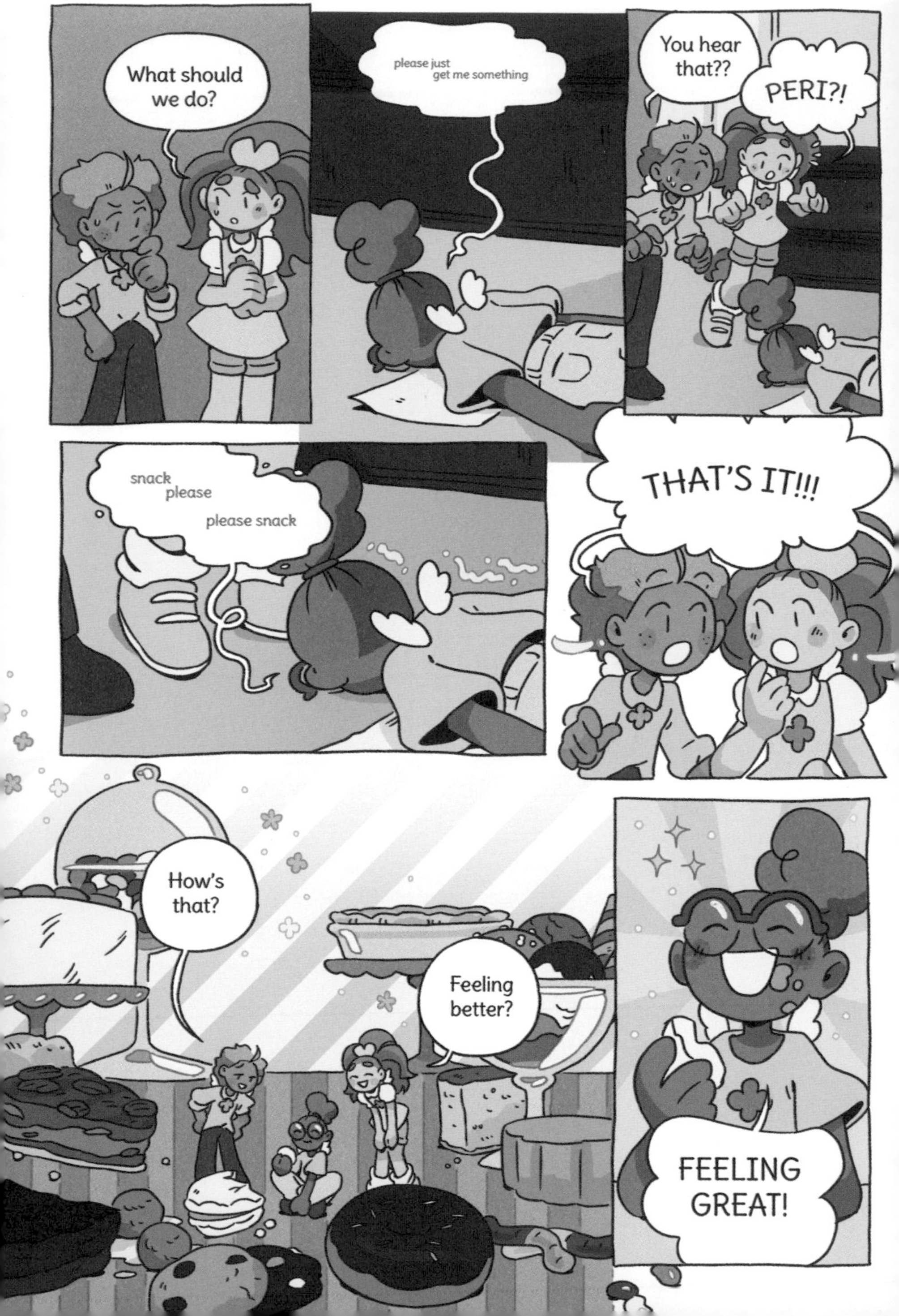
What should we do?
please just get me something
You hear that??
PERI?!
snack please
please snack
THAT'S IT!!!
How's that?
Feeling better?
FEELING GREAT!

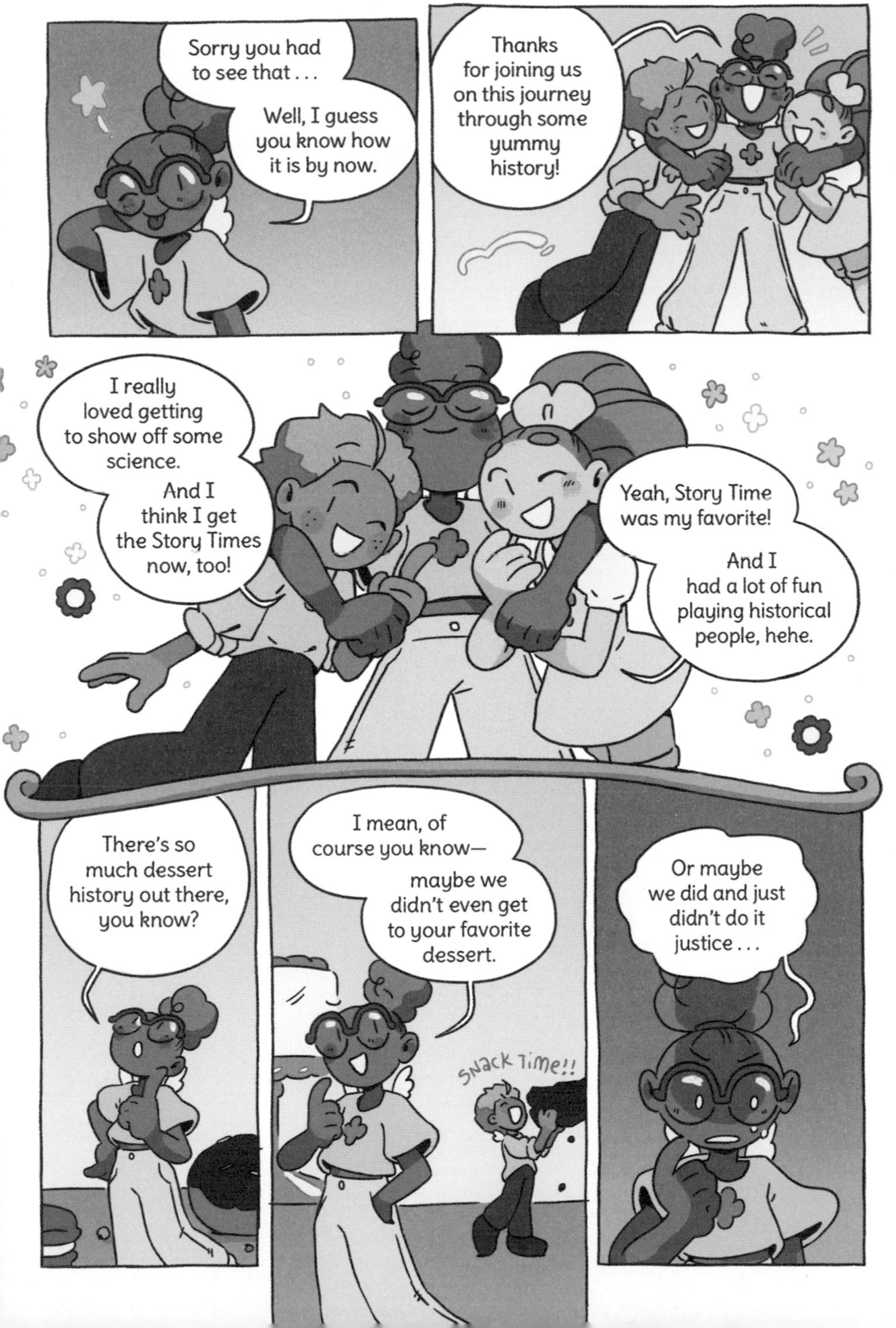
Sorry you had to see that . . .
Well, I guess you know how it is by now.
Thanks for joining us on this journey through some yummy history!
I really loved getting to show off some science.
And I think I get the Story Times now, too!
Yeah, Story Time was my favorite!
And I had a lot of fun playing historical people, hehe.
There's so much dessert history out there, you know?
I mean, of course you know—
maybe we didn't even get to your favorite dessert.
SNACK TIME!!
Or maybe we did and just didn't do it justice . . .

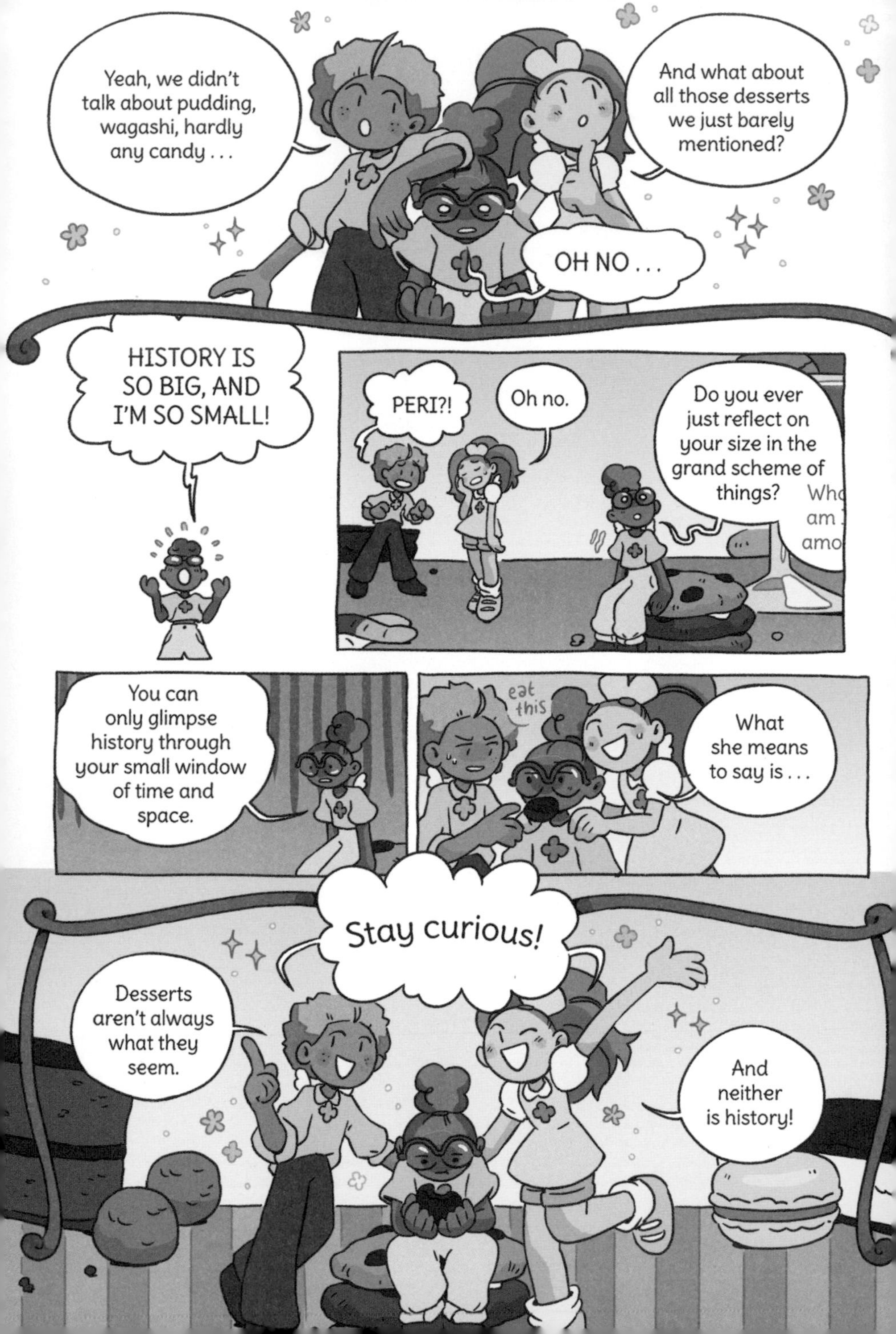
Yeah, we didn't talk about pudding, wagashi, hardly any candy . . .
And what about all those desserts we just barely mentioned?
OH NO . . .
HISTORY IS SO BIG, AND I'M SO SMALL!
PERI?!
Oh no.
Do you ever just reflect on your size in the grand scheme of things?
You can only glimpse history through your small window of time and space.
eat this
What she means to say is . . .
Stay curious!
Desserts aren't always what they seem.
And neither is history!

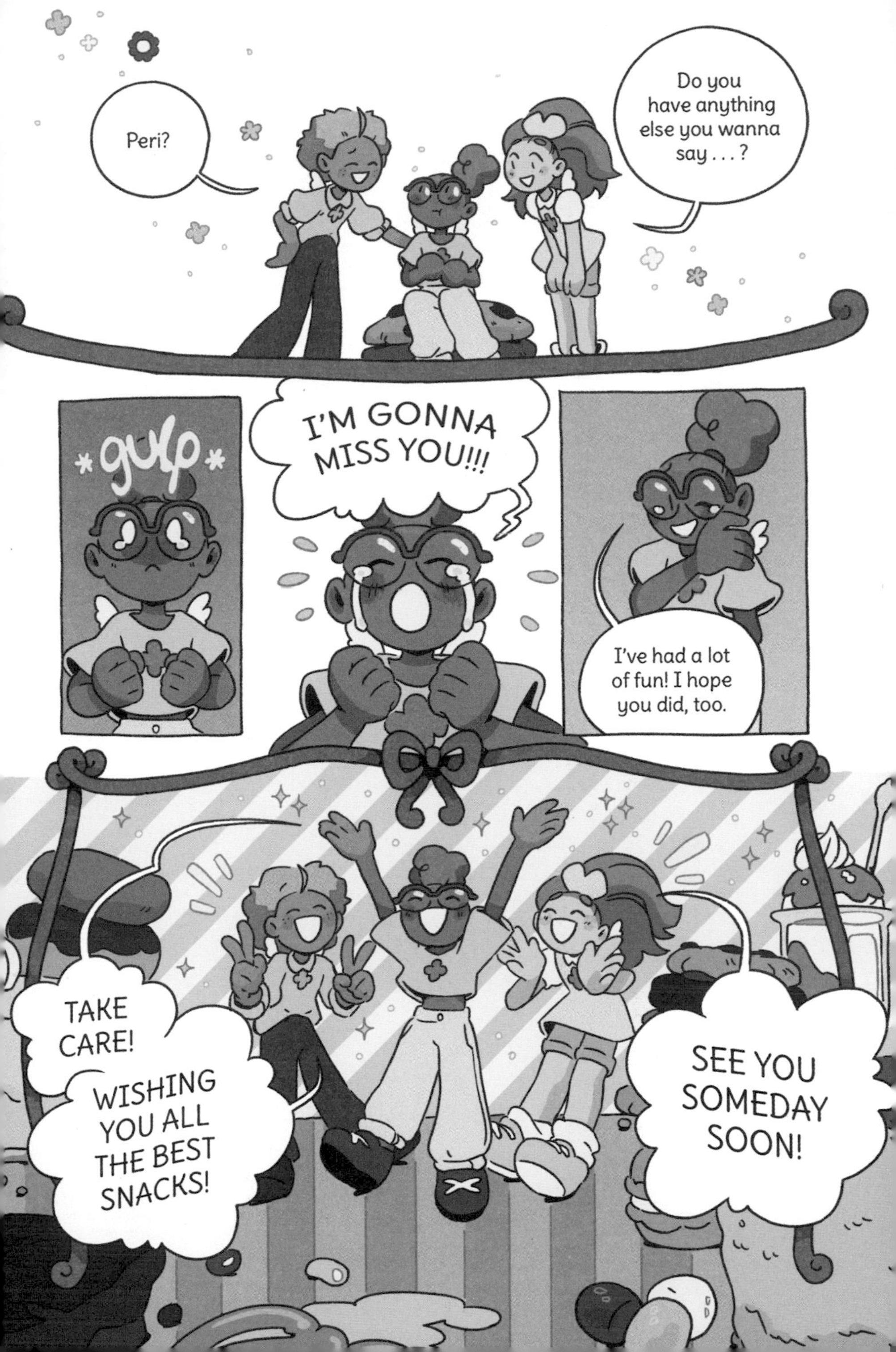
Peri?
Do you have anything else you wanna say . . . ?
*gulp*
I'M GONNA MISS YOU!!!
I've had a lot of fun! I hope you did, too.
TAKE CARE!
WISHING YOU ALL THE BEST SNACKS!
SEE YOU SOMEDAY SOON!

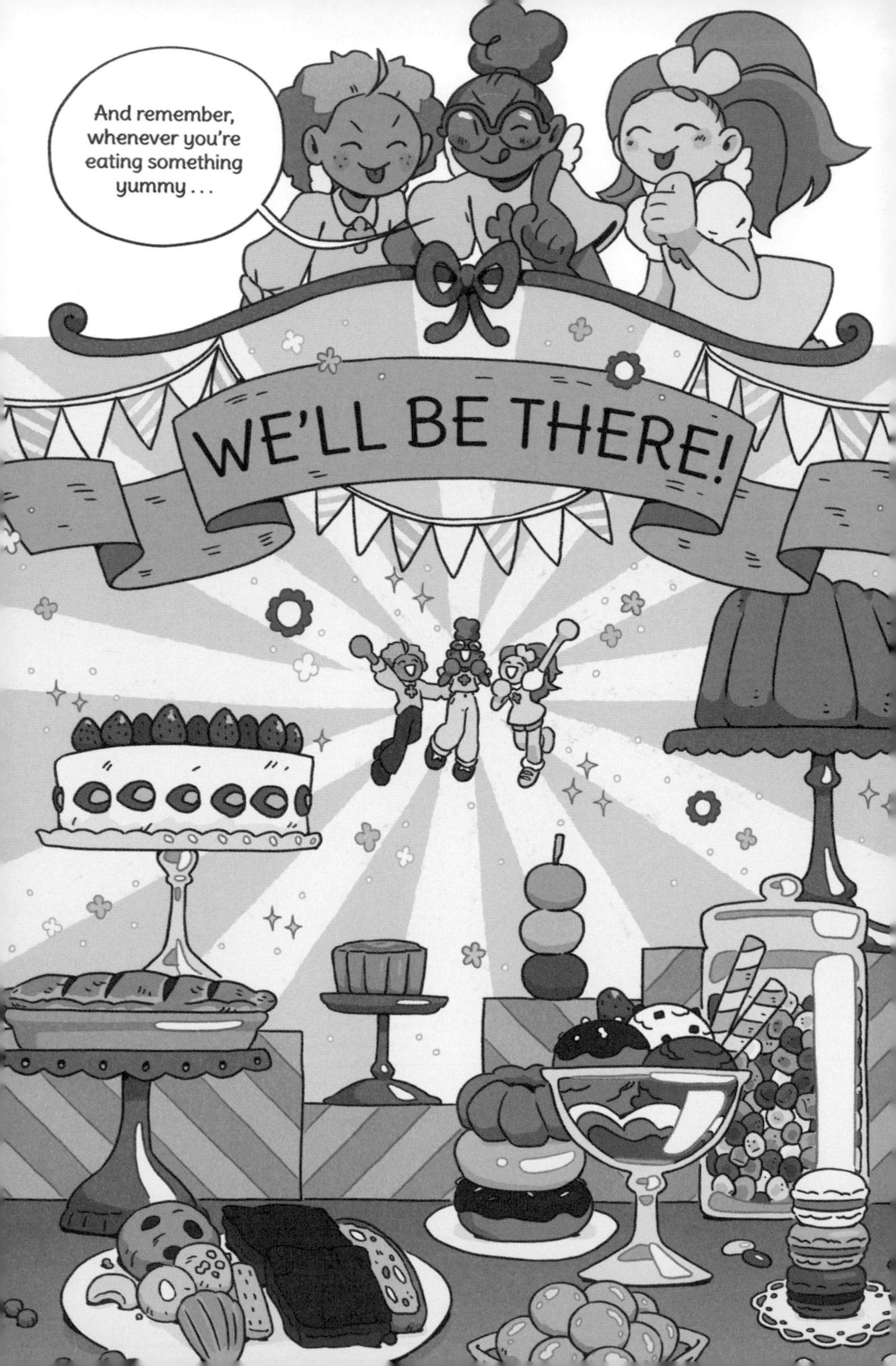
And remember, whenever you're eating something yummy . . .
WE'LL BE THERE!

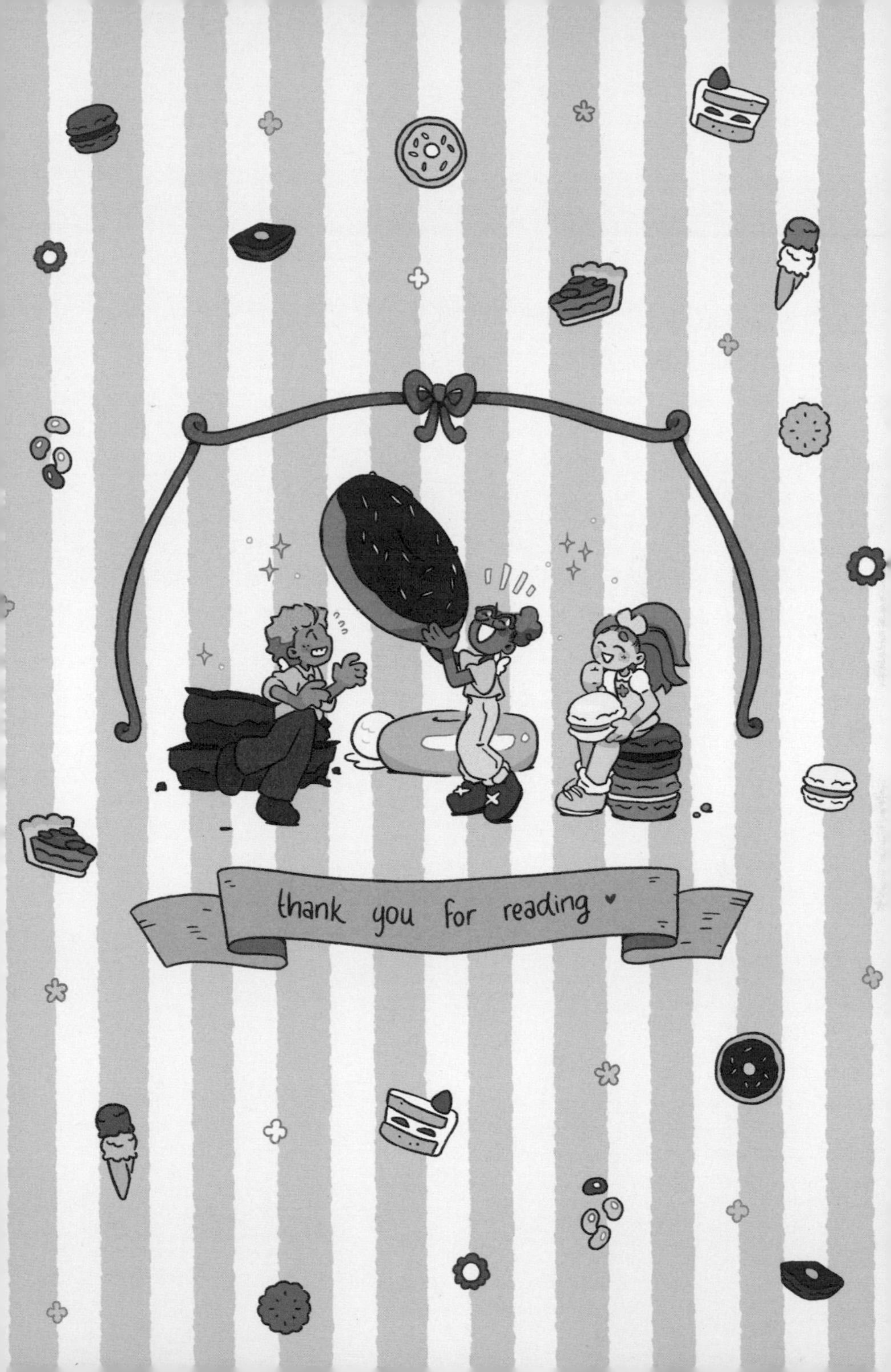
thank you for reading

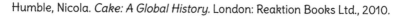

# Bibliography

Adriano, Joel D. "By Popular Demand: This Native Delicacy Shop Has Established Itself as a Dominant Buko Pie Maker." *Entrepreneur Philippines.* web.archive.org/web/20170515032701/http://www.entrepreneur.com.ph/startup-tips/by-popular-demand

Balachandran, Mohit. "Nankhatai–The Dying Indian 'Biskoot.'" NDTV Food. food.ndtv.com/opinions/nankhatai-the-dying-indian-biskoot-696071

Byrn, Anne. *American Cookie: The Snaps, Drops, Jumbles, Tea Cakes, Bars & Brownies That We Have Loved for Generations.* New York: Rodale, 2018.

Clarkson, Janet. *Pie: A Global History.* London: Reaktion Books Ltd., 2009.

Corning Museum of Glass. cmog.org

David, Elizabeth. *Harvest of the Cold Months: The Social History of Ice and Ices.* New York: Viking, 1994.

Davidson, Alan. *The Oxford Companion to Food.* New York: Oxford University Press, 2014.

Donati, Silvia. "Taste the History of Gelato." *Italy Magazine.* italymagazine.com/featured-story/taste-history-gelato

Gage, Mary. "History of Brownies (Chocolate)." New England Recipes. newenglandrecipes.org/History_of_Brownies.pdf

Goldstein, Darra. *The Oxford Companion to Sugar and Sweets.* New York: Oxford University Press, 2015.

"The History of Macaron Sisters." Macaron de Nancy. macaron-de-nancy.com/en/history

Hochman, Karen. "The History of Brownies." The Nibble. thenibble.com/reviews/main/cookies/cookies2/history-of-the-brownie.asp

Humble, Nicola. *Cake: A Global History.* London: Reaktion Books Ltd., 2010.

Kiriyama, Iku. "Haru Hashimoto: Matriarch of Mikawaya." Discover Nikkei: Nanka Nikkei Voices. discovernikkei.org/en/journal/2015/2/2/haru-hashimoto-mikawaya/

Krondl, Michael. *Sweet Invention: A History of Dessert.* Chicago: Chicago Review Press, 2011.

Krondl, Michael. *The Donut: History, Recipes, and Lore from Boston to Berlin.* Chicago: Chicago Review Press, 2014.

Levene, Alysa. *Cake: A Slice of History.* New York: Pegasus Books, 2016.

Marlowe, Jack. "Zalabia and the First Ice-Cream Cone." *Aramco World.* archive.aramcoworld.com/issue/200304/zalabia.and.the.first.ice-cream.cone.htm

The Met. metmuseum.org

Padden, Kathy. "This Day in History: June 22nd–Captain Gregory and the Invention of the Doughnut." Today I Found Out: Feed Your Brain. todayifoundout.com/index.php/2015/06/this-day-in-history-june-22nd-captain-gregory-and-the-invention-of-the-doughnut

Quinzio, Geraldine M. *Of Sugar and Snow: A History of Ice Cream Making.* Berkeley, CA: University of California Press, 2009.

Robertson, Amy E. "Maamoul: An Ancient Cookie That Ushers in Easter and Eid in the Middle East." NPR: *The Salt.* npr.org/sections/thesalt/2017/04/11/522771745/maamoul-an-ancient-cookie-that-ushers-in-easter-and-eid-in-the-middle-east

Shapiro, Laura. *Something from the Oven: Reinventing Dinner in 1950s America.* London: Penguin Books, 2005.

Starr, Ben. "REAL Red Velvet Cake." *Have YOU Ben Starr Struck?* benstarr.com/blog/real-red-velvet-cake-with-no-food-coloring-or-beet-juice

Watanabe, Teresa. "Frances Hashimoto Dies at 69; Little Tokyo Leader, Mochi Ice Cream Creator." *LA Times.* latimes.com/local/obituaries/la-xpm-2012-nov-07-la-me-frances-hashimoto-20121107-story.html

Zheng, Limin. "Zhu Yuanzhang and Moon Cake Uprising." China Central Television. english.cctv.com/2016/09/14/ARTILP1KMo4BtfYKI6gOB2Q2160914.shtml

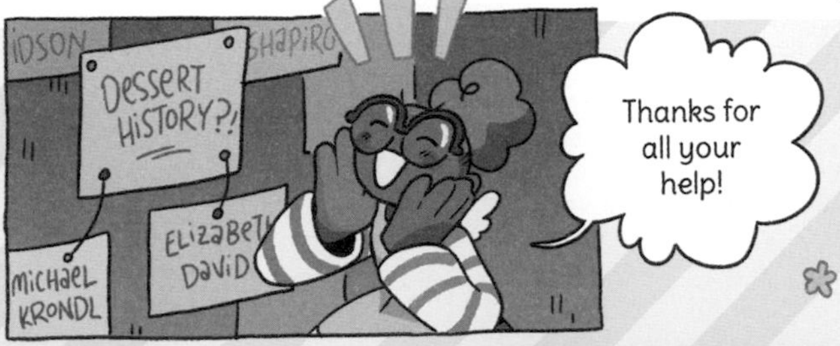
IDSON
SHAPIRO
DESSERT HISTORY?!
ELIZABETH DAVID
MICHAEL KRONDL
Thanks for all your help!

# WHAT ARE FOOD SPRITES?

Food sprites are everywhere you find tasty food! They all gravitate toward different flavors and ingredients . . . After all, they have favorites, too! Their true names are usually very complicated. For example, Peri's real name is the first sweet snack given to you by a friend. But since most people have trouble remembering what that was, she uses her nickname Peri instead!

## PERI

**FAVE ICE CREAM:**
bastani nooni

**FAVE CAKE:**
carrot cake

**FAVE PIE:**
PECAN!

**FAVE COOKIE:**
macarons

## FEE

**FAVE ICE CREAM:**
mochi ice cream

**FAVE CAKE:**
strawberry shortcake

**FAVE PIE:**
apple with ice cream

**FAVE COOKIE:**
GINGERBREAD!

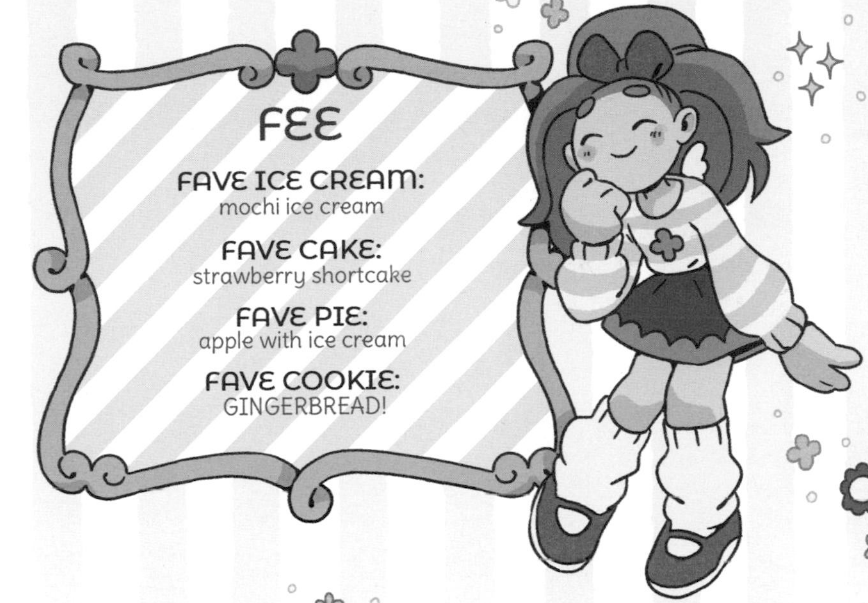

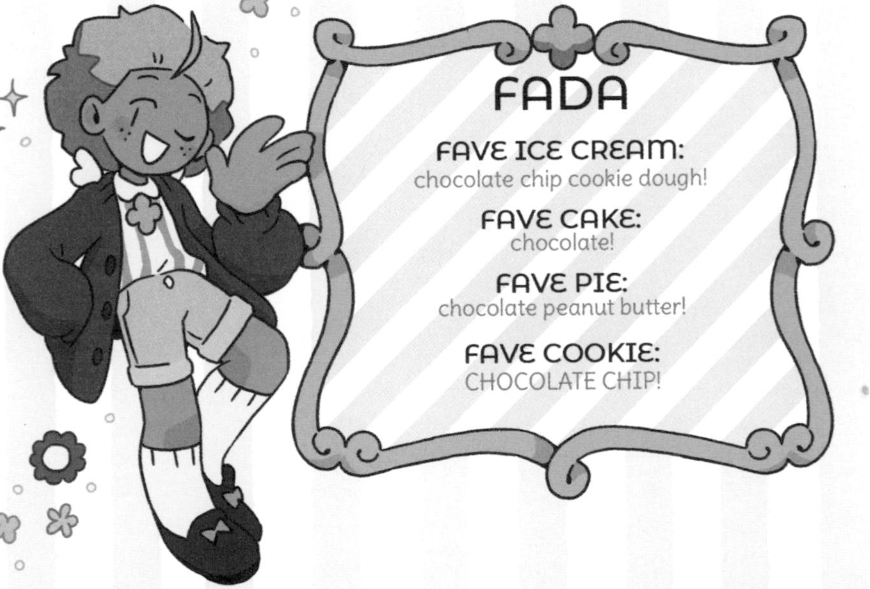

## FADA

**FAVE ICE CREAM:**
chocolate chip cookie dough!

**FAVE CAKE:**
chocolate!

**FAVE PIE:**
chocolate peanut butter!

**FAVE COOKIE:**
CHOCOLATE CHIP!

# NOTES AND ACKNOWLEDGMENTS

In researching for this book, I recognize the political nature of food, both in its origin and spread. Many times, more often than not with European heritage foods, colonization and slavery are at the center of their histories. As such, I'd like to acknowledge that this book was written and drawn in Austin, Texas, on the traditional land of the Jumanos, Tonkawa, Nʉmʉnʉʉ, and Sana people, the rightful stewards of this beautiful land, where I am grateful to live.

I'd like to thank the team at RHG—particularly Whitney, Patrick, and Gina—and my wonderful agent, Steven Salpeter, for helping me make this book a reality. Thank you to my friend Gaby for all your suggestions, feedback, and encouragement.

Thank you to my lovely partner, Sergio, for always believing in my dreams, being my partner in life, and listening to me endlessly ramble on about whatever it is I'm into . . . in this case, dessert history.

I could pour out endless thanks and love to all my friends and family, those who worked with me, those who shared meals and holidays and boba with me, those who said they'd buy dozens of copies of this book (I'm holding you to it), and those who sent love and support from afar. Without you, I'd truly be eating desserts alone in my house. Thank you so, so much.

And, of course, thank you, dear reader. You're the reason I'm here!

This is my first book and first time publishing research. While *Yummy* is as thorough as I could make it with the resources available to me, it is by no means a definitive or flawless global history. Rather, it's more like dipping your toes into dessert history. Are you curious about the history of your favorite food? I hope this book encourages you to keep an open mind and think of history as a constantly growing, changing thing. Like the food sprites said, stay curious!

# ABOUT THE AUTHOR

I'm Victoria Grace Elliott, a comic artist living in Austin, Texas. I love desserts (eating them, looking at them, making them, learning more about them), watching soap operas, and singing karaoke.

@fridayafternoon

# FIND YOUR VOICE
## WITH ONE OF THESE EXCITING GRAPHIC NOVELS

## PRESENTED BY RH GRAPHIC

@RHKIDSGRAPHIC

### A GRAPHIC NOVEL ON EVERY BOOKSHELF

1447